Third Canadian Edition

THE GENDERED SOCIETY READER

Edited by
MICHAEL KIMMEL
AMY ARONSON
AMY KALER

OXFORD
UNIVERSITY PRESS

Oxford University Press is a department of the University of Oxford.
It furthers the University's objective of excellence in research, scholarship,
and education by publishing worldwide. Oxford is a registered trade mark of
Oxford University Press in the UK and in certain other countries.

Published in Canada by
Oxford University Press
8 Sampson Mews, Suite 204,
Don Mills, Ontario M3C 0H5 Canada

www.oupcanada.com

Original edition published by Oxford University Press, Inc.,
198 Madison Avenue, New York, N.Y. 10016-4314, USA.
Copyright © 2005 Oxford University Press, Inc
The Gendered Society Reader, Fourth Edition was originally published in English in 2011.
This edition is published by arrangement with Oxford University Press, Inc.

First Canadian Edition published in 2007
Second Canadian Edition published in 2011

Library and Archives Canada Cataloguing in Publication

The gendered society reader / edited by Michael S. Kimmel,
Amy Aronson, Amy Kaler.—Third Canadian edition.

Includes bibliographical references and index.
ISBN 978-0-19-900697-7 (pbk.)

1. Sex role—Textbooks. 2. Sex differences (Psychology)—
Textbooks. 3. Gender identity—Textbooks. 4. Sex discrimination—
Textbooks. 5. Equality—Textbooks. I. Kaler, Amy, 1966-, editor
II. Kimmel, Michael S., editor III. Aronson, Amy, editor

HQ1075.G467 2015 305.3 C2015-900381-4

Cover image: suedhang/Getty Images

Oxford University Press is committed to our environment.
Wherever possible, our books are printed on paper which comes from
responsible sources.

Printed and bound in Canada
7 8 9 — 23 22 21

Contents

Preface to the Canadian Edition

Editing the third Canadian edition of *The Gendered Society Reader* has been a pleasure and a challenge. The pleasure rested in the chance to read widely and to familiarize myself with the liveliness and curiosity that characterizes the best gender research in Canada today. The challenge lay in the difficulty of choosing among the wide array of relevant texts. For every text included, many others could have easily been chosen. This was especially true for the two new sections on media and on social movements.

The challenge also lay in moving into a textual space already delineated by Michael Kimmel, one of the most prominent international figures in gender studies. My changes to this book have inevitably altered this space in directions of my own choosing, but I believe I've been able to retain his sense of gender as something that saturates the social world, differentiating the experiences of men and women and manifesting itself in actions, relationships, ideas, and dreams. I also believe I've retained Dr Kimmel's sense of hope and possibility for the transformation of gender, creating a better, more humane world for everyone, male and female alike.

The third edition contains 12 completely new articles, chosen in response to feedback from students and instructors about what they found most compelling and most valuable in the classroom. In selecting these new articles, I paid particular attention to finding work that addresses the social construction of masculinity in Canada, as well as work that engages gender and the intersection of other social categories, particularly "race" and ethnicity. The latter concern also led to the creation of an entirely new section on gender and race. In addition, I have added chapter introductions for all 42 chapters, to supplement the introductions at the beginning of each part. Finally, the questions for critical thought have been increased and updated.

In editing the Canadian version, I used several criteria in choosing texts to include. The most obvious criterion was that the texts had to be Canadian; they had to deal with the lives and experiences of Canadians, and ideally also be written by a Canadian author. I focused on the nationality of the texts not because I wanted to fill some arbitrary quota for Canadian content, but because I wanted to enable students to take a critical, analytical look at the country in which their own gendered subjectivities are being formed. I wanted to avoid the problem my own students often complain about: the tendency to universalize American experiences and to treat the United States as the norm for the entire world.

This concern on my part is consistent with the broader feminist imperative to question all universalizing tendencies and to attempt to decentre the centres of power—including academic power—in our writing, thinking, and teaching. There is no question that Canada and the United States are similar in many ways when it comes to the workings of gender, but it's important not to take this similarity for granted and to look for gender at work in the social world around us, rather than just gazing across the border.

Along the same lines, I have prioritized qualitative accounts of lived experience over heavily quantitative texts. I don't think that qualitative research is somehow better or truer than quantitative studies, but I do think that qualitative work offers undergraduates a way, at least partially, to get inside the life-worlds of gendered subjects, including those who are gendered differently from the students themselves. Qualitative work also enables readers to get a sense of the complex intersections of gender and other social categories, such as race, socioeconomic class, sexuality, and bodily status, all of which shape the experience of being gendered in subtle but powerful ways.

I was graced with an excellent team at Oxford University Press Canada. Many thanks to Suzanne Clark, Tanuja Weerasooriya, Amy Gordon, and Amy Hick for all their work on behalf of this book. I'd also like to acknowledge the students in my Sociology of Gender classes at the University of Alberta, from whom I am slowly learning what teaching gender can be, at its best. I hope this book intrigues, entertains, and possibly enlightens its readers.

Introduction

Amy Kaler and Michael S. Kimmel

Every day there's another story about how women and men are different. They say we have different brain chemistries, different brain organization, and different hormones, different bodies, and different selves. They say we have different ways of knowing, that we listen to different moral voices, and that we have different ways of speaking and hearing each other.

Some stories even hold that we come from different planets, women from Venus and men from Mars. In his bestselling series of books on this theme, pop psychologist John Gray informs us that not only do women and men communicate differently, "but they think, feel, perceive, react, respond, love, need, and appreciate differently" (Gray, 1995: 5). It's a miracle of cosmic proportions that we ever understand one another!

Yet we're all here together in the same classes, eating in the same dining halls, walking on the same campuses, reading the same books, being subject to the same criteria for grading. When we're not at school, we live in the same houses, eat the same meals, surf the same Internet, read the same magazines, and watch the same TV shows. How can we be so different and yet lead lives that are so similar?

This is just one of the enduring puzzles of gender. In the past three decades, the pioneering work of feminist scholars, both in traditional disciplines and in women's studies, has made us increasingly aware of how gender affects individual life experiences and how individuals collectively create gender. We know that gender is changeable, that some experiences are more strongly gendered than others, and that gender interacts with other forms of categorization, such as race, class, sexuality, and religion, to influence individual identities. Today, people are probably more conscious of gender as a social force than at any other time in history.

Three decades ago, social scientists would have listed only social class and race as the master statuses that defined and prescribed social life. When groundbreaking British sociologist Ann Oakley was a PhD student in the mid-1970s and wanted to do her doctoral research on the unpaid work women do in their homes (also known as housework), her academic supervisor argued that such a study would not be considered a legitimate part of the social sciences. Sociology was not about women's trivial preoccupations! But today, thanks to the stubbornness of Oakley and other pioneering sociologists, gender can't be dismissed as a minor add-on to the real business of sociology. Although individual experiences of gender are diverse, there are two near-universal phenomena that define gender in almost every culture we have ever known. First: *virtually every single society differentiates people on the basis of gender.* Why are women and men perceived as different in every known society? What are the differences that are perceived? Why is gender such an important way of differentiating who does what work, under what conditions, and gets what rewards (also known as the division of labour)? And, second: *virtually every known society is also based on male domination.* Why are social, political, ideological, material, and economic resources divided unequally between men and women? Why do men end up with more money, leisure time, prestige, and possessions than women do, time and time again?

It's important to note that we are talking about broad social trends here. Not every individual man has more power than every individual woman. Other social categories, such as race, class, and religion, also influence the distribution of the good things in life. Nonetheless, when looking at societies at the collective level, men, as a group, almost always hold more power and resources, on average, than do women as a group.

Of course, there are dramatic differences across societies regarding the ways in which men and women are thought to be different, the levels of gender inequality, and the amount of power (including violence) that is used to maintain systems of difference and domination. But the basic fact remains: *virtually every society known to us is founded upon assumptions of gender difference and the politics of gender inequality.*

Most of the arguments about gender difference begin, as will this book, with biology. Women and men *are* biologically different, after all. Our reproductive anatomies are different. Our brain structures differ; our brain chemistries differ. Our musculature is different. We have different levels of different hormones circulating through our different bodies. Surely, these add up to fundamental, intractable, and universal differences, and these differences provide the foundation for male domination, don't they? You can't argue with Mother Nature, can you?

In these models, biological "sex"—by which we mean the chromosomal, chemical, anatomical apparatuses that make us either male or female—leads inevitably to "gender," by which we mean the cultural and social meanings, experiences, and institutional structures that are defined as appropriate for those men and women. "Sex" is male and female; "gender" refers to cultural definitions of masculinity and femininity—the meanings of maleness or femaleness.

In the age-old question of whether nature or nurture defines our personalities, biological models of sex difference come down on the "nature" side. Our biological sex provides the raw material for our social and psychological development—all those different chromosomes hormones and body parts certainly have some effect on who we are and who we become. Of course, most sensible people recognize that both nature *and* nurture are necessary for gender development.

But biological sex varies very little from society to society, and yet experiences of gender vary enormously. And it has been the task of the social and behavioural sciences to explore the variations in gender. Biological universalism can't explain this diversity. This is the point at which the social and behavioural sciences—anthropology, history, psychology, sociology—have all had an important role to play in our understanding of gender.

What they suggest is that what it means to be a man or a woman will vary in four significant ways. First, the *meanings* of gender differences vary from one society to another. What it means to be a man or a woman differs—whether in nineteenth century Alberta, among Aboriginal peoples in the Australian outback today, in rural Norway a decade ago, or in medieval Japan. It has been the task of anthropologists to specify some of those differences, to explore the different meanings that gender has in different cultures. Some cultures, like our own, encourage men to be stoic and to prove their masculinity, and men in other cultures seem even more preoccupied with demonstrating sexual prowess than North American men seem to be. Other cultures prescribe a more relaxed definition of masculinity, based on civic participation, emotional responsiveness, and the collective provision for the community's needs. Some cultures encourage women to be decisive and competitive; others insist that women are naturally passive, helpless, and dependent.

Second, the experiences of being masculine or feminine vary within any one culture *over time*. The experience of being a man or a woman in seventeenth-century Quebec is probably very different from what it might mean there today. Dr Kimmel's own research has suggested that the meanings of manhood have changed dramatically from the founding of America in 1776 to the present (see Kimmel, 1996).

Third, gender is never simply gender, all by itself. Our experiences as gendered people are shaped by our experiences with other forms of social categorization, such as race, religion, or class. Since the 1970s, social scientists have come to realize that it is impossible to isolate gender and study it in a vacuum, detached from other forms of identity. Early sociologists who did so fell into the error of assuming that the experiences of certain gendered people with high visibility and social power—in North America, typically white middle-class Anglophones—can be generalized to all men or women.

Feminist scholars of colour have provided a strong corrective to the tendency to simply extrapolate from the experiences of the white middle class—tendencies that unfortunately have not disappeared from the social sciences. These scholars have argued that gender should be seen as "intersectional," in the words of Kimberle Crenshaw. Intersectionality means that gender is one of many ways in which people categorize and come to understand themselves and others, and that these different ways of understanding influence one another. Activists in broad-based social movements have called the same phenomenon "unbreakapartability,"[1] recognizing that all forms of inequality and oppression are connected, so that we cannot study inequalities of gender, for instance, without taking into consideration the effects of race or sexual orientation or economic class.

What does intersectionality mean for individuals? In everyday life, this means that being a young, white Canadian man (for example) is both similar to and different from being a man of colour, or an immigrant man, or an older man. All these men share an identification with masculinity, but the ways in which they "do" masculinity, and the ways in which others interact with them, may be very different. It also means that when we look at stratification or hierarchy through a gender lens, we see more than simply men and women, as two distinct groups. For instance, while men still out-earn women in Canada, when we look at average salaries for full-time, full-year work, the gender picture becomes more nuanced when we broaden our lens to include racial categories. White women, on average, out-earn men of colour, while men (and women) of different racial categories are distributed unevenly across the Canadian workforce. We are never purely or simply just men or just women.

Fourth, the meaning of masculinity and femininity will change *over the life course* as any individual person grows. Growing up and growing older brings new challenges and new opportunities for individuals to experience life as gendered beings, from early childhood through adolescence, adulthood, midlife, and the senior years. Accepting the idea that individuals face different developmental tasks as they grow and develop, psychologists have examined the ways in which the meanings of masculinity and femininity change over the course of a person's life. The issues confronting a man about proving himself and feeling successful and the social institutions in which he will attempt to enact those experiences will change, as will the meanings of femininity for prepubescent women, women in child-bearing years, and post-menopausal women, or for women entering the labour market or those retiring from it.

Finally, the meanings of gender will vary *among* different groups of women and men within any particular culture at any particular time. Simply put, not all Canadian men and women are the same. Our experiences are also structured by class, race, ethnicity, age, sexuality, and region of the country. Each of these axes modifies the others. When we focus on gender in this book, we don't assume that it is consistent in the face of all these other kinds of differences. Imagine, for example, an older, black, gay man in Montreal and a young, white, heterosexual male farmer in southern Saskatchewan. Wouldn't they have different definitions of masculinity? Or imagine a 22-year-old lesbian, Somali-Canadian in Toronto and a wealthy, white, Irish Catholic widow in Newfoundland. Wouldn't their experiences of being female be very different? One of the important elements of a sociological approach is to explore the differences *among* men and *among* women, since, as it turns out, these are often more decisive than the differences between women and men.

If gender varies across cultures, over historical time, over the life course, and among men and women within any one culture, this means we really cannot speak of masculinity or femininity as though they were constant, universal essences, common to all women and to all men. Rather, gender is an ever-changing assemblage of meanings, behaviours, opportunities, and resources. It's more appropriate, and more realistic, to think of *masculinities* and *femininities*, rather than simple *masculinity* and *femininity* as though these words meant the same thing everywhere and all the time.

At the same time, we can't forget that all masculinities and femininities are not created equal. Some expressions of masculinity and femininity are more powerful and persuasive than others. In North American society, almost everyone can point to models of idealized femininity and masculinity, standards to which individuals learn to compare themselves (and thereby find themselves wanting).

We also learn what is considered *unfeminine* or *unmasculine*. In fact, some sociologists and psychologists would argue that North Americans are less preoccupied with emulating the models of their own gender than they are with avoiding excessive resemblance to the other gender. Think of the horror with which small boys recoil from being called a "sissy." And while women may admire the androgynous style and range of gender expression available to women at the beginning of the twenty-first century, very few would actually embrace the label "mannish." Men, in particular, are often under pressure to make it clear—eternally, compulsively, decidedly—that they are not like women.

For both women and men, this is the hegemonic definition—the one that is most powerful in our society, although not without its critics and dissenters. Sociologist Erving Goffman once described this hegemonic definition of masculinity as follows:

> In an important sense there is only one complete unblushing male: a young, married, white, urban, northern, heterosexual, Protestant, father, of college education, fully employed, of good complexion, weight, and height, and a recent record in sports. . . . Any male who fails to qualify in any one of these ways is likely to view himself—during moments at least—as unworthy, incomplete, and inferior. (Goffman, 1963: 128)

Women also must contend with such an exaggerated ideal of femininity. The sociologist Raewyn Connell calls it "emphasized femininity." Emphasized femininity is organized around compliance with gender inequality and is "oriented to accommodating the interests and desires of men." One sees emphasized femininity in "the display of sociability rather than technical competence, fragility in mating scenes, compliance with men's desire for titillation and ego-stroking in office relationships, [and] acceptance of marriage and child care as a response to labour-market discrimination against women" (Connell, 1987: 183, 188, 187). Emphasized femininity exaggerates gender difference as a strategy of "adaptation to men's power" stressing empathy and nurturance; "real" womanhood is described as fascinating and women are advised that they can wrap men around their fingers by knowing and playing by the rules.

Parts I and II of this book recapitulate the nature/nurture tensions in sociological approaches to gender. Part I, on biological differences and similarities, presents some evidence of distinct and categorical biological differences, and a couple of critiques of that research from a neurobiologist and a psychologist, respectively. Cross-cultural research by anthropologists offered a way to critique the claims of biological inevitability and universality lodged in those biological arguments. It falls to sociologists and anthropologists to explore the variations among different groups of women and men, and also to specify the ways in which some versions of masculinity or femininity become hegemonic, and are thus the models against which all other versions of gender are arrayed and measured. As illustrated in Part II, sociologists today are concerned less with the fixed and limiting concept of sex roles, the term favoured in the mid-twentieth century, and more with understanding *gender relations*—the social and political dynamics that shape our conceptions of "appropriate" sex roles. Thus, sociologists are interested not only in gendered individuals, and the ways in which we each acquire our gendered identities, but also in gendered institutions. By institutions here, we mean not buildings of stone or concrete, but recurrent patterns of interactions connected through shared agendas and goals, even when these goals may not be explicit or obvious. In this way, a baby shower may be considered a social institution (and a very gendered one, at that!) and so may the United Nations, the café where you get your morning coffee, or a AAA hockey team. Some institutions are extremely gendered, by which we mean that men's and women's experiences in these institutions are very different—just think about a traditional white wedding—and that they strongly reinforce ideas about gender. Other institutions may be less gendered—think about an organic chemistry class, for instance—in that gender is not a prominent feature of the institution, although gender may be present in subtle, unexpected ways.

Sociologists thus return us to the original framing questions—the near-universality of assumptions about gender difference and the near-universality of male domination over women. They argue that male domination is reproduced not only by socializing women and men differently, but also by placing them in organizations and institutions in which specifically gendered norms and values predominate and by which both women and men are then evaluated and judged. Gendered individuals do not inhabit gender-neutral social situations, they contend; both individual and institution bear the mark of gender.

In Part III, we extend these insights on the socially constructed nature of gender to other social categories, specifically to the processes and dynamics that constitute racialization, the creation and maintenance of different racial categories.

In Parts IV and V, we begin to explore institutions and individuals. We begin in Part IV with the most basic unit of social life, the body itself, and demonstrate that bodies bear the signs of both physical sex and social gender. Through our bodies, we express some of the most intimate and important relationships in our lives, and Part V explores these gendered intimacies.

For most people, the primary social institution through which we learn gender is the family. In Part VI, we examine families as institutions that are both gendered *and* gendering, from which individuals go forth to engage with bigger, broader institutions. For most people, school provides the first encounter with the world beyond the family, and the process of learning (both the formal classroom subjects and the "hidden curriculum" of the playgrounds, halls, and cafeterias) is often deeply gendered. This gendering is explored in Part VII, where we investigate educational institutions.

After, or often during, formal education, most individuals work, whether for money in the paid workforce or without pay in the tasks of raising children and running households. Part VIII examines both the work*place* and the work*force* as institutions structured by gender.

Family, school, and work—is that all there is in a gendered life? Most people would quickly point out the pervasive, even saturating, influence of media. Thanks to new technologies, words and images of gender, carrying explicit and implicit messages, are inescapable, and Part IX, on media, explores some of these representations of gender.

In Part X, we examine the most blatant and poisonous manifestation of gender inequalities—gender violence. This type of violence is perpetrated by people who believe that some aspect of their gender (usually, but not always, some aspect of masculinity) legitimates their use of violence against others who appear to threaten their gendered world. In the future, the real measure of gender transformation will be the extent to which gender violence is eradicated so that individuals' sex no longer determines their likelihood of perpetrating or experiencing violence.

Fortunately, movements for the transformation of gender are thriving. Despite the pervasive gendering influences of all these institutions, human beings are not passive recipients of ideas about gender who create and recreate inegalitarian social structures without thinking. Part XI, on gendered social movements explores some of the ways in which people have rethought and reworked gender, with varying degrees of success and with not a little controversy.

Although this book adopts some of the conventions of thinking about gender in terms of differences between men and women, we hope that astute readers will see the profound similarities underlying the differences. As a statistician might put it, within-group variation consistently exceeds between-group variations. As someone more versed in pop culture might add, men aren't from Mars and women aren't from Venus—in the end, we are all from Earth.

Note

1. LA Crew. 2009. "Ideas in Action: An LA Story," *Left Turn* 31 (Jan/Feb): 54.

References

Connell, R.W. 1987. *Gender and Power*. Stanford, CA: Stanford University Press.

Goffman, E. 1963. *Stigma*. Englewood Cliffs, NJ: Prentice-Hall.

Gray, J. 1995. *Men Are from Mars, Women Are from Venus*. New York: Harper Collins.

Kimmel, M. 1996. *Manhood in America: A Cultural History*. New York: The Free Press.

PART I

Anatomy and Destiny

Biological Arguments about Gender Difference

Many people believe that anatomy is destiny and that the constitution of our bodies determines our social and psychological disposition. In other words, they think that biological sex decides our gendered experiences. The idea that gender is part of sex is so deep-seated that many people are not even aware that they have conflated the two in their minds.

Biological theories offer the tidiest and easiest explanations for both gender difference and gender inequality. According to this way of thinking, the observable differences between males and females derive from different anatomical organization, which makes us different as men and women, and those anatomical differences are the origin of gender inequality. Biologists rely on three different sets of evidence. Evolutionists, such as sociobiologists and evolutionary psychologists, argue that sex differences derive from the differences in our reproductive anatomies, which lead to divergences in the sorts of behaviour that lend themselves to success in reproduction, often referred to as different reproductive strategies. Females produce only one egg at a time, have a narrow window in which that egg may be fertilized, and must invest much energy and time in ensuring the survival of one baby. Thus, the theory goes, their "natural" instincts have evolved toward high sexual selectivity and monogamy, to obtain the best genetic material for fertilizing their few precious eggs, and to capture men's resources and their ability to provide food, shelter, and protection. Males, by contrast, are naturally promiscuous, since they have no shortage of sperm, nor any reproductive windows that must be utilized. They also are not burdened by the physical costs of carrying and bearing an infant. Thus, their reproductive success depends upon fertilizing as many eggs as possible without tying themselves to only one woman. Out of the many pregnancies that may result from this strategy, some are likely to survive and perpetuate the male's genes. A second source of evidence of biological difference focuses on some differences in brain function and brain chemistry. In the late nineteenth century, studies showed that men's brains were heavier, or more complex, than women's, and thus, women ought not to seek higher education or vote. (Similar studies also "proved" that the brains of white people were heavier and more complex than those of black people.) Today, such studies are largely discredited, but studies of sex differences in the brain continue. We now read about how men and women rely more on different halves of their brains, or that they use the two halves differently, or that the two halves are differently connected.

Finally, some biologists focus on the ways in which hormonal differences determine the dramatically divergent paths that males and females take from puberty onwards, when the amounts and activities of those hormones increase dramatically. Testosterone causes aggression, and since males have far more testosterone than females, male aggression—and social, political, and economic dominance—is thus explained.

To the social scientist, though, this biological "evidence" obscures as much as it reveals, telling us more about our own cultural need to find these differences than about the differences themselves. Biological explanations collapse all other sources of difference—race, ethnicity, and age—into one single dichotomous variable that exaggerates the differences between women and men, and also minimizes the similarities between them. "Believing is seeing," notes sociologist Judith Lorber in the title of her essay in this section, and a view of these differences as decisive is often used as a justification for gender inequality.

The readings in this section offer a cross-section of the main biological arguments. David M. Buss summarizes the evidence from evolutionary psychology that different reproductive strategies determine different psychological dispositions. Neurobiologist Robert Sapolsky suggests that the research on hormonal differences does not make a convincing case, while Judith Lorber challenges the assumptions of biological research, arguing that biology's inherent conservatism—justifying existing inequalities by reference to observed differences and ignoring observed similarities—is more than bad politics: it's also bad science. Fausto-Sterling presents perhaps the most audacious challenge to the idea that physical sex produces social gender; she argues that the very idea that there are two distinct and unambiguous human sexes is wrong.

Questions for Critical Thought

1. Imagine waking up tomorrow and reading in the newspaper that a team of scientists has proven conclusively, emphatically, and beyond all doubt that all gender differences are based in biology and that men and women are biologically

"programmed" to behave as they do. How might this change the way you think about your life?

2. Sapolsky argues that attributing male aggression to testosterone is a misleading oversimplification of a complex set of biological processes. Do you know of any other biological processes that have been subject to similar oversimplification?
3. Why has so much time, money, and effort been invested in trying to determine whether gender differences are attributable to biology? Why has this particular research area been so active and so controversial?
4. What do you think about Buss's argument that physical asymmetries between the sexes in reproductive capacities have produced major differences in gendered behaviour?
5. Do you believe that the differences between men and women have been exaggerated, as Lorber does? Or do you believe that these differences have not been sufficiently appreciated? Or are you not sure?
6. Fausto-Sterling imagines a utopian world in which intersexuality would be viewed not as a deviation from a rigid two-sex model but as just one of the many variations in human bodies. How might this world be different from the one in which you currently live?
7. How much faith do you put in explanations for human behaviour that rely on genes or hormones or other physiological explanations? Do you believe human beings are "hardwired" or predisposed to certain behaviours?
8. Imagine that you lived in a world in which there were no genders—in which "men" and "women" were not recognized as two distinct types of people, and instead individual differences were all that mattered. How might that world be different from the one in which you currently live?
9. How might human societies be different if we reproduced by laying eggs?
10. Think of all the physical characteristics that you possess. Which ones do you believe have been the most influential in shaping your life experiences?

Chapter 1

Overview

Why are men and women physically different? And what do these differences mean for personality and behaviour? Psychologist David Buss argues that reproductive biology is the key to understanding how men and women differ. He claims that because women undergo pregnancy, childbirth, and lactation, and men do not, over the course of thousands of generations men and women have developed different ways of being in the world.

Women face the challenge of identifying male partners who will support them and provide for them through the risky time of pregnancy and early motherhood. Because reproduction is so potentially dangerous, women cannot afford to take up with just any man because the consequences of choosing an inadequate mate are huge. By contrast, men do not face risk in reproduction. They have no incentive to select the most dependable and reliable provider as a mate; in fact, there is no downside for men in having sex with as many women as possible because they do not carry the consequences of pregnancy and birth.

Men, however, do have a challenge that women do not—paternity uncertainty. A man cannot be sure that the offspring of a particular woman are biologically his, unless he can be sure that no other man has had the opportunity to have sex with her. Buss argues that we who are alive today are the descendants of early humans who successfully resolved these challenges—women who caught and held the attention of male providers, and men who either impregnated a wide range of women or who were able to deny other men access to "their" women.

These successful strategies are preserved today as the different preferences and values expressed by men and women, which Buss illustrates with reference to psychological surveys in which women, for example, express a desire to have fewer sexual partners than men do or to find wealthy and successful mates. However, Buss does not explore the extent to which men's and women's preferences overlap, nor does he explore the tremendous range in preferences that exist within gender groups, as distinct from the difference *between* them.

Buss is a proponent of evolutionary psychology and sociobiology—bodies of thought that stress that the causes of human behaviour can be found in our biological adaptations to survival challenges in early human history. But as the articles in Chapters 2 and 3 show, relying on biology to explain social behaviour is full of pitfalls.

Psychological Sex Differences through Sexual Selection

David M. Buss

Evolutionary psychology predicts that males and females will be the same or similar in all those domains in which the sexes have faced the same or similar adaptive problems. Both sexes have sweat glands because both sexes have faced the adaptive problem of thermal regulation. Both sexes have similar (although not identical) taste preferences for fat, sugar, salt, and particular amino acids because both sexes have faced similar (although not identical) food consumption problems. Both sexes grow calluses when they experience repeated rubbing on their skin because both sexes have faced the adaptive problem of physical damage from environmental friction.

In other domains, men and women have faced substantially different adaptive problems throughout human evolutionary history. In the physical realm, for example, women have faced the problem of childbirth; men have not. Women, therefore, have evolved particular adaptations that are absent in men, such as a cervix that dilates to 10 centimetres just prior to giving birth, mechanisms for producing labour contractions, and the release of oxytocin in the bloodstream during childbirth.

Men and women have also faced different information-processing problems in some adaptive domains. Because fertilization occurs internally within the woman, for example, men have faced the adaptive problem of uncertain paternity in putative offspring. Men who failed to solve this problem risked investing resources in children who were not their own. All people descend from a long line of ancestral men whose adaptations (i.e., psychological mechanisms) led them to behave in ways that increased their likelihood of paternity and decreased the odds of investing in children who were putatively theirs but whose genetic fathers were other men. This does not imply, of course, that men were or are consciously aware of the adaptive problem of compromised paternity.

Women faced the problem of securing a reliable or replenishable supply of resources to carry them through pregnancy and lactation, especially when food resources were scarce (e.g., during droughts or harsh winters). All people are descendants of a long and unbroken line of women who successfully solved this adaptive challenge—for example, by preferring mates who showed the ability to accrue resources and the willingness to provide them for particular women. Those women who failed to solve this problem failed to survive, imperiled the survival chances of their children, and hence failed to continue their lineage.

Evolutionary psychologists predict that the sexes will differ in precisely those domains in which women and men have faced different sorts of adaptive problems. To an evolutionary psychologist, the likelihood that the sexes are psychologically identical in domains in which they have recurrently confronted different adaptive problems over the long expanse of human evolutionary history is essentially zero. The key question, therefore, is not whether men and women differ psychologically. Rather, the key questions about sex differences, from an evolutionary psychological perspective, are (1) In what domains have women and men faced different adaptive problems? (2) What are the sex-differentiated psychological mechanisms of women and men that have evolved in response to these sex-differentiated adaptive problems? and (3) Which social, cultural, and contextual inputs moderate the magnitude of expressed sex differences?

Sexual Selection Defines the Primary Domains in Which the Sexes Have Faced Different Adaptive Challenges

Although many who are not biologists equate evolution with natural selection or survival selection, Darwin (1871) sculpted what he believed to be a second theory of evolution—the theory of sexual selection. Sexual selection is the causal process of the evolution of characteristics on the basis of reproductive advantage, as opposed to survival advantage. Sexual selection occurs in two forms. First, members of one sex can successfully outcompete members of their own sex in a process of intrasexual competition. Whatever characteristics lead to success in these same-sex competitions—be they greater size, strength, cunning, or social skills—can evolve or increase in frequency by virtue of the reproductive advantage accrued by the winners through increased access to more numerous or more desirable mates.

Second, members of one sex can evolve preferences for desirable qualities in potential mates through the process of intersexual selection. If members of one sex exhibit some consensus about which qualities are desirable in the other sex, then members of the other sex who possess the desirable qualities will gain a preferential mating advantage. Hence, the desirable qualities—be they morphological features such as antlers or plumage or psychological features such as a lower threshold for risk-taking to acquire resources—can evolve by virtue of the reproductive advantage attained by those who are preferentially chosen for possessing the desirable qualities. Among humans, both causal processes—preferential mate choice and same-sex competition for access to mates—are prevalent between both sexes, and probably have been throughout human evolutionary history.

Hypotheses about Psychological Sex Differences Follow from Sexual Asymmetries in Mate Selection and Intrasexual Competition

Although a detailed analysis of psychological sex differences is well beyond the scope of this article, a few of the most obvious differences in adaptive problems include the following.

Paternity Uncertainty

Because fertilization occurs internally within women, men are always less than 100 per cent certain (again, no conscious awareness implied) that their putative children are genetically their own. Some cultures have phrases to describe this, such as "Mama's baby, papa's maybe." Women are always 100 per cent certain that the children they bear are their own.

Identifying Reproductively Valuable Women

Because women's ovulation is concealed and there is no evidence that men can detect when women ovulate, ancestral men had the difficult adaptive challenge of identifying which women were more fertile. Although ancestral women would also have faced the problem of identifying fertile men, the problem is considerably less severe both because most men remain fertile throughout their life span, whereas fertility is steeply age graded among women, and because women invest more heavily in offspring, making them the more "valuable" sex and more intensely competed for by men seeking sexual access. Thus, there is rarely a shortage of men willing to contribute the sperm necessary for fertilization, whereas from a man's perspective, there is a pervasive shortage of fertile women.

Gaining Sexual Access to Women

Because of the large asymmetry between men and women in their minimum obligatory parental investment—nine months gestation for women versus an act of sex for men—the direct reproductive benefits of gaining sexual access to a variety of mates would have been much higher for men than for women throughout human evolutionary history. Therefore, in social contexts that allowed some short-term mating or polygynous mating, men who succeeded in gaining sexual access to a variety of women—other things being equal—would have experienced greater reproductive success than men who failed to gain such access.

Identifying Men Who Are Able to Invest

Because of the tremendous burdens of a nine-month pregnancy and subsequent lactation, women who selected men who were able to invest resources in them and their offspring would have been at a tremendous advantage in survival and reproductive currencies compared to women who were indifferent to the investment capabilities of the men with whom they chose to mate.

Identifying Men Who Are Willing to Invest

Having resources is not enough. Copulating with a man who had resources but who displayed a hasty post-copulatory departure would have been detrimental to the woman, particularly if she became pregnant and faced raising a child without the aid and protection of an investing father. A man with excellent resource-accruing capacities might channel resources to another woman or pursue short-term sexual opportunities with a variety of women. A woman who had the ability to detect a man's willingness to invest in her and her children would have an adaptive advantage compared to women who were oblivious to a man's willingness or unwillingness to invest.

These are just a few of the adaptive problems that women and men have confronted differently or to differing degrees. Other examples of sex-linked adaptive problems include those of coalitional warfare, coalitional defense, hunting, gathering, combating sex-linked forms of reputational damage, embodying sex-linked prestige criteria, and attracting mates by fulfilling the differing desires of the other sex—domains that all have consequences for mating but are sufficiently wide-ranging to span a great deal of social psychology. It is in these domains that evolutionary psychologists anticipate the most pronounced sex differences—differences in solutions to sex-linked adaptive problems in the form of evolved psychological mechanisms.

Psychological Sex Differences Are Well Documented Empirically in the Domains Predicted by Theories Anchored in Sexual Selection

When Maccoby and Jacklin (1974) published their classic book on the psychology of sex differences, knowledge was spotty and methods for summarizing the literature were largely subjective and interpretive. Since that time, there has been a veritable explosion of empirical findings, along with quantitative meta-analytic procedures for evaluating them. Although new domains of sex differences continue to surface, such as the recently documented female advantage in spatial location memory, the outlines of where researchers find large, medium, small, and no sex differences are starting to emerge more clearly.

A few selected findings illustrate the heuristic power of evolutionary psychology. Cohen (1977) used the widely adopted d statistic as the index of magnitude of effect to propose a rule of thumb for evaluating effect sizes: 0.20 = "small," 0.50 = "medium," and 0.80 = "large." In *Sex, Power, Conflict: Feminist and Evolutionary Perspectives* (Buss and Malamuth, 1996), J.S. Hyde has pointed out that sex differences in the intellectual and cognitive ability domains tend to be small. Women's verbal skills tend to be slightly higher than men's ($d = -0.11$). Sex differences in math also tend to be small ($d = 0.15$). Most tests of general cognitive ability, in short, reveal small sex differences.

The primary exception to the general trend of small sex differences in the cognitive abilities domain occurs with spatial rotation. This ability is essential for successful hunting, in which the trajectory and velocity of a spear must anticipate correctly the trajectory of an animal as each moves with different speeds through space and time. For spatial rotation ability, $d = 0.73$. Other sorts of skills involved in hunting also show large magnitudes of sex differences, such as throwing velocity ($d = 2.18$), throwing distance ($d = 1.98$), and throwing accuracy ($d = 0.96$; Ashmore, 1990). Skilled hunters, as good providers, are known to be sexually attractive to women in current and traditional tribal societies.

Large sex differences appear reliably for precisely the aspects of sexuality and mating predicted by evolutionary theories of sexual strategies. Oliver and Hyde (1993), for example, documented a large sex difference in attitudes toward casual sex ($d = 0.81$). Similar sex differences have been found with other measures of men's desire for casual sex partners, a psychological solution to the problem of seeking sexual access to a variety of partners. For example, men state that they would ideally like to have more than 18 sex partners in their lifetimes, whereas women state that they would desire only 4 or 5. In another study that has been replicated twice, 75 per cent of the men but 0 per cent of the women approached by an attractive stranger of the opposite sex consented to a request for sex.

Women tend to be more exacting than men, as predicted, in their standards for a short-term mate ($d = 0.79$). Women tend to place greater value on good financial prospects in a mate—a finding confirmed in a study of 10,047 individuals residing in thirty-seven cultures located on six continents and five islands from around the world (Buss, 1989). More so than men, women especially disdain qualities in a potential mate that signal an inability to accrue resources, such as lack of ambition ($d = 1.38$) and lack of education ($d = 1.06$). Women desire physical protection abilities more than men, both in short-term mating ($d = 0.94$) and in long-term mating ($d = 0.66$).

Men and women also differ in the weighting given to cues that trigger sexual jealousy. Buss, Larsen, Westen, and Semmelroth (1992) presented men and women with the following dilemma: "What would upset or distress you more: (a) imagining your partner forming a deep emotional attachment to someone else or (b) imagining your partner enjoying passionate sexual intercourse with that other person?" (252). Men expressed greater distress about sexual than emotional infidelity, whereas women showed the opposite pattern. The difference between the sexes in which scenario was more distressing was 43 per cent ($d = 0.98$). These sex differences have been replicated by different investigators with physiological recording devices and have been replicated in other cultures.

These sex differences are precisely those predicted by evolutionary psychological theories based on sexual selection. They represent only a sampling from a larger body of supporting evidence. The sexes also differ substantially in a wide variety of other ways that are predicted by sexual selection theory, such as in thresholds for physical risk-taking, in frequency of perpetrating homicides, in thresholds for inferring sexual intent in others, in perceptions of the magnitude of upset that people experience as the victims of sexual aggression, and in the frequency of committing violent crimes of all sorts. As noted by Donald Brown (1991), "It will be irresponsible to continue shunting these [findings] aside, fraud to deny that they exist" (156). Evolutionary psychology sheds light on why these differences exist.

Conclusions

Strong sex differences occur reliably in domains closely linked with sex and mating, precisely as predicted by psychological theories based on sexual selection. Within these domains, the psychological sex differences are patterned in a manner that maps precisely onto the adaptive problems men and women have faced over human evolutionary history. Indeed, in most cases, the evolutionary hypotheses about sex differences were generated a decade or more before the empirical tests were conducted and the sex differences discovered. These models thus have heuristic and predictive power.

The evolutionary psychology perspective also offers several insights into the broader discourse on sex differences. First, neither women nor men can be considered "superior" or "inferior" to the other, any more than a bird's wings can be considered superior or inferior to a fish's fins or a kangaroo's legs. Each sex possesses mechanisms designed to deal with its own adaptive challenges—some similar and some different—and so notions of superiority or inferiority are logically incoherent from the vantage point of evolutionary psychology. The meta-theory of evolutionary psychology is descriptive, not prescriptive—it carries no values in its teeth.

Second, contrary to common misconceptions about evolutionary psychology, finding that sex differences originated through a causal process of sexual selection does not imply that the differences are unchangeable or intractable. On the contrary, understanding their origins provides a powerful heuristic to the contexts in which the sex differences are most likely to be manifested (e.g., in the context of mate competition) and hence provides a guide to effective loci for intervention if change is judged to be desirable.

Third, although some worry that inquiries into the existence and evolutionary origins of sex differences will lead to justification for the status quo, it is hard to believe that attempts to change the status quo can be very effective if they are undertaken in ignorance of sex differences that actually exist. Knowledge is power, and attempts to intervene in the absence of knowledge may resemble a surgeon operating blindfolded—there may be more bloodshed than healing.

The perspective of evolutionary psychology jettisons the outmoded dualistic thinking inherent in much current discourse by eliminating the false dichotomy between biological and social. It offers a truly interactionist position that specifies the particular features of social context that are especially critical for processing by our evolved psychological mechanisms. No other theory of sex differences has been capable of predicting and explaining the large number of precise, detailed, patterned sex differences discovered by research guided by evolutionary psychology. Evolutionary psychology possesses the heuristic power to guide investigators to the particular domains in which the most pronounced sex differences, as well as similarities, will be found. People grappling with the existence and implications of psychological sex differences cannot afford to ignore their most likely evolutionary origins through sexual selection.

References

Brown, D. 1991. *Human Universals*. Philadelphia: Temple University Press.

Buss, D.M. 1989. "Sex Differences in Human Mate Preferences: Evolutionary Hypotheses Tested in 37 Cultures," *Behavioural and Brain Sciences* 12: 1–49.

Buss, D.M., R. Larsen, D. Westen, and J. Semmelroth. 1992. "Sex Differences in Jealousy: Evolution, Physiology, and Psychology," *Psychological Science* 3: 251–5.

Cohen, J. 1977. *Statistical Power Analysis for the Behavioural Sciences*. San Diego, CA: Academic Press.

Darwin, C. 1871. *The Descent of Man and Selection in Relation to Sex*. London: Murray.

Hyde, J.S. 1996. "Where Are the Gender Differences? Where Are the Gender Similarities?," in D.M. Buss and Malamuth, eds., *Sex, Power, Conflict: Feminist and Evolutionary Perspectives*. New York: Oxford University Press.

Maccoby, E.E., and C.N. Jacklin. 1974. *The Psychology of Sex Differences*. Stanford, CA: Stanford University Press.

Oliver, M.B., and J.S. Hyde. 1993. "Gender Differences in Sexuality: A Meta-analysis," *Psychological Bulletin* 114: 29–51.

Chapter 2

Overview

Much has been made about testosterone, the "masculinity hormone," but what does it really do for men? As Robert Sapolsky points out, men like him, although less than 50 per cent of the human population, perpetrate much more than half the violence. Can male hormones be to blame?

Aggressive behaviour does seem to rise with levels of testosterone. But, says Sapolsky, the assumption that hormones drive aggression is misleading. True, some amount of testosterone appears to be necessary for aggressive behaviour in animals. However, he points out that in settings with groups of male primates, displays of aggressive dominance behaviour actually precede changes in testosterone levels—in other words, one could argue that aggression increases testosterone, that social behaviour can drives biology.

More complex studies with primates suggest that testosterone has a "permissive effect," in that injections of testosterone lead to amped-up displays of dominance by the test subject towards other males that are lower in the social hierarchy but don't lead the test subjects to challenge higher-status males. Testosterone can amplify pre-existing tendencies to violence and dominance behaviour, but it can't create the propensity for this behaviour.

Sapolsky's work is a good corrective to "biological reductionism," the tendency to ascribe all variation in human behaviour to genes, hormones, or physiology. As he points out, social interactions create biological outcomes as much as biology creates social behaviour. Violence, in this case, cannot be written off as simply "in the genes" or the result of too much testosterone. We are social animals, not just biological ones.

Testosterone Rules

Robert M. Sapolsky

Face it, we all do it—we all believe in stereotypes about minorities. These stereotypes are typically pejorative and false, but every now and then they have a core of truth. I know, because I belong to a minority that lives up to its reputation. I have a genetic abnormality generally considered to be associated with high rates of certain socially abhorrent behaviours: I am male. Thanks to an array of genes that produce some hormone-synthesizing enzymes, my testes churn out a corrosive chemical and dump the stuff into my bloodstream, and this probably has behavioural consequences. We males account for less than 50 per cent of the population, yet we generate a huge proportion of the violence. Whether it is something as primal as having an axe fight in a rain forest clearing or as detached as using computer-guided aircraft to strafe a village, something as condemned as assaulting a cripple or as glorified as killing someone wearing the wrong uniform, if it is violent, we males excel at it.

Why should this be? We all think we know the answer: something to do with those genes being expressed down in the testes. A dozen millennia ago or so, an adventurous soul managed to lop off a surly bull's testicles, thus inventing behavioural endocrinology. It is unclear from the historical records whether the experiment resulted in grants and tenure, but it certainly generated an influential finding: that the testes do something or other to make males aggressive pains in the ass.

That something or other is synthesizing the infamous corrosive chemical, testosterone (or rather, a family of related androgen hormones that I'll call testosterone for the sake of simplicity, hoping the androgen specialists won't take it the wrong way). Testosterone bulks up muscle cells—including those in the larynx, giving rise to operatic basses. It makes hair sprout here and there, undermines the health of blood vessels, alters biochemical events in the liver too dizzying to contemplate, and has a profound impact, no doubt, on the workings of cells in big toes. And it seeps into the brain, where it influences behaviour in a way highly relevant to understanding aggression.

Genes are the hand behind the scene, directing testosterone's actions. They specify whether steroidal building blocks are turned into testosterone or estrogen, how much of each, and how quickly. They regulate how fast the liver breaks down circulating testosterone, thereby determining how long an androgenic signal remains in the bloodstream. They direct the synthesis of testosterone receptors—specialized proteins that catch hold of testosterone and allow it to have its characteristic effects on target cells. And genes specify how many such receptors the body has, and how sensitive they are. Insofar as testosterone alters brain function and produces aggression, and genes regulate how much testosterone is made and how effectively it works, this should be the archetypal case for studying how genes can control our behaviour. Instead, however, it's the archetypal case for learning how little genes actually do so.

Some pretty obvious evidence links testosterone with aggression. Males tend to have higher testosterone levels in their circulation than do females, and to be more aggressive. Times of life when males are swimming in testosterone—for example, after reaching puberty—correspond to when aggression peaks. Among many species, testes are mothballed most of the year, kicking into action and pouring out testosterone only during a very circumscribed mating season—precisely the time when male–male aggression soars.

Impressive though they seem, these data are only correlative—testosterone found on the scene, repeatedly, with no alibi when some aggression has occurred. The proof comes with the knife, the performance of what is euphemistically known as a subtraction experiment. Remove the source of testosterone in species after species, and levels of aggression typically plummet. Reinstate normal testosterone levels afterward with injections of synthetic testosterone, and aggression returns.

The subtraction and replacement paradigm represents pretty damning proof that this hormone, with its synthesis and efficacy under genetic control, is involved in aggression. "Normal testosterone levels appear to be a prerequisite for normative levels of aggressive behaviour" is the sort of catchy, hum-able phrase the textbooks would use. That probably explains why you shouldn't mess with a bull moose during rutting season. But it's not why a lot of people want to understand this sliver of science. Does the action of testosterone tell us anything about individual differences in levels of aggression, anything about why some males—some human males—are exceptionally violent? Among an array of males, are the highest testosterone levels found in the most aggressive individuals?

Generate some extreme differences and that is precisely what you see. Castrate some of the well-paid study subjects, inject others with enough testosterone to quadruple the normal human levels, and the high-testosterone males are overwhelmingly likely to be the more aggressive ones. Obviously, extreme conditions don't tell us much about the real world, but studies of the normative variability in testosterone—in other words, seeing what everyone's natural levels are like without manipulating anything—also suggest that high levels of testosterone and high levels of aggression tend to go together. This would seem to seal the case that interindividual differences in levels of aggression among normal individuals are probably driven by differences in levels of testosterone. But that conclusion turns out to be wrong.

Here's why. Suppose you note a correlation between levels of aggression and levels of testosterone among normal males. It could be because (a) testosterone elevates aggression; (b) aggression elevates testosterone secretion; or (c) neither causes the other. There's a huge bias to assume option a, while b is the answer. Study after study has shown that if you examine testosterone levels when males are first placed together in the social group, testosterone levels predict nothing about who is going to be aggressive. The subsequent behavioural differences drive the hormonal changes, rather than the other way around.

Because of a strong bias among certain scientists, it has taken forever to convince them of this point. Suppose you're studying what behaviour and hormones have to do with each other. How do you study the behavioural part? You get yourself a notebook, a stopwatch, and a pair of binoculars. How do you measure the hormones and analyze the genes that regulate them? You need some gazillion-dollar machines; you muck around with radiation and chemicals, wear a lab coat, and maybe even goggles—the whole nine yards. Which toys would you rather get for Christmas? Which facet of science are you going to believe in more? The higher the technology, the more scientific the discipline. Hormones seem to many to be more substantive than behaviour, so when a correlation occurs, it must be because hormones regulate behaviour, not the other way around.

This is a classic case of what is often called physics envy, a disease that causes behavioural biologists to fear their discipline lacks the rigour of physiology, physiologists to wish for the techniques of biochemists, biochemists to covet the clarity of the answers revealed by molecular geneticists, all the way down until you get to the physicists who confer only with God. Recently, a zoologist friend had obtained blood samples from the carnivores he studies and wanted some hormones in the samples tested in my lab. Although inexperienced with the technique, he offered to help in any way possible. I felt hesitant asking him to do anything tedious, but since he had offered, I tentatively said, "Well, if you don't mind some unspeakable drudgery, you could number about a thousand assay vials." And this scientist, whose superb work has graced the most prestigious science journals in the world, cheerfully answered, "That's okay. How often do I get to do real science, working with test tubes?"

Difficult though scientists with physics envy find it to believe, interindividual differences in testosterone levels don't predict subsequent differences in aggressive behaviour among individuals. Similarly, fluctuations in testosterone levels within one individual over time don't predict subsequent changes in the levels of aggression in that one individual—get a hiccup in testosterone secretion one afternoon and that's not when the guy goes postal.

Look at our confusing state: normal levels of testosterone are a prerequisite for normal levels of aggression. Yet if one male's genetic makeup predisposes him to higher levels of testosterone than the next guy, he isn't necessarily going to be more aggressive. Like clockwork, that statement makes the students suddenly start coming to office hours in a panic, asking whether they missed something in their lecture notes.

Yes, it's going to be on the final, and it's one of the more subtle points in endocrinology—what's referred to as a hormone having a "permissive effect." Remove someone's testes and, as noted, the frequency of aggressive behaviour is likely to plummet. Reinstate pre-castration levels of testosterone by injecting the hormone, and pre-castration levels of aggression typically return. Fair enough. Now, this time, castrate an individual and restore testosterone levels to only 20 per cent of normal. Amazingly, normal pre-castration levels of aggression come back. Castrate and now introduce twice the testosterone levels from before castration, and the same level of aggressive behaviour returns. You need some testosterone around for normal aggressive behaviour. Zero levels after castration, and down it usually goes; quadruple levels (the sort of range generated in weight lifters abusing anabolic steroids), and aggression typically increases. But anywhere from roughly 20 per cent of normal to twice normal and it's all the same. The brain can't distinguish among this wide range of basically normal values.

If you knew a great deal about the genetic makeup of a bunch of males, enough to understand how much testosterone they secreted into their bloodstream, you still couldn't predict levels of aggression among those individuals. Nevertheless, the subtraction and reinstatement data seem to indicate that, in a broad sort of way, testosterone causes aggressive behaviour. But that turns out not to be true either, and the implications of this are lost on most people the first 30 times they hear about it. Those implications are important, however—so important that it's worth saying 31 times.

Round up some male monkeys. Put them in a group together and give them plenty of time to sort out where they stand with each other—grudges, affiliative friendships. Give them enough time to form a dominance hierarchy, the sort of linear ranking in which number 3, for example, can pass his day throwing around his weight with numbers 4 and 5, ripping off their monkey chow, forcing them to relinquish the best spots to sit in, but numbers 1 and 2 still expect and receive from him the most obsequious brown-nosing.

Hierarchy in place, it's time to do your experiment. Take that third-ranking monkey and give him some testosterone. None of this within-the-normal-range stuff. Inject a ton of it, way higher than what you normally see in rhesus monkeys, give him enough testosterone to grow antlers and a beard on every neuron in his brain. And, no surprise, when you check the behavioural data, he will probably be participating in more aggressive interactions than before.

So even though small fluctuations in the levels of the hormone don't seem to matter much, testosterone still causes aggression, right? Wrong. Check out number 3 more closely. Is he raining aggressive terror on everyone in the group, frothing with indiscriminate violence? Not at all. He's still judiciously kowtowing to numbers 1 and 2 but has become a total bastard to numbers 4 and 5. Testosterone isn't causing aggression, it's exaggerating the aggression that's already there.

Another example, just to show we're serious. There's a part of your brain that probably has lots to do with aggression, a region called the amygdala. Sitting near it is the Grand Central Station of emotion-related activity in your brain, the hypothalamus. The amygdala communicates with the hypothalamus by way of a cable of neuronal connections called the stria terminalis. (No more jargon, I promise.) The amygdala influences aggression via that pathway, sending bursts of electrical excitation that ripple down the stria terminalis to the hypothalamus and put it in a pissy mood.

Once again, do your hormonal intervention: flood the area with testosterone. You can inject the hormone into the bloodstream, where it eventually makes its way to the amygdala. You can surgically microinject the stuff directly into the area. In a few years, you may even be able to construct animals with extra copies of the genes that direct testosterone synthesis, producing extra hormone that way. Six of one, half a dozen of the other. The key thing is what doesn't happen next. Does testosterone make waves of electrical excitation surge down the stria terminalis? Does it turn on that pathway? Not at all. If, and only if, the amygdala is already sending an excited volley down the stria terminalis, testosterone increases the rate of such activity by shortening the resting time between bouts. It's not turning on the pathway, it's increasing the volume of signalling if it is already turned on. It's not causing aggression, it's exaggerating the pre-existing pattern of it, exaggerating the response to environmental triggers of aggression.

In every generation, it is the duty of behavioural biologists to try to teach this critical point, one that seems a maddening cliché once you get it. You take that hoary old dichotomy between nature and nurture, between intrinsic factors and extrinsic ones, between genes and environment, and regardless of which behaviour and underlying biology you're studying, the dichotomy is a sham. No genes. No environment. Just the interaction between the two.

Do you want to know how important environment and experience are in understanding testosterone and aggression? Look back at how the effects of castration are discussed earlier. There were statements like "Remove the source of testosterone in species after species and levels of aggression typically plummet." Not "Remove the source . . . and aggression always goes to zero." On the average it declines, but rarely to zero, and not at all in some individuals. And the more social experience an individual had, being aggressive prior to castration, the more likely that behaviour persists "sans cojones." In the right context, social conditioning can more than make up for the complete absence of the hormone.

A case in point: the spotted hyena. These animals are fast becoming the darlings of endocrinologists, sociobiologists, gynecologists, and tabloid writers, because of their wild sex reversal system. Females are more muscular and more aggressive than males, and are socially dominant to them; rare traits in the mammalian world. And get this: females secrete more of certain testosterone-related hormones than the males do, producing muscles, aggression, and masculinized private parts that make it supremely difficult to tell the sex of a hyena. So high androgen levels would seem, again, to cause aggression and social dominance. But that's not the whole answer.

High in the hills above the University of California at Berkeley is the world's largest colony of spotted hyenas, massive bone-crunching beasts who fight each other for the chance to have their ears scratched by Laurence Frank, the zoologist who brought them over as infants from Kenya.

Various scientists are studying their sex reversal system. The female hyenas are bigger and more muscular than the males and have the same weirdo genitals and elevated androgen levels as their female cousins back in the savanna. Everything is just as it is in the wild—except the social system. As those hyenas grew up, there was a very significant delay in the time it took for the females to begin socially dominating the males, even though the females were stoked on androgens. They had to grow up without the established social system to learn from.

When people first realize that genes have a great deal to do with behaviour—even subtle, complex, human behaviour—they are often struck with an initial evangelical enthusiasm, placing a convert's faith in the genetic components of the story. This enthusiasm is typically reductive—because of physics envy, because reductionism is so impressive, because it would be so nice if there were a single gene (or hormone or neurotransmitter or part of the brain) responsible for everything. But even if you completely understood how genes regulate all the important physical factors involved in aggression—testosterone synthesis and secretion, the brain's testosterone receptors, the amygdala neurons and their levels of transmitters, the favourite colour of the hypothalamus—you still wouldn't be able to predict levels of aggression accurately in a group of normal individuals.

This is no mere academic subject. We are a fine species with some potential, yet we are racked by sickening amounts of violence. Unless we are hermits, we feel the threat of it, often every day, and should our leaders push the button, we will all be lost in a final global violence. But as we try to understand this feature of our sociality, it is critical to remember the limits of the biology. Knowing the genome, the complete DNA sequence, of some suburban teenager is never going to tell us why that kid, in his after-school chess club, has developed a particularly aggressive style with his bishops. And it certainly isn't going to tell us much about the teenager in some inner city hellhole who has taken to mugging people. "Testosterone equals aggression" is inadequate for those who would offer a simple biological solution to the violent male. And "testosterone equals aggression" is certainly inadequate for those who would offer the simple excuse that boys will be boys. Violence is more complex than a single hormone, and it is supremely rare that any of our behaviours can be reduced to genetic destiny. This is science for the bleeding-heart liberal: the genetics of behaviour is usually meaningless outside the context of the social factors and environment in which it occurs.

Chapter 3

Overview

Most non-scientists (and many scientists themselves) cling fondly to the belief that science is objective and that scientists observe, record, and analyze data without any personal biases. Judith Lorber argues that in fact scientists often "discover" evidence that confirms their pre-existing beliefs about the world and that nowhere is this more true than in the biology of sex differences.

In medieval and Renaissance Europe, philosophers believed that men and women were physically identical—women's reproductive organs were simply men's turned inside out.

In the twentieth and twenty-first centuries, the pendulum has swung the opposite way, to the presumption that men and women are completely different in every conceivable way. Research and popular culture exaggerate these supposed "sex differences" and ignore the overlap between the categories of "male" and "female" people. Social institutions go to great lengths to reinforce the idea that there are two distinct and exclusive sex categories, as shown by the emphasis on "sex tests" at the Olympics for athletes whose bodies appear to violate the presumption that there are only two categories of humans.

Along with this insistence that men and women are completely physically different is the often unstated presumption that men's bodies are the standard against which women's bodies should be judged and that women are intrinsically weaker, smaller, needier, and less competent. Just look at measurements of physical fitness, where the activities chosen to exemplify "fitness" tend to be those that stress areas in which men have some physiological advantage, such as upper body strength. The characteristics that are most highly valued in a society tend to be the ones associated with men, such that women are left playing catch-up in many areas, trying to show that they are just as good or almost as good as men. Perhaps this is why we see so much media hype about the so-called First Woman phenomenon—the first woman astronaut, the first woman head of a Top Five bank, the first woman Nobel physicist—and almost nothing about First Men.

Believing Is Seeing: Biology as Ideology

Judith Lorber

Until the eighteenth century, Western philosophers and scientists thought that there was one sex and that women's internal genitalia were the inverse of men's external genitalia: the womb and vagina were the penis and scrotum turned inside out (Laqueur, 1990). Current Western thinking sees women and men as so different physically as to sometimes seem to be two species. The bodies, which have been mapped inside and out for hundreds of years, have not changed. What have changed are the justifications for gender inequality. When the social position of all human beings was believed to be set by natural law or was considered God-given, biology was irrelevant; women and men of different classes all had their assigned places. When scientists began to question the divine basis of social order and replaced faith with empirical knowledge, what they saw was that women were very different from men in that they had wombs and menstruated. Such anatomical differences destined them for an entirely different social life from men.

In actuality, the basic bodily material is the same for females and males, and except for procreative hormones and organs, female and male human beings have similar bodies (Naftolin and Butz, 1981). Furthermore, as has been known since the middle of the nineteenth century, male and female genitalia develop from the same fetal tissue, and so infants can be born with ambiguous genitalia (Money and Ehrhardt, 1972). When they are, biology is used quite arbitrarily in sex assignment. Suzanne Kessler (1990) interviewed six medical specialists in pediatric intersexuality and found that whether an infant with XY chromosomes and anomalous genitalia was categorized as a boy or a girl depended on the size of the penis—if a penis was very small, the child was categorized as a girl, and sex-change surgery was used to make an artificial vagina. In the late nineteenth century, the presence or absence of ovaries was the determining criterion of gender assignment for hermaphrodites because a woman who could not procreate was not a complete woman (Kessler, 1990: 20).

Yet in Western societies, we see two discrete sexes and two distinguishable genders because our society is built on two *classes* of people, "women" and "men." Once the gender category is given, the attributes of the person are also gendered: Whatever a "woman" is must be "female"; whatever a "man" is must be "male." Analyzing the social processes that construct the categories we call "female and male," "women and men," and "homosexual and heterosexual" uncovers the ideology and power differentials congealed in these categories (Foucault, 1978). This article will use two familiar areas of social life—sports and technological competence—to show how myriad physiological differences are transformed into similar-appearing, gendered social bodies. My perspective goes beyond accepted feminist views that gender is a cultural overlay that modifies physiological sex differences. That perspective assumes either that there are two fairly similar sexes distorted by social practices into two genders with purposefully different characteristics or that there are two sexes whose essential differences are rendered unequal by social practices. I am arguing that bodies differ in many ways physiologically, but they are completely transformed by social practices to fit into the salient categories of a society, the most pervasive of which are "female" and "male" and "women" and "men."

Neither sex nor gender are pure categories. Combinations of incongruous genes, genitalia, and hormonal input are ignored in sex categorization, just as combinations of incongruous physiology, identity, sexuality, appearance, and behaviour are ignored in the social construction of gender statuses. Menstruation, lactation, and gestation do not demarcate women from men. Only some women are pregnant and then only some of the time; some women do not have a uterus or ovaries. Some women have stopped menstruating temporarily, others have reached menopause, and some have had hysterectomies. Some women breast-feed some of the time, but some men lactate (Jaggar, 1983: 165 fn). Menstruation, lactation, and gestation are individual experiences of womanhood (Levesque-Lopman, 1988), but not determinants of the social category "woman," or even "female." Similarly, "men are not always sperm-producers, and in fact, not all sperm producers are men. A male-to-female transsexual, prior to surgery, can be socially a woman, though still potentially (or actually) capable of spermatogenesis" (Kessler and McKenna, [1978] 1985: 2).

When gender assignment is contested in sports, where the categories of competitors are rigidly divided into women and men, chromosomes are now used to determine in which category the athlete is to compete. However, an anomaly common enough to be found in several women at every major international sports competition are XY chromosomes that have not produced male anatomy or physiology because of a genetic defect. Because these women are women in every way significant to the sports competition, the prestigious International Amateur Athletic Federation has urged that sex be determined by simple genital inspection (Kolata, 1992). Transsexuals would pass this test, but it took a lawsuit for Renée Richards, a male-to-female transsexual, to be able to play tournament tennis as a woman, despite his male sex chromosomes (Richards, 1983). Oddly, neither basis for gender categorization—chromosomes nor genitalia—has anything to do with sports prowess (Birrell and Cole, 1990).

In the Olympics, in cases of chromosomal ambiguity, women must undergo "a battery of gynecological and physical exams to see if she is 'female enough' to compete. Men are not tested" (Carlson, 1991: 26). The purpose is not to categorize women and men accurately, but to make sure men don't enter women's competitions, where, it is felt, they will have the advantage of size and strength. This practice sounds fair only because it is assumed that all men are similar in size and strength and different from all women. Yet, in Olympic boxing and wrestling matches, men are matched within weight classes. Some women might, similarly, successfully compete with some men in many sports. Women did not run in marathons until about 20 years ago. In 20 years of marathon competition, women have reduced their finish times by more than 90 minutes; they might catch up with men's running times in races of other lengths within the next 50 years because they are increasing their fastest speeds more rapidly than are men (Fausto-Sterling, 1985: 213–18).

The reliance on only two sex and gender categories in the biological and social sciences is as epistemologically spurious as the reliance on chromosomal or genital tests to group athletes. Most research designs do not investigate whether physical skills or physical abilities are really more or less common in women and men (Epstein, 1988). They start out with two social categories ("women," "men"), assume they are biologically different ("female," "male"), look for similarities among them and differences between them, and attribute what they have found for the social categories to sex differences (Gelman, Collman, and Maccoby, 1986).

These designs rarely question the categorization of their subjects into two and only two groups, even though they often find more significant within-group differences than between-group differences (Hyde, 1990). The social construction perspective on sex and gender suggests that instead of starting with the two presumed dichotomies in each category—female, male; woman, man—it might be more useful in gender studies to group patterns of behaviour and only then look for identifying markers of the people likely to enact such behaviours.

What Sports Illustrate

Competitive sports have become, for boys and men, as players and as spectators, a way of constructing a masculine identity, a legitimated outlet for violence and aggression, and an avenue for upward mobility (Dunning, 1986; Kemper, 1990, 167–206; Messner, 1992). For men in Western societies, physical competence is an important marker of masculinity (Fine, 1987; Majors, 1990; Glassner, 1992). In professional and collegiate sports, physiological differences are invoked to justify women's secondary status, despite the clear evidence that gender status overrides physiological capabilities. Assumptions about women's physiology have influenced rules of competition; subsequent sports performances then validate how women and men are treated in sports competitions.

Gymnastic equipment is geared to slim, wiry, prepubescent girls and not to mature women; conversely, men's gymnastic equipment is tailored for muscular, mature men, not slim, wiry, prepubescent boys. Boys could compete with girls, but are not allowed to; women gymnasts are left out entirely. Girl gymnasts are just that—little girls who will be disqualified as soon as they grow up (Vecsey, 1990). Men gymnasts have men's status. In women's basketball, the size of the ball and rules for handling the ball change the style of play to "a slower, less intense, and less exciting modification of the 'regular' or men's game" (Watson, 1987: 441). In the 1992 Winter Olympics, men figure skaters were required to complete three triple jumps in their required program; women figure skaters were forbidden to do more than one. These rules penalized artistic men skaters and athletic women skaters (Janofsky, 1992). For the most part, Western sports are built on physically trained men's bodies:

> Speed, size, and strength seem to be the essence of sports. Women *are* naturally inferior at "sports" so conceived.
>
> But if women had been the historically dominant sex, our concept of sport would no doubt have evolved differently. Competitions emphasizing flexibility, balance, strength, timing, and small size might dominate Sunday afternoon television and offer salaries in six figures. (English, 1982: 266, emphasis in original)

Organized sports are big businesses and, thus, who has access and at what level is a distributive or equity issue. The overall status of women and men athletes is an economic, political, and ideological issue that has less to do with individual physiological capabilities than with their cultural and social meaning and who defines and profits from them (Slatton and Birrell, 1984; Messner and Sabo, 1990). Twenty years after the passage of Title IX of the US Civil Rights Act, which forbade gender inequality in any school receiving federal funds, the goal for collegiate sports in the next five years is 60 per cent men, 40 per cent women in sports participation, scholarships, and funding (Moran, 1992).

How access and distribution of rewards (prestigious and financial) are justified is an ideological, even moral, issue (Hargreaves, 1982; Birrell, 1988: 473–6). One way is that men athletes are glorified and women athletes ignored in the mass media. Messner and his colleagues found that in 1989, in TV sports news in the United States, men's sports got 92 per cent of the coverage and women's sports 5 per cent, with the rest mixed or gender-neutral (Messner, Duncan, and Jensen, 1993). In 1990, in four of the top-selling newspapers in the United States, stories on men's sports outnumbered those on women's sports 23-to-1. Messner and his colleagues also found an implicit hierarchy in naming, with women athletes most likely to be called by first names, followed by black men athletes, and only white men athletes routinely referred to by their last names. Similarly, women's collegiate sports teams are named or marked in ways that symbolically feminize and trivialize them—the men's team is called Tigers, the women's Kittens (Eitzen and Baca Zinn, 1989).

Assumptions about men's and women's bodies and their capacities are crafted in ways that make unequal access and distribution of rewards acceptable (Hudson, 1978; Messner, 1988). Media images of modern men athletes glorify their strength and power, even their violence (Hargreaves, 1986). Media images of modern women athletes tend to focus on feminine beauty and grace (so they are not really athletes) or on their thin, small, wiry, androgenous bodies (so they are not really women). In coverage of the Olympics,

> loving and detailed attention is paid to pixie-like gymnasts; special and extended coverage is given to graceful and dazzling figure skaters; the camera painstakingly records the fluid movements of swimmers and divers. And then, in a blinding flash of fragmented images, viewers see a few minutes of volleyball, basketball, speed skating, track and field, and alpine skiing, as television gives its nod to the mere existence of these events. (Boutilier and SanGiovanni, 1983: 190)

Extraordinary feats by women athletes who were presented as mature adults might force sports organizers and audiences to rethink their stereotypes of women's capabilities, the way elves, mermaids, and ice queens do not. Sports, therefore, construct men's bodies to be powerful and women's bodies to be sexual. As Connell (1987: 85) says,

> The meanings in the bodily sense of masculinity concern, above all else, the superiority of men to women, and the exaltation of hegemonic masculinity over other groups of men which is essential for the domination of women.

In the late 1970s, as women entered more and more athletic competitions, supposedly good scientific studies showed that women who exercised intensely would cease menstruating because they would not have enough body fat to sustain ovulation (Brozan, 1978). When one set of researchers did a year-long study that compared 66 women—21 who were training for a marathon, 22 who ran more than an hour a week, and 23 who did less than an hour of aerobic exercise a week—they discovered that only 20 per cent of the women in any of these groups had "normal" menstrual cycles every month (Prior et al., 1990). The dangers of intensive training for women's fertility therefore were exaggerated as women began to compete successfully in arenas formerly closed to them.

Given the association of sports with masculinity in the United States, women athletes have to manage a contradictory status. One study of women college basketball players found that although they "did athlete" on the court, "pushing, shoving, fouling, hard running, fast breaks, defense, obscenities and sweat" (Watson, 1987: 441), they "did woman" off the court, using the locker room as their staging area:

> While it typically took fifteen minutes to prepare for the game, it took approximately fifteen minutes after the game to shower and remove the sweat of an athlete, and it took another thirty minutes to dress, apply make-up and style hair. It did not seem to matter whether the players were going out into the public or

> getting on a van for a long ride home. Average dressing time and rituals did not change. (Watson, 1987: 443)

Another way women manage these status dilemmas is to redefine the activity or its result as feminine or womanly (Mangan and Park, 1987). Thus women bodybuilders claim "flex appeal is sex appeal" (Duff and Hong, 1984: 378).

Such a redefinition of women's physicality affirms the ideological subtext of sports that physical strength is men's prerogative and justifies men's physical and sexual domination of women (Willis, 1982; Hargreaves, 1986; Theberge, 1987; Olson, 1990; Messner, 1992). When women demonstrate physical strength, they are labelled unfeminine:

> It's threatening to one's takeability, one's rapeability, one's femininity, to be strong and physically self-possessed. To be able to resist rape, not to communicate rapeability with one's body, to hold one's body for uses and meanings other than that can transform what *being a woman means*. (MacKinnon, 1987: 122, emphasis in original)

Resistance to that transformation, ironically, was evident in the policies of American women physical education professionals throughout most of the twentieth century. They minimized exertion, maximized a feminine appearance and manner, and left organized sports competition to men (Mangan and Park, 1987; Birrell, 1988).

Dirty Little Secrets

As sports construct gendered bodies, technology constructs gendered skills. Meta-analyses of studies of gender differences in spatial and mathematical ability have found that men have a large advantage in ability to mentally rotate an image, a moderate advantage in a visual perception of horizontality and verticality and in mathematical performance, and a small advantage in ability to pick a figure out of a field (Hyde, 1990). It could be argued that these advantages explain why, within the short space of time that computers have become ubiquitous in offices, schools, and homes, work on them and with them has become gendered: men create, program, and market computers, make war and produce science and art with them; women microwire them in computer factories and enter data in computerized offices; boys play games, socialize, and commit crimes with computers; girls are rarely seen in computer clubs, camps, and classrooms. But women were hired as computer programmers in the 1940s because

> the work seemed to resemble simple clerical tasks. In fact, however, programming demanded complex skills in abstract logic, mathematics, electrical circuitry, and machinery, all of which . . . women used to perform in their work. Once programming was recognized as "intellectually demanding," it became attractive to men. (Donato, 1990: 170)

A woman mathematician and pioneer in data processing, Grace M. Hopper, was famous for her work on programming language (Perry and Greber, 1990: 86). By the 1960s, programming was split into more and less skilled specialties, and the entry of women into the computer field in the 1970s and 1980s was confined to the lower-paid specialties. At each stage, employers invoked women's and men's purportedly natural capabilities for the jobs for which they were hired (Zimmerman, 1983; Cockburn, 1983, 1985; Hartmann, Kraut, and Tilly, 1986; Hartmann, 1987; Wright et al., 1987; Donato, 1990; Kramer and Lehman, 1990).

It is the taken-for-grantedness of such everyday gendered behaviour that gives credence to the belief that the widespread differences in what women and men do must come from biology. To take one ordinarily unremarked scenario: In modern societies, if a man and woman who are a couple are in a car together, he is much more likely to take the wheel than she is, even if she is the more competent driver. Molly Haskell calls this taken-for-granted phenomenon "the dirty little secret of marriage: the husband-lousy-driver syndrome" (1989: 26). Men drive cars whether they are good drivers or not because men and machines are a "natural" combination (Scharff, 1991).

But the ability to drive gives one mobility; it is a form of social power.

In the early days of the automobile, feminists co-opted the symbolism of mobility as emancipation: "Donning goggles and dusters, wielding tire irons and tool kits, taking the wheel, they announced their intention to move beyond the bounds of women's place" (Scharff, 1991: 68). Driving enabled them to campaign for women's suffrage in parts of the United States not served by public transportation, and they effectively used motorcades and speaking from cars as campaign tactics (Scharff, 1991). Sandra Gilbert also notes that during the First World War, women's ability to drive was physically, mentally, and even sensually liberating:

> For nurses and ambulance drivers, women doctors and women messengers, the phenomenon of modern battle was very different from that experienced by entrenched combatants. Finally given a chance to take the wheel, these post-Victorian girls raced motorcars along foreign roads like adventurers exploring new lands, while their brothers dug deeper into the mud of France. . . . Retrieving the wounded and the dead from deadly positions, these once-decorous daughters had at last been allowed to prove their valor, and they swooped over the wastelands of the war with the energetic love of Wagnerian Valkyries, their mobility alone transporting countless immobilized heroes to safe havens. (1983: 438–9)

Not incidentally, women in the United States and England got the vote for their war efforts in the First World War.

Social Bodies and the Bathroom Problem

People of the same racial ethnic group and social class are roughly the same size and shape—but there are many varieties of bodies. People have different genitalia, different secondary sex characteristics, different contributions to procreation, different orgasmic experiences, different patterns of illness and aging. Each of us experiences our bodies differently, and these experiences change as we grow, age, sicken, and die. The bodies of pregnant and non-pregnant women, short and tall people, those with intact and functioning limbs and those whose bodies are physically challenged are all different. But the salient categories of a society group these attributes in ways that ride roughshod over individual experiences and more meaningful clusters of people.

I am not saying that physical differences between male and female bodies don't exist, but that these differences are socially meaningless until social practices transform them into social facts. West Point Military Academy's curriculum is designed to produce leaders, and physical competence is used as a significant measure of leadership ability (Yoder, 1989). When women were accepted as West Point cadets, it became clear that the tests of physical competence, such as rapidly scaling an eight-foot wall, had been constructed for male physiques—pulling oneself up and over using upper-body strength. Rather than devise tests of physical competence for women, West Point provided boosters that mostly women used—but that lost them test points—in the case of the wall, a platform. Finally, the women themselves figured out how to use their bodies successfully. Janice Yoder describes this situation:

> I was observing this obstacle one day, when a woman approached the wall in the old prescribed way, got her fingertips grip, and did an unusual thing: she walked her dangling legs up the wall until she was in a position where both her hands and feet were atop the wall. She then simply pulled up her sagging bottom and went over. She solved the problem by capitalizing on one of women's physical assets: lower-body strength. (1989: 530)

In short, if West Point is going to measure leadership capability by physical strength, women's pelvises will do just as well as men's shoulders.

The social transformation of female and male physiology into a condition of inequality is well illustrated by the bathroom problem. Most buildings that have gender-segregated bathrooms have an equal number for women and for men. Where there are crowds, there are always long lines in front of women's bathrooms but rarely in front of men's bathrooms. The cultural, physiological, and demographic combinations of clothing, frequency of urination, menstruation, and childcare add up to generally greater bathroom use by women than men. Thus, although an equal number of bathrooms seems fair, equity would mean more women's bathrooms or allowing women to use men's bathrooms for a certain amount of time (Molotch, 1988).

The bathroom problem is the outcome of the way gendered bodies are differentially evaluated in Western cultures: men's social bodies are the measure of what is "human." Gray's *Anatomy*, in use for 100 years, well into the twentieth century, presented the human body as male. The female body was shown only where it differed from the male (Laqueur, 1990). Denise Riley says that if we envisage women's bodies, men's bodies, and human bodies "as a triangle of identifications, then it is rarely an equilateral triangle in which both sexes are pitched at matching distances from the apex of the human" (1988: 197). Catharine MacKinnon also contends that in Western society, universal "humanness" is male because

> virtually every quality that distinguishes men from women is already affirmatively compensated in this society. Men's physiology defines most sports, their needs define auto and health insurance coverage, their socially defined biographies define workplace expectations and successful career patterns, their perspectives and concerns define quality in scholarship, their experiences and obsessions define merit, their objectification of life defines art, their military service defines citizenship, their presence defines family, their inability to get along with each other—their wars and rulerships—define history, their image defines god, and their genitals define sex. For each of their differences from women, what amounts to an affirmative action plan is in effect, otherwise known as the structure and values of American society. (1987: 36)

The Paradox of Human Nature

Gendered people do not emerge from physiology or hormones but from the exigencies of the social order, mostly, from the need for a reliable division of the work of food production and the social (not physical) reproduction of new members. The moral imperatives of religion and cultural representations reinforce the boundary lines among genders and ensure that what is demanded, what is permitted, and what is tabooed for the people in each gender is well known and followed by most. Political power, control of scarce resources, and, if necessary, violence uphold the gendered social order in the face of resistance and rebellion. Most people, however, voluntarily go along with their society's prescriptions for those of their gender status because the norms and expectations get built into their sense of worth and identity as a certain kind of human being and because they believe their society's way is the natural way. These beliefs emerge from the imagery that pervades the way we think, the way we see and hear and speak, the way we fantasize, and the way we feel. There is no core or bedrock human nature below these endlessly looping processes of the social production of sex and gender, self and other, identity and psyche, each of which is a "complex cultural construction" (Butler, 1990: 36). The paradox of "human nature" is that it is always a manifestation of cultural meanings, social relationships, and power politics—"not biology, but culture, becomes destiny" (Butler, 1990: 8).

Feminist inquiry has long questioned the conventional categories of social science, but much of the current work in feminist sociology has not gone beyond adding the universal category "women" to the universal category "men." Our current debates over the global assumptions of only two categories and the insistence that they must be nuanced to include race and class are steps in the direction I would like to see feminist research go, but race and class are also global categories (Spelman, 1988; Collins, 1990). Deconstructing sex, sexuality, and gender reveals many possible categories embedded in the social experiences and social practices of what Dorothy Smith calls the "everyday/everynight world" (1990). These emergent categories group some people together for comparison with other people without prior assumptions about who is like whom. Categories can be broken up and people regrouped differently into new categories for comparison. This process of discovering categories from similarities and differences in people's behaviour or responses can be more meaningful for feminist research than discovering similarities and differences between "females" and "males" or "women" and "men" because the social construction of the conventional sex and gender categories already assumes differences between them and similarities among them. When we rely only on the conventional categories of sex and gender, we end up finding what we looked for—we see what we believe, whether it is that "females" and "males" are essentially different or that "women" and "men" are essentially the same.

References

Birrell, S.J. 1988. "Discourses on the Gender/Sport Relationship: From Women in Sport to Gender Relations," in K. Pandolf, ed., *Exercise and Sport Science Reviews*, Vol. 16. New York: Macmillan.

Birrell, S.J., and S.L. Cole. 1990. "Double Fault: Renee Richards and the Construction and Naturalization of Difference," *Sociology of Sport Journal* 7: 1–21.

Boutilier, M.A., and L. SanGiovanni. 1983. *The Sporting Woman*. Champaign, IL: Human Kinetics.

Brozan, N. 1978. "Training Linked to Disruption of Female Reproductive Cycle," *New York Times*, 17 April.

Butler, J. 1990. *Gender Trouble: Feminism and the Subversion of Identity*. New York and London: Routledge & Kegan Paul.

Carlson, A. 1991. "When Is a Woman Not a Woman?," *Women's Sport and Fitness* (March): 24–9.

Cockburn, C. 1983. *Brothers: Male Dominance and Technological Change*. London: Pluto.

———. 1985. *Machinery of Dominance: Women, Men, and Technical Know-How*. London: Pluto.

Collins, P.H. 1990. *Black Feminist Thought: Knowledge, Consciousness, and the Politics of Empowerment*. Boston: Unwin Hyman.

Connell, R.W. 1987. *Gender and Power*. Stanford, CA: Stanford University Press.

Donato, K.M. 1990. "Programming for Change? The Growing Demand for Women Systems Analysts," in B.F. Reskin and P.A Roos, eds., *Job Queues, Gender Queues: Explaining Women's Inroads into Male Occupations*. Philadelphia: Temple University Press.

Duff, R.W., and L.K. Hong. 1984. "Self-images of Women Bodybuilders," *Sociology of Sport Journal* 2: 374–80.

Dunning, E. 1986. "Sport as a Male Preserve: Notes on the Social Sources of Masculine Identity and Its Transformations," *Theory, Culture, and Society* 3: 79–90.

Eitzen, D.S., and M.B. Zinn. 1989. "The De-athleticization of Women: The Naming and Gender Marking of Collegiate Sport Teams," *Sociology of Sport Journal* 6: 362–70.

English, J. 1982. "Sex Equality in Sports," in M. Vetterling-Braggin, ed., *Femininity, Masculinity, and Androgyny*. Boston: Littlefield, Adams.

Epstein, C.F. 1988. *Deceptive Distinctions: Sex, Gender, and the Social Order*. New Haven, CT: Yale University Press.

Fausto-Sterling, A. 1985. *Myths of Gender: Biological Theories about Women and Men*. New York: Basic Books.

Fine, G.A. 1987. *With the Boys: Little League Baseball and Preadolescent Culture*. Chicago: University of Chicago Press.

Foucault, M. 1978. *The History of Sexuality: An Introduction*. R. Hurley, trans. New York: Pantheon.

Gelman, S.A., P. Collman, and E.E. Maccoby. 1986. "Inferring Properties from Categories versus Inferring Categories from Properties: The Case of Gender," *Child Development* 57: 396–404.

Gilbert, S.M. 1983. "Soldier's Heart: Literary Men, Literary Women, and the Great War," *Signs: Journal of Women in Culture and Society* 8: 422–50.

Glassner, B. 1992. "Men and Muscles," in M.S. Kimmel and M.A. Messner, eds., *Men's Lives*. New York: Macmillan.

Hargreaves, J.A., ed. 1982. *Sport, Culture, and Ideology*. London: Routledge & Kegan Paul.

———. 1986. "Where's the Virtue? Where's the Grace? A Discussion of the Social Production of Gender Relations in and through Sport," *Theory, Culture, and Society* 3: 109–21.

———, ed. 1987. *Computer Chips and Paper Clips: Technology and Women's Employment*, Vol. 2. Washington, DC: National Academy Press.

Hargreaves, J.A., R.E. Kraut, and L.A. Tilly, eds. 1986. *Computer Chips and Paper Clips: Technology and Women's Employment*, Vol. 1. Washington, DC: National Academy Press.

Haskell, M. 1989. "Hers: He Drives Me Crazy," *New York Times Magazine* (24 September): 26, 28.

Hudson, J. 1978. "Physical Parameters Used for Female Exclusion from Law Enforcement and Athletics," in C.A. Oglesby, ed., *Women and Sport: From Myth to Reality*. Philadelphia: Lea and Febiger.

Hyde, J.S. 1990. "Meta-analysis and the Psychology of Gender Differences," *Signs: Journal of Women in Culture and Society* 16: 55–73.

Jaggar, A.M. 1983. *Feminist Politics and Human Nature*. Totowa, NJ: Rowman & Allanheld.

Janofsky, M. 1992. "Yamaguchi Has the Delicate and Golden Touch," *New York Times*, 22 February.

Kemper, T.D. 1990. *Social Structure and Testosterone: Explorations of the Sociobiosocial Chain*. New Brunswick, NJ: Rutgers University Press.

Kessler, S.J. 1990. "The Medical Construction of Gender: Case Management of Intersexed Infants," *Signs: Journal of Women in Culture and Society* 16: 3–26.

Kessler, S.J., and W. McKenna. [1978] 1985. *Gender: An Ethnomethodological Approach*. Chicago: University of Chicago Press.

Kolata, G. 1992. "Track Federation Urges End to Gene Test for Femaleness," *New York Times*, 12 February.

Kramer, P.E., and S. Lehman. 1990. "Mismeasuring Women: A Critique of Research on Computer Ability and Avoidance," *Signs: Journal of Women in Culture and Society* 16: 158–72.

Laqueur, T. 1990. *Making Sex: Body and Gender from the Greeks to Freud*. Cambridge, MA: Harvard University Press.

Levesque-Lopman, L. 1988. *Claiming Reality: Phenomenology and Women's Experience*. Totowa, NJ: Rowman & Littlefield.

MacKinnon, C. 1987. *Feminism Unmodified*. Cambridge, MA: Harvard University Press.

Majors, R. 1990. "Cool Pose: Black Masculinity in Sports," in M.A. Messner and D.F. Sabo, eds., *Sport, Men, and the Gender Order: Critical Feminist Perspectives*. Champaign, IL: Human Kinetics.

Mangan, J.A., and R.J. Park. 1987. *From Fair Sex to Feminism: Sport and the Socialization of Women in the Industrial and Post-industrial Eras*. London: Frank Cass.

Messner, M.A. 1988. "Sports and Male Domination: The Female Athlete as Contested Ideological Terrain," *Sociology of Sport Journal* 5: 197–211.

———. 1992. *Power at Play: Sports and the Problem of Masculinity*. Boston: Beacon Press.

Messner, M.A., M.C. Duncan, and K. Jensen. 1993. "Separating the Men from the Girls: The Gendered Language of Television Sports," *Gender & Society* 7: 121–37.

Messner, M.A., and D.F. Sabo, eds. 1990. *Sport, Men, and the Gender Order: Critical Feminist Perspectives*. Champaign, IL: Human Kinetics.

Molotch, H. 1988. "The Restroom and Equal Opportunity," *Sociological Forum* 3: 128–32.

Money, J., and A.A. Ehrhardt. 1972. *Man & Woman, Boy & Girl*. Baltimore, MD: Johns Hopkins University Press.

Moran, M. 1992. "Title IX: A 20-year Search for Equity," *New York Times* (Sports Section), 21–23 June.

Naftolin, F., and E. Butz, eds. 1981. "Sexual Dimorphism," *Science* 211: 1263–324.

Olson, W. 1990. "Beyond Title IX: Toward an Agenda for Women and Sports in the 1990s," *Yale Journal of Law and Feminism* 3: 105–51.

Perry, R., and L. Greber. 1990. "Women and Computers: An Introduction," *Signs: Journal of Women in Culture and Society* 16: 74–101.

Prior, J.C., Y.M. Yigna, M.T. Shechter, and A.E. Burgess. 1990. "Spinal Bone Loss and Ovulatory Disturbances," *New England Journal of Medicine* 323: 1221–7.

Richards, R., with J. Ames. 1983. *Second Serve*. New York: Stein and Day.

Riley, D. 1988. *Am I That Name? Feminism and the Category of Women in History*. Minneapolis: University of Minnesota Press.
Scharff, V. 1991. *Taking the Wheel: Women and the Coming of the Motor Age*. New York: Free Press.
Slatton, B., and S. Birrel. 1984. "The Politics of Women's Sport," *Arena Review* 8 (July).
Smith, D.E. 1990. *The Conceptual Practices of Power: A Feminist Sociology of Knowledge*. Toronto: University of Toronto Press.
Spelman, E. 1988. *Inessential Woman: Problems of Exclusion in Feminist Thought*. Boston: Beacon Press.
Theberge, N. 1987. "Sport and Women's Empowerment," *Women Studies International Forum* 10: 387–93.
Vecsey, G. 1990. "Cathy Rigby, Unlike Peter, Did Grow Up," *New York Times* (Sports Section), 19 December.
Watson, T. 1987. "Women Athletes and Athletic Women: The Dilemmas and Contradictions of Managing Incongruent Identities," *Sociological Inquiry* 57: 431–6.
Willis, P. 1982. "Women in Sport in Ideology," in J.A. Hargreaves, ed., *Sport, Culture, and Ideology*. London: Routledge & Kegan Paul.
Wright, B.D., M.M. Ferree, G.O. Mellow, L.H. Lewis, M.-L.D. Samper, R. Asher, and K. Claspell, eds. 1987. *Women, Work, and Technology: Transformations*. Ann Arbor, MI: University of Michigan Press.
Yoder, J.D. 1989. "Women at West Point: Lessons for Token Women in Male-dominated Occupations," in J. Freeman, ed., *Women: A Feminist Perspective*, 4th ed. Palo Alto, CA: Mayfield.
Zimmerman, J., ed. 1983. *The Technological Woman: Interfacing with Tomorrow*. New York: Praeger.

Chapter 4

Overview

Biologist Ann Fausto-Sterling's work builds on Judith Lorber's assertion that there is much more "overlap" between male and female than is frequently assumed. As Fausto-Sterling documents, human history is filled with accounts of individuals who possess physical characteristics associated with both males and females. These individuals, collectively known as intersexed people, cannot be sex-typed on the basis of biology alone, even though in societies built on a two-sex social system they are frequently required to live as one sex or the other. Fausto-Sterling makes the provocative claim that if scientists were truly interested in mapping the physical world, they would abandon their claims to a two-sex model in the face of evidence that human physiology comes in many different shapes and forms and instead assert that sex is, in her words, "a vast, infinitely malleable continuum." At the very least, she argues, medical science should recognize five sexes, rather than the common two.

Historically, intersexed people have been treated as medical and social problems that need to be managed through surgery. Fausto-Sterling argues that this is unnecessary and stigmatizing—the "unruly bodies" of the intersexed are part of natural human variation and should not be a source of anxiety or shame. In the years since this piece was first published, an "intersex rights" movement has arisen, consisting of people who assert their right to live with bodies that do not fit neatly into the two boxes that society has created for them. This movement is important not only because it enhances the lives of intersexed people but also because it helps to liberate everyone—intersexed and otherwise—from the mistaken notion that there are only two biological sexes.

It is important to remember here that "sex" and "gender" are not synonymous. Even if we were to become more accepting of a multiplicity of physical sexes, the question of gender would still remain. "Gender" is a social phenomenon, and does not simply follow from our knowledge of physical sex, as the readings in Part II demonstrate.

The Five Sexes: Why Male and Female Are Not Enough

Anne Fausto-Sterling

In 1843 Levi Suydam, a 23-year-old resident of Salisbury, Connecticut, asked the town board of selectmen to validate his right to vote as a Whig in a hotly contested local election. The request raised a flurry of objections from the opposition party, for reasons that must be rare in the annals of American democracy: it was said that Suydam was more female than male and thus (some 80 years before suffrage was extended to women) could not be allowed to cast a ballot. To settle the dispute a physician, one William James Barry, was brought in to examine Suydam. And, presumably upon encountering a phallus, the good doctor declared the prospective voter male. With Suydam safely in their column the Whigs won the election by a majority of one.

Barry's diagnosis, however, turned out to be somewhat premature. Within a few days he discovered that, phallus notwithstanding, Suydam menstruated regularly and had a vaginal opening. Both his/her physique and his/her mental predispositions were more complex than was first suspected. S/he had narrow shoulders and broad hips and felt occasional sexual yearnings for women. Suydam's "feminine propensities, such as a fondness for gay colors, for pieces of calico, comparing and placing them together, and an aversion for bodily labor, and an inability to perform the same, were remarked by many," Barry later wrote. It is not clear whether Suydam lost or retained the vote, or whether the election results were reversed.

Western culture is deeply committed to the idea that there are only two sexes. Even language refuses other possibilities; thus to write about Levi Suydam I have had to invent conventions—*s/he* and *his/her*—to denote someone who is clearly neither male nor female or who is perhaps both sexes at once. Legally, too, every adult is either man or woman, and the difference, of course, is not trivial. For Suydam it meant the franchise; today it means being available for, or exempt from, draft registration, as well as being subject, in various ways, to a number of laws governing marriage, the family, and human intimacy. In many parts of the United States, for instance, two people legally registered as men cannot have sexual relations without violating anti-sodomy statutes.

But if the state and the legal system have an interest in maintaining a two-party sexual system, they are in defiance of nature. For biologically speaking, there are many gradations running from female to male; and depending on how one calls the shots, one can argue that along that spectrum lie at least five sexes—and perhaps even more.

For some time medical investigators have recognized the concept of the intersexual body. But the standard medical literature uses the term *intersex* as a catch-all for three major subgroups with some mixture of male and female characteristics: the so-called true hermaphrodites, whom I call herms, who possess one testis and one ovary (the sperm- and egg-producing vessels, or gonads); the male pseudohermaphrodites (the "merms"), who have testes and some aspects of the female genitalia but no ovaries; and the female pseudohermaphrodites (the "ferms"), who have ovaries and some aspects of the male genitalia but lack testes. Each of those categories is in itself complex; the percentage of male and female characteristics, for instance, can vary enormously among members of the same subgroup. Moreover, the inner lives of the people in each subgroup—their special needs and their problems, attractions, and repulsions—have gone unexplored by science. But on the basis of what is known about them, I suggest that the three intersexes, herm, merm, and ferm, deserve to be considered additional sexes each in its own right. Indeed, I would argue further that sex is a vast, infinitely malleable continuum that defies the constraints of even five categories.

Not surprisingly, it is extremely difficult to estimate the frequency of intersexuality, much less the frequency of each of the three additional sexes: it is not the sort of information one volunteers on a job application. The psychologist John Money of Johns Hopkins University, a specialist in the study of congenital sexual-organ defects, suggests intersexuals may constitute as many as 4 per cent of births. As I point out to my students at Brown University, in a student body of about 6,000, that fraction, if correct, implies there may be as many as 240 intersexuals on campus—surely enough to form a minority caucus of some kind.

In reality though, few such students would make it as far as Brown in sexually diverse form. Recent advances in physiology and surgical technology now enable physicians to catch most intersexuals at the moment of birth. Almost at once such infants are entered into a program of hormonal and surgical management so that they can slip quietly into society as "normal" heterosexual males or females. I emphasize that the motive is in no way conspiratorial. The aims of the policy are genuinely humanitarian, reflecting the wish that people be able to "fit in" both physically and psychologically. In the medical community, however, the assumptions behind that wish—that there be only two sexes, that heterosexuality alone is normal, that there is one true model of psychological health—have gone virtually unexamined.

The word *hermaphrodite* comes from the Greek names Hermes, variously known as the messenger of the gods, the patron of music, the controller of dreams, or the protector of livestock, and Aphrodite, the goddess of sexual love and beauty. According to Greek mythology, those two gods parented Hermaphroditus, who at age fifteen became half male and half female when his body fused with the body of a nymph he fell in love with. In some true hermaphrodites the testis and the ovary grow separately but bilaterally; in others they grow together within the same organ, forming an ovo-testis. Not infrequently, at least one of the gonads functions quite well, producing either sperm cells or eggs, as well as functional levels of the sex hormones—androgens or estrogens. Although in theory it might be possible for a true hermaphrodite to become both father and mother to a child, in practice the appropriate ducts and tubes are not configured so that egg and sperm can meet.

In contrast with the true hermaphrodites, the pseudohermaphrodites possess two gonads of the same kind along with the usual male (XY) or female (XX) chromosomal makeup. But their external genitalia and secondary sex characteristics do not match their chromosomes. Thus merms have testes and XY chromosomes, yet they also have a vagina and a clitoris, and at puberty they often develop breasts. They do not menstruate, however. Ferms have ovaries, two X chromosomes and sometimes a uterus, but they also have at least partly masculine external genitalia. Without medical intervention they can develop beards, deep voices and adult-size penises.

Intersexuality itself is old news. Hermaphrodites, for instance, are often featured in stories about human origins. Early biblical scholars believed Adam began life as a hermaphrodite and later divided into two people—a male and a female—after falling from grace. According to Plato there once were three sexes—male, female, and hermaphrodite—but the third sex was lost with time.

Both the Talmud and the Tosefta, the Jewish books of law, list extensive regulations for people of mixed sex. The Tosefta expressly forbids hermaphrodites to inherit their fathers' estates (like daughters), to seclude themselves with women (like sons), or to shave (like men). When hermaphrodites menstruate they must be isolated from men (like women); they are disqualified from serving as witnesses or as priests (like women), but the laws of pederasty apply to them.

In Europe a pattern emerged by the end of the Middle Ages that, in a sense, has lasted to the present day: hermaphrodites were compelled to choose an established gender role and stick with it. The penalty for transgression was often death. Thus in the 1600s a Scottish hermaphrodite living as a woman was buried alive after impregnating his/her master's daughter.

For questions of inheritance, legitimacy, paternity, succession to title, and eligibility for certain professions to be determined, modern Anglo-Saxon legal systems require that newborns be registered as either male or female. In the United States today, state laws govern sex determination. Illinois permits adults to change the sex recorded on their birth certificates should a physician attest to having performed the appropriate surgery. The New York Academy of Medicine, on the other hand, has taken an opposite view. In spite of surgical alterations of the external genitalia, the academy argued in 1966, the chromosomal sex remains the same. By that measure, a person's wish to conceal his or her original sex cannot outweigh the public interest in protection against fraud.

During this century the medical community has completed what the legal world began—the complete erasure of any form of embodied sex that does not conform to a male–female, heterosexual pattern. Ironically, a more sophisticated knowledge of the complexity of sexual systems has led to the repression of such intricacy.

In 1937 the urologist Hugh H. Young of Johns Hopkins University published a volume titled *Genital Abnormalities, Hermaphroditism and Related Adrenal Diseases*. The book is remarkable for its erudition, scientific insight, and open-mindedness. In it Young drew together a wealth of carefully documented case histories to demonstrate and study the medical treatment of such "accidents of birth." Young did not pass judgment on the people he studied, nor did he attempt to coerce into treatment those intersexuals who rejected that option. And he showed unusual even-handedness in referring to those people who had had sexual experiences as both men and women as "practising hermaphrodites."

One of Young's more interesting cases was a hermaphrodite named Emma who had grown up as a female. Emma had both a penis-size clitoris and a vagina, which made it possible for him/her to have "normal" heterosexual sex with both men and women. As a teenager Emma had had sex with a number of girls to whom s/he was deeply attracted; but at the age of nineteen s/he had married a man. Unfortunately, he had given Emma little sexual pleasure (though he had had no complaints), and so throughout that marriage and subsequent ones Emma had kept girlfriends on the side. With some frequency s/he had pleasurable sex with them. Young describes his subject as appearing "to be quite content and even happy." In conversation, Emma occasionally told him of his/her wish to be a man, a circumstance Young said would be relatively easy to bring about. But Emma's reply strikes a heroic blow for self-interest:

> Would you have to remove that vagina? I don't know about that because that's my meal ticket. If you did that, I would have to quit my husband and go to work, so I think I'll keep it and stay as I am. My husband supports me well, and even though I don't have any sexual pleasure with him, I do have lots with my girlfriends.

Yet even as Young was illuminating intersexuality with the light of scientific reason, he was beginning its suppression. For his book is also an extended treatise on the most modern surgical and hormonal methods of changing intersexuals into either males or females. Young may have differed from his successors in being less judgmental and controlling of the patients and their families, but he nonetheless supplied the foundation on which current intervention practices were built.

By 1969, when the English physicians Christopher J. Dewhurst and Ronald R. Gordon wrote *The Intersexual Disorders*, medical and surgical approaches to intersexuality had neared a state of rigid uniformity. It is hardly surprising that such a hardening of opinion took place in the era of the feminine mystique—of the post–Second

World War flight to the suburbs and the strict division of family roles according to sex. That the medical consensus was not quite universal (or perhaps that it seemed poised to break apart again) can be gleaned from the near-hysterical tone of Dewhurst and Gordon's book, which contrasts markedly with the calm reason of Young's founding work. Consider their opening description of an intersexual newborn:

> One can only attempt to imagine the anguish of the parents. That a newborn should have a deformity . . . [affecting] so fundamental an issue as the very sex of the child . . . is a tragic event which immediately conjures up visions of a hopeless psychological misfit doomed to live always as a sexual freak in loneliness and frustration.

Dewhurst and Gordon warned that such a miserable fate would, indeed, be a baby's lot should the case be improperly managed; "but fortunately," they wrote, "with correct management the outlook is infinitely better than the poor parents—emotionally stunned by the event—or indeed anyone without special knowledge could ever imagine."

Scientific dogma has held fast to the assumption that without medical care hermaphrodites are doomed to a life of misery. Yet there are few empirical studies to back up that assumption, and some of the same research gathered to build a case for medical treatment contradicts it. Francis Benton, another of Young's practising hermaphrodites, "had not worried over his condition, did not wish to be changed, and was enjoying life." The same could be said of Emma, the opportunistic hausfrau. Even Dewhurst and Gordon, adamant about the psychological importance of treating intersexuals at the infant stage, acknowledged great success in "changing the sex" of older patients. They reported on 20 cases of children reclassified into a different sex after the supposedly critical age of 18 months. They asserted that all the reclassifications were "successful," and they wondered then whether re-registration could be "recommended more readily than [had] been suggested so far."

The treatment of intersexuality in this century provides a clear example of what the French historian Michel Foucault has called biopower. The knowledge developed in biochemistry, embryology, endocrinology, psychology, and surgery has enabled physicians to control the very sex of the human body. The multiple contradictions in that kind of power call for some scrutiny. On the one hand, the medical "management" of intersexuality certainly developed as part of an attempt to free people from perceived psychological pain (though whether the pain was the patient's, the parents', or the physician's is unclear). And if one accepts the assumption that in a sex-divided culture, people can realize their greatest potential for happiness and productivity only if they are sure they belong to one of only two acknowledged sexes, modern medicine has been extremely successful.

On the other hand, the same medical accomplishments can be read not as progress but as a mode of discipline. Hermaphrodites have unruly bodies. They do not fall naturally into a binary classification; only a surgical shoehorn can put them there. But why should we care if a "woman," defined as one who has breasts, a vagina, a uterus and ovaries, and who menstruates, also has a clitoris large enough to penetrate the vagina of another woman? Why should we care if there are people whose biological equipment enables them to have sex "naturally" with both men and women? The answers seem to lie in a cultural need to maintain clear distinctions between the sexes. Society mandates the control of intersexual bodies because they blur and bridge the great divide. Inasmuch as hermaphrodites literally embody both sexes, they challenge traditional beliefs about sexual difference: they possess the irritating ability to live sometimes as one sex and sometimes the other, and they raise the spectre of homosexuality.

But what if things were altogether different? Imagine a world in which the same knowledge that has enabled medicine to intervene in the management of intersexual patients has been placed at the service of multiple sexualities. Imagine that the sexes have multiplied beyond currently imaginable limits. It would have to be a world of shared powers. Patient and physician, parent and child, male and female, heterosexual and homosexual—all those oppositions and others would have to be dissolved as sources of division. A new ethic of medical treatment would arise, one that would permit ambiguity in a culture that had overcome sexual division. The central mission of medical treatment would be to preserve life. Thus hermaphrodites would be concerned primarily not about whether they can conform to society but about whether they might develop potentially life-threatening conditions—hernias, gonadal tumours, salt imbalances caused by adrenal malfunctions—that sometimes accompany hermaphroditic development. In my ideal world, medical intervention for intersexuals would take place only rarely before the age of reason; subsequent treatment would be a co-operative venture between physician, patient, and other advisers trained in issues of gender multiplicity.

I do not pretend that the transition to my utopia would be smooth. Sex, even the supposedly "normal," heterosexual kind, continues to cause untold anxieties in Western society. And certainly a culture that has yet to come to grips—religiously and, in some states, legally—with the ancient and relatively uncomplicated reality of homosexual love will not readily embrace intersexuality. No doubt the most troublesome arena by far would be the rearing of children. Parents, at least since the Victorian era, have fretted, sometimes to the point of outright denial, over the fact that their children are sexual beings.

All that and more amply explains why intersexual children are generally squeezed into one of the two prevailing sexual categories. But what would be the psychological consequences of taking the alternative road—raising children as unabashed intersexuals? On the surface, that tack seems fraught with peril. What, for example, would happen to the intersexual child amid the unrelenting cruelty of the schoolyard? When the time came to shower in gym class, what horrors and humiliations would await the intersexual as his/her anatomy was displayed in all its nontraditional glory? In whose gym class would s/he register to begin with? What bathroom would s/he use? And how on earth would Mom and Dad help shepherd him/her through the minefield of puberty?

In the past 30 years those questions have been ignored, as the scientific community has, with remarkable unanimity, avoided contemplating the alternative route of unimpeded intersexuality. But modern investigators tend to overlook a substantial body of case histories, most of them compiled between 1930 and 1960, before surgical intervention became rampant. Almost without exception, those reports describe children who grew up knowing they were intersexual (though they did not advertise it) and adjusted to their unusual status. Some of the studies are richly detailed—described at the level of gym-class showering (which most intersexuals avoided without incident); in any event, there is not a psychotic or a suicide in the lot.

Still, the nuances of socialization among intersexuals cry out for more sophisticated analysis. Clearly, before my vision of sexual multiplicity can be realized, the first openly intersexual children and their parents will have to be brave pioneers who will bear the brunt of society's growing pains. But in the long view—though it could take generations to achieve—the prize might be a society in which sexuality is something to be celebrated for its subtleties and not something to be feared or ridiculed.

Postscript

For an account of developments that occurred in the decade after I wrote this article, please see my 10-year follow-up piece, "The Five Sexes, Revisted," which is available online at www.researchgate.net/profile/Anne_Fausto-Sterling/publications/2.

PART II
Cultural Constructions of Gender

If gender is not just a gloss on physical sex differences, what is it? To say that gender differences and relations are cultural is to state the very obvious. However, no one has yet come up with an uncontested definition of what "culture" is. Sociologists and anthropologists have wrestled over the term, defining it variously as, among other things, a learned system of assigning meanings to experiences; the collective concepts and ideas with which individuals interpret their world; and the sum total of behaviour patterns, values, ideas, and preferences that characterize a society. In decades past, anthropologists tended to focus more on the intangible, conceptual aspects of culture, such as religious beliefs or kinship systems, while sociologists focused more on how power was exercised in very material ways, through studies of criminology and "deviance" or through studying changes in forms of economic production. However, this distinction no longer holds, as both sociologists and anthropologists study the interaction of symbolic systems with the distribution of power.

Within gender studies, the central contribution of "culture," regardless of how it is defined, is that masculinity and femininity are enacted in very different ways, in different times and places. There are some broad tendencies, to be sure—such as the disproportionate responsibility women bear for maintaining the health and well-being of family members or the relatively greater sexual latitude accorded to men—but for every one of these generalizations, exceptions can be found.

Twenty anthologies the size of this one could be devoted to gender and culture, without even beginning to scratch the surface of the subject. The readings in this section are intended to give you some insight into how one might think about the ways in which culture creates gender and vice versa.

We open with one of the classic statements on gender and culture. Candace West and Don Zimmerman's foundational article on gender as something that is enacted in everyday life clarifies and develops the concept of "doing gender." From this perspective, gender is not a way of dividing the human race into two groups, nor is it a quality possessed by individuals, objects, or situations. Instead, gender exists as interpersonal actions; an infinite set of interpersonal encounters through patterns and variations emerge, related to the gender of the actor.

Tabassum Ruby examines the symbolic meanings assigned to the *hijab*, the veil worn by some devout Muslim women. Wearing *hijab* is clearly a gendered behaviour, one of many rules and practices that mark out the difference between genders. However, Ruby demonstrates that this powerful cultural symbol carries multiple meanings for the women who adopt it. Wearing *hijab* is undoubtedly doing femininity, but for the women who take it up, the gendered meanings of the veil are diverse and variable.

The transgender individuals studied by Patricia Gagné, Richard Tewksbury, and Deanne McGaughey have to do gender in a way that is much more deliberate and self-conscious than it is for most non-transgender people. Their efforts to pass as members of their desired gender demonstrate how much work is involved in maintaining the cultural architecture of gender and how difficult it is to "cross the line" into the territory of the other gender.

In a twist on the "doing gender" approach to studying daily life, the women interviewed by Nancy Theberge insist that they do not in fact do gender when they are on the ice and that they are emphatically not creating a feminized version of hockey. By distancing themselves from the idea of "women's hockey," these players may be unintentionally reinforcing a binary opposition of gendered sport, in which the "feminized" variant is an inferior knock-off of the original. This is especially salient for hockey, which, Theberge argues, has come to symbolize the idealized form of Canadian sport (and of Canadian masculinity).

Questions for Critical Thought

1. Is it possible to live in the world without "doing gender"? Or perhaps more accurately, is it possible to live in the world without being interpreted by others as a gendered person?

2. West and Zimmerman contend that most of our "doing gender" is done unconsciously—that is, men and women are not constantly trying to conform to an idealized idea of gender norms, but rather have internalized concepts of what is appropriate for members of their sex category and deploy these concepts

unconsciously. Can you recall times in which you have been conscious of "doing gender," where you have deliberately shaped your behaviour, appearance, or interactions to be consistent with generally accepted norms for your sex category?

3. Imagine that you woke up one morning to discover that your best friend had changed his or her gender. How do you think he or she might be different? How might he or she be the same?
4. Ruby describes the *hijab* as an article of clothing that has a wide variety of meanings for the women who wear it. What other examples of clothing or other personal items that carry multiple gendered meanings can you think of?
5. Gagné and colleagues describe the process of creating a transgender identity as "coming out," yet they make it clear that "coming out" as transgender is not the same as coming out as queer or homosexual. What do you think are the differences between these experiences? How is being gay, lesbian, bisexual, or queer different from being transgender?
6. Some transgender people choose to "pass" as a member of a particular gender, while others choose to disrupt the assumption of a two-gender social system. What does a transgender person have to do to pass in a society that is based on the assumption that there are two and only two genders? How might transgender people disrupt the two-gender system through the choice not to pass?
7. Could you successfully pass as a member of a different gender if you wanted to do so?
8. Theberge's hockey players are divided as to whether there are (or should be) distinctive "masculine" and "feminine" ways to play hockey. Can you think of other activities or behaviours that have identifiable "masculine" and "feminine" forms?
9. Theberge describes a situation in which women are entering into previously male-dominated spaces, in the world of elite hockey. Can you think of examples of men's entry into spaces (physical or social) that have historically been dominated by women?
10. Many scholars following West and Zimmerman have argued that the social censure men face for not doing gender in an approved way—for "acting like a girl" or "being a sissy"—is much stronger than the social censure women face for not doing femininity in conventional ways. Has this been true in your experience? If so, why do you think this asymmetry exists?

Chapter 5

Overview

By now, you will have become familiar with the idea that sex and gender are not the same thing—that our physical bodies do not always determine what course our lives as gendered individuals will take. So if gender is not sex, what is gender? This classic essay is an early attempt by prominent sociologists to grapple with that question. They define gender as an "accomplishment"—something that is done or achieved, not a trait or personality characteristic, or a label stuck on people with particular types of bodies. We "do gender" through our gender displays, which are visible and (usually) intelligible to others.

Using the experience of Agnes, a male-to-female transsexual, West and Zimmerman differentiate between sex (our biological hardware), sex category (the social systems for classifying bodies based on that hardware, or on the presumption that individuals possess that hardware), and gender: the "ongoing task" of being a woman or man, and fitting one's actions to social expectations about how members of particular sex categories will behave in given situations. West and Zimmerman emphasize that doing gender is always improvisational—there is no set "gender script" that dictates how a man or woman ought to act, so we are continually reinventing gender as we go, through our interactions with others. How exactly we do this is still unclear, so West and Zimmerman lay out a research agenda for understanding how humans become competent gender actors.

By focusing on the improvisational quality of gender and by emphasizing that it is accomplished through interactions with, and in response to, the actions of our fellow gendered humans, West and Zimmerman moved beyond the confines of gender-as-role, which had dominated much sociological and psychological thinking in the twentieth century, and paved the way for the emergence of postmodern and post-structural ways of thinking about gender.

Doing Gender

Candace West and Don H. Zimmerman

In the beginning, there was sex and there was gender. Those of us who taught courses in the area in the late 1960s and early 1970s were careful to distinguish one from the other. Sex, we told students, was what was ascribed by biology: anatomy, hormones, and physiology. Gender, we said, was an achieved status: that which is constructed through psychological, cultural, and social means. To introduce the difference between the two, we drew on singular case studies of hermaphrodites and anthropological investigations of "strange and exotic tribes."

Inevitably (and understandably), in the ensuing weeks of each term, our students became confused. Sex hardly seemed a "given" in the context of research that illustrated the sometimes ambiguous and often conflicting criteria for its ascription. And gender seemed much less an "achievement" in the context of the anthropological, psychological, and social imperatives we studied—the division of labour, the formation of gender identities, and the social subordination of women by men. Moreover, the received doctrine of gender socialization theories conveyed the strong message that while gender may be "achieved," by about age five, it was certainly fixed, unvarying, and static—much like sex.

Since about 1975, the confusion has intensified and spread far beyond our individual classrooms. For one thing, we learned that the relationship between biological and cultural processes was far more complex—and reflexive—than we previously had supposed. . . .

Our purpose in this article is to propose an ethnomethodologically informed, and therefore distinctively sociological, understanding of gender as a routine, methodical, and recurring accomplishment. We contend that the "doing" of gender is undertaken by women and men whose competence as members of society is hostage to its production. Doing gender involves a complex of socially guided perceptual, interactional, and micropolitical activities that cast particular pursuits as expressions of masculine and feminine "natures."

When we view gender as an accomplishment, an achieved property of situated conduct, our attention shifts from matters internal to the individual and focuses on interactional and, ultimately, institutional arenas. In one sense, of course, it is individuals who "do" gender. But it is a situated doing, carried out in the virtual or real presence of others who are presumed to be oriented to its production. Rather than as a property of individuals, we conceive of gender as an emergent feature of social situations: both as an outcome of and a rationale for various social arrangements and as a means of legitimating one of the most fundamental divisions of society. . . .

To elaborate our proposal, we suggest that important but often overlooked distinctions be observed among *sex*, *sex category*, and *gender*. *Sex* is a determination made through the application of socially agreed upon biological criteria for classifying persons as females or males. The criteria for classification can be genitalia at birth or chromosomal typing before birth, and they do not necessarily agree with one another. Placement in a *sex category* is achieved through application of the sex criteria, but in everyday life, categorization is established and sustained by the socially required identificatory displays that proclaim one's membership in one or the other category. In this sense, one's sex category presumes one's sex and stands as proxy for it in many situations, but sex and sex category can vary independently; that is, it is possible to claim membership in a sex category even when the sex criteria are lacking. *Gender*, in contrast, is the activity of managing situated conduct in light of normative conceptions of attitudes and activities appropriate for one's sex category. Gender activities emerge from and bolster claims to membership in a sex category. . . .

We begin with an assessment of the received meaning of gender, particularly in relation to the roots of this notion in presumed biological differences between women and men.

Perspectives on Sex and Gender

In Western societies, the accepted cultural perspective on gender views women and men as naturally and unequivocally defined categories of being, with distinctive psychological and behavioural propensities that can be predicted from their reproductive functions. Competent adult members of these societies see differences between the two as fundamental and enduring—differences seemingly supported by the division of labour into women's and men's work and an often elaborate differentiation of feminine and masculine attitudes and behaviours that are prominent features of social organization. Things are the way they are by virtue of the fact that men are men and women are women—a division perceived to be natural and rooted in biology, producing, in turn, profound psychological, behavioural, and social consequences. The structural arrangements of a society are presumed to be responsive to these differences. . . .

Taking a different tack, role theory has attended to the social construction of gender categories, called "sex roles" or, more recently, "gender roles" and has analyzed how these are learned and enacted. . . . Role theory has emphasized the social and dynamic aspect of role construction and enactment. But at the level of face-to-face interaction, the application of role theory to gender poses problems of its own. Roles are *situated* identities—assumed and relinquished as the situation demands—rather than *master identities*, such as the sex category, that cut across situations. Unlike most roles, such as "nurse," "doctor," and "patient," or "professor" and "student," gender has no specific site or organizational context.

Moreover, many roles are already gender marked, so that special qualifiers—such as "female doctor" or "male nurse"—must be added to exceptions to the rule. Thorne (1980) observes that conceptualizing gender as a role makes it difficult to assess its influence on other roles and reduces its explanatory usefulness in discussions of power and inequality. Drawing on Rubin (1975), Thorne calls for a reconceptualization of women and men as distinct social groups, constituted in "concrete, historically changing—and generally unequal—social relationships" (Thorne, 1980: 11).

We argue that gender is not a set of traits, nor a variable, nor a role, but the product of social doings of some sort. What then is the social doing of gender? It is more than the continuous creation of the meaning of gender through human actions. We claim that gender itself is constituted through interaction. . . .

Sex, Sex Category, and Gender

Garfinkel's (1967) case study of Agnes, a transsexual raised as a boy who adopted a female identity at age 17 and underwent a sex reassignment operation several years later, demonstrates how gender is created through interaction and, at the same time, structures interaction. Agnes, whom Garfinkel characterized as a "practical methodologist," developed a number of procedures for passing as a "normal, natural female" both prior to and after her surgery. She had the practical task of managing the fact that she possessed male genitalia and that she lacked the social resources a girl's biography would presumably provide in everyday interaction. In short, she needed to display herself as a woman, simultaneously learning what it was to be a woman. Of necessity, this full-time pursuit took place at a time when most people's gender would be well-accredited and routinized. Agnes had to consciously contrive what the vast majority of women do without thinking. She was not "faking" what "real" women do naturally. She was obliged to analyze and figure out how to act within socially structured circumstances and conceptions of femininity that women born with appropriate biological credentials come to take for granted early on. As in the case of others who must "pass" . . . , Agnes's case makes visible what culture has made invisible—the accomplishment of gender. . . .

Sex

Agnes did not possess the socially agreed-upon biological criteria for classification as a member of the female sex. Still, Agnes regarded herself as a female, albeit a female with a penis, which a woman ought not to possess. The penis, she insisted, was a "mistake" in need of remedy (Garfinkel, 1967). Like other competent members of our culture, Agnes honoured the notion that there are "essential" biological criteria that unequivocally distinguish females from males. However, if we move away from the commonsense viewpoint, we discover that the reliability of these criteria is not beyond question. Moreover, other cultures have acknowledged the existence of "cross-genders" and the possibility of more than two sexes.

More central to our argument is Kessler and McKenna's (1978) point that genitalia are conventionally hidden from public inspection in everyday life; yet we continue, through our social rounds, to "observe" a world of two naturally, normally sexed persons. It is the *presumption* that essential criteria exist, and would or should be there if looked for, that provides the basis for sex categorization. Drawing on Garfinkel, Kessler and McKenna argue that "female" and "male" are cultural events—products of what they term the "gender attribution process"—rather than some collection of traits, behaviours, or even physical attributes. Illustratively, they cite the child who, viewing a picture of someone clad in a suit and a tie, contends,

"It's a man, because he has a pee-pee" (Kessler and McKenna, 1978: 154). Translation: "He must have a pee-pee [an essential characteristic] because I see the *insignia* of a suit and tie." . . . Kessler and McKenna note [that] we operate with a moral certainty of a world of two sexes. We do not think, "Most persons with penises are men, but some may not be" or "Most persons who dress as men have penises." Rather, we take it for granted that sex and sex category are congruent—that knowing the latter, we can deduce the rest.

Sex Categorization

Agnes's claim to the categorical status of female, which she sustained by appropriate identificatory displays and other characteristics, could be *discredited* before her transsexual operation, if her possession of a penis became known, and after by her surgically constructed genitalia. In this regard, Agnes had to be continually alert to actual or potential threats to the security of her sex category. Her problem was not so much about living up to some prototype of essential femininity but preserving her categorization as female. This task was made easy for her by a very powerful resource, namely, the process of commonsense categorization in everyday life.

The categorization of members of society into indigenous categories such as "girl" or "boy," or "woman" or "man," operates in a distinctively social way. The act of categorization does not involve a positive test, in the sense of a well-defined set of criteria that must be explicitly satisfied prior to making an identification. Rather, the application of membership categories relies on an "if–can" test in everyday interaction. This test stipulates that if people *can be seen* as members of relevant categories, *then categorize them that way*. That is, use the category that seems appropriate, except in the presence of discrepant information or obvious features that would rule out its use. This procedure is quite in keeping with the attitude of everyday life, which has us take appearances at face value unless we have special reason to doubt. . . .

Agnes's initial resource was the predisposition of those she encountered to take her appearance (her figure, clothing, hair style, and so on) as the undoubted appearance of a normal female. Her further resource was our cultural perspective on the properties of "natural, normally sexed persons." Garfinkel (1967) notes that in everyday life, we live in a world of two—and only two—sexes. This arrangement has a moral status, in that we include ourselves and others in it as "essentially, originally, in the first place, always have been, always will be, once and for all, in the final analysis, either 'male' or 'female'" (Garfinkel, 1967: 122). Consider the following case:

> This issue reminds me of a visit I made to a computer store a couple of years ago. The person who answered my questions was truly a *salesperson*. I could not categorize him/her as a woman or a man. What did I look for? (1) Facial hair: She/he was smooth skinned, but some men have little or no facial hair. (This varies by race; Native Americans and Blacks often have none.) (2) Breasts: She/he was wearing a loose shirt that hung from his/her shoulders. And, as many women who suffered through a 1950s adolescence know to their shame, women are often flat-chested. (3) Shoulders: His/hers were small and round for a man, broad for a woman. (4) Hands: Long and slender fingers, knuckles a bit large for a woman, small for a man. (5) Voice: Middle range, unexpressive for a woman, not at all the exaggerated tones some gay males affect. (6) His/her treatment of me: Gave off no signs that would let me know if I were of the same or different sex as this person. There were not even any signs that he/she knew his/her sex would be difficult to categorize and I wondered about that even as I did my best to hide these questions so I would not embarrass him/her while we talked of computer paper. I left still not knowing the sex of my salesperson, and was disturbed by that unanswered question (child of my culture that I am). (Diane Margolis, personal communication)

What can this case tell us about situations such as Agnes's or the process of sex categorization in general? First, we infer from this description that the computer salesperson's identificatory display was ambiguous, since she or he was not dressed or adorned in an unequivocally female or male fashion. It is when such a display *fails* to provide grounds for categorization that factors such as facial hair or tone of voice are assessed to determine membership in a sex category. Second, beyond the fact that this incident could be recalled after "a couple of years," the customer was not only "disturbed" by the ambiguity of the salesperson's category but also assumed that to acknowledge this ambiguity would be embarrassing to the salesclerk. Not only do we want to know the sex category of those around us (to see it at a glance, perhaps), but we also presume that others are displaying it for us, in as decisive a fashion as they can.

Gender

Agnes attempted to be "120 per cent female" (Garfinkel, 1967: 129)—that is, unquestionably in all ways and at all times feminine. She thought she could protect herself from disclosure before and after surgical intervention by comporting herself in a feminine manner, but she also could have given herself away by overdoing her performance. . . . Her problem was to produce configurations of behaviour that would be seen by others as normative gender behaviour.

Agnes's strategy of "secret apprenticeship," through which she learned expected feminine decorum by carefully attending to her fiancé's criticisms of other women, was one means of masking incompetencies and simultaneously acquiring the needed skills (Garfinkel, 1967). It was through her fiancé that Agnes learned that sunbathing on the lawn in front of her apartment was "offensive" (because it put her on display to other men). She also learned from his critiques of other women that she should not insist on having things her way and that she should not offer her opinions or claim equality with men (Garfinkel, 1967: 147–8). (Like other women in our society, Agnes learned something about power in the course of her "education.")

Popular culture abounds with books and magazines that compile idealized depictions of relations between women and men. Those focused on the etiquette of dating or prevailing standards of feminine comportment are meant to be of practical help in these matters. However, the use of any such source *as a manual of procedure* requires the assumption that doing gender merely involves making use of discrete, well-defined bundles of behaviour that can simply be plugged into interactional situations to produce recognizable enactments of masculinity and femininity. The man "does" being masculine by, for example, taking the woman's arm to guide her across a street, and she "does" being feminine by consenting to be guided and not initiating such behaviour with a man.

. . . To be successful, marking or displaying gender must be finely fitted to situations and modified or transformed as the occasion demands. Doing gender consists of managing such occasions so that, whatever the particulars, the outcome is seen and seeable in context as gender-appropriate or, as the case may be, gender-*in*appropriate—that is, *accountable*.

Gender and Accountability

As Heritage (1984: 136–7) notes, members of society regularly engage in "descriptive accountings of states of affairs to one another," and such accounts are both serious and consequential. . . .

. . . [S]ocietal members orient to the fact that their activities are subject to comment. Actions are often designed with an eye to their accountability—that is, how they might look and how they might be characterized. The notion of accountability also encompasses those actions undertaken so that they are specifically unremarkable and thus not worthy of more than a passing remark, because they are seen to be in accord with culturally approved standards.

Heritage observes that the process of rendering something accountable is interactional in character:

> [This] permits actors to design their actions in relation to their circumstances so as to permit others, by methodically taking account of circumstances, to recognize the action for what it is. (1984: 179)

The key word here is *circumstances*. One circumstance that attends virtually all actions is the sex category of the actor. As Garfinkel comments:

> [T]he work and socially structured occasions of sexual passing were obstinately unyielding to [Agnes's] attempts to routinize the grounds of daily activities. This obstinacy points to the *omnirelevance* of sexual status to affairs of daily life as an invariant but unnoticed background in the texture of relevances that compose the changing actual scenes of everyday life. (1967: 118, emphasis added)

If sex category is omnirelevant (or even approaches being so), then a person engaged in virtually any activity may be held accountable for performance of that activity as a *woman* or a *man*, and their incumbency in one or the other sex category can be used to legitimate or discredit their other activities. Accordingly, virtually any activity can be assessed as to its womanly or manly nature. And note, to "do" gender is not always to live up to normative conceptions of femininity or masculinity; it is to engage in behaviour *at the risk of gender assessment*. While it is individuals who do gender, the enterprise is fundamentally interactional and institutional in character, for accountability is a feature of social relationships and its idiom is drawn from the institutional arena in which those relationships are enacted. If this be the case, can we ever *not* do gender? Insofar as a society is partitioned by "essential" differences between women and men and placement in a sex category is both relevant and enforced, doing gender is unavoidable.

Resources for Doing Gender

Doing gender means creating differences between girls and boys and women and men, differences that are not natural, essential, or biological. Once the differences have been constructed, they are used to reinforce the "essentialness" of gender. In a delightful account of the "arrangement between the sexes," Goffman (1977) observes the creation of a variety of institutionalized frameworks through which our "natural, normal sexedness" can be enacted. The physical features of social setting provide one obvious resource for the expression of our "essential" differences. For example, the sex segregation of North American public bathrooms distinguishes "ladies" from "gentlemen" in matters held to be fundamentally biological, even though both "are somewhat similar in the question of waste products and their elimination" (Goffman, 1977: 315). These settings are furnished with dimorphic equipment (such as urinals for men or elaborate grooming facilities for women), even though both sexes may achieve the same ends through the same means (and apparently do so in the privacy of their own homes). To be stressed here is the fact that:

> The *functioning* of sex-differentiated organs is involved, but there is nothing in this functioning that biologically recommends segregation; that arrangement is a totally cultural matter. . . . [T]oilet segregation is presented as a natural consequence of the difference between the sex-classes when in fact it is a means of honoring, if not producing, this difference. (Goffman, 1977: 316)

Standardized social occasions also provide stages for evocations of the "essential female and male natures." Goffman cites organized sports as one such institutionalized framework for the expression of manliness. There, those qualities that ought "properly" to be associated with masculinity, such as endurance, strength, and competitive spirit, are celebrated by all parties concerned—participants, who may be seen to demonstrate such traits, and spectators, who applaud their demonstrations from the safety of the sidelines (1977: 322).

Assortative mating practices among heterosexual couples afford still further means to create and maintain differences between women and men. For example, even though size, strength, and age tend to be normally distributed among females and males (with considerable overlap between them), selective pairing ensures couples in which boys and men are visibly bigger, stronger, and older (if not "wiser") than the girls and women with whom they are paired. So, should situations emerge in which greater size, strength, or experience is called for, boys and men will be ever ready to display it and girls and women, to appreciate its display. . . .

Many situations are not clearly sex categorized to begin with, nor is what transpires within them obviously gender relevant. Yet any social encounter can be pressed into service in the interests of doing gender. Thus, Fishman's (1978) research on casual conversations found an asymmetrical "division of labour" in talk between heterosexual intimates. Women had to ask more questions, fill more silences, and use more attention-getting beginnings in order to be heard. Her conclusions are particularly pertinent here:

> Since interactional work is related to what constitutes being a woman, with what a woman is, the idea that it is work is obscured. The work is not seen as what women do, but as part of what they are. (Fishman, 1978: 405)

We would argue that it is precisely such labour that helps to constitute the essential nature of women as women in interactional contexts.

Individuals have many social identities that may be donned or shed, muted or made more salient, depending on the situation. One may be a friend, spouse, professional, citizen, and many other things to many different people—or, to the same person at different times. But we are always women or men—unless we shift into another sex category. What this means is that our identificatory displays will provide an ever-available resource for doing gender under an infinitely diverse set of circumstances.

Some occasions are organized to routinely display and celebrate behaviours that are conventionally linked to one or the other sex category. On such occasions, everyone knows his or her place in the interactional scheme of things. If an individual identified as a member of one sex category engages in behaviour usually associated with the other category, this routinization is challenged. Hughes (1945: 356) provides an illustration of such a dilemma:

> [A] young woman . . . became part of that virile profession, engineering. The designer of an airplane is expected to go up on the maiden flight of the first plane built according to the design. He [sic] then gives a dinner to the engineers and workmen who worked on the new plane. The dinner is naturally a stag party. The young woman in question designed a plane. Her co-workers urged her not to take the risk—for which, presumably, men only are fit—of the maiden voyage. They were, in effect, asking her to be a lady instead of an engineer. She chose to be an engineer. She then gave the party and paid for it like a man. After food and the first round of toasts, she left like a lady.

On this occasion, parties reached an accommodation that allowed a woman to engage in presumptively masculine behaviours. However, we note that in the end, this compromise permitted demonstration of her "essential" femininity, through accountably "ladylike" behaviour.

Hughes (1945: 357) suggests that such contradictions may be countered by managing interactions on a very narrow basis—for example, "keeping the relationship formal and specific." But the heart of the matter is that even—perhaps, especially—if the relationship is a formal one, gender is still something one is accountable for. Thus a woman physician (notice the special qualifier in her case) may be accorded respect for her skill and even addressed by an appropriate title. Nonetheless, she is subject to evaluation in terms of normative conceptions of appropriate attitudes and activities for her sex category and under pressure to prove that she is an "essentially" feminine being, despite appearances to the contrary. Her sex category is used to discredit her participation in important clinical activities, while her involvement in medicine is used to discredit her commitment to her responsibilities as a wife and mother. Simultaneously, her exclusion from the physician colleague community is maintained and her accountability *as a woman* is ensured.

In this context, "role conflict" can be viewed as a dynamic aspect of our current "arrangement between the sexes" (Goffman, 1977), an arrangement that provides for occasions on which persons of a particular sex category can "see" quite clearly that they are out of place and that if they were not there, their current troubles would not exist. What is at stake is, from the standpoint of interaction, the management of our "essential" natures, and from the standpoint of the individual, the continuing accomplishment of gender. If, as we have argued, sex category is omnirelevant, then any occasion, conflicted or not, offers the resources for doing gender.

We have sought to show that sex category and gender are managed properties of conduct that are contrived with respect to the fact that others will judge and respond to us in particular ways. We have claimed that a person's gender is not simply an aspect of what one is, but, more fundamentally, it is something that one *does*, and does recurrently, in interaction with others.

What are the consequences of this theoretical formulation? If, for example, individuals strive to achieve gender in encounters with others, how does a culture instill the need to achieve it? What is the relationship between the production of gender at the level of interaction and such institutional arrangements as the division of labour in society? And, perhaps most important, how does doing gender contribute to the subordination of women by men?

Research Agendas

To bring the social production of gender under empirical scrutiny, we might begin at the beginning, with a reconsideration of the process through which societal members acquire the requisite categorical apparatus and other skills to become gendered human beings.

Recruitment to Gender Identities

. . . Cahill (1982, 1986a, 1986b) analyzes the experiences of preschool children using a social model of recruitment into normally gendered identities. Cahill argues that categorization practices are fundamental to learning and displaying feminine and masculine behaviour. Initially, he observes, children are primarily concerned with distinguishing between themselves and others on the basis of social competence. Categorically, their concern resolves itself into the opposition of "girl/boy" classification versus "baby" classification (the latter designating children whose social behaviour is problematic and who must be closely supervised). It is children's concern with being seen as socially competent that evokes their initial claims to gender identities:

> During the exploratory stage of children's socialization . . . they learn that only two social identities are routinely available to them, the identity of "baby," or, depending on the configuration of their external genitalia, either "big boy" or "big girl." Moreover, others subtly inform them that the identity of "baby" is a discrediting one. When, for example, children engage in disapproved behaviour, they are often told "You're a baby" or "Be a big boy." In effect, these typical verbal responses to young children's behaviour convey to them that they must behaviourally choose between the discrediting identity of "baby" and their anatomically determined sex identity. (Cahill, 1986a: 175)

Subsequently, little boys appropriate the gender ideal of "efficaciousness"—that is, being able to affect the physical and social environment through the exercise of physical strength or appropriate skills. In contrast, little girls learn to value "appearance"—that is, managing themselves as ornamental objects. Both classes of children learn that the recognition and use of sex categorization in interaction is not optional, but mandatory.

Being a "girl" or a "boy" then, is not only being more competent than a "baby," but also being competently female or male—that is, learning to produce behavioural displays of one's "essential" female or male identity. In this respect, the task of four- to five-year-old children is very similar to Agnes's:

> For example, the following interaction occurred on a preschool playground. A 55-month-old boy (D) was attempting to unfasten the clasp of a necklace when a preschool aide walked over to him.
>
> A: Do you want to put that on?
> D: No. It's for girls.
> A: You don't have to be a girl to wear things around your neck. Kings wear things around their neck. You could pretend that you're a king.
> D: I'm not a king. I'm a boy. (Cahill, 1986a: 176)

As Cahill notes in this example, although D may have been unclear as to the sex status of a king's identity, he was obviously aware that necklaces are used to announce the identity "girl." Having claimed the identity "boy" and having developed a behavioural commitment to it, he was leery of any display that might furnish grounds for questioning his claim.

In this way, new members of society come to be involved in a *self-regulating process* as they begin to monitor their own and others' conduct with regard to its gender implications. The "recruitment" process involves not only the appropriation of gender ideals (by the valuation of those ideals as proper ways of being and behaving) but also *gender identities* that are important to individuals and that they strive to maintain. Thus gender differences, or the sociocultural shaping of "essential female and male natures," achieve the status of objective facts. They are rendered normal, natural features of persons and provide the tacit rationale for differing fates of women and men within the social order.

Additional studies of children's play activities as routine occasions for the expression of gender-appropriate behaviour can yield new insights into how our "essential natures" are constructed. In particular, the transition from what Cahill (1986a) terms "apprentice participation" in the sex-segregated worlds that are common among elementary school children to "bona fide participation" in the heterosocial world so frightening to adolescents is likely to be a keystone in our understanding of the recruitment process.

Gender and the Division of Labour

Whenever people face issues of *allocation*—who is to do what, get what, plan or execute action, direct or be directed, incumbency in significant social categories such as "female" and "male" seems to become pointedly relevant. How such issues are resolved conditions the exhibition, dramatization, or celebration of one's "essential nature" as a woman or man.

Berk (1985) offers elegant demonstration of this point in her investigation of the allocation of household labour and the attitudes of married couples toward the division of household tasks. Berk found little variation in either the actual distribution of tasks or perceptions of equity in regard to that distribution. Wives, even when employed outside the home, do the vast majority of household and childcare tasks. Moreover, both wives and husbands tend to perceive this as a "fair" arrangement. Noting the failure of conventional sociological and economic theories to explain this seeming contradiction, Berk contends that something more complex is involved than rational arrangements for the production of household goods and services:

> Hardly a question simply of who has more time, or whose time is worth more, who has more skill or more power, it is clear that a complicated relationship between the structure of work imperatives and the structure of normative expectations attached to work as *gendered* determines the ultimate allocation of members' time to work and home. (Berk, 1985: 195–6)

She notes, for example, that the most important factor influencing wives' contribution of labour is the total amount of work demanded or expected by the household; such demands had no bearing on husbands' contributions. Wives reported various rationales (their own and their husbands') that justified their level of contribution and, as a general matter, underscored the presumption that wives are essentially responsible for household production.

Berk contends that it is difficult to see how people "could rationally establish the arrangements that they do solely for the production of household goods and services" (1985: 201)—much less, how people could consider them "fair." She argues that our current arrangements for the domestic division of labour support *two* production processes: household goods and services (meals, clean children, and so on) and, at the same time, gender. As she puts it:

> Simultaneously, members "do" gender, as they "do" housework and child care, and what [has] been called the division of labor provides for the joint production of household labor and gender; it is the mechanism by which both the material and symbolic products of the household are realized. (1985: 201)

It is not simply that household labour is designated as "women's work," but that for a woman to engage in it and a man not to engage in it is to draw on and exhibit the "essential nature" of each. What is produced and reproduced is not merely the activity and artifact of domestic life, but the material embodiment of wifely and husbandly roles, and derivatively, of womanly and manly conduct. What are also frequently produced and reproduced are the dominant and subordinate statuses of the sex categories.

How does gender get done in work settings outside the home, where dominance and subordination are themes of overarching importance? Hochschild's (1983) analysis of the work of flight attendants offers some promising insights. She found that the occupation of flight attendant consisted of something altogether different for women than for men:

> As the company's main shock absorbers against "mishandled" passengers, their own feelings are more frequently subjected to rough treatment. In addition, a day's exposure to people who resist authority in a woman is a different experience than it is for a man. . . . In this respect, it is a disadvantage to be a woman. And in this case, they are not simply women in the biological sense. They are also a highly visible distillation of middle-class American notions of femininity. They symbolize Woman. Insofar as the category "female" is mentally associated with having less status and authority, female flight attendants are more readily classified as "really" females than other females are. (1983: 175)

In performing what Hochschild terms the "emotional labor" necessary to maintain airline profits, women flight attendants simultaneously produce enactments of their "essential" femininity.

Sex and Sexuality

What is the relationship between doing gender and a culture's prescription of "obligatory heterosexuality"? As Frye (1983: 22) observes, the monitoring of sexual feelings in relation to other appropriately sexed persons requires the ready recognition of such persons "before one can allow one's heart to beat or one's blood to flow in erotic enjoyment of that person." The appearance of heterosexuality is produced through emphatic and unambiguous indicators of one's sex, layered on in ever more conclusive fashion (Frye, 1983: 24). Thus, lesbians and gay men concerned with passing as heterosexuals can rely on these indicators for camouflage; in contrast, those who would avoid the assumption of heterosexuality may foster ambiguous indicators of their categorical status through their dress, behaviours, and style. But "ambiguous" sex indicators are sex indicators nonetheless. If one wishes to be recognized as a lesbian (or heterosexual woman), one must first establish a categorical status as female. Even as popular images portray lesbians as "females who are not feminine" (Frye, 1983: 129), the accountability of persons for their "normal, natural sexedness" is preserved.

Nor is accountability threatened by the existence of "sex-change operations"—presumably, the most radical challenge to our cultural perspective on sex and gender. Although no one coerces transsexuals into hormone therapy, electrolysis, or surgery, the alternatives available to them are undeniably constrained:

> When the transsexual experts maintain that they use transsexual procedures only with people who ask for them, and who prove that they can "pass," they obscure the social reality. Given patriarchy's prescription that one must be *either* masculine or feminine, free choice is conditioned. (Raymond, 1979: 135, emphasis added)

The physical reconstruction of sex criteria pays ultimate tribute to the "essentialness" of our sexual natures—as women *or* as men.

Gender, Power, and Social Change

Let us return to the question: Can we avoid doing gender? Earlier, we proposed that insofar as sex category is used as a fundamental criterion for differentiation, doing gender is unavoidable. It is unavoidable because of the social consequences of sex category membership: the allocation of power and resources not only in the domestic, economic, and political domains but also in the broad arena of interpersonal relations. In virtually any situation, one's sex category can be relevant, and one's performance as an incumbent of that category (i.e., gender) can be subjected to evaluation. Maintaining such pervasive and faithful assignment of lifetime status requires legitimation.

But doing gender also renders the social arrangements based on sex category accountable as normal and natural—that is, legitimate—ways of organizing social life. Differences between women and men that are created by this process can then be portrayed as fundamental and enduring dispositions. In this light, the institutional arrangements of a society can be seen as responsive to the differences—the social order being merely an accommodation to the natural order. Thus if, in doing gender, men are also doing dominance and women are doing deference, the resultant social order, which supposedly reflects "natural differences," is a powerful reinforcer and legitimator of hierarchical arrangements. Frye observes:

> For efficient subordination, what's wanted is that the structure not appear to be a cultural artifact kept in place by human decision or custom, but that it appear *natural*—that it appear to be quite a direct consequence of facts about the beast which are beyond the scope of human manipulation. . . . That we are trained to behave so differently as women and men, and to behave so differently toward women and men, itself contributes mightily to the appearance of extreme dimorphism, but also, the *ways* we act as women and men, and the *ways* we act toward women and men, mold our bodies and our minds to the shape of subordination and dominance. We do become what we practice being. (Frye, 1983: 34)

If we do gender appropriately, we simultaneously sustain, reproduce, and render legitimate the institutional arrangements that are based on sex category. If we fail to do gender appropriately, we as individuals—not the institutional arrangements—may be called to account (for our character, motives, and predispositions).

Social movements such as feminism can provide the ideology and impetus to question existing arrangements, and the social support for individuals to explore alternatives to them. . . . To be sure, equality under the law does not guarantee equality in other arenas. As Lorber (1986: 577) points out, assurance of "scrupulous equality of categories of people considered essentially different needs constant monitoring." What such proposed changes can do is provide the warrant for asking why, if we wish to treat women and men as equals, there needs to be two sex categories at all. . . .

Gender is a powerful ideological device, which produces, reproduces, and legitimates the choices and limits that are predicated on sex category. An understanding of how gender is produced in social situations will afford clarification of the interactional scaffolding of social structure and the social control processes that sustain it.

References

Berk, S.F. 1985. *The Gender Factory: The Apportionment of Work in American Households*. New York: Plenum.

Cahill, S.E. 1982. "Becoming Boys and Girls." PhD dissertation, Department of Sociology, University of California, Santa Barbara.

———. 1986a. "Childhood Socialization as Recruitment Process: Some Lessons from the Study of Gender Development," in P. Adler and P. Adler, eds., *Sociological Studies of Child Development*, pp. 163–86. Greenwich, CT: JAI Press.

———. 1986b. "Language Practices and Self-Definition: The Case of Gender Identity Acquisition," *The Sociological Quarterly* 27: 295–311.

Connell, R.W. 1985. "Theorizing Gender," *Sociology* 19: 260–72.

Fishman, P. 1978. "Interaction: The Work Women Do," *Social Problems* 25: 397–406.

Frye, M. 1983. *The Politics of Reality: Essays in Feminist Theory*. Trumansburg, NY: The Crossing Press.

Garfinkel, H. 1967. *Studies in Ethnomethodology*. Englewood Cliffs, NJ: Prentice-Hall.
Goffman, E. 1976. "Gender Display," *Studies in the Anthropology of Visual Communication* 3: 69–77.
———. 1977. "The Arrangement between the Sexes," *Theory and Society* 4: 301–31.
Heritage, J. 1984. *Garfinkel and Ethnomethodology*. Cambridge, UK: Polity Press.
Hochschild, A.R. 1983. *The Managed Heart. Commercialization of Human Feeling*. Berkeley: University of California Press.
Hughes, E.C. 1945. "Dilemmas and Contradictions of Status," *American Journal of Sociology* 50: 353–59.
Kessler, S.J., and W. McKenna. 1978. *Gender: An Ethnomethodological Approach*. New York: Wiley.
Komarovsky, M. 1946. "Cultural Contradictions and Sex Roles," *American Journal of Sociology* 52: 184–9.
———. 1950. "Functional Analysis of Sex Roles," *American Sociological Review* 15: 508–16.
Linton, R. 1936. *The Study of Man*. New York: Appleton-Century.
Lorber, J. 1986. "Dismantling Noah's Ark," *Sex Roles* 14: 567–80.
Parsons, T. 1951. *The Social System*. New York: Free Press.
Parsons, T., and R.F. Bales. 1955. *Family, Socialization and Interaction Process*. New York: Free Press.
Raymond, J.G. 1979. *The Transsexual Empire*. Boston: Beacon.
Rossi, A. 1984. "Gender and Parenthood," *American Sociological Review* 49: 1–19.
Rubin, G. 1975. "The Traffic in Women: Notes on the 'Political Economy' of Sex," in R. Reiter, ed., *Toward an Anthropology of Women*, pp. 157–210. New York: Monthly Review Press.
Stacey, J., and B. Thorne. 1985. "The Missing Feminist Revolution in Sociology," *Social Problems* 32: 301–16.
Thorne, B. 1980. "Gender . . . How Is It Best Conceptualized?" Unpublished manuscript.

Chapter 6

Overview

The *hijab* is clearly a gendered marker in multiethnic communities—wearing the *hijab* is what West and Zimmerman would term a "gender display," announcing the wearer as a woman. But what does this gendered display signify, other than the presumed sex of the wearer? Ruby talks with Muslim women, some of whom wear the *hijab*, to uncover the multiple gendered meanings of wearing a headscarf.

For all the women with whom she speaks, the meaning of the *hijab* is bound up with their ideas about what it means to be a Muslim woman, but the *hijab* signifies different things in different settings to different women. The thought and consideration that her participants give to their choices make it clear that they are doing "identity work," as well as following their interpretation of their religion's sacred texts. For some women, wearing the *hijab* shows their membership in a global religious community; for others, it signifies a woman who does not feel obligated to make herself up in order to appeal to male viewers. On the other hand, some of Ruby's participants were Muslim women who did not wear the *hijab*. For them, the choice not to wear it is also a way of crafting their identities as Muslim women, believing that in Canadian society the *hijab* draws attention in a way that is not consistent with Koranic teachings about modesty.

Whatever their interpretations of *hijab*, Ruby's participants are agreed that the way the headscarf is portrayed in the Western press—as a symbol of oppression or an indicator of terrorist sympathies—is very narrow. The gendered meanings that Muslim women ascribe to their decisions to wear or not wear the *hijab* are much more complex and individualized than simply conforming to religious dictates. Gender displays such as *hijab* are not always simple and straightforward.

Listening to the Voices of *Hijab*

Tabassum F. Ruby

With the increasing number of *muhajibah*[1] around the globe, the issue of the *hijab* has become a topic of debate among Muslim and non-Muslim scholars. Researchers such as Nasser (1999) have pointed out that the "new *hijab* phenomenon" initially began two decades ago in countries such as Egypt, and Muslim women around the globe have since embraced the practice. In Canada, the *hijab* is often seen as a symbol of Muslim women's oppression and a restriction to their mobility, particularly in the media.[2] Many Muslim women, however, claim that the *hijab* empowers them in numerous ways: making their identities[3] distinct; taking control of their bodies; and giving them a sense of belonging to a wider Muslim world. Thus, the discussion on the *hijab* is contentious, revealing the complexity of the issue.

The intricacy of the issue of *hijab*, nonetheless, is not limited to whether the *hijab* oppresses a Muslim woman or liberates her. Most often, the Muslim community and the dominant culture recognize the *hijab* as clothing that is used to cover the female body (i.e., a headscarf and/or long coat). This research, however, indicates that immigrant Muslim women[4] perceive the *hijab* in a variety of ways and associate it with diverse meanings that range from covering of the head to modest behaviour. As a result, the participants often negotiate their places in the larger community, as well as in the Muslim community, because they feel pressure whether wearing or not wearing the *hijab*.

Methodology and Sampling

There is a small population of immigrant Muslim women in Saskatoon (the geographical location of my research), and most of them know each other. I have personal contact with many of these Muslim women, and through the use of the "snowball technique," I was able to identify participants. The "snowball" or "chain" method occurs when "sampling identifies cases of interest from people who know other people with relevant cases" (Bradshaw and Straford, 2000: 44). In recruiting the sample, the Islamic Association of Saskatchewan played a particularly important role. Along with Friday prayers, weekly gatherings in the mosque facilitated meetings with diverse groups of women and provided opportunities to talk with them about my research project.[5]

Using focus groups, I interviewed 14 women who came from 12 different countries. I conducted three interview sessions and divided my participants into two groups of five based on whether or not they wore a headscarf. I conducted one interview session with participants who did not wear a headscarf and one with those who did. Each interview session was 90 minutes long. My third group consisted of a mix of participants, some of whom wore the headscarf and some who did not. The session with the mixed group, which had four participants, lasted 110 minutes. With the participants' permission, the interviews were audiotaped.

In order to protect the anonymity of my participants, personal details such as place of birth, age, and occupation cannot be fully described here, but general characteristics are as follows. The participants' countries of origin include Afghanistan, Bangladesh, Brunei, Burma, Egypt, Guyana, India, Iran, Jordan, Kuwait, Pakistan, and Turkey. The women's ages range from just under 20 to 60. The participants' occupations vary from physician to accountant, writer to insurance officer, and students. Their immigrant experiences range from arrival in Canada within the last few years to immigration more than two decades ago. Some informants have lived in other cities such as Toronto and Edmonton; others have resided in Saskatoon since they emigrated. Six participants did not wear the *hijab*, and eight were *muhajibah*. As the overall number of participants is quite small, the results of this study may best serve as a "case study."

Before illustrating the participants' views about the *hijab*, I would like to outline some of the basic concepts of the *hijab* in the Muslim context, because many participants referred to them. The Qur'anic verses that are traditionally cited to describe women's dress code are as follows:

> And say to the believing women that they should lower their gaze and guard their modesty; that they should not display their beauty and ornaments except what (must ordinarily) appear thereof; that they should draw their veils over their bosoms and not display their beauty. . . . And that they should not strike their feet in order to draw attention to their hidden ornaments. (24:31)

> O Prophet! Tell thy wives and daughters, and the believing women, that they should cast their outer garments over their persons (when abroad): this is most convenient, that they should be known (as such) and not molested. And God is oft forgiving, most merciful. (33:59)

The scholars' explanation that women should cover their bodies is not only based on the interpretation of the cited verses, but also on *hadith*[6] literature. However, many *hadiths* that are often cited as justification for women's covering have been challenged, with researchers arguing that these *hadiths* are not authentic[7] (*sahih'*). Ibe-al-Jawzi (d. 1201), as cited in Roald (2001), argues that women should stay at home and, if they need to go out, should wear the *hijab* because they can cause *fitnah* (temptation).[8] Ibe-al-Jawzi bases his argument on a *hadith* that reads: the Prophet says that "the best mosque for woman is her home." Contrary to Ibe-al-Jawzi, however, Al-Ghazzali (1989) argues that there are many *hadiths* that provide evidence that women used to pray at the mosque during the Prophet's time and that those *hadiths* are stronger than the one cited (Roald, 2001).

Khaled (2001) argues that the debate on the *hijab* among classical and contemporary scholars is fundamentally rooted in the previously mentioned idea of *fitnah*[9] (temptation). He states that the Qur'an uses the word *fitnah* for non-sexual temptations, such as "money and severe trials and tribulations" (Khaled, 2001: 233). Nonetheless, scholars often associate the notion of *fitnah* with women's sexuality, which is signalled, in part, by an uncovered appearance in public. Khaled writes that women are prohibited from attending mosques or driving cars, and that "every item and colour of clothing is analyzed under the doctrine of *fitnah*" (Khaled, 2001: 235). He argues, however, that these restrictions are misplaced, and that *fitnah* reflects men's fantasies of uncontrollable lust, which they have associated with women's sexuality.

Khaled further argues that the injunction that women need to cover their bodies to avoid bringing on *fitnah* is not in harmony with Islam's message; the Qur'an does not use the word to imply women's temptation, and does not view women's bodies as *fitnah*. Moreover, Islam requires lowering of the gaze and guarding modesty for both men and women; thus, a covered female body will not lead to a modest society (the essence of the *hijab*) until men behave in a similar manner.

What Is the *Hijab*? The Discussion among the Participants

> That is a question that I ask myself. (Almas)[10]

The extent to which Muslim women should cover their bodies is not only a controversial issue among scholars, but also emerged as a contentious matter among the participants in this study, where the meanings of the *hijab* are interpreted in a variety of ways. The *hijab,* in the form of physical garments, signifies headscarves (as worn by some of the women interviewed), but also modest clothing that does not include the covering of the head. Equally important, the *hijab* in this research also refers to modest behaviour.

Some participants indicated that although the Qur'an requires head covering, "the instructions are not clear, and people have diverse views about the *hijab.*" Scholars such as Asad (1980) have pointed out that there are sound reasons for not stating precise rules regarding the covering of women's bodies. He argues that human circumstances vary over time, and that the verses are moral guidelines that could be observed against the ever-changing background of time and social environment. Similarly, Dilshad', one of the participants, recognized the purpose of the vague regulations of Islam, and stated that the religion accommodates people's cultural differences. She remarked:

> Islam defines certain [rules] very strictly, because you have to follow them throughout your life. Even till the end of the world . . . these rules will remain the same. But some things are [a] little flexible, because you have to adjust with time, culture, and country.

The idea of the *hijab* with reference to headscarves or covering of the body, however, is only one element of the *hijab*. Most participants reported that physical articles such as clothing would not serve the purpose of the *hijab* unless women believe in the practice. Islam requires lowering the gaze, avoiding seeing what is forbidden, and not inviting the male gaze. For these reasons, many participants mentioned that whether a woman wears a headscarf or not, modest behaviour is a fundamental aspect of the *hijab*. Raheelah, for example, remarked that the *hijab* is not limited to head covering; conducting life unpretentiously is also significant in fulfilling the requirements of the *hijab*. "To me," she stated, "the *hijab* is not just covering of your head . . . it is your life, your portrayal of yourself as a person. As long as you dress decently, and you do not draw attention to yourself, that to me is the *hijab*." Raheelah does not wear a headscarf, but her concept of the *hijab* dictates modesty of dress, such as not wearing miniskirts or tight dresses that could be seen as bringing attention to oneself. She also believes that moral behaviour is part of the *hijab*. This indicates that she sees the *hijab* not as a material garment, but as an ethical belief. Raheelah then, while not wearing the headscarf, feels that she is maintaining the boundaries of the *hijab*.

Why or Why Not Wear the *Hijab?*

> It keeps the society pure in many, many ways. (Dilshad')

Following the discussion of the concept of the *hijab*, some participants mentioned the rationale of the Qur'an in requiring the *hijab*. For example, Farza'nah' argues that the *hijab*[11] sets a boundary between men and women that helps them avoid premarital relationships, which are not permissible in Islam. She commented that a woman's beauty needs to be concealed, because beauty brings a "lot of other things . . . freedom, the kind that we see here." Farza'nah' identifies the *hijab* as a means of minimizing easy interaction between men and women, which in turn promotes chastity. However, according to Farza'nah's views, chastity is not restricted to women's behaviour, but it is extended to society, where women's modesty grants chaste society.

Contrary to Farza'nah's opinion, Dilshad' did not think that women's bodies should be covered simply because they are eye-catching. She believes that the *hijab* is a tool that diminishes sexual appeal and, as a result, promotes a virtuous public domain. She stated that women need to wear the *hijab* because "it keeps the society pure in many, many ways." Despite the seeming differences about the attractiveness of women's bodies, both Farza'nah' and Dilshad' linked the *hijab* with women's sexuality. Underlying their views is a concept of women's bodies as either tempting (their beauty will seduce men) or polluting (their immodest behaviour can corrupt society). The status of women's bodies, in turn, is seen as a sign of the moral status of the nation, because women are perceived as the cultural carriers of their society (Yuval-Davis, 1994). Thus, a chaste, moral, or pure society is dependent upon the condition of women's bodies according to Farza'nah' and Dilshad'.

Farza'nah's and Dilshad's reasoning also indicates that because they see women's bodies as *fitna*, their views contradict the Qur'an as discussed earlier. In verse 33:59, already mentioned, the Qur'an states that women should cover themselves so as not to be "molested." The context of the verse indicates that at the time this verse was revealed, men treated slave women very disrespectfully, and there were incidents in Medina[12] when the men assaulted Muslim women. The offenders' excuse was that they did not know that these were Muslim women. In order to protect Muslim women, it was stated that they should dress modestly so that they could be recognized. Implied in the Qur'an is the idea that men are the aggressors and women the victims, whereas according to these participants, women are the actors and men the victims (Roald, 2001). Thus, as Roald (2001) points out, many Muslims have turned the Qur'anic view around to suggest that women are responsible for a corrupted and unchaste society.

While some women wear the *hijab* because they feel responsible for a moral society, others wear it because it offers them respect, dignity, and protection. Almas, for example, is just under 20 and away from her country of origin, as well as her family, for the first time. She reported that because she is living by herself, the *hijab* has become a security measure, that men are respectful towards *muhajibah* and do not treat them like sexual objects. She remarked that "to me now it's like protection . . . I wear the *hijab* and people do not treat you the way they treat other girls here. They are more respectful." Although she had difficulty explaining why men respect *muhajibah*, for Almas the *hijab*, as it desexualizes her body, is a device for earning respect and ensuring her safety from potential male viewers. Many studies, such as Read and Bartkowski (2000), have found that many women wear the *hijab* because they think men will respect them. These researchers did not discuss why men respect *muhajibah*, and it was difficult for me to speculate about the reason(s). Nonetheless, Almas's remarks indicate that she feels that the *hijab* gives her the status of a respectable person, which shows that the *hijab* has a significant impact on its wearer regarding her social relationships and her perception of her "self."

Since people often recognize the *hijab*[13] as a religious sign that offers its wearers respect and dignity, many Muslims look negatively upon women who do not wear it, and non-wearers often feel community pressure to conform. Despite the dominant view that the *hijab* is a symbol of religious commitment, non-wearers of headscarves[14] argue that a woman not wearing a headscarf still could be a dedicated *muslimah*.[15] Bilqis', for instance, remarked:

> Within the Muslim community, if you are not wearing the *hijab*, then you know you are not Muslim or you are not Muslim enough, when . . . it's a totally personal choice, you know. My relationship as a Muslim and my spiritual development is between me and God, and that's it.

The participants who did not wear headscarves perceived the *hijab* as a cultural dress code rather than as a religious symbol. These women indicated that wearing the *hijab* is a new cultural phenomenon, locally and globally, and that it does not have a religious connotation. Ati'yah, for example, remarked, "I think it's more like a culture that is the way they are raised there ['back home']. . . . I do not think it is taken as a religion when they started." According to Ati'yah, women are taught traditionally to cover their bodies with the *hijab*, and they do not wear it because of religious requirement.

Although non-wearers of the headscarves ascribed different reasons for wearing the *hijab* from those who did wear it, both group categories felt that the *hijab* was a way of demonstrating the difference between Muslim and Western values. Mali'hah, for instance, commented that morality is declining in Canadian society, and wearing the *hijab* shows people that its wearers do not subscribe to immoral values; also, she added, *muhajibah* are afraid, because they do not have control over these undesired values.

The *Hijab* as an Identity Symbol

> In the global context, if I see a woman in the *hijab* I know she is a Muslim and it creates a sense of community in that respect, which is a nice feeling, I think. (Bilqis')

The reasons for wearing it can be diverse, but the *hijab* has become a very powerful, pervasive symbol of Muslim women's identity, particularly in the West. Ibrahim (1999) states that it is a growing feeling on the part of Muslim women that they no longer wish to identify with the West, and that reaffirmation of their identities as Muslims requires the kind of visible sign that the adoption of traditional clothing implies. For these women, the issue is not that they have to dress traditionally, but that they choose to embrace the *hijab* as a marker of their Muslim identities.

Similarly, many participants who wear the *hijab*[16] claimed that it was a mark of their Muslim identities, ensuring that people immediately recognize them as Muslim women. Sima, for example, who wears a headscarf, commented that her distinct clothing symbolizes Muslim identities, and that the *hijab* makes her visible in a non-Muslim society. Being visible as a Muslim, however, also means encountering the negative stereotypes that are linked with Muslims, and Sima is aware of that. She remarked:

> Nothing else tells them that I am a Muslim, just my *hijab*. And . . . if they have the idea, oh, Muslims are terrorists, they might look at me like [that], and if they have the idea that, oh, Muslims are good people, they might look at me [with] respect. But still it gives me . . . identity.

Nasser (1999: 409) writes that adoption of the *hijab* "conveys a public message/statement, both about the wearer and about the relationship between the wearer and potential viewers." Accordingly, Sima's response shows that she recognizes her *hijab* as a public statement. However, whether she would be identified as a "terrorist" or a "good" person in Canada is a secondary consideration for her. The significant element to her is that she will be known as a Muslim in a non-Muslim country. Sima thus uses her *hijab* as a tool for declaring her Muslim identities.

The concept of the *hijab* is not limited to personal identity; it has also become the symbol of the Muslim *ummah*, or community. An immigrant Muslim woman's attempt to identify herself as a Muslim by wearing a headscarf is an acknowledgment of general support for the attitudes, values, and beliefs of Islam and her culture that links her to the broader community of believers (Daly, 1999; Read and Bartkowski, 2000). Some participants in this study also saw the *hijab* as representative of the Muslim community, and argued that the *hijab* helped them to stay away from un-Islamic practices. Farza'nah' stated that the practice of the *hijab* defined boundaries for her, and that she would not do anything that could portray the religion negatively:

> The *hijab* limits me from doing certain things. When I have the *hijab* on . . . as a Muslim woman, I consider myself basically representative of the whole Muslim community. So, I do not go to bars with my *hijab* on. I do not go to strip clubs with my *hijab* on because I know [that] by wearing the *hijab*, I am not representing only myself . . . it's the whole Muslim community, basically.

The *hijab* not only links the wearers with a larger community, but it is also a symbol of rites of passage. In Iran, reported Pervin', when a young woman begins to wear the *hijab*, the family celebrates it. It is a "memorable" event and "part of the life of a girl as a graduation party." According to Sima,[17] it signifies that a young woman is now a responsible person, and family and friends rejoice in her honour. In this cultural context, the *hijab* appears as a sign of adulthood and offers the wearer prestige and appreciation from friends and family members.

The participants in this study who have maintained the practice of wearing headscarves in Canada indicated that they are stricter in the use of their *hijab* in Canada than are those "back home." Shaffir (1978) states that usually people become more loyal to their traditions and customs if their identities are threatened by the larger society:

> A feature common to groups that perceive the outside world as a threat is the belief that they must resist the assimilative influence of the larger society. . . . [This helps the] group members to feel more committed and increases their awareness of their separate identity. (Shaffir, 1978: 41)

Confirming Shaffir's observations, a number of informants in this study reported that they have embraced the *hijab* in Canada more enthusiastically than have people in their country of origin. Pervin', for instance, stated, "I find that our *hijab* here is better than people are wearing in Iran . . . and I think the reason is [that] . . . somehow we need more to do this here than there." The *hijab* helps Pervin' keep her distinct identities in a non-Muslim country, and it appears as a sign of resistance to the assimilative influence of the larger society.

In comparing the practice of wearing the *hijab* in Canada to its usage "back home," the wearers of headscarves are crafting their Muslim identities not only in relation to the dominant values of their residing country, but also to the values of their country of origin. Many informants held a static view of their places of birth, and on their occasional visits they were surprised that the societies had changed. They argued that there is now a tendency "back home" for women to dress in tight clothes and not to wear "proper" *hijab*. The contrast of two different places allows these informants to notice differences in the *hijab*, and "improper" *hijab* emerges as a symbol of the loss of Islamic values. Thus, the *hijab* for these participants stands as a guardian of Muslim standards, and they thought that "back home" people were careless in not maintaining it.

The *Hijab*, Body, and Gaze

> The study of dress as situated practice requires moving between, on the one hand, the discursive and representational aspects of dress, and the way the body/dress is caught up in relations of power, and on the other, the embodied experience of dress and the use of dress as a means by which individuals orientate themselves to the social world. (Entwistle, 2000: 39)

Many prominent scholars, such as El Saadawi (1980) and Mernissi (1987, 1991), have situated the practice of veiling as an act of controlling women, both physically and psychologically. These writers argue that veiling represents, and is a result of, oppressive social hierarchies and male domination (Read and Bartkowski, 2000; Roald, 2001); therefore, it should be condemned. Mernissi (1991), for instance, states "all debates on democracy get tied up in the woman question and that piece of cloth [the *hijab*] that opponents of human rights today claim to be the very essence of Muslim identity" (188). Mernissi views the *hijab* as a hindrance to accessing human rights and, consequently, inherently oppressive. Equally important, she denies the lived experiences of many of those women who recognize the *hijab* as a positive experience that empowers them and grants them Muslim identities.

For the wearers of the headscarves in this study, the *hijab* is a tool that confers power and, contrary to the above writers' opinions, helps many of them to take control of their bodies. Many of the participants seem to be utilizing the *hijab* to set boundaries between themselves and the outside world. Di'ba, for example, commented that she likes keeping her curtains closed when she has the lights on, because otherwise people walking down the street can see her. One of Di'ba's friends, however, finds her precautions odd, and argues that Islam is not that strict, that she can relax without the *hijab* while she is in her home.

For Di'ba, putting a barrier between herself and potential viewers is not due to Islamic restrictions; rather, she wants to create a space where she feels free from the male gaze. Di'ba reported her friend's reaction:

> What's the big deal? Like, you are in your house. . . . Allah is not going to punish you for what you are doing in your own house, you know. And I am, like, but it is not about being punished . . . I do not know how Allah is going to view this, but I do not want people, like [some] guy, [looking in]. . . that's the thing.

Secor (2002) writes that veiling, as a form of dress, is a spatial practice embedded in relations of power and resistance. Accordingly, extending the idea of the *hijab* from headscarf to the creation of "safe" space, Di'ba uses her curtains to assert power and resistance, her freedom from the undesired gaze.

The notion that the *hijab* liberates women from the male gaze and helps them to be in charge of their own bodies is a very prominent claim by those Muslim women who wear it. They argue that the *hijab* is not a mark of oppression; rather, it is a sign of liberation that protects them from a sexist society. The *hijab* allows Muslim women physical mobility because they feel free from the male gaze. Consequently, they move in the public sphere more comfortably (Hoodfar, 1993; Odeh, 1993; Khan, 1995). Noreen's story of being released from the gaze by wearing the *hijab* is particularly significant, because she suffered heavily from the "inspecting gaze." Noreen was 18 years old when she got married and came to Canada. When her husband did not let her wear the *hijab*, she reports, "it got [her] into real trouble." She and her husband ran a store where she often worked by herself. After being harassed in her workplace by some non-Muslim men, her husband consented to allowing her to wear the *hijab*.

From the conversation in other parts of my interview with Noreen about her experience of harassment, she was not only the victim of harassment, but her response to the harassers was also inspected by her husband. The behaviour of Noreen's spouse indicates that he blamed the victim, as if Noreen were responsible for the harassment. The *hijab*, however, elevated her position from the "observed" to the "observer," as she felt free from the male gaze. This granted Noreen the protection that otherwise might not have been possible for her.

Contrary to the opinions of those women who perceive the *hijab* as protection, the non-wearers of the headscarves argued that the *hijab* is not an appropriate dress in Canada. These participants stated that while the basic purpose of the *hijab* is not to draw attention to oneself, in Canada, where it is not customary dress, people often scrutinize women who wear the *hijab*. Citing the example of her daughters who wear the *hijab*, Ati'yah reported that whenever she goes out with her daughters, she notices that people stare at them, which "is the opposite of what the *hijab* is supposed to be." Ati'yah's observation indicates that the *hijab* is a marker of difference in Canada, as people find it "strange." Equally important, since it draws attention to the wearer, Ati'yah sees it as contrary to the teachings of the Qur'an.

While some women in this study retain their distinct Muslim identities by wearing the *hijab*, Ati'yah, in order to be more anonymous in mainstream society, did not wear the *hijab*. Both wearers and non-wearers are crafting their identities and negotiating a place as Muslim women immigrants in a Western society.

As noted earlier, the sample of this study is very small and the results cannot be generalized to the larger population of Muslim women in Saskatoon. Nonetheless, the results indicate that the reasons for wearing or not wearing the *hijab* are varied and complex, and cannot be reduced simply to religious or cultural reasons.

Western Perception of the *Hijab*

> Veiling—to Western eyes, the most visible marker of the differentness and inferiority of Islamic societies—became the symbol now of both the oppression of women (or, in the language of the day, Islam's degradation of women) and the backwardness of Islam, and it became the open target of colonial attack and the spearhead of the assault on Muslim societies. (Ahmed, 1992: 152)

The formation of identities is not only restricted to the ways in which we relate and present ourselves to others; it also depends on how others perceive us. One avenue for understanding the ways in which a society views different people or cultures is to study media representations, because the media often play a powerful role in suggesting and shaping national and personal identities. Studies such as Bullock and Jafri (2000), Jafri (1998), and Kutty (1997) show that mainstream North American media have consistently portrayed an image of "the Muslim woman" as an oppressed and passive *hijab* wearer. Bullock and Jafri (2000) argue that Muslim women are presented by the media as "others," members of a religion that does not promote "Canadian" values but, rather, anti-Canadian values such as indiscriminate violence and gender oppression.

In mainstream society, the negative stereotypes of Muslim women have become more visible since the attacks in New York on 11 September 2001, and the *hijab* has become a sign of a "terrorist" woman. There are a number of incidents in Canada where *muhajibah* were harassed after September 11[18] and some participants mentioned that they also had encountered racist harassment. Pervin', for instance, who has also experienced racism in Canada, reported that someone has since called her a "terrorist," and she inferred that it was because she wore the *hijab*. "Some guy said 'Terrorist,' because I wear the *hijab*," she remarked. "Some people stare at me. They think that if you have the *hijab*, you are a 'terrorist' . . . really, some of them think so." Pervin's experience reveals the powerful and negative stereotypes that have linked the *hijab*—the sign of Muslim identity—with terrorism, resulting in verbal, racial, and ethnic assaults like the one cited above. These racist incidents demonstrate that Muslim women (and men) are often seen as "other" in Canadian society and, despite claims that it is a multicultural country, many Muslims face difficulties living in Canada.

The participants not only mentioned the negative stereotype of the *hijab*, but they also recognized that many Western-style clothes could be construed as oppressive. Bilqis', for example, remarked that many North American women wear short dresses and expose their bodies, but this is not perceived as an act of oppression in Canada, whereas covering the body is interpreted as a sign of subjugation. She commented:

> Western women, when they see a Muslim woman in the *hijab*, they think, ah, oppression. But you know, ten-inch heels and a miniskirt is not seen as oppressive. To me it is more oppressive than putting a scarf on your head.

Wolf (1991) has demonstrated that the "beauty myth" has often resulted in the objectification of women, and the expenditure of large amounts of money to achieve the ideal body. Wolf (1991: 13) writes that there is no justification for the beauty myth: "What it is doing to women today is a result of nothing more exalted than the need of today's power structure, economy, and culture to mount a counteroffensive against women." Similarly, Bilqis' argues that the Western style of wearing scanty outfits is a form of women's oppression.

Conclusion

This article discussed the concept of the *hijab* and its meanings to immigrant Muslim women. Wearing the *hijab* in the last two decades has become a popular phenomenon, locally and globally; however, to what extent Muslim women need to cover is a debatable question among scholars as well as among the participants. The idea of the *hijab* ranges from wearing headscarves to demonstrating modest behaviour, depending on one's understanding of religious precepts. The participants described the *hijab* in a variety of ways; some linked it with the moral Muslim society and others thought that it was a sign of opposing immoral values. For those informants who wear the *hijab*, it is a religious obligation. The non-wearers of the headscarves view it as a cultural symbol. The *hijab* as a mark of identity is a persistent theme and the *muhajibah* use the *hijab* to assert agency, which in turn confers status and dignity to its wearers. At the same time, however, the *hijab* disempowers non-wearers because the Muslim community does not perceive them as "good" *muslimah*.

While the *hijab* holds multiple meanings for Muslim women, mainstream North American society's perception of the *hijab* is usually negative, and the practice is often presented in the Canadian media without proper cultural and historical reference. Unlike the participants' views, the depiction of the *hijab* in Canada suggests that there is only one form of the *hijab*—that is, as a symbol of the oppression of Muslim women. Canadian attitudes towards the *hijab* suggest that Westerners "know the Orient better than the Orient can know itself" (Khan, 1995: 149).

In some situations the *hijab* may indeed be imposed on Muslim women, but in this study many of the participants chose to wear it. Living in Canada, where the connotation of the *hijab* is often negative, has a strong impact on those immigrant Muslim women who wear it, as they consequently face negative stereotypes of Muslim women such as being labelled "terrorists." In spite of these racist acts, the *muhajibah* wear the *hijab* as a sign of their Muslim identities and in opposition to "immodest" Western values. Those who do not identify with the visible marker recognize that the *hijab* is not an acceptable dress code in Canada. In fact, their refusal to wear the *hijab* could be read as a symbol of assimilation, but in not drawing attention to themselves and by wearing modest clothes (without the headscarf) these women, nonetheless, maintain the practice of the *hijab*. Thus, the non-wearers of the headscarves may not confront the racism that wearing the *hijab* can prompt; however, they usually encounter criticism within the Muslim community. The *hijab*, therefore, in the form of Muslim woman's clothing, emerges as a device to negotiate spaces within the Muslim community, as well as in the dominant western culture.

Notes

1. A woman who wears a *hijab*, such as a headscarf, is called *muhajibah*.
2. Media is defined here as any form of written text (i.e., books, magazines, journal articles, reports or articles in newspapers) and audio or visual productions (i.e., radio, television shows, and documentary films).
3. The use of the word "identities" in plural form is more appropriate here because a person's identity is multi-faceted. For instance, a Muslim woman living in Saskatoon is not only viewed as a woman, but also as a woman of colour, an immigrant, and a member of an ethnic, as well as a religious, group.
4. The term refers here to any Muslim woman born outside Canada, but currently is residing in Canada with any kind of official documents, such as a Canadian passport or student visa.
5. Please note that men's and women's gatherings are held separately in the mosque.
6. A collection of the Prophet's sayings and actions is called *hadiths*.
7. There is a science of knowledge that studies the authenticity of *hadiths*.
8. I will discuss this issue below. The idea of *fitnah* is also found in the Judeo-Christian veiling tradition, where it was thought that an uncovered female head aroused sexual desire in men (Bronner, 1993; D'Angelo, 1995).
9. Please note that he discusses the *hadith* literature in reference to the fitnah, and argues that they are not authentic *hadiths*.
10. Please note that all participants have been given pseudonyms.
11. The *hijab* here signifies a headscarf.
12. Geographical location where the Prophet was residing.
13. Here the *hijab* is identified by the form of headscarf and/or long coat.
14. I used the word headscarf here to make a distinction between those whose concept of the *hijab* includes the physical article, such as a headscarf, and those who view the *hijab* as modest clothing (without the head covering) and modest behaviour.
15. *Muslimah* is the feminine for a Muslim woman.
16. The *hijab* here particularly refers to the material article; nonetheless, modest behaviour is not excluded.
17. As stated earlier, please note that as I conducted focus groups, the participants talked among themselves and commented on each other's views.
18. See for instance, the *Globe and Mail* (15 October 2001), and Jain (2001).

References

Al-Ghazzali, M. 1989. *as-sunna an-anbawiya bayna ahl al-fiqh wa ahl al-hadith*. Cairo: Dar ash-Shuruq.

Asad, M., trans. 1980. Gibraltar: Dar Al-Andalus.

Bradshaw, M., and E. Straford. 2000. "Qualitative Research Design and Rigour," in Iain Hay, ed., *Qualitative Research Methods in Human Geography*, pp. 37–49. South Melbourne: Oxford University Press.

Bronner, L.L. 1993. "From Veil to Wig: Jewish Women's Hair Covering," *Judaism* 42, 4: 465–77.

Bullock, K., and J. Jafri. 2000. "Media (Mis) Representations: Muslim Women in the Canadian Nation," *Canadian Woman Studies* 20(2, Summer): 35–40.

Daly, C.M. 1999. "The 'Paarda' Expression of Hejaab among Afghan Women in a Non-Muslim Community," in L. Arthur, ed., *Religion, Dress and the Body*, pp. 147–61. Oxford: Berg.

D'Angelo, R.M. 1995. "Veils, Virgins, and the Tongues of Men and Angels: Women's Heads in Early Christianity," in H. Eilberg-Schwartz and W. Doniger, eds., *Off with Her Head! The Denial of Women's Identity in Myth, Religion, and Culture*, pp. 131–64. Berkeley, CA: University of California Press.

El Saadawi, N. 1980. *The Hidden Face of Eve: Women in the Arab World*, Hetata, trans. London: ZED Press.

Entwistle, J. 2000. *The Fashioned Body: Fashion, Dress, and Modern Social Theory*. Cambridge: Polity Press; Malden, MA: Blackwell.

Hoodfar, H. 1993. "The Veil in Their Minds and on Our Heads: The Persistence of Colonial Images of Muslim Women," *Resources for Feminist Research* 22(3/4): 5–18.

Ibrahim, B.S. 1999. *Women in Islam: Hijab*. Aalim: Islamic Research Foundation (IRF).

Jafri, G.J. 1998. "The Portrayal of Muslim Women in Canadian Mainstream Media: A Community-based Analysis." Online Afghan Women's Organization. Project report. Available at www.fmw.org/political_activities.htm.

Khaled, A. 2001. *Speaking in God's Name: Islamic Law, Authority and Women*. Oxford: Oneworld.

Khan, S. 1995. "The Veil as a Site of Struggle: The Hejab in Quebec," *Canadian Woman Studies* 15(2/3): 146–52.

Kutty, S. 1997. "Speaking for Her: The Representation of the Muslim Woman in Popular Culture." Canadian Muslim Civil Liberties Association. Pamphlet.

Mernissi, F. 1987. *Beyond the Veil: Male–Female Dynamics in Modern Muslim Society*. London: Al Sagi Books.

———. 1991. *Women and Islam: A Historical and Theological Enquiry*, M.J. Lakeland, trans. Oxford: B. Blackwell. Basil.

Nasser, M. 1999. "The New Veiling Phenomenon—Is It an Anorexic Equivalent? A Polemic," *Journal of Community & Applied Social Psychology* 9: 407–12.

Odeh, L.A. 1993. "Post-colonial Feminism and the Veil: Thinking the Difference," *Feminist Review* 43(Spring): 26–37.

Read, G., and P.J. Bartkowski. 2000. "To Veil or Not to Veil? A Case Study of Identity Negotiation among Muslim Women in Austin, Texas," *Gender and Society* 14(3, June): 395–417.

Roald, S.A. 2001. *Women in Islam: The Western Experience*. London: Routledge.

Shaffir, W. 1978. "Canada: Witnessing as Identity Consolidation: The Case of the Lubavitcher Chassidim," in H. Mol, ed., *Identity and Religion: International, Cross-cultural Approaches*, pp. 39–57. Beverly Hills, CA: Sage Publications.

Wolf, N. 1991. *The Beauty Myth*. Toronto: Vintage Books.

Yusuf, A.A., trans. 1946. *The Holy Qur'an*. Durban: Islamic Propagation Center International.

Yuval-Davis, N. 1994. "Identity Politics and Women's Ethnicity," in V. Moghadam, ed., *Identity Politics and Women: Cultural Reassertions and Feminism in International Perspective*, pp. 408–24. Boulder, CO: Westview Press.

Chapter 7

Overview

The previous articles in Part II have focused on "identity work" involved in gender display. Here, Gagné and colleagues focus on a particularly intense and complex form of identity work, as undertaken by people whose identities and daily lives are not defined by conventional notions of gender. Gagné and colleagues use the term " transgenderists," by which they mean not only transgender individuals who have chosen to live as members of a sex category different from the one that they were assigned at birth but also cross-dressers, drag queens, and others who "live outside the dominant gender system." The particular individuals in this article are "masculine to feminine," in that they were considered male by their families and communities when they were born but later came to challenge that identification and to associate themselves more closely with femininity in various forms, such as dressing like women or undergoing surgical operations to reshape their bodies.

Gagné and colleagues study how transgenderists "came out"—how they identified, first to themselves and later to friends and family, that they did not conform to the simple categorization of male or female. This coming out is superficially similar to coming out as gay or lesbian, but, unlike gay, lesbian, bisexual, or queer people, the participants in this study questioned not only their sexual desires but their understanding of themselves as men or boys. They experienced internal and externally imposed stigma for being "girlish" and reported shame or embarrassment associated with their unconventional gender displays. For many, a catalyst in their evolving gender identity was learning that they were not the only individuals in the world to have experienced such tension between their sex category and their gender, and that there were other transgender people like themselves. The discovery of a collective identity enabled their passage to a more authentic sense of self.

Others in the subjects' lives did not always appreciate the physical and psychological transformations they experienced, and their life stories include accounts of being considered an outsider or a deviant in a social world that is oriented to two and only two sexes with corresponding genders. Perhaps ironically, many of the participants in this study did not wish to challenge this sex-gender binary—they simply wanted to cross over to the other side of it and be accepted as feminine women; in other words, to "pass." For a minority, however, the entire concept of two genders tied to two sexes is innately oppressive, and they asserted their desire to live outside the sex-binary as individuals who escape easy categorization.

Coming Out and Crossing Over: Identity Formation and Proclamation in a Transgender Community

Patricia Gagné, Richard Tewksbury, and Deanna McGaughey

Much of the social scientific focus on transgendered individuals has derived from an interest in understanding "deviation" from the "normal" and "natural" two-sex system. . . . Within this literature, there has been little examination of sexuality (but see Herdt, 1994) and a virtual absence of research on the coming-out experiences of transgendered individuals.

In this article, we examine the coming-out experiences of . . . individuals who were members of the transgender community at the time we solicited volunteers for our project. Transgenderism refers to "the lives and experiences of diverse groups of people who live outside normative sex/gender relations" (Namaste, 1994: 228). Persons who enact alternative gender presentations or who have internalized alternative gender identities are referred to as "transgenderists" (Tewksbury and Gagné, 1996). When looking at the experiences of transgenderists, identity management concerns are at least as complex as those of bisexuals, gay men, and lesbians, if not more so. While there are some similarities between the coming-out processes of transgenderists and gay men, lesbians, and bisexuals, there are also salient differences. . . .

While transgenderism is an issue of sex and gender, it does entail aspects of sexual *reorientation*. Thus, sexually active transgenderists must recognize, tolerate, and learn to accept an alternative gender identity; develop a repertoire of coping strategies to manage public presentations of gender; and, in some cases, manage the actual transformation of permanent identity and anatomy. Whether gender transformations are temporary or permanent, the sense that one really is the sex associated with the gender portrayed involves a reexamination of sexual identity. For example, some anatomically male transsexuals and cross-dressers, in the process of establishing a feminine self, engage in sexual activity with other anatomical male persons. While the observers may morphologically define the experience as *homosexual* or *same sexed*, the social women experiencing the interaction tend to define it as *heterosexual*. . . .

. . . Whereas lesbians, gay men, and bisexuals are able to carefully control information dissemination, transgenderists, because of changes in gender or biological appearance, are often forced out of the closet, creating awkward—or even dangerous—situations. Transgenderists provide an opportunity to examine the private and public dimensions of achieving a new gender through interaction with others and the emergence and management of alternative sex, gender, and sexual identities.

Method

We completed 65 semi-structured, in-depth, tape-recorded interviews with masculine-to-feminine individuals from several points along the transgender spectrum (see Tewksbury and Gagné, 1996). *Transgenderism* . . . encompasses a variety of identities—including transsexual; fetish and non-fetishistic cross-dresser; drag queen, and other terms—as devised by individuals who live outside the dominant gender system. In this study, we have categorized individuals on the basis of the identity they proclaimed to us. . . .

Included in our sample are individuals who self-identify as pre- (n = 27), post- (n = 10), and non-operative (n = 4) transsexual. Transsexuals are people who believe themselves to be female and who wish to, or do, live full-time as women. Preoperative transsexuals are those who desire to have, but have not yet had, SRS [sex reassignment surgery]. Post-operative transsexuals are those who have had SRS. Non-operative transsexuals are those who live full-time or nearly full-time as women but who do not wish to have SRS. Some have availed themselves of other medical and cosmetic procedures—including female hormones, breast implants, and electrolysis, whereas others alter their gender presentations without bodily alteration. During childhood (before age 10), about one-third ($n = 16$) felt a strong desire to become a girl or believed themselves to be female. The remainder began to recognize a desire to be female during adolescence ($n = 15$) or adulthood ($n = 10$). They self-identified as heterosexual, bisexual, lesbian, and asexual. Although our sample included many male individuals who had had sexual relationships or encounters with other male persons, no one in our sample self-identified as gay at the time of the interview or at any time during their lives.

A small number of persons ($n = 5$) who cross-dressed and had no desire for SRS referred to themselves in more politically oriented terms. While there are subtle differences in politics, all five of these people have used transgenderism to challenge binary assumptions about sex, gender, and sexuality. Their intent is not to "pass" as women but to challenge the idea that gender is a "natural" expression of sex and sexuality. . . . In our discussions of the transgendered people in our sample, we have self-consciously adhered to the self-identifications used by our volunteers, with the exception of the final group of five. For purposes of clarity, we refer to this group as gender radicals. We have taken the liberty of doing this because all of them emphasized their desire to eliminate the existing system of gender, rather than just their own gender.

Our research was conducted over a one-year period, spanning 1994 and 1995. Early in the research process, we made a conscious decision to include all full-time or nearly full-time transgenderists who volunteered. We solicited volunteers through 14 transgender support groups, transgender online services, and by responding to personal ads in a national transgender publication. People in every region of the contiguous 48 states volunteered for interviews, making our research national in scope. Participants resided in large urban areas, small towns, suburbs, and rural areas. Our sample includes 4 African Americans, 2 Asians, 1 Hispanic, and 58 Caucasians. Participants ranged in age from 24 to 68 years, with a mean age of 44. Occupationally, they were diverse with jobs ranging from doctors, airline pilots, computer systems analysts, engineers, college professors, schoolteachers, enlisted members of the military, police officers, welders, mechanics, food service and clerical workers, and janitors. Although our sample was occupationally diverse, the majority was well educated and had long employment histories in the skilled trades and professions. Most members of our sample were either employed or voluntarily unemployed (i.e., retired or student) at the time we talked with them. Nonetheless, one post-operative and eight preoperative transsexuals were unemployed, and the majority of those who lived full-time as the gender into which they were not assigned at birth were vastly underemployed.[1]

Respondents were guided through several areas of inquiry, including their earliest transgender experiences or feelings; being discovered cross-dressed; acquiring girls' or women's clothing, makeup, and wigs; learning about and refining a feminine appearance or persona; participating in transgender support groups or online communities; finding therapists and surgeons and experiences with the medical community; identifying and labelling emotions, feelings, behaviours, and identity; telling others; transformations or stability in sexual fantasy, behaviour, and identity; and political and gender attitudes. Interviews ranged from 45 minutes to eight hours in length, averaging about three hours.

Early Transgendered Experiences

Examination of the earliest recollections that transgendered individuals have of feeling that either their sex or gender was "wrong" or did not "fit" for them are useful in providing insight into the earliest manifestations that become alternative identities. Many recollections of childhood may, in fact, be reconstructed biographies. Nonetheless, these are materials from which individuals mould current identities and, therefore are valid and significant.[2] This is the process in which the collective creation of biographical stories brings phenomenologically real "true selves" into being (Mason-Schrock, 1996).

Gender constancy—a sense that a person's gender is a permanent aspect of self—is acquired between the ages of three and five years (Kohlberg, 1966; Kohlberg and Ulian, 1974). In our sample, 16 transsexuals recalled wanting to be girls or knowing that they really were girls during early childhood. For all but one of the remainder, feelings of being or wanting to be a woman emerged during adolescence or adulthood. Among cross-dressers, all reported knowing they were boys in early childhood and throughout adolescence, but four said they remembered wishing they could be girls during early childhood, and two reported knowing they were male but wishing they could become female during adolescence. . . . Feminine behaviours and feelings of being or wanting to be girls created confusion for young children and adolescents, particularly when they received messages that they could not be or act that way.

For transsexuals and cross-dressers, one way of making sense of the incongruity between sex and gender was to explore whether a feminine boy might actually be able to become a girl. For example, one cross-dresser explained that at about the age of five, "I remember . . . asking my mother out in the backyard, 'Am I always going to be a boy? Could I change and be a girl someday?'" Such questions are undoubtedly common among young children. For most children, clothing and other expressions of gender are signifiers of maleness or femaleness. Cross-dressers explained that they were satisfied with explanations that they could not change their anatomy and become female but that they continued to want to temporarily "become" girls by wearing feminine clothing, makeup, and wigs. As adults, all but four cross-dressers (who were exploring the possibility they might be transsexual) reported knowing they were male and being happy with their sex and gender identity. Throughout their lives, they were able to conceal their transgenderism much more easily than were transsexuals, who felt compelled to act and be feminine at all times.

Among transsexuals, confusion over gender, desires to be female, or feelings of being female were commonly reported in childhood and over the life course. Many of the transsexuals in our sample thought they really were girls (in the dominant cultural sense) until they began to receive messages to the contrary. For example, one postoperative transsexual explained her earliest understanding of gender and the way in which it started to be corrected. She said,

> I was probably three or four years old. . . . I remember playing with paper dolls and Barbie dolls and stuff with my sisters and wearing their clothes. I didn't even know I wasn't a girl until [at school] I was told it was time to line up for a restroom break.

Differentiating themselves from girls did not come easily for these 16 transsexuals. Socializing messages might be gentle and subtle, as the ones above, or more laden with overt hostility and anger. For example, another preoperative transsexual explained,

> I can remember begging my mother to let me wear her clothes. . . . I kicked and screamed. . . . Another time she was ironing and I wanted my own ironing board and iron and be just like mommy. This time she got really angry and I guess I was becoming aware of the fact that I wasn't ever going to be a little girl, that it was socially unacceptable . . . because she said, "You want to be a little girl? Well, we'll put you in a little dress and tie your hair up in ribbons." . . . She became aggressive about it and at that point I understood that it was socially unacceptable.

In early childhood, cross-dressing and cross-gender behaviour appear to have been tolerated. However, as children advanced beyond the "toddler" stage, they were pressured by adults and other children to recognize and adhere to traditional conceptualizations of gender and conform to masculine stereotypes. Pressures to conform to the gender binary were often based on homophobic assumptions about gender "deviants." For example, a non-operative transsexual said,

> Around the time I was 9 or 10 years old, there was one boy in the neighborhood . . . [who] was never allowed to spend the night at my house. . . . All he would tell me is, "My dad won't let me." One afternoon I approached his dad about it. . . . This man turned an incredible red-purple color and shaking and pointing a finger in my face [said], "Because you're a fucking queer!" I didn't know what those words meant, but it was clear from his body language that whatever those words were tied to was not ok.

The pressure to adhere to the masculine stereotype was strong, and many in our sample tried to conform. Cross-dressers hid their dressing, segmenting it off from the rest of their lives. Among transsexuals, such segmentation of the feminine aspect of self was more difficult. The majority felt more comfortable playing with girls, participating in "girls" activities, and expressing and presenting themselves in more feminine ways. For those whose transgender feelings and behaviours began in early childhood, pressures to "fit" into the masculine stereotype and "act" like boys created confusion about identity, an internalized sense of deviance, and frequently strong self-loathing. For example, a preoperative transsexual said, "I didn't know it was transsexual. I just didn't feel like a male. Everyone was telling me I was and I felt I had to act that way. . . . I felt it was something very, very wrong."

After an initial period of confusion about sex and gender, most children recognized that cross-dressing and feminine behaviour were deviant and, therefore, they tried to repress it and keep it secret. This suggests that as children begin to understand the binary gender system, they become ashamed of feminine or transgendered feelings, learn to hide their behaviours, and become confused about who they are and how they fit into the world. Many in our sample talked about becoming addicted to alcohol or drugs later in life, in an effort to numb the emotional pain they experienced and to repress the "true self," which did not fit and, therefore, needed to be repressed. Throughout adolescence and adulthood, most went through periods of "purging," when they would stop engaging in transgendered behaviour and throw out feminine clothing, makeup, and wigs. Despite the stigma attached to transgenderism, however, the need to "be themselves" was strong. Even as they tried to stop, and as their feminine attributes were criticized and sanctioned, they found it impossible to stop and learned to become more and more secretive. For example, a preoperative transsexual explained,

> I was being beat up, called sissy. . . . I didn't feel normal. I felt like, "Why are you doing this? This isn't right. You're a boy." But I couldn't stop. . . .

Coming Out to One's Self

. . . When individuals fail to adhere to the gender binary, they are often told they are wrong or bad, so they tend to initially think of themselves as sick or deviant. Until they find similar others who have rejected stigma, self-blame and the internalization of deviance are common. As the transgenderists in our sample became aware that there were others in the world like them, they experienced a sense of self-recognition, and most quickly aligned themselves with new potential identities. The refinement and adoption of relatively stable identities occurred within the possibilities offered by the transgender subculture, which has been heavily influenced by medical models of transgenderism.

Most transsexuals and a minority of the cross-dressers in our sample reported being labelled "sissies" by parents, siblings, and schoolmates. Those labelled "sissy" or "girl-like" experienced extreme stigmatization, isolation, and at times abuse. Derogative comments from family members seemed to affect the self-esteem and self-concept more than insults from peers or other non-relatives. One non-operative transsexual married to a woman recounted how her parents and friends pressured her to be more masculine. She said,

> The kids in the neighborhood that I wanted to be friends with . . . were the girls. . . . I wanted my own doll and remember the boys in the neighborhood seemed to have a real problem with that. . . . In that same time period, my dad came into my bedroom one night and he took all the dolls out of my bed. He said I could keep the animals but the dolls had to go because, "You're a little boy and little boys don't sleep with dolls." . . .

Just as children tried to conceal transgenderism or conform to the expectations of family and other socializing agents, adults were likely to engage in similar coping strategies until they began to accept themselves as transgenderists. Transsexuals tended to react to negative messages by being hypermasculine. As adults, many in our sample went into physically strenuous or high-risk occupations where they could prove their masculinity. [One participant] said, "I would avoid doing anything that someone might see as being a remotely feminine kind of thing. I wouldn't even help my ex-[wife] plant a flower garden." Out of our entire sample, 18 had served in the military. Most said they hoped the experience would make men out of them. Although an extreme example of this sentiment, another preoperative transsexual explained,

> I knew there was something wrong with me and I wanted to do whatever I could to make a real man out of myself. So I joined the army. Voluntarily went to Vietnam. Voluntarily carried a machine gun in the jungle. I was a paratrooper. I was a Green Beret. I did everything I could do in that three-year period to make a man out of myself.

Cross-dressers were less likely to react in hypermasculine ways, primarily because they kept their feminine side hidden.

Throughout childhood, adolescence, and early to mid-adulthood most transgenderists in our study experienced shame and confusion for not being "right." They lived in a social region for which there was no idiom. Because they were sanctioned for feminine attributes and behaviour, they learned that there was no place for feminine boys or men in society. Feeling more comfortable with girls, they began to understand gender and sex within the social options presented to them. The socially constructed aspects of reality were so strong that believing they were born with the wrong genitals seemed more plausible than violating the gender binary. Even in adulthood, transsexuals frequently made efforts to conceal their genitals, even from themselves, by tucking them between the legs or taping them up. While relatively uncommon in our sample (during adulthood, $n = 2$), when transsexuals were unaware of available medical options or were unable to afford SRS, they attempted self-castration. These efforts indicate the degree to which gender is signified by genitalia.

It was common in our sample for transgenderists to experience sexual attractions to other men, to have sexual fantasies about men, or both. At the same time, they experienced social sanctions and pressures to conform to dominant conceptualizations of gender. While they worried they might be gay, they began to experience and explore sexuality within the binary system and its ancillary compulsory heterosexuality (Rich, 1989). As a 36-year-old bisexual cross-dresser explained, "You're getting all kinds of messages that men are men and women are women. Sissy boys and fags. The adolescent years are really, really hard on homosexuals and anything not mainstream sexually." Within our sample, adolescent male persons and adult men in the early stages of identity formation were frequently confused about the implications feminine behaviour had for their sexuality. As men, they knew sex with male individuals was unacceptable; but as women, it was a source of validation. Most reacted by repressing attractions to men, at least until they began to go out in public as women, when sexual interactions with men were indicative of passage into social womanhood.

None of the people in our sample adopted a gay identity, even temporarily, although sexual experimentation with male persons was a common aspect of the coming-out experience. Because of an understanding that transgenderism, homosexuality, and femininity were wrong, all but two transgenderists made efforts to conceal, to purge, to deny, and to cure themselves in order to avoid acceptance of their transgenderism.

Most commonly, the triggering event for acceptance of an identity came when, either accidentally or intentionally, the individual encountered others who served as symbols for available identities. However, role models who challenged binary conceptualizations of gender were largely unavailable because "there is no place for a person who is neither a woman or a man" (Lorber, 1994: 96), finding role models and formulating an identity outside the gender binary is virtually impossible. Thus, alternative identities were restricted to those available within the gender binary, usually found among those who had crossed *from* one gender *to* the only other one known to be legitimately available. . . .

Finding others who felt as they did helped to alleviate, but not remove, the sense of isolation experienced by transgendered individuals. Nonetheless, through such initial exposures, many individuals learned that there were alternatives to living in confusion and shame, if one was willing to transform (either temporarily or permanently) to the other gender. Simply learning that SRS was possible led some to reconfigure their identities and reassess their place in the world.

In today's information age, online computer services appear to be emerging as a primary location for finding both virtual and real mentors. It was common for transgenderists who deciphered and accepted their identities in the 1990s to have done so with the assistance of online bulletin boards and personal conversations with already-identifying transgenderists. Here, in the privacy of one's home or work area, contacts could be made that allowed both experimentation with identities and informational inquiries that did not jeopardize existing identities or social, occupational, and familial relationships. In addition, online services allowed individuals to access information beyond that concerning the strictly erotic aspects of cross-dressing. For some transgenderists, this was a critical factor, as tabloid media and sensationalist reports have created a common misperception of cross-dressing as primarily an erotic activity. A self-identified radical transgenderist credits his subscription to one online service with helping him understand that cross-dressing need not be sexually charged. He said, "It wasn't until I got a hold of [online service] that I got exposed to aspects other than the erotic aspects, which are all over the place." . . .

Coming Out to Others

Accepting an identity for one's self was one thing; proclaiming and working to get others to accept it was quite different. Going public with a transgendered identity could be an intimidating experience, to say the least. The degree to which transgenderists were intimidated about revealing their transgenderism may be heard in the words of a 10-month, post-operative transsexual, who said,

> For somebody who's been a freak, a hippie, and a marijuana dealer, . . . and a flamboyant dresser, and somebody who refuses to get a conventional job and all this, somebody who's not been afraid of public opinion, it's, I think, notable that the gender area of my life and the social expectations were the one area I was afraid of public opinion.

Intimidation came from two fronts: (1) fears about how one would be treated by others and (2) anxieties about how others would cope with what was certainly seen by many as "non-traditional" behaviour. . . . These concerns typically centred on one's family, both nuclear and extended.

According to the accounts of those who have proclaimed their transgender identities to significant others, the fears about negative reactions were largely exaggerated, but not altogether unwarranted. . . . They consciously selected individuals to come out to those who were, in fact, sympathetic to the alternative identity. Who would be accepting was ascertained through discussions of various potentially volatile issues. In that way, transgenderists learned if there was a need for caution or preparatory education of the recipient. Those who received negative reactions to their proclamations were least likely to have gathered information or to have laid the necessary groundwork. Instead, they simply announced the new identity. For example, a preoperative transsexual decided to tell an 18-year-old daughter, who did not even know that her father had been cross-dressing, when the daughter moved back home. She said,

> After a week or two there, it seemed inappropriate not to tell my daughter. The girl lives in the house. For crying out loud, she's 18 years old. So I told her and I didn't really build up to it or anything. . . . She was always in the bathroom, doing hair and makeup and stuff. I stopped in to chat. I suppose it was like a bomb or something like that. "By the way . . . I'm going to have a sex change." She turned into an ice cube.

Although the experience of telling one's first "other" was not necessarily a negative experience, fears remained, and careful, often painful, decisions were made regarding with whom to share an emergent identity. Interestingly, two factors stand out about these early disclosures. First, they were usually done only out of a sense of responsibility, when someone was perceived as "needing to know." Second, the individuals with whom this information was shared were almost always female, most often a significant other. This was true among all groups of transgenderists in our sample. . . .

The arena where transgenderists (usually transsexuals) were least likely to receive positive reactions was at work. Although there were a few people who were permitted to transition on the job, it was more common for transsexuals to be fired, demoted, pressured to quit, and harassed by other workers. Some found employment in unskilled, low-wage jobs, such as janitors or in fast-food restaurants; others worked for temporary agencies. A few in our sample went back to college, transitioning as students. The loss of identity and the structure of one's daily routine that comes with a career was more difficult for transsexuals to cope with than the actual loss of income. After accepting a severance package in exchange for her silence about her job termination, one post-operative transsexual wrote to the first author, "I have spent my entire life becoming the best [job title] I could be. Today I sold myself for 50 pieces of silver." Frequently, the loss of professional identity and income came at the same time that relationships with old friends and family members were being risked and sometimes lost.

Early excursions into the public domain were commonly as frightening as coming out to significant others or on the job. While going out and passing in public may be thought to be different from coming out, it is important to recognize that for the majority of transgenderists, the goal is to be perceived and accepted as a woman, not a transgenderist. Telling others about their transgenderism is done primarily to lay the groundwork for greater expression, acceptance, and legitimation of a feminine identity, and this was accomplished in public and in private interactions. Although there was variation between going out in public or telling a significant other first, every person in our sample felt a need to expand their spheres of interaction with others. While control over access to information about the transgendered identity remained important, this became less salient as the need to interact with others publicly increased. Because of the fear of the danger inherent in negative public reactions, most transgenderists carefully planned and carried out their initial public excursions in limited-access locations.

When transgenderists began to go out in public, they did so because of a need to receive reactions from others to legitimate identity. While some have undoubtedly been driven back into the closet by their initial forays into public places, in our sample, such excursions served to increase commitment to the emergent identity. Selection of safe places for public ventures meant that transgenderists looked for locations where they could make quick and easy entrances and exits and where they are unlikely to encounter disapproving others. Transgenderists most commonly reported that their first ventures were to gay community events or locations, simply driving in their cars, or going to known meeting places for transgenderists. The most common site for first ventures was gay bars. Here, among other marginalized community members, individuals could try out their new identities. Despite a strong desire to avoid being perceived as homosexual, gay bars were defined as safe havens (Levine, Shaiova, and Mihailovic, 1975). For example, a preoperative transsexual, who had been living as a woman full-time for seven months, related that "while I was working on coming out full-time, I needed a safe place to go while I practised. The bar was it. I know the drag queens might not like that. It was still a safe place for me though."

Typically, successful ventures provided the impetus and courage for transgenderists to move forward and present themselves face-to-face with others; however, these steps were taken slowly and carefully. Movement was usually into either a gay bar or a gathering of other transgenderists. For example, a preoperative transsexual who is fully out only to one family member and acquaintances in the transgender community, explained her first time out in public as follows:

> About 10 years ago. . . . I was out very late one night, got in my car, drove downtown to the north side of the city which is known for its gays, lesbians, and an occasional transvestite. Walked to what I thought was a bar where transvestites hung out and sat down, had a couple of drinks, couple cigarettes. . . . I did things like get dressed and drove around. I'd go for a short walk around the block or something. I didn't think I was good enough yet to go out in daylight and try to pull it off as a woman.

In gay bars and neighbourhoods, transgenderists were most likely to be interpreted as marginal members of the queer subculture. Such settings provide a place where one who is "neither woman nor man" (Lorber, 1994: 96) is most likely to find a social place that does not disturb the social order.

For others, the impetus to appear in public for the first time surfaced when opportunities arose to meet other transgenderists in the context of a support group. Support groups were one location where the most important identity tests occurred, when the individual encountered other transgenderists. As they entered such groups, transgenderists commonly reported a feeling of total acceptance and freedom to be themselves, often for the first time in their lives. If these supposedly similar others were willing to accept the individual, and the individual felt safe in the group, this communicated that she or he truly was transgendered. The value of support groups, online services, organizations, and publications becomes most clear in this context. . . .

Resolution of Identity

After a lifetime of being stigmatized and feeling as if they did not fit, the transgenderists in our sample engaged in a long process of identity exploration. The majority in our sample explained that they had arrived at a "true" identity, with which they felt they could "be themselves." Only a minority of men who cross-dressed, but were exploring transsexualism, had not yet resolved their identities. In their efforts to resolve and establish an identity that was comfortable, the individuals in our sample shared diverse goals and visions for themselves and the community. Transsexuals sought to "completely" transform and live convincingly as their true (female) selves. Cross-dressers sought only to have opportunities to temporarily vary their public identity presentations, express their femininity, and be recognized and treated as women. Only the gender radicals in our sample wished to live and be recognized as transgendered. Significant differences appeared among specific transgender identities. Among most transsexuals and cross-dressers, there was an overwhelming desire that femininity and treatment as a woman were achieved. For a minority, as experience and confidence were gained, passing was a desirable, but no longer essential, aspect of going out in public. These people tended to recognize that physical stature, including height and musculature, made it difficult, if not impossible, for them to pass. Among gender radicals, concerns with presenting a convincing appearance as a woman were secondary, if at all important for them. The goal was to challenge dominant conceptualizations of gender and create new possibilities.

Among transsexuals, because of the internalized identity as women, it was most common to find an aspiration to be seen and identified by others as real women. When discussing this feeling, transsexuals expressed a need to "pass" in their daily interactions. This desire was paramount for such individuals and taken as a symbolic testament of final arrival at their desired self and socially constructed identity. One divorced, preoperative transsexual summarized this sentiment well when she commented, "[Passing] to me is the most important aspect of the whole thing. If you can't do that, I don't see the point of living this way." Enduring the internal and social struggles encountered in the process of recognizing and accepting a new identity and introducing oneself to the outside world was valued only if there could be a non-stigmatizing, "normal" resolution to the process. Transsexuals did not wish to challenge the gender binary, although most perceived their transitions as very radical actions. Rather, their goal was to "become" the women they "truly are" and to pass from being their masculine selves into full womanhood. Often, after learning to pass and completing the transformation process, transsexuals dropped out of the transgender community and assumed their place as women in society. . . .

Although most transgenderists were concerned with passing as well as possible, there is an emergent group within the community that seeks a free expression of gender, outside of the binary system. For example, the ambigenderist in our sample explained that she had moved beyond such concerns, focusing on her own welfare and identity, not the perceptions of others.

> At one time, [passing] was important. I don't care anymore. A lot of times I'll go out in a dress . . . no makeup on. I'm not trying to pass and I know I'm not going to pass. I am who I am. . . . It is political, everything's political. A social statement about who I am and I'm going to express myself.

For both those who were and were not seeking to pass when in public, the most common, overwhelming desire was to simply be accepted. This was difficult unless they could find ways to fit within the binary and symbolically communicate identity within the idiomatic system of gender expression. To "blend in" to society as a woman was something most transgenderists, especially transsexuals, saw as an ultimate goal. The ultimate resolution was an identity that was not wrapped in the language of transgenderism. To be known as simply just another person was desirable. . . .

Conclusion

Gender is so pervasive that it is taken for granted and often completely overlooked, until the norms of gender presentation, interaction, or organization are inadvertently violated or deliberately challenged (Lorber, 1994). . . .

Individuals who attempt to challenge the binary conceptualization of sex and gender, by living androgynously between genders, are likely to be ridiculed and stigmatized (see Gagné and Tewksbury, 1996). Those who attempt to live outside of the sex/gender binary, for example, by publicly confessing that they are male persons with (or who would like to have) breasts or vaginas, are also likely to be ostracized. Those who are willingly or unwittingly unconvincing in their gender presentations and interactions are subject to greater levels of emotional and physical abuse than are those who are able to pass. It is those who are publicly perceived as "not women/not men" who pose the greatest challenge to the binary system. Nonetheless, the goal of most is to be perceived as a woman and treated like a lady. Those who pass are perceived as women, and any challenge they might have posed to the gender system goes unnoticed.

As we have shown, the recognition, exploration, establishment, and final resolution of an identity outside cultural understandings is a difficult, complex, and for some, impossible process. Despite the policing of gender that was experienced by the transgenderists in our sample, the need to express a "true self" was an overwhelming urge that could not be denied. Although many tried to hide their femininity through hypermasculine activity or self-isolation, and most tried to deny transgendered feelings and urges, all eventually found the urge to "be themselves" overwhelmingly undeniable. Among our sample, others" reactions to them playing with girls, engaging in "girls" activities, cross-dressing, wearing makeup, and other expressions of a feminine self caused confusion, anxiety, and a deep sense of shame. Only when they discovered that there were others like them were they able to begin to make sense of what they were experiencing and who they were. Entering into a community of supportive others allowed for an exploration and resolution of identity. Our data suggest that gender is not a natural and inevitable outgrowth of sex. Those who are not comfortable expressing gender that is congruent with genital configuration experience an overwhelming urge to express gender in alternative ways. Nonetheless, the vast majority stay within the gender binary as masculine men and feminine women. The tendency to stay within the binary gender system is so strong that as Hausman (1993) has asserted, gender determines sex, rather than the reverse. Given the limited range of identities available to them, it is interesting, but not surprising, that the overwhelming majority of transgendered individuals adhere to traditional conceptualizations of sex and gender.

Notes

1. We recognize that there is a transgender community within the impoverished class, but we were unable to solicit volunteers from that segment of the population through the routes we used.
2. This view, however, is disputed by others who believe that retrospective biography construction is actually a search for ways "to fashion this information into a story that leads inexorably to the identity" that is being constructed (Mason-Schrock, 1996: 176–7).

References

Adam, B. 1995. *The Rise of a Gay and Lesbian Movement*, rev. ed. New York: Twayne.

Altman, D. 1982. *The Homosexualization of America*. Boston: Beacon.

Bornstein, K. 1994. *Gender Outlaw. On Men, Women, and the Rest of Us*. New York: Random House.

Bullough, V.L., and B. Bullough. 1993. *Cross Dressing, Sex, and Gender*. Philadelphia: University of Pennsylvania Press.

D'Emilio, J. 1983. *Sexual Politics, Sexual Communities: The Making of a Homosexual Minority in the United States, 1940–1970*. Chicago: University of Chicago Press.

Epstein, S. 1994. "A Queer Encounter: Sociology and the Study of Sexuality," *Sociological Theory* 12: 188–202.

Foucault, M. [1978] 1990. *The History of Sexuality: An Introduction*. Vol. 1, R. Hurley, trans. New York: Vintage.

Gagné, P., and R. Tewksbury. 1996. "No "Man's" Land: Transgenderism and the Stigma of the Feminine Man," in M. Texler Segal and V. Demos, eds., *Advances in Gender Research*. Vol. 1. Greenwich, CT: jai Press.

Gecas, V. 1991. "The Self-Consent as a Basis for a Theory of Motitvation," in J.A. Howard and P.L. Callero, eds., *The Self–Society Dynamic*. Cambridge, UK: Cambridge University Press.

Goffman, E. 1963. *Stigma: Notes on the Management of a Spoiled Identity*. Englewood Cliffs, NJ: Prentice-Hall.

Hausman, B.L. 1993. "Demanding Subjectivity: Transsexualism, Medicine and the Technologies of Gender," *Journal of the History of Sexuality* 3: 270–302.

Herdt, G. 1994. "Introduction: Third Sexes and Third Genders," in G. Herdt, ed., *Third Sex, Third Gender: Beyond Sexual Dimorphism in Culture and History*. New York: Zone Books.

Kohlberg, L. 1966. "A Cognitive-Developmental Analysis of Children's Sex-role Concepts and Attitudes," in E.E. Maccoby, ed., *The Development of Sex Differences*. Stanford, CA: Stanford University Press.

Kohlberg, L., and D.Z. Ulian. 1974. "Stages in the Development of Psychosexual Concepts and Attitudes," in R.C. Friedman, R.M. Richard, and R.L. Vande Wiele, eds., *Sex Differences in Behavior*. New York: Wiley.

Laqueur, T. 1990. *Making Sex: Body and Gender from the Greeks to Freud*. Cambridge, MA: Harvard University Press.

Levine, E.M., C.H. Shaiova, and M. Mihailovic. 1975. "Male to Female: The Role Transformation of Transexuals," *Archives of Sexual Behavior* 5: 173–85.

Lorber, J. 1994. *Paradoxes of Gender*. New Haven, CT: Yale University Press.

Mason-Schrock, D. 1996. "Transsexuals' Narrative Construction of the 'True Self,'" *Social Psychology Quarterly* 59: 176–92.

Morris, J. 1974. *Conundrum*. Faber & Faber.

Namaste, K. 1994. "The Politics of Inside/Out: Queer Theory, Poststructuralism, and a Sociological Approach to Sexuality," *Sociological Theory* 12: 220–31.

Pauly, I.B. 1990. "Gender Identity Disorders: Evaluation and Treatment," *Journal of Sex Education & Therapy* 16: 2–24.

Raymond, J.G. 1994. *The Transsexual Empire: The Making of the She-male*. New York: Teachers College Press.

Rich, A. 1989. "Compulsory Heterosexuality and Lesbian Existence," in L. Richardson and V. Taylor, eds., *Feminist Frontiers II: Rethinking Sex, Gender, and Society*. New York: Random House.

Rothblatt, M. 1995. *The Apartheid of Sex: A Manifesto on the Freedom of Gender*. New York: Crown.

Seidman, S. 1994. "Symposium: Queer Theory/ Sociology: A Dialogue," *Sociological Theory* 12: 166–77.

———, ed. 1996. *Queer Theory/Sociology*. Cambridge, MA: Blackwell.

Stein, A., and K. Plummer. 1994. "'I can't even think straight': Queer Theory and the Missing Sexual Revolution in Sociology," *Sociological Theory* 12: 1778–87.

Stoller, R.J. 1971. "The Term 'Transvestism,'" *Archives of General Psychiatry* 24: 230–7.

Stone, G.P. 1975. "Appearance and the Self," in D. Brissett and C. Edgley, eds., *Life as Theatre: A Dramaturgical Sourcebook*. Chicago: Aldine.

Talamini, J.T. 1981. "Transvestism: Expression of a Second Self," *Free Inquiry in Creative Sociology* 9: 72–4.

———. 1982. *Boys Will Be Girls: The Hidden World of the Heterosexual Male Transvestite*. Lanham, MD: University Press of America.

Taylor, V., and N. Whittier. 1992. "Collective Identity and Social Movement Communities: Lesbian Feminist Mobilization," in A.D. Morris and C. McClurg Mueller, eds., *Frontiers in Social Movement Theory*. New Haven, CT: Yale University Press.

Tewksbury, R., and P. Gagné. 1996. "Transgenderists: Products of Non-normative Intersections of Sex, Gender, and Sexuality," *Journal of Men's Studies* 5: 105–29.

Weinberg, R.S. 1978. "On 'Doing' and 'Being' Gay: Sexual Behavior and Homosexual Male Self-identity," *Journal of Homosexuality* 4: 563–78.

West, C., and D.H. Zimmerman. 1987. "Doing Gender," *Gender & Society* 1: 125–51.

West, C., and S. Fenstermaker. 1995. "Doing Difference," *Gender & Society* 9: 8–37.

Woodhouse, A. 1989. *Fantastic Women: Sex, Gender and Transvestism*. New Brunswick, NJ: Rutgers University Press.

Chapter 8

Overview

The transgender individuals interviewed by Gagné and colleagues have undertaken a particularly arduous and intense form of gender transformation as they "cross over" from one gender presentation to another. Theberge examines a different form of gender transformation, as members of one gender enter social and cultural settings that have historically been the territory of the other gender. Sports is the ideal setting to see these transformations in action, as women move into historically masculine sports, such as ice hockey.

Theberge followed a women's hockey team for three years and observes how ideas about femininity and womanhood become interwoven with discussions about the future direction of the sport. In particular, the physical aggression associated with hockey comes under scrutiny. Body checking marks the border between men's hockey and women's—it is permitted in the former but not the latter—and so body checking becomes a symbol of debate over whether women's hockey is as good as the "real thing" or whether it is a feminized imitation of the men's game. Theberge reveals a range of opinions on the desirability of body checking. For some women players, the "feminization" of hockey by means of the ban on body checking means that they are playing a lesser form of hockey. For others, the ban on body checking allows a different game to emerge, more based on speed and skating skills than on aggression, which they see as an improvement on the game played by men. At the same time as women's hockey is challenging some of the pillars of the men's game, Theberge argues that some women athletes also accept uncritically many of the other aspects of men's hockey, such as the necessity of "playing hurt" and enduring bodily damage for the sake of the sport.

As Theberge points out, debates about hockey are not merely debates about the rules of a team sport. She argues that men's hockey has been treated as the hegemonic, or dominant, form of the game, and so challenges to the rules of play from women's hockey are challenges to masculine hegemony in the world of organized sport. She poses the intriguing question of whether, in the gender transformations occasioned by women's participation in hockey, women are changing the game, or the game is changing women, by immersing them in a sports culture that normalizes injury and pain.

"It's Part of the Game": Physicality and the Production of Gender in Women's Hockey

Nancy Theberge

Perhaps as much as any social setting in the contemporary period, the world of sport is seeing considerable change regarding the condition of women and gender relations. To be sure, professional sport remains largely a male preserve in which the majority of opportunities and rewards go to men. In other contexts, including school and university sport and international competitions, including most notably the Olympics, opportunities for women are expanding, performances are improving, and public interest is rising. These developments pose a challenge to ideologies of gender and to the historical association between gender, physicality, and power.

A particularly significant challenge to gender ideologies is the increased involvement of women in sports that Bryson (1990: 174) calls "flag carriers" of masculinity. These are sports that "quintessentially promote hegemonic masculinity and to which a majority of people are regularly exposed" (Bryson, 1990: 174). Writing from an Australian setting, Bryson cites as examples cricket and football (i.e., soccer). In the North American context, the best examples are football and ice hockey. In these sports, which celebrate force and toughness and involve direct confrontation between competitors, it is "dominate or lose" (Whitson, 1994: 359).

This article provides an analysis of challenges to hegemonic masculinity posed by women's participation in the "flag carrier" sport of ice hockey. Data are taken from fieldwork and interviews with players and coaches participating at the highest levels of the sports in Canada. The analysis begins with a discussion of the satisfaction players derive from the physicality of sport. This is followed by a detailed examination of the material and ideological conditions that structure the experience of physicality. A key determinant of the practice of women's hockey is rules that limit—but by no means eliminate—body contact. Debates about the place of contact in women's hockey and its relationship to injury occur within a framework in which men's sport is positioned as the "real" thing. The conclusion contrasts the transformative potential of sports organized within the dominant model of masculine sport with possibilities presented by activities organized outside the framework of institutionalized sport.

Data and Methodology

Women's hockey is now experiencing a period of growth and development, with the most notable event in this regard being its inclusion in the Olympic program for the 1998 games in Nagano, Japan. The first World Championships were held in 1990, with subsequent events in 1992 and 1994. Canada has won all three of these competitions.

In Canada, the sport is growing; the number of female players registered with the Canadian Hockey Association increased from 8,146 in 1990–1 to 19,050 in 1994–5. These figures do not include girls playing on boys' teams, for which there are no reliable statistics (Etue and Williams, 1996). While school and university programs are expanding, the sport is primarily organized in clubs that are affiliated with provincial associations, which in turn are affiliated with the national governing body, the Canadian Hockey Association.

The analysis presented here is part of a broader study of women's ice hockey in Canada. The primary focus of the research is a team I call the Blades, which plays in a league located in a large Canadian metropolitan area. The league in which the Blades play is generally considered to be the strongest in the country. As an indication of this strength, several players from the Blades and from other teams in its league were members of one or more Canadian national teams that won World Championships in 1990, 1992, and 1994.

The research began when I attended the Annual General Meeting of the Provincial Women's Hockey Association in May 1992, where I met a woman who plays on the Blades and also operates a girls' hockey camp. In July I spent several days at the camp, where I met the Blades coach and told him of my interest in doing research in women's hockey. He was supportive, and in November, shortly after the start of the season, I attended a practice during which the coach introduced me to the team. I then met with the players in the coach's absence, explained my interests, and asked for permission to spend time with the team for the purpose of doing research.

Following this meeting, I began to attend games, practices, and other events such as the annual Christmas party. The fieldwork continued from November 1992 until the completion of the season in April 1993 and through the following season, from October 1993 until April 1994. I had complete access to team activities, including access to the team change room where I spent time with the players before and after games and practices. I also accompanied the team to out-of-town tournaments, including the provincial and national championships. Following each game, practice, or other events, I wrote field notes. The field notes cover a range of issues concerned with the practice and organization of the sport, team activities, and team dynamics.

To provide some perspective on experiences of players from elsewhere in the sport, I interviewed an additional eight players from three provinces, all of whom played at an elite level. I also interviewed eleven coaches from three provinces, all of whom also have experience at the highest levels of women's hockey. These additional interviews, conducted between 1993 and 1995, focused on the practice of the sport and the organization of women's hockey in Canada. All of the interviews were tape-recorded and transcribed.

There is no professional women's hockey in Canada, and the women who are the subject of this research have "day jobs" or are students. Their involvement in hockey is nonetheless of a very high calibre, and they are committed athletes. For the purpose of the analysis provided here, it is important to note that the data are taken from athletes who participate at the highest level of the sport.

Playing the Game: The Construction of Women's Hockey

The rules of play in men's and women's ice hockey are substantially the same, with one major difference: the rules on women's hockey prohibit intentional body checking—that is, intentional efforts to hit, or "take out," an opposing player. To be sure, there is still considerable use of the body and body contact in women's hockey, both intentional and unintentional. To watch a game is to see players constantly try to outmanoeuvre and outmuscle one another. At the same time, women's games are noticeably different from the full-contact game played at the higher levels of the men's sport.

Interviews with players and coaches reveal a variety of views about the elimination of body checking from women's hockey. Respondents generally agree this results in a game in which speed, strategy, and playing skills are featured more prominently than in a full-contact game, which emphasizes power and force. Beyond this point of agreement, however, lies greater debate about the construction of women's hockey, with contrasting assessments of the relation of women's and men's hockey.

Until the late 1980s, the rules regarding body contact in women's hockey varied across Canada. The sample of women interviewed for this research includes a number who have played both full contact and the current game, which prohibits body checking. These players see advantages to both versions. While most acknowledge the attraction of the game that favours speed and playmaking, a number of these same players also express a sense of pleasure and accomplishment in playing the full-contact game and in receiving and taking a body check well. In interviews, these women describe body checking as "part of the game," "the way it should be," and "part of the fun." In this view, body checking is a skill, one among a repertoire of abilities that players can master. The following statement by a player is a representative account:

> It's a certain aggressiveness. You're putting your strength against, your technique against. It's still a technique. It's not somebody, to me it's not go and kill that person, they hurt me, I'm going to get them back. It's nothing like that. It's a technique that you've learned and you can complete, and maybe you can complete it better than they can. You can prove your flexibility and your stamina, your stability on the ice.

Other players support the limitations on contact. One woman, who has never played the full-contact game, said:

> I prefer it without. Maybe just because I've always played without. You know the women's game being a bit different from the men's game, it may actually be better without it. I like to think of it as more of a finesse game. And I don't know if body contact has any part in it, really if it would enhance it in any way. I mean I think

> maybe the reason for having the body contact in the men's game is possibly just to make it more exciting to watch. I don't know. It's hard to say when you haven't really played that much.

Coaches also express a range of views. Some indicate that the women's game, as it is played today, is ideal—it is physical, sometimes very physical, and "just right" in this regard. Some see the inclusion of body checking as the "wedge" that leads to the unacceptably rough play that characterizes men's hockey. One coach offered the following comments:

> I ask myself sometimes, "Would body contact be a good thing?" It could be good if they stay within the limits, which seems very hard to do. And if the guys didn't do it, we're not smarter than the guys. . . . Women's hockey, if you were allowed body contact, to me, we'll end up as guys' hockey with slashing and cross checking. In my head, it's hard to believe it won't happen.

Other coaches have reservations about, or actively disagree with, the current formulation. Like some players, these coaches say checking is "part of the game" and a skill that can be—and should be—taught and used effectively. The argument that body checking is responsible for the violence that plagues the men's game is also disputed. Several respondents noted that women's hockey already has severe penalties—usually suspension for several games—that limit the incidence of dirty play. So long as these sanctions are in place, it is argued, introducing body checking will not lead to an increased incidence of other, undesirable features of men's hockey.

A number of players recognized the dilemma of playing an alternative version of the sport. The player quoted above on the technique of body checking had extensive experience playing boys' hockey before moving to women's hockey in late adolescence. She commented on the women's game:

> It is a different game and there are different rules. . . . I think a lot of women think it's better. But I prefer the game where you're allowed contact. I grew up playing that game. I just think it's different and why make it different . . . I want to be able to say I play hockey and [people] understand it's the same hockey. But now I have to say I play girls' hockey. It's not the same game as boys' hockey. . . . They're changing the game.

Another player, whose only experience is in women's hockey, offered further commentary. She described her reaction to a seminar she attended during which an official from the Canadian Hockey Association emphasized the uniqueness of the game:

> When you're playing a sport, you don't go out there saying, "Ok, I'm a woman. Ok, I have to play like one." You go out there and you play aggressive, you play your game and that's that, whereas people are trying, I think, to give the image that it's just an all-skill game and it's a woman's game kind of thing. Basically they were saying that you know women don't compare to men. Which is true, when you get to the older ages. I mean there's no NHL calibre women in the game right now and that's fine. Strength factor and everything, I mean people are going to know that no matter what. But you don't have to go around saying that this is a woman's sport, there's no contact, it's totally skill, and make it sound like it's a nothing sport either. I think that's part of the reason why women's hockey went nowhere for so many years.

A third player, who played women's hockey when body checking was allowed, also expressed cynicism about efforts to de-emphasize the physical aspects and to promote women's hockey on the basis of its difference from the men's game. This player explicitly acknowledged a connection between the rules of play in women's hockey and concerns about its image:

> It doesn't make any sense to me. If they want to say, I don't know, the words feminine, I don't like those types of terms, masculine, feminine, all that crap. If they want to do it [promote women's hockey], that's not the way to do it, for my view. Hitting doesn't make you any more of a boy than non-hitting. I just don't know what they are trying to do.

The relationship between the risk of injury and the place of body checking is one of the contested features of the debate about the construction of women's hockey. Some coaches and players believe that a main reason for eliminating body checking is to reduce the risk of injury. Others dispute this association and believe that eliminating body checking has actually increased the risk of injury.[1] The explanation is that without checking, there is more illegal contact and stick work. One player who said, "I think I've had more injuries with the no intentional body checking rule in," explained the effect of the rule on the practice of the game:

> I think because [with no body checking] I'm not expecting some of the hits that I'm getting because some people don't play within the rules. And if they can hit you or hurt you and hit you and put you into the boards or whatever when you're not expecting it, which usually I don't because I think, no, we play within the rules, they don't want to get a penalty, they don't want to hurt me. You know I'm a nice person [she laughs]. So I don't expect it.

Another player offered further explanation:

> I think most of the players at first liked the idea of no checking, no intentional body checking. Some of them I think have come around and said, "Hey, yeah, less stick work." So okay, say you get frustrated out there and you hit somebody clean and you know it's coming, like if you know it's coming you're not going to get hurt. That's the way I always feel. If . . . there's body checking I know I'm going to get hurt. Fine. I know how to go into the boards a little differently. . . . So with that in mind, yeah, I prefer the body checking, myself. It's the game.

When asked why players seem to see an inevitable trade-off between checking and illegal stick work, she explained:

> Well because you've got to slow them down somehow. You've got to get in front of them somehow and usually if you can't hit them or at least take a piece of them, that's the only thing left. And that's your stick to slow them down. Myself—unless you can outskate them. Well, that's not me.

This player's comments speak to the view that checking is part of the repertoire of a hockey player's skills. When it is not available, players resort to other tactics to accomplish their task. These tactics include illegal and sometimes dangerous practices.

Other players who spoke of the risks of body checking attributed these risks to the fact that players are not taught to receive and take checks.

One player said that when there was body checking:

> It wasn't clean at all. Girls aren't taught how to hit. 'Cause you don't hit all the way up. Then all of a sudden you get to senior A and there's contact. No one knows how to hit; sticks are up, hands are up.

A second player provided a similar analysis. When asked about playing the game when there was body checking, she said:

> Well to be honest with you checking was fine but I believe that the women weren't taught properly how to check. And there was a lot of injuries, like I was pretty scared of a few people out there just because I know, they were going to hit you like this [demonstrates], with their fists up or whatever. If checking had been taught, you know properly at a young age, just like the boys, they learn checking at a young age up, then maybe it wouldn't be so bad. Like you know, to take a hit on the boards is fine. It's just, I don't think women know how to check properly.

Conclusion: Women's Hockey and the Challenge to Masculine Hegemony

This discussion has focused on two aspects of the debate around physicality in women's hockey: the risk of injury and the appeal of a full-contact version of the sport versus one that prohibits body checking but is nonetheless very physical. Debate over these issues occurs within a material and ideological context that conditions the practice of the sport.

Suggestions that a "problem" with body checking is that girls are not taught this skill complement the observation that eliminating checking improves the game by making it easier to officiate. Both imply that the "problem" with checking is not the practice, per se, but limitations in the organization of the sport regarding training and skill development of athletes and officials.

Some respondents likened their support for the inclusion of body checking in women's hockey to the professionalization of the sport. When asked about reasons for the prohibition of body checking, a coach and a player both responded, "These people [we] aren't being paid to play" and "They [we] have to get up and go to work the next day." Another coach who endorsed the inclusion of body checking went on to note that it would only be feasible if the game were organized professionally and women could earn a living by their efforts. In effect, he was arguing for a structure that offers material rewards to athletes commensurate with their own investment and commitment.

Gender equality has received increased attention in many sports, including hockey, in recent years (Williams, 1995). Calls for better training of players, coaches, and officials, and improved material conditions, including medical support, are an important aspect of the struggle within women's hockey to gain legitimation. At the same time, this struggle heightens the significance of the debate around the construction of the sport. As women players become bigger, stronger, and more skilled and as the practices of the game become more intense and physical, the question "How should women play hockey?" raises the ideological stakes.

Women's hockey is played in a cultural context in which men's sport is hegemonic. This view that body checking is an integral "part of the game" is emblematic of hockey as it has historically been conceptualized, practised, and epitomized by the National Hockey League. Debates about what version of the game is most appealing, and the relation between physicality and the incidence of dirty play, occur in a context in which this version has been positioned as the "real" game and the model against which others have been compared and evaluated (Theberge, 1995).

The dominance of the "NHL model" of hockey is under challenge today, not only from women's hockey, but also from within boys' hockey, about which parents and officials have expressed concern. Targets of criticism in boys' hockey are the style of play, which emphasizes intimidation and domination, and the competitive and elitist system that eliminates boys by early adolescence, boys who are unable to perform by these standards. In response to these concerns, some provincial and local hockey associations have implemented programs that prohibit body checking, reduce the emphasis on winning, and stress the enjoyment of participation (Gruneau and Whitson, 1993). Other alternatives to the dominant model are recreational men's leagues that prohibit body checking in the interests of safety and make the game more attractive to participants. As Gruneau and Whitson (1993: 162) note, however, "NHL-style customs and values remain those ones that really "count" in the subculture of Canadian hockey."

The dominance of men's hockey provides the background for much of the debate over the construction of the women's game. Against this background, to argue that women's hockey need not be the same as men's is to position the women's game as not only different from but inferior to the "real" game. Alternatively, to argue women should play the same game as men is to capitulate to the violence and other problems that plague men's hockey. Within the confines of a debate structured by the model of the "NHL style" of play, the challenge posed by women's hockey to dominant views of how the game should be played is severely diminished.

As noted, some of the players and coaches interviewed for this research dispute the contention that playing by the same rules as men will inevitably lead to the reproduction of the problems in men's hockey. They argue that women's hockey can be constructed, and the rules enforced, in a way that eliminates the violence and other unacceptable features of the men's game while including full body contact. Some contest the view that body checking increases the rate of injury. These views are significant because they suggest that debate about the construction of the women's game should not be contained by the practices and experiences of men's hockey. These arguments, however, are rarely part of the public discussion of women's hockey.

The prohibition of body checking is central to a strategy to promote women's hockey by emphasizing its differences from the men's game.[2] While the game clearly is different from men's hockey in the absence of body checking, evidence of troubling similarities is provided in the discussion of pain and injury in women's hockey. A growing body of literature examines the violence inflicted on athletic bodies through the routinization of pain and injury in sport. Initial interest in this issue focused on male athletes (Messner, 1990; Curry, 1993; Young 1993; Young, White, and McTeer, 1994). More recent work has extended the discussion to women. Young and White (1995) examined experiences of pain and injury among a sample of elite women athletes who had incurred a variety of injuries, including broken bones, separated shoulders, dislocated knee caps, and herniated disks. These athletes normalized the presence of pain in their lives, through strategies of denial and "disrespect" or indignation toward painful injuries. Citing comparisons with earlier work they conducted with male athletes, Young and White (1995: 51) identify similarities in the acceptance of physical danger and injury and conclude that "if difference exists between the way male and female athletes in our projects appear to understand pain and injury, it is only a matter of degree." In a study of university students, Nixon (1996) found higher pain thresholds among athletes than non-athletes and no significant gender differences in their acceptance of pain.

Injury and pain were routine features of the lives of the hockey players examined here. For these athletes, overcoming injury and pain is a measure of both ability and commitment. Like the athletes Young and White (1995) studied, the hockey players in this study showed little critical awareness of the physical dangers of their sport participation. In interviews, players were asked to comment on the element of risk in women's hockey. Most denied that it was risky, often following this assessment with rationalizations about the presence of danger in everyday life—for example, the possibility of being hit by a car while crossing a street. The increasing evidence that women athletes readily accept violence inflicted on their bodies in competitive sport suggests an incorporation of, rather than resistance to, the dominant model of men's sport.

Testimony provided at the outset of this discussion indicates the satisfaction and sense of accomplishment women hockey players derive from their sport participation. These sentiments are directly tied to the physicality of sport and the possibility for the exercise of skill and force in athletic competition. A number of writers (MacKinnon, 1987; Theberge, 1987; Whitson, 1994) have identified these features as the basis of sport's potential to challenge traditional ideologies of gender and empower women. While women hockey players experience empowerment from their sport participation, the challenge to masculine hegemony posed by the sport is diminished in two key ways.

The transformative possibilities of women's sport are seriously compromised by the uncritical adoption of a "sport ethic" (Hughes and Coakley, 1991) that celebrates toughness in the face of physical violence. One of the troubling ironies of improved material resources in women's hockey is that players now have greater affinities with a system that normalizes injury and pain.

Ideologically, the challenge to masculine hegemony is weakened by the location of the debate about the practice of women's hockey within a framework that positions men's hockey as the "real" game. While women's hockey provides clear and compelling refutation of the myth of female frailty, the potential of the sport to challenge traditional ideologies of gender is diminished by its construction as a milder version of the sport that "really counts."

The analysis presented here suggests the complexities inherent in women's involvement in "flag carrier" sports such as ice hockey. Drawing from Connell's (1983) observation that every sport involves a balance between force and skill, Whitson (1994) suggests that the more force is decisive, the more a physically dominating hegemonic masculinity can be celebrated and the more likely it is that the culture of sport will be part of the defence of the existing gender order. Whitson acknowledges that sports such as hockey and football do allow for empowerment in the absence of domination and cites testimony from former NHL player Eric Nesterenko (in Terkel, 1974) on the pleasure of performing the skills required in ice hockey. This pleasure, however, was never allowed to be the central purpose of participation and usually was subordinated by the quest for victory, a quest that demanded an emphasis on force and domination. This quest, Whitson argues, becomes the norm in organized male sport at an early age.

Possibilities for challenge to masculine hegemony do exist within the context of team sports. An example is provided in Birrell and Richter's (1987) account of a women's recreational softball league. The women Birrell and Richter interviewed consciously rejected the view that the dominant model of sport, which many referred to as the "male model," is the only "real" version. Informed by this belief, they rejected an excessive emphasis on winning and domination and an ethic of endangerment that values performance over safety. Instead, they actively worked to construct and practise their own vision of sport, which emphasized the pleasure and satisfaction of participation and the development of physical skills in a supportive context.

In an analysis of the historical significance of sport for the politics of gender relations, Messner (1988) argues women's increasing athleticism represents a genuine quest for equality. This quest, however, is marked by contradictions and ambiguities over the socially constructed meanings of sport and gender. Messner concludes that in the contemporary period the women athlete is "contested ideological terrain."

The cultural struggle in women's hockey is conditioned by its relation to the dominant male model. Unlike the recreational softball community studied by Birrell and Richter (1987), in which participants consciously challenged the "male model," the struggle within elite-level women's hockey occurs largely within a value system regulated by this model. While women's hockey provides participants with pleasure and a sense of personal empowerment, it does so in a context that reproduces the problems of institutionalized sport. A more fully transformative vision of hockey would offer empowerment in a setting that rejects violence and the normalization of injury in favour of an ethic of care.

Notes

1. Interviews with women who played full contact hockey during the 1980s reveal that part of the collective memory of the league in which the Blades compete is stories of particular hits and players who had an especially forceful game. While these stories are an important part of the history of the sport, there are no data to test the relationship between playing full-contact hockey and rates of injury. Some believe that to the extent body checking increases injuries, this is "limited" to serious injuries such as broken bones.
2. The main challenge to the prohibition against body checking comes not domestically but within the International Ice Hockey Federation, in which some countries argue for the inclusion of body checking in international women's hockey. Proponents of the rule change generally are from countries where development lags behind that in Canada and the United States, the dominant countries in the sport. Because the inclusion of body checking is generally agreed to slow the game down and reduce the advantage of superior playing skills, body checking is thought to offer an advantage to weaker teams. (My thanks to Elizabeth Etue for information on this issue.) It should be noted that it is unlikely that Canadian support for prohibiting body checking arises out of a concern for a loss of competitive dominance should the rules be changed. The first World Championships in 1990 were played with body checking. Canada won this tournament, as well as subsequent tournaments in 1992 and 1994 played without body checking.

References

Birrell, S., and D. Richter. 1987. "Is a Diamond Forever? Feminist Transformations of Sport," *Women's Studies International Forum* 10: 395–409.

Bryson, L. 1990. "Challenges to Male Hegemony in Sport," in M. Messner and D. Sabo, eds., *Sport, Men and the Gender Order*. Champaign, IL: Human Kinetics.

Connell, R.W. 1983. "Men's Bodies," in R.W. Connell, ed., *Which Way Is Up?* Sydney: Allen & Unwin.

Curry, T. 1993. "A Little Pain Never Hurt Anyone: Athletic Career Socialization and the Normalization of Sport Injury," *Symbolic Interaction* 16: 273–90.

Etue, E., and M. Williams. 1996. *On the Edge: Women Making Hockey History*. Toronto: Second Story.

Gruneau, R., and D. Whitson. 1993. *Hockey Night in Canada*. Toronto: Garamond.

Hughes, R., and J. Coackley. 1991. "Positive Deviance among Athletes: The Implications of Over-conformity to the Sport Ethic," *Sociology of Sport Journal* 8: 307–25.

MacKinnon, C. 1987. "Women, Self-possession, and Sport," in C. MacKinnon, ed., *Feminism Unmodified*. Cambridge, MA: Harvard University Press.

Messner, M. 1988. "Sports as Male Domination: The Female Athlete as Contested Ideological Terrain," *Sociology of Sport Journal* 5: 197–211.

———. 1990. "When Bodies Are Weapons: Masculinity and Violence in Sport," *International Review for the Sociology of Sport* 25: 203–18.

Nixon, H. 1996. "The Relationship of Friendship Networks, Sports Experiences, and Gender to Expressed Pain Thresholds," *Sociology of Sport Journal* 13: 78–86.

Terkel, S. 1974. *Working*. New York: Avon Books.

Theberge, N. 1987. "Sport and Women's Empowerment," *Women's Studies International Forum* 10: 387–93.

———. 1995. "Sport, Caractere Physicque et Differenciation Sexuelle," *Sociologie et Societés* 27: 105–16.

Whitson, D. 1994. "The Embodiment of Gender: Discipline, Domination, and Empowerment," in S. Birrell and C. Cole, eds., *Women, Sport, and Culture*. Champaign, IL: Human Kinetics.

Williams, M. 1995. "Women's Hockey: Heating Up the Equity Debate," *Canadian Woman Studies* 15: 78–81.

Young K. 1993. "Violence, Risk, and Liability in Male Sports Culture," *Sociology of Sport Journal* 10: 373–97.

Young, K., and P. White. 1995. "Sport, Physical Danger, and Injury: The Experiences of Elite Women Athletes," *Journal of Sport and Social Issues* 19: 45–61.

Young, K., P. White, and W. McTeer. 1994. "Body Talk: Male Athletes Reflect on Sport, Injury, and Pain," *Sociology of Sport Journal* 11: 175–94.

PART III

Gender, Race, and Racialization

In this section, we examine the intersection of gender and racialization. We use the term "racialization" rather than the more familiar "race" in order to stress the human actions involved in creating and maintaining the categories we call "races" or "ethnicities." Although race is often described in terms of physical characteristics, scientific consensus now holds that race itself has no biological meaning—there are no hard-and-fast markers that can be used to divide humans up into a finite number of groups called races. In a purely biological sense, race does not exist.

However, this has not stopped humans from creating such categories and assigning membership in these categories to individuals, based on their physical appearance or their parentage. Race thus becomes what social theorists call a "floating signifier," a word that does not have an actual physical referent (unlike, say, "tree" or "Ottawa"), but that carries great power to shape social life. More importantly, the biological non-existence of race has not stopped us from ascribing social characteristics or traits to individuals, based on their perceived membership in racial categories. This is what we refer to as "racialization"—the ways in which racial differences are created and reinforced through social interactions. Racialization is a profoundly gendered process, as different qualities and characteristics are ascribed to men and women within the same racial category.

The process of racialization is also a process of differentiation and stratification. Membership in certain racial categories is associated with greater economic and political power, a phenomenon we call racial privilege. Those with racial privilege may find that their way in the world has been smoothed by positive stereotypes associated with their race, and when they look around at the powerful people in society, they see people who look quite a bit like themselves. In Canada, racial privilege is still associated with whiteness, as can be seen by the composition of Parliament, by leaders of industry, and even by the composition of the faculty of many universities. White individuals may not even be aware of the power associated with whiteness, because they are accustomed to seeing themselves as the norm or the standard in Canadian society.

Being racialized as white is not necessarily a ticket to an easy life—many white individuals experience downward mobility, or struggle to get ahead, or find they have less power than other racialized individuals. Yet whiteness remains the colour of privilege in twenty-first-century Canada, the colour of the racial majority.

The process of racialization is also a process of "othering"—defining a group or groups of individuals as being in some ways different from or exceptions to a norm. "Othering" typically involves exclusion or subordination and is part of the conceptual apparatus of hierarchy and injustice. When we think of people primarily in terms of what they are not—not white, not English-speaking, not male, not affluent, not heterosexual—it is easy to see their difference as forms of lack or the absence of positive qualities. Racism, like sexism, builds on the "othering" of individuals and groups.

People who are racialized in other ways are often much more conscious of the power of race to shape their experiences. Some people are constantly reminded of their status as a racialized minority by their everyday interactions, while for others race is not a major influence in their lives. Still others find that both race and gender become a salient category under specific circumstances—when interacting with the police, for instance, or when dating or marrying someone of a different racial category.

In the readings that follow, Sherene Razack offers a powerful indictment of the "unbreakapartability" of racism and sexism in her well-known analysis of the 1995 murder of Pamela George, an Aboriginal woman who worked in the sex trade in Saskatoon, by two white men. Razack interrogates whiteness as a form of privilege and shows how it worked to lessen the consequences of homicide for the killers.

Tamari Kitossa and Katerina Deliovsky also examine the ways in which race inflects gender in their study of "racial profiling" experienced by mixed-race couples. While profiling is most often associated with law enforcement, Kitossa and Deliovsky argue that it describes daily life for men and women who are in relationships with partners of a different race. The combination of race and gender produces very different encounters for their participants, depending on whether they are male or female, white people or people of colour.

Angela Aujla demonstrates that men and women are not simply passive objects of racialization but are also observers, critics, and change agents in our own lives. Her study of young South Asian women's experiences, as expressed in their poetry and autobiographical writing, suggests creativity and resistance to oppressive racial stereotypes.

Finally, Gillian Creese illustrates the intersection of race and gender among African immigrants to Vancouver. Boys and young men are much more likely to experience their racialization in an oppressive way, as a result of negative experiences with police and other law enforcement agencies, and as a result are more likely to identify strongly with oppositional and defiant aspects of African-American popular music and culture. Women of African origin, although subject to negative attention because of their race, experience this racism differently because they are female, not male.

Questions for Critical Thought

1. When you hear the word "race," what does it mean to you?
2. How are racial categories similar to sex categories? How are they different?
3. What is racism? How similar is it to sexism?
4. Do you consider yourself a member of a particular racial or ethnic category? What qualities do you associate with that category? What qualities do you think other people associate with that category?
5. Razack argues that gender and race intersect such that the deaths or disappearances of some people are treated as less important than the deaths or disappearances of others. Can you think of any other examples of the devaluing of particular people based on their gender or race?
6. Have you ever been "profiled," as Kitossa and Deliovsky describe? If so, do you think your gender was an issue in the profiling?
7. Both Aujla and Creese discuss the complexities faced by young people who are pressured to both maintain a distinct racial or ethnic identity, and to conform to "white" or "mainstream" society. How are these pressures different depending on the gender of the young people concerned?
8. Do you think your racial category has been as important as your gender in shaping your life so far?
9. All the authors here demonstrate the unbreakapartability of gender and race. Are there other forms of intersectionality beyond the race/gender nexus? Have these other forms of intersectionality had a significant impact on your life?
10. Razack and other scholars assert that "white privilege" exists and is powerful, yet not all white people feel that they are individually powerful, indeed, many white people feel disempowered in many aspects of their lives. How can these two situations coexist?

Chapter 9

Overview

In 1996, Steven Kummerfield and Alex Ternowetsky, two young white Saskatchewan men, were found guilty of manslaughter after beating to death Pamela George, an Aboriginal woman. The facts of the case are horrifying in themselves, and public outcry went up when the defendants were convicted on manslaughter rather than the more serious charge of murder and given a comparatively light sentence of six and a half years. In this famous piece, Sherene Razack delves into Canadian history to explore how gender and race came together to shape the trial—in particular, the relatively lenient treatment afforded to the white defendants for the crime of killing an Aboriginal woman.

Razack argues that this is not only a case of extreme male violence against women but also one where the violence was historically and geographically racialized. She explores the history of sexual violence against Aboriginal women and the devaluation of Aboriginal women's lives.

However, Aboriginal women are not the only racialized subjects here, and Razack explores the historical construction of white privilege, which, she argues, enabled Kummerfield and Ternowetsky to believe they could get away with their crime and which underlay the defense's argument that they should be treated as decent young men who had made a terrible mistake.

Razack also argues that not only individuals but places and spaces are subject to gendering and racialization. She explores the places associated with the George murder, examining how some spaces are understood as suitable only for undervalued members of society (such as Aboriginal sex workers) with the result that the people who inhabit these places are treated as less valuable than their counterparts in different locations.

Razack's challenge to readers is to understand cases like the George murder, or other instances of racialized violence against women, not only as tragedies in their own right but also as historically overdetermined by gendered racialization. Ideas about gender and race mark out these women as "dispensable" in the eyes of their killers; and too often the killers themselves are protected by white privilege.

Gendered Racial Violence and Spatialized Justice: The Murder of Pamela George

Sherene H. Razack

> To unmap literally is to denaturalise geography, hence to undermine world views that rest upon it.
>
> —Richard Phillips, *Mapping Men and Empire*

On Easter weekend, April 17, 1995, Pamela George, a woman of the Saulteaux (Ojibway) nation and a mother of two young children, was brutally murdered in Regina, Saskatchewan. Beyond the fact that Pamela George came from the Sakimay reserve on the outskirts of the city, and that she occasionally worked as a prostitute, something she was doing that weekend, few details of her life or the life of her community are revealed in the court records of the trial of the two white men accused of her murder or in the media coverage of the event. More is known about her two murderers—young middle-class white men. Easter marked the first weekend since the end of their university exams. There was a week or so of freedom before summer jobs began, and nineteen-year-old university athletes Steven Kummerfield and Alex Ternowetsky set out to celebrate the end of term. They went out drinking in isolated areas under bridges and behind hockey arenas, and then cruised "the Stroll," the city's streets of prostitution. Eventually, after failing to persuade one Aboriginal woman working as a prostitute to join the two of them in the car, one man hid in the trunk. Approaching her twice and being refused twice, they finally succeeded in persuading another Aboriginal woman, Pamela George, to enter the car.

The two men drove George to an isolated area outside the city, a place littered with bullet casings and condoms. Following oral sex, they took turns brutally beating her and left her lying with her face in the mud. They then drove to a fast-food restaurant and later to a cabin on Saskatchewan Beach, which belonged to one of their grandfathers. The next morning, upon returning to town, they heard a radio report describing a body found outside the city. After both first confided their involvement in the murder to a number of friends and to one of their parents, one man left town to take up his summer job planting trees in the northern forests of British Columbia. The other man flew to the mountain resort of Banff, Alberta, where he joined other white male university athletes celebrating the end of term. In early May, nearly one month later, after following a tip and having exhausted the list of suspects who were mostly Aboriginal or of the "streets" of the Stroll, the Royal Canadian Mounted Police (RCMP) arrested both men for the murder of Pamela George. The arrest of two young middle-class white men for the murder of an Aboriginal woman working as a prostitute sent shock waves through the white population of this small prairie city. Pamela George's own family endured the pain of losing a loved one violently.

At the trial two years later, the defence at first tried to argue that Pamela George managed to walk away from the isolated field and was killed by someone else, an Aboriginal man. They also argued that since both men were highly intoxicated, they bore diminished responsibility for the beating. The boys did "pretty darn stupid things," but they did not commit murder. Both the Crown and the defence maintained that the fact that Pamela George was a prostitute was something to be considered in the case.[1] The judge sparked a public furor when he instructed the jury to bear this in mind in their deliberations. The men were convicted of manslaughter and sentenced to six-and-a-half years in prison, having already spent twenty months in prison. The objections of the Native community and some members of the white community stemmed from their belief that the crime was, at the very *least*, one of second-degree murder and that the judge acted improperly in directing the jury to a finding of manslaughter.[2] Alex Ternowetsky was paroled in 2000 after having served only two-thirds of his sentence. In August 2001, he faced new charges of assault, robbery, mischief, impaired driving, and refusing to take a Breathalyzer test.[3] . . .

. . . I deliberately write against those who would agree that this case is about an injustice but who would de-race the violence and the law's response to it, labelling it as generic patriarchal violence against women, violence that the law routinely minimizes. While it is certainly patriarchy that produces men whose sense of identity is achieved through brutalizing a woman, the men's and the court's capacity to dehumanize Pamela George came from their understanding of her as the (gendered) racial Other whose degradation confirmed their own identities as white—that is, as men entitled to the land and the full benefits of citizenship. . . .

. . . In examining the transcripts of the case, one can hardly miss the spatiality of the violence and its relationship to identity as well as to justice.

The men leave the university and their families' and girlfriends' middle-class homes in the suburbs to spend time with each other, in places that are "outside" civilized society. From drinking under bridges, beside airports, and behind hockey arenas, they proceed to the Stroll, the streets of prostitution occupied by racial Others, and ultimately to the murder scene. In the elite spaces of middle-class life (the university, suburban homes, chalets, and cottages), they learn who they are, and, more important, who they are not. Moving from respectable space to degenerate space and back again is an adventure that confirms that they are indeed white men in control who can survive a dangerous encounter with the racial Other and who have an unquestioned right to go anywhere and do anything.

. . . I propose to unmap these journeys. That is to say, I want to denaturalize the spaces and bodies described in the trial in an effort to uncover the hierarchies that are protected and the violence that is hidden when we believe such spatial relations and subjects to be naturally occurring. To unmap means to historicize, a process that begins by asking about the relationship between identity and space.[4] What is being imagined or projected on to specific spaces, and I would add, on to bodies? Further, what is being enacted in those spaces and on those bodies? In the first section of this chapter, I discuss the factors that brought Pamela George to the Stroll and those that brought two white men to it. I suggest that the encounter between the white men and Pamela George was fully colonial—a making of the white, masculine self as dominant through practices of violence directed at a colonized woman. In the second section, I explore how various legal and social constructs naturalized these spatial relations of domination, highlighting in the process white respectability and entitlement and Aboriginal criminality. In the conclusion, I explore how we might contest these practices of domination through a resurrection of historical memory of colonization and its continuing effects. In essence, I suggest that we insist that in law, as in life, we inhabit histories of domination and subordination for which we are accountable.

Space, Gendered Racial Violence, and the Making of White Settler Societies

. . . Two white men who buy the services of an Aboriginal woman in prostitution, and who then beat her to death, are enacting a quite specific violence perpetrated on Aboriginal bodies throughout Canada's history, a colonial violence that has not only enabled white settlers to secure the land *but to come to know themselves as entitled to it.* In the men's encounter with Pamela George, these material (theft of the land) and symbolic (who is entitled to it) processes shaped both what brought Pamela George to the Stroll and what white men from middle-class homes thought they were doing in a downtown area of prostitution on the night of the murder. These processes also shaped what sense the court made of their activities. . . .

Regina, a city of almost two hundred thousand people in which Aboriginal peoples make up approximately 8 per cent of the population,[5] is estimated to have a higher urban Aboriginal population per capita than all other major Canadian cities. The Aboriginal population is also the youngest one in Canada—43 per cent of Aboriginals are fifteen years old or younger.[6] However, the presence of a significant Aboriginal population in an urban centre is a relatively recent historical development. Canada's colonizing endeavours confined the majority of Aboriginal peoples to reserves by the second half of the nineteenth century, establishing in the process the geographical configuration of Regina today as a primarily white city in the midst of the reserves of the Qu'appelle Valley. This nineteenth-century spatial containment of a subject population was never secure and often required brutal policing and settler violence. In 1885, for example, white settlers of Regina who were fearful of Native rebellions organized a Home Guard and pressed vigorously for the North West Mounted Police (NWMP) to police Natives and to hang Native leaders arrested after the Riel Rebellion.[7]

Sexual violence towards Aboriginal women was an integral part of nineteenth-century settler strategies of domination. In her research on the appearance during this time of captivity narratives (stories about the abduction of white women and children by Aboriginal peoples), Sarah Carter documents the important role that stereotypical representations of Aboriginal women played in maintaining the spatial and symbolic boundaries between settlers and Natives. Prior to 1885 there had been relative co-existence between fur traders and Aboriginal peoples, but the Metis rebellion and general Aboriginal resistance to their spatial confinement, as well as the increasing presence of white women on the Prairies, led to powerful negative images of Aboriginal women that portrayed them as licentious and bloodthirsty. These images helped to justify the increasing legal regulation of Aboriginal women's movements and their confinement to reserves. As Carter demonstrates, "the squalid and immoral 'squaw'" helped to deflect criticism away from the brutal behaviour of government officials and the NWMP, and it enabled government officials to claim that the dissolute character of Aboriginal women and the laziness of the men explained why reserve land was not used to capacity and were pockets of poverty.

After 1885, the pass system was introduced and required Aboriginal peoples to obtain a pass from a government employee before leaving the reserve. One rationale was that the system would limit the numbers of Aboriginal women "of abandoned character" entering the towns. Relying on diaries of policemen, newspapers, and court records, Carter discusses a variety of oppressive practices towards Aboriginal women. For example, government agents sometimes withheld rations to reserve communities unless Aboriginal women were made available to them. The NWMP often turned a blind eye to such practices, engaging in their own coercive relations with Aboriginal women. White men in positions of authority often beat Aboriginal women, sometimes fatally. Oral narratives of late-nineteenth-century Lakota women suggest that the NWMP had easy sexual access to Aboriginal women whose families were starving.[8]

Newspaper records of the nineteenth century indicate that there was a conflation of Aboriginal woman and prostitute and an accompanying belief that when they encountered violence, Aboriginal women simply got what they deserved. Police seldom intervened, even when the victim's cries could be clearly heard.[9] In one case explored by Sarah Carter, which bears an uncanny parallel to the trial of Ternowetsky and Kummerfield for the murder of Pamela George, a Cree woman, referred to in the newspapers as a squaw named Rosalie who was working as a prostitute, was murdered by William Fisk, a white man of a well-established family. Even when Fisk confessed to the murder, the Crown expressed his sympathy for Fisk as a man whose activities in capturing rebellious Natives clearly marked him as a patriot and an upstanding citizen. . . .

There are perhaps no better indicators of continuing colonization and its accompanying spatial strategies of containment than the policing and incarceration of urban Aboriginal peoples, a direct continuation of the policing relationship of the nineteenth century. Between the late 1960s and the early 1970s, the number of Aboriginal peoples in Regina's jails increased by 10 per cent. In 1971 the city stepped up downtown patrols, and in 1975 created a special task force for the purpose of policing Aboriginal peoples. By 1994, the province of Saskatchewan (of which Regina is the capital) had the highest level of incarceration of Aboriginal peoples in Canada: 72 per cent of the population in the province's jails were Aboriginal.[10] According to a "One-Day Snapshot" survey taken in October of 1996, 76 per cent of Saskatchewan's inmates on register in adult correctional facilities were Aboriginal.[11] In 1999, Patricia Monture-Angus tells us that Aboriginal men made up approximately 80 per cent of the population at Saskatchewan Penitentiary.

The rates of incarceration are even more dramatic for Aboriginal women. Ten years ago it was estimated that in Saskatchewan a treaty Indian woman was 131 times more likely to be incarcerated than a non-Aboriginal woman, while Metis women were twenty-eight times more likely to be incarcerated. According to Jim Harding's 1993 testimony to the Royal Commission, Aboriginal women then made up 80 to 90 per cent of the prison population at Pinegrove, a correctional facility in Regina. Thus, while the number of admissions to correctional centres increased in Saskatchewan by 46 per cent between 1976 and 1992, the rate of increase for Aboriginal women was 111 per cent for the same period.[12] Looking to a national scale, and to more recent statistics, First Nations women (registered or "Status" Indians) made up only 1 to 2 per cent of the Canadian population in 1997, but represented 19 per cent of federally sentenced women.[13] . . .

The evidence that Aboriginal peoples live in a state of colonization as direct and coercive as prevailed two centuries ago is nowhere better demonstrated than in the high rate of suicide among Aboriginal peoples in Canada. As a government report concludes, the suicide rate, one of the highest in the world and four times higher than that of the non-Aboriginal population, is an expression of the "collective anguish" of three hundred years of colonial history. . . .

Although there is no systematic study of the sexual violence Aboriginal women endure today on the streets at the hands of white men,[14] the cases that do surface suggest that the nineteenth-century perception of the Aboriginal woman as a licentious and dehumanized squaw . . . continues to prevail. The Aboriginal Justice Inquiry's discussion of the 1971 murder of Helen Betty Osborne in The Pas, Manitoba, elaborates on its prevalence. Brutally murdered by two white men, Osborne, an Aboriginal student who was walking along a downtown street, was picked up in town and driven to a more secluded spot where she was assaulted and killed. As the Commissioners of the Aboriginal Justice Inquiry concluded, Osborne's attackers "seemed to be operating on the assumption that Aboriginal women were promiscuous and open to enticement through alcohol or violence. It is evident that the men who abducted Osborne believed that young Aboriginal women were objects with no human value beyond [their own] sexual gratification."[15]

Such assumptions often appear to be operating when the police fail to respond to the disappearance of Aboriginal women, citing their involvement in prostitution and their practices of moving from place to place. In the early 1990s, John Crawford, a white man, was convicted of murdering three Aboriginal women—Calinda Waterhen, Shelley Napope, and Eva Taysup. In each case, Crawford and another white friend began by drinking and having sex with the woman in question who was possibly working as a prostitute. The women's disappearance attracted little attention. When their families reported them missing, police appeared to assume that such women were simply transients on the move. As police sergeant Dave Kovach told a reporter, the police don't look for transient adults because such individuals often go missing and often don't want to be found.[16] Crawford's victims were indeed, as Denise McConney has written, "caught up in the ongoing displacement, relocation, and search for a safe place that is a consistent theme in the lives of most native women."[17] Ironically, it is their very dispossession that is held against them when Aboriginal women encounter violence on the streets.

The Making of White Man: The Two Accused

Alex Ternowetsky and Steven Kummerfield's histories begin in the colonial practices described above. In their everyday life, they would have had almost no chance of encountering an Aboriginal person. Absent from the university, the ordered suburbs of their families, the chalets and cottages, Aboriginal bodies had to be sought out in the marginal spaces of the city. Why would white men seek out these bodies? Why would they leave their own spaces of privilege? How do young white men such as Alex Ternowetsky and Steven Kummerfield come to know themselves as beings for whom the definition of a good time is to travel to the parts of the city inhabited by poor and mostly Aboriginal peoples and there to purchase sexual services from an Aboriginal woman? I argue that the subject who must cross the line between respectability and degeneracy and, significantly, return unscathed, is first and foremost a colonial subject seeking to establish that he is indeed in control and lives in a world where a solid line marks the boundary between himself and racial/gendered Others. For this subject, violence establishes the boundary between who he is and who he is not. It is the surest indicator that he is a subject in control. . . .

. . . The men's behaviour bears some resemblance to the young hockey athletes researched by Laura Robinson in her book *Crossing the Line: Violence and Sexual Assault in Canada's National Sport*. Robinson describes the masculinity that is actively fostered in the world of young athletes as one where violence and sexual aggression, and a hatred of the softness that is female, are positive signs of masculinity. The normalizing of abusive relationships and male-bonding rituals designed to foster team relationships help to produce men for whom relationships with other men become the primary source of intimacy. Drawing on the work of scholars researching sports and masculinity, notably Peggy Reeves Sanday, Robinson suggests that sexual violence collectively enacted enables the men to get as close to each other as they can without endangering their sense of themselves as heterosexuals. To debase and degrade a woman in the presence of other men secures the masculinity that must be aggressive and that must disavow sexual feelings for other men.[18] . . .

Kummerfield and Ternowetsky inhabited a world in which the homosocial bonding, drinking, and aggression were important features. Their counsel presented a unified picture of boys who started drinking at fourteen and who steadily progressed into a regular pattern of weekend and summer drinking. Both of the accused noted that as the youngest members of their university sports teams, they were initiated into more serious drinking by older teammates. . . .

On the weekend of the murder, both men indulged in extensive drinking with their friends. Ternowetsky's account of his activities over the Easter weekend prior to the murder provides some idea of his social world. Arriving via Edmonton, he contacted a friend, Rod MacLeod, with whom he went drinking at one of their old haunts behind the Balfour hockey arena. Later, at a bar, his friend Eric Willrich got into a fight with a man he assumed was harassing Ternowetsky. Eric broke his leg during the fight. The following day, Ternowetsky continued drinking with MacLeod on the roof of the Optimist's arena.[19] Nostalgically sharing a bottle of rye in memory of a good time the summer before, the two also went drinking behind Massey Pool. Finally, when neither Willrich nor Macleod was available to continue partying, Ternowetsky arranged to meet Kummerfield at Rainbow Bridge and took a cab there, stopping at a bank machine en route to withdraw money for the night's activities. . . .

The sense of identity that both accused gained from their activities with other men was premised on a shared whiteness. . . . [E]vidence of their shared whiteness is most apparent in their own and their friends' and families' responses to Pamela George and to the Stroll. The men told several of their friends about the events the night of the murder and received considerable support and advice. Alex Ternowetsky told at least four of his friends. One of these, Rodney McLeod, with whom he had been drinking at Massey Pool and whose fleece jacket he was wearing the night of the murder, reassured him that no one would find out. To another, Tyler Harlton, he confided that he had killed "an Indian hooker." Ryan Leier, with whom Ternowetsky had been in trouble before and to whom he confided the full details of the night while both were in a hot tub at a chalet in Banff, reassured his friend with the advice "you shouldn't assume you killed her." Finally, Ternowetsky told his friend Eric Willrich, whose jeans he was wearing the night of the murder and at whose house he is alleged to have washed the blood stains off.[20]

Steven Kummerfield confided to his best friend Tyler Stuart, with whom he had once gone to the area of prostitution, that "we beat the shit" out of "an Indian hooker." In Tyler Stuart's account, Kunlmerfield also elaborated that he said to Pamela George, "If you don't give us head, we're going to kill you." Stuart, apparently mostly concerned about the transmission of disease to Kummerfield's white girlfriend, advised his friend to break up with her if he hadn't worn a condom the night of the murder.[21] In none of these conversations was there any indication that the men acknowledged that a woman had been brutally murdered; her death seemed almost incidental and simply inconvenient. The men seemed to possess a collective understanding of Pamela George as a thing, an objectification that their exclusively white worlds would have given them little opportunity to disrupt. . . .

The testimonies of the men . . . suggest that, at least in the all-male spaces, sexual aggression was normalized. Ternowetsky's drunken talk at the chalet did not strike his listeners as unusual. (He is reported as saying eight times in a half-hour period that "I want to go find a hooker and beat and rape her," and replying to a question about whether he had ever done this with "Yeah . . . it was fun and it was a rush.") They objected to his loudness but, as Curtis Doell testified, nothing struck him as unusual. The normal pattern was to ski and follow this up by eight hours or more of drinking. It was also typical to bring white women picked up in bars to the chalet.[22] Presumably, this talk about women and "Indians" was entirely normal.

In this all-white masculine world of privilege, the Stroll, the area of prostitution described in the trial as encompassing St. John and Ottawa Streets and involving a specific set of streets and hotels in between, represented the dangerous world of racial Others, a frontier on the edge of civilization. Police described the Stroll as a world of drugs and prostitution, and most of all, as a space of Aboriginality. Steven Kummerfield and his friends visited the Stroll "out of curiosity." Alex Ternowetsky and his friends took their girlfriends on an adventure to the Stroll, "sort of seeing who was there," as his lawyer put it.[23] The young women hid under blankets while the young men negotiated for the services of an Aboriginal prostitute: a thrilling excursion to the slums that would have helped these young white people to know their own place in the world. . . .

When young white men enter racialized urban spaces their skin clearly marks them as out of place. They are immediately read as johns, as rich white men who have come "slumming." This visibility no doubt contributes to white (particularly more affluent) city dwellers' tendency to perceive themselves as likely targets of robbery or violence in racialized urban space.[24] Steven Kummerfield once paid for the services of a prostitute and alleged that she disappeared with the money without providing her service. Such perceptions of white vulnerability frequently exist in a manner disproportionate to actual documented incidence of crimes, violent crimes in particular.[25] It is perhaps the men's perception that they were marked and at risk on the Stroll that prompted them to drive Pamela George outside the city to a borderland between the country and the city, a no-man's-land that offers greater anonymity.[26] In this no-man's-land, violent acts can be committed without meaningful consequence. Although the accused both maintained that they did not know the area, the RCMP and the neighbouring farmers testified that it was isolated and that it was routine for prostitution to occur there.[27] . . .

It is difficult to avoid both the historical and contemporary racial and spatial parallels between the murders of Helen Betty Osborne and Pamela George. Equally, newspaper reports in 1999 calling attention to cases of Aboriginal men found frozen to death after Saskatoon police apparently dropped them outside the city limits in the dead of winter, outline the tremendous violence of the eviction of Aboriginal peoples from urban space.[28] In each instance, white men forcibly and fatally removed Aboriginal bodies from the city space, a literal cleansing of the white zone. The violence is itself cleansing, enabling white men to triumph over their own internal fears that they may not be men in control. The evictions are to areas where white men are able to evade responsibility for their violent acts, areas where there are few witnesses and where, significantly, the norms of civility are suspended and violence by contract is known to occur.

Although there are several instances which neither of the accused can recall, they generally agreed that once at the country field, Pamela George was frightened and tried to defend herself. They talked to her and gave her false names. She ultimately agreed to perform oral sex and all three remained in the front seat of the car while this was in progress. While George was performing oral sex on Ternowetsky (having finished with Kummerfield), Kummerfield announced that they should leave. Ternowetsky asked that George be allowed to finish but a short time later, Kummerfield dragged her from the car and hit her.

Ternowetsky, at first surprised, joined in. Neither recalled the extent of the violence but each remembered her face in the mud and the fact that she tried to defend herself. They later claimed that when they drove off (after having bent the license plate to conceal the numbers), Pamela George was still standing.[29]

During the trial, the murder scene and the Stroll were described as spaces somehow innately given to illicit and sexual activity. The bodies of Charlene Rosebluff, Pamela George, and a number of Aboriginal men were represented variously as bodies that naturally belonged to these spaces of prostitution, crime, sex, and violence. This degenerate space, into which Kummerfield and Ternowetsky ventured temporarily, was juxtaposed to the spaces of respectability. Each space required a different legal response. In racialized space, violence may occur with impunity. Bodies from respectable spaces may also violate with impunity, particularly if the violence takes place in the racialized space of prostitution.

Unmapping Law: Gendered Racial Violence in Anomalous Zones

. . . Apart from a few moments, such as when Charlene Rosebluff remembered her as a nice person and a mother with two children, and when her mother and sister recalled that she liked doing crafts, could cook anything and was a good mother to her ten- and five-year-old, Pamela George never left the racially bounded space of prostitution and degeneracy during the trial, a space that marked her as a body to be violated. We never learn of the Sakimay reserve and the extensive familial networks of her life there, nor do we learn anything about why she resorted to prostitution a few times a month, and why she left the reserve in the first place. It is only in newspaper articles that we learn that she helped her father through his crisis with alcohol abuse, supporting him in his journey to become an addictions counsellor. When details of her life emerged, such as the fact that Pamela George had a cousin in prison, and her father had himself been falsely accused of a crime,[30] they only confirmed the equation of Aboriginality with violence, a state of affairs that remained unconnected to the violence of the colonizers. In place of details that might have given her personhood, there were a myriad of other details that instead reassured the court of her belonging to spaces of violence. The needle marks on her arm, the tattoos on her body with the words "Ed" and "I love Mom," the stories of her ripping off clients (stories the police report they heard from Lenny Hall), the mention of her sister who was also a prostitute, and the detailed descriptions of how prostitutes conducted their business (but not how clients participate) leave a powerful image of degeneracy. . . .

Perhaps most telling of all were the accused's sense of the crime they committed. Ternowetsky told his friend Tyler Harlton that they picked up an Indian hooker, got kind of mad at her, started to hit her and did it too much and so probably killed her. Tyler was asked on the witness stand how Ternowetsky regarded the murder, to which he replied: "He kind of glanced over it, looked at it sexually." When asked to clarify, he explained that his friend did not describe the sexual act but instead made a noise like grunting. Ternowetsky did not apologize to the George family until relatively late in the trial. Questioned by the Crown attorney as to why he felt he had to leave town quickly if all he thought he had done was hit someone a few times, Steven Kummerfield replied:

> I was basically disgusted with what took place that evening, and I really didn't want to be arrested or anything like that just because there are so many opportunities I had, you know, to be successful and stuff and, you know, I just felt so ashamed and things like that.[31]

Lost opportunities weighed more heavily on Kummerfield's mind than the thought that he might have severely injured if not killed a woman. Kummerfield's response to the violence parallels those of hockey players like Jarret Reid, who described in his statements to the court the tragedy of the loss of his hard-won hockey career and his reputation as an adored and respected athlete.[32] . . .

It is no small irony that racism, so rarely named during the trial, only emerged explicitly during sentencing. The defence reported that Alex Ternowetsky had taken a course on Native literature while in prison and had written a paper on Aboriginal–white relations that proved that he had "no clear motive of hatred towards someone of a particular racial origin."[33] Racelessness was pursued to the bitter end, however. When there were complaints made against him after the trial, Mr. Justice Malone confirmed (in a letter to Chief Justice Allan McEachern) that race overdetermined the trial, but noted that only a strategy of racelessness (ignoring everyone's race) countered it:

> I suspect the real basis for most of the complaints, including the two that I have dealt with, is the underlying feeling that because the two accused were white and the victim was a First Nations person they received special treatment and the jury's verdict [of manslaughter and not murder] was based on racism. This was certainly the reaction of several First Nations spokesmen and extensive media coverage was given to their remarks in this regard. Furthermore, both accused came from financially secure homes and enjoyed the material benefits associated therewith. Their position in life was in striking contrast to the position of the victim. Every effort was made during the trial by counsel and myself to deal with the case strictly on the basis of relevant evidence and not on the financial and social positions of the accused and their victim or their race.[34]

Here, colour-blindness as a legal approach, the belief that justice can only be achieved by treating all individuals as though they *were* the same, held full sway.

Race, social position, and, I would add, gender were indeed made to disappear during the trial and in sentencing. The social meaning of spaces and bodies was deliberately excluded as evidence that would contaminate the otherwise pure processes of law, evidence that was not relevant. It was not then possible to interrogate what white men thought they were doing in journeying to the Stroll to buy the services of an Aboriginal prostitute. It was also not possible to interrogate the meaning of consent and violence in the space of prostitution and between white and Aboriginal bodies. Since bodies had no race, class, or gender, the constructs that ruled the day, heavily inflected with these social relations, coded rather than reveal them explicitly. Thus "prostitute" and people of "the street" came to signify the racial Other and the spaces of violence. In contrast, the university, the chalet, the cottage, the suburban home, the isolated spaces in which the men socialized were unmarked. When Pamela George's mother Ina and her sister Denise respectively commented in their victim impact statements, "so what if she was a prostitute" and "it felt she was on trial because she was a prostitute," they were identifying two domains of law—the domain of justice and the domain beyond it.[35] This spatial configuration was explicitly geographical and quite deliberately mapped. It was also explicitly raced, classed, and gendered. Bodies that engage in prostitution and the spaces of prostitution are racialized, as I have argued elsewhere, regardless of the actual race of the prostitute. In this sense, it is possible, as Ternowetsky's lawyer suggested at sentencing, that Pamela George's race made no difference, but only in the sense that any woman engaging in prostitution loses her status as white. What a spatial analysis reveals is that bodies in degenerate spaces lose their entitlement to personhood through a complex process in which the violence that is enacted is naturalized. Even when the trial judge at sentencing acknowledged that Pamela George was the victim of mindless violence and that her murderers "cast her aside as if she were something less than human," these observations did not alter his ultimate position that the accused deserved a punishment of six and a half years, given the time of twenty months already served.[36] . . .

. . . What would it mean to deliberately introduce history and social context into this trial? In the first instance, we would have to ask questions about the activities of the accused. How did they routinely conduct themselves? What is the role of violence against women in their activities? Who were the women who were seen as targets of the violence? These questions would have to be raised within the historical and social context of Aboriginal–white relations in Regina. Secondly, to appreciate that a person has been brutally murdered, details about Pamela George's life, once again historically contextualized, would have to be on the record to counter the historically produced response to her as a woman whose life was worth very little. Efforts to introduce these two lines of evidence would be thwarted by the notion that prostitution is a contract and not violence, and the notion that individuals must be judged as though they were not embedded in historical and contemporary relations of domination. These approaches would also be resisted by the deeply entrenched notion that colonization simply happened a long time ago, if at all, and that it has ended, without colonizers enacting it and benefiting from it and, most of all, without their continuing to do so. If this exploration of Pamela George's murder trial does anything at all, my hope is that it raises consciousness about how little she mattered to her murderers, their friends and families, and how small a chance she had of entering the court's and Canadian society's consciousness as a person.

Notes

1. *R. v. Kummerfield and Ternowetsky*, "Transcript of 12–15, 18–22, 25–28 November, and 2–5, 9–12, and 17–20, December 1996" [1997] (Regina, Sask. Prov. Ct. [Crim. Div.]), 3469, 4755 (hereinafter "Transcript").
2. B. Pacholik, "Relief, and Anger. Aboriginal Spokesman Demands Appeal," *Leader Post* (Regina), December 21, 1996, p. A1.
3. B. Pacholik, "Ternowetsky in Ontario Jail, Facing New Charges," *Leader Post*, October 3, 2001, p. A1.
4. R. Phillips, *Mapping Men and Empire: A Geography of Adventure* (New York: Routledge, 1997), p. 338.
5. *Canada, Profile of Census Tracts in Regina and Saskatoon* (Ottawa: Statistics Canada, 1999). Regina's total population for 1996 was 193,652. Of that total 14,565 persons identified as Aboriginal. On the problems associated with Aboriginal census data, see J. Saku, "Aboriginal Census Data in Canada: A Research Note," *Canadian Journal of Native Studies* 19, 2 (1999). In coming years Saskatchewan is expected to have a greater proportion of population with Aboriginal identity: 13 per cent by 2016. See M.J. Norris, D. Kerr, and F. Nault, *Projections of the Population with Aboriginal Identity, Canada, 1999–2016* (Ottawa: Statistics Canada and Population Projections Section, Demography Division, 1996).
6. D. Anaquod and V. Khaladkar, "Case Study: The First Nations Economy in the City of Regina," in *For Seven Generations: An Information Legacy of the Royal Commission on Aboriginal Peoples*, CD-ROM (Ottawa: Libraxus, 1997), p. 6.
7. J.W. Brennan, *Regina: An Illustrated History* (Toronto: James Lorimer and Company and the Canadian Museum of Civilization with the Secretary of State, 1989), p. 37; Sarah Carter, *Capturing Women: The Manipulation of Cultural Imagery in Canada's Prairie West* (Montreal: McGill-Queen's Press, 1997), pp. 20–1. The brutality of the NWMP and the RCMP towards Aboriginal peoples and their sexual brutality towards Aboriginal women is described in L. Brown and C. Brown, *An Unauthorized History of the RCMP* (Toronto: James Lewis and Samuel, 1973), pp. 143–81.
8. Carter, *Capturing Women*, pp. 179–82, 187. In 1894, amendments to the *Indian Act* racially encoded the suspect morality of the Aboriginal woman, as well as the suspect obedience to spatial confinement of the Aboriginal man. That year Indian agents regained their criminal law authority over certain sexual offences committed by Aboriginal persons (first articulated in 1890), and two additional offences became law: Indian prostitution and Indian vagrancy. Canada, *Report on the Royal Commission on Aboriginal Peoples: Looking Forward, Looking Back*, vol. 1 (Ottawa: Supply and Services Canada, 1996), p. 289.
9. Carter, *Capturing Women*, p. 181.
10. Harding, "Presentation to the Royal Commission on Aboriginal Peoples"; Brennan, *Regina*, p. 165; J. Hylton cited in *Royal Commission on Aboriginal Peoples, Bridging the Cultural Divide: A Report on*

Aboriginal People and Criminal Justice in Canada (Ottawa: Supply and Services Canada, 1996), p. 31 n. 41.

11. A. Finn et al., "Female Inmates, Aboriginal Inmates, and Inmates Serving Life Sentences: A One Day Snapshot," *Juristat* 19, 5 (Ottawa: Canadian Centre for Justice Statistics/Statistics Canada, 1999), p. 9. In addition, "at the provincial/territorial level, a larger proportion of Aboriginal than non-Aboriginal inmates were segregated from the rest of the inmate population (11 per cent versus 4 per cent)."
12. P. Monture-Angus, "Women and Risk: Aboriginal Women, Colonialism, and Correctional Practice," *Canadian Woman Studies* 19, 1 and 2 (1999), p. 28 n. 3; Manitoba, *Report of the Aboriginal Justice Inquiry of Manitoba: The Justice System and Aboriginal People*, vol. 1 (Winnipeg: Queen's Printer, 1991), p. 498. In describing the Saskatchewan situation, Manitoba's commissioners were highlighting the fact that the disproportionate rate of Aboriginal women represented in Manitoba's Portage Correctional Institution (at that time 70 per cent) was by no means unique, particularly when considered within the prairie regional context; Harding, "Presentation to the Royal Commission on Aboriginal Peoples," p. 323: Hylton cited in *Royal Commission on Aboriginal Peoples, Bridging the Cultural Divide*, pp. 31–2 (notes omitted).
13. "Fact Sheets: Alternatives to Incarceration." Elizabeth Fry Society. www.elizabethfry.ca/facts1_c.htm. July 21, 2000. According to the Society, in 1998 "41 percent of federally sentenced women who are classified as maximum security women are Aboriginal, whereas Aboriginal women represent only 18.7 percent of the total population of federally sentenced women, and less than 2 percent of the population of Canada." See "Position of the Canadian Association of Elizabeth Fry Societies (CAEFS) Regarding the Classification and Carceral Placement of Women Classified as Maximum Security Prisoners." Elizabeth Fry Society, www.elizabethfry.ca/maxe.htm. July 21, 2000.
14. Of course, Aboriginal women also endure considerable violence from the men of their own communities. I would argue that such violence is of a different order than the violence discussed here, although the obvious link is that both emerge out of conditions of colonization. As Emma LaRocque so insightfully commented in her testimony to the Aboriginal Justice Inquiry of Manitoba, the squaw stereotype regulates relations between Aboriginal men and women as it does between Aboriginal women and white society. Emma LaRocque, "Written Presentation to Aboriginal Justice Inquiry Hearings, 5 February 1990," cited in Manitoba, *Report of the Aboriginal Justice Inquiry*, p. 479. See also Sherene Razack, *Looking White People in the Eye: Gender, Race and Culture in Courtrooms and Classrooms* (Toronto: University of Toronto Press, 1998), p. 69.
15. Manitoba, *Report of the Aboriginal Justice Inquiry of Manitoba: the Deaths of Helen Betty Osborne and John Joseph Harper*, vol. 2 (Winnipeg: Queen's Printer, 1991), p. 52.
16. J.L. Sheane, "Life and Death on the Edge of Nowhere," *Star Phoenix* (Saskatoon), June 8, 1996, p. C3.
17. Denise McConney, "Differences for Our Daughters: Racialized Sexism in Art, Mass Media, and the Law," *Canadian Woman Studies* 19, 1 and 2, (1999), p. 212.
18. L. Robinson, *Crossing the Line: Violence and Sexual Assault in Canada's National Sport* (Toronto: McClelland and Stewart, 1998), pp. 39, 120, 151–2.
19. "Transcript", pp. 3818, 3821, 3824.
20. "Transcript," pp. 315–24, 457, 595–615.
21. "Transcript," pp. 846–910.
22. "Transcript," pp. 470–95, 3494.
23. "Transcript," pp. 892, 3760.
24. At Public Hearings in Saskatoon for RCAP, Robin Bellamy contrasted this fear typical of (white) suburbanites ("people say that they are concerned about coming down there on a Saturday night at midnight") with Aboriginal citizens' fear of entering the "better parts of Saskatoon." Steven Bellamy, "Saskatoon Friendship Inn, 'Discussion Paper C,'" May 13, 1992, Saskatoon, Saskatchewan, *For Seven Generations*, p. 366.
25. "Transcript," p. 3933. Recall Harding's assertion that the typical victim of violent crime in racialized urban space is young, female, and Aboriginal, not white and male. In 1990–91, Aboriginal persons comprised 31 per cent of the victims or reported crime In Regina, while they represented approximately 5 percent of the population. Harding, "Presentation to the Royal Commission," p. 331.
26. This interpretation was suggested to me by Carol Schick.

27. "Transcript," pp. 262, 304.
28. Following press coverage of this incident, the Assembly of First Nations for the prairie region received nearly six hundred calls from Aboriginal men and women describing similar acts of violence towards them. M. O'Hanlon. "RCMP Investigate Deaths of Saskatoon Aboriginal's," The *Toronto Star*, February 17, 2000, p. A3.
29. "Transcript," pp. 3574, 3888.
30. T. Sutter, "'She Was My Baby,'" *Leader Post* (Regina), May 13, 1995, p. l.
31. "Transcript," pp. 457, 3763.
32. Robinson, *Crossing the Line*, p. 44.
33. *R. v. Kumnrerfield and Ternowetsky*, "Transcript of Sentencing 30 January 1997" [1997] (Regina, Sask. Prov. Ct. [Crim. Div.]), (hereinafter "Transcript of Sentencing"), p. 40.
34. Justice Malone, "Response to the Honourable Chief Justice Allan McEachern." Emphasis added.
35. "Transcript," p. 5023.
36. "Transcript," p. 60. While I do not take a position on the value of long prison terms, I note here that they have been traditionally understood by society as an indicator of the severity of the crime.

Chapter 10

Overview

What is it like to be "racially profiled"? Do men and women experience this profiling differently? In this article Kitossa and Deliovsky examine the practice of applying negative stereotypes to individuals based on their perceived membership in racialized groups, and extend that concept beyond its customary usage in criminology to describe the experience of interracial mixed-sex couples in everyday life.

Canada prides itself on being a multicultural, non-racist society, and many people point to the increasing numbers of mixed-race couples, both married and otherwise, as evidence that we have truly moved beyond the stereotypes of the past. However, Kitossa and Deliovksy's interviews with ten mixed-race heterosexual couples suggest that the embrace of multiculturalism can coexist with suspicion and hostility. They use early sociologist Herbert Marcuse's notion of "repressive tolerance" to describe this apparently paradoxical situation.

Their work demonstrates the interaction of gender and race in shaping social experiences. The men of colour they interviewed had all undergone extra scrutiny by police or law enforcement, which they connected to their racialized appearance. Interestingly, however, the men differed as to whether this was unwarranted, with some of them seeing racial profiling as a "necessary evil" for crime control. Women of colour were much less likely to experience racial profiling by the police but were also subject to scrutiny by both officials and neighbours.

For white women in interracial relationships, the revelation of racist beliefs held by others often came as an uncomfortable shock. They came to see that they were regarded differently as women because of their connections to men of colour. The authors refer to this as "stigma transference" and define it as social sanctions meted out to white women who are perceived as transgressing a hierarchy of race and gender that reserves white women for white men. Racial profiling affected these women indirectly, through their relationships; they often felt it as a potential threat to their husbands, boyfriends, or sons.

Interracial Unions with White Partners and Racial Profiling: Experiences and Perspectives

Tamari Kitossa and Katerina Deliovsky

Introduction

Racial profiling in Canada has received considerable public attention over the past decade. The term describes a practice of applying criminal stereotypes to negatively racialized[1] groups by police agencies and society (Harris, 2003; Tanovich, 2006). It is a means of effectively controlling and regulating those marginalized populations. On one end the concept is narrowly defined to encapsulate forms of racial stereotyping that law enforcement/security forces use as a routine practice for criminal suspicion (e.g., drug trafficking = young Black and Latino men; drug courier = Black and Latino women; drunk = "Indians"; terrorist = Arab males). On the other end of the continuum, the term reflects Eurocentric societal assumptions about the criminal propensity of entire ethno-racial groups (Welch, 2007; Kitossa, 2005; Gabbidon, 2003). Regardless of whether the definition describes law enforcement specifically or popular cultural stereotypes, racial profiling is a new name for a long established practice in which racial stereotypes are vital components of "criminal" suspicion and the "discovery" of crime among racially devalued groups (Coke, 2003; Willis-Esquida, 2007). . . .

Our pilot study suggests that young Black men and White women report being racially profiled as a couple, and so it is likely the age of couples and the historic patterns of defacto prohibition may be factors in their experience. However, indicative of the experience of young Black men/White women unions, a substantial number of our research sample contend racial profiling is much broader than its manifestation in law enforcement. Rather, in the case of interracial couples, racial profiling is a manifestation of a "repressive" regime of discrimination, surveillance, and regulation thinly obfuscated by the multiculturalist discourse of "tolerance." In addition, the multicultural discourse of "tolerance" conceals a wide range of repressive regulatory tactics deployed by a broad range of communities. In effect, this research suggests racial profiling and repressive tolerance have points of convergence in how interracial couples make sense of law enforcement and their place in Canadian society.

Interracial Coupling: A Short Social History

In Canada, and for that matter the Caribbean and elsewhere in North and South America, there is a long-standing history of interracial coupling. The history of their moral and social regulation is almost as long (Dua, 1999; Perry, 2001; Thompson, 2009; Valverde, 1991). From the very inception of conquering indigenous peoples and the enslaving of Africans, European males took partners from these populations by force, necessity, and sometimes affection without duress (though in case of the latter it is questionable whether indigenous and African women confronted by a violently patriarchal and foreign regime were in fact making "free" choices). During the mercantile and early colonial period in British and French pre-Confederation Canada, interracial relationships between European male fur traders and First Nation women were encouraged by trading companies and colonial administrations for economic and political purposes (Perry, 2001). With White settler colonialism and the introduction of White women into the Americas, the rise of chattel slavery, the passage of anti-miscegenation laws and the nation building project in North America, attitudes and policies on race mixing underwent uneven renovations between the mid-17th on into the mid-20th century. As miscegenation became linked to the nation building project and maintaining the perceived moral and physical superiority of the "Anglo-Nordic race," regulating interracial unions became paramount in the context of increasing the racial, economic, patriarchal, and political power of White settlers. This history was not uniform and had regional valences to be sure. . . .

Currently, there are no legal prohibitions against race mixing, but there remains deep aversion in various communities though their reasons are not all the same nor on the same plane of significance. Despite latent opposition, recent data from Statistics Canada indicates the numbers of interracial unions are increasing and that within this increase White women and men "of colour" are the leading edge of these numbers (Statistics Canada, 2008: 16). Great care, however, must be taken not to conclude this is evidence of greater acceptance of these unions. Indeed, the increase in interracial unions is in absolute terms and there is no evidence the increase is statistically significant relative to the overall national population. Significantly, given what is known about the new or enlightened racism, few have conducted qualitative studies that elicit the experiences and stories of these couples.

Interracial Coupling and Multiculturalism

. . . Even with the increasing numbers, interracial unions are still a minority of all intimate unions in Canada, the US, and elsewhere in the Americas. While their statistical percentage of all unions is small—3.2 per cent in Canada[2] versus 2.2 per centin the US (Milan and Hamm, 2004)—their symbolic importance as a perceived measure of integration (Zebronski, 1999: 123) and multiculturalism (Milan and Hamm, 2004) far outweigh their number. Yet, interracial unions stand in an ambivalent societal location. On one hand their existence is trumpeted as evidence Canadian society has passed the litmus test for public "tolerance" and that integration policies are successfully reducing racial antagonism. On the other hand these unions are discomforting for many in the communities from which the partners are drawn (Deliovsky, 2010). To explain this paradox we have borrowed Herbert Marcuse's (1965) phraseology of "repressive tolerance." Our usage of Marcuse's terminology has nothing of his complex and counterintuitive theory on political liberation. Rather, we suggest that despite the very public celebration of the increase in interracial unions repressive tolerance aptly describes a lived contradiction in the public and private lives of Canadians. If we are to make sense of the experiences and perceptions of partners in interracial unions, we need to theorize how they are situated in the nation's imaginary.

As we use it, the concept of repressive tolerance reflects Erica Chito Childs' observation that despite the increase in the interracial unions opposition remains and is encoded in colour blind language (2004). Our usage of this concept in part draws on Rima Berms-McGown's observation that while "tolerance" is not without merit, in the context of a deeper form of multiculturalism it is less than desirable. She contends multiculturalism has a self-reinforcing discursive and practical power reality that: a) creates a differentiated hidden/unnamed centre ("we") and a visible/named periphery ("you"); b) assumes an air of White self-congratulatory moral superiority in "putting-up-with" with the Others' racial "difference"; and c) implies a recognition of the racial Other that is conditional upon their appropriate performance of implied behaviours (Berms-McGown, 2007: 9). We agree that multiculturalism presents a paradox in its lived reality. At a symbolic level, the discourse promotes practices of ethno-racial group maintenance and celebration of difference that easily transit into group siloing. Simultaneously at the level of political culture, multiculturalism aims toward producing a unified social domain wherein group plurality and social intercourse maintains the status quo of capitalism, patriarchy and White supremacy (Bannerji, 2000). The aim of the latter is to pacify and wield the difference of the racial Other into a workably pluralistic ethno-racial democracy in which group boundaries are porous, never solidifying into enmity since the principles of equality, fairness, and opportunity applies to all ethno-racial groups. . . .

Sample, Methodology, and Theoretical Framework

. . . In the summer of 2009, we conducted in-depth qualitative interviews with 10 heterosexual interracial couples in three southern Ontario cities. We used purposive sampling to locate a diverse range of interracial couples.[3] For each couple we required one partner to be of European descent. The latter was important for this pilot study for three reasons. First, given the purpose of racial profiling is to aggrandize White supremacy, we imagined a greater probability of finding couples who experienced racial profiling in cases where the woman was White and their partners' men "of colour." Second, and here the Hawthorn effect must be fully considered, polls have found 68 per cent of White Torontonians believe the police are biased against "racial minorities" (Wortley, 2008) and in the US 81 per cent of White peoples said they disapproved of racial profiling (Gross, 2007: 52). Finally, we imagined that by virtue of their participation in an interracial union White interracial partners may be more likely to have high degrees of racial literacy and genuinely oppose racial profiling. Among the White participants we wanted both men and women. While we did not imagine White partners would experience racial profiling, given our discussion of the gendered nature of repressive tolerance that White women would more likely be in situations to witness racial profiling. Among the participants "of colour" we sought men and women from one of the Statistics Canada census groups, for example: Black, Aboriginal,[4] Chinese, South East Asian, Latin American, Arab, etc. The couples' ages range from 19 to 73. The objective for this broad range was to capture longitudinal distinctions in how couples experienced racial profiling. We sought interviewees from diverse socio-economic backgrounds and educational levels.

The interviews were transcribed, coded, and contextually analyzed to arrive at the following themes: a) men "of colour" and critical engagement with racial profiling; b) men "of colour" and provisional concurrence; c) perspectives and experiences of White males; d) perspectives and experiences of women "of colour"; e) perspectives and experiences of White women. The analysis was grounded in critical race and feminist theory. Both formulations use narrative as a tool to uncover systems of racial and gender power and inequity. They offer a critique of contemporary social structures through historically grounded analyses of society and the law, and they hold that gender does not act independently of race and class. These theories contextualize oppressive relations and appreciate their multi-dimensionality in creating marginalization and privilege. This multifaceted theoretical orientation is important because it allows us to apprehend that within interracial unions with White partners are lived experiences, world views and social positions that are simultaneously dominant and oppositional. Indeed, in terms of class, gender, race, colonialism, and imperialism the partners in these relationships embody different social and historical trajectories.

Men "Of Colour" and Critical Engagement with Racial Profiling

Among the research participants the news media played an important role in shaping their understanding of racial profiling. . . . For some participants, though, the media's pedagogic function was less so educative than providing a vocabulary with which to name their experience. In other words they did not learn from the news media what their experience, and in some cases their parental socialization, had not already taught them—that as negatively racialized persons they may be treated with suspicion. This was the case for the Cambodian and all African Canadian males in our study.

Roger, the most senior of our research participants, for instance pointed out he first became aware of the term racial profiling and particularly "driving while black" through reading about the Kingston racial profiling study (Wortley, 2005). News of Wortley's study resonates with Roger because he experienced racial profiling while working in New Brunswick in the mid-1980s—he was stopped and questioned under the pretext of mistaken identity. His other most salient experience came in 2005 when he and Diane, his partner, were to fly out of Buffalo airport to a southern destination. He recounts:

> I was the only Black man in the shuttle bus at customs and the only Black man getting on the plane at Buffalo Airport. Both times, they zeroed on me alone of all the other passengers. It was very uncomfortable. It didn't seem random to me.

. . . In Wayne's case his father recounted experiences of job discrimination and the many times he was stopped by the police. Wayne's father drives high end cars and based on his experience of being stopped frequently warned him to expect to be stopped also. He recalls, "[m]y dad told us a lot about the discrimination he encountered in Jamaica and Canada and I think he did this to show us that although things like racial profiling exist it should not suppress you completely." In spite of his father's encouragement that educational and economic success is the antidote to racism, Wayne was paradoxically cautioned that material success might inspire White envy. Consistent with this, Wayne noted that in a number of the instances he was stopped he was asked: "whose car is this and what do you do?" Confronted with such questions Wayne contends, "[the police] see a Black person driving a nice car and maybe they get jealous."

Throughout his adolescent life, Albert was reminded by his parents to behave in a manner that was beyond reproach, especially with White girls. The explicit message was that he was already criminalized by his race, and so it would take little for him to be subject to undue surveillance and punishment for a sexual offence. His parents' chief concern was less about his being stopped by police and more about the regulation of African Canadian male sexuality. The implied message was that dating White girls had risks. While Albert did not take the myth of the Black rapist too seriously, he was forced to rethink the merits of his parents' wisdom on a visit to a city in Michigan. He describes that while he and his partner Amelia were in a shopping mall looking for a parking spot, they were flashed by a cruiser requiring them to stop. Albert describes his epiphany of feeling sick in his stomach when he said to himself: "Oh my God. I think they pulled me over because I have her in the car." Albert is convinced that while racial profiling exists, he is unwilling to judge all police officers by the conduct of a few. Nonetheless, he is concerned that racial profiling prevents police from seeing African Canadians as people first and criminals second. For Albert the key issue is, "how can [the police] build partnerships with people who [they] are . . . branding as criminals?" . . .

The Perspectives and Experience of White Males

As we expected, we did not have any White men that experienced racial profiling in Canada or elsewhere in their travels. They were not, however, uniform in their views on racial profiling and racial discrimination. Two of the three men, Andrew and Goran, were not only aware of racial profiling but maintained it is was unworkable, ineffective, racist, and an unjustified abrogation of the civil liberties of marginalized groups. Like the men "of colour" who were critical of racial profiling, Andrew and Goran argued that White men are the beneficiaries of white skinned privilege and this reduces their surveillance burden. For example, pointing to themselves as beneficiaries of this privilege, they noted their partners, Anne and Nira and the communities of which they are a part, have fallen under the gaze of White suspicion.

Andrew in particular, agreeing with Nira's contention that racial profiling constitutes a mode of power that personally and socially disables its targets, noted that "Middle Eastern men have joined Black, Aboriginal men, and others as a kind of a main target" for racial profiling. He was concerned that the same principle that justifies racial profiling and its abrogation of civil liberties is based on a similar logic that sees the West "going into a country and killing half a million people . . . it isn't worth it." On grounds of its futility in Western led wars in Muslim countries abroad, Andrew was not hopeful for the prospects of racial profiling at home. Goran like Andrew concludes that racial profiling is not only civilly and morally wrong, he felt it adds to social conflict because "it will turn people against one another. They will have no social solidarity with one another."

John's perspective on racial profiling differed markedly from Andrew and Goran's views. His views closely approximated Jason's actuarial assumption. A key distinction for John, however, was that racial profiling should be based on crime rates and "crime mapping." In taking an actuarial approach, John suggested targeted policing would apply to a particular urban geography and criminal profile in which race and dress styles are criteria for suspicion. Assuming the effectiveness of "crime mapping," John believed racial profiling would be one tool, among others, at the disposal of law enforcement in the fight against crime. John's one caveat, though, is that racial profiling does not justify police brutality, such as with the beating of Rodney King by LAPD officers.

While all three men consistently demonstrated competence in their articulation of racial literacy, their perspectives on racial profiling revealed an important distinction in their understanding of how racism works. The potential of John's racial literacy was undermined by his uncritical acceptance that criminal and racial profiles can be de-linked and that the latter does not saturate the former. His account shared much in common with Jason's and Gamal's and largely rested on the assumptions that racial profiling has a logical terminus and it does not justify institutional abuses of authority. For their part, Andrew and Goran shared much in common with men "of colour" who critically rejected racial profiling. The level of their racial literacy was such that they contended racial profiling would not only lead to counter-intuitive consequences but also provide a justification for the police to practise racial discrimination in the guise of law enforcement.

The Perspectives and Experiences of Women "Of Colour"

Among women "of colour," awareness, perceptions, and experience differed markedly. Although neither of the women had any harrowing experiences with law enforcement as described by some of the men "of colour," two of the three described experiences that fit the criteria for racial profiling. For all three women, the media was their chief source of awareness rather than parents who attempted to "race proof" them. Anne, for example, a Canadian born woman of Caribbean heritage, had at least two experiences that might qualify as "shopping while Black." Interestingly she did not append the label of racial profiling to these experiences. Importantly, she noted her parents did not raise her or her sisters with a race-proofing discourse that might have enabled a more cogent discourse on racism.

Nira, a woman of Turkish heritage, who lived in Germany before taking up residency in Canada and is now a PhD candidate, had little reluctance to define her experience at Munich airport as an instance of racial profiling. Here the crucial issue is how the comparative privilege conferred on Andrew and her daughter illuminated her differential treatment:

> In terms of racial profiling after September 11, I experience this every time at the airport as a woman. One time, we stopped over in Munich when we were going to Turkey. They did not even look at Andrew and my daughter's which were Canadian passports. The guy looked at my passport, every page and looks up . . . tries to see if it is fake. That is racial profiling.

Nira extends racial profiling to a broader range of social experiences than law enforcement. For her racial profiling is a production of "larger social perceptions." She contends that while racial stereotypes contain a kernel of truth, it "gets out of hand and becomes the whole picture telling us what a group of people are like." For Nira, law enforcement cannot be founded on half-truths. Instead, she sees in racial profiling a tool of racial domination that enables the majoritarian culture of whiteness to use stereotypes and discrimination as weapons to "put the person who is profiled into the position of being disempowered and disabled. They can't do anything about it."

Jennifer, a woman of South East Asian descent, reported no experience with racial profiling. She did report, however, that while travelling in the wake of the 2001 asymmetrical attacks in the US, her brother was frequently subjected to searches at airports. Beyond this, she describes experiences of feeling racially Othered in her home city and middle class neighbourhood; both of which are overwhelmingly White though there is increasing demographic change. In response to being mistaken for her children's nanny and to signal she is not out of place, she is conscious about using middle class styles of dress that would modulate her racial difference.

Perspectives and Experiences of White Women

Of all the participants in this study, White women shared a striking number of characteristics in common even when [their] perspectives and experiences differed. The first of these commonalities relate to "colour blind" ideology and how their experiences as partners and parents in an interracial family contradicted this view. Colour blind ideology can be understood as the belief that race is no longer a salient issue because post-civil rights progress renders racism a thing of the past (Sweeney, 2008). For most of the women, as a consequence of their vicarious experience with racism directed at their partners and children, "colour blindness" gave way to [what] France Winddance Twine calls "racial literacy" (2004). The women who demonstrated a complex and critical appraisal of racial profiling also narrate an evolution of consciousness paralleling their attainment of higher education. Finally, the partners of the men of "colour" who provisionally accommodated themselves or were not concerned about being racially profiled demonstrated the highest level of anxiety about the impact of racial profiling on their partners and children.

For the White women who became aware of racial profiling or were able to name it when witnessing it, this was an act of becoming consciously aware of and naming racism, White privilege, and the experience of repressive tolerance. An aspect of this consciousness meant becoming aware of and questioning "colour blind" ideology or rejecting it altogether so that White privilege could be challenged. To be sure, not all of the White women in our sample fully transitioned into this on-going stance of awareness. Here, Diane is a stand-out. Despite contradictory evidence, she held onto the mystique of colour blindness and in the process undermined Roger's accounts of racism and racial profiling saying that he was "sometimes overly sensitive."

Elise's socialization stood in stark contrast to that of Diane's. She was raised to believe in social and racial equality. But, her family's negative reaction to her marrying Jason because of his Asian heritage revealed to her that "colour blindness" was a myth. Now estranged from her father and brother, she is also doubtful of continued contact with her sister because of her proclivity for using racial slurs. Elise points out her parents promoted a rhetoric of tolerance for others but "[it] turned out they did not actually mean it." Also, expressions of negative societal reaction to her union attuned her to the ways in which racial profiling constitutes a form of White privilege that is subsidized by a preoccupation with the criminalization of the Other. Elise reasoned this was not only unfair and unjust, but also that the exemption of White people from suspicion undermined more effective public safety measures such as random searches.

Despite Elise taking a different position on racial profiling to her partner Jason, she understands that what we term "provisional accommodation" is a survival technique for him. And, while she believes he is eminently capable of handling himself in a situation of racial profiling she does not believe he would be so sanguine if his children were subject to the same behaviour. For her part, should her children be subject to racial profiling, she remarks "that would make me very angry."

Like Elise, Amelia was raised with the discourse of colour blindness. Her family, however, raised no serious objections to her relationship with Albert. In fact, her father, an Italian immigrant who experienced significant discrimination as a youth in Northern Ontario, more than tolerated Albert, he fully embraced him. Having initially accepted the discourse of "colour blindness," vicariously experiencing racial profiling, and now confronting issues having to do with navigating the racial identity of their son, Amelia is open to exploring issues of racism and whiteness: "I am just beginning to become aware of racism. And, it does kind of scare me."

Elizabeth shares in common with Elise a partner who provisionally welcomes racial profiling. Elizabeth, however, does not share Gamal's sanguine view on racial profiling. She points to three central reasons why this is the case. First of these is her appreciation that Gamal's identity as a new immigrant does not predispose him to make the same civil liberty claims as someone born in Canada. Elizabeth's concern for Gamal centres on the experience of Maher Arar who was subjected to "extraordinary rendition" by the US with the consent of CSIS. Though they have yet to cross into the US together she imagines that if they do and are detained in ways that appear consistent with racial profiling, she says that "I would not be as patient as him. I could imagine us doing a border crossing and my getting very angry and upset quite quickly and him not."

Elizabeth was concerned, in part, around how gender and masculinity might be articulated in racial profiling. Citing the movie *Crash*, where White police officers dehumanized an African American man by fondling his wife, tempting him to offer some resistance, she theorized that racial profiling might enable White men to regulate the sexuality of White women and men "of colour." While Gamal had no tales to tell of racial profiling, Elizabeth's prior marriage to a Nigerian man and having two children with him radically shaped her awareness and perspective of racial profiling. She describes, while with her former partner, being stopped, their identity checked, and sent on their way without being ticketed on a number of occasions. She is particularly concerned that her teenage son's experience with being racially profiled in school continues with police and airport security who label him as a drug trafficker.

Like Elizabeth, Deborah is concerned for her partner, particularly where international travel is concerned. For his part, Joseph's concern was initially stimulated by the post–September 2001 moral panic; but with time and having travelled to the US without incident his personal concerns have waned. Rather than direct experience, the Western reaction to the asymmetrical attacks on the US and the Arar case are Deborah's points of reference. She remains concerned for Joseph, in part because of his Pakistani heritage and also because of her professional experience with the courts and the police: "I am concerned in Canada for how he may be treated by the cops. I just know too many cops who are morons." More prosaically, she points out that whereas she and other White women in the women's assault movement have and continue to critically confront their "invisible knapsacks of white privilege," she believes the courts, Crown, and the police are demonstrably resistant to anti-racist and diversity education and training that may eliminate or reduce the use of racial profiling. Her concerns, however, are not only professional and for Joseph but also for her youngest son, who she describes as both "the darker skinned" "and also . . . the mouthiest . . ." of her children.

As opposed to other women in our sample (excluding Diane) who were raised with the rhetoric of "colour blindness," Vesna and Dina received subtle and overt messages from their families and communities which disparaged interracial unions and criminalized people "of colour." For example, upon learning of Vesna's pregnancy her father replied, "you are carrying a monkey in your stomach . . . I am never going to talk to you again if you have this baby." His central rationalization rested on the proposition that "Cambodians are worse than Black people" and hence more criminogenic. Because in Vesna's experience repressive tolerance and the criminalization of Asians were closely linked, she believed racial profiling was but one manifestation of a wider pattern of discrimination she encountered because of her participation in an interracial union.

Unlike Vesna, Dina had the benefit of some family members coming around to accept Jason though they were vehemently opposed at the start. That said, she remains estranged from her father who insisted that "you are going to marry . . . a Serbian man. That is the way it is, the way it was, and the way it should be." Dina does not, however, connect her experience with repressive tolerance to the discourse and practice of racial profiling. Her conception of racial profiling is, instead greatly informed by her experience as a criminology student and her own experience with being with Wayne when he was racially profiled by campus police. In our sample, racial literacy or the absence thereof seemed to determine White women's understanding of racial profiling and not whether their spouses described being racially profiled.

Conclusion

Gender and race, but class in more subtle ways, played defining roles in the participants' perceptions and experiences of racial profiling. These perceptions and experiences were in no way racially uniform. For example, there was provisional concurrence with racial profiling from one White, one Asian, and one Arabic male. In none of these cases though was racial profiling condoned *carte blanche*. These participants emphasized that due process rights must be strictly adhered to and that actuarial assumptions and "crime mapping" would enable criminal profiling to trump racial profiling. Interestingly, the majority of the White men in this study concurred with the men "of colour" who opposed racial profiling on two important points: racial profiling was perceived as a racial subsidy for White men and that it provoked racial antagonism. Whereas all the White men were aware of how racism impacted their partners, none experienced the phenomenon of what Deliovsky calls "stigma transference" (2002), which is the spoiling of the White partner's social identity because of their intimate association with a negatively racialized individual (Goffinan, 1963). On the other hand for White women with men "of colour" stigma transference is a racially gendered directive to regulate their sexuality in service of whiteness and patriarchy (Deliovsky, 2010).

Among our participants, educationally accomplished White women seemed cognizant of the duality of White privilege and racial oppression and how their choice of racial partner compounded gender oppression by casting them out of the White "fold." Their narratives suggest there are multiple reasons for their awareness. In part, for those with a strong anti-oppression discourse, they were able to make parallels between gender and racial oppression. In many instances, witnessing their partners' being racially profiled or discriminated against made them thoughtful about what their partners or children may experience. In addition to stigma transference, those White women exposed to postsecondary education and anti-oppression workshops had a language that enabled a critique of the implications of racial profiling for themselves, their families, and society.

A question arises as to why women "of colour" in our sample had little to say about explicit experiences with racial profiling. There are a variety of reasons for this. First, this is a pilot study and the sample is small. Second, we did not have poor and working class women in our sample. This is important given the criminalization of poverty. And, third, criminality in the public imagination is associated with men "of colour" thus criminalizing stereotypes for women "of colour" is more contingent on context, space, and place. Hence, on their own, women "of colour" might attract some degree of suspicion but depending on space and place, not on the order of danger and threat that surrounds the bodies of some men "of colour." In our study, the African-Canadian men and the Cambodian-Canadian man had the most consistent and stark experiences with racial profiling. For Wayne and Albert racial profiling was experienced irrespective of class. And, taking Roger's experience into account, it appears the more youthful our African Canadian sample was the more likely racial surveillance will occur. In view of the way that slavery has built a normative anti-African racial bias into the law, this experience suggests the long standing history of the criminalization of African men bears upon these contemporary experiences. With respect to Ang the image of Asian males as perpetual "foreigners," aiming to take the jobs of White Canadians, and heavily involved in gangs and marijuana grow ops are the background factors through which to understand his experience.

Among our 10 participant couples, two couples felt singled out by law enforcement and security guards *because* they were an interracial couple. Key to this is that these couples were composed of young Black men and White women. Being targeted as a couple, however, was not a salient feature of their narratives. Rather, the major concern is that the male partners were persistent targets of racial profiling, racial discrimination, and repressive tolerance.

Beyond racial profiling, however, all participants described one instance or another of repressive tolerance. The salient feature here is that White women who entered their unions with notions of racelessness developed discursive awareness of racism and White privilege. Very troubling is that the young women of Eastern European heritage were the recipients of threats and punitive sanctions from their families and community. Our study indicates that while White participants articulated awareness of racism and racial profiling, and most opposed it, their level of consciousness and critical analysis varied. Some believed they would have demonstrated this critical awareness even if they were not with partners "of colour." Yet, most held beliefs of "colour blindness" before entering into their unions and were disabused of this notion only as they were witness to incontrovertible instances of racism and racial profiling. All the partners in our study related instances in which family members or others in society expressed mild disapproval, threatened physical violence and discriminated against them. Most couples, however, seemed unable to resolve the contradiction between multiculturalism and the reality of their experiences. . . .

Notes

1. Racialization as defined by Miles properly describes being raced as a continuous process. The problem, however, is that being raced has differential and contingent terminals if one is the racial Other as opposed to the Occidental norm. Thus, racialization assumes a radical relativity that undermines whatever meaningful descriptive power the term may have. To leave racialization at the level of generic description reifies the universalism of whiteness as a default racial category. Thus, to ensure whiteness is not obfuscated the concept of racialization requires the prefix of "negative" or "positive" so that the provisional terminus and its attendant conditions of advantage and disadvantage can be named.
2. This number includes couples from "visible minority" groups as well as couples who are from "non-visible minority" groups and "visible minority" groups.
3. All participants are Canadian citizens: 1. Chinese/Filipino man and English/German woman; 2. Bulgarian man and African Caribbean woman; 3. Scottish/English man and Turkish woman; 4. Pakistani man and Polish-Jewish woman; 5. English man and Indian woman; 6. Moroccan man and English woman; 7. Trinidadian man and English/French woman; 8. Jamaican man and Italian woman; 9. Jamaican/Syrian man and Serbian Canadian woman; 10. Cambodian man and Croatian woman.
4. We arranged to interview two Aboriginal/White couples, but at the last minute these interviews fell through.

References

Bannerji, H. 2000. *The Dark Side of the Nation: Essays on Multiculturalism, Nationalism, and Gender*. Toronto: Canadian Scholars' Press.

Berms-McGown, R. 2007. "What It Means to Belong: Reframing 'Accommodation' in a Multicultural Liberal Democracy," Immigration, Minorities and Multiculturalism In Democracies Conference Ethnicity and Democratic Governance MCRI project. www.edg-gde.ca. October 25–27, 2007. Montreal, QC, Canada.

Childs, E.C. 2004. "Families on the Color-line: Patrolling Borders and Crossing Boundaries." *Race & Society* 5: 139–61.

Coke, T.E. 2003. "Racial Profiling Post-9/11: Old Story, New Debate," in C. Brown, ed., *Lost Liberties: Ashcroft and the Assault on Personal Freedom*, New York: New Press.

Deliovsky, K. 2010. *White Femininity: Gender, Race and Power*. Black Point, NS: Fernwood Press.

Gabbidon, S.L. 2003. "Racial Profiling by Store Clerks and Security Personnel in Retail Establishment: An Exploration of 'Shopping While Black,'" *Journal of Contemporary Criminal Justice* 19(3): 345–64.

Gross, S.R. 2007. "The Rhetoric of Racial Profiling," in R.L. Weiner, B.H. Bornstein, R. Schopp, and S.L. Willborn, eds., *Social Consciousness in Legal Decision Making: Psychological Perspectives*, pp. 35–60. New York: Springer.

Harris, D.A. 2003. *Profiles in Injustice: Why Racial Profiling Cannot Work*. New York: The New Press.

Kitossa, T. 2005. "Malleus Maleficarum Africanus: The Criminalization of African Canadians and 'Due Process' as a Property of Whiteness," in L. Visano, ed., *Law and Criminal Justice: A Critical Inquiry*. Toronto: The Athenian PolicyForum Inc.

Marcuse, H. 1965. "Repressive Tolerance," in R.P. Wolff, B. Moore, Jr., and H. Marcuse, eds., *A Critique of Pure Tolerance*, pp. 81–123. Boston: Beacon Press.

Milan, A., and B. Ham. 2004. "Mixed Unions," *Statistics Canada-Catalogue* No. 11-008.

Perry, A. 2001. *On the Edge of Empire: Gender, Race, and the Making of British Columbia, 1849–1871*. Toronto: University of Toronto Press.

Statistics Canada. 2008. *Canada's Ethnocultural Mosaic, 2006 Census*. Catalogue no. 97-562-X. Retrieved April 7, 2008. www12.statcan.ca/census-recensement/2006/as-sa/97-562/pdf/97-562-XIE2006001.pdf

Sweeney, K.A. 2008. "Contact and the Continuum of White Women's Racial Awareness," *Spaces for Difference: An Interdisciplinary Journal* 1(1):42–64.

Tanovich, D. 2006. *The Colour of Justice: Policing Race in Canada*. Toronto: Irwin Law.

Thompson, D. 2009. "Racial Ideas and Gendered Intimacies: The Regulation of Interracial Relationships in North America," *Social and Legal Studies* 18(3): 353–71.

Twine, F.W. 2004. "A White Side of Black Britain: The Concept of Racial Literacy," *Ethnic and Racial Studies* 27(6): 878–907.

Valverde, M. 1991. *The Age of Light, Soap, and Water: Moral Reform in English Canada, 1885–1925*. Toronto: McClelland and Stewart Inc.

Welch, K. 2007. "Black Criminal Stereotypes and Racial Profiling," *Journal of Contemporary Criminal Justice* 23(3): 276–88.

Willis-Esquida, C. 2007. "Racial Profiling as a Minority Issue," in R.L. Weiner, B.H. Bomstein, R. Schopp, and S.L. Willbom, eds., *Social Consciousness in Legal Decision Making: Psychological Perspectives*, pp. 76–87. New York: Springer.

Wortley, S. 2005. *Bias Free Policing: The Kingston Data Collection Project; Preliminary Results*. Retrieved June 25, 2010. www.cantraining.org/BTC/research.php.

Wortley, S. 2008. "Addressing Issues of Racial Diversity in the Criminal Justice System." Paper presented at Dialogue on Diversity: Making Diversity Real in our Workplaces. Toronto. January 30, 2008.

Zebroski, S.A. 1999. "Black-white Intermarriages the Racial and Gender Dynamics of Support and Opposition," *Journal of Black Studies* 30(1): 123–32.

Chapter 11

Overview

Like Kitossa and Deliovsky, Angela Aujla questions the notion that the official Canadian policy of multiculturalism reflects a colour-blind society. In a departure from standard social science methodology, she looks at the poetry and creative writing produced by South Asian Canadian women, in which they grapple with pressures to assimilate to "mainstream," presumably white, Canadian society, while at the same time recognizing that they cannot (and do not wish to) shed their South Asianness.

Like Razack, Aujla historicizes the experience of South Asian Canadian women, pointing out the ways in which South Asian women have been positioned within popular representations as simultaneously threatening and desirable to white men. As a result, the racist attention reported by the women in her study has strong overtones of gender stereotyping. The "beauty myth" also illustrates the intersection of race and gender in the lives of South Asian women. As their poetry and stories relate, they are keenly conscious that whiteness is associated with attractiveness. This association is reinforced by the casual comments of others and is internalized as dislike for one's own appearance.

As the other authors in this section describe, assimilation to "white" "mainstream" society is often easier for racialized women than for men. However, the gendered possibilities of assimilation bring their own discontents for the women in Aujla's study. They describe being positioned as an "honorary white person," who is seen as somehow distinct from other Asians, a stance that singles out the individual woman as well as denigrating the state of being Asian.

Aujla avoids a simplistic equation of racialized minority status with oppression and victimization through her attention to the creative works of South Asian women. Poetry, prose, and other narratives can be a form of resistance to gendered and racialized prejudices, as well as a way to assert the value of cultural difference. Aujla's participants are not just objects of gendered racialization; they are also keen observers and active creators of their own intercultural identities.

Others in Their Own Land: Second Generation South Asian Canadian Women, Racism, and the Persistence of Colonial Discourse

Angela Aujla

"Go back to where you came from!"

"Where are you *actually* from?"

"Paki!"

Though born and raised in Canada, the national identity of multigenerational South Asian Canadian women is subject to incessant scrutiny and doubt, as reflected in the phrases above. They are othered by a dominant culture which categorizes them as "visible minorities," "ethnics," immigrants, and foreigners—categories considered incommensurable with being a "real" Canadian, despite the promises of multiculturalism. Never quite Canadian enough, never quite white enough, these women remain "others" in their own land. Not only are they excluded from national belonging, they are haunted by a discourse which has historically constructed non-white women as a threat to the nation-state. Contemporary constructions of South Asian Canadian women are situated in a larger racist, sexist, and colonial discourse which cannot be buried under cries of "unity in diversity."

In this article, I focus on how the gendered racialization of multigenerational South Asian Canadian women excludes them from national belonging and pressures them to assimilate. The literary production of these women reflects the deep repercussions of this exclusion. and provides a location where issues of identity, otherness, and racism may be articulated and resisted. I will look at poetry and personal narratives by multigenerational South Asian Canadian women as points of intervention into these issues. Beginning with a brief overview of racism against South Asians in Canada, I will discuss how racist and colonial discourses of the past continue to influence dominant discourses and perceptions of South Asian Canadian women today.

Unity against Diversity

Despite the many differences among multigenerational South Asian Canadian women, similar experiences can be identified. These include experiences of racism, feelings of being "other" and not belonging, colonialism, patriarchy, sexism, and living in a diasporic culture. I use the term "South Asian" because it challenges the geographical locatedness of cultures and identities through its wide scope of reference. Generally, the category "South Asian" refers to those who trace their ancestry to places including India, Pakistan, Sri Lanka, Bangladesh, Bhutan, Tanzania, Uganda, South Africa, and the Caribbean (Henry et al; Agnew). Terms such as "East Indian" and "Indo-Canadian" are problematic because of their narrow reference. Both refer directly to the Indian subcontinent, excluding other South Asian regions. They also refer to nation states and nationalities, implying the idea that ethnicity, identity, and "race" are neatly confined within the borders of homogenous states.

Much in the same spirit as colonial cartography, South Asians have been "mapped" and inscribed by the dominant culture through racialized discourse and state practices since they began immigrating to Canada in the late nineteenth century (Buchnigani and Indra). Surrounded by an imposed mythos of being deviant, threatening. Undesirable, and inferior to the white "race," South Asians were constructed as "other" to the dominant Canadian culture who could not even bear to sit beside them on trains (Henry et al.). This attitude is evident in the contemporary phenomena of "white flight" in certain BC municipalities where some white residents have chosen to move rather than live alongside the South Asians who are "ruining the neighbourhood." In the early 1900s, they were not permitted to participate as full citizens, the Canadian state controlled where they could live, where they could work, and even what they could or could not wear. Though they were British subjects, they could not vote federally until 1947 (Henry et al.). Though in a less overt form, the traces of this mapping continue to effect South Asian bodies today. Dominant representations of South Asian Canadians are largely stereotypical and impose static notions of culture and identity on them, whether they are immigrants or multigenerational.

The history of media images of South Asians attests to this. In the early [twentieth] century, the South Asian presence in British Columbia was referred to as "a Hindu Invasion" by the news media; a proliferation of articles in BC newspapers stressed the importance of maintaining Anglo-Saxon superiority[1] (Henry et al.). Negative media portrayal of South Asians still persists. As Yasmin Jiwani states ". . . even contemporary representations cohere around an 'us' versus 'them' dichotomy that ideologically sediments a notion of national identity that is clearly exclusionary" (1998: 60).

Canadian Sikhs for example, have been depicted as over-emotional religious extremists predisposed to violence. Used repeatedly, these images reinforce prejudice against all South Asians, both male and female. The *Vancouver Sun* headlines "Close Watch on City Sikhs" and "Sikh Militancy Grows" have not strayed very far from the cry of "Hindu Invasion" in the early part of the twentieth century. Representations of South Asian Canadian women in the media portray them as the meek and pitiful victims of arranged marriages and abusive husbands or uses them as colourful, orientalized exotica to be fawned over (Jiwani, 1998). Such media images subtly exclude South Asian Canadians from national belonging. Their cultures are represented as barbaric and backwards, as "clashing" and "conflicting" with civilized and modern Canadian society. These portrayals imply that South Asians do not "fit in" here, and that they are certainly not "real" Canadians. Edward Said states,

> [The] imaginative geography of the "our land/ barbarian land" variety does not require that the barbarians acknowledge the distinction. It is enough for "us" to set up these boundaries in our own minds; "they" become "they" accordingly, and both their territory and their mentality are designated as different from "ours." (54)

Said describes how the us–them boundary and its accompanying mythos about "others" mentalities has historically been constructed by the dominant culture and imposed onto "others" regardless of their consent. Though Said was referring to relations between colonizer and colonized, his idea remains just as relevant when applied to contemporary relations between South Asian Canadians and the dominant Canadian culture.

Feel-good, multicultural goals of unity in diversity and ending racism are simplistic and certain to fail because they do not acknowledge the deeply rooted racist, sexist, and colonial discourse that has constructed Canada and "Canadian identity." As Ann Laura Stoler argues, "the discourse of race was not on parallel track with the discourse of the nation but part of it" (93). Historically, Canadian identity has not been a First Nations identity, or even a French identity. It has been, and continues to be a white, British, Anglo-Saxon identity. As in other white-settler colonies, and in Britain, the civility and superiority of blood and nation was constructed against the "backwardness" and inferiority of the "darker races" (Stoler; Jiwani, 1998; Dua). For example, the modernity of the Canadian state was juxtaposed to the pre-modern South Asian woman, the blood of the superior Anglo Saxon race was juxtaposed to the degenerate blood of non-white races (Henry et al.). White, Anglo-Canadian unity was constructed in opposition to non-white "diversity." But now, with the introduction of multiculturalism, we are suddenly expected to make the very unrealistic leap from unity against "diversity," to unity *in* diversity.

The Persistence of Colonial Discourse

South Asian women have been both sexualized and racialized through colonial discourse as oppressed, subservient, tradition-bound, and pre-modern (Dua). They are also constructed as seductive, exotic objects of desire. In another construction they are considered overly-fertile, undesirable, smelly, and oily-haired (Jiwani, 1992; Brah). The legacy of colonial discourse is evident in contemporary racialized and sexualized constructions of South Asian women. In a *Guardian* article published September 5, 1985, a 19-year-old South Asian woman in London recounts the sexualized racist comments she faces walking home from college:

> . . . if I'm on my own with other girls it's, "Here comes the Paki whore, come and fuck us Paki whores, we've heard you're really horny." Or maybe they'll put it the other way around, saying that I am dirty, that no one could possibly want to go to bed with a Paki . . . (qtd. in Brah 79)

These co-existing sentiments of desire and revulsion can be seen as remnants of British colonial attitudes towards South Asian women. While their colonizers considered non-white women savage, and backwards, they were also thought to possess a "sensual, enticing and indulgent nature" (Smits 61). According to Yasmin Jiwani, in British imperialist fiction by authors including Rudyard Kipling, the Indian woman was characterized by her rampant sexuality and her abundant fertility (1992). As can be inferred from the comments yelled at the 19-year-old South Asian woman walking home from college, contemporary stereotypes of multigenerational South Asian women remain deeply rooted in the colonial tradition.

Race, blood, and nation have historically been deeply interconnected and overlapping concepts in the West. Historically, the immigration and presence of women of colour in Canada, and other Western countries was seen as a threat to the nation-state. They brought with them the danger of increasing the non-white population and the possibility of miscegenation—a danger all the more immanent given their "overly fecund" nature. Dua comments that "In Canada, as well as other settler colonies, racial purity was premised on the Asian peril—the danger of Anglo-Saxons being overrun by more fertile races" (252). Non-white women endangered Western "civility" and national identity; the proliferation of non-white babies was not just a threat to the racial purity of Western societies, but to their dominance and very existence. It was thought that miscegenation and too many non-white births could lead to the demise of the Anglo-Saxon race, and therefore, the demise of the nation state itself. As Dua writes,

> . . . the submissiveness of Hindu women was linked to a decline into pre-modern conditions. While white bourgeois women were racially gendered as mothers of the nation, colonized women were racially gendered as dangerous to the nation-state. (254)

Similarly, in everyday the racist/xenophobic discourse of this country, the "real" Canadians complain that immigrants are invading their neighbourhoods, cities, and the country itself. The *Globe and Mail* warns, "soon there will be more visible minorities than whites in Vancouver and Toronto," and that their number "is the highest in history." Feeding into fears of non-white women's limitless fertility, they also report that the number of visible minorities born in Canada is rising steadily and that they are younger than "the total Canadian population" (Mitchell). Such articles reflect the persistence of colonial discourse; while the white woman's regulated fecundity was supposed to ensure the reproduction of the social body, the non-white woman's "limitless fertility" was seen as endangering the reproduction of the social body. Non-white and "mixed race" bodies signalled a danger to the State.

I Am Canadian?

> "Are you Fijian by any chance?" the stranger asked.
>
> "No," I replied.
>
> "Are you from India?"
>
> "No."

During this brief encounter on Vancouver's Robson Street in 1997, various thoughts quickly ran through my head: do I reply with the answer that I know he wants to hear? Or do I explain that I'm Canadian only to be met with the standard reply of "Where are you really from?" or "But where are you from *originally?*" I walked away frustrated, glad I didn't give him the answer he expected, but upset that I didn't take the opportunity to challenge his preconceptions further by stating that not all brown people are immigrants, or saying "why do you ask?" taking the spotlight off me and hopefully inciting him to question the motivation behind his intrusive inquiry. Kamala Visweswaran states,

> Certainly the question "Where are you from?" is never an innocent one. Yet not all subjects have equal difficulty in replying. To pose a question of origin to a particular subject is to subtly pose a question of return, to challenge not only temporally, but geographically, one's place in the present. For someone who is neither fully Indian nor wholly American, it is a question that provokes a sudden failure of confidence, the fear of never replying adequately. (115)

Even in "multicultural" Canada, skin colour and ethnicity continue to act as markers of one's place of origin, markers which are used to ascertain traits and behaviours which are associated with certain "races." It is a question that left me with an acute sense of being out of place and being "other"—if I seemed out of place to the man who asked the question, I must appear so to the people around me. Underlying such (frequently asked) questions are racist assumptions about what a "real" Canadian looks like. In that brief encounter, the stranger automatically linked me to a far away land that I have never seen, a place where I would surely be considered an outsider, and certainly not be considered Indian. His question served as a reminder of my "visible minority" status—that I was not quite Canadian and could never be so.

The "other" does not necessarily have to be "other" in terms of exhibiting strange or "exotic" language and behaviour. Time and time again, the dominant culture reduces identity down to imaginary racial categories. The fact that multigenerational South Asian Canadians are treated as other, as not-quite Canadians, attests to this. At what point do multigenerational South Asian Canadians cease being seen as from somewhere else? As Himani Bannerji comments, "[t]he second generation grows up on cultural languages which are not foreign to them, though they are still designated as foreigners" (1993: 186). South Asian Canadian women are in a predicament of perpetual foreigness—constantly being asked where they are from and having stereotypical characteristics assigned to them despite their "Canadianness." Though they are in their country of origin, they are not *of* it.

Presentation of self is one way in which we demonstrate our personal identities and recognize those of others. This holds true if we encountered someone who had inscribed her body with tattoos, multiple body-piercings, and blue hair. However, it is quite a different situation when a South Asian Canadian woman tries to ground her personal identity in this way; regardless of whether her hair is covered by a *hijab* or is short and chic, regardless of whether she is wearing a *salwaar-kameez* or jeans, she is still subject to an otherization based on an imaginary "South Asian other" constructed through racist ideology. Her own body inscriptions are ignored, as the only signifier needed for recognition from the dominant culture seems to be phenotypical. These phenotypical characteristics stand, as they have in the past, though perhaps to a lesser extent, as signifiers of difference and inferiority.

In Farzana Doctor's poem "Banu," the narrator traces her changing responses and attitudes towards racism at different stages throughout her life. During childhood and as a young adult, assimilation is her response. Eventually she rejects assimilation in favour of resistance. In "Banu," the racist interpellation "Paki go home" (218) is directed at the little girl in the poem. According to the *Oxford English Dictionary*, "Paki" is an abbreviation for Pakistani, and is also described as a slang word. In "Banu," however, the common use of the term does not reflect its literal or etymological meaning. The term has become imbued with racist emotions and signifies detest, hatred, and intolerance towards all South Asians, regardless of their geographical place of origin.

A generically used term in places such as Canada, Great Britain, and the United States, "Paki" is a common racist insult directed toward those who appear to be of South Asian ancestry (Bannerji, 1993; Sheth and Handa). Unlike racist insults against South Asians that are based on food or dress such as "curry-eater" or "rag-head," the insult "Paki" is based simply on one's "foreign/other" appearance. The insult "Paki" does not simply express disgust at aspects of South Asian cultures as the previously mentioned insults do. Rather, it expresses disgust or hatred based directly toward one's "race" or ethnic background. For a multigenerational South Asian Canadian to be told "Paki go home" is particularly disturbing because she is told that Canada is not her home, but a far away land which she may have never set foot on. Regardless of being Canadian by citizenship and birth, she remains, under racist eyes, simply a "Paki." When the South Asian *Canadian* girl in the poem is told to "go home," she is not only told that she does not belong in Canadian society, but is also told that she should leave. The man who uttered the slur obviously felt he was a "real" Canadian with the right to tell the "foreigner" what to do. The popularity of this term in racist discourse not only reflects an ignorance about South Asian cultures and their diversity, but also reinforces the opinion that Canada does not have room for non-white "others."

Others in Their Own Land

In looking at Canadian multiculturalism and its promotion of diversity and tolerance, one would not find any overt pressures promoting assimilation. If anything, it seems that assimilation is not an issue—they tell us that we can all co-exist harmoniously within our respective tile of the mosaic. Yet, unstated, implied, and subtle pressures to assimilate remain a powerful force. As Michel Foucault stated, "[t]here is no need for arms, physical violence, material constraints, just a gaze" (155). While official

Canadian multiculturalism may promote the acceptance of diversity, the lived experience of multiculturalism is quite a different thing. For many South Asian Canadian women the strong desire to "fit in," as a result of being discriminated against, culminates in an internalization of the gendered racism they receive. Frantz Fanon argues that the consequence of racism from the dominant group to the minority group is guilt and inferiority. The inferiorized group attempts to escape these feelings by "proclaiming his [sic] total and unconditional adoption of the new cultural models, and on the other, by pronouncing an irreversible condemnation of his own cultural style" (38–9).

This is a process multigenerational South Asian Canadian women undergo in their attempts to reject South Asian culture and assimilate. Assimilation has often been used as a coping mechanism not only by South Asian Canadians, but by all visible minorities where the majority of the dominant culture is white. Obvious forms of assimilation include speaking English and wearing Western-style clothing. A less obvious form is the desire to change one's physical appearance (Bannerji, 1990; Sheth and Handa; James; Karumanchery-Luik). Based on personal experiences and literature by multigenerational South Asian Canadian women, the desire to be white or possess typically Western features is, unfortunately, quite common. The impact of this is compounded for multigenerational South Asian Canadian women who have been socialized into the Western beauty ideal.

Internalized racism is a theme common to much of the literature by multigenerational South Asian Canadian women. One manifestation of this is illustrated by the proliferation of ads for "Fair and Lovely" skin cream and skin bleaches aimed at South Asian women, and the desire expressed in matrimonial ads for light-skinned wives. Sheth comments that light skin is so desirable in India that "the cosmetics industry continually pitch skin-lightening products to women" (Sheth and Handa 86). Various cosmetic products promising to do this are also found in Vancouver and Surrey's South Asian shops.

The desire for whiteness is demonstrated in second generation South Asian Canadian activist and theatre artist Sheila James' personal narrative about how she unnaturally became a blond because "All the sex objects on TV, film and magazines were blond-haired and blue eyed. I figured I could adjust the colour in my head to fit the role" (137). Underlying the desire for "whiteness" is a racist ideology which interprets the world associated with the dark skin of Indian and African people with danger, savagery, primitiveness, intellectual inferiority, and the inability to progress beyond a childlike mentality. Meanwhile whiteness is equated with purity, virginity, beauty, and civility (Ashcroft et al.; Arora).

Assimilation pressures and internalized racism experienced by the second generation are captured quite forcefully in Himani Bannerji's short story "The Other Family" (1990: 140–145) in which the second-generation South Asian protagonist of the story draws what is supposed to be a picture of her family for a school project. The picture, however, bears very little resemblance to her own family. She draws her family as white with blond hair and blue eyes, and herself as having a button nose and freckles. The drawing can be interpreted as an illustration of the little girl's desire to belong and to be like the other children—to fit in at the cost of the negation of her own body, of her own physical appearance. An essay by a multigenerational South Asian Canadian woman, Nisha Karumanchery-Luik, reflects a similar theme:

> When I was younger, I hated my brown skin. I had wished that I was not so dark, that my skin would somehow magically lighten. When I was younger, I was ashamed and embarrassed of my Indian heritage and the "foreigness" that my skin betrayed. I developed creative strategies of denial and pretense to cope with and survive in a racist environment. (54)

Her choice of phrase that her skin "betrayed" her "foreigness" and Indian heritage is a significant one. It speaks to the circumstance that many multigenerational South Asian Canadian women and other multigenerational visible minorities are in—though they may act "Canadian" in the mainstream-white-Anglo-Saxon-Protestant sense of the word (language, clothes, behaviour), their skin colour and phenotypical characteristics, signifying them as "other," never fail to give them away. Being different from the mainstream is, of course, not a problem in and of itself. It becomes one as the resulting of the othering, gendercd racism, and exclusion that multigenerational South Asian Canadian women are subject to. In the following excerpt of a poem by Reshmi J. Bissessar, she reveals the shame she felt over being Guyanese:

> I was there last in '86
> At age fourteen
> Eleven years ago
> When I would say
> Thank you
> If someone told me that I didn't look
> *Guyanese.*
> My, how loyalties change. (22)

Often, multigenerational South Asian Canadian women try to hide and mask what it is that singles them out for racist taunts and prying gazes. For example, in another poem, the parent of a young South Asian Canadian woman asks the daughter "why do you cringe when seen by white folks in your sari? / why are you embarrassed when speaking Gujurati in public?" (Shah 119). Thus the pressures to assimilate and "belong" result in denying aspects of South Asian culture—even to the point of internalizing the dominant ideology and seeing themselves as inferior. Thinking that their food "stinks," that their physical characteristics are less beautiful and undesirable according to Western standards, embarrassment over being seen in Indian clothing, or by the accents of their parents, are all aspects of their inferiorization.

At the Borders of National Belonging

Multigenerational South Asian Canadian women's efforts at masking their ethnicity are, of course, in vain. The closest they come is to be mistaken for a less marginalized ethnic group or to be bestowed with the status of "honorary white," through comments to the effect of "you're different. . . . you're not like the *rest* of them." I was given this status when deciding where to go for dinner with a group of people. One white woman asked me if I ate meat, implying that I must have "strange" eating habits as a South Asian. Before I could answer, another white woman exclaimed, "Oh of course she does, she's *just like us!*" But despite the "acceptance" of being just like them, I was still othered by the initial curiosity of "do you eat meat?" If I was "just like them" why was I the only one to whom that question was posed? Thus, even the "honorary white" status given to some South Asians fails to appease a sense of not belonging. Suparana Bhaskaran outlines the limiting typology of the "assimilated South Asian" and the "authentic South Asian" which can be applied to the phenomena of the "honorary white" discussed above:

> The logic of purity allows South Asians to be conceptually defined in only two ways: as authentic South Asians or assimilated South Asians. The "authentic South Asian" may range from being conservative, lazy and poor to being spiritual, brilliant, non-materialistic and religious. By this definition, the assimilated South Asian . . . pursues the promise of the "postcultural" full citizenship of Anglo life. (198)

Though some multigenerational South Asian Canadian women may, by the above typology, be considered "assimilated South Asians" and therefore subject to the discrimination faced by the "authentic South Asian," we see in the literature by South Asian Canadian women that seeking this identification and inclusion into "Anglo-life" is, for the most part, unattainable and continues to be fraught with othering and a sense of exclusion.

Being singled out as "other" and the consequent pressures to assimilate has a particularly strong effect on multigenerational South Asian Canadian women. They have been socialized in Canadian society from birth and have thus, unlike their parents, lived their entire lives as "ethnic/other," and different from the dominant culture. For the second generation, the assimilation process begins much earlier and in the more formative years. Therefore, racism and being othered by the dominant culture has a deeper, more detrimental impact on multigenerational South Asian Canadians than it does on their parents who did not grow up in Canada. Though the parents of second-generation South Asian Canadians may be more "othered" due to their accents, the fact that they wear Indian clothing, and from having been socialized in a non-Western culture, they have come to Canada with some pre-established sense of identity (though it changes through their experiences in their new country), which is not the case for their children.

It is likely that many Canadians would be quite content if South Asian Canadians and other "visible minorities" simply integrated into Anglo-Canadian society instead of making a fuss about racist immigration policies or their right to wear *hijabs*. Of course, assimilation can no longer be overtly legislated, although it continues to be suggested in more subtle ways, as reflected in the literature by South Asian women. Because of "subtle" pressures to assimilate, many South Asian Canadian women have interiorized the inspecting gaze of the dominant culture to the point that they are exercising surveillance over themselves. Foucault argues that physical violence and constraints are no longer needed to control a population once they have interiorized the inspecting gaze—"a gaze which each individual under its weight will end by interiorizing to the point that he is his own overseer, each individual thus exercising this surveillance over, and against himself" (155).

The inspecting gaze in this context, are the judgmental eyes of the dominant culture—state officials, journalists, neighbours, teachers, and peers. The pressure to assimilate is no longer over, it is embedded in everyday language and stereotypes used to describe and "other" South Asian Canadian women, in popular culture and media depictions, and in structures such as institutional racism. The content of the literature by multigenerational South Asians discussed earlier reveals that they have interiorized the inspecting gaze of the dominant culture, though it is a gaze which many of them have come to reject. Over and over again, these writers express the desire they have or once had to belong, to be accepted, and to "fit" into the dominant culture.

Conclusion

Though I have concentrated on how multigenerational South Asian Canadians have been "raced" and gendered through the dominant ideology, it is important to note that those constructed as other are not merely the passive recipients of power. In many cases, they are remapping themselves by challenging dominant representations of "their kind" through subversive forms of literary production. I would argue that in the tension between imposed identities and those asserted by multigenerational South Asian Canadian women, spaces of resistance have formed in the anthologies and other venues in which they publish, and in the act of writing itself. These venues provide a forum for South Asian Canadian women to creatively express their insights, anger, pain, and reflections. It is a textual space created by and for multigenerational South Asian Canadian women in which their marginalization and repression is both articulated and resisted.

Multigenerational South Asian Canadian women's literature is considered a new, diasporic form of cultural production. It is new in that these women are writing as both insiders and outsiders to Canadian society. Their literature demonstrates an ongoing negotiation of two intertwined cultural contexts and influences. The positionality of these women allows for a unique vantage point from which to comment on Canadian racism, sexism, and other repressions. Their writing poses an important challenge to the idea that culture and identity arc fixed within certain national borders.

Note

1. The *Daily Colonist* wrote: "To prepare ourselves for the irrepressible conflict, Canada must remain a White Man's country. On this western frontier of the Empire will be the forefront to the coming struggle. . . . Therefore we ought to maintain this country for the Anglo-Saxon and those races which are able to assimilate themselves to them. If this is done, we believe that history will repeat itself and the supremacy of our race will continue" (Henry et al. 71).

References

Agnew, V. 1996. *Resisting Discrimination: Women from Asia, Africa, and the Caribbean and the Women's Movement in Canada*. Toronto: University of Toronto Press.

Arora, P. 1995. "Imperilling the Prestige of the White Woman: Colonial Anxiety and Film Censorship in India," *Visual Anthropology Review* 11(2): 36–49.

Ashcroft, B., G. Griffiths, and H. Tiffin. 1998. *Key Concepts in Post-Colonial Studies*. London: Routledge.

Bannerji, H. 1990 "The Other Family," in L. Hutcheon and M. Richmond, eds., *Other Solitudes: Canadian Multicultural Fictions*. Toronto: Oxford University Press.

Bannerji, H. 1993. "Popular Images of South Asian Women," in H. Bannerji, ed., *Returning the Gaze*. Toronto: Sister Vision Press.

Bhaskaran, S. 1993. "Physical Subjectivity and the Risk of Essentialism," in Women of South Asian Descent Collective, eds., *Our Feet Walk the Sky: Women of the South Asian Diaspora*. San Fransisco: Aunt Lute Books.

Bisessar, R.J. 1997. "Struggle," in S.K. Chatree, ed., *Shaktee Kee Awaaz: Voices of Strength*. Toronto: Shakti Kee Chatri.

Brah, A. 1996. *Cartographies of Diaspora: Contesting Identities*. London: Routledge.

Buchnigani, N., and D. Indra. 1985. *Continuous Journey: A Social History of South Asians in Canada*. Toronto: McLelland and Stewart.

"Close Watch on City Sikhs." *Vancouver Sun*, 20 October 1985a.

Doctor, F. 1995. "Banu," in F. Rafiq, ed., *Aurat Durbar*. Toronto: Second Story Press.

Dua, E. 1999. "Beyond Diversity: Exploring the Ways In Which the Discourse of Race Has Shaped the Institution of the Nuclear Family," in E. Dua and A. Robertson, eds., *Scratching the Surface: Canadian Anti-Racist Feminist Thought*. Toronto: Women's Press.

Fanon, F. 1967. *Toward the African Revolution*. New York: Grove Press.

Foucault, M. 1980. *Power/Knowledge*. New York: Pantheon.

Henry, F., C. Tator, W. Mattis, and T. Rees. 1995. *The Colour of Democracy*. Toronto: Harcourt, Brace and Co.

James, S. 1995. "From Promiscuity to Celibacy," in F. Rafiq, ed., *Aurat Durbar*. Toronto: Second Story Press.

Jiwani, Y. 1992. "The Exotic, Erotic, and the Dangerous: South Asian Women in Popular Film," *Canadian Woman Studies* 13(1): 42–46.

Jiwani, Y. 1998. "On the Outskirts of Empire: Race and Gender in Canadian TV News," in V. Strong-Boag et al., eds., *Painting the Maple: Essays on Race, Gender and the Construction of Canada*. Vancouver: University of British Columbia Press.

Karumanchery-Luik, N. 1997. "The Politics of Brown Skin," in S.K. Chatree, ed., *Shaktee Kee Awaaz: Voices of Strength*. Toronto: Shakti Kee Chatri.

Mitchell, A. 1998. "Face of Big Cities Changing," *Globe and Mail*, 18 February: A1, A3.

Said, E.W. 1994. *Orientalism*. New York: Vintage.

Shah, S. 1997. "The Interrogation," in S.K. Chatree, ed., *Shaktee Kee Awaaz: Voices of Strength*. Toronto: Shakti Kee Chatri.

Sheth, A., and A. Handa. 1993. "A Jewel in the Frown: Striking Accord Between Indian Feminists," in H. Bannerji, ed., *Returning the Gaze*. Toronto: Sister Vision Press.

"Sikh Militancy Grows," *Vancouver Sun*, 7 November 1985b.

Smits, D. 1987. "Abominable Mixture," *The Virginia Magazine of History and Biography* 95(2): 227–61.

Stoler, A.L. 1995. *Race and the Education of Desire: Foucault's History of Sexuality and the Colonial Order of Things*. Durham: Duke University Press.

Visweswaran, K. 1994. *Fictions of Feminist Ethnography*. Minneapolis: University of Minnesota Press.

Chapter 12

Overview

This article, taken from a much larger project by Gillian Creese, examines how young African immigrants in Vancouver shape their personal sense of identity from the cultural resources available to them. As racialized men and women, they can never partake of "middle-class whiteness"; as immigrants, their experiences are not the same as those of the African-Americans whose music and style is so prominent in popular culture; and as Africans, they must negotiate their connection to a homeland that is both spatially and socially distant. As Creese demonstrates, both men and women experience downward social mobility when they immigrate to Canada, and both face negative reactions from non-African Canadians based on accent and appearance.

However, says Creese, gender mediates the experience of being a diasporic African in Vancouver. Young men are more likely to experience negative attention in the form of surveillance and policing by legal authorities and, perhaps in consequence, are more likely to adopt the defiant, oppositional stance found in much African-American music and style. At the same time, their families and particularly their fathers expect these young men to show respect for elders, achieve well, and stay out of trouble.

Creese finds that young women are less torn between street culture and the expectations of their families and communities. Young women and girls typically have fewer oppressive encounters with the police and other authorities than their male counterparts, so adopting a stance of defiance and opposition is less appealing. Where diasporic girls and women do oppose authority, says Creese, is more often by confronting teachers and educators who underrate their potential to achieve. Diasporic girls' identity-work and practices are closer to those valued by their parents, so girls are more easily assimilated into the institutions and communities of the African diaspora.

However, as Creese notes, age and passage through the life course shape the ways that gender and race are experienced. As the young people of the African generation grow older, how will they come to see themselves?

Gendered Diasporas across Generations: The New African Diaspora in Vancouver

Gillian Creese

Introduction

. . . Vancouver is a diverse metropolis where 40 per cent of the population are immigrants and an equal number identify as people of colour, and yet migrants from diverse nations within sub-Saharan Africa constitute only about 1 per cent of the population. This new African diaspora navigates the social geography of the city and practices of (un)belonging in the context of local nation-building discourses and the historic African-American diaspora across the border.

Although the latter does not overlap in spatial terms, it does culturally and in the social imaginary. A central element of the migration process from Africa to Canada involves "becoming Black."[1] This process of racialization is mediated through dominant representations of the historic African-American diaspora, and contemporary forms of African-American cultural production, particularly among young Black men, that celebrates a culture of resistance emerging from the dual practices of ghettoizing and imprisoning significant numbers of African Americans.[2] Such practices and cultural productions are highly gendered, and speak differently to African immigrants and to their children raised in Canada, shaping gendered and generational practices within Vancouver's new African diaspora.

Identity, Racialization, and Migration

Whether they came as independent immigrants or as refugees, adult migrants from sub-Saharan Africa experience considerable downward economic and social mobility in Canada. In everyday interactions, in workplaces, schools, shops, and on street corners, African migrants are differentiated from other Canadians. Two key practices demonstrate these processes of othering: pervasive queries about origins and responses to African English accents. The frequent refrain "where are you from" greets those from Africa on an almost daily basis. This simple question reinforces, time and again, that Black bodies must be from somewhere else because they cannot be from here. Compulsory narratives of difference and foreign origins undermine belonging, and so too do local reactions to African English accents. Even for fluent English speakers from Commonwealth African countries, African accents are typically met with a mixture of incomprehension and public reproach. As Bizima,[3] a landed immigrant who came from Zambia, observed: "since we can't talk like them, it's really hard to convince them that you can talk sense, when they find out what accent you have."[4] As Pierre Bourdieu has observed, accents are indexes of authority that authorize or impede the right to speak and be heard.[5] Local accents are routinely privileged in Canada such that African English accents possess little authority or ability to be heard.

African migrants to Canada enter a social imaginary where they are "already constructed, imagined and positioned" through centuries of White privilege and discourses about Blackness.[6] Pejorative discourses about Black masculinity, in particular, circulate widely through the US domination of local media and popular culture.[7] Not surprisingly, racialization, marginalization, and downward mobility produce very ambivalent subjectivities of Canadianness even for those who have long resided there and have Canadian citizenship. As Bangila, a Canadian citizen originally from the Democratic Republic of Congo, commented, travelling on a Canadian passport is an advantage, but at home in Canada he is treated as second class:

> Travelling with a Canadian passport. That is the only time you feel good about being a Canadian. But once you are in Canada, there is nothing good about being a Canadian. I am truly a Black person.[8]

Indeed, learning to be Black in the context of White privilege is central to the formation of the new African diaspora in Vancouver. Facing similar challenges, with educational credentials unrecognized, underemployment, disparaging of African English accents and foreign Black bodies, various claims making practices are enacted to construct an African diaspora across differences of national origins, ethnicity, language, and religion. Discourses of common African values—grounded in extended families, hierarchical gender relations, and deference to elders and fathers—are drawn on to forge links across differences in the African continent.[9] For parents, efforts to instil African cultural values in their youngsters means actively rejecting liberal individualism that dominates public discourse in Canada, and resisting the glorification of street life and opposition to authority so prevalent in African-American youth culture.

Gendered Practices and the Diaspora

Migration unsettles gender relations and identities so it should not be surprising that gender shapes diasporic claims making practices.[10] To some degree gender differences resemble divisions between public and private realms, distinguishing formal community development from family and neighbourly networks of mutual aid. Equally important, however, gendered diasporic practices involve divergent orientations toward Africa and the homeland versus Canada and homemaking.

Much of women's community organizing is linked to homemaking within Canada by providing support to negotiate everyday realities of settlement. These supports range from helping new mothers or bereaved families with food and financial support, to providing information and strategies that help newer migrants negotiate unfamiliar institutions. Women form the backbone of a growing number of African settlement workers employed in non-profit immigrant agencies that provide integration supports through government funded programs. These are crucial forms of community building that give material substance to the idea of a local African community, but take second place to the arena of formal political organizations dominated by men.

Many formal organizations have been created that focus on specific African nations with mandates of "upholding and preserving their culture."[11] These organizations, run by men, are oriented more toward developments in the homeland than to settlement issues in Canada. In addition, there are half a dozen local non-profit organizations geared directly toward supporting development initiatives in different African countries.[12] These bodies are also led mainly by men and are closely connected to maintaining ties and status within homeland communities.

Men face a crisis in masculinity linked to downward class mobility and loss of social status in Canada, compounded by lessened authority over wives and children. Remaining involved in politics and development work in Africa, and sending remittances home to relatives, maintains men's social standing within their homelands while positioning them as leaders within the local African community. Hence focusing on ties with the homeland can also reaffirm positive masculine identities in Canada. Women also face downward class mobility, combined with less access to family-based or affordable childcare and domestic support, and negotiate unfamiliar dangers facing their children. These pressures heighten women's focus on homemaking in Canada as they simultaneously struggle to renegotiate more equitable domestic relationships by drawing on local discourses of women's rights. Women are more likely to define new ways of mothering without fearing that this might undermine their identities as good mothers. For men, in contrast, identities as good fathers are firmly tied to exercising authority, leading to more intense conflicts between fathers and offspring, particularly with sons who bear the brunt of public surveillance that accompanies being young, Black, and male in North America.

Generational Shifts: Children of Immigrants Negotiating the African Diaspora

Members of the African community who grew up in Vancouver, develop hybrid identities and diasporic practices that are quite distinct from their parents.[13] The divergent emphasis on the homeland and homemaking come together in local spaces, and hyphenated, though often no less ambivalent, identities as African-Canadian are more common. The next generation negotiates their place in the local African diaspora from three distinct locations: 1) through the values, beliefs, and practices expressed within their families and the local African community; 2) through immersion in colloquial Canadian culture and institutions; and 3) through engagement with the historic African-American diaspora.

Parenting in the context of migration is always unsettling since familiar parenting strategies often do not work well in a new environment. Expectations around authority, deference, and respect for elders, and fathers in particular, are presented as core African values that collide with the more individualistic orientation of Canadian society. Hence it is hard for youth to live up to parents' expectations of what it is to be African, leading many parents to lament that their own children's behaviour suggests they are "lost," and to question the Africanness of the next generation.[14] Jane, a Canadian-born woman in her mid-twenties, for example, notes that her father calls her "whitewashed."[15] Distance between immigrant parents and the next generation is further exacerbated, for many, by lack of fluency in their parent's ancestral languages, impeding deeper forms of cultural understanding about the homeland.

The children of African immigrants not only question their own Africanness, they also question their Canadianness. For those born or raised in Canada, the quest to be recognized as Canadian is a critical element of belonging that simultaneously distances them from the immigrant diaspora. At the same time, being Black in Vancouver renders tenuous any straightforward claim to Canadian identity and re-establishes the centrality of their African ancestry. Canadianness, like Africanness, is both asserted and doubted in the same breath. Danielle, a university student who was born in metro Vancouver commented: "I sometimes felt a little like I wasn't part of either world, the Canadian or African." Language separated her from the local African world, while being "the only Black child at school, in my church" made her stand out when she "wanted so badly to be like everyone else."[16]

Local institutions have a formative influence on children in ways that are embraced by the next generation and often resisted by immigrant parents. The values of western liberal individualism are explicitly inculcated through schools and enforced through other social institutions. Emphasis on individualism clashes with family-centred identities, and discourses of children's rights conflict with expectations of stronger parental authority and discipline. As a result of such tensions, both parents and offspring perceive that "the school criticizes everything that [African] parents do."[17] Equally important, schools are a central site of interface with North American youth culture, and negotiating relations with peers may be even more critical to school experiences than anything in the formal curriculum. North American youth culture is saturated with forms of popular culture that normalize early (hetero) sexuality, glorify risk-taking activities, particularly drug and alcohol consumption, encourage conspicuous consumption and materialism, and valorise adolescent autonomy, all of which are antithetical to the idealized visions of adolescent experience in their homelands that migrants bring with them.

For the children of migrants from Sub-Saharan Africa, like other adolescents, learning to fit in and be accepted by their peers is a central preoccupation.[18] Mediating relations with peers is both racialized and gendered, and central to connections with the new Vancouver-based and historical African-American diasporas. For adolescent boys and young men, negotiating masculinity means earning respect from other boys and learning to stand up for themselves under imminent threat of aggression from other young men ever ready to put them in their place.[19] For young Black men, adolescent masculinity is negotiated in a space in which images of Black masculinity are saturated with pejorative associations of violence and criminality embedded in North American popular culture, historical legacies, and contemporary marginalization.[20] Youthful confrontations are played out on a field of White privilege in which young men in the African diaspora describe learning to walk a fine line between defending themselves and "earning respect," and simultaneously learning to be "humble," "mellow," and "cautious" so as not to arouse the interest of authorities. Harassment by the police, border guards, or others in authority, challenges about the right to occupy public spaces, and being perceived as the trouble-makers when youthful confrontations do occur, are all routine parts of learning to live through the devalued status of young Black men in Canada.[21]

Young women in the local African diaspora face different pressure to embody particular forms of heterosexual femininity. Images of Black femininity in North America coalesce around hyper-sexuality and masculinized forms of domination and strength.[22] Young African-Canadian women find it nearly impossible to measure up to norms rooted in White middle-class femininity. Though threats of violence are less often a means of policing relations among women and girls, exclusion, gossip, and other psychological forms of harassment can be equally problematic.[23]

Like their male counterparts, African-Canadian adolescent girls struggle to fit in and stand up for themselves. For girls, however, the double-edge of Black femininity provides few routes for earning respect since sexual double standards mark hyper-sexuality as a means of denigrating young women. Instead, earning respect is mediated through greater attention to academic performance, leading girls to stand up more to their teachers when they are underestimated, and enlisting the support of allies, whether other teachers or parents, to pursue grievances.[24]

Hence young African-Canadians of both genders must negotiate oppressive racialized scripts linked to the historical African-American diaspora as they try to fit in and stand up for themselves, scripts that run counter to gendered norms in the local African diaspora and conventional (White middle class) Canadian culture. Yet they navigate these tensions differently. In turning to academic achievement and building support networks, young women lean closer to their parents and further away from the images of Black femininity in American popular culture. Young men, on the other hand, even those who value academic achievement, negotiate masculinity in more solitary ways. Routine racialized encounters with police and other authorities, which young African-Canadian women do not experience in the same way, reinforces similarities between young Black men's lives in Vancouver and in the United States.

Hence the oppositional stance of African-American youth culture, fostered out of intense marginalization of young Black men in the United States, has a strong resonance for many of the sons of African immigrants in Vancouver. They are more likely to conceive of themselves as part of a larger Black diaspora, and hence further removed from their father's notions of proper African masculinity. In contrast, the intense misogyny of so much African-American youth culture mutes its appeal to their sisters. Jane sees these gendered differences as central to the continuing estrangement between her brothers and her father. Her father, she says, "hates African-American culture [and is] always trying to differentiate himself" as an African.[25] Her brothers, in contrast, embrace a streetwise Black masculinity as a way of negotiating a local space of respect. She acknowledges that her brothers face more coercive forms of racism than she encounters because they are young, Black, and male, and this shapes their affinity with African-American identities.

Moreover, young women tend to identify more with the local African community as they begin to contemplate raising their own children in Canada. Parenting practices that instil respect for authority and the importance of extended family networks—the very things most rebelled against as adolescents—are being reclaimed by young women as culturally appropriate ways to parent the third generation of African-Canadian youngsters. Young women are drawing together home making and homeland with explicit reference to the need to connect their own future children to the local African community and to larger extended families in Africa. For young men who embrace the scripts of oppositional masculinity, it remains to be seen whether similar shifts occur as they age and may become fathers, or whether the gendered experiences of being young, Black, and male in Canada continue to mitigate rebuilding stronger connections and identities with the local African community in ways that their sisters are already envisioning.

Notes

1. Awad El Karim Ibrahim. 1999. "Becoming Black: Rap and Hip-Hop, Race, Gender, Identity, and the Politics of ESL Learning," *TESOL Quarterly* 33: 349–369.
2. Patricia Hill Collins. 2005. *Black Sexual Politics: African Americans, Gender, and the New Racism*. New York: Routledge.
3. Pseudonyms are used to refer to all interviewees.
4. Gillian Creese, *The New African Diaspora in Vancouver: Migration. Exclusion and Belonging* (Toronto: University of Toronto Press, 2011).
5. Pierre Bourdieu. 1977. "The Economics of Linguistic Exchanges," *Social Science Information* 16: 645–68.
6. Ibrahim, "Becoming Black", 353.
7. For example see Gamal Abdel-Shehid, 2005, *Who da Man? Black Masculinities and Sporting Culture* (Toronto: Canadian Scholars Press); Collins, *Black Sexual Politics*; and Ibrahim, "Becoming Black."
8. Creese, *The New African Diaspora in Vancouver*, 203.
9. John Arthur. 2000. *Invisible Sojourners: African Immigrant Diaspora in the United States*. Westport: Praeger; and Atsuko Matsuoka and John Sorenson, 2001, *Ghosts and Shadows: Construction of Identity and Community in an African Diaspora*. Toronto: University of Toronto Press.
10. Katherine Donato, et al. 2006. "A Glass Half Full? Gender in Migration Studies," *International Migration Review*, 40: 3–26; Patricia Pessar. 2003. "Engendering Migration Studies: The Case of New Immigrants in the United States" in P. Hondagneu-Sotelo, ed., *Gender and US Immigration: Contemporary Trends*, Berkeley: University of California Press: 20–42.
11. Mambo Masinda and Edith Ngene Kambere. 2008. *Needs Assessment and Services Delivery Plan for African Immigrants and Refugees in Vancouver Metropolitan Area, British Columbia*. Vancouver: United Way of the Lower Mainland and Umoja Operation Compassion Society, 43.
12. Creese, *The New African Diaspora in Vancouver*, 218.
13. For the purposes of this paper the term second generation will be used to refer to those born in Africa and raised largely in Canada (the 1.5 generation) and the Canadian born (2nd generation proper). I have not yet conducted enough interviews with the 1.5 and 2nd generation to delineate differences that may exist among these groups, but that will form part of an ongoing analysis.
14. Creese, *The New African Diaspora in Vancouver*; and Gillian Creese, Edith Ngene Kambere, and Mambo Masinda, 2011, "'You Have to Stand Up For Yourself': African Immigrant and Refugee Teens Negotiate Settlement in Vancouver," *Metropolis British Columbia Working Paper Series*, No 11–16.
15. Where only a pseudonym of an interviewee appears without a citation, these are interviews that are part of my ongoing and unpublished research project on the second generation.
16. Unpublished interview data on the second generation.
17. Gillian Creese, Edith Ngene Kambere, and Mambo Masinda. in press. "Voices of African Immigrant and Refugee Youth: Negotiating Migration and Schooling in Canada," in Immaculee Harushimana et al., eds., *African-born Educators and Students in Transnational America: Reprocessing Race, Language, and Ability*. New York: Peter Lang.
18. Creese, Kambere, and Masinda, "Voices of African Immigrant and Refugee Youth"; and Creese, Kambere, and Masinda, "You Have to Stand Up For Yourself."
19. R.W. Connell. 1995. *Masculinities*. Berkeley: University of California Press.
20. Collins, *Black Sexual Politics*.
21. Creese, Kambere, and Masinda, "Voices of African Immigrant and Refugee Youth."
22. Collins, *Black Sexual Politics*.
23. Dawn Currie, Deirdre Kelly, and Shuana Pomerantz. 2009. *"Girl Power": Girls Reinventing Girlhood*. New York: Peter Lang.
24. Creese, Kambere and Masinda, "Voices of African Immigrant and Refugee Youth."
25. Unpublished interview data on the second generation.

References

Abdel-Shehid, G. 2005. *Who da Man? Black Masculinities and Sporting Cultures*. Toronto: Canadian Scholars Press.

Arthur, J. 2000. *Invisible Sojourners: African Immigrant Diaspora in the United States*. Westport: Praeger.

Bourdieu, P. 1977. "The Economics of Linguistic Exchanges," *Social Science Information* 16: 645–68.

Brubaker, R. 2005. "The 'Diaspora' Diaspora," *Ethnic and Racial Studies* 28: 1–19.

Clifford, J. 1994. "Diasporas," *Cultural Anthropology* 9: 302–38.

Collins, P.H. 2005. *Black Sexual Politics: African Americans, Gender, and the New Racism*. New York: Routledge.

Connell, R.W. 1995. *Masculinities*. Berkeley: University of California Press.

Creese, G. 2011. *The New African Diaspora in Vancouver: Migration, Exclusion and Belonging*. Toronto: University of Toronto Press.

Creese, G., E.N. Kambere, and M. Masinda. 2011. "'You Have to Stand Up For Yourself' African Immigrant and Refugee Teens Negotiate Settlement in Vancouver," *Metropolis British Columbia Working Paper Series*, No. 11–16.

———, in press. "Voices of African immigrant and Refugee Youth: Negotiating Migration and Schooling in Canada," in I. Harushimana, C. Ikpeze, and S. Mthethwa-Sommers, eds., *African–born Educators and Students in Transnational America: Reprocessing Race, Language, and Ability*. New York: Peter Lang.

Currie, D., D. Kelly, and S. Pomerantz. 2009. *"Girl Power": Girls Reinventing Girlhood*. New York: Peter Lang.

Donato, K., D. Gabaccia, J. Holdaway, M. Manalansan, and P. Pessar. 2006. "A Glass Half Full? Gender in Migration Studies," *International Migration Review* 40: 3–26.

Fumanti, M., and P. Werbner. 2010. "The Moral Economy of the African Diaspora: Citizenship, Networking and Permeable Ethnicity," *African Diaspora* 3: 3–12.

Gregoire, N. 2010. "Identity Politics, Social Movement and the State: 'Pan-African' Associations and the Making of an 'African Community' in Belgium," *African Diaspora* 3: 160–82.

Hall, S. 1990. "Cultural Identity and Diaspora," in J. Rutherford, ed., *Identity: Community, Culture, Difference*, pp. 222–37. London: Lawrence and Wishart.

Ibrahim, A.E.K. 1999. "Becoming Black: Rap and Hip-Hop, Race, Gender, Identity, and the Politics of ESL Learning," *TESOL Quarterly* 33: 349–69.

Masinda, M., and E.N. Kambere. 2008. *Needs Assessment and Services Delivery Plan forAfrican Immigrants and Refugees in Vancouver Metropolitan Area, British Columbia*. Vancouver: United Way of the Lower Mainland and Umoja Operation Compassion Society.

Matsuoka, A., and J. Sorenson. 2001. *Ghosts and Shadows: Construction of Identity and Community in an African Diaspora*. Toronto: University of Toronto Press.

Morawska, E. 2011. "'Diaspora' Diasporas" Representations of their Homelands: Exploring the Polymorphs," *Ethnic and Racial Studies* 34: 1029–48.

Pessar, P. 2003. "Engendering Migration Studies: The Case of New Immigrants in the United States" in P. Hondagneu-Sotelo, ed., *Gender and US Immigration: Contemporary Trends*, pp. 20–42. University of California Press.

Werbner, P. 2010. "Many Gateways to the Gateway City: Elites, Class and Policy Networking in the London African Diaspora," *African Diaspora* 3: 132–59.

Zeleza, P.T. 2005. "Rewriting the African Diaspora: Beyond the Black Atlantic," *African Affairs* 104: 35–68.

PART IV
The Gendered Body

Perhaps nothing is more deceptive than the "naturalness" of our bodies. We experience what happens to our bodies, and what happens *in* our bodies, as utterly natural, physical phenomena.

Yet to the social scientist, nothing could be farther from the truth. Our bodies are both shaped and interpreted in entirely gendered ways. How our bodies look, what our bodies feel, and what we think about how our bodies look and feel, are filtered through cultural lenses that make some kinds of bodies seem desirable and other kinds seem unacceptable. However, these lenses are not "natural" or universal. Cultural standards of health, beauty, musculature, and aesthetics are constantly changing. Take, for example, women's notions of beauty. Fortunes are made by companies that purvey the beauty myth—as feminist writer Naomi Wolf called it—reminding women that they do not measure up to these cultural standards and then providing products that will help them try. By such logic, women who experience eating disorders are not deviant non-conformists, but rather over-conformists to unrealizable norms of femininity. Feminist philosopher Susan Bordo's essay reminds us of the ways in which the types of female bodies valorized in contemporary North American society articulate with particular forms of femininity.

While many people feel pressured to consume body-enhancing products, for a minority, their bodies are themselves the products. For example, the figure skaters described by Karen McGarry are used to "sell" excitement, beauty, and Canadian pride. In order to do this, their bodies must be easily readable as both gender-normative and hetero-normative. The skaters and other entrepreneurs of the body experience an intensified form of the same pressures that "ordinary" men and women confront.

However, "ordinary" men and women are not merely passive templates, uncritically receiving and accepting cultural messages about "good" and "bad" bodies. Pamela Wakewich's work shows how people can, and do, create their own ideas about what it means to have a "good" body, ideas that have more to do with health and well-being than with unrealizable standards of beauty.

Women, of course, are not the only people who grapple with the gendered challenges of living in bodies. As Michael Atkinson describes, men too may seek to modify their bodies through surgery, among other means. Men who use cosmetic surgery, however, need to navigate the apparent contradiction between cosmetic surgery and hegemonic forms of masculinity, which suggest that concern with one's appearance marks one as "feminine."

Questions for Critical Thought

1. How much do you depend on the appearances of bodies to shape your interactions with other people? Do you react differently to different kinds of bodies?
2. Do you agree with Bordo that practices that are seen as pathological, such as eating disorders, can also be a form of resistance to gendered pressures?
3. Bordo emphasizes the impact of media on the body image of young women, while the women Wakewich interviewed do not appear to base their own body image on what they see in media. How influential are the representations of male and female bodies we see in magazines, on TV, and on the Internet? What other forces influence how people think about their bodies?
4. Do you think there is one dominant or hegemonic ideal of beauty for women today? What about for men?
5. McGarry describes a group of people who function as "public bodies"—whose physical appearance is made available as a product to be consumed by the public. Think of other public bodies. Do all public bodies share any common traits?
6. As social interaction is increasingly mediated by technologies, such as Facebook or text, as distinct from face-to-face encounters, do you think the significance of embodiment has changed?
7. The women in Wakewich's study claim that their satisfaction with their own bodies has changed significantly over their life cycle, from young adulthood to middle age. What motivates individuals to change the way they perceive their bodies? How does ageing affect the experience of embodiment?

8. Is there such a thing as a "perfect" body? If so, what does it look like?
9. Why did the men in Atkinson's study seek cosmetic surgery? Are their reasons different from the reasons that women seek out these procedures?
10. How might people use their bodies to express resistance to dominant ideas about gender?

Chapter 13

Overview

This classic piece by Susan Bordo leverages the powerful insights of Michel Foucault to argue that bodies—female bodies, in her examples—become "texts" of gender, manifesting the contradictions and complexities of being feminine. West and Zimmerman, in an earlier section, also focused on bodies, but they were primarily interested in how the social interactions that create gender are made possible by the way people display and use their bodies. Bordo goes a step further by examining how gender is written on bodies themselves.

She does so by focusing on bodily practices that are often viewed as pathological—hysteria, agoraphobia, and anorexia. Rather than separating these conditions off as abnormal or extreme, Bordo argues that they are the logical extensions of dominant ideas about femininity—the idealization of the domestic homemaker in the 1950s or the valorization of slenderness, self-effacement, and restraint for women in later decades. The anorexic body is a manifestation of the idea that women's hungers—whether for food, for sex, or for presence in the world—must be controlled and restrained. At the same time, the anorexic body demonstrates the self-mastery and orientation to achievement that Bordo argues became a desirable goal for both men and women in twentieth century North America.

So are we condemned to be merely "texts" for gender, living examples of dominant ideas? No, says Bordo. Bodily practices that express extreme forms of femininity also, paradoxically, express resistance to and protest against those very forms. Agoraphobic housewives refused to do the shopping and other domestic tasks expected of them, while anorexic women compel the attention of others in a culture in which women and girls are expected to be passive and invisible. This is a controversial claim, and Bordo has been charged by other scholars with romanticizing these disorders by reading political meaning into them.

Nonetheless, Bordo's work places bodies—how we shape them, what we do with them, and how we think about them—squarely at the centre of theorizing about gender. Theory is not only about abstractions like society, culture, or power; it is also about the very corporeal bodies through which we encounter the world.

The Body and the Reproduction of Femininity[1]

Susan Bordo

Reconstructing Feminist Discourse on the Body

The body—what we eat, how we dress, and the daily rituals to which we attend—is a medium of culture. The body, as anthropologist Mary Douglas has argued, is a powerful symbolic form, a surface on which the central rules, hierarchies, and even metaphysical commitments of a culture are inscribed and thus reinforced through the concrete language of the body (Douglas, 1966, 1982). The body may also operate as a metaphor for culture. From quarters as diverse as Plato and Hobbes to French feminist Luce Irigaray, an imagination of body morphology has provided a blueprint for diagnosis and/or vision of social and political life.

The body is not only a text of culture. It is also, as anthropologist Pierre Bourdieu and philosopher Michel Foucault (among others) have argued, a practical, direct locus of social control. Banally, through table manners and toilet habits, through seemingly trivial routines, rules, and practices, culture is "made body," as Bourdieu puts it—converted into automatic, habitual activity. As such, it is put "beyond the grasp of consciousness . . . [untouchable] by voluntary, deliberate transformations" (Bourdieu, 1977: 94). Our conscious politics, social commitments, and strivings for change may be undermined and betrayed by the life of our bodies—not the craving, instinctual body imagined by Plato, Augustine, and Freud, but what Foucault calls the "docile body," regulated by the norms of cultural life.[2]

Throughout his later "genealogical" works (*Discipline and Punish*, *The History of Sexuality*), Foucault constantly reminds us of the primacy of practice over belief. Not chiefly through ideology, but through the organization and regulation of the time, space, and movements of our daily lives, our bodies are trained, shaped, and impressed with the stamp of prevailing historical forms of selfhood, desire, masculinity, and femininity. Such an emphasis casts a dark and disquieting shadow across the contemporary scene. Women, as study after study shows, are spending more time on the management and discipline of our bodies than we have in a long, long time. In a decade marked by a reopening of the public arena to women, the intensification of such regimens appears diversionary and subverting. Through the pursuit of an ever-changing, homogenizing, elusive ideal of femininity—a pursuit without a terminus, requiring that women constantly attend to minute and often whimsical changes in fashion—female bodies become docile bodies—bodies whose forces and energies are habituated to external regulation, subjection, transformation, and "improvement." Through the exacting and normalizing disciplines of diet, makeup, and dress—central organizing principles of time and space in the day of many women—we are rendered less socially oriented and more centripetally focused on self-modification. Through these disciplines, we continue to memorize on our bodies, the feel and conviction of lack, of insufficiency, of never being good enough. At the farthest extremes, the practices of femininity may lead us to utter demoralization, debilitation, and death.

Viewed historically, the discipline and normalization of the female body—perhaps the only gender oppression that exercises itself, although to different degrees and in different forms, across age, race, class, and sexual orientation—has to be acknowledged as an amazingly durable and flexible strategy of social control. In our own era, it is difficult to avoid the recognition that the contemporary preoccupation with appearance, which still affects women far more powerfully than men, even in our narcissistic and visually oriented culture, may function as a backlash phenomenon, reasserting existing gender configurations against any attempts to shift or transform power relations.[3] . . .

This essay will focus on the analysis of one particular arena where the interplay of these dynamics is striking and perhaps exemplary. It is a limited and unusual arena—that of a group of gender-related and historically localized disorders: hysteria, agoraphobia, and anorexia nervosa.[4] I recognize that these disorders have also historically been class- and race-biased, largely (although not exclusively) occurring among white middle- and upper-middle-class women. Nonetheless, anorexia, hysteria, and agoraphobia may provide a paradigm of one way in which potential resistance is not merely undercut but *utilized* in the maintenance and reproduction of existing power relations.[5]

The central mechanism I will describe involves a transformation (or, if you wish, duality) of meaning, through which conditions that are objectively (and, on one level, experientially) constraining, enslaving, and even murderous, come to be experienced as liberating, transforming, and life-giving. I offer this analysis, although limited to a specific domain, as an example of how various contemporary critical discourses may be joined to yield an understanding of the subtle and often unwitting role played by our bodies in the symbolization and reproduction of gender.

The Body as a Text of Femininity

The continuum between female disorder and "normal" feminine practice is sharply revealed through a close reading of those disorders to which women have been particularly vulnerable. These, of course, have varied historically: neurasthenia and hysteria in the second half of the nineteenth century; agoraphobia and, most dramatically, anorexia nervosa and bulimia in the second half of the twentieth century. This is not to say that anorectics did not exist in the nineteenth century—many cases were described, usually in the context of diagnoses of hysteria (Showalter, 1985: 128–9)—or that women no longer suffer from classical hysterical symptoms in the twentieth century. But the taking up of eating disorders on a mass scale is as unique to the culture of the 1980s as the epidemic of hysteria was to the Victorian era.[6]

The symptomatology of these disorders reveals itself as textuality. Loss of mobility, loss of voice, inability to leave the home, feeding others while starving oneself, taking up space, and whittling down the space one's body takes up—all have symbolic meaning, all have political meaning under the varying rules governing the historical construction of gender. Working within this framework, we see that whether we look at hysteria, agoraphobia, or anorexia, we find the body of the sufferer deeply inscribed with an ideological construction of femininity emblematic of the period in question. The construction, of course, is always homogenizing and normalizing, erasing racial, class, and other differences and insisting that all women aspire to a coercive, standardized ideal. Strikingly, in these disorders, the construction of femininity is written in disturbingly concrete, hyperbolic terms: exaggerated, extremely literal, at times virtually caricatured presentations of the ruling feminine mystique. The bodies of disordered women in this way offer themselves as an aggressively graphic text for the interpreter—a text that insists, actually demands, that it be read as a cultural statement, a statement about gender.

Both nineteenth-century male physicians and twentieth-century feminist critics have seen, in the symptoms of neurasthenia and hysteria (syndromes that became increasingly less differentiated as the century wore on), an exaggeration of stereotypically feminine traits. The nineteenth-century "lady" was idealized in terms of delicacy and dreaminess, sexual passivity, and a charmingly labile and capricious emotionality (Vicinus, 1972, x–xi). Such notions were formalized and scientized in the work of male theorists from Acton and Krafft-Ebing to Freud, who described "normal," mature femininity in such terms.[7] In this context, the dissociations, the drifting and fogging of perception, the nervous tremors and faints, the anesthesias, and the extreme mutability of symptomatology associated with nineteenth-century female disorders can be seen to be concretizations of the feminine mystique of the period, produced according to rules that governed the prevailing construction of femininity. Doctors described what came to be known as the hysterical personality as "impressionable, suggestible, and narcissistic; highly labile, their moods changing suddenly, dramatically, and seemingly for inconsequential reasons . . . egocentric in the extreme . . . essentially asexual and not uncommonly frigid" (Smith-Rosenberg, 1985: 203)—all characteristics normative of femininity in this era. As Elaine Showalter points out, the term hysterical itself became almost interchangeable with the term *feminine* in the literature of the period (Showalter, 1985: 129).

The hysteric's embodiment of the feminine mystique of her era, however, seems subtle and ineffable compared to the ingenious literalism of agoraphobia and anorexia. In the context of our culture this literalism makes sense. With the advent of movies and television, the rules for femininity have come to be culturally transmitted more and more through standardized visual images. As a result, femininity itself has come to be largely a matter of constructing, in the manner described by Erving Goffman, the appropriate surface presentation of the self (Goffman, 1959). We are no longer given verbal descriptions or exemplars of what a lady is or of what femininity consists. Rather, we learn the rules directly through bodily discourse: through images that tell us what clothes, body shape, facial expression, movements, and behaviour are required.

In agoraphobia and, even more dramatically, in anorexia, the disorder presents itself as a virtual, though tragic, parody of twentieth-century constructions of femininity. The 1950s and early 1960s, when agoraphobia first began to escalate among women, was a period of reassertion of domesticity and dependency as the feminine ideal. Career woman became a dirty word, much more so than it had been during the war, when the economy depended on women's willingness to do "men's work." The reigning ideology of femininity, so well described by Betty Friedan and perfectly captured in the movies and television shows of the era, was childlike, non-assertive, helpless without a man, "content in a world of bedroom and kitchen, sex, babies and home" (Friedan, 1962: 36).[8] The housebound agoraphobic lives this construction of femininity literally. "You want me in this home? You'll have me in this home—with a vengeance!" The point, upon which many therapists have commented, does not need belabouring. Agoraphobia, as I.G. Fodor has put it, seems "the logical—albeit extreme—extension of the cultural sex-role stereotype for women" in this era (Fodor, 1974: 119; see also Brehony, 1983).

The emaciated body of the anorectic, of course, immediately presents itself as a caricature of the contemporary ideal of hyper-slenderness for women, an ideal that, despite the game resistance of racial and ethnic difference, has become the norm for women today. But slenderness is only the tip of the iceberg, for slenderness itself requires interpretation. "*C'est le sens qui fait vendre*," said Barthes, speaking of clothing styles—it is meaning that makes the sale (Culler, 1983: 74). So, too, it is meaning that makes the body admirable. To the degree that anorexia may be said to be "about" slenderness, it is about slenderness as a citadel of contemporary and historical meaning, not as an empty fashion ideal. As such, the interpretation of slenderness yields multiple readings, some related to gender, some not. For the purposes of this essay I will offer an abbreviated, gender-focused reading. But I must stress that this reading illuminates only partially, and that many other currents not discussed here—economic, psychosocial, and historical, as well as ethnic and class dimensions—figure prominently.[9]

We begin with the painfully literal inscription, on the anorectic's body, of the rules governing the construction of contemporary femininity. That construction is a double bind that legislates contradictory ideals and directives. On the one hand, our culture still widely advertises domestic conceptions of femininity, the ideological moorings for a rigorously dualistic sexual division of labour that casts woman as chief emotional and physical nurturer. The rules for this construction of femininity (and I speak here in a language both symbolic and literal) require that women learn to feed others, not the self, and to construe any desires for self-nurturance and self-feeding as greedy and excessive.[10] Thus, women must develop a totally other-oriented emotional economy. In this economy, the control of female appetite for food is merely the most concrete expression of the general rule governing the construction of femininity: that female hunger—for public power, for independence, for sexual gratification—be contained, and the public space that women be allowed to take up be circumscribed, limited. Figure 13.1, which appeared in a women's magazine fashion spread, dramatically illustrates the degree to which slenderness, set off against the resurgent muscularity and bulk of the current male body-ideal, carries connotations of fragility and lack of power in the face of a decisive male occupation of social space. On the body of the anorexic woman such rules are grimly and deeply etched.

On the other hand, even as young women today continue to be taught traditionally "feminine" virtues, to the degree that the professional arena is open to them, they must also learn to embody the "masculine" language and values of that arena—self-control, determination, cool, emotional discipline, mastery, and so on. Female bodies now speak symbolically of this necessity in their slender spare shape and the currently fashionable men's-wear look. (A contemporary clothing line's clever mirror-image logo, shown in Figure 13.2, offers women's fashions for the "New Man," with the model posed to suggest phallic confidence combined with female allure.) Our

Figure 13.1

Figure 13.2

Figure 13.3

bodies, too, as we trudge to the gym every day and fiercely resist both our hungers and our desire to soothe ourselves, are becoming more and more practised at the "male" virtues of control and self-mastery. Figure 13.3 illustrates this contemporary equation of physical discipline with becoming the "captain" of one's soul. The anorectic pursues these virtues with single-minded, unswerving dedication. "Energy, discipline, my own power will keep me going," says ex-anorectic Aimee Liu, re-creating her anorexic days. "I need nothing and no one else. . . . I will be master of my own body, if nothing else, I vow" (Liu, 1979: 123). . . .

In the pursuit of slenderness and the denial of appetite, the traditional construction of femininity intersects with the new requirement for women to embody the "masculine" values of the public arena. The anorectic, as I have argued, embodies this intersection, this double bind, in a particularly painful and graphic way.[11] I mean *double bind* quite literally here. "Masculinity" and "femininity," at least since the nineteenth century and arguably before, have been constructed through a process of mutual exclusion. One cannot simply add the historically feminine virtues to the historically masculine ones to yield a New Woman, a New Man, a new ethics, or a new culture. . . . Explored as a possibility for the self, the "androgynous" ideal ultimately exposes its internal contradiction and becomes a war that tears the subject in two—a war explicitly thematized, by many anorectics, as a battle between male and female sides of the self.

Protest and Retreat in the Same Gesture

In hysteria, agoraphobia, and anorexia, then, the woman's body may be viewed as a surface on which conventional constructions of femininity are exposed starkly to view, through their inscription in extreme or hyperliteral form. They are written, of course, in languages of horrible suffering. It is as though these bodies are speaking to us of the pathology and violence that lurks just around the corner, waiting at the horizon of "normal" femininity. It is no wonder that a steady motif in the feminist literature on female disorder is that of pathology as embodied *protest*—unconscious, inchoate, and counterproductive protest without an effective language, voice, or politics, but protest nonetheless. . . .

Robert Seidenberg and Karen DeCrow, for example, describe agoraphobia as a "strike" against "the renunciations usually demanded of women" and the expectations of housewifely functions such as shopping, driving the children to school, accompanying their husband to social events (1983: 31). Carroll Smith-Rosenberg presents a similar analysis of hysteria, arguing that by preventing the woman from functioning in the wifely role of caretaker of others, of "ministering angel" to husband and children, hysteria "became one way in which conventional women could express—in most cases unconsciously—dissatisfaction with one or several aspects of their lives" (1985: 208). A number of feminist writers, among whom Susie Orbach is the most articulate and forceful, have interpreted anorexia as a species of unconscious feminist protest. The anorectic is engaged in a "hunger strike," as Orbach calls it, stressing that this is a political discourse, in which the action of food refusal and dramatic transformation of body size "expresses with [the] body what [the anorectic] is unable to tell us with words'—her indictment of a culture that disdains and suppresses female hunger, makes women ashamed of their appetites and needs, and demands that women constantly work on the transformation of their body (Orbach, 1985).[12]

The anorectic, of course, is unaware that she is making a political statement. She may, indeed, be hostile to feminism and any other critical perspectives that she views as disputing her own autonomy and control or questioning the cultural ideals around which her life is organized. Through embodied rather than deliberate demonstration she exposes and indicts those ideals, precisely by pursuing them to the point at which their destructive potential is revealed for all to see.

The same gesture that expresses protest, moreover, can also signal retreat; this, indeed, may be part of the symptom's attraction. Kim Chernin, for example, argues that the debilitating anorexic fixation, by halting or mitigating personal development, assuages this generation's guilt and separation anxiety over the prospect of surpassing our mothers, of living less circumscribed, freer lives (Chernin, 1985). Agoraphobia, too, which often develops shortly after marriage, clearly functions in many cases as a way to cement dependency and attachment in the face of unacceptable stirrings of dissatisfaction and restlessness.

Although we may talk meaningfully of protest, then, I want to emphasize the counterproductive, tragically self-defeating (indeed, self-deconstructing) nature of that protest. Functionally, the symptoms of these disorders isolate, weaken, and undermine the sufferers; at the same time they turn the life of the body into an all-absorbing fetish, beside which all other objects of attention pale into unreality. On the symbolic level, too, the protest collapses into its opposite and proclaims the utter capitulation of the subject to the contracted female world. The muteness of hysterics and their return to the level of pure, primary bodily expressivity have been interpreted, as we have seen, as rejecting the symbolic order of the patriarchy and recovering a lost world of semiotic, maternal value. But at the same time, of course, muteness is the condition of the silent, uncomplaining woman—an ideal of patriarchal culture. Protesting the stifling of the female voice through one's own voicelessness—that is, employing the language of femininity to protest the conditions of the female world—will always involve ambiguities of this sort. Perhaps this is why symptoms crystallized from the language of femininity are so perfectly suited to express the dilemmas of middle-class and upper-middle-class women living in periods poised on the edge of gender change, women who have the social and material resources to carry the traditional construction of femininity to symbolic excess but who also confront the anxieties of new possibilities. The late nineteenth century, the post–Second World War period, and the late twentieth century are all periods in which gender becomes an issue to be discussed and in which discourse proliferates about "the Woman Question," "the New Woman," "What Women Want," "What Femininity Is."

Collusion, Resistance, and the Body

The pathologies of female protest function, paradoxically, as if in collusion with the cultural conditions that produce them, reproducing rather than transforming precisely that which is being protested. In this connection, the fact that hysteria and anorexia have peaked during historical periods of cultural backlash against attempts at reorganization and redefinition of male and female roles is significant. Female pathology reveals itself here as an extremely interesting social formation through which one source of potential for resistance and rebellion is pressed into the service of maintaining the established order. . . .

Here, examining the context in which the anorexic syndrome is produced may be illuminating. Anorexia will erupt, typically, in the course of what begins as a fairly moderate diet regime, undertaken because someone—often the father—has made a casual critical remark. Anorexia *begins in*, emerges out of, what is, in our time, conventional feminine practice. In the course of that practice, for any number of individual reasons, the practice is pushed a little beyond the parameters of moderate dieting. The young woman discovers what it feels like to crave and want and need and yet, through the exercise of her own will, to triumph over that need. In the process, a new realm of meanings is discovered, a range of values and possibilities that Western culture has traditionally coded as "male" and rarely made available to women: an ethic and aesthetic of self-mastery and self-transcendence, expertise, and power over others through the example of superior will and control. The experience is intoxicating and habit-forming.

At school the anorectic discovers that her steadily shrinking body is admired, not so much as an aesthetic or sexual object, but for the strength of will and self-control it projects. At home she discovers, in the inevitable battles her parents fight to get her to eat, that her actions have enormous power over the lives of those around her. As her body begins to lose its traditional feminine curves, its breasts and hips and rounded stomach, it begins to feel and look more like a spare, lanky male body, and she begins to feel untouchable, out of reach of hurt, "invulnerable, clean and hard as the bones etched into my silhouette," as one student described it in her journal. She despises, in particular, all those parts of her body that continue to mark her as female. "If only I could eliminate [my breasts]," says Liu, "cut them off if need be" (1979: 99). For her, as for many anorectics, the breasts represent a bovine, unconscious, vulnerable side of the self. Liu's body symbolism is thoroughly continuous with dominant cultural associations. Brett Silverstein's studies on the "Possible Causes of the Thin Standard of Bodily Attractiveness for Women" (1986) testify empirically to what is obvious from every comedy routine involving a dramatically shapely woman: namely, our cultural association of curvaceousness with incompetence. The anorectic is also quite aware, of course, of the social and sexual vulnerability involved in having a female body; many, in fact, were sexually abused as children.

Through her anorexia, by contrast, she has unexpectedly discovered an entry into the privileged male world, a way to become what is valued in our culture, a way to become safe, to rise above it all—for her, they are the same thing. She has discovered this, paradoxically, by pursuing conventional feminine behaviour—in this case, the discipline of perfecting the body as an object—to excess. At this point of excess, the conventionally feminine deconstructs, we might say, into its opposite and opens onto those values our culture has coded as male. No wonder anorexia is experienced as liberating and that the anorectic will fight family, friends, and therapists in an effort to hold onto it—fight them to the death, if need be. The anorectic's experience of power is, of course, deeply and dangerously illusory. To reshape one's body into a male body is not to put on male power and privilege. To *feel* autonomous and free while harnessing body and soul to an obsessive body-practice is to serve, not transform, a social order that limits female possibilities. And, of course, for the female to become male is only for her to locate herself on the other side of a disfiguring opposition. The new "power look" of female bodybuilding, which encourages women to develop the same hulk-like, triangular shape that has been the norm for male body-builders, is no less determined by a hierarchical, dualistic construction of gender than was the conventionally "feminine" norm that tyrannized female body-builders such as Bev Francis for years.

Although the specific cultural practices and meanings are different, similar mechanisms, I suspect, are at work in hysteria and agoraphobia. In these cases too, the language of femininity, when pushed to excess—when shouted and asserted, when disruptive and demanding—deconstructs into its opposite and makes available to the woman an illusory experience of power previously forbidden to her by virtue of her gender. In the case of nineteenth-century femininity, the forbidden experience may have been the bursting of fetters—particularly moral and emotional fetters. John Conolly, the asylum reformer, recommended institutionalization for women who "want that restraint over the passions without which the female character is lost" (Showalter, 1985: 48). Hysterics often infuriated male doctors by their lack of precisely this quality. S. Weir Mitchell described these patients as "the despair of physicians," whose "despotic selfishness wrecks the constitution of nurses and devoted relatives, and in unconscious or half-conscious self-indulgence destroys the comfort of everyone around them" (Smith-Rosenberg, 1985: 207). It must have given the Victorian patient some illicit pleasure to be viewed as capable of such disruption of the staid nineteenth-century household. A similar form of power, I believe, is part of the experience of agoraphobia.

This does not mean that the primary reality of these disorders is not one of pain and entrapment. Anorexia, too, clearly contains a dimension of physical addiction to the biochemical effects of starvation. But whatever the physiology involved, the ways in which the subject understands and thematizes her experience cannot be reduced to a mechanical process. The anorectic's ability to live with minimal food intake allows her to feel powerful and worthy of admiration in a "world," as Susie Orbach describes it, "from which at the most profound level [she] feels excluded" and unvalued (1985: 103). The literature on both anorexia and hysteria is strewn with battles of will between the sufferer and those trying to "cure" her; the latter, as Orbach points out, very rarely understand that the psychic values she is fighting for are often more important to the woman than life itself.

Textuality, Praxis, and the Body

The "solutions" offered by anorexia, hysteria, and agoraphobia, I have suggested, develop out of the practice of femininity itself, the pursuit of which is still presented as the chief route to acceptance and success for women in our culture. Too aggressively pursued, that practice leads to its own undoing, in one sense. For if femininity is, as Susan Brownmiller has said, at its core a "tradition of imposed limitations" (1984: 14), then an unwillingness to limit oneself, even in the pursuit of femininity, breaks the rules. But, of course, in another sense the rules remain fully in place. The sufferer becomes wedded to an obsessive practice, unable to make any effective change in her life. She remains, as Toril Moi has put it, "gagged and chained to [the] feminine role," a reproducer of the docile body of femininity (1985: 192).

This tension between the psychological meaning of a disorder, which may enact fantasies of rebellion and embody a language of protest, and the practical life of the disordered body, which may utterly defeat rebellion and subvert protest, may be obscured by too exclusive a focus on the symbolic dimension and insufficient attention to praxis. As we have seen in the case of some Lacanian feminist readings of hysteria, the result of this can be a one-sided interpretation that romanticizes the hysteric's symbolic subversion of the phallocentric order while confined to her bed. This is not to say that confinement in bed has a transparent, univocal meaning—in powerlessness, debilitation, dependency, and so forth. The "practical" body is no brute biological or material entity. It, too, is a culturally mediated form; its activities are subject to interpretation and description. The shift to the practical dimension is not a turn to biology or nature, but to another "register," as Foucault puts it, of the cultural body, the register of the "useful body" rather than the "intelligible body" (Foucault, 1979: 136). The distinction can prove useful, I believe, to feminist discourse.

The intelligible body includes our scientific, philosophic, and aesthetic representations of the body—our cultural *conceptions* of the body, norms of beauty, models of health, and so forth. But the same representations may also be seen as forming a set of practical rules and regulations through which the living body is "trained, shaped, obeys, responds," becoming, in short, a socially adapted and "useful body" (Foucault, 1979: 136). Consider this particularly clear and appropriate example: the nineteenth-century hourglass figure, emphasizing breasts and hips against a wasp waist, was an intelligible *symbolic* form, representing a domestic, sexualized ideal of femininity. The sharp cultural contrast between the female and the male form, made possible by the use of corsets and bustles, reflected, in symbolic terms, the dualistic division of social and economic life into clearly defined male and female spheres. At the same time, to achieve the specified look, a particular feminine *praxis* was required—straitlacing, minimal eating, and reduced mobility—rendering the female body unfit to perform activities outside its designated sphere. This, in Foucauldian terms, would be the "useful body" corresponding to the aesthetic norm.

The intelligible body and the useful body are two arenas of the same discourse; they often mirror and support each other, as in the above illustration. Another example can be found in the seventeenth-century philosophic conception of the body as a machine, mirroring an increasingly more automated productive machinery of labour. But the two bodies may also contradict and mock each other. A range of contemporary representations and images, as noted earlier, have coded the transcendence of female appetite and its public display in the slenderness ideal in terms of power, will, mastery, and the possibilities of success in the professional arena. These associations are carried visually by the slender superwomen of prime-time television and popular movies and promoted explicitly in advertisements and articles appearing routinely in women's fashion magazines, diet books, and weight-training publications. Yet the thousands of slender girls and women who strive to embody these images and who in that service suffer from eating disorders, exercise compulsions, and continual self-scrutiny and self-castigation are anything *but* the "masters" of their lives. . . .

This is not to deny the benefits of diet, exercise, and other forms of body management. Rather, I view our bodies as a site of struggle, where we must work to keep our daily practices in the service of resistance to gender domination, not in the service of docility and gender normalization. This work requires, I believe, a determinedly skeptical attitude toward the routes of seeming liberation and pleasure offered by our culture. It also demands an awareness of the often contradictory relations between image and practice, between rhetoric and reality. Popular representations, as we have seen, may forcefully employ the rhetoric and symbolism of empowerment, personal freedom, "having it all." Yet female bodies, pursuing these ideals, may find themselves as distracted, depressed, and physically ill as female bodies in the nineteenth century were made when pursuing a feminine ideal of dependency, domesticity, and delicacy. The recognition and analysis of such contradictions, and of all the other collusions, subversions, and enticements through which culture enjoins the aid of our bodies in the reproduction of gender, require that we restore a concern for female praxis to its formerly central place in feminist politics.

Notes

1. Early versions of this essay, under various titles, were delivered at the philosophy department of the State University of New York at Stony Brook, the University of Massachusetts conference on Histories of Sexuality, and the twenty-first annual conference for the Society of Phenomenology and Existential Philosophy. I thank all those who commented and provided encouragement on those occasions. The essay was revised and originally published in Alison Jaggar and Susan Bordo, eds., *Gender/Body/Knowledge: Feminist Reconstructions of Being and Knowing* (New Brunswick: Rutgers University Press, 1989).
2. On docility, see Michel Foucault, *Discipline and Punish* (New York: Vintage, 1979), 135–69. For a Foucauldian analysis of feminine practice, see Sandra Bartky, "Foucault, Femininity, and the Modernization of Patriarchal Power," in her *Femininity and Domination* (New York: Routledge, 1990); see also Susan Brownmiller, *Femininity* (New York: Ballantine, 1984).
3. During the late 1970s and 1980s, male concern over appearance undeniably increased. Study after study confirms, however, that there is still a large gender gap in this area. Research conducted at the University of Pennsylvania in 1985 found men to be generally satisfied with their appearance, often, in fact, "distorting their perceptions [of themselves] in a positive, self-aggrandizing way" ("Dislike of Own Bodies Found Common Among Women," *New York Times*, 19 March 1985: C1). Women, however, were found to exhibit extreme negative assessments and distortions of body perception. Other studies have suggested that women are judged more harshly than men when they deviate from dominant social standards of attractiveness. Thomas Cash et al., in "The Great American Shape-Up," *Psychology Today* (April 1986): 34, report that although the situation for men has changed, the situation for women has more than proportionally worsened. Citing results from 30,000 responses to a 1985 survey of perceptions of body image and comparing similar responses to a 1972 questionnaire, they report that the 1985 respondents were considerably more dissatisfied with their bodies than the 1972 respondents, and they note a marked intensification of concern among men. Among the 1985 group, the group most dissatisfied of all with their appearance, however, were teenage women. Women today constitute by far the largest number of consumers of diet products, attenders of spas and diet centres, and subjects of intestinal by-pass and other fat-reduction operations.
4. On the gendered and historical nature of these disorders: the number of female to male hysterics has been estimated at anywhere from 2:1 to 4:1, and as many as 80 per cent of all agoraphobics are female (Annette Brodsky and Rachel Hare-Mustin, *Women and Psychotherapy* [New York: Guilford Press, 1980], 116, 122). Although more cases of male eating disorders have been reported in the late eighties and early nineties, it is estimated that close to 90 per cent of all anorectics are female (Paul Garfinkel and David Garner, *Anorexia Nervosa: A Multidimensional Perspective* [New York: Brunner/Mazel, 1982], 112–13). For a sophisticated account of female psychopathology, with particular attention to nineteenth-century disorders but, unfortunately, little mention of agoraphobia or eating disorders, see Elaine Showalter, *The Female Malady: Women, Madness and English Culture, 1830–1980* (New York: Pantheon, 1985). For a discussion of social and gender issues in agoraphobia, see Robert Seidenberg and Karen DeCrow, *Women Who Marry Houses: Panic and Protest in Agoraphobia* (New York: McGraw-Hill, 1983). On the history of anorexia nervosa, see Joan Jacobs Brumberg, *Fasting Girls: The Emergence of Anorexia Nervosa as a Modern Disease* (Cambridge: Harvard University Press, 1988).
5. In constructing such a paradigm I do not pretend to do justice to any of these disorders in its individual complexity. My aim is to chart some points of intersection, to describe some similar patterns, as they emerge through a particular reading of the phenomenon—a political reading, if you will.
6. On the epidemic of hysteria and neurasthenia, see Showalter, *The Female Malady;* Carroll Smith-Rosenberg, "The Hysterical Woman: Sex Roles and Role Conflict in Nineteenth-Century

America," in her *Disorderly Conduct: Visions of Gender in Victorian America* (Oxford: Oxford University Press, 1985).

7. See Carol Nadelson and Malkah Notman, *The Female Patient* (New York: Plenum, 1982), 5; E.M. Sigsworth and T.J. Wyke, "A Study of Victorian Prostitution and Venereal Disease," in Vicinus, *Suffer and Be Still*, 82. For more general discussions, see Peter Gay, *The Bourgeois Experience: Victoria to Freud*. Vol. 1: *Education of the Senses* (New York: Oxford University Press, 1984), esp. 109–68; Showalter, *The Female Malady*, esp. 121–44. The delicate lady, an ideal that had very strong class connotations (as does slenderness today), is not the only conception of femininity to be found in Victorian cultures. But it was arguably the single most powerful ideological representation of femininity in that era, affecting women of all classes, including those without the material means to realize the ideal fully. See Helena Mitchie, *The Flesh Made Word* (New York: Oxford, 1987), for discussions of the control of female appetite and Victorian constructions of femininity.
8. Betty Friedan, *The Feminine Mystique* (New York: Dell, 1962), 36. The theme song of one such show ran, in part, "I married Joan . . . What a girl . . . what a whirl . . . what a life! I married Joan . . . What a mind . . . love is blind . . . what a wife!'
9. For other interpretive perspectives on the slenderness ideal, see "Reading the Slender Body" in [*Unbearable Weight: Feminism, Western Culture, and the Body*]; Kim Chernin, *The Obsession: Reflections on the Tyranny of Slenderness* (New York: Harper and Row, 1981); Susie Orbach, *Hunger Strike: The Anorectic's Struggle as a Metaphor for Our Age* (New York: W.W. Norton, 1985).
10. See "Hunger as Ideology," in [*Unbearable Weight: Feminism, Western Culture, and the Body*], for a discussion of how this construction of femininity is reproduced in contemporary commercials and advertisements concerning food, eating, and cooking.
11. Striking, in connection with this, is Catherine Steiner-Adair's 1984 study of high-school women, which reveals a dramatic association between problems with food and body image and emulation of the cool, professionally "together," and gorgeous superwoman. On the basis of a series of interviews, the high schoolers were classified into two groups: one expressed skepticism over the superwoman ideal, the other thoroughly aspired to it. Later administrations of diagnostic tests revealed that 94 per cent of the pro-superwoman group fell into the eating-disordered range of the scale. Of the other group, 100 per cent fell into the non-eating-disordered range. Media images notwithstanding, young women today appear to sense, either consciously or through their bodies, the impossibility of simultaneously meeting the demands of two spheres whose values have been historically defined in utter opposition to each other.
12. When we look into the many autobiographies and case studies of hysterics, anorectics, and agoraphobics, we find that these are indeed the sorts of women one might expect to be frustrated by the constraints of a specified female role. Sigmund Freud and Joseph Breuer, in *Studies on Hysteria* (New York: Avon, 1966), and Freud, in the later *Dora: An Analysis of a Case of Hysteria* (New York: Macmillan, 1963), constantly remark on the ambitiousness, independence, intellectual ability, and creative strivings of their patients. We know, moreover, that many women who later became leading social activists and feminists of the nineteenth century were among those who fell ill with hysteria and neurasthenia. It has become a virtual cliché that the typical anorectic is a perfectionist, driven to excel in all areas of her life. Though less prominently, a similar theme runs throughout the literature on agoraphobia. One must keep in mind that in drawing on case studies, one is relying on the perceptions of other acculturated individuals. One suspects, for example, that the popular portrait of the anorectic as a relentless over-achiever may be coloured by the lingering or perhaps resurgent Victorianism of our culture's attitudes toward ambitious women. One does not escape this hermeneutic problem by turning to autobiography. But in autobiography one is at least dealing with social constructions and attitudes that animate the subject's own psychic reality. In this regard the autobiographical literature on anorexia, drawn on in a variety of places in [*Unbearable Weight: Feminism, Western Culture, and the Body*], is strikingly full of anxiety about the domestic world and other themes that suggest deep rebellion against traditional notions of femininity.

References

Bourdieu, P. 1977. *Outline of a Theory of Practice*. Cambridge: Cambridge University Press.

Brehony, K. 1983. "Women and Agoraphobia," in V. Franks and E. Rothblum, eds., *The Stereotyping of Women*. New York: Springer.

Brownmiller, S. 1984. *Femininity*. New York: Ballantine.

Chernin, K. 1985. *The Hungry Self: Women, Eating, and Identity*. New York: Harper and Row.

Clément, C., and Cixous, H. 1986. *The Newly Born Woman*, B. Wing, trans. Minneapolis: University of Minnesota Press.

Culler, J. 1983. *Roland Barthes*. New York: Oxford University Press.

Douglas, M. 1966. *Purity and Danger*. London: Routledge and Kegan Paul.

———. 1982. *Natural Symbols*. New York: Pantheon.

Fodor, I.G. 1974. "The Phobic Syndrome in Women," in V. Franks and V. Burtle, eds., *Women in Therapy*. New York: Brunner/Mazel.

Foucault, M. 1979. *Discipline and Punish*. New York: Vintage.

———. 1980. *The History of Sexuality*. Volume 1: *An Introduction*. New York: Vintage.

Friedan, B. 1962. *The Feminine Mystique*. New York: Dell.

Goffman, E. 1959. *The Presentation of the Self in Everyday Life*. Garden City, NJ: Anchor Doubleday.

Hunter, D. 1985. "Hysteria, Psychoanalysis and Feminism," in S. Garner, C. Kahane, and M. Sprenger, eds., *The (M)Other Tongue*. Ithaca, NY: Cornell University Press.

Liu, A. 1979. *Solitaire*. New York: Harper and Row.

Mitchie, H. 1987. *The Flesh Made Word*. New York: Oxford University Press.

Moi, T. 1985. "Representations of Patriarchy: Sex and Epistemology in Freud's Dora," in C. Bernheimer and C. Kahane, eds., *In Dora's Case: Freud—Hysteria—Feminism*. New York: Columbia University Press.

Orbach, S. 1985. *Hunger Strike: The Anorectic's Struggle as a Metaphor for Our Age*. New York: W.W. Norton.

Poster, M. 1984. *Foucault, Marxism, and History*. Cambridge: Polity Press.

Showalter, E. 1985. *The Female Malady: Women, Madness and English Culture, 1830–1980*. New York: Pantheon.

Siedenberg, R., and K. DeCrow. 1983. *Women Who Marry Houses: Panic and Protest in Agoraphobia*. New York: McGraw-Hill.

Silverstein, B. 1986. "Possible Causes of the Thin Standard of Bodily Attractiveness for Women," *International Journal of Eating Disorders* 5: 907–16.

Smith-Rosenberg, C. 1985. "The Hysterical Woman: Sex Roles and Role Conflict in Nineteenth-Century America," in C. Smith-Rosenberg, *Disorderly Conduct: Visions of Gender in Victorian America*. Oxford: Oxford University Press.

Vicinus, M. 1972. "Introduction: The Perfect Victorian Lady," in M. Vicinus, *Suffer and Be Still: Women in the Victorian Age*, pp. x–xi. Bloomington: Indiana University Press.

Chapter 14

Overview

The mass media present us with millions of images of gendered bodies every day. These bodies may be judged more or less appropriately feminine or masculine. They speak not only of gender but also of other social categories, such as nation or religion.

Karen McGarry examines some very visible bodies—high-performance figure skaters, whose art and athleticism are shown by their appearance on ice. Both male and female skaters' bodies are texts that can be "read," to borrow Bordo's terminology, by coaches, sponsors, and TV audiences. An inadequate or inappropriate gender performance not only would be held against the skater but also would be understood as reflecting badly on Canada, given figure skating's status as a "flagship" sport in international competitions.

Kurt Browning and Elvis Stojko are examples of flag-bearers for this gendered nationalism, as both manifest a form of skating that exaggerates stereotypical masculinity, as contrasted with other skaters such as Toller Cranston who, while equally talented, used cosmetics and ballet-inspired moves. Masculinity is conflated with heterosexuality, McGarry argues, so that male skaters must engage in these displays of masculinity so that they will not be regarded as gay. Female skaters also come under the same sort of scrutiny and have their gendered performances judged against ideals of what a properly feminine body should look like.

Mass Media and Gender Identity in High Performance Canadian Figure Skating

Karen McGarry

Introduction

This paper is based upon qualitative, anthropological fieldwork conducted between 2000 and 2002 among Canadian journalists, high performance (i.e., National, World, and Olympic level) figure skaters, coaches, sponsors, and others involved in the production of mediated representations of figure skating for mainstream Canadian television networks and other print media. With the permission of various organizations, I conducted participant observation and field work in skating arenas and in the media centres of major competitions to understand the role of figure skating in shaping a sense of Canadian national identity. As standard practice in anthropology, the names of those interviewed are withheld to protect their anonymity. The goal of this paper is to highlight the role of the media in promoting particular gendered images of figure skaters for public consumption, thereby drawing attention to two issues: (1) the socially constructed nature of various representations of men and women in the sport, and (2) the ways in which particular gendered images of sports figures are promoted in the interests of nationalism.

Figure Skating, the Media, and Canadian Culture

Figure skating is viewed by many Canadians as an integral part of Canadian culture. Records of ice-skating date back to at least the 1700s, and figure skating, along with hockey, receives prime-time television coverage on major Canadian television networks. Figure skating, in fact, is ranked second only to hockey in terms of television spectatorship, government funding, and corporate sponsorship (Skate Canada, 2002). Its popularity among fans is heightened by the fact that since the 1940s, Canadians have won more than 500 international medals, making it one of the nation's most competitively successful amateur sports. Skaters such as Elvis Stojko, Kurt Browning, Elizabeth Manley, Barbara Ann Scott, Toller Cranston, Jamie Salé and David Pelletier, to name a few, have become household names and national icons in Canada.

Given figure skating's high spectatorship levels, it is not surprising that Skate Canada, the sport's amateur governing body, and CTV, Canada's self-declared "official figure skating network" have opportunistically marketed figure skating as a distinctly "Canadian" sport and a sport of national significance:

> Figure Skating is a sport of national significance to Canadians and is part of our heritage. Canadians have excelled in figure skating, achieving international success and celebrity status. (Skate Canada Fact Sheet, 2002)

> It's part of our Canadian heritage. That's why CTV—"Canada's Figure Skating Network"—is committed to bringing you the best figure skating in the world. CTV has been partnered with the sport since 1961, and makes figure skating its core sports property. (CTV website, 16 July 2001)

For Skate Canada and its top skaters, sponsorships are relatively easy to obtain (in comparison with other amateur sports). In fact, Skate Canada has become a primarily self-sustaining organization over the years, thanks mainly to lucrative sponsorship opportunities. While the organization continues to receive government funding, this represents a small portion (7 per cent) of its annual operating budget (Skate Canada, 2002). This means that the task of promoting a sense of national identity among Canadians has, in the case of figure skating, moved increasingly into the hands of non-state actors, and particularly the mass media and its sponsors and advertisers. Throughout my research, I learned that there exist powerful alliances of interest between skating sponsors and various Canadian media outlets, both of which have a vested economic interest in promoting various national representations that appeal to entertainment spectacles. These alliances, in turn, indirectly influence the gendered representations upheld for Canadian audiences. For example, at one event, I talked with a television sports network executive from a major media outlet. Very excited to be there, she had this to say about her company's agreement with Skate Canada:

> *Executive:* When they [Skate Canada] approached us, we were excited to be a part of it all. We were looking for the best sports ambassadors for Canada to support. What's better than figure skating? They're good, clean-cut kids. We're proud too of our association with skating and our advertisers have really supported Elvis Stojko over the years.
>
> *Karen:* What was it about Elvis that makes him appealing?
>
> *Executive:* He's successful and a champion. And he's such a strong, masculine presence.

Top skaters recognize the importance of their sport to the country, and they rarely doubt that their image will not be promoted favourably. Their bodies have become commodified to the point where, as one skater confidently told me, "I'm not trying to be arrogant here, but they [the network] would have my people [his sponsors] down their throats if I got criticized. I'm worth a lot to them." In many ways then, figure skating represents an opportunity for understanding how the Canadian media and television, in conjunction with advertisers, influence the production of gendered, commodified identities on ice, and in doing so, produce highly specific gendered bodily representations of the nation.

Gender and Figure Skating

The gendered categories of "masculinity" and "femininity" are socially constructed concepts and societal ideals about an appropriate masculine or feminine behaviour vary spatially, from culture to culture, and temporally, depending upon various socio-historical circumstances (e.g., Butler, 1990). In other words, what is considered "socially appropriate" behaviour for a female or male (today) is not the same as a century ago. Given the lucrative sponsorship potential of the sport, it is not surprising that the Canadian mainstream media and its sponsors and advertisers have sought to endorse "clean cut," mainstream, heterosexual images of masculinity and femininity for public consumption.

While figure skating is rumoured to have the highest proportion of homosexual men of any amateur competitive sport (Pronger, 1999), it is ironically a sport in which men must exhibit the most blatantly heterosexual signs to be successful and to receive commercial endorsements. Since the late 1980s, Skate Canada, the media, and its sponsors have made a concerted effort to de-emphasize figure skating's balletic heritage, a tradition that was strengthened in the 1970s by skaters such as Canadian Olympian Toller Cranston, an openly homosexual competitor who introduced flamboyant costumes, cosmetics, ballet, and choreography into men's skating. Male homosexuality, it seems, is considered a financial liability to the sport. In 1998, for example, the two-time Olympic silver medallist, Brian Orser, was "outed" in the media during a palimony lawsuit. Orser was devastated by the media exposure and claimed that such allegations of homosexuality would threaten his economic livelihood. Similarly, at the 2001 World Championships in Vancouver when a well-known male Canadian skater was contacted by a gay magazine about the possibility of doing a feature story on him, he was told by Skate Canada that he must decline the request. As one coach said to me, "that is not the sort of picture that Skate Canada wants to paint for the country, especially in an international forum." Every effort is made to construct such skaters as heterosexual.

The heterosexual masculine images of World Champion skaters like Kurt Browning and Elvis Stojko were endorsed enthusiastically in the media throughout the 1990s, a point also noted by Adams (1997). Usually skating to rock and roll music, or adopting the traditionally masculine personas of characters like ninjas, Scottish warriors, or karate experts, Stojko was constructed in the media as "Canada's Terminator." At one competition I attended, I watched Stojko warm up backstage with balletic exercises, but the camera technician, who was instructed to film Stojko's pre-competitive routine, waited until he decided to jog to film him. As he said to me, "Elvis is such a macho guy; we want to show that side of him." By emphasizing male skaters' athletic abilities in media portrayals, links are made between the supposed "strength" of the male figure skating body, and the "strength" of the nation. As one sponsor said to me, "We want to promote strong images of our male skaters to show the Americans and other nations that we are an important force to contend with." The bottom line is that images of male heterosexuality sell to a broader, and hence more lucrative, spectator demographic.

Similar sorts of gender expectations and pressures exist for Canada's female skaters. Women are expected to emulate a soft, delicate femininity reminiscent of, as one coach told me, "an Audrey Hepburn or Grace Kelly era." The competitive future of female skaters who fail to project such images may, in some cases, be threatened. One female skater I spoke with, for example, told me that, subsequent to a competition, she was informed by a judge that her earring (she had three piercings in each ear), her nose ring, and her weight, were "unfeminine" and that she might fare better in the future should she comport herself "more accordingly and ladylike." She also suggested that the skater should lose five pounds, as this would make her more attractive to the media.

Clearly then, the gendered images performed in figure skating are culturally constructed images, oftentimes produced in conjunction with the media. Some skaters I spoke with, for instance, informed me that they consult their agents and media organizations for input before deciding upon their annual costume and program themes.

Social Implications/Conclusion

The gendered images favoured in figure skating are important to discuss here because they have a variety of negative consequences for the sport. First, the persistence of idealized representations of gender can lead to the onset of debilitating emotional and physical disabilities among skaters. For women in particular, figure skating is notorious for the existence of eating disorders and a variety of other physical and psychological ailments (e.g., Ryan, 1995; Davis, 1997) as a result of the desire to achieve an "idealized femininity." The narrow range of opportunities for gendered identities also hampers the individual creative talents and artistic abilities of skaters, coaches, and choreographers, many of whom feel limited in the range of options available. Also, it is somewhat surprising, in the supposedly tolerant, multicultural, and inclusive environment of a nation like Canada, that such a rigid and narrow definition of gendered identities is accepted and promoted (oftentimes unconsciously) for public consumption. Clearly, this is a growing concern within the sport due to the increasing power and hegemony of the mainstream media and its powerful position in shaping modern identities. As nation-states gradually begin to lose control over the production of national identities in increasingly globalized contexts, non-state entities like the mass media are taking over or supplanting the state's role in nation-building. As this article has suggested, this has important connotations for the future of increasingly mediated sports like figure skating, where the bodies of skaters are heavily commodified and mainstream representations of national bodies dominate.

References

Adams, M. 1997. "To Be an Ordinary Hero: Male Figure Skaters and the Ideology of Gender," *Avante* 3(3): 93–110.

Butler, J. 1990. *Gender Trouble: Feminism and the Subversion of Identity*. New York: Routledge.

CTV. 2001. *CTV and Figure Skating*. Available at www.ctv.ca/sport (accessed 16 July 2001).

Davis, C. 1997. "Eating Disorders and Hyperactivity: A Psycho-biological Perspective," *Canadian Journal of Psychiatry* 42: 168–75.

Pronger, B. 1999. *The Arena of Masculinity: Sport, Homosexuality, and the Meaning of Sex*. New York: St Martin's Press.

Ryan, J. 1995. *Little Girls in Pretty Boxes: The Making and Breaking of Elite Gymnasts and Figure Skaters*. New York: Doubleday.

Skate Canada. 2002. *Skate Canada Fact Sheet*. Ottawa: Skate Canada.

Chapter 15

Overview

Most of us will never be high-performance skaters or elite athletes. So what is it like to live in a gendered body as an ordinary man or woman? Pamela Wakewich interviewed 40 women and men in North Bay about their ideas about body image, health, and ageing (in this excerpt, we focus on the interviews with women). These interviews reveal a much wider range of ideas about bodies than the stereotypes commonly invoked in the media. While Wakewich's interviewees are aware that their bodies do not match the slender, ultra-fit ideals of the media, this discrepancy is not a source of significant distress. The women are critical readers of media images, rather than passive consumers. For them, a "good" body is a healthy one that can carry out their many responsibilities.

Wakewich's work also illustrates the diversity of embodiments and the ways in which people's sense of their own embodiment changes over time. Women recall how their concerns with being thin and conventionally attractive have changed over time, towards a greater concern with being healthy and capable. Changes in friendship groups and life partnerships also lead to changes in body image and self-perception. Weight is a significant concern for many of the women, but it does not over-determine their feelings about their bodies.

These participants experience their gendered embodiment quite differently from the anorexics studied by Bordo or the elite skaters studied by McGarry. Their efforts to conform to conventional ideals of femininity are moderated by their social networks and ultimately subordinated to the goal of having a healthy body, even though it might be an "imperfect" one when judged against cultural ideals.

Contours of Everyday Life: Women's Reflections on Embodiment and Health over Time

Pamela Wakewich

> Written on the body is a secret code only visible in certain lights; the accumulations of a lifetime gather there. In places the palimpsest is so heavily worked that the letters feel like Braille. I keep my body rolled up away from prying eyes. Never unfold too much, tell the whole story.
>
> —Jeanette Winterson, *Written on the Body*

> People have to inhabit their bodies, and their physical identity is part of themselves. Particularly as they grow older, they have a need to account for this identity, to draw together all that they have experienced. This body is their inheritance, it is the result of the events of their life, and it is their constraint.
>
> —Mildred Blaxter, "The Causes of Disease: Women Talking"

While efforts to incorporate the body into social theory have become prolific in the past decade, it is only recently that writers have begun to explore the ways in which people actively constitute and experience the body in everyday life.[1] Analysts have tended to focus upon representations of the female body in the professional discourses of medicine and science or the popular discourses of media and advertising, and to presume a direct link between these representations and women's experiences of the body.[2] Even where authors seek to present alternative frameworks, their analysis generally remain framed by the scientific and biomedical categories and language that they wish to challenge. Body and identity are presented as static notions with the presumption that they remain fixed and homogeneous through time and place.

A similar limitation is evident in much contemporary feminist literature that addresses the relationship between media and women's body image dissatisfaction. Largely influenced by writers like Foucault, analysts have carefully documented the ways in which media and advertising serve to promote and normalize disciplinary practices of the female body towards the achievement of unhealthy ideals. Susan Bordo's much cited essay "Reading the Slender Body" brilliantly deconstructs the pathologized, individuated image that both medicine and media present us with—the woman who "succeeds" in achieving these ideals only to damage her own health and perhaps risk her life in the process. Bordo's analysis clearly shows the importance of seeing the "everyday-ness" of these disciplinary practices and how they inscribe on the surface (and increasingly the interior) of women's bodies the "bulimic personality" of contemporary American capitalist society. This society requires, at one and the same time, unrestrained consumption to achieve health and happiness and intense repression of desire and body boundaries to meet narrowly prescribed moral and cultural standards (Bordo, 1990).

Yet Bordo's analysis, along with those of many others who address this topic, leaves us with little, if any, indication of how women "read" and respond to—or perhaps even resist—these dominant ideals. We get little sense of the extent to which these dominant ideals may or may not be significant or predominant in women's identity construction and how this may shift over time and in different social contexts, as well as in relation to other aspects of the multiple-subject positions women hold (such as class, ethnicity, age, sexuality, regional identity, and so on).

Studying Health and Body Perceptions in Northwestern Ontario

These concerns were the points of departure for a research project that I conducted in northwestern Ontario between 1996 and 1999. Comparing the experiences of white working-class and middle-class women and men, I explored how ideas about health and the body are shaped and reshaped over time, as well as how identities of gender, class, sexuality, culture, region (in this case "northern-ness") are constituted within and through discourses on health and the body.[3] The decision to interview both women and men was in part motivated by my desire to "de-problematize" the female body, a problem that is evident in many current medico-scientific and feminist analyses.

In conducting this research, I used techniques of feminist oral history to elicit what Barbara Duden calls "bio-logies," or body stories, in order to bring into view the everyday processes and social relations through which ideas about health and the body are constituted and experienced.[4]

My research was carried out in the city of Thunder Bay, in northwestern Ontario, a community whose own identity is in many ways negotiated and liminal.[5] By "liminal," I mean it is at once northern (officially considered part of the provincial north), and yet not northern (being located only 50 kilometres from the American border). It is urban (having a population of some 120,000), and yet rural (being physically isolated from other large centres by at least a full day's drive in either direction). It is an important regional business and service centre, and yet, residents feel largely ignored and insignificant in provincial terms. Its population is culturally diverse, comprising a mix of various Northern and Eastern European roots, a significant First Nations population as well as recent migrants from Latin America and South East Asia, and yet conformity of style, speech, and even behaviour is valued and remarked upon. As several of the women interviewed noted, straying too far from the accepted norms of dress and appearance may meet with social sanctions such as public commentary or ridicule. Although the primary resource industries (such as the paper mills and grain elevators) are no longer as significant to the local economy as they once were, and even though women make up an increasingly large share of the city's labour force, the city maintains an image in the eyes of both residents and outsiders of being a "lunch-bucket" or "workingman's" town (Dunk, 1991).

Interviews were conducted with 40 women and men between the ages of 30 and 65. In choosing this age range, I anticipated that participants would be old enough to have a "history" of body experiences to reflect upon, and yet young enough to not be preoccupied with significant gerontological concerns. To address the dimension of social class, equal numbers of working-class and middle-class women and men were included. As Robert Crawford's research on working-class notions of health and white middle-class discourses on AIDS has suggested (Crawford, 1994), attentiveness to class enables a comparison of both gender and class discourses on the language and representation of health and the body, and the extent to which they are invoked in the constitution of identity. For working-class women, I expected that there might not be a distinctly positive association between the nature of work and body image. The exigencies of work, family, and limited income experienced by working-class women might be seen as antithetical to the possibility of "cultivating" the ideal female body promoted by popular cultural representations. My interest here was to examine whether working-class women define their health and body experiences in relation to the middle-class norms represented in popular culture and medico-scientific discourse on the "healthy" body, or whether alternative identities are constructed.

The 20 women interviewed ranged in age from 33 to 53, with a median age of 43. Sixteen of the women were currently married, one was living common-law, another was single, and two were divorced. All but five of the women had children or dependents living at home. Some of these children were in their late teens and early twenties; however, the women still thought of them as dependents financially, emotionally, and in terms of household labour. The working-class women's occupations included clerical work, grocery clerk, letter carrier, homemaker, babysitter, kitchen worker, union representative, and diploma nurses. The middle-class women's occupations included nurse administrators, lawyer, teacher, university professor, homemaker, small business owner/workers, and office administrator. Four of the women combined part-time work with primary childcare responsibilities, while the remainder were employed full-time, and most reported some additional responsibility for children or dependents. Nine of the women had more than one paid occupation—either a combination of part-time jobs, or a full-time job and a part-time job (such as union representative).

In broad terms, the interviews focused on the participants' past and current perceptions of health and embodiment with particular attention to the ways in which these have changed or remained stable through the course of their lives. Interviews explored the role of body image in the women's perceptions of health and well-being, construction of self and "other," and the significance attributed to popular culture, family socialization, employment, medical interactions, and other aspects of the social environment in shaping ideas about health and the body.

The interview schedule focused on four main themes: (1) background information on family, education, employment, and social class; (2) definitions of health; (3) gender, work, family, leisure, and their relationship to health and identity; and (4) ideas about body and body image, and their relationship to gender, work, family, health, and identity.

Defining Health and Healthiness

For the majority of the women interviewed, ideas about health and body image are intimately interlinked and have changed over their lives. For many, ideas about health and healthiness have evolved from a more conventional biomedical notion of health as the absence of disease (adhered to at an earlier age), to the assessment of well-being in more environmental or holistic terms. The women's notions of health discuss levels of physical energy, comfort in carrying out and balancing multiple roles, satisfaction with quality of work and family relations, and concerns about time for self and leisure.

When asked whether her idea of what it is to be healthy had always been the same, Carol, a 41-year-old university professor, responded this way: "No. I'd say now, getting older that . . . there is no doubt that my sense of health is becoming much less separate from how I look, and much more to do with how I feel." Laura, a 43-year-old nurse administrator and part-time graduate student, said, "Probably as I have grown older my expectations for being healthy have actually increased rather than decreased. . . . To me now, being healthy does not just mean being free of disease or not on any medication, but being in the best state I can be in, mentally and physically." Janet, also 43 and a teaching administrator, agreed that her notions of health had changed over time. As she notes: "I used to think before that you had to be like five foot five, 120 pounds [and] go to the gym every day. That was my image of what it was to be healthy. I think now it's more like how you feel on the inside. Mentally, as well as physically. The two kind of go together." Similarly, Debbie, a 44-year-old clerical worker, responded, "I don't think that I thought about stress when I was [younger]. I don't think that I thought about assessing my health I that way. It is different now."

The women generally evaluated their health in terms of coping with multiple roles and the quality of family relations.[6] In contrast to many of the men who discussed the importance of physical endurance and a perceived sense of strength when evaluating their appearance, several expressed a sentiment of being "overweight" even though they generally felt healthy.

Behaviours associated with staying healthy had also changed over the course of the women's lives. Many indicated that they did little consciously to stay healthy when they were younger, but now were much more conscientious about eating well, getting regular exercise, and rest. For most, time was the more important constraint to achieving optimal health. They cited the difficulties of finding time for themselves (for leisure or exercise) while juggling multiple work and family roles.

Reflecting on her past and present health practices in response to my question "Do you consider yourself a healthy person?" Mildred, a 49-year-old co-owner/worker in a small family business, replied:

> *Sigh*. . . well, I would like to think I was. There certainly was a time when I had a lot more time to spend on getting myself that way, [such as] all the time [we were] raising the children and everything. I still make all our own bread and pastries, cookies and those things. I think that counts. I buy meat from the farmer that I know doesn't use steroids or penicillin. We raise our own chickens, eggs and stuff like that. I try working at it. I try to get exercise. Years ago I got tons more than I do now. I would have to say the working thing has just cramped my style considerably. I'm overweight, of course, and I don't get as much exercise as I should. Years ago when I was home I would walk for three hours a day. I love walking. I love being outside. I also feel at times, I've narrowed it down, I know what it is—it is nature deprivation. I feel nature deprivation if I don't get outside enough—you know, the less you do [exercise], the less you can do it. You get home and you're tired. You don't feel like going out.

I asked Mildred, "When would you say you used to do more? Was it when your kids were younger?" and she replied:

> Yeah. And I babysat, and I was at home. We had the business out of the house for a while too. When we started doing it [establishing the business], the transitional period, I could just be out more. It was easier to do it. . . . If I could afford somebody full time [to help with the business], I would be out of there in a flash. I would be home feeding the chickens and raising the pigs and things like that. Because that's what I enjoy doing.

Several of the women indicated that they didn't have a sense of entitlement of "time off." Women with younger children generally built their own leisure pursuits around activities that could include their children. Terri, a professional who had been very athletic in her youth, expressed frustration at trying to get a "workout" for herself while doing activities with her children. Having recognized that the desires to spend time with her children and to exercise for herself were working at cross-purposes, she temporarily "resolved" the issue by putting her own needs on hold until the children were older.

Class differences were also apparent in the women's definitions of health over the life course. Many middle-class women identified with current "healthiest" discourses that emphasize health as an individual phenomenon, and blamed themselves for failing to live up to the ideals of dietary and exercise regimes promoted in public health rhetoric. Ironically, even those who were professionals identified structural elements such as the exigencies of the double-work day and an unequal division of labour in the home as the major impediments to self-care. Working-class women tended to evaluate and discuss their own health in relational, rather than individual, terms. They assessed their own health in terms of their self-sufficiency and their ability to serve others (their family members, for example).

In general, the women were attentive to, and aware of, body image issues through the course of their lives, yet the importance and meanings attributed to them had changed significantly for most.[7] Many had previously dieted and monitored their weight carefully as adolescents and in their early twenties, yet most had abandoned these practices, either due to a sense of frustration with their lack of success, or emptily as a form of resistance to what they perceived as inappropriate medicalization and monitoring of their bodies by parents, doctors, partners, and others.

Laura, a 50-year-old clothing store owner and mother of two grown children, described how her ideas of body image and being healthy have changed over time in this way:

> I guess I was, as a baby boomer, probably on the leading edge of anorexia and bulimia and all that kind of stuff. I never had bulimia, but I'm sure I was one of the first anorexics [and this] was never diagnosed. Just from trying to starve yourself because society said you should be a thin person. If you weren't [thin] you felt you should be, so you tried anything to get there. That has changed for me drastically. I'm not unhealthy and I'm certain my body image is no longer an issue [for me]. If somebody doesn't like me because I am heavy that's their problem, not mine.

When I asked Laura whether there was something specific that changed her notion of health, she said:

> I think it was just finding out just after having my son that I couldn't starve myself every day. And why the heck should I have to—to be somebody else's image of what I should be? As long as I'm a good mother and a good person. Being in the [business of running a clothing store for large women] has certainly helped that too . . . if you're clean and your makeup's on and your clothes are nice and you keep yourself looking good, that's what people see.

Most of the women talked about having multiple body images. They emphasized the fluidity and contextualness of their own perceptions. Body image was different at home and in public spaces, in the company of friends and with strangers, at times of healthiness and during illness episodes, and often between work and leisure. Karen, a 33-year-old health administrator, described body image in the following way: "It's how you perceive yourself. How I perceive myself is not just my physical being. It's whether I am confident in a certain situation of feeling secure. It does change if you are in a situation that you don't feel as confident [in]."

Debbie pointed out that her consciousness of body image is affected by whether she is in the company of women or of men. She states: "I think I am more aware of what I look like and how I am perceived when I am with a bunch of women. Men are, even though you like to think men are fussy—they aren't fussy, they don't care. Women are much more critical. I think I worry about it more when I am with a bunch of women." Marg, a 45-year-old office administrator similarly observed: "I think it's different in different settings. . . . Okay, for instance when I'm dressed nicer and I look good. When I'm dressed in sloppy clothes around the house . . . I don't feel too powerful."

For many of the women, different body images were also related to the quality of relationships with their partners or their peer group. Rita, a 43-year-old small business owner who had divorced and remarried, described a very different sense of body image with her new partner whom she described as "comfortable with me as I am." Laura indicated that comfort with her body shifts in relation to contact with a group of female friends who are extremely physically active and concerned about appearance. Louise, a 38-year-old homemaker with three school-age children, described herself as a "borderline" anorexic in adolescence, but had overcome this during her early twenties. She found the weigh-in and fundus[8] measurement during routine pregnancy checkups very anxiety-provoking; it created for her a negative shift in body image that has taken many years to resolve.

The women's notions of body image were fluid and changing over time. Often defined as body shape or physical appearance in adolescence, for some, body image expanded to a larger sense of "presentation of self" (Goffman, 1959) as they aged. For professional and business women this incorporated not only appearance and styles of dress—or "dressing for success" as many described it—but also a sense of self-confidence, a feeling of accomplishment or skill in their field of work, and an improved sense of healthiness over time. For many of the working-class women, being successfully relied upon by others and being seen as coping, were important aspects of the assessment of body image. Some of their responses expressed a kind of idealization of a "northern" (almost akin to pioneer) women for whom strength and endurance were key dimensions of a positive body image.

Consciousness of the body was also described as situational and, again, varied along class and gender lines. Many of the women indicated that they were not conscious of their bodies on an ongoing basis. A few women who were particularly concerned about weight described their bodies as constraints (as the opening quote from Blaxter suggests), which they had difficulty transcending. However, most others indicated that body consciousness was situational, brought on by a particularly serious or sudden illness episode, by concerns about what to wear to a particular social event (for example, a class reunion or family gathering), by travelling to a large urban centre like Toronto where consciousness and monitoring of appearance seems more evident, or by shopping for clothing—especially the painful annual new bathing suit ritual. For many of the women, body consciousness and anxiety were also heightened by medical concerns and encounters (even routine checkups) that frequently raised concerns about unhealthy weight, independent of a women's own assessment of her state of healthiness.

Media and Other Representations of the Female Body and Health

Responses to predominant media images of the idealized female body had also changed in the women's reflections. They differed on opinions about the extent to which ideals of slenderness and feminine beauty were more predominant or widely circulated today than when they were younger. Many remembered routinely reading or "studying" the teen magazines of their youth, such as *Seventeen,* often with a sense of regret that the products and fashions advertised were not readily available in the North. While many continue to be avid magazine readers, the choice of magazines has changed from teen magazines to ones such as *Canadian Living* or *Woman's Day,* and the appeal cited was as much the recipes and advice columns as the clothing and fashion images.

When asked how they respond to or whether they "see" themselves in the images of women presented in these magazines, most indicated a strong sense that the images were largely unreal and sometimes almost amusing in their absurdity. A few noted an increased representation of "real" or average women in the magazines in recent years. They found this trend appealing and felt they paid much more attention to these ads or pictures because they could get a sense of how clothes might really look on them.

Medical information and advice columns in the magazines were frequently read by the women and taken much more seriously than fashion layouts. Many of the women found these columns to be an important source of personal and family health information and said they discussed them with friends. But even this information could be dismissed or resisted if the women didn't feel that it matched their own perspective.

Body and body image were seldom discussed in individual terms, but rather almost always constituted in relational terms. Constructing the self was done in relation to a constructed "other." Thus, norms or expectations of femininity were contrasted with norms of masculinity (and vice versa); middle-class concerns about presentation of self and success were presented as opposite to stereotypes of a working class lack of care or lack of discipline; and working-class concerns about the lack of time and money to pursue idealized health and body images were construed in relation to the presumption of generic middle-class investment in, and resources available to, achieve those ideals.

Contemporary senses of health and body image were referential to past notions and ideals and often made efforts to present an integrated or coherent history of embodiment. In some instances, where particularly troubling experiences of violence—such as sexual abuse or social stigma—were part of a woman's past, her efforts at providing an integrated narrative were contradictory or incomplete. The strong resonances of past experiences showed through the narrative surface, giving a texture much like the "palimpsest" that Winterson's opening quote to this chapter so eloquently describes.

These observations suggest that women's ideas about body and body image are fluid and contextual. They are shaped and re-shaped over time and placed in relation to other aspects of identity and subjectivity. Ideas about the body are interlinked with notions of health and well-being and evolve in relation to both individual and collective experiences. Science, medicine, and media may play an important role in shaping and normalizing our ideals and behaviours—particularly in our younger years—but they are often ignored or actively resisted when the images they present us with fail to match our own evolving sense of health or well-being. Thus the analysis and incorporation of body and embodiment in social theory and feminist research must attend to the fluidity and contextualness of women's experiences, and explore their constitution and reconstitution in specific times and places with particular attention to the quality and nature of the social relations in which they are shaped.

Notes

1. See, for example, Kathy Davis, ed., *Embodied Practices: Feminist Perspectives on the Body* (London: Sage, 1997); Frigga Haug, ed., *Female Sexualization* (London: Verso, 1987); Nicole Sault, ed., *Many Mirrors: Body Image and Social Relations* (New Brunswick, NJ: Rutgers University Press, 1994); and Sue Scott and David Morgan, ed., *Body Matters* (London: The Falmer Press, 1993).
2. See Diane Barthel, *Putting on Appearance* (Philadelphia: Temple University Press, 1988); Susan Bordo, "Reading the Slender Body," in Mary Jacobus and Evelyn Fox Keller, eds., *Body/Politics: Women and the Discourses of Science* (London: Routledge, 1990), 83–112; and Susie Orbach, *Hunger Strike: The Anorectic's Struggle as a Metaphor for Our Age* (New York: W.W. Northon, 1986).
3. This paper is drawn from portions of my PhD dissertation, "Contours of Everyday Life: Reflections on Health and Embodiment over the Life Course" (University of Warwick, UK, 2000). To study the ways in which ideas about health and embodiment change over the life course, I conducted in-depth interviews with 40 working- and middle-class women and men in northwestern Ontario. Interviewing both women and men allowed a close comparison of the similarities and differences of women and men's experiences of health and embodiment,

and the extent to which these were a potential source of gender consciousness. All but two of the respondents were "white." I use the term "white" here as a social construct following Richard Dyer, *White* (London: Routledge, 1997) and Ruth Frankenberg, *White Women, Race Matters: The Social Construction of Whiteness* (Minneapolis: University of Minnesota Press, 1993). While the research sample reflects the ethnic diversity of the region, as other analysts have noted, the primary distinction recognized by local residents is that between First Nations, or Aboriginal Peoples, and "whites." See, for example, Thomas Dunk, *It's a Working Man's Town: Male Working-Class Culture in Northwestern Ontario* (Montreal: McGill-Queen's University Press, 1991). The dissertation includes an analysis of the terrain and interpretations of "whiteness" as it is both visible and invisible in the participants' narratives of "healthy selves" and "unhealthy others."

4. Barbara Duden, *The Woman Beneath the Skin*, uses the concept of "bio-logies" or body stories to describe the changing understandings and representations of the body evident in the narratives given to eighteenth-century German physician Johannes Storch by his clients over the course of his professional relationship with them.
5. Liminality is valued by postmodern researchers because studying liminal or "in-between" categories highlights the ways in which differences are marked by people and given "presence" or value within a particular culture or subculture. See Sonya Andermahr, Terry Lovell, and Carol Wolkowitz, *A Concise Glossary of Feminist Theory* (London: Arnold, 1997) for a discussion of the use of liminality in postmodern research.
6. A similar point is raised by Nickie Charles and Vivienne Walters in their analysis of age and gender in South Wales' women's accounts of health. They point out, "Women's accounts demonstrate that their experiences and explanations of health, while showing certain commonalities, vary with age and stage in the life cycle and are shaped by wider structural changes in employment patterns and gendered divisions of labour. Thus structural and cultural changes shape the discourses that women call upon when talking about health and illness. . . ." "Age and Gender in Women's Accounts of Their Health: Interviews with Women in South Wales," *Sociology of Health and Illness* 20 (1998): 348.
7. By contrast, many of the men found it much harder to reflect on "body" history and required more prompting to make connections between a sense of embodiment and specific activities or instances of their youth. Most often, they talked about embodiment in terms of success or endurance in sporting activities, the ability to do physical labour (especially for working-class men) or in relation to illness of self or appearance norms. Those who did were primarily middle-class men who discussed presentation of self in terms of their leadership image at work and their embodiment of corporate imagery.
8. The fundus is the top of the uterus. Its changing position is measured throughout the pregnancy to assess the growth and position of the baby.

References

Blaxter, M. 1983. "The Causes of Disease: Women Talking," *Social Science and Medicine* 17: 69.

Bordo, S. 1990. "Reading the Slender Body," in M. Jacobus and E. Fox Keller, eds., *Body/Politics: Women and the Discourses of Science*, pp. 83–112. London: Routledge.

Charles, N., and V. Walters. 1998. "Age and Gender in Women's Accounts of Their Health: Interviews with Women in South Wales," *Sociology of Health and Illness* 20: 348.

Crawford, R. 1994. "The Boundaries of the Self and the Unhealthy Other: Reflections on Health, Culture and AIDS," *Social Science and Medicine* 38: 1347–65.

Dunk, T. 1991. *It's a Working Man's Town: Male Working-Class Culture in Northwestern Ontario*. Montreal: McGill-Queen's University Press.

Goffman, E. 1959. *The Presentation of Self in Everyday Life*. Garden City, NY: Doubleday.

Winterson, J. 1994. *Written on the Body*. New York: Vintage Books.

Chapter 16

Overview

When we read about cosmetic surgery in the media, the "patient" is often presumed to be a woman, seeking to look younger, sexier, or thinner. However, Michael Atkinson interviewed 44 men who opted to use their surgery to change their appearance. In some ways, this seems a counter-normative choice—aren't women supposed to be the ones who worry about looking old or unattractive?

Atkinson suggests, however, that men seek out these procedures in order to shore up their sense of masculinity—to acquire a bodily appearance that is visually congruent with gendered ideals of strength, confidence, and vigour. Atkinson situates these surgeries within the context of a "crisis" of masculinity, as he argues that men find it increasingly difficult to live up to what they believe they ought to be, do, or look like as men. He uses the conceptual tools of figurational sociology to present cosmetic surgery as a means through which men attempt to assert control over their bodies and their social lives in a world in which the achievement of masculine ideals constantly threatens to elude them.

Exploring Male Femininity in the "Crisis": Men and Cosmetic Surgery

Michael Atkinson

Cosmetic Surgery, Figurational Sociology

Since the year 2000, men's cosmetic surgery practices in Canada have mushroomed. Estimates suggest that over 10,000 Canadian men have received aesthetic surgery in the past 10 years, with participation rates rising sharply in the past three years alone—a 20 per cent increase in participation (Medicard, 2004). The collective willingness of men to experiment with surgical intervention in the pursuit of more youthful, vibrant, attractive, and healthy-looking bodies (especially around the face) perhaps signifies that these men's collective sensibilities, or habituses, are shifting; stated differently, it may symbolize how men are presently negotiating traditional parameters of "established" (Elias and Scotson, 1965) masculine identity performance to include cosmetic bodywork.

While there has been a reinvigorated interest in masculinity research (see Pronger, 2002), there is a paucity of extended, standpoint investigations of men's experiences with aesthetics and body modification that do not attempt to theoretically dissect the practice from either feminist or pro-feminist viewpoints—save, perhaps, for the literature on men and masculinity in the sociology of sport (Young, 2003), or within the burgeoning literature on gay/metro masculinities (Atkinson, 2003). The lack of theoretically innovative research symbolizes, as Connell (2005) suggests, a general tendency to view masculinity as a singularly constructed and unproblematic gender identity. Masculinity still tends to be framed by gender researchers along very narrow conceptual lines, as Grogan and Richards (2002) illustrate. Dominant constructions of masculinity are either interpreted as rigidly hegemonic/traditional (Garlick, 2004), or drastically alternative and deeply marginalized (Hise, 2004). Neither of these polar positions accurately captures how clusters of men often wrestle with and negotiate established constructions of masculinity in novel ways. . . .

. . . There is a noticeable dearth of empirical investigations of men's experiences with aesthetic body modification (Davis, 2002). Few have studied, for instance, how "everyday" men engage bodywork in order to appear "regular," or have responded to broader cultural fluctuations in masculine hegemony with scripted body ritual. Fewer still have inspected how men play with innovative forms of aesthetic masculinity (i.e., beyond the context of "gym work," tattooing or other stereotypically masculine body projects) to bolster their *self-perceived* social power in a context of felt crisis.

To explore how selected men in Canada fashion cosmetic surgery as a technique of bodywork, Elias's (1978) figurational analysis of social power balances and control mechanisms serves as a departure point.

In *What Is Sociology?* (1978), Elias outlined three basic social controls that are interwoven into figurational power dynamics. For Elias (1978, 2002), members of social figurations enact power and control:

1. over nature through technological advancements
2. over groups of individuals through institutional processes
3. over drives and desires through learned mechanisms of self-restraint

Elias argues in *The Civilising Process* (2002) that the collective history of Western nations reveals a common tendency for complex groups of densely interdependent agents (what he referred to as *figurations*) to rely upon the third source of social control over the long term. That is, while court-centred monarchies and then nation-states relied upon the threat of force as a main tool of control over citizenries, the course of civilizing processes paved the way (although unintentionally) for the development of self-restraint as the dominant social control mechanism. Of course, as a full range of gender theorists point out, the social groups responsible for dominating others first by force and later via codes of mannered conduct have been, over time, controlled by men.

Figurational sociologists have argued that a central task in civilizing processes has been to "tame" masculinity (Dunning, 1999). Indeed, the history of social discipline and punishment illustrates how aggressiveness and psychological/ affective orientations (typically described as "masculine" or attributed as essential characteristics of men) were transformed as complex social institutions took form. In such a theoretical meta-narrative, struggles for power and control in figurational life progress from hand-to-hand combat to symbolic power plays between men for knowledge, authority, and physical distinction enacted across institutional fields (Elias, 1978, 1996, 2002). Elias illustrates, for example, in *The Germans* (1996) that as physical violence becomes less pervasive in social life and inner restraint increases in importance as a means of revealing one's distinction (*qua* power) to others, the institutional control of productive forces and knowledge dissemination became more central. As Brinkgreve (2004) argues, these mechanisms of control tend to be dominated by men in Western figurations.

The emerging literature on contemporary masculine politics in Western nations like Canada suggests that the institutional sources of men's social control have been fractured, both materially and symbolically, by ongoing structural and cultural change (or what Elias, [2002] called "sociogenesis;" see also Mosse, 1996). Horrocks (1994) outlines how movements toward gender equality in families, educational sites, workplaces, religious institutions, and a full host of other institutional sites calls into question the very basis of masculine hegemony. As an extension of what Elias (2002) referred to as the "parliamentarisation of conflict," gender stratification and related power imbalances have been systematically disputed through highly institutionalized, formal, and rationalized rule systems. The splintering and redistribution of masculine control across institutional landscapes has spurred on a "crisis of masculinity," in that men are no longer certain about what constitutes men's roles and statuses, or how to enact properly gendered masculine identities (Whitehead, 2002). . . .

In sum, in this article I read the crisis of masculinity not as a cultural truth per se, but as a conceptual backdrop for interpreting why men may be selecting and inscribing aesthetic bodywork as an innovative technique of "male-feminine" biopower. Cosmetic surgery is configured by the men in this study as a tool for "re-establishing" a sense of empowered masculine identity in figurational settings that they perceive to be saturated by gender doubt, anxiety, and contest. In figurational terms, surgically altering the flesh is a return to a very basic technique of social control in a context of cultural uncertainty. Men, as de Certeau (1984) might predict, seize control over their bodies in order to "reframe" (White et al., 1995) their masculinity as revitalized and empowered. With diffuse ideological and material pressures to consume, commodify the body and perform scripted identity work through highly rationalized physical displays (Crewe, 2003; Featherstone, 2000), it is understandable why, at this historical juncture, Canadian men are finding "collective solutions" to common "status problems" (Cohen, 1955) via cosmetic surgery. The empirical evidence presented in this study suggests a pervasive but tactically managed "cultural victim" mentality among the men, and also why their habituses (Elias, 1991, 1996, 2002) may be underpinned by a sense of doubt regarding the concept of established masculine dominance.

Method

Although there exists a rather full literature on women's experiences with cosmetic surgery in North America and elsewhere (Sarwer and Crerand, 2004), incredibly few body theorists have empirically addressed men's embodied interpretations of the cosmetic surgery process (Davis, 2002). My own involvement with cosmetically altered men commenced when I first encountered a surgery patient named "Les" in southern Ontario. Les exercised in a local health club I attended, and learned about my previous research on tattooing. During the middle of a workout one day, Les approached me and inquired as to whether I had studied cosmetic surgery. Following a brief conversation, he disclosed his experiences with three cosmetic procedures: Botox injections, liposuction, and an eye lift procedure. Over the course of time I pondered Les's confessional narrative to me, and considered the viability of a study of men and cosmetic surgery. By the autumn of 2004, I sought out additional patients in the southern Ontario area (e.g., Toronto, Hamilton, Mississauga, London, and Burlington) for interviews.

Through Les's sponsorship, I encountered and subsequently interviewed 44 cosmetic surgery patients in southern Ontario. I asked Les to provide the names of several other patients he knew personally. At the time of his interview, Les offered five names of fellow patients in the city of Hamilton alone. Rather surprisingly, all of the patients agreed to be interviewed for the study. Subsequently, each patient provided the names of, on average, 2–4 other male patients, and the sample expanded progressively. . . .

Interviews with the men were conducted in a variety of settings such as my office at the university, a coffee shop, a local park, or a restaurant. In all but a few instances, I used a tape-recorder during the interviews and field notes were taken both during and after the interviews. Notes were then (within several hours or, at maximum, one day) transcribed onto computer files and filled in considerably as I conceptually analyzed the texts in a constant comparison process. With further regard to data analysis, the interview texts were coded holistically as conceptual types of narratives about the experience of body modification, and then open-coded separately and comparatively around emergent themes related to masculinity and its embodied performance. It is important to note that theoretical lines of inquiry related to the crisis of masculinity were neither prefigured into the interview schedule, nor crudely fitted onto the emergent data. Rather, the theoretical reading of crises in the men's narratives reflected how men, themselves, told stories about and ascribed meaning to their cosmetic surgery experiences. The narrative theme of "crisis" I outline in the article is one of the most consistently present themes, but not the only one woven across the men's narratives. . . .

Most of the discussions started with a basic request: "So, tell me about your cosmetic surgery." I wanted the men to craft narratives from the interpretive standpoints they wished, and from starting points they found to be sensible. Over the course of time, I tactically discussed my own personal doubts, interpretations, and scepticisms about cosmetic surgery, as a means of encouraging participants to share the more intimate details of their personal narratives. As a "bad cop" technique of narrative elicitation (Hathaway and Atkinson, 2003), I challenged the basis of cosmetic surgery as "appropriate" masculine bodywork. Here, I wanted to inspect how practitioners justify and tell stories about cosmetic surgery to outsiders. By engaging such interactive techniques with respondents I wanted our conversations to probe motivations for cosmetic surgery, emotional accounts of its performance, and elements of patients' social biographies.

Men, Cosmetics, and the Triad of Social Controls

> I looked at my neck droop for so long before I mustered up enough courage to have it fixed. . . . I look like I'm 20 again; well, at least around my neck. At least no one calls me "turkey neck" anymore . . . you have no idea how many times I wore a turtleneck sweater to avoid derision. I can't buy enough low-collared shirts to show off my work. (Tom, facelift)

Tom is a 46-year-old advertisement executive living in Toronto. Although one may never glance at him and suspect his "work," he is proud of his body for the first time in his life and exudes comfort in his "new skin." Tom's cosmetic surgery narrative is a typical one: he tells a story about cosmetic surgery as a pathway toward body enhancement, as a vehicle for fitting in, and as a technique for building self-esteem. As part of his narrative, Tom expresses a clear understanding of his own interest in body enhancement; he simply wants to be present, recognized, and very "commonly" male.

Among the select few men who choose to tell stories about cosmetic surgery, a common narrative theme similar to Tom's underpins their accounts. For these men, transforming the body into something socially "common" (and therefore something to show off as "common") motivates their aesthetic projects. The act of cosmetic surgery becomes a process of gaining power over others' negative stares and comments. Cosmetic surgery is not sought out by the men I interviewed egomaniacally, nor is it intended to draw the social gaze to the surgically enhanced flesh. The intervention is intended to achieve the opposite: to allow the individual to fade into a crowd as a "regular guy." With few exceptions, such as a hair transplant, collagen/Botox injections, or muscle implants, the most common forms of surgery men undertake physically and symbolically "remove" unwanted, stigmatizing features from their bodies. A liposuction patient named Patrick (37) described:

> There's a comfort every day in walking out of your house and knowing that people won't be looking at your gut when you pass by . . . when people ignore you, it's because you are the average person, the nondescript regular guy. I was a fat kid, and then a fat man, and all I ever wanted was to look regular. Yeah, when people ignore you, wow, what a great feeling.

Like many of the men interviewed in this research, Patrick's cosmetic surgery stories are replete with the idea of feeling "average," of looking "regular," and not being marginalized. The ability to do so, these patients articulate, is an act of biopower for them; a power to negotiate a portion of their public image through non-traditionally masculine work. As discussed below, however, the sense of being average deeply resonates with very traditional images and ideologies of established masculinity in Canada.

Physicality, Violence, and Masculine Bodies

In a poignant analysis of the gendering of power in Western figurations, Brinkgreve (2004) comments that men's social control has been challenged along a number of lines, especially men's ability to wield unfettered dominance as public practice. In adopting a figurational perspective, she argues that men's agency for expressing aggressive affect has been curtailed over the course of long-term civilizing processes, or showcased in contained manners in social forms like sport or theatre (see also Atkinson and Young, forthcoming). The massive cultural popularity among men of violent sports in Canada like ice hockey, lacrosse, football, and rugby, argue Atkinson and Young (forthcoming), is proportionately related to the degree to which aggression and violence are taboo in other social spheres. . . .

Yet some men, contends Godenzi (1999), interpret the ongoing and unfinished civilizing "attack" on aggression as a challenge to the very foundation of established masculinity. Labre (2002) examines how groups of men perceive the (external) restraint of men or male bodies as a critical condemnation of and attempt to control the very basis of the male psyche and/or the male social order. In perceiving masculinity as threatened through diffuse anti-authoritarian (read *anti-male*) social doctrines and politically correct "sensitivity policies," some Canadian men feel encouraged to reflexively engage in forms of bodywork to shore up their traditionally masculine images in socially "non-threatening" ways. The cosmetic surgery patient Allan (41) explains:

> I'd never looked like a handsome guy until I underwent the hair transplantation, you know. . . . I'm like every other man who's lived with teasing about being bald so young. Women find the look totally unsexy and not very strong looking, but all the same attack me as a chauvinist, just because I am male. I hear that all the time at work. If I became angry about being teased for my baldness, I would be called hothead or the Alpha male trying to vent his anger. What a joke. I could never win then, and now the only way people leave you alone and accept you now [as a man], is if you look good without "acting out" as a guy.

As Allan and like-minded peers explain, men may find novel forms of social power by reclaiming their "threatened" bodies and repackaging them as aesthetically desirable (i.e., as emotionally pacified). They tactically align with "new" or "metrosexual" images of "male femininity" through cosmetic surgery as a technique for illustrating their consent to late modern social codes about men (Atkinson, 2006). By drawing on current cultural preferences in Canada for the fit, toned, groomed, and non-aggressive body (Niedzviecki, 2004), the men, at least from their interpretive standpoints, negotiate their way through the contemporary crisis of masculinity.

For many of the men I interviewed, exploring one or another form of cosmetic surgery displays a willingness to submit the body to others. The late modern Canadian man "gives" his body to a corporeal professional such as a surgeon to be re-worked in stereotypically feminine ways; in the process, he acknowledges a central deficiency with his body. It is both an admission of weakness (i.e., the failure to physically live up to masculine cultural expectations) and a moral gesture of the desire for self-improvement. Such a "confessional" practice finds grounding not only in one's desire to explore masculinity in novel but power-building ways, but also in a traditional Canadian middle-class aesthetic (see White et al., 1995) that targets bodies as sites of strict monitoring and disciplining. Byron (28) comments:

> I haven't spoken to a lot of people about the face peel, because I'm so young and the reaction would probably be seriously negative. But the women I've told react in a similar way; they congratulate me for my body care. Some say it makes me sound more gentle and sensitive, and into looking beautiful. . . . I should have done this years ago. At this point in my life, I have no problem admitting I need help to be as attractive as possible, especially if I get something [accolades] out of it . . . people, at least from my perspective, appreciate a body that is maintained and controlled. A "tight" body communicates

> that I care about myself, and probably take care of things in my life in general.

. . . Men's involvement in cosmetic surgery, especially invasive and painful forms, might be configured as an ironically self-aggressive response to cultural stereotypes linking masculinity and violence. Davis (2002) has argued that acts of cosmetic surgery are implicitly self-violent. Yet, as noted elsewhere (Atkinson, 2006), involvement in painful forms of body modification can be (re)interpreted by men as a process of masculine character-building (i.e., as part of one's ability to withstand painful body ordeals with a quiet resolve) and a hyperbolically masculine solution to problems of cultural doubt. Kevin (39) suggests:

> When the doctor stripped away the layers of fat from around my waist, he removed 30 years of anguish from my soul. I'd always been the fat outsider, the little boy who never quite made the cut for anything. Being inside a body that is a gelatinous prison kills a tiny piece of you every moment of your life. . . . When I woke up after the surgery and looked down, I felt strong and confident as a man should. I could, never ever in my life, speak to anyone about how much being heavy hurt me emotionally, and now I don't have to. . . . Surgery is the best psychotherapy offered on the market. You have to go through hell and the pain [of surgery] to come out on top. Being beaten up through surgery is temporary, but being beaten up socially can last a lifetime.

Kevin's perspective teaches us that the current boom in Canadian men's cosmetic surgery might be, at least in part, viewed as an indicator of the cultural imperative for these men to engage in cosmetic, self-abusive forms of body work.

Institutional Control and Masculine Bodies

Although marked gaps continue to exist between the genders in relation to established-outsider power balances within most institutions, the men interviewed in this study believe their position as established authority figures has been dislodged by women's participation in the economic and political spheres. When telling stories about motivations underpinning cosmetic procedures, nearly three-quarters (74 per cent) of the men interviewed talked about feeling threatened at work by younger, smarter, and healthier women—especially in image-oriented business environments that equate outward appeal with intellectual competency and moral worth. It seems that as women have secured preliminary inroads to power sources in Western cultures like Canada, some men become rather fear-oriented in their disposition. For figurational sociologists, the sociogenic shifts in work patterns and relationships may impact men's habituses and corresponding body regimens. Peter (54) teaches us:

> Our company hired three new managers last year, and two of them didn't look any older than 25. What makes it worse is that they are well-spoken, bright, charming women who are gorgeous. So there is me, an ageing guy in a changing business environment who appears as if he's missed more nights of sleep than he should have. The superficiality of that realisation kind of makes you sick . . . but these people won't want me around unless I adapt, unless I change.

Important is that Peter's fear-orientation encourages him to consider self-aggressive cosmetic bodywork as a rational solution to his incompetence anxieties. Peter's masculinity, partly anchored in his ability to physically appear as competent in the workplace, as Sennett (1998) might predict, is reconciled through physical intervention. The outward ability to "look good" supersedes concerns about his ability to perform intellectually as a business administrator.

For other men, their ascribed social positions as established workers within dense chains of interdependency are threatened by subtle implications that their bodies appear decisively non-masculine, and therefore socially impotent. As Connell and Wood (2005) document through the study of masculine business cultures, one's sense of masculinity is often validated by peers' positive comments (or at least lack of mockery) regarding one's body image and style while "on the job." Therefore, when a man experiences persistent teasing about his body as lacking masculinity (i.e., the fat, unhealthy, powerless body), the passive ridicule may eventually manifest into a fear that others view him as inadequate socially. A man adopting such an interpretive mindset associates his peers' lack of public acknowledgement of him as a business "expert" as an indicator of their collective interpretation of his deficient body image. Andrew (33) explains:

> With my job, I don't have time to work out two or three hours a day, and I have to eat most meals on the run . . . and most of it is not healthy. And, it's hard to lose weight, so the liposuction gave a little kick-start to the process. Now I'm not the office fat guy everyone pokes fun at and ignores. People listen to me and consider my opinions on practically everything. No one looks at a fat guy and says, there's a real go-getter . . . they say the opposite, he's lazy, unmotivated and someone worth firing.

Andrew's cosmetic surgery narrative is filled with self-effacing accounts of his "bigness" and correlated social inferiority. For him, cosmetic surgery is an act of masculine "re-establishment," and a self-directed technique of threat management. Andrew is not concerned with his body as a potential health risk to him, but as a social symbol of inferiority. For men like Andrew, surgery is a more rational and controlled response to body problems than the styles of self-starvation among young men described by Braun et al. (1999). Aesthetic surgery is, then, a civilized and self-restrained response to long-term emotional distress.

The men who describe risk or threat at work as a motivator for cosmetic surgery strategically employ classic techniques of neutralization (Sykes and Matza, 1956) to account for their body projects. When interviewed and challenged about the source of their concerns at work, and the perceived lack of control experienced in the workplace, men typically respond by arguing that cosmetic bodywork is neither morally problematic nor physically dangerous. Further still, they highlight how the degree to which they are willing to sacrifice their bodies to look masculine jibes with a sense of worth and personal dedication to succeed—once more, their clearly habituated middle-class aesthetic. Buttressing these accounts is a stereotypically Western, consumeristic, and present-centred mentality, in that the solution to their lack of work control must be immediate and discoverable in a commodity/service form. Derrick, a 52-year-old marketing expert who regularly receives Botox and microdermabrasion treatments, says:

> I can't wait another 20 years to take action. I need to be a man who walks into the room and no one says, "Damn, he looks tired." If that continues to happen, I'll be out the door. I could have experimented with herbal remedies, creams or lotions to erase the years from my face, but it might take years, if it even works. Why wait when I can have better results from a doctor in only one day?

For Derrick, any risk or potential long-term effects of the procedures is secondary to the immediate gains received from medical intervention. The means–end, here-and-now mentality is directly reflective of the commodified and highly rationalized manner by which people come to approach bodies (and body problems) in "civilized" figurations (Elias, 2002). Any service that cures his problems of masculinity is thus justified as worthwhile, particularly when the service may be purchased from a qualified medical professional with celerity and precision.

What the above narratives underscore is the process by which men come to frame and reframe their bodies/identities as innovatively "male feminine" through surgical intervention. For the men in the current sample, actively responding to a perceived control threat through traditionally feminine bodywork is strategically interpreted as a very masculine endeavour: as a manoeuvre designed to make them appear culturally invested in new social constructions of masculinity. Surgery is, then, configured as a technique of biopower and control as it helps men respond to the fear of the masculinity crisis "head on" (Sargent, 2000) without resorting to "uncivilized" types of male aggression. Resonant with White et al.'s (1995) description of how male athletes reframe the injury process as a silent testing ground of masculine character-building, cosmetic surgery patients often tell stories about how their willingness to endure painfully invasive surgeries re-establishes their ability to meet social threats with "modern" masculine resolve.

Knowledge Production and Masculine Bodies

Compounding the threat some men perceive to exist regarding their masculinity in the workplace and across institutional settings is the type of work men are performing and the lack of spare-time exercise they undertake. With more men than ever in service or information-processing industries, the current generation of middle-class Canadian men are perhaps the most "stationary" workforce in the country's history. With decreasing amounts of spare-time, dietary habits revolving around high calorie fast-food choices, and leisure time dominated by consumption and inactivity, the physical toll on their bodies is evident (Critser, 2002). The post-industrial economy and associated lifestyles, it seems, are not easily reconciled with traditional images of the powerful, performing, and dominant male (Faludi, 1999).

Men interviewed in the present study express a sense of frustration with the form and content of their work responsibilities. For these men, ritually performing disembodied or virtual work (i.e., computer-facilitated) every day encourages a mind–body separation and neglect (Potts, 2002). Roger's (45) words are emblematic of the disaffection some men experience with their work:

> Sitting at a desk for 10 hours a day, then a car for 2, on then on your couch for 3 more wears your body down. Not to mention that my skin barely ever sees the light of day. At times, I can feel my face literally sagging because of my posture. . . . Looking in the mirror when you're 40 and having a road map for a face shouldn't be surprising. That's not who I am, that's not the image of my inside I want to project.

Men like Roger refuse to link marginalized external bodies with inner selves. Roger's body is further objectified and instrumentalized in the cosmetic surgery process, as he views his physical form as a site of much-needed management. Such an interpretation of the body only exacerbates existing fears about men's bodies as socially non-masculine. Cosmetic surgery provides a fast, efficient and highly rational way of alleviating these psychological strains and social discomfort:

> From the time I was 15 years old, I gained weight. I watched my diet and tried to work out, but I kept packing on inches. By the time I graduated school and started office work [computer programmer], it only grew worse . . . literally. Liposuction saved me from my self-hatred and the ridicule I faced from others. It's like having the clock re-set, or like a magic wand being waved and your troubles are gone. (Ray, 43)

Narratives about the role of cosmetic surgery in eliminating the unfortunate side effects of sedentary lifestyles are equally filled with constructions of the "male-feminine" body as "victimized" by established cultural expectations that men must labour for long hours. For men like Leo (37), a graphics designer living in Sarnia, Ontario, his "need" for facial surgeries results from a social pressure to work in support of his extended family:

> It's not like I can quit my job, or be there for less than 12 hours a day if I want to earn a living. No one pays me for sitting on my ass and doing nothing, they pay me for sitting on my ass and designing! If I choose not to work, I'm choosing not to feed my family. . . . We come from a very traditional Italian background, and it's not questioned that I'm the sole provider. . . . There's an unspoken rule that a man who cannot provide [for his family] isn't really a man.

For nearly 10 years, Leo's work habits have, in his terms, "weathered" his body. The three facial surgeries he has received temporarily remove the unwanted "marks of masculinity" from his appearance. Like other men, Leo configures his surgical preferences as a symbol of his dedication to looking his best, even in the context of incredible social/work pressure. Surgery, for Leo, is a decisively calculated male-feminine response to the social problems of "men's work" inherent in everyday life. . . .

. . . Alan, a 50-year-old office manager, re-directs criticism about "problematic" body practices back to the source:

> Everyone who picks on me for having my skin re-surfaced I bet never thinks about the million ways they change their bodies every day by going to the gym or eating low-carb, kill-yourself diets. . . . Don't call me less of a man because I do something to improve my looks that you are too afraid to do yourself.

Ironically, while men like Alan frequently position themselves as victims of work structures and expectations, through their cosmetic surgery storytelling they vehemently deny losing agency or possessing an inferior masculine status by undergoing the cosmetic surgery process. Quite predictably, as Davis (2002) mentions, these men never pathologize invasive body interventions as self-victimizing. Instead, they reframe surgical intervention as masculine character building. The courage associated with undergoing cosmetic surgery is highlighted as a powerfully decisive response to their identity/body problems.

Discussion

The men's narratives included in this article provide a conceptual composite of what a selection of men in Canada consider to be the "re-established" male-feminine body. It is a body that is at once firm, fit, flexible and fat-free, and open to exploring non-traditional (feminized) forms of bodywork in order to appear as innovatively male. But most importantly, as Frank (2003) notes, it is a body that exudes a cultural awareness and acceptance, a form articulating a deep sensibility toward changing roles, statuses and identities of "new men." The male's cosmetically altered body is one that is economically invested in the established cultural brand of masculinity (Schmitt, 2001). At the same time, it is an aesthetically contoured body validated by "muted" social recognition and kudos from admiring others. In these ways and others, the cosmetically altered body is interdependent with shifting constructions of masculinity and derives social meaning from extended social interaction across social settings.

Upon first glance, one might interpret the recent turn to cosmetic surgery among men as a stark indicator of shifting habituses among men. Indeed, the participation in quintessentially feminine forms of bodywork might indicate a fracturing of traditional notions of masculine physical manipulation and display. However, while men may respond to sociogenic change and contemporary ideological currents with heretofore non-traditional forms of masculine modification (Benwell, 2003), the narratives discussed in this article illustrate how men may tactically reframe cosmetic surgery along established masculine lines of power and authority.

First, involvement in cosmetic surgery reaffirms how bodies are employed by men as texts of strength, authority and power. The cosmetically altered male is readable as a signifier of power at a time when traditionally masculine bodies are perceived to be under siege (Niva, 1998). The surgically tucked, sharpened, minimized, or masculinized body provides men with a restored or re-established sense of social control—especially when other forms of institutional control and knowledge production are fragmented.

Second, the implicit risk-taking and objectification of the body in order to affirm one's sense of masculinity equally suggests how cosmetic surgery is incorporated into a wide range of men's "self-aggressive" or "risk-oriented" body practices. As Elias (2002) suggested, cosmetic instances of body performance are encoded communicative gestures of masculine distinction and ability to endure pain, further demarcating one's sense of social power and achieved cultural worth. The willingness to engage in surgery as self-aggressive risk may be, nevertheless, a civilizing turn in men's habituses. The social battle over gender power and the "fragmentation of masculinity" is turned inward and then inscribed on the skin rather than cast outward through aggressive physicality or dominance of others. Akin to Elias and Dunning's (1986) description of sport in the civilizing process, cosmetic surgery is a form of social mimesis for some men, as aesthetic alterations to the body become proxy representations of a social battle between genders.

Third, the men in the study comment on how cosmetic surgery tends to be quietly managed and privately experienced. At present, the men interviewed in this study do not openly discuss their cosmetic body projects with "outsiders." Men typically express how cosmetic surgery is not mainstream masculine performance in Canada, and how an air of stigma still hovers around the practice. The men perceive themselves as, in Goffman's (1963) terms, "discreditable deviants" whose predilections for surgical enhancement might jeopardize their status as "real" masculine men. In response, the men refrain from expressing emotion about the cosmetic surgery process and prefer to suffer the physical pains of surgery in silence. They do, however, relish the positive comments received regarding their "fresh"-looking faces, newly toned bodies, or magically reinvigorated senses of self.

Fourth, the widening use of cosmetic surgery among men may be a clever technique of masculine power attainment via collective image work. In a beauty/image-saturated and obsessed culture, these men glean significant attention and social accolades for their secretly "improved" physical forms. The beautification of men's bodies through cosmetic surgery might be considered as the poaching of a traditionally feminine technique of power attainment through the body, inasmuch as men are colonizing a site of social power traditionally dominated by women. . . .

. . . Men's narratives about cosmetic surgery allude to how established masculinity is reframed in innovative ways to reproduce traditional results: social power and distinction for men across the Canadian social landscape. In this way, the proverbial "song remains the same" for men, masculinity and social control.

References

Atkinson, M. 2003. *Tattooed: The Sociogenesis of a Body Art.* Toronto: University of Toronto Press.

Atkinson, M. 2006. "Masks of Masculinity: Cosmetic Surgery and (Sur)passing Strategies," in P. Vanni and D. Waskul, eds., *Body/Embodiment: Symbolic Interaction and the Sociology of the Body*, pp. 247–61. London: Ashgate.

Atkinson, M., and K. Young. forthcoming. *Sport, Deviance and Social Control.* Champaign, IL: Human Kinetics.

Benwell, B. 2003. *Masculinity and Men's Lifestyle Magazines.* Oxford: Blackwell.

Braun, D., S. Sunday, A. Huang, and K. Halmi. 1999. "More Males Seek Treatment for Eating Disorders," *International Journal of Eating Disorders* 25(4): 415–24.

Brinkgreve, C. 2004. "Elias in Gender Relations: The Changing Balance of Power Between the Sexes," in S. Loyal and S. Quilley, eds., *The Sociology of Norbert Elias*, pp. 67–88. Cambridge: Cambridge University Press.

Cohen. A. 1955. *Delinquent Boys: The Culture of the Gang.* New York: Free Press.

Connell, R. 2005. *Masculinities.* Berkeley, CA: University of California Press.

Connell, R., and J. Wood. 2005. "Globalisation and Business Masculinities," *Men and Masculinities* 7(4): 347–64.

Crewe, B. 2003. *Representing Men: Cultural Production and Producers in the Men's Magazine Market.* Oxford: Berg.

Critser, G. 2002. *Fat Land: How Americans Became the Fattest People in the World.* New York: Houghton Mifflin.

Davis, K. 2002. *Dubious Equalities and Embodied Differences: Cultural Studies and Cosmetic Surgery.* New York: Rowman and Littlefield.

de Certeau, M. 1984. *The Practice of Everyday Life.* Berkeley, CA: University of California Press.

Dunning, E. 1999. *Sport Matters: Sociological Studies of Sport, Violence, and Civilisation*. London: Routledge.

Elias, N. 1978. *What Is Sociology?* London: Hutchinson.

Elias, N. 1991. *The Society of Individuals*. Oxford: Basil Blackwell.

Elias, N. 1996. *The Germans: Studies of Power Struggles and the Development of Habitus in the Nineteenth and Twentieth Centuries*. Oxford: Polity Press.

Elias, N. 2002. *The Civilising Process*. Oxford: Blackwell.

Elias, N., and E. Dunning. 1986. *The Quest for Excitement: Sport and Leisure in the Civilising Process*. Oxford: Basil Blackwell.

Elias, N., and J. Scotson. 1965. *The Established and the Outsiders*. London: Sage.

Faludi, S. 1999. *Stiffed: The Betrayal of the American Man*. New York: William Morrow and Co.

Featherstone, M. 2000. *Body Modification*. London: Sage.

Frank, A. 2003. "Emily's Scars: Surgical Shapings, Technoluxe, and Bioethics," *Hastings Center Report* 34(2): 18–29.

Garlick, S. 2004. "What is a Man? Heterosexuality and the Technology of Masculinity," *Men and Masculinities* 6(3): 156–72.

Godenzi, A. 1999. "Style or Substance: Men's Response to Feminist Challenge," *Men and Masculinities* 1(4): 385–92.

Goffman, E. 1963. *Stigma*. New York: Prentice Hall.

Grogan, S., and H. Richards. 2002. "Body Image: Focus Groups with Boys and Men," *Men and Masculinities* 4(3): 219–32.

Hathaway, A., and M. Atkinson. 2003. "Active Interview Tactics in Research on Public Deviance: Exploring the Two Cop Personas," *Field Methods* 15(2): 161–85.

Hise, R. 2004. *The War against Men*. Oakland, CA: Elderberry Press.

Horrocks, R. 1994. *Masculinity in Crisis: Myths, Fantasies and Realities*. Basingstoke: St Martin's Press.

Labre, M. 2002. "Adolescent Boys and the Muscular Male Body Ideal," *Journal of Adolescent Health* 30(4): 233–42.

Medicard. 2004. *Report on Cosmetic Surgery in Canada*. Toronto.

Mosse, G. 1996. *The Image of Man: The Creation of Modern Masculinity*. Oxford: Oxford University Press.

Niedzviecki, H. 2004. *Hello, I'm Special*. New York: Penguin.

Niva, S. 1998. "Tough and Tender: New World Order Masculinity and the Gulf War," in M. Salewski and J. Parpart, eds., *The "Man" Question in International Relations*, pp. 109–28. Boulder, CO: Westview Press.

Potts, A. 2002. "The Essence of the Hard-on: Hegemonic Masculinity and the Cultural Construction of 'Erectile Dysfunction,'" *Men and Masculinities* 3(1): 85–103.

Pronger, B. 2002. *Body Fascism: Salvation in the Technology of Physical Fitness*. Toronto: University of Toronto Press.

Sargent, P. 2000. "Real Men or Real Teachers? Contradictions in the Lives of Men Elementary Teachers," *Men and Masculinities* 2(4): 410–33.

Sarwer, D., and C. Crerand. 2004. "Body Image and Cosmetic Medical Treatments," *Body Image: An International Journal of Research* 1: 99–111.

Schmitt, R. 2001. "Proud to be a Man?," *Men and Masculinities* 3(3): 393–404.

Sennett, R. 1998. *The Corrosion of Character*. New York: W.W. Norton.

Sykes, G., and D. Matza. 1956. "Techniques of Neutralisation," *American Sociological Review* 22: 664–70.

White, P., K. Young, and J. Gillett. 1995. "Bodywork as a Moral Imperative: Some Critical Notes on Health and Fitness," *Loisir et Société* 18(1): 159–82.

Whitehead, S.M. 2002. *Men and Masculinities: Key Themes and New Directions*. Cambridge: Polity Press.

PART V
Gendered Intimacies

Nowhere are the differences between women and men more emphasized than in our intimate lives: our experiences of love, friendship, and sexuality. It is our intimate relationships that give rise to the cliché that men and women are truly from different planets.

But gender is not necessarily destiny when it comes to intimacy. In heterosexual relationships, we find a mixed pattern of convergence and divergence between men and women in terms of the way they experience love and sex. As Lily Tsui and Elena Nicoladis demonstrate in their study of first intercourse experiences among Canadian university students, men and women have much more similar experiences of first intercourse than the men-are-from-Mars-women-are-from-Venus model of gender difference might lead us to expect.

Melanie Beres develops this theme further, suggesting that men and women use very similar presumptions and discourses to shape their experience of heterosexual casual sex—although, as Beres argues, these discourses tend to position men as active sexual pursuers and women as more passive participants in sexual activities. Nonetheless, some women manage to find ways to meet their own sexual desires, even without overtly challenging dominant ways of thinking about sex.

Nick Mulé takes on the question of "public intimacies," and the ways in which governments shape the way men and women experience sexuality, love, and relationships. Canada was one of the first countries in the world to legally recognize marriages between two people of the same sex, which most gender theorists have hailed as a major milestone. Mulé, however, provocatively suggests that the legalization of same-sex marriage is merely a reform of the traditional institution of marriage, and not a transformation.

Questions for Critical Thought

1. Is it possible to have sexuality without gender? Can physical attraction or desire exist in the absence of gender?
2. Sexual relationships are intensely intimate, individualized, and personal, yet they exist within a gender-differentiated world. How does gender influence the ways that men and women experience sexual intimacy and closeness?
3. Why is virginity very important to some people, and not so important to others? What are some of the different cultural and personal significances of virginity?
4. Beres identifies several gendered discourses that her participants invoked when they talked about their casual sex experiences. Have you seen these discourses or others presented elsewhere? Which ones appear in your experience to be most powerful?
5. In your experience, or in the experiences of people you know, are long-term, intimate relationships gendered differently from short-term, casual relationships?
6. Some theorists have criticized the idea of gender "scripts" as being too restrictive and standardized for the way that people actually act. This is why Beres uses the vocabulary of sexual "discourses," rather than roles or scripts, for instance. How "scripted" do you think sexuality is, in terms of gender?
7. What do you think about marriage between two people of the same sex? What are some arguments for and against it? Do you agree with Mulé that the entire institution of marriage is problematic?
8. In Canada today, more and more people are opting to live common-law or to remain single. Why is marriage still so symbolically important?
9. What do you think should be covered in a "sex education" curriculum for young people who are not yet sexually active?
10. How does an individual's gender influence the way that he or she expresses his or her sexuality?

Chapter 17

Overview

Lily Tsui and Elena Nikoladis provide a detailed empirical account of how virginity and sexual experience are gendered. When undergraduates in a psychology class are asked about their experiences of first intercourse, men's and women's accounts diverge in some respects, and converge in others. Men and women appear to be very similar in their accounts of their relationship status and the emotional impact of first intercourse.

However, women were significantly more likely to report that they believed they were in love with their partner at the time they had sex and that their male partner took the initiative leading up to sex. These accounts appear to hew quite closely to the old stereotypes of female sexuality—built on a foundation of romantic love and awakened by the actions of men.

Tsui and Nikoladis neither confirm nor reject the Mars-and-Venus way of looking at gender but suggest that what is emerging among younger generations in Canada is a mixed picture—when it comes to significant life experiences like having sex for the first time, men and women have some things in common, but other things remain different. Their sample is limited to heterosexual intercourse, raising the question of how men and women would report their sexual experiences if they were being asked about same-sex sexuality. How much of the gender differences we see here might be the result of interactions between men and women, which are intrinsic to heterosexuality, and how much might be apparent even if the people having sex were of the same gender?

Losing It: Similarities and Differences in First Intercourse Experiences of Men and Women[1]

Lily Tsui and Elena Nicoladis

Introduction

Historically, a woman's virginity was crucial to marriage in terms of both honour and value; women who were found not to be virgins on their wedding night (often determined by the presence of blood at first intercourse) were seen as worthless in many cultures. In contrast, "proof" of male virginity is unavailable physically and less important culturally. Such differences in how virginity has been perceived in society have created an environment in which men and women may have different perceptions of first intercourse and its meanings.

Quantitative studies have demonstrated gender differences in both attitudes toward and actual experience of first intercourse. For example, Carpenter (2001) found that women were twice as likely as men to think of their virginity as a gift to a future partner (61 per cent versus 36 per cent), while men were three times more likely than women to view their virginity as a stigma (57 per cent versus 21 per cent). Darling, Davidson, and Passarello (1992) found that a greater percentage of men than women perceived their first intercourse to be physiologically satisfying (81 per cent versus 28 per cent) and psychologically satisfying (67 per cent versus 28 per cent).

Qualitative studies based on feminist analyses of power differences between men and women have suggested possible explanations for such findings. For example, young adults' accounts of first sexual intercourse reveal that men gain an affirmation of manhood through first intercourse. It is thus primarily a young man's moment that marks his "coming of age" or his entry into manhood (Holland, Ramazanoglu, Sharpe, and Thomson, 2000). However, the dependence on women for this validation of men has taken on multiple social meanings, many of which are viewed by feminist thinkers as embedded in a patriarchal culture.

Holland et al. (2000) found that young men's accounts of first intercourse were mostly concerned with their own performance, orgasm, and sense of having reached a landmark. Their partners' pleasure or orgasm was seen as "icing on the cake." The problem with young men having this construction of first intercourse is that it leaves young women to cope with first intercourse experiences that may fail to meet their own expectations to affirm feelings of love and romance (Holland et al., 2000). In this view, sex differences in first intercourse experiences have their basis in different perceptions of its meaning and in constructions of sexuality.

Burr (2001) argues that the contemporary construction of men's sexuality as "active, dynamic, powerful, and, potentially uncontrollable," also portrays women's sexuality as essentially passive. In this construction, sex for women is not about active participation but about something that is received (Darling et al., 1992). Women may thus be seen as dependent on men for introducing them to the physical pleasure aspects of sexual activities because conventional femininity demands that a woman appear to be sexually unknowing, to desire not just sex but a relationship, to let sex "happen" without requesting it, to trust, to love, and to make men happy (Holland et al., 2000). Traditional dating scenarios reinforced this perspective in that the woman was expected to wait for the man to ask her out and the man was expected to handle details of cost, transportation, and activity (Allgeier and Royster, 1991).

Social discourses around sexuality, and particularly female sexuality, reflect and influence personal and educational perspectives on first intercourse. Fine (1997) identifies three such discourses. The first discourse, sexuality as violence, instills fear of sex by focusing on abuse, incest, and other negative outcomes of sexual activity. The second discourse, sexuality as victimization, identifies females as subject to the pressuring tendencies of male sexuality and focuses attention on the risk of women "being used" or coerced and thus on ways to avoid the physical, social, and emotional risks of sexual intimacy. Messages related to unintended pregnancy and sexually transmitted infections (STIs) may reinforce notions of risk and are used by some to pressure for classroom priority on strategies to avoid sex, "saying no," and "abstinence only" approaches to sexuality education. In this context, Fine's third discourse, sexuality as individual morality, would value women's choice about sexuality as long as the choice is premarital abstinence. Such discourses, Fine suggests, lead to a construction of sexuality where the male is in search of desire and the female is in search of protection. Largely absent from public sexual education is a fourth discourse, sexuality as desire. Fine notes that

> The naming of desire, pleasure, or sexual entitlement, particularly for females, barely exists in the formal agenda of public schooling on sexuality . . . a genuine discourse of desire would invite adolescents to explore what feels good and bad, desirable and undesirable, grounded in experiences, needs, and limits. (Fine, 1997)

The Present Study

Given the questions implicit in these background observations, the present study sought to identify university students' perspectives on various aspects of their first experience of consensual heterosexual sexual intercourse. The questionnaire designed for this purpose dealt with precursors to, experience of, and subsequent feelings about first intercourse. Students who had not had intercourse answered selected questions based on their expectations.

Apart from the anticipation arising from the literature review that men's and women's experiences would differ and that men's would be more positive, we refrained from making more specific hypotheses. This reticence was due to our perception that the literature had given a clearer picture of what to ask than what to expect. We consider the study to be a descriptive and exploratory step in determining if and how women's and men's experiences of first intercourse differ and to what extent the findings reflect the various constructions of sexuality portrayed in the literature.

Method

Questionnaire

Respondents who had experienced first intercourse answered questions about the context of their first intercourse, preparations prior to intercourse, actual circumstances of first intercourse, and feelings afterward. Those who had not experienced consensual first intercourse were asked about their expectations of first intercourse including preparation, anticipation of pain, orgasm, etc. The questionnaire is presented in Appendix A.

Definitions

This study defined first intercourse as the first time the person had consensual heterosexual intercourse. The four participants whose first experience of sexual intercourse happened in the context of a sexual assault therefore did not provide answers about their first intercourse based on this experience but rather on their first consensual experience, if that had occurred. If they had not had consensual intercourse, their responses were based on their expectations regarding first intercourse, as were those of others who had not had consensual intercourse.

Participants

Among the 358 introductory psychology undergraduate students who participated (114 men, 244 women), the mean age was 19.4 years (SD = 2.32, range 17–38). Participants who had not had intercourse were slightly but significantly younger on average than those who had (19.0 versus 19.73 years respectively) $t(356) = 2.99$; $p = .002$. Most participants were born in Canada (79 per cent). Grouping of free-response items on cultural background yielded six categories: "Canadian" (30 per cent); "European" (39 per cent); "Asian" (18 per cent); "Middle Eastern" (4 per cent); and "Other" (10 per cent). Religious affiliation grouped into five categories: "Christian (not Catholic)" (33 per cent); "Catholic" (31 per cent); "Hindu/Sikh/Muslim" (9 per cent); "Buddhist/Taoist" (3 per cent); and "No religious affiliation" (25 per cent).

Based on the definition of first intercourse as the first experience of consensual sexual intercourse, 55.6 per cent (n = 199) of the sample had experienced first intercourse and 44.4 per cent (n = 159) had not. Men and women did not differ in this respect (44.7 per cent of men and 44.3 per cent of women had not had first intercourse).

Results

Contextual Variables of First Intercourse

Age at first intercourse

All but one participant could recall their age at first intercourse. Mean age for first intercourse was 17.13 years (SD = 1.65; range 13–28) with no significant difference between the sexes (17.04 for women and 17.31 for men; see Table 17.1 for all age-related data).

Partner's age at participant's first intercourse

On average, women had first intercourse with partners who were significantly older than they were (mean of 17.04 years for women and 18.41 years for their partners) ($t(132) = -6.01$, $p < .001$, $d = -1.38$) whereas mean age at first intercourse for men (17.31 years) did not differ from that of their partners (17.6 years; see Table 17.1).

Relationship to partner at time of first intercourse

The great majority of both women and men (84 per cent overall) said they were in a couple/romantic relationship with their first intercourse

Table 17.1 Mean age and relationship status of participants and their partners at time of participants' first intercourse

	Men	Women
Age of Participant and Partner at First Intercourse		
Participant's Age	17.31	17.04*
Partner's Age	17.6	28.41*
Relationship Status with First Intercourse Partner		
Couple	83%	85%
Other Relationship	17%	15%
Length of Relationship and Time Known		
Mean Length of Relationship	5.74 months** (*SD* = 5.46)	8.14 months** (*SD* = 7.89)
Time Known Regardless of Relationship	26 months ns	34 months ns

* Difference for women and partners significant $p < .001$; *n*: men (63), partners (60); women (135), partners (130)

** Difference approaches significance at $p = .51$

ns indicates not significant

partner while 16 per cent were not in a romantic relationship. There was no significant sex difference in relationship status at first intercourse (see Table 17.1).

Duration of relationship with partner prior to first intercourse

Among the 84 per cent of participants who were in a relationship at the time of first intercourse, mean relationship duration was 7.4 months (SD = 7.29 months, range = less than one month to 36 months) with men approaching a significantly greater likelihood of having shorter duration than women (5.74 months for men, 8.14 months for women) ($t(163) = 1.97$, $p = .051$, $d = -2.40$). On average, all participants had known their partner for 31 months ($SD = 39.5$; range was less than one month to 2 years) with no significant difference between the sexes in this respect (see Table 17.1).

Intercourse experience of participant's first partner

Just over half of the participants reported that they were the first person with whom their partner had intercourse (52.3 per cent). The sexes did not differ in this respect.

Perceptions of being in love at first intercourse and in hindsight

Women were significantly more likely than men to report that they were in love with their partner at the time of first intercourse (63 per cent and 43 per cent respectively) ($\chi^2(2, N = 199) = 7.78$, $p = .02$). This difference was not present in hindsight (47 per cent and 41 per cent respectively) with men appearing to move from "unsure" to "no" and women from "yes" to "no" (see Table 17.2).

Decision to have intercourse

Participants were asked whether the decision to have first intercourse was mutual or whether one partner took the lead. While 57 per cent of men and 61 per cent of women said the decision was mutual, Chi-squared analysis showed a significant effect of gender on the decision to have first intercourse (see Table 17.3). In cases where women did not report a mutual decision, 79 per cent assigned the initiative to their partner and 21 per cent to themselves; for men, 42 per cent assigned the initiative to their partners, and 42 per cent to themselves (calculated from data in Table 17.3). Since these students were not reporting on first intercourse with other

Table 17.2 Participants' perception of being in love at time of first intercourse and in retrospect

	"In Love" at time of first intercourse? (%)		"In Love" in hindsight? (%)	
	Men (n = 63)	Women (n = 136)	Men (n = 63)	Women (n = 136)
Yes	43	63	41	47
No	35	25	48	42
Not sure	22	12	11	11
$\chi^2(2, N = 199)$	7.78*	ns		

* $p = .02$
ns indicates not significant

Table 17.3 Participant perceptions of their and their partners' role in decision to have first intercourse

Participants	Mutual Decision	Male Partner Suggested	Female Partner Suggested
Men (n = 63)	57%	25%	18%
Women (n = 136)	61%	31%	8%
$\chi^2(2, N = 199)$		12.53, $p = .002$*	

* When the decision was not identified as mutual, men were significantly more likely to have been the ones who suggested intercourse.

respondents, it is not possible to determine whether these sex differences in perception of who initiated would also be seen within couples.

Discussions prior to first intercourse

Among the six pre-intercourse discussion items listed in Table 17.4, participants were most likely to have discussed having sexual intercourse and condom use (63–73 per cent), somewhat less likely to have discussed other methods of birth control (48–58 per cent), and most unlikely to have discussed sexually transmitted infections, possible outcomes of pregnancy, and emotional implications of intercourse for them (32–40 per cent). The sexes did not differ significantly on any of these items (see Table 17.4).

Circumstances associated with first intercourse

Nine items in Table 17.4 assessed different aspects of the participants' actual first intercourse experience. Although less than half of respondents indicated that first intercourse had occurred when they expected it to (41 per cent of males, 46 per cent of females), condom use at first intercourse was common (75–80 per cent). Alcohol use by self or partner was less common (14–21 per cent), and drug use by self or partner was rare (0–2 per cent). The sexes did not differ on any of these items (see Table 17.4).

Women were much more likely than men to report pain at first intercourse (52 per cent versus 5 per cent), much less likely than men to report orgasm at first intercourse (12 per cent versus 76 per cent), and more likely to report partner orgasm than were men (73 per cent versus 32 per cent). Each of these differences was statistically significant (see Table 17.4). We did not ask about prior orgasm history of women in our sample but note that our female participants appear less likely to have had orgasm at first intercourse (12 per cent) than was reported by our male respondents of their first intercourse partners (32 per cent; see Table 17.4).

Table 17.4 Participants "yes" responses to questions about prior discussion, circumstances of, and follow-up to first intercourse (%)

	Men (n = 63)	Women (n = 136)	$\chi^2(1, 199)$
Pre-Intercourse Discussion			
Having intercourse	76	74	ns
Condom use	63	73	ns
Other methods of birth control	58	48	ns
Sexually transmitted infection	33	32	ns
Outcomes if pregnancy were to occur	33	37	ns
Emotional implications	33	40	ns
Circumstances Associated with First Intercourse			
Did intercourse occur when expected?	41	46	ns
Was a condom used?	75	80	ns
Were you drinking?	19	21	ns
Was your partner drinking?	14	18	ns
Were you using any drugs?	0	0	ns
Was your partner using any drugs?	2	2	ns
Was first intercourse painful?	5	52	41.49*
Did you have an orgasm?	76	12	81.91*
Did your partner have an orgasm?	32	73	30.18*
Feelings/Outcomes Subsequent to First Intercourse			
Physical satisfaction	62	35	12.39*
Emotional satisfaction	56	54	ns
Sex again with same partner?	87	89	ns
Stayed a couple or became a couple after?	83	86	ns
Pregnancy occur?	0	0	–

*$p < .001$
ns indicates not significant

Feelings and outcomes after first intercourse

Men were significantly more likely than women to report feeling physically satisfied after first intercourse (62 per cent versus 35 per cent). However, the sexes did not differ on reports of emotional satisfaction (56 per cent and 54 per cent), having had sex again with the same partner (87 per cent and 89 per cent), or staying as or becoming a couple after first intercourse (83 per cent and 86 per cent). None of the respondents reported pregnancy as a consequence of first intercourse. Men and women were similar in the extent to which they reported no regrets about first intercourse (76 per cent and 72 per cent) and in their perception that they had first intercourse at "the right age" (63 per cent and 65 per cent; see Table 17.4).

Overall assessment of first intercourse experience

Participants were asked to give an overall "rating" of their first intercourse experience based on six options (see Table 17.5). There was no statistically significant sex difference in these overall assessments with 72 per cent of men and 61 per cent of women rating the experience as either perfect, very good, or good in contrast to the 11 per cent and 13 per cent respectively who recalled their first intercourse as either "bad" or "very bad."

Slightly less than one quarter of all respondents chose the "neither good nor bad" option.

Expectations of first intercourse among participants who had not had intercourse

Participants who had not had intercourse (n = 159) answered 9 items from Table 17.4 based on their expectations of first intercourse. There responses are reported in the first two columns of Table 17.6. Students who had not had intercourse did not generally consider it important that their first intercourse partner would also have not had intercourse (36 per cent of men and 29 per cent of women said yes). We did not ask about current relationship status and thus cannot determine how many students in this subsample might, at the time of the study, have been in a relationship with an eventual first intercourse partner.

With respect to their expectations of discussion of particular topics prior to first intercourse, the sexes in this non-intercourse group differed significantly in their expectations about discussing methods of birth control other than condoms $\chi^2(2, n = 156) = 10.65, p = .005$. Women were more likely than men to expect such discussion (77 per cent versus 53 per cent respectively; see Table 17.6) and men more often unsure (41 per cent versus 17 per cent respectively). Men and women who had not had intercourse also differed significantly in their expectations about prior discussion of STIs, $\chi^2(2, n = 157) = 8.17, p = .017$ (57 per cent of women expected such discussion versus 36 per cent of men; 36 per cent of women and 46 per cent of men were unsure or did not know).

The sexes also differed in their expectation of pain at first intercourse, $\chi^2(2, n = 157) = 69.01, p < .001$, with a smaller percentage of men (4 per cent) than women (34 per cent) expecting to experience pain. Men and women also differed in expectations about their own and their future partner's likelihood of having orgasm at first intercourse, $\chi^2(2, n = 156) = 39.44, p < .001$, and $\chi^2(2, n = 156) = 7.80, p = .020$ respectively.

Comparison of expectations of participants who had not had intercourse with actual experiences of those who had first intercourse

Table 17.6 also provides an opportunity to compare the first intercourse expectations of the participants who had not had intercourse with the first intercourse experiences of those who had. A comparison of the experiences of the latter with the expectations of the former invites speculation about the extent to which expectations may or may not match experience. For example, women who had not had intercourse appeared more likely to expect pre-intercourse discussion of birth control methods other than condoms (77 per cent) than was actually experienced by women who had first intercourse

Table 17.5 Participants' overall ratings of their first intercourse experience (%)

Response	Men (n = 63)	Women (n = 136)	Total
Perfect, wouldn't change a thing	14	19	18
Very good	29	19	22
Good	29	23	25
Neither good or bad	18	26	23
Bad	8	10	10
Very bad	3	3	3

Table 17.6 Expectations of first intercourse among students who had not had intercourse and a comparison with those who had

	First Intercourse Expectations (students who had not had intercourse)		Reported First Intercourse Experiences (students who had had intercourse)	
Responses	**Men (n = 51)**	**Women (n = 108)**	**Men (n = 63)**	**Women (n = 136)**
Partners not having had intercourse before is important?	36	29		
Pre-Intercourse Discussion				
Discuss having intercourse	60	66	76	74
Discuss condom use	70	83	63	73
Discuss other methods of birth control	53	77	58	48
Discuss STIs	36	57	33	32
Discuss pregnancy	55	53	33	37
Discuss emotional implications	33	44	33	40
Physical Expectations				
Pain at first intercourse	4	34	5	52
Personal experience of orgasm	58	11	76	12
Partner's experience of orgasm	22	28	32	73

(48 per cent). The expected sex difference on this item experienced by those who had intercourse was in the reverse direction to that expected by those who had not. In the relation to the pre-intercourse discussion items as a whole, the trend appears to be for women who have not had intercourse to have higher expectations for such discussion than occurred in practice for those who had. Women's expectation of their own orgasm at first intercourse (11 per cent) matched that of women who had intercourse (12 per cent) but women's expectation of their partner's orgasm (28 per cent) was lower than that reported about their partners by women who had had intercourse (73 per cent; see Table 17.6).

Discussion

In contrast to other studies that highlighted differences between the sexes in their experience of first intercourse (Darling et al., 1992; Cohen and Shotland, 1996; Guggino, 1997; Holland et al., 2000; Carpenter, 2001), the present findings indicate that, with some exceptions, women's and men's reports of the experience were quite similar. The average age at first intercourse was the same for both sexes. Men and women were equally likely to have had first intercourse within the context of a romantic relationship, to have known their first intercourse partner for the same average length of time, and to have had a first partner who had previous intercourse experience. Women were as likely as men to report activities indicating that they had discussed preparations for and other aspects of first intercourse. In a majority of cases, the decision to have first intercourse was a mutual one. On average, men and women gave similar responses to questions about condom use (usually), alcohol use (seldom), drug use (almost never), and whether first intercourse was expected. The finding that 75 per cent of men and 80 per cent of women reported condom use at first intercourse is consistent with the relatively high levels of protection against unintended pregnancy and STI at first intercourse reported in other recent Canadian studies of young adults (e.g., Hampton, Smith, Jeffrey, and McWatters, 2001). In addition, the sexes did not differ significantly in their evaluation of their feelings and follow-up to first intercourse in relation to emotional satisfaction, subsequent intercourse with first partner, regret, timing, and overall rating.

The women and men in our study who had not had intercourse were also similar to each other on such items as whether it was important that their first partner had also not previously had intercourse (about one-third said yes) and on their expectation of discussion in advance of condom use (high) and possible outcomes if unintended pregnancy were to occur (slightly over half).

The degree of gender similarity in this sample of university students may not represent accurately what is going on in the general population. However, it is also possible that this sample reflects a shift in the sexual practice of young people towards more equally balanced engagement in discussions and decisions related to sexual activity in general and first intercourse in particular. Since the limited research that has been done on first intercourse experience is from the United States, it has been tempting to assume that the Canadian population is similar. However, strongly conservative political and religious influences in the US may reflect an environment that has been more hostile than Canada to premarital sexual activity and hence to the education that would support more informed, and perhaps egalitarian, decision making and experiences surrounding first intercourse.

Some of our findings do suggest gender differences in which men appear to have greater influence on sexual interactions in heterosexual relationships, at least when it comes to first intercourse. The greater age differences between women and their first intercourse partners could result in men having more power and control in the sexual relationship. On the other hand this could simply be a reflection of our society's tendency for younger women to be drawn to older partners and vice versa. The fact that men had known their first intercourse partners for a shorter period of time than women is consistent with Cohen and Shotland's (1996) report that men consider sexual intercourse acceptable earlier in a dating relationship than do women. Among the approximately 40 per cent of women and men in our study who said first intercourse had not been a "mutual decision," women were significantly more likely to say that their partner had suggested intercourse than were men. This fits with the traditional dating scenario in which men are more likely to take initiative with the sexual aspects of romantic relationships. However, our questions did not explore what these students meant by their partner "taking the initiative" nor did they explore other aspects of relationship dynamics.

On average, women were more likely than men to believe that they were in love at first intercourse (men were more likely to be unsure). These views converged, in retrospect, with both sexes being equally likely to believe that they were not in love. The greater tendency for women to believe they were in love at first intercourse may reflect greater internalization by women than men of the feeling that sex is about love. There may be a parallel here in the finding of Quackenbush, Strassberg, and Turner (1995) that the inclusion of romance in erotica can serve as a relationship buffer that make erotic material more acceptable to women. Similarly, the belief that they are "in love" might be viewed as the relationship buffer necessary for some women to justify first intercourse.

We think these findings have important implications for sexual health education although we are also aware that the study has a number of limitations that invite cautious interpretation of the results. The study was conducted on a convenience sample of introductory psychology students and cannot be generalized to other populations, including students who did not go to university or who left school early. The questionnaire was designed for this study and has not been validated. Participants were only asked about consensual first intercourse and not about other sexual activities such as oral sex. Thus, the study cannot shed light on participants' prior sexual behaviour or on the attitudes that may have shaped their perceptions of their first intercourse experience. That being said, socially constructed gender differences appear to permeate all levels of society and to that extent the findings may well have useful applications for educators and health professionals.

Notes

1. We would like to thank Jenn Mitchell, Kim Scott, and Hanna Wajda for their assistance in conducting this study. This research is partially supported by SSHRC funding to the second author.

References

Allgeir, E.R., and B.J.T. Royster. 1991. "New Approaches to Dating and Sexuality," in E. Grauerholz and M.A. Koralewski, eds, *Sexual Coercion: A Sourcebook On Its Nature, Causes, and Prevention*, pp. 133–47. Lexington, MA: Lexington Books.

Burr, J. 2001. "Women Have It. Men Want It. What Is It? Constructions of Sexuality in Rape Discourse," *Psychology, Evolution, & Gender* 3: 103–7.

Carpenter, L.M. 2001. "The Ambiguity of 'Having Sex': The Subjective Experience of Virginity Loss in the United States," *The Journal of Sex Research* 38: 127–39.

Cohen, L.L., and R.L. Shotland. 1996. "Timing of First Sexual Intercourse in a Relationship: Expectations, Experiences, and Perceptions of Others," *The Journal of Sex Research* 33: 291–9.

Darling, C.A., J.K. Davidson, and L.C. Passarello. 1992. "The Mystique of First Intercourse among College Youth: The Role of Partners, Contraceptive Practices, and Psychological Reactions," *Journal of Youth and Adolescence* 21: 97–117.

Fine, M. 1997. "Sexuality, Schooling, and Adolescent Females: The Missing Discourse of Desire," in M.M. Gergen and S.N. Davis, eds., *Toward a New Psychology of Gender*, pp. 375–402. New York, NY: Routledge.

Guggino, J.M., and J.J., Jr., Ponzetti. 1997. "Gender Differences in Affective Reactions to First Coitus," *Journal of Adolescence* 20: 189–200.

Hampton, M.R, P. Smith, B. Jeffery, and B. McWatters. 2001. "Sexual Experience, Contraception, and STI Prevention among High School Students: Results from a Canadian Urban Centre," *The Canadian Journal of Human Sexuality* 10: 111–26.

Holland, J., C. Ramazanoglu, S. Sharpe, and R. Thomson. 2000. "Deconstructing Virginity—Young People's Accounts of First Sex," *Sexual and Relationship Therapy* 15: 221–32.

Quackenbush, D.M., D.S. Strassberg, and C.W. Turner. 1995. "Gender Effects of Romantic Themes in Erotica," *Archives of Sexual Behavior* 24: 21–35.

Appendix A: Survey items and response categories

Questions	Response Categories
Relationship to Partner	
Were you a couple at the time?	Yes / No
Did you consider yourself to be "in love" with this person at the time when you had intercourse?	Yes / No / Not Sure
Looking back, do you think you were actually "in love" with this person when you had intercourse, regardless of your answer to the last question?	Yes / No / Not Sure
How long had you known this person in total, regardless of changes in your relationship to this person?	___ months and ___ years
Were you the first person with whom your partner has had intercourse?	Yes / No
What is your relationship to this person now?	Partner or Spouse / Friend / Acquaintance / No relationship / Other
Preparations Prior to Intercourse	
Did you and your partner talk about having intercourse beforehand?	Yes / No / Not Sure

Appendix A (*Continued*)

Questions	Response Categories
Did you and your partner discuss condom use before having first intercourse?	Yes / No / Not Sure
Did you and your partner discuss other methods of birth control before having first intercourse?	Yes / No / Not Sure
Did you and your partner discuss STIs before having first intercourse?	Yes / No / Not Sure
Did you and your partner discuss what to do if you / your partner became pregnant before having first intercourse?	Yes / No / Not Sure
Did you and your partner discuss the emotional implications of having intercourse before having first intercourse?	Yes / No / Not Sure
Do you think that you and your partner decided to have intercourse together, or did one of you take the lead?	Decided together / You took the initiative / Partner took the initiative
Circumstances of First Intercourse	
Did first intercourse occur when you expected it to?	Yes / No / Not Sure
Where did you have intercourse for the first time?	Your home / Partner's home / Hotel or motel / Vehicle / Other
Did you / your partner use a condom?	Yes / No
Did you / your partner use any other form of contraceptive?	Yes / No
At the time you had intercourse, was there alcohol in your system?	Yes / No / Don't remember or know
Was there alcohol in your partner's system?	Yes / No / Don't remember or know
Were you on any drugs?	Yes / No / Don't remember or know
Was your partner on any drugs?	Yes / No / Don't remember or know
Did you find your first intercourse experience to be physically painful in any way?	Yes / No / Not Sure
Did you achieve orgasm?	Yes / Not / Not Sure / Don't Remember
Did your partner achieve orgasm?	Yes / Not / Not Sure / Don't Remember
Feelings / Outcomes Subsequent to First Intercourse	
Did you feel physically satisfied with your first intercourse experience?	Yes / No / Not Sure
Did you feel emotionally satisfied with your first intercourse experience?	Yes / No / Not Sure
Did you and this particular partner ever have sex again?	Yes / No / Don't Remember
Did you and this partner stay together as a couple, or, if you were not a couple at the time you had intercourse, did you and this partner become a couple?	Yes / No
Do you regret having shared your first intercourse experience with this person?	Yes / No / Don't Remember
Looking back, what do you think about the timing of your first intercourse experience?	I was about the right age / I was too young / I was too old / Not Sure
Did you or your partner become pregnant as a result of your first intercourse experience?	Yes / No / I don't know

(*Continued*)

Appendix A (*Continued*)

Questions	Response Categories
Did you or your partner get an STI as a result of your first intercourse experience?	Yes, I caught something from him or her / Yes, s/he caught something from me / No / Not Sure
Overall, how would you rate your first intercourse experience?	Perfect, wouldn't change a thing / Very Good / Good / Neither Good or Bad / Bad / Very Bad
Expectations About First Intercourse by Respondents who had not had Intercourse	
Will it be important to you that the person with whom you have intercourse for the first time is also having intercourse for the first time?	Yes / Maybe / No / Don't Know
Do you think you and your future partner will talk about having intercourse beforehand?	Yes / Maybe / No / Don't Know
Do you think you and your future partner will discuss condom use before having first intercourse?	Yes / Maybe / No / Don't Know
Do you think you and your future partner will discuss other methods of birth control before having first intercourse?	Yes / Maybe / No / Don't Know
Do you think you and your future partner will discuss STIs before having first intercourse?	Yes / Maybe / No / Don't Know
Do you think you and your future partner will discuss what to do if you / your partner became pregnant after having first intercourse?	Yes / Maybe / No / Don't Know
Do you think you and your future partner will discuss the emotional implications of having first intercourse before having first intercourse?	Yes / Maybe / No / Don't Know
Do you think your first intercourse experience will be physically painful in any way?	Yes / Maybe / No / Don't Know
Do you think you will achieve orgasm at first intercourse?	Yes / Maybe / No / Don't Know
Do you think your future partner will achieve orgasm at first intercourse?	Yes / Maybe / No / Don't Know

Chapter 18

Overview

Melanie Beres takes a detailed and perhaps eye-opening look at the micropolitics of sexual negotiation. Her account complements Tsui and Nikoladis' broad-brush picture of heterosexuality among Canadian young people, as she gets up close and personal, asking how people identify a potential sexual partner and communicate their intentions and desires, through verbal and non-verbal means.

Beres goes beyond moralizing about "hookup culture" to reveal how this culture actually works. She identifies four distinct "discourses," or powerful beliefs, about sexuality that men and women use to understand and describe their experiences. These discourses are highly gendered—in contrast to the more gender-neutral patterns described by Tsui and Nikoladis—as men and women are described as having different kinds of sexual drives, orientations to relationships, and sexual agency.

"It Just Happens": Negotiating Casual Heterosexual Sex

Melanie Beres

In the summer of 2005, Melanie Beres spent several months in Jasper, Alberta, interviewing young people who had come to Jasper for seasonal work in the tourist industry. Her intent was to understand the negotiating of sexual consent in short-term heterosexual encounters ("hooking up" or "one night stands"). Beres chose Jasper because of the dense population of transients and seasonal workers. The youth culture that grew up around this population perceived recreational sex as a common activity. In this chapter, Beres discusses the different ways in which men and women in Jasper talk about casual sex, and how they depict the process of consenting to a sexual encounter.

I begin this chapter by highlighting ways that the negotiation of casual sex in Jasper is dominated by discourses that privilege male sexual desire. I discuss the three discourses of heterosexuality as outlined by Hollway (1984) and I argue for a fourth discourse within casual sex; I label it the "it just happens" discourse. Through this discourse, casual sex is constructed as something that "just happens" and is beyond the control of the partners. I end with an analysis of the ways that women find spaces of power and agency within these discourses. Women do this by placing limits on casual sex, disrupting the "coital imperative" and taking the typically "male" position within the discourse and actively seeking casual sex.

The (Male) Models of Heterosexual Casual Sex in Jasper

"It Just Happens" Discourse

When I approached young adults in Jasper (YAJs) and told them about my study I explained that I was interested in learning about how casual sex happens in Jasper, and how partners communicate their willingness to participate in casual sex. I began interviews by asking them about their lives in Jasper and about their past dating and sexual experiences. At some point during the interview I inevitably asked some version of the question "How does casual sex happen?" or "How do two people come to the understanding that they are going to have sex?" At this point many of the participants stopped and stared at me with perplexed looks on their faces. I interpreted their reactions as saying "Have you never had sex?" The presumption seemed to be that if I had sex at some point, then I would have known how it happened. The answer would have been obvious. The answer (of course) is that "it just happens." Almost all of the women and a few of the men responded with some version of this statement.

Samantha: So you're like kind of like making eye contact, smiling at each other, and then all of a sudden we're like standing by each other talking. And just like . . . I don't know how it happened but we like; all of a sudden we were . . . (laughs) . . . we were just like talking and we were talking about that and like he started kissing me and we went back to my house. And it wasn't even a question of "would you like to come to my house?" You know what I mean? It was just like that. That's what happened. (laughs) And then in the middle of it, it was just like, oh my God!

Anne: He, he just kissed me. Like he just, we were holding hands and dancing then he kissed me and I kissed him back and then it just . . . Yeah, we were hugging and kissing. I was, it was not . . . I don't know, it just happened.

James: That's a really interesting question, because you don't really, I don't really analyze how it happens really, it just kind of happens.

This discourse of "it just happens" reflects a sense that there is a force greater than and external to the two people involved in casual sex that is ultimately responsible for instigating sex. . . . Gwen provides a particularly poignant example.

> Yeah. And then so, yeah, and then he just kept talking. Like we didn't dance or anything. We just sat by the bar and talked for like two hours and he just kept feeding me drinks. (laughs) But he was just drinking just as much as I was so it wasn't that big of a deal. So every time I'd get a drink, he would get a drink. And um . . . yeah, and then . . . And then I went to the washroom and then when I came out, he wasn't there. It was like okay, I'm just going to go home. And then I was walking outside and he like got a cab and stuff. And he was like do you need a ride? Like I'll give you a cab and I'll give you a ride home. And then like sure, whatever. It was raining. It was ugly out. And then um . . . his friend was with him too and he said well why don't you just come over for a couple of beer? And I was like okay, I don't have to work until 3:30 the next day. I can do that. And um . . . so I went over. We had some beer. And then I was like okay, I'm going to go home. And he was like well no, let's just talk for a bit. And I was like okay, and then one thing led to another . . .

The way that Gwen tells the story, she sees it as a series of events that took place, finishing with "and one thing led to another." She does not see the man's behaviour as orchestrating her going home with him for casual sex. She dismisses his buying her lots of drinks, because he too is drinking. She does not think anything of him arranging a cab for her, or asking her home. She does not say anything to imply that his actions may have been planned—that he may be buying her alcohol to get her drunk so she would be more likely to go home with him. She ends the story with "and one thing led to another" implying that neither one of them was in control of what was happening.

. . . James is one of the few men who also expresses this sense of "it just happens."

> It's just something that happens, and you don't really know how it happened, but it happened. And ah, I've never had an experience where it's happened and then she's been like "I really didn't want that to happen" which I'm very thankful for. But you know, you go to an after party or something, right like you're already just hard-core making out on the dance floor let's say, right and you're doing dry humping and bumping and grinding and hanging off each other as you leave the bar. You get to the guy's party house or wherever you're at right, you're sitting around. The next thing you know, nobody's in the room and you're lying on each other and one thing leads to another. Right like, that's really the only way to put it, you start making out that leads to nakedness that leads to sex.

James was thankful that no woman has ever told him afterwards that she did not want to have sex. He said this as though he cannot control the situation or outcome—as though he has no access to the woman's comfort levels, interests, or desires. If sex can just happen, and he has no control over what happens, he then has no control over any potential consequences of the interaction. This use of the "it just happens" discourse assumes that they are not responsible for negotiating casual sex. This results in a failure for men to take responsibility for their actions and the potential for these actions to create harm.

Agnes, among others, connected the "it just happens" discourse with alcohol. "Alcohol is a huge key, like huge, and it really makes you, it really limits you, your ability to make good, clear, conscious decisions." I spoke with only one person who said that most often his casual sex hook-ups occur in the absence of alcohol, often with people he meets in coffee shops or on the street. All other participants mentioned that alcohol plays an important part in their casual sex experiences. When I asked Susan how casual sex happens, alcohol was the first thing she mentioned.

> Go to the bar. Start buying other people drinks and start drinking yourself. It's really really . . . it's all related to alcohol, I think. And for a lot of other people drugs, but I don't see that side of it because I've never been a part of that side of it. Um, but yeah, well it depends, well as a girl if that's what you're looking for when you come to Jasper. You dress really skanky and you get out on the dance floor and you drink lots. And there's gonna be a guy there. Guaranteed. . . .

. . .

Male Sexual Drive Discourse

While most women and a few men began talking about casual sex through the "it just happens" discourse, this was not the only way that hookups were conceptualized.

Many men said they went out to parties or bars with an intention of hooking up, and they pay particular attention to what types of things women may want in men, or particular things to do to get women interested in them. For these men, casual sex does not just happen; it is something that they have to work for, and something they practise. Robert, a bouncer in one of the local bars said that he often sees men going from one group of women to another until they find someone willing to talk with them. Don said that he approaches a lot of women when he's looking for sex and that he knows he will get turned down frequently.

This fits in with what Hollway (1984) describes as the male sexual drive discourse in which men's sex drive is insatiable and that women's role in sexual activity is to be passive and go along with men's desires. Within this discourse men are sexual subjects acting in ways to fulfill their desire for sex. Through this discourse men also secure their masculinity, by reinforcing their ever-present sex drive. Conversely, women are positioned as sexual objects, necessary for men to satiate their desire for sex without any desires of their own. Men reported many strategies that they used in order to find a sexual partner. For instance, some men said that they will often approach many women, with the idea that the more women they approach, the greater the likelihood that they will find one who will have sex with them.

Even once men were in conversation, or dancing with a particular woman, it was important for them to continue to monitor women's behaviours in ways that would increase the chance of "getting laid." For instance, it was important that women should feel as though the situation was not threatening, and to feel comfortable and cared for.

> *Don:* You just give her a sense of security like, making them the focal point, and just looking out for them like, just simple sayings like, like obviously getting the door for them, like putting on their jacket but like actually pulling their hair back so it doesn't go under their jacket, like little things like that, and just looking out for them, even if it's just like creating some space for them, like in a crowded club or something like that just little things like that seemed to go a long way . . . you have to really play it by ear because it can be overdone . . . you have to give her her space and be relaxed then the same time just be conscientious and make her feel comfortable, you know offer them like something to drink, right. I'm not saying offering them a shot or something like that, but like can I get you a drink, would you like my jacket, are you cold, and something like that.

Don is very deliberate in his approach with women; he sees himself in pursuit of sex and sees it as challenging to get women to have sex with him. He is quite aware of his actions and how they may help him reach his goal. While on the surface he seems concerned about women's comfort level, this is a means to an end, a way to get women to go to bed with him. . . .

In order to satiate his "natural" sexual desires, Don learned and implemented specific strategies that enabled him to have casual sex. In this version of the male sexual drive discourse Don positioned himself in a way that relinquishes both partners from responsibility. Here, Don accepts that he is responsible for learning how to quench his ever-present desire. His drive is "natural" and thus it is "inevitable" that he must have casual sex throughout the summer; however, by becoming skilled at the "arts" of "courting" he increases the likelihood and frequency that he will be able to satisfy these desires.

He talked in detail about monitoring women's behaviour to gauge their comfort level and willingness to have sex. In particular, a woman's breathing was very important.

> It is all about the girl's breathing, and that's like, a lot of guys don't realize that, but that's like, that's your like light signal that's your red, yellow, green, right there it's her breathing and just playing that off and so you just gradually sort of progress things forward to taking off clothes.

For Don, it was important that he maintain control over the situation and over casual sex. He talked positively about situations where women initiated casual sex, as long as the woman was not too direct.

> The odd time that I get approached by a girl it works, like it's nice to see a girl of confidence and stuff like that but you can't be too direct because then it's just too easy, it kills it, like you know unless I was just slumming it you know, and going for raunchy sex.

Several other men talked in similar ways about women who are actively seeking sex.

> *Colin:* If they come on too strong, then you can kind of tell that they're kinda skanky. But if they come on sort of in a shy manner, then, then it's a good thing. Good cause it gives you room to open them up. You know what I mean? Like you've got to make them feel comfortable obviously or else it's just going to be stupid and suck. . . . If they're really aggressive, it's just like no; I don't want to do this. Cause it's not really giving you a challenge. Cause if they're really aggressive, it's just like well okay, I'll just take my shorts off and let's go.

Thus, the chase becomes a "natural" part of casual sex, and courtship and seduction becomes the property of men. . . .

Women were far less likely to articulate ways that casual sex happens. Even in cases where the women were interested in particular men, women waited for men to initiate contact.

> *Samantha:* It's usually the guy who makes the first move I guess, towards me if they can see I'm attracted to them or whatever.

Even when women initiate sex, they still take up the male sexual drive discourse by assuming that the men will be willing to engage in sex.

> *Agnes:* And I think it's more the girl to . . . be the one that decides whether or not it's going to happen because from my experiences, there's not very many times when a guy won't have sex. In fact, more often than not, that's all they're in it for is and not like looking for a relationship or just somebody to snuggle with.

Men also articulated this aspect of the male sexual drive discourse. When I asked men how they indicated their willingness for sex to their partners, many responded by saying that they do not have to demonstrate willingness.

> *Colin:* I just like I'm, I'm a guy. I'm ready, willing and able anywhere anytime.
>
> *Gary:* I think it's probably pretty rare that the guy says stop. I mean, I don't know with other guys

for sure but . . . from, from what I know, then I say that the guy's not going to say stop. Unless there's something else like he has a girlfriend or something like that.

This male sexual drive discourse was the discourse most frequently referred to by both women and men as they talked about casual sex. The male sexual drive discourse is different from the "it just happens" discourse in that both men and women who take up this discourse recognize that men actively pursue casual sex. This is viewed as the "normal" and "natural" way to engage in casual sex. It remained unquestioned by all but one female participant.

Stacy: It's, it's so unfair that it's really assumed in our society that it's the guy's job to [initiate sex]. You know what I mean. It's the guy's job to invite the girl out on a date. It's the guy's job to initiate this. It's the guy's job to initiate that. Yeah, it's the guy's job to initiate sex. It's the guy's job to do everything. The girl's kind of the passive like you know? Passive partner who goes along with everything or doesn't. But is always like you know, things happen to her, she doesn't, you know what I mean? . . . Like don't treat me like some idiot! Like some damsel in fucking distress. So I think that that goes a long way into the bedroom too where like I don't expect him, you know what I mean? Like I'm willing to go out on a limb and face rejection, you know what I mean?

Have/Hold Discourse

While the male sexual drive discourse was the most frequently taken up, other discourses described by Hollway (1984) were alluded to by participants. Many women and a few men took up the have/hold discourse, which Hollway describes as the belief that sex comes with a committed and ongoing relationship. In this discourse women are positioned as the sexual subjects who were trying to establish a committed relationship with a man. Men are positioned as the objects of this discourse. Thus, the have/hold discourse works with the male sexual drive discourse; men are attempting to satiate their sexual desires, and women participate in sex to build and maintain a committed relationship.

It was surprising to see this discourse taken up when women and men were talking about casual sex. Although both women and men were aware that many casual sex experiences do not lead to lasting and committed relationships, some women reported that one reason they engage in casual sex is because they may be interested in a relationship. Samantha and Agnes both said that some of the partners they chose were people they were interested in developing a relationship with. Most of these casual sex experiences did not lead to a relationship. Agnes said that she learnt that if she wanted a relationship that she should not sleep with a man the first night they are together because she found that after she slept with a man on the first "date," he would no longer speak to her.

> We ended up sleeping together and woke up the next morning, and we slept together again and then he like, never talked to me after that. And we were supposed to hang out on New Year's Eve together, cuz it was like two nights after that and umm, I phoned him on New Year's Eve, and asked him what he was doing, and he was like "oh I think I'm just going to stay home." He totally blew me off.

. . . Agnes told stories about hooking up with people for casual sex, and said "I'm totally, like, fine to have casual sex with people, but like if they're under one impression and I'm under another and it's not the same then that kind of makes me mad." In Agnes's version of this discourse, she is looking for more than just one night of sex. This commitment does not have to be in the form of an exclusive and romantic relationship. It could also be a casual affair that lasts several weeks.

Agnes is not the only woman who spoke of similar ideas. Jane recounts a story where she met a man she was interested in. At first she thinks he is a real "gentleman" because he does not try to sleep with her the first night they are together. They did, however, have sex the second night they were together. Afterwards she was angry because he is no longer speaking to her. She called him a "really big slut" and a liar. She sees his actions as being dishonest because, for her, having sex with someone is a sign that there is at least some interest and some commitment.

Even for some women who actively sought out one-night-stands, their subject position was at least partially constructed through the have/hold discourse. After seeking out casual sex with a particular man Anne turned off her answering machine and purposely spent a lot of time out of the house for the following few days. She did not want to know if he had called or not.

> So it was not like I was expecting anything out of it, but I still, I do have like, like, I had like little fantasies about him, like staying or something like that, or like us continuing the relationship, so there must be, and I went into it totally like chasing him. I just wanted to have, to basically have casual sex, but I still have the future flashes.

Anne has purposely tried to disregard and shed the have/hold discourse and went out looking for a one-night-stand. Yet she still finds that she has what she calls "future flashes" and that she fantasizes about a possible future with the man. She also mentioned a few times that she saw no reason why they could not be friends, or at least talk with one another after having casual sex.

> I had one one-night-stand . . . and I just, I thought, like okay, well, you have sex with someone, and to me it doesn't matter, like sex . . . ok, I never felt like a slut when I do it, so I don't see other people . . . like I can never imagine other people thinking of me as a slut, but like, so I thought that we could just hang out with these guys afterwards and be friends, but it's weird, like once you've done the act, it's, there's like very like a lack of interest. . . . How are you supposed to meet anybody in this stupid town to hang out with, you know what I mean?

Here Anne takes up a different form of the have/hold discourse. She is not concerned with creating or maintaining a sexual or romantic relationship. However, she expects that she should be able to maintain a friendly relationship with men with whom she has had sex. She views the men as potential people to hang out with and party with, people who can be part of her larger social network. She resents that most often after she has sex with them, she is excluded from their social network.

Men do not take up this discourse as it relates to casual sex. Almost all the men expected not to engage in any sort of relationship with someone after they had sex, unless there was a relationship established before they had sex. A few men mentioned that they would delay having sex with a woman if they wanted to have a relationship with her.

> *Colin:* Well if you have a connection with this person and you're super attracted to them and you can see yourself being with them, then you won't fuck them the first date. Like if you really want a relationship with them, you're not going to spoil it by screwing them.
>
> *Don:* Like a really good one is going home to smoke pot or to do blow but like I've cut blow out of my life, that was like a high school thing. But like blow's really good because it shows that you really wanna talk to them because when you do a lot of blow your dick is like a limp spaghetti, and it's just like useless for sex and so shows that you care about conversation and bullshit like that.

For men, the have/hold discourse comes into play only when they want to develop a relationship with a woman, whereas for women, they often take it up whenever they are engaging in casual sex.

This discourse operates along with the male sexual drive discourse to enable casual sex among YAJs. Men engage in casual sex because of their "natural" and insatiable drive for sexual gratification. Conversely, women participate in casual sex with the hope of developing a lasting and committed relationship.

Sexual Permissiveness Discourse

Both men and women deployed the sexual permissiveness discourse, according to which casual sexual activity is considered normal and expected. Many of the men and women I spoke with were surprised at how many women in Jasper initiate and seek out casual sex. Robert said, "When I lived in [another province], it was the guys. But like here, it's anybody who's you know, guys or girls making the first move for sure." . . .

Casual sex for women is accepted, rather than stigmatized, in Jasper (although if they are "too" assertive or aggressive they risk being labelled a slut). Without this discourse, and the feeling that it is acceptable for women to have casual sex, it would be much more difficult for men to find willing partners. This discourse, which on the surface seems to support women's sexual desires, is necessary for men to engage in a lot of casual sex. This discourse can also obscure sexual double standards. It appears as though it is acceptable for both women and men to engage in casual sex. However, this is only acceptable if they are engaging in a "masculine" version of casual sex and if women are adhering to normative constructions of femininity created through the male sexual drive discourse.

Women's Sexual Agency

The discourses discussed above create depictions of casual sex that benefit male sexual desires and needs and are subject to male initiation. However, within these discourses women carve out spaces to exercise agency over their own sexuality and engage in heterosexual casual sex. Women create different degrees of agency during their casual sex experiences. First, women take advantage of the perception that more men are interested in casual sex than women, and therefore women have more choice about with whom they have sex. Second, women exercise agency by interrupting sexual activity before they engage in casual sex. Third, they actively seek out and orchestrate casual sex to satisfy their own sexual desires.

Women exercise agency by taking advantage of the perception that there are a lot more men seeking casual sex than there are women, creating a situation where women have a lot of choice regarding with whom they go home.

> *Teresa:* There's so many men looking for sex that, you know, women really have their pick and choose of the litter. If they're just looking for a one-night-stand [the men I've talked to] said that you really have to stick out like a sore thumb or like be right there.

Men and women sometimes argue that women have more power than men when it comes to casual sex, because they have the power of choice. Jane says that "girls have a lot of power in whether they go home with a man or not. Guys just kind of take their chance and hope they get lucky." If women are looking for casual sex, it is much easier for them to find someone with whom to go home. In a sense they are taking advantage of the male sexual drive discourse and using it to their advantage to have casual sex when they desire it.

Additionally, women exercise agency within and around the male sexual drive discourse by placing limits on the sexual activity—getting what they want out of it and stopping the interaction when they are satisfied. Agnes says that "I think too because the girl ultimately usually decides on . . . if there's going to be sex or not." Thus, while casual sex operates on the presumption of a male model of sexuality, women and men perceive that women act as the "gatekeepers" and determine whether or not casual sex will happen.

Men, as well as women, reported that women often act as limit-setters. Tim mentioned that sometimes women will be totally "into making out," but they will not let him take off their pants. He reads this as an indication that they are menstruating; he suggests that many women get particularly "horny" while they are menstruating. Regardless of whether or not these women are menstruating, taking up this strategy, or going along with his suggestion that they are menstruating gives them a chance to engage in casual sexual activity that does not lead to penetration. James mentioned similar strategies used by a few women.

> Like, you'll be with the girl and you'll be making out and she'll stop and be like, you know, "I really like you but I don't wanna go all the way because of this reason." Right, like, there

are still virgins out there, believe it or not, who are like, saving themselves for marriage, it's a really romantic concept that I really still enjoy, but you . . . it's a rarity I'll say . . . but they'll still have tonnes and tonnes of fun, but they just won't go all the way.

By being up front and telling men their limits, these women are opening up possibilities for casual sexual activity that do not include penetration. James mentioned that often they would engage in oral sex or genital touching. When men mentioned these strategies, they did not mind that the women were placing limits on sexual activity. James mentioned later on that "realistically again, you know, a lot of them are tourists they're not gonna be around the next day, so you have bad luck that night you always go out a couple nights later and maybe your luck's changed." If one woman is not willing to participate fully in a male model of casual sex that includes sexual penetration, then another one will be later on.

Thus, these women are able to negotiate the "coital imperative" (Jackson, 1984) of heterosexual sex by placing boundaries and limits around the sexual activity. This way, women are able to indirectly satisfy their own sexual desires while operating within normative heterosexual discourses. They do this without completely rejecting the coital imperative. By saying that they want to wait until marriage to have sex or that they are having their period, they imply that they would otherwise be willing to engage in intercourse and are recognizing the central role that intercourse plays in heterosexual relations.

While the women I interviewed did not talk about strategies that included claiming they were menstruating or that they wanted to remain virgins, many of them mentioned setting limits as a way to ensure control over their casual sex.

Agnes: I just don't let it happen. I say no, like when they try to go that direction, I'm like "no, I don't sleep with guys on the first date."

Many women have a sense that they are in control of placing limits on sexual activity. Of course they do have to be careful about how they approach setting these limits.

Laurie: Well I guess, I would just, I don't know, I guess I would try to keep it kind of light and stuff, cause I don't want to piss them off right? Some guys could be weird and psycho (laughs) and so, I don't know I'd probably try to keep it light, put clothes on or whatever if I took my clothes off, and be like, "oh, can you go?" or "I'm gonna go home" or whatever.

While women exercised agency by setting limits and interrupting sexual activity prior to penetration, the reaction of the men they were with varied. In the examples discussed above, the women's excuses were considered "legitimate" by the men. However, if a man did not consider the excuses "legitimate" he often became frustrated and women were labelled "teases." These consequences acted as constraints and the men attempted to limit women's access to these strategies to create their own agency.

While many women set sexual limits, others reported orchestrating their own casual sex experiences focused on their own pleasure. Anne's story is a good example of this type of agency and of the tension between a male-oriented discursive construction of heterosexual casual sex and women's space for agency within that discourse. Anne carefully sought out and chose a man to have casual sex with.

He's not young young, he's 19, but like I haven't been with a 19-year-old guy since I was 17, so it was really weird, but um it's so sad but it seems to be safer to me, to go for someone who wasn't like, living in Jasper for so long, than for someone new and innocent, it sounds so dirty! (laughs) . . . but it's that attitude. Like he was a really good-looking boy, but he probably didn't know how good-looking quite yet you know what I mean . . . and I knew when I met him that he was like, how old he was and I knew he was leaving in August.

Anne carefully chose a man whose social position enabled her more control over the situation. She liked the idea that Jack was young and new to Jasper. To her, this meant that he was likely not very experienced and that he had not yet developed an attitude like many other men she met in Jasper. This gave her greater control over the situation. She went out with Jack and a few friends one night to go partying. Both of them got quite drunk, but the whole night she was focused on getting him to go home with her. At one point they tried to go to a different bar, but Jack was so drunk that the bouncers would not let him in; he said that he would just go home.

> I was like, no, the whole point of going out with you guys is because of you, you can't go home, so, but I didn't say that, I'm like oh no no no, we can't leave one person out that's so wrong. And I asked the bouncer if we take him to the park and he sobers up can we come back in an hour, and they said as long as he can walk straight or something like that then we'll let him in. So that, so we ended up doing that.

Anne ensured that Jack would stay with the rest of the group until the end of the night so she could take him home with her. They did end up back at that bar. Anne and Jack were dancing and kissing on the dance floor. One of Jack's friends was leaving the bar and came up and shook Jack's hand to congratulate him on successfully picking up Anne.

> Like when the guy shook the guy's hand and like I don't care cause like, congratulations to me too, you know what I mean, that was my goal for the night, to go home with him. So like, and then we did, and he is so much fun.

Anne felt that she too should be congratulated; she was taking up the typically male role in casual sex. She took up the active role seeking sex, and he took on the more passive role by going along with it. When they did end up back at her place she was concerned about him, and his willingness to participate in sex.

> I know I wanted to have sex, like that was something that was going to happen for me. But I did ask him because I kinda felt . . . just because I was so forward with it all the time, I just wanted to make sure he was along for the, like was there as well. . . . Cause yeah, cause a lot of times I probably haven't been with the guy, and it just happened anyways, you just kind of follow along with the progression of things. . . . Like I asked him before we had sex, are you sure you're okay with this? And he was like, yeah! Like what the fuck, like why are you asking that question?

She knew that she was not always really into the casual sex that took place previously, and she did not like the feeling that gave her. Therefore, she made a point of ensuring that Jack was a willing participant. Jack almost took offence to her question. Her question subverts the male sexual drive discourse by questioning his desire. He took this as also questioning his masculinity as framed within the male sexual drive discourse.

Throughout the sexual activity, Anne ensured that her desires would be met.

> I don't mind like, like helping myself get off when I'm having sex cause some guys are good at it, some guys know how to do it and you don't have to worry about it, but some guys are totally clueless, especially, maybe not so experienced guys and so I don't have an issue at all with for me it's for me and I know that I don't have a problem with I want to do this I want to do that. . . . Like when I was with Jack I did say it. I have no problem saying certain things like, like just stuff like getting on top, different positions and like can you move over here can you move over there.

Anne had no problem taking control over her sexual pleasure. During casual sex, she will pleasure herself if she is not getting what she wants from sex. She is also comfortable enough to ask for what she wants, a switch in position, or for Jack to shift to a different position. Anne uses her sense of agency to get what she wants; at the same time she recognizes that the model of casual sex is a male model and so she has learned how to temporarily manipulate the model to fit her desires.

> Like guys are assholes, I had no idea, no one told me, and it's not that I'm not angry at them,

> because I just see it, as that's the way they are, you just have to know that. I think girls should be given that knowledge, so that and then they can make their own decisions and what they want. If they want to participate in it or not, because sometimes I do, sometimes I'm like, I want to, and I'm up for it but you have to be really aware of what you're getting into, because you can get really hurt like otherwise.

She feels that now that she knows more about what casual sex is all about, she can choose when and how she participates in it. For Anne, casual sex is deliberately engaged in, which contrasts with many other women's experiences of casual sex as something that "just happens."

Women who take up sexual agency in this way move beyond the permissiveness discourse because they are not just giving themselves permission to participate in sex. They are creating experiences and situations to satisfy their own sexual desires. They do this not by changing the dominant discourses that govern heterosexual casual sex, but by creating spaces within those discourses and subtly challenging them to allow them to cater to their own needs.

The negotiation of heterosexual casual sex is a nuanced process laden with hegemonic and often contradictory discourses. Often, there is the sense that casual sex is not really negotiated at all, that it just happens when two people are together at the bar drinking. Running parallel to this discourse are the male sexual drive discourse and the sexual permissiveness discourse. The male sexual drive discourse is used to create a model of casual sex governed by notions of male sexual desire as being ever-present and never satisfied. This discourse simultaneously silences women's sexual desires and assumes that women play a passive role in sexual relations. For casual sex to take place, the sexual permissiveness discourse is deployed, allowing women to desire and participate in sex as long as it is the version of sex in the male sexual drive discourse—that is, penetrative sex with "no strings attached." A few women however, position themselves within the have/hold discourse and expect that after casual sex the possibility for a friendship or relationship still exists.

Within these discourses that privilege male desire, women have been able to carve out ways to negotiate casual sex that takes into consideration their own desires. Women will place limits on the sexual activity or leave after their needs have been met. Sometimes women will take an even more active role in designing and orchestrating their own casual sex experiences that satisfy their desires. Women are adapting by recognizing that casual sex is often controlled by male sexual desire, then choosing when and how they participate in casual sex to get their own desires met.

Conclusion

When discussing issues of casual sex, YAJs first turn to a discourse of "it just happens" and suggest that casual sex is a serendipitous event. However, through their stories the male sexual drive discourse is the dominant discourse operating in this environment. Casual sex is driven by the assumption that men are perpetually in search of sex. Perhaps surprisingly, the women deploy the have/hold discourse and report that one reason they engage in casual sex is for the possibility of developing a relationship with their casual partner. Finally, casual sex is dependent on the sexual permissiveness discourse that suggests that casual sex is permissible for both women and men (at least within the confines of the male sexual drive discourse). Finally, within these discourses women exert power through their choice in partners, by setting limits and by taking what may be considered a typically masculine role and actively pursuing casual sex.

References

Hollway, W. 1984. "Gender Difference and the Production of Subjectivity," in J. Henriques, W. Hollway, C. Urwin, C. Venn, and V. Walkerdine, eds., *Changing the Subject: Psychology, Social Regulation and Subjectivity*, pp. 227–63. New York: Routledge.

Chapter 19

Overview

Historically, sexual activity has been legitimated and privileged if it happens within the context of marriage. With the legalization of same-sex marriage in Canada in 2005, we joined a growing group of countries that have effectively de-gendered the legal institution of marriage, granting political recognition to same-sex couples who seek equality with their heterosexual peers. While this has been hailed as a major milestone in human rights, and is widely supported in Canadian public opinion, Nick Mulé suggests that we may want to think a bit harder about some of the implicit assumptions that are validated by the legalization of same-sex marriage.

Mulé positions himself as a "critical liberationist," who believes individuals should be able to freely choose how they live their lives, without hierarchies and exclusions. He argues that the legalization of same-sex marriage effectively reinforces a two-tier structure: privileging married people (regardless of the gender of their partner) while excluding others who do not or choose not to marry, or who have other forms of intimate relationships. Simply removing the gendered component of marriage does not produce a better or more just society in itself, as long as the conjugal (married) couple is assumed to be the most important social unit. While not everyone would agree with Mulé, his arguments make us think about the unintended consequences and unspoken assumptions in different forms of social change.

Same-Sex Marriage and Canadian Relationship Recognition: One Step Forward and Two Steps Back. A Critical Liberationist Perspective

Nick Mulé

Introduction

Same-sex marriage in Canada brought forth an important legal sanctioning of same-sex couples with social implications for their public recognition and legitimacy. The purpose of this paper is to deconstruct the platforms posited by sexually diverse proponents of same-sex marriage and their allies from a critical liberationist perspective. Arguments put forth on this issue in the literature are reviewed, and how the debate was restricted in Canada to focus exclusively on traditional/couplist and neo-liberal views is exposed. Injecting a critical liberationist perspective expands the narrowed frameworks of the debate, deepening the discourse in Canada and beyond. By moving beyond equality-based arguments, the very platforms utilized by the proponents of same-sex marriage are interrogated in light of a broader social justice approach that highlights and questions the privileges of marriage (LaSala, 2007; Mulé, 2006) and seeks recognition of a variety of relationships.

Proponents argue that extending marital rights to same-sex couples achieves equality, whereas I argue that this "achievement" is at the expense of equity in recognizing many other kinds of relationships—an outcome that is contrary to the ideals of social justice.

A Critical Liberationist Perspective

The analysis herein is guided by a critical liberationist perspective utilizing a queer lens. By critical, I mean there is an obligation to deconstruct existing social structures in order to interrogate degrees of equality, equity, and benefits, and then provide options to address any levels of oppression found therein (Mulé, 2008). A liberationist ethos speaks to individuals having the right to define for themselves who they are and how they live their lives with the impact of contributing to society's diversity (Hay & Roscoe, 1996; Warner, 2002), rather than being shaped by society to fit hegemonic roles and expectations and thus being marginalized if they fail to do so (Altman, 1971; Mulé, 2006). The queer lens being applied comes from a non-heterosexual and non-gender binary approach, in which the lived experiences of lesbians, gays, bisexuals, transgender, transsexual, two-spirit, intersex, queer, and/or questioning is an acknowledged reality despite society's heterosexist structures.

Institution of Marriage Questioned

"Marriage creates a two-tier system that allows the state to regulate relationships" (Ettelbrick, 1997, p. 167). In essence, by extending marriage to Canadian same-sex couples the state has been invited back into their bedrooms. Proponents of same-sex marriage, in effect, accept the regime of marriage and thus its monopoly, rather than reject "the regime of marriage . . . [as] a means of transcending the traditional church/state monopoly on relationship options" (Butler, 2001a, p. 58).

During the debates on same-sex marriage in Canada, alternative ideas about relationship recognition were advanced by some organizations. The Law Commission of Canada (LCC) (2001) acknowledged that although recognition and support of personal adult caring and interdependent relationships is an important objective of the state (which has expanded rights and obligations for adult relationships), the state's legal recognition of relationships has focused on conjugal relationships only. LCC espoused broader values in calling for a more expanded approach to relationships: "Instead of focusing mainly on married couples and couples deemed to be 'marriage-like,' governments should establish registration schemes to facilitate the private ordering of both conjugal and non-conjugal relationships" (LCC, 2001, p. 131). LCC proposed civil registration for adults regardless of relationship type that would require subscribing to a series of associated legal rights and obligations.

Similarly, the Coalition for Lesbian and Gay Rights in Ontario (CLGRO) proposed that the state should exit the business of marriage and that the institution of marriage continue to exist under the auspices of religious institutions, thus challenging marriage's state sanctioning. This would result in marriages having no legal implications, privileges, or special status (CLGRO, 2003). This proposal questions the institution of marriage, and shifts the systemic structure from the couple to the individual as the core unit, with allowance made for dependents (e.g., children, the aged, and people with (dis)abilities), thereby undercutting traditional epistemological perspectives in the process. CLGRO called for the system to be reformed by placing the individual at the core, choosing who they would register as their significant other(s), without restrictions as to relationships being sexual, conjugal, or limited to two people. CLGRO advocated for a systemic reformation that would both legally and socially recognize diverse forms of relationships, which would end the current two-tier system of relationship recognition. "there should be no hierarchy of legally recognized relationships, such as placing marriage at a higher level than common-law relationships or non-conjugal relationships" (CLGRO, 2003, p. 2). Proposed is a broader analysis that goes beyond equality, illuminating the pursuit of same-sex marriage as contributing to the privileging of those that choose to marry, while marginalizing those that do not.

Extending Marriage to Same-Sex Couples

Varying themes have been used in arguing for the extension of marriage to same-sex couples. Marital status and its continuity between private and public spheres, hierarchy, and power are similarly understood in family and society and have been argued from both pre-modern (Smith & Windes, 2000) and modern (Sullivan, 1995) perspectives. By exposing heterosexual extended family and friends to a same-sex marital coupling, traditional concepts of marriage are challenged (Cox, 1997). Others argue liberationist concepts exist within same-sex marriage. For example, the disruption of traditional gendered and hierarchical definitions of marriage (Hunter, 1995) and the ushering in of same-sex partners both in public and in private societal realms challenges heterosexist concepts of the family (Calhoun, 2000). Such perspectives are problematic for their oversight of class and power differentials within same-sex relationships and for centralizing marriage and family in their concepts of citizenship (Boyd & Young, 2003). Same-sex marriage nevertheless remains enframed in traditional heterosexual couplist structures of marriage. In other words, within the familiar institution of marriage, the structuring of the couple remains, with the only change being from opposite to same-sex parties.

These arguments may challenge traditional conceptualizations based on man/woman but they do not challenge general society as other types of relationships are simply not part of the equation. Critical liberationist perspectives assist us in understanding the breadth and depth of relationships recognition. Warner (1999) posits three liberationist principles regarding same-sex marriage: that the institution of marriage is idealized; that a variety of intimate relationships need to be affirmed and respected; and the application of straight cultural norms to queer lives needs to be resisted. Clearly, same-sex marriage will not address sexual prejudice, nor achieve social acceptance or broad personal fulfillment. Furthermore, a queer theoretical approach calls us to address sexual minority oppression by destabilizing gender and sexual categories (Butler, 2001a); therefore, some suggest a resistance to domestication by highlighting uniqueness of difference over assimilationism (Robson, 1998). Also, a counter-cultural perspective reveals how same-sex marriage contributes to a heteronormative discourse, which impacts on gay male identity that is queer-based and distinguished from the heteronormative male (Grindstaff, 2003).

One Step Forward, Two Steps Back: Equality Arguments versus Critical Liberationist Perspectives

Internationally, Canada became the fourth country to legislatively permit same-sex couples to marry, preceded by the Netherlands, Belgium, and Spain (EGALE Canada, 2006). The process to arrive at such legislation was driven by the work of activist organizations such as EGALE Canada (a Canadian LGBT lobby group) and its offshoot, Canadians for Equal Marriage—proponents of the initiative within Canadian sexually diverse communities. On the surface, allowing same-sex couples to marry paints a picture of a progressive piece of legislation that lifts a blatant form of discrimination from a marginalized population—one step forward. For sexually diverse populations it represents recognition of same-sex relationships equal to that of opposite-sex relationships with added material benefits found in tax law, spousal benefits, survivor pensions, and so on. To many Canadians, this decision symbolically represented Canada's commitment to a more inclusive society. The world generally views Canada as a progressive country. When viewing the issue from an equality perspective, within which the debates were framed, the outcome is a significant one, with implications for the recognition of relationships and how families are constituted within Canadian society, sexually diverse populations therein as well as at the international level conceptually.

However, applying a critical examination from a liberationist perspective reveals that the equality arguments and strategy in effect sets Canada's recognition of relationships two steps back. This transpired through the polarized public debates that were limited to an equality framework. An equality framework is premised on equal treatment of all people, in this case permitting same-sex couples access to the heterosexually defined institution of marriage. Proponents were made up largely of vocal members of sexually diverse communities and their supporters, and opponents generally consisted of those on the right wing of the political spectrum and/or of traditional religious views. Canadian sexually diverse proponents of same-sex marriage argued their cause via four equality-based platforms: a human rights issue narrowly defined; equality for some; inclusion, personhood, and internalized homophobia; and pro-choice for others—but problematic.

A Human Rights Issue Narrowly Defined

The argument "It's a fight for human rights" was promulgated by the Canadians for Equal Marriage campaign, further suggesting Canada could take the lead in international human rights with the legalization of same-sex marriage ("It's a Fight for Human Rights," n.d., p. 1). Bourassa and Varnell (2002, p. 16), both active members of this campaign, also see the issue as one of human rights with discriminatory implications, for which "homosexuals were second-class citizens" in the absence of being able to marry.

The extent of the human rights argument is questioned by a critical liberationist perspective as to why only certain kinds of couples (read: same-sex conjugal)—as opposed to other kinds of relationships—are elevated to a privileged status warranting the "human rights" marriage offers. A helpful distinction between the "rights" stance (to marry for those who choose to) and the "justice" stance (that would capture all, including those who choose not to marry) is posited by Ettelbrick (1997). Attaining rights for a few and not correcting the power imbalances between the married and unmarried (regardless of sexual orientation) fails to serve justice (Ettelbrick, 1989).

Equality for Some

The issue of same-sex marriage has been presented in a sweeping fashion. According to Heale (2003), "this is an issue of equality as protected by the Canadian Constitution" (p. 5), premising merely one kind of relationship recognition on equality. "It is about fairness, mutual respect and equality," said Gilles Marchildon, Executive Director of EGALE Canada (Canadians for Equal Marriage, 2004). A closer examination reveals that the pursuit of same-sex marriage was not about achieving equality for same-sex relationships, but rather about achieving equality for same-sex relationships most closely resembling those of the traditional/pre-modern heterosexual model. Hence, the assimilated minority members gain the advantages of an acquiescing majority, while those who refuse to assimilate are further marginalized (Eskridge, 2003). Yet, by using such sweeping language, a discourse is created within sexually diverse communities urging support for an issue of "equality." However, restricting the human rights perspective to liberal ideals of equality does not address how same-sex marriage generates new inequalities and negates equity in the process.

Inclusion, Personhood, and Internalized Homophobia

For many people, a sense of personhood is based upon being included in the mainstream with the majority, and that such a feeling can contribute to combating a form of internalized homophobia. Access to the institution of marriage addresses this, particularly for those who revere the social status of marriage without question. Quebec pro-same-sex marriage and gay activist Michael Hendricks called marriage the "gold standard of social respectability" (cited in Brown, 2002, p. 12). Thus, by entering such an institution, a special and powerful social status is bestowed (Ettelbrick, 1997), elevating the couple by their mere membership: "I feel like I've been admitted into membership of some kind of club," said Toronto city councilor Kyle Rae, upon marrying his same-sex partner (CityTV, 2004). The enduring status of marriage (Goldberg-Hiller, 2002) backed by legal recognition has caused some to perceive domestic partnership agreements as a discursive tension between the status of the former and contractual obligations of the latter. A heightened validity is associated with marital relationships (Ettelbrick, 1997), which is substantiated by legally sanctioned and culturally supported legitimacy. This was exemplified by Metropolitan Community Church of Toronto (MCCT) in their submission to the Parliamentary Panel on Same-sex Marriage:

> Marriage also confers a status with well-recognized social significance that, rightly or wrongly, is perceived by many to be the commitment of the highest order of one person to another. As with many other Canadians, for gays and lesbians the capacity to marry and the right to marry the person of their choice are an incident of full membership in society. For gays and lesbians, a group that has been historically marginalized, marriage is also the recognition before and by the society of their "full personhood." (2003, p. 12)

Right from the outset of this quotation, it is made clear that the status marriage has in our society is not to be interrogated, but rather they are centring their position on acquiescence and acquisition for relational purposes and the benefit of assigning elevated status to personhood. By permitting access to the institution of marriage, some same-sex marriage proponents generalize its benefits to sweeping levels, as when gay activist Michael Leshner declared, "Homophobia is dead legally as of today" (Mackenzie, 2003, p. 12).

Usage of terms and phrases such as "gold standard of social respectability," "membership," and "social significance" submits to a socio-cultural ideology of marriage, contributing to and sustaining its elevated status in society unquestionably. A discourse is created that extends to individuals and couples with terminology such as "full personhood," constructing a false sense of self-worth, devaluing those outside the institution. Such discourse contributes to a form of subordination to heteronormativity, underscored by internalized homophobia that serves to further marginalize individuals who have the strength to be non-conformist.

Pro-Choice for Others—But Problematic

Not all sexually diverse proponents of same-sex marriage want marriage for themselves, but have put forth the strong argument to support the choice of others to marry. Kevin Bourassa and Joe Varnell state, "Our goal is to ensure that couples have the equal right to marry if they choose, not to advocate that all couples get married. We recognize that many people will choose not to formalize their relationship, through civil or religious marriage" (Equal Marriage, n.d.). Again, this perspective falls short of recognizing or extending benefits to relationships that are located outside of the institution of marriage. The lack of consensus on the issue in sexually diverse communities, which was rarely reported on in mainstream media, is addressed by Canadians for Equal Marriage campaign Co-chairperson, Mary Woo Sims:

> I think that even in our own community the issue is not very well understood, in that this is not about forcing individuals to get married, it's about giving people in our community who wish to marry the same choices that other Canadians have. . . . [Let's] be clear [on] what this debate is all about. (MacMullin, 2004, p. 4)

Sims provides a classic example of how to restrict the debate. By framing the context within one of confusion as to why sexually diverse communities have not reached unanimity on the issue, she attempts to clarify via the argument of choice, simultaneously curtailing the discussion within the confines of a liberal perspective. Such a reductionist approach serves to fence out a more expansive appraisal of the debate as would be taken by a liberationist perspective.

By extending choice to others, the hierarchy of relationships, which holds marital ones at the top, is maintained, not questioned. The following quotation from an "older lesbian" attests to how effective the campaign was in its influence on sexually diverse communities: "It's funny, I know a number of people, myself included, who support the marriage thing, but would never want it personally, and so feel we're letting down the team if we say so" (Mackenzie, 2003, p. 12). Proponents who take a pro-choice position for others, yet do not personally opt for marriage, on the outset, present as altruistic, but, simultaneously and usually unbeknownst to the proponents, contribute to the further marginalization of those who do not enter this privileged status, including themselves.

Conclusion

The legalization of same-sex marriage in Canada is seen by many as a step forward on the equality front. Yet the reductionist approach to the issue undertaken by Canadian sexually diverse proponents and their allies during the debates limited the discourse to conjugal relationships that most closely matched marital heterosexual relationships on the basis of "equality." This focus sent the queer movement two steps back, for it fails to encompass a broader range of relationship recognition in multicultural Canada from an equity perspective. A deconstruction of five platforms that sexually diverse proponents of same-sex marriage utilized during the debates reveals an assimilationist position that ultimately provided access into a two-tiered system that privileges marital relationships over all others. A critical analysis with a liberationist lens expands the discourse on broader relationship recognition in Canada, questioning the special status ascribed to marital relationships. According to liberationists, all relationships need to be recognized equitably, legally, economically, and socioculturally if we are to create a level playing field.

References

Alderson, K.G. 2004. "A Phenomenological Investigation of Same-Sex Marriage," *The Canadian Journal of Human Sexuality* 13(2): 107–22.

Altman, D. 1971. *Homosexual Oppression and Liberation*. New York: Outerbridge & Deinstfrey.

Auchmuty, R. 2004. "Same-Sex Marriage Revived: Feminist Critique and Legal Strategy," *Feminism & Psychology* 14(1): 101–26.

Auger, J.A. 2003. *Passing Through: The End-of-life Decisions of Lesbians and Gay Men*. Halifax, NS: Fernwood.

Bourassa, K., and J. Varnell. 2002. *Just Married: Gay Marriage and the Expansion of Human Rights*. Ontario: Doubleday Canada.

Boyd, S.B. 1999. "Family, Law and Sexuality: Feminist Engagements," *International Journal of Social & Legal Studies* 8(3): 369–90.

Boyd, S.B., and C.F.L. Young. 2003. "'From Same-Sex to No Sex'?: Trends Towards Recognition of (Same-sex) Relationships in Canada," *Seattle Journal for Social Justice* 1(3): 757–93.

Brown, E. 2002, June 20. "Civil Unions, How Romantic." Toronto: *fab*., pp. 12.

Butler, J. 2001a. "There Is a Person Here: An Interview with Judith Butler," compiled by M.S. Breen, W.J. Blumenfeld, with S. Baer, R.A. Brookey, L. Hall, V. Kirby, D.H. Miller, R. Shail, and N. Wilson. *International Journal of Sexuality and Gender Studies* 6(1/2): 7–23.

Butler, J. 2001b. *Is Kinship Always Already Heterosexual? Inaugural Lecture Presented to the Center for the Study of Sexual Culture*. April 25. Berkeley: University of California.

Calhoun, C. 2000. *Feminism, the Family, and the Politics of the Closet: Lesbian and Gay Displacement*. Oxford and New York: Oxford University Press.

Canadians for Equal Marriage. 2004, April 28. *News Release: Canadians for Equal Marriage to Respond to Opponents. Big Bucks Campaign*. Ottawa: Canadians for Equal Marriage.

Canadians for Equal Marriage. n.d. "Abolishing Civil Marriage: Nobody Wins." Retrieved April 19, 2004, from www.equal-marriage.ca/info/abolish.pdf.

Canadians for Equal Marriage. n.d. "It's a Fight for Human Rights." Retrieved April 19, 2004, from www.equal-marriage.ca/releases/Canadians_for_Equal_Marriage_Campaign.pdf.

Christopher, M.C. 2005. "Is Marriage Obsolete?," *Law Now* 29: 6.

CityTV. 2004, April 3. *Pride and Joy*. Toronto: CityTV.

Coalition for Lesbian and Gay Rights in Ontario (CLGRO). (2002). August. *News Release: The State Has No Business in the Marriages of the Nation*. Toronto: Author.

Coalition for Lesbian and Gay Rights in Ontario (CLGRO). 2003, April 10. *Presentation to the Federal Consultation on Same-Sex Marriage*. Toronto: Author.

Coalition for Lesbian and Gay Rights in Ontario (CLGRO). 2004. *Lesbian, Gay and Bisexual Liberation in the 2000s*. Toronto: Author.

Coates, J., and R. Sullivan. 2005. "Achieving Competent Family Practice with Same-Sex Parents: Some Promising Directions," *Journal of GLBT Family Studies* 1(2): 89–113.

Cox, B.J. 1997. "A (Personal) Essay on Same-Sex Marriage," in R.M. Baird and S.E. Rosenbaum, eds., *Same-Sex Marriage: The Moral and Legal Debate*, pp. 27–29. Amherst, NY: Prometheus Books.

Donovan, C. 2004. "Why Reach for the Moon? Because the Stars Aren't Enough," *Feminism & Psychology* 14(1): 24–29.

EGALE Canada. 2003, August 14. *News Release: Abolishing Civil Marriage: Nobody Wins*. Retrieved April 19, 2004, from www.egale.ca/printer.asp?lang=E&item=205&version=EN.

EGALE Canada. (2006). *Equal Marriage*. Retrieved April 29, 2006, from www.egale.ca/index.asp?lang=E&menu=30&item=983.

Equal Marriage for Same-Sex Couples. n.d. Introduction. Retrieved April 19, 2004, from www.samesexmarriage.ca/introduction.htm.

Eskridge, W.N., Jr. 1996. *The Case for Same-Sex Marriage: From Sexual Liberty to Civilized Commitment*. New York: The Free Press.

Eskridge, W.N., Jr. 2002. *Equality Practice: Civil Unions and the Future of Gay Rights*. London: Routledge.

Eskridge, W.N., Jr. 2003. "The Same-Sex Marriage Debate and Three Conceptions of Equality," in L.D. Wardle, M. Strasser, W.C. Duncan, and D. Orgon Coolidge, eds., *Marriage and Same-Sex Unions: A Debate*, pp. 167–85. Westport, CT: Praeger Publishers.

Ettelbrick, P. 1989. "Since When Is Marriage a Path to Liberation?," in A. Sullivan, ed., *Same-Sex Marriage: Pro and Con*, pp. 121–28. New York: Random House.

Ettelbrick, P.L. 1992. "Since When Is Marriage a Path to Liberation?," in S. Sherman, ed., *Lesbian and Gay Marriage*, pp. 20–26. Philadelphia: Temple University Press.

Ettelbrick, P.L. 1997. "Since When Is Marriage a Path to Liberation?," in R.M. Baird, and S.E. Rosenbaum, eds., *Same-Sex Marriage. The Moral and Legal Debate*, pp. 164–68. New York: Prometheus Books.

Goldberg-Hiller, J. 2002. *The Limits to Union: Same-Sex Marriage and the Politics of Civil Rights*. Ann Arbor, MI: The University of Michigan Press.

Grindstaff, D. 2003. "Queering Marriage: An Ideographic Interrogation of Heteronormative Subjectivity," *Journal of Homosexuality* 45(2/3/4): 257–75.

Hay, H., and W. Roscoe, eds. 1996. *Radically Gay: Gay Liberation in the Words of Its Founder*. Boston: Beacon Press.

Heale, R. 2003. "Divided We Fall," *OutLooks*, October: 5.

Hunter, N.D. 1995. "Marriage, Law and Gender: A Feminist Inquiry," in L. Duggan and N.D. Hunter, eds., *Sex Wars: Sexual Dissent and Political Culture*, pp. 107–22. New York and London: Routledge.

Janson, G.R. 2002. "Family Counseling and Referral with Gay, Lesbian, Bisexual, and Transgendered Clients: Ethical Considerations," *The Family Journal* 10: 328–33.

LaSala, M.C. 2007. "Too Many Eggs in the Wrong Basket: A Queer Critique of the Same-Sex Marriage Movement" (Commentary), *Social Work* 52(2): 181–83.

Law Commission of Canada. 2001. *Beyond Conjugality: Recognizing and Supporting Close Personal Adult Relationships*. Ottawa: Law Commission of Canada.

Mackenzie, I. 2003. "Canadians Cheer US Decision," *Xtra!*, November 27: 13.

MacMullin, G. 2004. "Hoping to Woo the Voters," *OutLooks* February: 4.

Maynard, S. 2000. "Modernization or Liberation?" *Capital Xtra!* March 17: 19.

McClellan, D.L. 1997. *Second Parent Adoption in Lesbian Families: Legalizing the Reality of the Child*. Brandeis University: Unpublished.

Metropolitan Community Church of Toronto (MCCT). 2003. *Submission of the Metropolitan Community Church of Toronto Executive Summary*. Toronto: Author.

Mohr, R.D. 1997. "The Case for Gay Marriage," in R.M. Baird and S.E. Rosenbaum, eds., *Same-Sex*

Marriage: The Moral and Legal Debate, pp. 84–104. Amherst, NY: Prometheus Books.

Mossman, M.J. 1994. "Running Hard to Stand Still: The Paradox of Family Law Reform," *Dalhousie Law Journal* 17: 5–34.

Mulé, N.J. 2006. "Equality's Limitations, Liberation's Challenges: Considerations for Queer Movement Strategizing," *Canadian Online Journal of Queer Studies in Education* 2(1). Available at http://jqstudies.oise.utoronto.ca/journal/viewarticle.php?id=26.

Mulé, N.J. 2008. "Demarcating Gender and Sexual Diversity on the Structural Landscape of Social Work," *Critical Social Work* 9(1). Available at www.criticalsocialwork.com/units/socialwork/critical.nsf/982f0e5f06b5c9a285256d6e006cff78/ebb5ace61ebf5d368525744c00802bdf?OpenDocument.

Ontario Association of Social Workers (OASW) & Canadian Association of Social Workers (CASW). 2003. *Statement of Support for Legal Recognition of Same-Sex Unions*. Toronto: Author.

Phelan, S. 2001. *Sexual Strangers: Gays, Lesbians and Dilemmas of Citizenship*. Philadelphia: Temple University Press.

Robinson, S. 2004, January 15. *News Release: Robinson Slams Martin and Cotler "Backtracking" on Equality for Gay and Lesbian Couples; Calls for Liberals to Respect Court Rulings on Same-Sex Marriage and Pension Rights*. Ottawa: Author.

Robson, R. 1998. *Sappho Goes to Law School*. New York: Columbia University Press.

Rubin, G.S. 1993. "Thinking Sex: Notes for a Radical Theory of the Politics of Sexuality," in H. Abelove, M.A. Barale, and D.M. Halperin, eds., *The Lesbian and Gay Studies Reader*, pp. 3–44. New York: Routledge.

Smith, R.R., and R.R. Windes. 2000. *Progay/Antigay: The Rhetorical War Over Sexuality*. Thousand Oaks, CA: Sage.

Sullivan, A. 1995. *Virtually Normal: An Argument about Homosexuality*. New York: Knopf.

Tully, C.T. 1994. "To Boldly Go Where No One Has Gone Before: The Legalization of Lesbian and Gay Marriages," *Journal of Gay and Lesbian Social Services* 30(2): 73–87.

Vallee, D. 2003. "Same-Sex Marriage: Why Knot? Here's Why Not," *The Toronto Star*, June 23: A21.

Walters, S.D. 2001. "Take My Domestic Partner, Please: Gays and Marriage in the Era of the Visible," in M. Bernstein and R. Reinmann, eds., *Queer Families, Queer Politics: Challenging Culture and the State*, pp. 338–57. New York: Columbia University Press.

Warner, M. 1999. "Normal and Normaller: Beyond Gay Marriage," *GLQ: A Journal of Lesbian and Gay Studies* 5: 119–71.

Warner, T. 2002. *Never Going Back: A History of Queer Activism in Canada*. Toronto: University of Toronto.

Webb, R.A. 2005. "Overview of Same-Sex Marriage in the U.S.: The Struggle for Civil Rights and Equality," National Association of Social Workers (NASW). Retrieved October 21, 2007, from www.socialworkers.org/diversity/lgb/062005.asp.

Yep, G.A., K.E. Lovaas, and J.P. Elia. 2003. "A Critical Appraisal of Assimilationist and Radical Ideologies Underlying Same-Sex Marriage in LGBT Communities in the United States," *Journal of Homosexuality* 45(1): 45–64.

PART VI
The Gendered Family

Are families "in crisis"? Are traditional arrangements collapsing under the weight of contemporary trends ranging from relaxed sexual attitudes, increased divorce, and women's entry into the labour force to rap music and violence in the media? The persistence of public argument about family values, the idea that "the family" is somehow in decline, the emergence of new family forms: all of these phenomena underscore the centrality of families to the reproduction of social life and to gender identity. In 1985, S.F. Berk described families as "gender factories," and while the factory metaphor is perhaps a bit too mechanical for the complex and often contradictory gender work that goes on in families, it does emphasize the important role families play in the creation and constant re-creation of gender.

Although the "typical" family represented in 1950s television sitcoms—composed of breadwinner father, housewife mother, and 2.5 happy, well-adjusted children—is the empirical reality for less than 10 per cent of all households, it remains the cultural ideal against which contemporary family compositions are measured. And some would like to see us "return" to as close as possible an approximation of that imagined idealized model—perhaps by restricting access to easy divorce or restricting women's entry into the labour force or by promoting sexual abstinence and delegitimating homosexuality.

Others, though, view the problems with the family differently. The disjunctures between the demands of the workplace and the demands (and desires) of home are evident in Gillian Ranson's account of women engineers who find that motherhood marks a major turning point in their relationship with their high-intensity, high-skill careers. Childbearing and raising children do not fit easily into the professional world—at least not the intensive-mothering form of child-raising that most North Americans have learned to value.

Mothers are not the only ones who struggle with the contradictions and tensions of parenthood. The fathers in Dominelli and colleagues' study face a different set of challenges—establishing themselves as responsible, credible parents, despite having children who are in the public child welfare system. The spectre of the "bad dad" haunts these men as they attempt to sustain relationships with their children.

Family life consists of more than just caring for children, of course. As Anne Martin-Mathews demonstrates, caregiving work in families is often needed to help the elderly and the ill, as well as the young. For many families, the actual activities of caregiving and care-receiving do not fit neatly into stereotypes about women as the caring sex. The physical maintenance of the home has also been an arena of contestation between men and women, although this is an arena in which changes are happening. Sociologist Scott Coltrane discusses the relationship between housework, childcare, and the status of women in society: the more housework and childcare women do, the lower their status. As a result, he suggests that sharing housework and childcare is not only a way for husbands and wives to enact more egalitarian relationships but also a way to ensure that the next generation will maintain egalitarian attitudes.

Questions for Critical Thought

1. What is your vision of ideal family life? Would your parents, siblings, and peers share that vision?
2. Ranson suggests that taking care of children is at odds with the demands of paid work, especially for women. Do you share her implicit pessimism about combining childcare and paid work?
3. Have you seen evidence of women whose work or family lives require them to become "conceptual men," as in Ranson's study? Are there any circumstances under which men might be treated as "conceptual women"?
4. The men in Dominelli et al. want to be seen as "good enough dads," making positive contributions to their children's lives despite difficult circumstances. What does it mean to be a "good enough dad"? Is it different from being a "good enough mom"?
5. Think about a parent (yours, or another parent you know) with whom you share a gender. In what ways do you think your life will be different from his or hers? In what ways would you like your life to be different from his or hers?
6. How is space "gendered" in the homes of your family (or families) of origin?

7. As the Canadian population ages, more and more adults will face caregiving scenarios like those depicted by Martin-Matthews. How does caring for elderly parents differ from caring for children? How do you think gender might shape the relationships between the parents who receive care and the children who give it?

8. The men in Coltrane's study who aspired to equal parenting found themselves singled out, in both positive and negative ways, by their friends and neighbours. What are some other ways in which atypical gendered behaviour within families gets noticed?

9. The domestic division of labour still favours men with more leisure time than women, despite significant changes in recent decades. Why don't men do more around the house? What are the costs and rewards—for both men and women—of a lopsided distribution of household work?

10. Can you foresee a future in which all Canadian families will be shared-parenting families as described by Coltrane? What social changes would have to happen for this to become a reality?

Chapter 20

Overview

Engineering is one of the last bastions of male dominance in the professional world. Women who enter this profession, however, do not necessarily face isolation or discrimination—until family life enters the picture. Gillian Ranson argues that women enter the profession as "conceptual men," who fit easily into the engineering mainstream. However, when this illusion of being conceptual men can no longer be sustained—when pregnancy, childbirth, and child rearing enter the picture—women find that they can no longer be "one of the boys." Women without children believe that if they were to become parents their career options would be narrowed, and they are right, judging by the experiences of their peers who did go on to become mothers.

The women in Ranson's study understand their circumstances as the result of choices that they had made as individuals—to pursue engineering as a career, to move into part-time or consulting work, or to seek out more time at home with their children. Their experiences contrast with the experiences of fathers who are engineers, whom Ranson interviewed in an earlier study. These men were able to hew out their own compromises and work schedules with the assistance of a partner who either worked part-time or was not in paid employment. The experiences of the women in this study call into question the very organization of engineering as a profession. It is predicated on the existence of a workforce made up of individuals with no pressing commitment or family priorities that might interfere with the job. Parenthood—more specifically, motherhood—disrupts the presumption that all workers can and should fit into this mould. However, gendered divisions of unpaid labour, such as those discussed in other articles in this section, mean that the brunt of this disruption is borne by women.

No Longer "One of the Boys": Negotiations with Motherhood, as Prospect or Reality, among Women in Engineering[1]

Gillian Ranson

Women who train and work as professional engineers in Canada and other industrialized countries are women operating on male turf. Unlike professions such as medicine and law, both of which are much closer to gender parity, engineering remains "archetypically masculine" (Wajcman, 1991: 145). In spite of nearly two decades of "women into engineering" campaigns supported by government and industry, the numbers of women entering engineering have been described as "derisory in most countries" (Faulkner, 2000: 92). The Canadian Council of Professional Engineers (CCPE) notes that, though the proportion of women in Canadian engineering schools increased annually after 1972, in the last few years it has levelled off at about 20 per cent (CCPE, 2003). While hardly derisory, these numbers fall far short of gender parity.

Retention of women in engineering over the long haul is also likely to be a problem given that the growth in numbers of those actually practising the profession is among women in their late twenties and early thirties (CCPE, 1998). These women are also at the age where family formation becomes salient. The arrival of children seems to be one critical point at which women, but not men, leave the profession, move to part-time work, and in many other ways put their careers "on the back burner" (Ranson, 1998, 2000).

Motherhood, it seems clear, is a significant watershed, and one that policy-makers and others concerned about retaining women in engineering should take seriously. But the reasons why it is such a watershed—and hence what needs to be done to compensate for its effects—may be more complicated than the conventional explanations about work and family balance suggest. A more elaborated explanation is that motherhood, as embodied and as material experience, exposes a major fallacy inherent in the liberal discourses of equality and gender neutrality, which establish the terms for women's entry into male-dominated occupations and workplaces in the first place. These terms allow women to enter, not as women, but as conceptual men (Snitow, 1990: 26). This conceptual cover is blown when they become, or think about becoming, mothers. For many women (especially those who themselves internalize the gender neutrality discourse), actual or prospective motherhood compels them to confront identities as "engineer" and "mother" that may be "mutually incongruous" (Jorgenson, 2000: 7) and require complex negotiation and management.

In this paper I examine this more nuanced explanation, and explore its implications for all women in male-dominated occupations and workplaces who face the challenges of being "travellers in a male world" (Marshall, 1984; Gherardi, 1996).

Women in a Man's World

Recent women entrants to male-dominated occupations have had more legal, and, increasingly, cultural support for their presence on male turf. But while the terms of their participation have changed somewhat, difficulties persist. A 1992 report by the Canadian Committee on Women in Engineering cited many stories of sexism, systemic discrimination and workplace inequality, and a series of "common and difficult" barriers faced by women engineers (Canadian Committee on Women in Engineering, 1992: 60).

Why should such barriers persist, especially in a discursive climate of gender equality and "family-friendly" workplaces? Acker (1990) contends that organizations are not gender-neutral spaces that women may enter on the same footing as men; neither can a "job" be defined as abstract and gender-neutral, performed by an abstract and disembodied "worker" who exists only in relation to the job. Acker's widely cited argument is that in the real world of actual workers, the closest approximation to the disembodied worker who exists only for the job is "the male worker whose life centers on his full-time, life-long job, while his wife or another woman takes care of his personal needs and his children" (Acker, 1990: 149).

Acker's description was, until recently, a good fit for most engineers. Recent initiatives to get women into engineering have usually been predicated on the assumption that "women must be modified to fit into engineering, not the other way round" (Faulkner, 2000: 93). In ethnographic research on engineering women in a variety of educational and work settings, Eisenhart and Finkel (1998) found that organizational expectations regarding commitment to workplace activities and the worker identity favoured people who were able to put work demands first. At the same time, these expectations were perceived by everyone concerned, women and men alike, as gender-neutral. The researchers came to view gender neutrality as a socially and culturally constructed discourse that "confers legitimacy on women's professional contribution only when they act like men" and "makes discussion of women's distinctive issues virtually impossible" (Eisenhart and Finkel, 1998: 181).

Mothers in a Man's World

Motherhood as a barrier to women's career progress in engineering is demonstrated in much research through the 1990s. Studies in the United States (McIlwee and Robinson, 1992), Britain (Devine, 1992; Evetts, 1994, 1996; Corcoran-Nantes and Roberts, 1995; Wajcman, 1998) and Canada (Ranson, 1998, 2000) all point to the challenges for women in combining "masculine" professional work and motherhood. They may find themselves, as noted earlier, in workplaces in which a discourse of gender neutrality masks clearly masculinist expectations about work performance and career progress. At the same time, they confront cultural expectations about mothers, framed around a dominant ideology of "intensive mothering" (Hays, 1996; Arendell, 2000) that directly contradicts workplace expectations.

In contrast, the men with whom these women work are not subject to the same expectations regarding their family involvement. These men are much more likely than their women colleagues to have partners who can take on the bulk of family responsibilities (Wajcman, 1998; Ranson, 2000).[2] For most men, the prevailing cultural expectation is that they will be responsible for their family's financial provision, whether or not their contribution is supplemented by working partners, and whether or not they are also involved caregivers (Christiansen and Palkovitz, 2001; Ranson, 2001).

Organizational responses in the form of "family-friendly" policies and programs would seem to be the way to overcome this under-resourcing. But research evidence suggests they are not helping nearly as much as company rhetoric and popular discourse would suggest. While policies like parental leave or flexible work schedules are generally couched in gender-neutral terms, and are purported to be directed to both women and men, in practice their take-up by men has been minimal (Andrews and Bailyn, 1993; Pleck, 1993; Rapoport and Bailyn, 1996; Hochschild, 1997). This constitutes women as the prime beneficiaries of such policies, and further entrenches the idea that they are special concessions or benefits for women (Jones and Causer, 1995; Lewis, 1997) rather than rights to which all workers are entitled.

Managing Gender

If women's entry to male occupational turf is largely based on liberal assumptions that women are for practical purposes the same as men, it follows that women themselves will need to "manage gender" in order to fit themselves into existing organizational cultures and structures (Rubin, 1997: 31). Whatever their standing as "conceptual men," real-life embodied women must negotiate feminine subjectivity as well.[3] This is neatly illustrated by one of Miller's (2004) interviewees, a woman engineer working in the same city as the women in this study:

> When you go to the field, you don't take a purse because you're really rubbing that female helplessness thing in, and you put all your junk—the female hygiene stuff—in your little pockets. Another thing you do when you work downtown is you always wear wide skirts because sometimes you're going to be going to the field in the afternoon. And you can wear high heels to the office but keep a pair of flat loafers there. . . . (Miller, 2004: 54)

While some of the women engineers in a 1999 study by Kvande did indeed, as noted above, strive to be "one of the boys," others drew on other discourses (or, in Kvande's terms, constructed other femininities) that corresponded to a view of themselves as *different from*, not the same as, their male colleagues. Kvande found that the women who saw themselves in this way were invariably women with children. Jorgenson, whose research (2000, 2002) focused particularly on the ways women engineers with children managed the potentially contradictory discourses of motherhood and engineering, found similar complexity. Sometimes the women positioned themselves as competent career-oriented professionals, sometimes as caring mothers, but usually with an awareness of the incompatibility of the mother–engineer identities. As one of her interviewees commented, "I didn't want to try to be the perfect engineer because I knew I wanted a family" (Jorgenson, 2002: 370).

Jorgenson's work summarizes the position outlined at the start of the paper, that women enter engineering work as "conceptual men," and that motherhood is, in many cases, a "defining moment," separating mothers from others.

"Conceptual Men," Alternative Subjectivities, and Motherhood in Engineering

Women without Children

Sally, who was 41 and childless, provides a good example of the sort of long-term engineering careers available to competent and highly motivated women able to be single-minded about their professional work. This was not the case for the younger women, who still needed to confront the possibility of motherhood. Among these women, particular understandings both of motherhood and of engineering work framed talk that was also significantly shaped by age and family or relationship circumstance.

The experience of Sally—a senior manager in a major oil company—provides a link to the issue of motherhood because she attributed her career success to the fact that—not from choice—she didn't have children. Sally noted that despite her company's public claims to being "family-friendly," the "day-to-day business environment" included the perception that to get ahead "you've got to put in the long hours" and be "willing to sacrifice." Asked if she thought more women in the organization would make a difference, she said: "I think that may be the sort of thing that *keeps* women from making a difference." She was explicit about the difference it had made to her career: "Because I don't have the child connection . . . I have been able to, if need be, go the extra mile, every time they've asked."

The single women's responses to the prospect of motherhood were provisional and speculative, since all saw a permanent relationship as a prerequisite. For example, Rosemary, four years post-graduation, commented:

> I'm probably indifferent either way, you know. I think it would depend on my spouse. Like, if I met somebody and they wanted kids, then I would be open to having one, maybe two. And hopefully maybe they would like to adopt children rather than (laughter) . . . I just can't see myself just, just staying home and being a mom. . . . So, but if, hey, my previous boyfriend, he was more than happy to be a stay-at-home dad. So that, that's a fit for me as well.

In this way, at the hypothetical level at least, she constructed a family scenario that would allow her to remain "one of the boys." This scenario did not challenge the "intensive" version of mothering that would remove her from the workplace. Instead, Rosemary discursively nominated her hypothetical partner as the full-time caregiver, and gave herself a family role similar to those of her male colleagues. In other words, she positioned herself as a conceptual "father."

Like Rosemary, Julia was also 27 and four years past graduation. Though she did not self-identify as "one of the boys" in the way Rosemary did, she was relishing the hands-on, technical, outdoor nature of her fieldwork job. But she also saw this way of working as contingent:

> [N]ow I don't have the five-year to ten-year plan. I mean, between you and I, I would love to be a stay-at-home mom. . . . But, I'm not married. And I don't have any kids. So *until then*, I'm going to do the best job that I can, and follow my career, and if it happens, it happens. If it doesn't, it doesn't (emphasis added).

Julia's vision of motherhood included the view that "if you have children . . . somebody should be at home"—and she was clear that, in her family, unlike Rosemary's, she would be that somebody. She presented this version of mothering as incompatible with engineering work: "If I could work from home, or if I could work part-time, then that would be my ideal. But in engineering, you don't seem to be able to do that. . . ."

Other single, childless women, with more work experience than Julia, took her story to another level: children needed care that mothers should provide and that they, as mothers, would potentially be willing to provide; in the absence of these family obligations, they were devoting their energies to engineering work; this engineering work was getting to be of a kind and at a level that would not easily accommodate maternal responsibilities. Thus, for example, Sarah—a 34-year-old engineer who had recently been promoted to manage a major energy project for her company—expressed excitement that this project could be "a stepping stone" to "a lot more exciting projects." Asked if she thought she would be able to combine her present job with children and family responsibilities, Sarah said:

> I think I would. I know women that do do that here but they have to have a very understanding spouse that's more flexible. It's very difficult to do this job and have a spouse that's doing exactly the same thing with exactly the same sort of aspirations, I think.

Sarah's immediate qualification of the possibility of a work–family balance in her current job (by positioning herself, like Rosemary, as a father) was qualified still further by her comment later that she "couldn't go on maternity leave in the next two years" even if she wanted to, and that she had "sort of accepted the fact that [having children] might not happen." Sarah had recognized, in Wajcman's (1996) terms, the "domestic basis for the managerial career."

Different versions of the engineering–motherhood balance came from women who were in permanent relationships with men, and who were all anticipating having children sooner or later. These women were in two groups. When interviewed, four were recent graduates, within six years of graduation, and all were in their twenties. Three were a little older and more experienced (all were 34 and had 12 years of engineering experience behind them).

Among the younger four, the ideology of intensive mothering appeared in comments rejecting nannies or daycare as strategies enabling full-time work while having young children. But they also rejected the stay-at-home mother option; all planned to work part-time when their children were young. They all assumed that part-time work would be viable, even when—as in Sheila's case—there was some evidence from a colleague working an 80 per cent schedule that it might be hard to manage. (Sheila commented, "I honestly think that she's a little bit less organized and that I could probably handle it a little better.") These women also expressed a strong sense of entitlement with respect to what their employer ought to do for them. And they were united in their conviction that their partners—all of whom were also engineers—would share the childcare responsibilities, likely also moving to part-time work to do so. This conviction was striking, given their collective experience of working in resoundingly masculinist workplace cultures where men, for the most part, were able to delegate their family responsibilities, and where male engineers working less than full-time were almost unheard of.

The three older women were characteristic of many women in male-dominated occupations in having deferred childbearing (see Ranson, 1998). All three spoke about their work, and their current workplaces, in terms that clearly indicated career success: a raise or stock options whenever she thought about leaving (Marcie); promotion from a junior position to the same grade as her male colleagues (Helen); a senior management position in a company she had helped to grow (Shelley). All three intended to keep working after having children, and all three, in different ways, planned to make their experience and seniority work for them as they thought about accommodating their jobs to family responsibilities. As Shelley said:

> I've been with the company for a long time and I've always been a very good employee. As a result I'm paid well now, and I have a lot of responsibility and respect [within] the company. And, you know, that's my money to cash in when I need to negotiate a deal. . . . A position of strength to bargain from is always a good thing.

What seems to be the case is that this position of strength is achieved by proof of successful career performance according to male standards—in other words, by women paying their dues as "conceptual men." This is not to suggest that these women achieved their success by aligning themselves with men. For example, some of the experience that earned Helen her current job was gained in an overtly sexist work environment that she was "not ever going to be a part of." It is also not to suggest that "male standards" are uniform. For example, most of Shelley's male colleagues and superiors were about her age; she suggested that their relative youth made them less conventional. But in every case, the standards in place were standards established by men. Having met those standards, women felt freer to negotiate as women for changes they needed to accommodate their family responsibilities.

To summarize, the women without children produced a number of different scenarios for the way motherhood might combine with engineering: motherhood viewed as incompatible with engineering, and chosen as its alternative; motherhood refused, delegated, or privatized to enable the continuation of the engineering career; motherhood and engineering combined by means of modified work arrangements (earned by male-defined career success), and the equal participation of husbands and partners. Of these scenarios, only the first assumed that motherhood and engineering were truly "mutually incongruous," and this was not a common position. But the "strong" view of intensive mothering it implied appeared in more diluted form in all the accounts. This, in turn, shaped how women thought they would need to accommodate their work. Unless (as in Rosemary's case) they planned to become "fathers," motherhood was seen as putting an end to business as usual.

Women with Children

The choices and accommodations anticipated by the childless women turned out to be a generally accurate summary of the routes the mothers took. As with the mothers in Kvande's study, though, they were generally more likely to position themselves as women, differently situated from their current or former male colleagues.

Five of the women gave up full-time engineering work at or shortly after the arrival of their children. At the time they were interviewed, two were not in paid employment at all, and spoke as if a return to engineering was unlikely. Holly commented: "As soon as I had a baby, my total perspective changed." For Jenny, the other stay-at-home mother, her first baby's arrival signalled not so much a change of perspective as the opportunity to retreat gratefully from a world she had never wholeheartedly embraced. Jenny's choice was motherhood over engineering:

> It's not a door that I've closed and I don't have bad memories. Although what I hear about engineering now . . . I think, oh, man, I don't want to get into that any more. I really don't.

The others had had longer and more conventionally successful careers as engineers before having children. All undertook intermittent consulting contracts, but at the time they were interviewed, none were working more than a day or so a week. Kate, at home with her first child, (aged nine months at the time of the interview) framed her stay-at-home-mom status as "a wonderful break" after having worked in engineering for 15 years. The baby was long-awaited. She commented: "I didn't sort of have huge expectations of it but when we finally did [have] him, I just thought, oh, why wouldn't I just kind of stay and enjoy him?" Kate had worked long enough, and recently enough, that the engineer identity was still strong ("even though I'm not working I'll always be an engineer"). But asked whether she would be an engineer 10 years down the road, she replied, "Probably not."

Lisa's work history was similar to Kate's. She had worked full-time for 10 years for one company, then switched to part-time with the birth of her first child. But half-time work with a second child heightened the tension between work and family responsibilities:

> I wasn't doing a good job with anything. . . . If it had gone on any longer I would have regretted it and you can't live your life like that. You've just got to do what you know you can.

Like Julia, cited earlier, Lisa had broader aspirations about family and motherhood, to which this decision conformed:

> I really wanted to be the one with the babies. I wanted to nurse them, I wanted to raise them. . . . It would have been a sacrifice to not be home with them, to me. I really wanted to do that. It was the life experience I wanted to have.

While for all four women, the commitment to motherhood rather than engineering could be construed as voluntary, for Ellie, the fifth woman in the group, it was not. At the time she was interviewed she was recovering from two very difficult pregnancies, residual physical problems following childbirth, and an extremely demanding second baby. ("I think I literally lost my mind," she commented.) In Rothman's (1994) terms, she was experiencing the "embodied challenges" to working like a man—challenges she resisted as much as she could. Echoes of the energetic and driven women engineers described by Kate appeared in her talk of working while pregnant and sick, or doing from her hospital bed the work her (female) replacement was supposed to be doing. Ellie spoke optimistically about returning to work: "I do want to work. I really enjoy working. I never wanted really to be a stay-at-home." The clear implication was that when she was physically able, she would pick up her working life.

Six of the women with children continued to work full-time, or close to full-time, in engineering jobs. But the conscious downplaying of career goals in order to accommodate family responsibilities expressed by Lisa was evident in the talk of these women as well. It was also reflected in their practices—a shift in the kind of work being done to something perceived to be less stressful (Linda), a refusal of promotion in order to remain in a familiar and manageable work environment (Joanne), a move from permanent employment to consulting as a means to achieve flexibility (Kelly), the use of a pregnancy to signal a shifting of gears after a successful corporate career (Hilary), cutting back to four instead of five days a week (Shauna). These work arrangements were accompanied by talk that linked them to family benefits.

The third group of mothers is those whose careers appeared on the surface to have been less affected by motherhood. Given the way these women were working, and the jobs they were doing, they could be described as mothers in careers more often associated with men. The nine women in this group had all reached senior levels of management and/or technical specialty. But in this group also, the balance of motherhood and career was complicated and fluid. It was also in this group that the most vivid images of "conceptual men" becoming mothers emerged. Cassie was one example. As a woman who had always been able to work as "one of the boys," Cassie downplayed issues of gender in the workplace, noting that she had never experienced "discrimination, or anything like that," and was "not a supporter of affirmative action–type programs." She said she thought "opportunities go to those people who are willing to work for them." But this perspective was challenged by an unplanned pregnancy at a time when she was making dramatic career progress.

Carla's case is worth noting because it is such a good example of the discursive positioning of the "professional engineer" and the (very much embodied) mother. When Carla returned to work after her first maternity leave, she tried to breastfeed her baby during her lunch break as a way to continue nursing. She said:

> Well, I tried it for two weeks, but then my milk supply was so big, it was just like . . . you know, here I am a professional engineer and my boobs are leaking all over the place and I just couldn't, couldn't do that.

Asked if those around her at work were supportive, she replied, "Well, I didn't really talk about it with anybody. It was kind of a private thing." Carla's acknowledgment of the incongruity of "professional engineers" breast-feeding, and of breast-feeding itself as belonging in the private domain, hinted at the subjective shifts she also negotiated. Carla's career choices were constrained by her family's need for her income. Like many men also, she was the family breadwinner, in a position to delegate family work to her partner.

Unlike most men, however, she expressed unease about this arrangement. Her interview was interspersed with comments that clearly indicated what Smith (1987) would call a bifurcated consciousness, divided between a focus on her work (which she enjoyed), and preoccupation with a domestic life over which she had reluctantly surrendered control. "There are really times that I long to be the stay-at-home parent," she commented.

For other women, there was a more conscious crossing over from a family focus to a more explicit career orientation. Zoe responded to an appeal by a friend to leave her flexible consulting arrangement and lead a small company; Ingrid's long-time male mentor asked her to return to work part-time, two months after her second child was born. Ingrid spoke of having planned not to return to work until the children were in school. But the part-time work quickly turned to full-time, then a partnership. Her account combined expressions of her enjoyment of her job with regrets about its costs.

> I think once a woman works, it's hard not to work. It's hard to stay home and not have that challenge. . . . Knowing that other people are advancing, advancing, advancing. . . . The downside is the time. You don't know (if you raised) your kids yourself. I don't consider, myself, that I've raised my kids . . . I consider that they spend more time with their babysitter than they do with me, right? I consider that and now it's more time at school than with me, right? So I consider myself kind of the secondary raiser, kind of in their lives, my husband and I.

But in this group of mothers there were also those whose accounts were much less conflicted. For example, Denise had her first and only child, at 35. She took 20 weeks of maternity leave, the maximum her company allowed—"and honestly, I was dying to get back to work." She commented:

> It didn't change much in my life. I still worked the same hours. I was still the same person at work as I was before. Just because I have a full-time nanny during the day, I was pretty uninterrupted, having a child, compared to what it could be.

To summarize, the 20 women with children followed fairly closely the paths anticipated by the childless women engineers described earlier with respect to the combination of engineering and motherhood. A very few voluntarily "chose" motherhood. All the others negotiated a balance between being an engineer and being a mother that was both discursive and practical. For some of these negotiators, the balance was achieved by a conscious gearing down on the work side—but usually only after careers had been established and dues paid. For the others, it was achieved (as just noted) by means of privatizing and delegating family responsibilities in order to maintain career progress.

Conclusion

This study has proceeded from the assumption that motherhood is a watershed for women in engineering, and has explored what was described at the start of the paper as a more nuanced explanation for why this might be the case: that women enter engineering jobs as "conceptual men," and that problems arise because mothers can't *be* conceptual men.

What it means to work as a "conceptual man" is not self-evident. In this paper I chose to see women engineers working in this way if they were doing the same kind of work, in the same conditions, for the same hours, and with the same general expectations about quality of performance as their male colleagues. Another part of the definition was that this work was done in workplaces dominated by men—a condition that was more than met in every case. I also tried to distinguish between *working as* a conceptual man, and *aligning oneself*, or *discursively positioning oneself*, with men. On the basis of this definition, all of the women without children were working as conceptual men. Often, though not invariably, they also positioned themselves as "one of the boys"—though this positioning was seldom sustained and consistent. Nine of the 20 women with children were also working as conceptual men—though they were much less likely to position themselves with "the boys."

In my discussion of these nine, and in comments about the plans of some of the childless women also proposing to delegate to partners or otherwise privatize their family responsibilities, I have suggested that these women were or would become "fathers." This proposition is not entirely theoretical. In a separate study (Ranson, 2001) I explored the ways the men with children interviewed for the same engineering project balanced work and family responsibilities. Serious accommodation to family responsibilities generally took two forms: a choice of work (generally office, rather that field-based, with predictable hours); or downshifting from an intensive work focus to a more relaxed pace—usually the choice of men who had achieved considerable career success first. But for all of these men, the balance of work and family still typically involved working days of 8–10 hours, and in almost every case, also involved a partner working part-time or not in paid employment, and available to pick up the slack. Access to this private infrastructure of support characterized almost all the fathers. For those mothers who have access to something similar, the "father" analogy has some merit.

For the mothers, "downshifting" to accommodate children went much further: an opting out of engineering, temporarily or permanently, or a reduction in work hours. Fathers never employed these strategies; indeed, men with young families working less than full-time never emerged in the larger study. This is why such strategies come to be identified with women, and why so-called "family-friendly" organizational policies purporting to help employees balance work and family responsibilities come to be perceived as helping women fit in to men's workplaces. As noted by researchers cited earlier (Jones and Causer, 1995; Lewis, 1997; Rubin, 1997; Liff and Ward, 2001), these policies may become another organizational device for differentiating women from "the boys"—and mothers from fathers.

Notes

1. The author would like to thank Marilyn Porter and the CRSA reviewers for very helpful comments on an earlier version of the paper. This manuscript was first submitted in September 2003 and accepted in March 2005.
2. In the larger project from which the present study is drawn, only 25 per cent of fathers in engineering jobs had partners who also worked full-time, compared to 92 per cent of the engineering mothers.
3. I am grateful to the anonymous reviewer who urged that this point be made more explicit.

References

Acker, J. 1990. "Hierarchies, Jobs, Bodies: A Theory of Gendered Organizations," *Gender & Society* 4(2): 139–58.

Andrews, A., and L. Bailyn. 1993. "Segmentation and Synergy: Two Models of Linking Work and Family," in J. Hood, ed., *Men, Work and Family*, pp. 262–75. Newbury Park, CA: Sage.

Arendell, T. 2000. "Conceiving and Investigating Motherhood: The Decade's Scholarship," *Journal of Marriage and Family* 62(4): 1192–207.

Canadian Committee on Women and Engineering. 1992. *More Than Just Numbers*. Fredericton: University of New Brunswick.

Canadian Council of Professional Engineers. 1998. *National Survey of the Canadian Engineering Profession in 1997*. Ottawa: Canadian Council of Professional Engineers.

———. 2003. "Women in Engineering." Available at www.ccpe.ca/e/prog_women_1.cfm.

Christiansen, S., and R. Palkovitz. 2001. "Why the 'Good Provider' Role Still Matters: Providing as a Form of Paternal Involvement," *Journal of Family Issues* 22(1): 84–106.

Corcoran-Nantes, Y., and K. Roberts. 1995. "'We've got one of those': The Peripheral Status of Women in Male-dominated Industries," *Gender, Work and Organization* 2(1): 21–33.

Devine, F. 1992. "Gender Segregation in the Engineering and Science Professions: A Case of Continuity and Change," *Work, Employment and Society* 6(4): 557–75.

Eisenhart, M., and E. Finkel. 1998. *Women's Science*. Chicago, IL: University of Chicago Press.

Evetts, J. 1994. "Women and Career in Engineering: Continuity and Change in the Organisation," *Work, Employment and Society* 8(1): 101–12.

———. 1996. *Gender and Career in Science and Engineering*. London: Taylor & Francis Ltd.

Faulkner, W. 2000. "The Power *and* the Pleasure? A Research Agenda for 'Making Gender Stick' to Engineers," *Science, Technology, & Human Values* 25(1): 87–119.

Gherardi, S. 1996. "Gendered Organizational Cultures: Narratives of Women Travellers in a Male World," *Gender, Work and Organization* 3(4): 187–201.

Hays, S. 1996. *The Cultural Contradictions of Motherhood*. New Haven, CT: Yale University Press.

Hochschild, A. 1997. *The Time Bind*. New York: Metropolitan Books.

Jones, C., and G. Causer. 1995. "'Men Don't Have Families': Equality and Motherhood in Technical Employment," *Gender, Work and Organization* 2(2): 51–62.

Jorgenson, J. 2000. "Interpreting the Intersections of Work and Family: Frame Conflicts in Women's Work," *The Electronic Journal of Communication* 10: 3–4.

———. 2002. "Engineering Selves: Negotiating Gender and Identity in Technical Work," *Management Communication Quarterly* 15(3): 350–80.

Kvande, E. 1999. "'In the Belly of the Beast': Constructing Femininities in Engineering Organizations," *European Journal of Women's Studies* 6(3): 305–28.

Lewis, S. 1997. "'Family-friendly' Employment Policies: A Route to Changing Organizational Culture or Playing About at the Margins?," *Gender, Work and Organization* 4,(1): 13–23.

Liff, S., and K. Ward. 2001. "Distorted Views through the Glass Ceiling: The Construction of Women's Understandings of Promotion and Senior Management Positions," *Gender, Work and Organization* 8(1): 19–36.

Marshall, J. 1984. *Women Managers: Travellers in a Male World*. Chichester: John Wiley and Sons.

McIlwee, J., and J. Robinson. 1992. *Women in Engineering*. Albany, NY: SUNY Press.

Miller, G. 2004. "Frontier Masculinity in the Oil Industry: The Experience of Women Engineers," *Gender, Work and Organization* 11(1): 47–73.

Pleck, J. 1993. "Are 'Family-supportive' Employer Policies Relevant to Men?," in J. Hood, ed., *Men, Work and Family*, pp. 217–37. Newbury Park, CA: Sage.

Ranson, G. 1998. "Education, Work and Family Decision Making: Finding the 'Right Time' to Have a Baby," *Canadian Review of Sociology and Anthropology* 35(4): 517–33.

———. 2000. "The Best of Both Worlds? Work, Family Life and the Retention of Women in Engineering." Paper presented at the 8th annual conference of the Canadian Coalition of Women in Engineering, Science, Trades and Technology, St. John's, Newfoundland, 6–8 July.

———. 2001. "Men at Work: Change—or No Change?—in the Era of the 'New Father'," *Men and Masculinities* 4(1): 3–26.

Rapoport, R., and L. Bailyn. 1996. *Relinking Life and Work: Toward a Better Future*. New York: Ford Foundation.

Rothman, B. 1994. "Beyond Mothers and Fathers: Ideology in a Patriarchal Society," in E.N. Glenn, G. Chang, and L.R. Forcie, eds., *Mothering: Ideology, Experience and Agency*, pp. 139–57. New York: Routledge.

Rubin, J. 1997. "Gender, Equality and the Culture of Organizational Assessment," *Gender, Work and Organization* 4(1): 24–34.

Smith, D. 1987. *The Everyday World as Problematic: A Feminist Sociology*. Toronto: University of Toronto Press.

Snitow, A. 1990. "A Gender Diary," in M. Hirsch and E.F. Keller, eds., *Conflicts in Feminism*. New York: Routledge.

Wajcman, J. 1991. *Feminism Confronts Technology*. Cambridge: Polity Press.

———. 1996. "The Domestic Basis for the Managerial Career," *Sociological Review* 44(4): 609–29.

———. 1998. *Managing Like a Man*. University Park, PA: Pennsylvania State University Press.

Chapter 21

Overview

If parenting is a tough gig for female engineers, it's at least as stressful—if in different ways—for fathers whose children are in the care of the family welfare system. Dominelli and colleagues interviewed a group of these men without making judgments as to the merits of their cases or the reasons why their children were "in the system." These fathers believe that they are either invisible as parents in a system that regards mothers as the primary caregivers, or hyper-visible, in that they are regarded as the source of the family's problems. These fathers adopt different narratives to explain their situations, ranging from the "survivor dad" to the "misrepresented dad."

The fathers also maintain often tense and complex relationships with the social workers who function as gatekeepers and overseers for their relationship with their children. While the dads acknowledge that the social workers are right to be wary of them, given their checkered histories, the dads insist they are using all the resources available to them to build strong relationships with their children.

Of particular interest from the perspective of gender analysis, are the dads who define themselves in relation to mothers, seeing themselves as "better than moms." Women's parenting activities become the standard against which these men judge themselves or against which they believe they are being judged by others.

"Here's My Story": Fathers of "Looked After" Children Recount Their Experiences in the Canadian Child Welfare System

Lena Dominelli, Susan Strega, Chris Walmsley, Marilyn Callahan, and Leslie Brown

Introduction

Fathers of "looked after" children occupy problematic terrain in the child welfare system (Scourfield, 2003) while practitioners configure their status around the "good dad"–"bad dad" binary articulated by Pleck (2004). . . . We investigated how fathers of "looked after" children described their experiences of being fathers within the child welfare system of a middle-sized city in western Canada. Their stories were moving and complex. Fathers described their experiences of being fathers and highlighted the strategies they used to convince (not always effectively) child welfare practitioners that they were "good enough" fathers who could be trusted to care for children. . . . Hearing directly from fathers interacting with child protection systems is unusual. To break this invisibility, the fathers we interviewed speak for themselves without us passing judgment on their stories.

The research took place in Canada, a federated state that gives each province constitutional authority for social services provision. Indigenous peoples are a federal responsibility. . . . This study included indigenous and mainstream agencies. Fathers, aware of their different mandates and services, engaged with those they felt best met their families' needs. . . .

Indigenous or First Nations peoples have complex relationships with non-indigenous Canadians, especially those of British and French origins. A history of racism, colonization, poverty, abuse in residential schools has undermined their well-being, traditional languages, cultures, and resilience and brought forth stereotypes based on violence and substance misuse. As one in three of those in care, First Nations' children are over-represented in Canada's child welfare system (Blackstock et al., 2004; Walmsley, 2005).

Research Method

. . . Our earlier narrative analyses revealed that the theme of fathers' resistance to being configured as "bad dads" was significant (Rutman et al., 2002; Dominelli et al., 2008). For this article, we revisited interview transcripts to examine how fathers configured themselves as worthy of caring for children and challenged child welfare stories of them as "bad dads." The typologies and stories describing fathers' interactions with social workers emerged from this subsequent analysis.

It showed that fathers employed a range of strategies to get social workers to accept that they were responsible enough to play significant roles in children's lives, whether biologically theirs or not (Flood, 2005). They configured their accounts around resistance to social workers' depiction of them as "risky" fathers and sought recognition for being "good enough dads" within trying circumstances. There were many storylines in the fathers' narratives grouped around: "I'm a hero, but you don't see me"; "I'm a survivor"; "I denied my identity to get by"; "I was the mother"; and "I'm a role model dad." From these, we developed the typologies of the "misrepresented dad," "survivor dad," "mothering dad," "denied identity dad," and "citizen dad." . . . We suspect that child welfare professionals might question these accounts or their relevance to decision-making processes. However, we think they can use fathers' claim that becoming a father is a life-changing event to work with them and make caring for children a more equally shared responsibility between men and women.

Qualitative In-Depth Interviews

We interviewed 11 fathers who volunteered following publicity about the project in child care agencies and/or being told about it by child welfare workers. We used narrative approaches to analyse detailed in-depth interviews of fathers and subjected the transcripts to comprehensive and lengthy processes of analysis to unearth different stories recounted by diverse actors (Reissman, 2002). Narrative approaches to these data are apt because they allow subjugated stories told by "ordinary people" (Fraser, 2004) to become part of public discourses and turn their invisible experiences into visible ones (Devault, 1999). Narrative analyses also enable researchers to uncover the layered contexts of "race," class, and gender (Reissman, 2002). We recognize that as researchers, we become involved in the story-telling process by interpreting what was said and through our commitment to improving child welfare policy and practice (Fraser, 2004).

We sought a purposive sample. To be interviewed, fathers had to have children who either were or had been in the child protection system. The fathers ranged between 24 and 50 years of age at the time of interview. All had cared for the children who either had been or were being processed by the child welfare system. The fathers were either First Nations (six) or white European (five) in origin. All First Nations fathers and three white European-origined ones had problems with substance misuse, either currently or in the past. Five fathers had served time in prison. Nine fathers had quit school early, having achieved grade eight (the level reached at age 13) or less. Most were on benefit, a few in low-paid work. Four fathers had full-time care and custody of children; seven were actively seeking this, jointly with the mother or on their own. We use fictitious names—Tony, Todd, Ben, Peter, Trevor, Darren, Alex, Tom, Gerald, Darryl, Mark—to retain anonymity and enable readers to track their stories. We quote their own words. . . .

Discourses about Fathers

There is a considerable literature on fathers in general written from sociological, psychological, social policy, and legal perspectives. . . . The literature, seldom based on fathers' own voices when discussing their experiences of child protection (Walmsley et al., forthcoming), leaves an important gap for researchers to tackle. We contribute towards filling this by interviewing one excluded group—fathers of "looked after" children—to hear their stories, better understand their situations, and improve practice with them.

We do not examine the validity of the views fathers expressed when interviewed or compare their stories to those of social workers. These fathers were aware that practitioners sought to lower risks for children, but complained that they showed "no respect" for them in the process. Our findings contradicted discourses around the range of roles that fathers occupy in wider society to reveal that the "good dad"–"bad dad" binary (Pleck, 2004) framed practice. The fathers might accept, challenge, or contradict it. But they knew they had to overcome being seen as "bad" dads if they were to convince social workers they were "good dads" who could relate effectively and safely to children. . . .

None of the fathers interviewed wanted sympathy for his "hard luck" story. Some wanted others to know of their successes in surviving the system and strategies for coping with it. Several offered this as a reason for giving interviews. Fathers were aware of the system's concern to protect children and problems faced by overloaded workers (Scourfield and Welsh, 2003). Sympathy with their plight failed to prevent their being fearful of the enormous amount of power that practitioners exerted over their lives (Strega et al., 2008). Mark, for example, states: "You're never free. Once you're in the system, you stay in the system your whole life. They take your children. They take your grandchildren." This fear motivates fathers to fight to care for children. Confronting powerful welfare workers for the system's failure to meet children's needs is "scary," says Alex.

Most fathers acknowledged the aptness of social workers' scepticism. Their past behaviours included violence, substance misuse, and, for some, a history of being in care. Their realism about their position within child protection meant they relied on lawyers or other professionals to uphold their fathering roles (Strega et al., 2002). They insisted that they be given a chance to look after children based on their current capacity to adapt, change, and act in accordance with practitioners' demands. These fathers often cast social workers as "the enemy"—professionals to stay away from—a finding replicated in Ashley et al. (2006).

Fathers were critical of the constant pressures to which social workers subjected them and the hurdles they encountered to "look promising" (Callahan et al., 2005), behave appropriately by eschewing drugs, alcohol, or violence, and prove they could be trusted with caring for children. Their stories conveyed a complex graduated picture because they maintained that social workers also supported fathers with an array of programmes and insights into their progress—as suggested by Tony, whose performance improves through agency inputs. However, Tony wants daycare to be publicly funded to reduce the pressures of combining work, going to college, and looking after children. . . .

Fathers' Typologies When Recounting Narratives of Fathering in the Child Welfare System

Fathers' self-profiles indicate that they lead complicated lives (Milner, 2004). Those we interviewed disclosed complex, constantly changing existences as they engaged in a perpetual dance to challenge social workers' depiction of them as "bad dads." Persistence in becoming accepted as "good dads" figured strongly in their narratives, as did resilience and coping strategies in confronting a system they perceived as distant, invisible, and dis-empowering. They identified the key stories defining their lives as:

- "misrepresented dad"—*I'm a good dad, but not seen as such*;
- "survivor dad"—*I was expected to fail, but I didn't*;
- "mothering father"—*I act as a (good) mother would*;
- "denied my identity dad"—*I had to play the game of being someone other than myself*; and
- "good role model" or "citizen dad"—*I am a good citizen . . . I join community groups . . . and look after my children.*

We explore how fathers use these descriptions as they struggle to prove their worthiness as fathers, although Pleck's (2004) "good dad"–"bad dad" binary remained embedded in fathers' complex and nuanced understandings of their actual interactions with social workers. They described specific experiences ranging from "I'm a ghost" to "I didn't want to be an aboriginal."

Those who admitted they had problems that needed sorting out rejected social workers' views of them as "bad" dads, thereby highlighting different objectives between social workers and fathers. Practitioners were rightly concerned with minimizing potential risks to children while fathers focused on the hardship and suffering they endured in the child welfare system and skated hurriedly over their limitations and contributions to environments not conducive to raising children. Even problematic fathers amplified resilience and strengths in developing relationships with children, as Todd indicates below. Some stories did not have "happy endings," as child welfare workers had valid reasons for being sceptical of their intentions.

Misrepresented Dad

. . . Fathers saw becoming a father as a life-changing event, a source of identity and pride. The "misrepresented father" was configured when practitioners did not acknowledge men's skills as "good fathers." Mark highlighted how social workers do not appreciate fathers' strengths as carers, focusing instead on making fathers work to pay for meeting children's needs when "it's not in the budget." Mark found practitioners' behaviour unhelpful and arbitrary: "She wasn't returning my calls. . . . when she did talk to me, her attitude sucked because she was telling me . . . if the mom is involved in drugs . . . the other parent is too." Whether social workers cast them as misusing drugs and alcohol or economic providers, fathers had difficulty being heard as "good dads" and felt "misrepresented."

Ben felt mistreated by being denied contact with his child when told to "hang in there" and misrepresented when falsely accused of violence and his drinking was "blown way out of proportion." His unsuccessful attempts to gain custody make him conclude that fathers are hurt when treated as "bad dads" because "they are probably good fathers and all they are doing is trying to see their kids." Ben worries that he will be unable to build a relationship with the child and asks, "how long can people hide her from me?"

Darren and Gerald were "misrepresented" dads because their willingness to change was misbelieved. Darren's partner used his violent history to falsely accuse him of violence to "get him out of the picture." Gerald, a First Nations man, had a restraining order imposed when his partner called the police and alleged he assaulted her brother while planning her father's funeral. He was imprisoned for a few days and their five-week-old baby taken into care. Gerald thought he was a "good dad" and fought a system that assumed allegations of assault were true. He minimized his violence, blaming his ex-partner and social workers for exaggerating his contributions to his predicament.

Victimhood and blaming others featured in misrepresented fathers' stories. For Gerald, this encompassed difficulties in controlling his temper and drinking. Gerald justifies feeling the victim with:

> I didn't want her to go party . . . she called the cops. It was my house. I paid the rent. All of the bills and everything were in my name, but I went to jail.

Child welfare professionals configured misrepresented dads around rigorous assessments that allayed mistrust of their behaviour. Gerald knew that risk assessments could jeopardize his chances of gaining custody of "the baby":

> I had to prove they were wrong now . . . assault with a weapon. That makes me a high risk father right off the bat.

Gerald describes social workers' surveillance practice over misrepresented dads as:

> I had to do all my visits under a glass. They had a two way mirror and a speaker. . . . No matter what I said, it's all being recorded. I had somebody watching me at [sic.] all the times.

Becoming a father, a life-changing event, motivated Gerald, like others, to change. He claims to be "the happiest man alive." Having a baby and looking after it "makes it all worthwhile. It gives you reason to get up. It makes you ten feet tall." Gerald turned his life around after being supported by an indigenous voluntary agency, attending anger management groups and parenting classes, and rejecting alcohol. He demonstrates that supportive interventions are effective in altering behaviour and earns custody of the child by strategizing how to escape the "invisible" category; getting child welfare workers to transcend the "misrepresented dad" label, listen to his views, and see his strengths; and learning from the groups he attended. His decision to "fight me" by not drinking and acquire skills that engaged his worker gave him confidence in getting the practitioner onside. Gerald explains:

> I changed the focus of the whole thing. Instead of . . . taking the full force and running me through the wringer, I switched it so that the focus was now on baby.

By creating a defining moment that began when visiting his child and asking the worker why "baby had a diaper rash," Gerald demonstrated that he could place the baby's interests and well-being above his own. This led the child welfare worker to listen to him, eventually becoming convinced that he was "fit enough" to have custody. Gerald encourages workers to accept "good enough" parenting rather than overwhelm fathers with endless demands and programs for becoming better fathers when they cannot quite meet the white middle-class, heterosexual standards. . . .

Survivor Dad

Todd exemplifies the "survivor dad" who is resilient, overcomes adversity, and becomes a "good" father. He was a "struggler and survivor"; "miracle" baby who should have died at birth; sexually abused child who survived; survivor of a serious motor vehicle accident; and survivor of a suicide attempt. Todd presented himself as a caring provider who made sure children in his relationship (one being his biological child) followed a "nightly routine"; worked; and paid bills. Since he split up with his partner, he has struggled to gain access to the children and be heard as a father who has contributed to their well-being and still can. He feels *entitled* to be with them, but social workers remain unconvinced.

Social workers thought Todd was "a boyfriend" who came and went. His relationship with practitioners was mediated by his ex-partner, a gatekeeper with the power to deny his presence. She configured him as invisible by ensuring that practitioners remained unaware of his involvement with the children. They had an "open" file on the oldest child (not biologically his) under the mother's name. She had not declared income obtained from renting to Todd and others. Todd thought the system encouraged this invisibility because otherwise she would lose "money." He acknowledges being "suicidal and . . . end[ing] up in the rubber room," but downplays her exclusion of him for being risky by recounting her saying:

> I am keeping you out of the picture for the safety of the children because of [your] emotional state.

He survives invisibility by contacting practitioners with concerns about the oldest child's welfare and demanding access. Social workers did not engage directly with Todd, speak to or interview him about his child or demands for access. Practitioners relied on the mother for information and presumed its accuracy. Without a formal gate-keeping contract, she was expected to report Todd's presence in her life. . . . Social workers did not assess Todd as "looking promising" and the biological father got custody. The mother refused contact when he requested it. His nine-month-old biological child remained with her, with social workers "coming in and checking up on how things were." As the invisible man fighting for custody, Todd said:

> This is so out of whack . . . me not being able to see the children . . . so off the wall.

Darren, asked if he wanted "to be the father," replied "I am the father." He rose to the challenge, saying he could take care of his daughter better than her substance-misusing mother. Social workers helped him become "survivor dad" by configuring him as a deserving father and giving him extensive support. They brought the baby to visit him in prison. Once out, practitioners supported him to get custody, form a good bond with his daughter, become a better father, and stop smoking. His narrative reveals he is not fully trusted, and surveillance systems monitor his performance. He knows that if he "screws up," the child will be removed. He feels the system is "working with me, working at me" and is constantly on guard. Workers also watch how he behaves with a second child, although he was not given information about her medical condition. He constantly feels "spied on" while claiming foster-parents retain their privacy by not discussing the child's allergy with him. Despite expectations of failure, he is "going to prove them wrong." He succeeds as "survivor dad" and social workers are preparing him to receive another child currently in care. Darren thinks he has become "a better person" by becoming a father. He survived by becoming a "good dad" in contrast to the "bad mom" who wanted him to do all the parenting tasks.

Alex can gain custody "as long as we have our support in place and . . . don't drink." His plan to become "survivor dad" fails when a promising working relationship slips as his worker is replaced by one who is unsupportive. Staff turnover can produce decisions that fathers experience as arbitrary in the child welfare dance of surveillance and support that enmeshes them when caring for children.

Mothering Father

A "mothering father" is a better parent than the mother. Scourfield (2003) found this category, too. This role is expressed in diverse ways. Practitioners tell Darren "he is better than most women." Gerald comments on the inadequate mother that allows him to become the "mothering father." He says: "[S]he stood back and wasn't doing anything . . . knowing that if it wasn't for me, baby would have nobody." He reprimands the social worker for inadequate parenting—not knowing about a diaper rash:

> You're going to tell me how to be a mother. You're going to tell me how to be a father and you don't know enough to check if she's got a . . . diaper rash.

Peter would "come home from work, . . . bathe and feed [the child]." He thought he was doing better than the mother, who left the baby "with a bottle propped up and . . . ignored most of the day." As a lone father providing through waged work, looking after a sick child was tough. He lacked "the extra person to fall back on when she's sick at the daycare." His parenting work remained unrecognized: child-care workers did not return his calls, were rude, or hung up.

Trevor cannot establish his right to care for the children. His proof that he is a better mother than the mother—that the children no longer want to stay with her—is not accepted by practitioners. He states: "They have a child-friendly home and everything I do is for them." This includes controlling their behaviour and disciplining them if they do wrong. A key aim of his relationship with his son was to help him acquire self-esteem and self-pride. When chastising his son for getting into the wrong crowd, he goes over the top and assaults him. He calls child welfare to tell them before someone reports him and uses this to request further assistance.

Tony and partner were HIV-positive. As "mothering dad," Tony explains:

> . . . a regular routine day would be for me to get up . . . in the . . . night to make the bottles, heat them up . . . because we're HIV positive there's no breastfeeding . . . I was doing that . . . as well as trying to attend college and . . . keep up my studies.

He feels the system excluded him by removing the children because his "wife pass[ed] out on the lawn" and his mothering efforts are discounted. When refused custody, he attributes it to discrimination for being HIV-positive:

> I had [social workers] that didn't like the fact that I'm HIV positive. . . . They tried to screw with my cheque because they don't think I should have a kid.

The system configured *this* family as problematic because the mother, a First Nations woman, had been under its gaze earlier; both parents had been in care, were HIV-positive, and thought to be abusing alcohol. Social workers' initial reactions labelled both "unfit" parents:

> You know when that doorbell rang you became scared. Is that the Ministry at the door even though your house is clean and there is nothing you have to worry about?

Tony configures his story within an "all-powerful and unaccountable" system:

> I remember crying like a baby because I never knew they had so much power to seize my child.

He believes cautious workers concluded that an HIV-positive father who looks tired is "on drugs" and takes tests to refute this. Tony was upset by the lack of apology for this mistreatment and lack of respect for him and his family. He feels pushed to succeed as a "father with all the odds against me."

Tony finds the system capricious. Continuing to fight for his child, Tony regrets that his words were twisted by a worker when he gave a life history:

> . . . just for the records so that they could better handle the case, . . . better understand my family dynamics and situations we're coping with. I [was] honest about . . . being an ex-junkie . . . fighting with the police. You think once you fly straight, . . . go to college, they're never going to screw you around, so you tell them the truth.

Sometimes, Tony thought the tricks were more obvious:

> They'd ask me the same questions four or five different ways to try to trip me up. . . . it was just basically undermining.

Tony interprets child welfare workers' queries about reconciliation with his wife as tricks because "had I answered the wrong way, my daughter would have been seized . . . nor was I planning to reconcile." Tony was prepared to "jump through the hoops" to get his daughter back. He finally succeeds and reports his wife for hitting her. He threw his wife out, saying "my daughter is not going to end up in care because you choose not to do anything." When the child is returned, he is under constant surveillance. Anonymous tip-offs lead to his being checked for alcohol and drug misuse, even when tests clear him. Being a mothering father is hard.

Denied My Identity Dad

Proving an identity as a "good enough father" was problematic and required men to behave according to white, middle-class, heterosexual norms consistent with being a Canadian citizen. Tony thought that racism underpinned workers' perceptions of his wife as a First Nations woman who misused substances. Like other First Nations peoples, Daryl resists racist configurations of his family by hiding the impact of residential schools, fights, and substance misuse, and denying his aboriginal identity:

> I was so ashamed of my family . . . of what I was . . . I didn't want to be an aboriginal. My best friends were not aboriginal. . . . Everybody thought we weren't aboriginal. So I pretended I wasn't till I messed up one time.

He had eight children. Most were taken into care, some permanently. Daryl's story gives readers insights into why this is so. At one point, Daryl encountered friendly social workers who supported him to change, find "a different way," and become a "fit" parent. His wife, initially involved, dropped out. Daryl persevered by changing himself, becoming comfortable with asking professionals for help. As "mothering father," he does what was necessary to keep the children. His main strategy was to become "citizen dad," "look promising," continue caring for six children and ensure they did not get into trouble. He controls their behaviour by getting them to school, keeping them out of gangs, and being a good role model. As Daryl explains:

> . . . my children see me . . . at the school working, at home sleeping, getting up, making . . . breakfast . . . putting a movie on for them, being there for them, not being drunk, not being violent, not hanging around with gang members.

His progress was not straightforward. He got into difficulty when relatives stayed overnight because social workers constructed them as stereotypical aboriginals and potential risks, involved in alcohol, drugs, and violence. Living in an indigenous neighbourhood increased these risks despite his lifestyle being at odds with that of many around him. People jumped to conclusions about his parenting abilities, raising questions for social workers to investigate. Constantly under surveillance (Beck, 1992), his ex-wife creates problems by repeatedly phoning, promising to visit the children, then not showing up. As citizen dad, he lives with the constant fear of not "looking promising" if he steps out of line (Callahan et al., 2005).

Daryl learns to defend himself when challenged. He gives his ex-wife $20 to stay away from the children for a month so she is not "around them when she's high." Nor does he allow her to stay overnight. He draws tight boundaries around the children's "best interests" and keeps to these. These include leaving a "bad" neighbourhood; being proactive about his children's behaviour at school; and acting the "good citizen" through membership of community boards like the Parents Council. He wants his children to know "that I'll be there for them no matter what. I want them to find different avenues than what I did." They have to move out of an "aboriginal identity" and become well behaved, decent kids. He configures himself as the "good dad" who is "involved with them." Helping his disabled son exceed the system's expectations is another crucial parenting ambition. He protects him from "rough kids" and equips him for a "good job." As model dad complying with society's norms, Daryl is:

> . . . very proud of him. . . . I don't want to give up on him. . . . I want my son to be able to do something when he goes to grade seven.

Daryl experiences the system's capriciousness: "I always seem to run into a worker that wants to make it hard." He attends different programs, has a part-time job that fits in with the children's schooling, and social assistance workers want him to get a night-time job! This devalues his work in looking after children, as the system does for women, and ignores the extra childcare costs entailed in someone being home to keep children safe at night. Although a support worker proclaims, "He's got all his kids back and he's doing wonderful," Daryl is aware that he cannot stop having to prove himself as a "good" father within a framework dominated by a white child welfare system, even if indigenous agencies in the locality support him. At times, he challenges representatives of this structure as he does police officers who question his caring potential by saying his son is hanging around with gang members. He asks them:

> Why don't you go see the parents? . . . If you're definitely sure that they're gang members why can't you do something about it?

For Daryl, their reply—"it's not our job"—depicts a racialized system of justice that endangers First Nations children "already in the system." He does not complain in case they place his children for "adoption" and jeopardize his fathering role.

Mistrust exists on both sides, with power struggles between the child welfare system and fathers. Alex thinks his family is labelled as "nothing but trouble" because:

> They just want to keep my children. . . . I don't understand why they gave us a hard time. . . . I've been fighting with them over the years. . . I won't back down . . . but it's taking a toll on me.

Alex's hopes of getting his children back are arbitrarily raised and dashed by workers who constantly undervalue his identity as a father. He says: "They keep giving promises and . . . back out of them." He assumes he has been set up to fail to "start drinking again," thereby proving lack of fitness to parent. . . .

Conclusions

Stories uncovered by this study reveal that although the "good dad"–"bad dad" binary frames fathers' relationships with social workers, these are difficult and complicated because social workers do not completely trust fathers to care for children. The typologies of "misrepresented dad," "survivor dad," "denied my identity dad," "mothering father," or "citizen dad" represent fathers' views of this interaction. The categories overlap and have positive dimensions in exposing fathers' struggles to become "good dads" despite being trapped by social workers' expectations about safeguarding children; scepticism about their endeavours to change their behaviours; and constant demands to "look promising." Fathers, under surveillance, have to act as white heterosexual "citizen dad" to prove they are "good enough" to be entrusted with caring for children.

Practitioner responses to fathers of "looked after" children require sensitivity, courage, and approaches that do not undermine the rights of mothers and children. Fathers argued that the system can better support them in taking a full share of responsibilities in an equal partnership (not necessarily a live-in one) with mothers if social workers:

- listened actively to their views and trusted that they, too, have the best interests of their children at heart;
- had appropriate training, especially for children with fetal alcohol syndrome; and
- provided more continuity and stability in client–worker relationships.

"Trust," flexibility, and sound professional judgments are important ingredients in relationships that promote children's interests and enable practitioners to support fathers. Workers need training for effective intervention in fetal alcohol syndrome cases to enable fathers to change their behaviour and look after such children. Fathers suggested that practitioners learn how to handle problematic, assertive fathers and work with their strengths to help them become better fathers. Their stories indicate that workers can both control and support them. . . .

Acknowledgement

The study on which this article is based was funded by the Social Sciences and Humanities Research Council of Canada.

References

Ashley, C., B. Featherstone, M. Ryan, C. Roskill, and S. White, S. 2006. *Fathers Matter: Research Findings on Fathers and their Involvement with Social Care Services.* London: Family Rights Group.

Beck, U. 1992. *Risk Society: Towards a New Modernity.* London: Sage.

Blackstock, C., N. Trocmé, and M. Bennett. 2004. "Child Maltreatment Investigations among Aboriginal and Non-Aboriginal Families in Canada: A Comparative Analysis," *Violence Against Women* 10(8): 901–16.

Callahan, M., L. Dominelli, D. Rutman, and S. Strega. 2005. "Looking Promising: Contradictions and Challenges for Young Mothers in Child Welfare," in D.L. Gustafson, ed., *Unbecoming Mothers: The Social Production of Maternal Absences.* New York: Haworth Press.

Devault, M. 1999. "Talking and Listening from Women's Standpoint: Feminist Strategies for Interviewing and Analysis," in M. Devault, ed., *Liberating Method: Feminism and Social Research.* Philadelphia: Temple University Press.

Dominelli, L., L. Brown, M. Callahan, S. Strega, and C. Walmsley. 2008. "Reconfiguring the Fathers," *Trabajo Social* 74: 107–16.

Flood, M. 2005. "Fathers' Rights and the Defense of Paternal Authority in Australia," *Violence Against Women* 16(3): 328–47.

Fraser, H. 2004. "Doing Narrative Research: Analysing Person Stories Line-by-Line," *Qualitative Social Work* 3(2): 179–201.

Milner, J. 2004. "From 'Disappearing' to 'Demonised': The Effects on Men and Women of Professional Interventions Based on Men Who Are Violent," *Critical Social Policy* 24(1): 79–101.

Pleck, E. 2004. "Two Dimensions of Fatherhood: A History of the Good Dad–Bad Dad Complex," in M. Lamb, ed., *The Role of the Father in Child Development,* 4th edn. New York: Wiley and Sons, first published in 1997.

Reissman, C. 2002. "Narrative Analysis," in M. Huberman and M.B. Miles, eds., *Qualitative Researcher's Companion.* Thousand Oaks: Sage.

Rutman, D., S. Strega, M. Callahan, and L. Dominelli. 2002. "'Undeserving' Mothers? Practitioners' Experiences Working with Young Mothers in/from Care," *Child and Family Social Work* 7(3): 149–60.

Scourfield, J. 2003. *Gender and Child Protection.* London: Palgrave.

Scourfield, J., and I. Welsh. 2003. "Risk, Reflexivity and Social Control in Child Protection: New Times or Same Old Story?," *Critical Social Policy* 23(3): 398–420.

Strega, S., M. Callahan, L. Dominelli, and D. Rutman. 2002. "Undeserving Mothers: Social Policy and Disadvantaged Mothers," *Canadian Review of Social Policy/Revue Canadienne de Politique Sociale* 40(5): 175–94.

Strega, S., C. Fleet, L. Brown, M. Callahan, L. Dominelli, and C. Walmsley. 2008. "Connecting Father Absence and Mother Blame in Child Welfare Policies and Practice," *Children and Youth Services Review* 30: 705–16.

Walmsley, C. 2005. *Protecting Aboriginal Children.* Vancouver: University of British Columbia Press.

Walmsley, C., L. Brown, L. Dominelli, S. Strega, and M. Callahan. Forthcoming. "Where's Waldo? Fathering in Social Work Education," submitted to the *Canadian Social Work Review.*

Chapter 22

Overview

Children are not the only ones who need care in families. As the Canadian population ages, the care of the elderly will become a pressing issue for their adult sons and daughters. Anne Martin-Matthews studies how elderly men and women are cared for in their homes, by a combination of kin and paid care workers. In doing so, she focuses on the concept of "home" as a social as well as a physical space, and examines how the use of this space is gendered.

The home of the elderly parent receiving care looks quite different to sons and to daughters. The sons Martin-Matthews interviewed are acutely conscious of zones of privacy within the home and of not wanting to intrude on the personal spaces of parents, especially mothers. By contrast, daughters (and female care workers), perhaps because they are more used to navigating domestic terrain, are more comfortable working in the homes of the elderly.

Martin-Matthews also brings out the voices of the care workers, all women, who form emotional bonds with their clients as well as providing services. The interactions between the care workers and the families appear to also be gendered, as the care workers receive instructions, training, and feedback from the female relatives of the care recipients.

Situating "Home" at the Nexus of Public and Private Spheres: Aging, Gender, and Home Support Work in Canada

Anne Martin-Matthews

Introduction

This article considers issues of gender in the relationship between elderly clients and home support workers and in the triangulated relationship between an old person, their family member(s) and home support workers.

Home Care and Home Support Work in Canada

In recent decades, Canada's health care system, like that of much of the world, has embraced the concept of community and home care (Shapiro, 2002, 2003). The transition from hospital and institution-based care for both post-acute and chronic health conditions has involved "sending care closer to home" (Armstrong and Armstrong, 2004: 21–3), making relatively routine the proffering of a public service in a private place.

It is estimated that one million people in Canada use home care services annually (Shapiro, 2002). Several distinct groups of workers are included under the heading of home care workers. Many have professional training and qualifications as nurses, care managers, physiotherapists, occupational therapists and social workers. However, most home care workers are "unregulated workers" who provide non-professional services in the form of personal assistance with daily activities, such as bathing, dressing, grooming, and light household tasks that help to maintain a safe and supportive home. They are variously known across Canada as home support workers, personal care workers, home helps, and, until recently, "homemakers." These workers are the focus of this article, and are referred to as home support workers throughout.

The estimated 32,000 home support workers in Canada in 2001 provided approximately 70–80 per cent of home care needs, including both personal care (bathing, toileting) and instrumental needs (food preparation, laundry). Despite ongoing problems with low pay, little or no job progression, lack of pay for travel time between clients and often unpredictable hours of work, home support workers in Canada average eight to nine years of employment in this sector (The Home Care Sector Study Corporation, 2003).

Home Care Research and Family Biography

In the 1990s, I conducted research through four home support agencies in rural and small-town Ontario, Canada.

However, in 1999, my research interest in home support workers shifted dramatically when home care became part of my family biography. With my mother's experience of a debilitating stroke, and the building of a new home to accommodate her new life as a person with left side flaccid paralysis, confined to a wheelchair, and dependent on others for all her physical needs, home care workers entered my family life. My mother receives home care services up to 30 hours a week, every week of the year—supplementing the care provided also at home by my father and two sisters (one co-residing, one living nearby) and, periodically as distance permits, my brothers and me. I live 3000 miles away on the opposite coast of Canada.

Throughout a six-year biography that now includes the community-based health care service that I had previously studied, I have reflected anew on the research questions and issues relevant to an understanding of home as the site of care work, both paid and unpaid. I have had many private conversations with a succession of home support workers about their training, their motivations for employment in this sector, the challenges and rewards of their work, and their concerns as women and as workers. I have listened to my mother grapple with how to approach these strangers who attend to her in the most intimate settings. I have heard my father lament the loss of autonomy in his own home and its "invasion" by a succession of women employed to care. I have spent countless hours talking with my sisters about how to manage the home care situation, the turnover of workers, their variation in abilities, and the impact of their personalities on the home life experience of my parents and others in my family. I have also had the experience of making telephone calls to "home," and having a home support worker answer the call. With this stranger (to me) then telling me about how *my* family members are doing, at such times I have thought to myself: who *is* this person?

In this process, the focus of my research enquiries has changed. I now have new lenses with which to look again at my own data, at those earlier studies I conducted. Looking now with the lens of autobiography and personal experience.

Through these new lenses, my focus has shifted to explore the meaning of home as the site of care, not just as a physical structure but also as a complex symbolic concept. Looked at in this way, the data reveal issues of possession and control of the territory of home, giving rise to concerns about boundaries and spatial familiarity and attendant efforts to make sense of the "stranger" in private places. Issues of gendered care and gendered space emerge as important to this focus. The context and frame for these enquiries is the recognition of home care as situated at the intersections of the public and private spheres and of paid and unpaid labour (Martin-Matthews and Phillips, 2003).

A Focus on Home and the Lens of Gender

A unique aspect of home care is that the workplace of the care provider is the home of the care recipient. While the implications of locale are rarely noted in texts about home care in the health and medical sciences or even in policy discussions of home and community-based services, sociology and social geography understand the significance of the locus of activity. In the context of postmodernity, Giddens argues that "locales are thoroughly penetrated by and shaped in terms of social influences quite distant from them. What structures the locale is not simply that which is present on the scene; the 'visible form' of the locale conceals the distanciated relations which determine its nature" (Giddens, 1991: 18–19). With home care now dominating my family biography, I have observed how the penetration into the place of "home" of public policies as interpreted by local health authorities, agencies, and case managers, occurs through the behaviours and practices of home care workers whose work locale is the client's home. The offering of a public service in private space exemplifies these distanciated relations that determine the nature of home care from the perspective of the older person.

Although the interpersonal dimension of home involves social interaction within and across its physical boundaries, the concepts of privacy and familiarity are inherently part of what home means: "a haven and place of order, 'insideness' and belonging" (Dill, 1991: 230). My approach has also been informed by interpretations of home as a refuge from the outside world, "a place where one can control the level of social interaction, and a place for privacy and independence" (Després, 1991: 98).

Methods

First, interviews were conducted with home care workers and their elderly clients in Ontario, Canada, at two points in time in the 1990s, 12–18 months apart. The study involved 150 home care workers interviewed in Phase I, with 137 of them reinterviewed in Phase II. Of these 137 women, 33 were no longer employed in home support at the second interview, but were included in the study because of their insights into retention issues in home care employment. Second, 155 elderly clients of home care services were interviewed in Phase I, with 118 of them interviewed again in Phase II (14 of these 118 were former clients of home care services by the time of the second interview). These home care clients ranged in age from 57 to 95 years, with an average age of 78 years. They had lived in their present community for an average of 35 years and had been receiving home care services from one month to eight years.

Third, as part of the thesis research project of a graduate student, interviews were conducted with 39 adult children identified as primary caregivers to an elderly parent who had participated in the home care client interviews (von Hof, 1991). There were 26 daughters, 7 daughters-in-law, and 6 sons in that study, ranging in age from 23 to 63, with an average age of 51 years.

Finally, data are drawn from participant observation and field notes collected in Newfoundland, Canada, in interactions and meetings with home support workers, case managers, elderly home care recipients, and family members. The analysis is also informed by meetings with individual home care supervisors and agencies as part of a project currently being launched in British Columbia, Canada (www.nexushomecare.arts.ubc.ca).

Gender is relevant to these analyses in a number of ways that are both implicit and explicit. It is implicit in terms of the context of home support services delivery, since all the case managers, agency personnel and home support workers participating in these studies are women. Gender is therefore difficult to interrogate in this context largely because it is so overwhelmingly *assumed* that women deliver these services. In the accounts of the clients of these services, gender is relevant because, as Twigg (2004: 65) notes, "deep old age is predominantly female." Reflecting this, 77 per cent of the elderly clients were women. Most of these women (58 per cent) were widowed and had lived alone an average of 14 years. Among the men, all but two were married and co-resided with their wives.

Home as the Site of Care: The Meaning of Place and Space

Perspectives of Elderly Clients: Boundary Control and the Significance of Home

Three broad themes were identified by elderly clients in their references to home as the site of care: issues of territory and boundary; control and co-operation; and the symbolic significance of home.

Issues of territory and boundary were typically expressed in terms of the necessity of bringing "strangers" into one's own home, giving over one's privacy and sharing of the physical place:

> I think homemakers are a wonderful idea. I know my family wouldn't want to be bothered by this—having strangers around their home for hours every week—but they haven't been laid up as much as I have. (Woman, age 80, home care received seven years)

Control and co-operation also emerged as themes. Reflecting Russell's observations . . . about gender differences in the meaning of home as a "psychosocial bastion," it is notable that none of the comments concerning this issue is made by men, even though men constitute 23 per cent of the respondents in the study of elderly clients of home support services:

> The lack of privacy [does bother me]. I had two homemakers who eavesdropped every time the phone rang. (Woman, age 57, home care received two years)

For many elderly home care clients, however, there is a trade-off: by having someone come into their own home to work, they are enabled to remain in their home for longer than they would otherwise. Issues of boundary, territory, control and co-operation are dealt with in this larger context:

> Having a homemaker helps keep people in their own homes. It's worth it—the training new people, the constant revolving door with new people coming into my home and my having to explain everything to each one all over again. I don't like that, but I know what the alternative is. (Woman, age 79, home care received three years)

As the literature on home as a haven indicates, there are dimensions of inside- and outside-ness in individual accounts of having individuals come "into" the private space of home. Although some women did comment on what the home support workers bring into the home from "outside," it is noteworthy that the two men who were solitary inhabitants of their homes both mentioned this:

> They are cheerful. They are pleasant when they come in. They tell me what is happening outside. They go ahead and do the work. (Man, age 69, receiving home care for three years)

The theme of the symbolic significance of and attachment to home is also evident in the accounts of many elderly home care clients. It is particularly notable when these individuals speak positively about their home support worker: the highest praise for the labour of home support workers invokes the language of pride of place and "home." However, none of the men made reference to this:

> She does everything she can to make me comfortable. . . . Mary is a very devoted person. It is like her own home, she takes very good care of it. (Woman, age 75, home care received one-and-a-half years)

In these accounts, issues of boundary, territory, and sharing of physical space with a home support worker were more frequently expressed as problematic by older women than by men. For men, references to space and place were not framed in terms of privacy and control, but rather in terms of what home support workers were able to bring into the home from the outside world.

Perspectives of Family Members: Gendered Care and Gendered Space

Among the family members interviewed, the verbatim accounts of adult sons identified the relationship between gendered filial care and the territoriality of certain types of space when home is the site of care. No women (daughters and daughters-in-law) made such comments, and we can speculate that this was because no space within the dwelling is "off limits" for them in their roles as carers. Just as care is gendered, spatial access within the dwelling is also frequently gendered (particularly in terms of who else is occupying the space at a particular time). In answer to a question about what impact the presence of a home care worker had had on the kind of assistance provided by the adult child, several sons noted this:

> It's my mother's house, even though I grew up in it. I haven't been in her bedroom or bathroom for years, not since she needed that personal care. My sisters and the home care women go in there. They do what they need to do to help Mom with that kind of stuff. That's all off-limits to me. Fine with me. I help out with the yard work and the kitchen stuff, like when the fridge breaks. That's my territory. (Son, age 51, mother receiving home care nine years)
>
> My mother's pretty private about herself, and she doesn't get me involved in the personal care. Good thing too. I don't even go near that part of her place, her apartment when she's in there with the worker. Fixed the plumbing in there once, that's all. (Son, age 47, mother receiving home care three years)

These gendered patterns of access to these private spheres within the home reflect the range of care that women, typically, provide to other women. Twigg (2004) has observed that care work is quintessentially gendered work in that it is performed predominantly by women, and constructed around gendered identities. The verbatim accounts of these sons reflect my own observation that because "bodywork," as described by Twigg (2004), is typically performed by women as home support workers and women as daughters and daughters-in-law, they have differential access (than do men, and especially sons) to those private spheres of the home in which this body work occurs.

Reflecting the findings of earlier studies of the gendered nature of filial care (Campbell and Martin-Matthews, 2003; Martin-Matthews and Campbell, 1995), sons and sons-in-law largely confined their helping behaviours to the outside, to yard work, and to the more public spaces within the home. By their own accounts, the more private spaces in the dwelling (spaces connected to body work) were not within the sons' realm of activities because they did not (and were not expected to) provide this type of care. In the verbatim accounts from the interviews and in my own participant observations, there were implicit gender taboos about care (especially body work) and of gendered access to private space that were equally self-imposed by female caregivers and the home support workers.

It is clear that there are psychological, social, and emotional boundaries to be negotiated as family members move beyond the give-and-take of "typical" family relationships over the life course, to assume responsibilities that are defined as "caregiving." So too are there physical boundaries—and access to physical spaces imbued with meaning—to be negotiated (and renegotiated) within families. When home is the site of care, new boundaries may emerge within domestic spaces; these boundaries reflect a system of (gendered) meanings about spaces within the household and private spaces within the home.

Home as the Site of Care: Negotiating (Contingent) Relationships

Home as the site of care is about more than the meaning of and utilization of space. Analyses of the verbatim accounts of older home care clients, home support workers and family members identified other issues: the definition of the worker–client relationship; its contingent nature; issues of isolation, security, and constraints when home is the site of care; and blurring the boundaries of paid/unpaid and trained labour. Issues of gender figure in a number of these accounts.

Perspectives of Elderly Clients: Friendship and the Boundaries of Paid Labour

In the interviews with elderly clients, they were asked whether they saw the home support worker as an employee, as a friend, or as some combination of both. Fully 39 per cent considered the home support worker to be primarily a friend; 18 per cent as an employee; 27 per cent as both employee and friend; 3 per cent "like family"; 6 per cent indicated all three; and 6 per cent identified at least one of their home support workers as both a friend and "like family." The men receiving services were significantly more likely to consider the home support worker as an employee and no men saw her primarily as a friend (although several noted that she was a "friend" to their wives). However, several men used the language of a family tie in describing their home support worker, describing her as "like my own daughter" (man, age 85, receiving home care for two years). Nevertheless, for the majority of male clients, interaction with the home support worker was mediated by their wives.

Among elderly women who described their home care worker either as a friend or a combination of employee and friend, there were issues to be negotiated in the interaction however. Some were more equivocal than others:

> It depends on the day. Most of the time we get along, and I call her Jody. But some days, I want to let her know to keep her distance and I call her by her married name, Mrs S___. I depend on her, so what else can I do to let her know that she's in my house and some days I just need . . . my space, I suppose. (Woman, age 77, receiving home care six years)

Others were clear as to the nature of the relationship as outside the bounds of friendship:

> I like her enough. She's good to me, and kind, and she works hard. But she's not the sort of person I would choose as a friend, to go on an outing with, that sort of thing. (Woman, age 76, receiving home care five years)

For others, an awareness of the power differential between the dependent client and the worker characterized the relationship:

> She's always eager to go rushing out the door. I'm not as important to her as other things in her life. (Woman, age 76, receiving home care one year)

For elderly clients, therefore, the relationship between home support workers and the client is a complex one. The presence of a stranger in the household is frequently made sense of through a refraining to the language of friendship or fictive kin. But, nevertheless, there are frequent reminders of the limits of this refraining, especially when workers rotate and the paid work period ends.

Perspectives of Home Support Workers: Couple and Gender Dynamics

Among the elderly clients interviewed, in only 15 per cent of the households were the husband and wife both clients of home care services, whereas home support workers had many situations where a client and a non-client spouse or family member co-resided. When home is the site of care, the relationship between the client and the home support worker is highly contingent on the dynamic between the couple, and between the home support worker and the non-client spouse. Gender factored into these relationships. In the verbatim accounts of the home support workers, the only references to difficult relations with non-client spouses involved the husbands of female clients:

> I had to leave one couple. He screamed at me while I was washing her hair; said I'd pushed her, which was just not true. I'd had to intervene several times during a fight between the husband and wife. The husband interfered with everything I did, said I used too much water doing laundry. There was no pleasing him. I asked to be relieved. (Woman, age 43, employed in home care three-and-a-half years)

However, male clients were not uniformly viewed as more difficult. For example, one worker noted that "Men are easier to please. They usually appreciate what you do for them" (woman, age 37, employed in home care four years).

The non-client spouse or co-resident family member plays a pivotal role in the contingent relationship between the client and the home support worker. While agencies may see the non-client co-resider as essentially "neutral" in the delivery of services to the client, in practice (and in my own experience as participant observer) the non-client plays a role within the home that home support workers find facilitating, hindering or ambivalent:

> I don't know what I would do if Mrs M___ wasn't there to help me cajole him into the bath tub and to let me do the bathing of him. She jollies him too when he's out of sorts. Makes a real difference to my day. It helps me get the job done in the time it's supposed to take. (Woman, age 41, employed in home care nine years)

Other family members who were not co-resident also influenced both the nature of the care work and the relationship between the client and home support worker:

> It really bothers me when sometimes Mrs R___ asks me to do some extra cooking or washing and I know it is not for her, it's for her daughter who's having company over or something, or needs an extra hand with the laundry. (Woman, age 47, employed in home care three years)

Home support workers spoke at length about their relationships with their elderly clients, identifying a range of issues reflecting care and concern for clients, and a keen sense of the contingent nature of the relationship:

> You get so attached to these elderly people. It will kill me when this dear old lady I am caring for dies. (Woman, age 46, employed in home care two years)

Other workers see their relationship extending beyond the elderly client to include a role in bridging between the elder and his or her kin:

> I inform the children . . . you act as a liaison officer or a colleague between the person you're caring for and their relatives. Some relatives really appreciate it. (Woman, age 55, employed in home care two years)

However, others invoke the language of space and territory, in proceeding more cautiously in relation to family members:

> You're in their home, and their sphere, so knowing your place is an issue sometimes. With one client, . . . I felt she should be in a nursing home because the family just kept her in a chair in front of the TV. When I bathed her, she was so frail (bones cracking), etc. But the home support worker is not to advise the family caregiver that it's time to place their parent in a nursing home. It's a difficult situation. I know that she needs better care. (Woman, age 40, employed in home care five years)

Perspectives of Home Support Workers: Boundaries of Labour and Training

In the interviews, a quarter of the elderly clients reported contact with their home support worker outside the worker's official hours of employment. Most of this interaction took place as social visits or outings. The remainder were for a variety of reasons: when they wanted the worker to pick up groceries for them; to ask the worker for transportation; and, on occasion, when the worker phoned the client to check on the client's health:

> The cutback in hours is a problem. I know she needs more help than she's getting. She relies on me. So sometimes I go back on weekends on my own, and run errands for her. This puts me in a dilemma because if the agency knew . . . and my husband thinks I'm just being taken advantage of . . . but what am I to do, if she's got no one else to do it? (Woman, age 47, employed in home care seven years)

Home support workers in Canada contribute an average of 2.6 hours of unpaid work per week (The Home Care Sector Study Corporation, 2003). While this assistance may be voluntarily given, these personal arrangements may also be exploitative for either the provider or the recipient, especially if there are no other options (Armstrong and Armstrong, 2004). Issues of gender are implicit in the clients' accounts of these unpaid contributions by women who are "really nice girls" who "treat me like their mother." For some clients, this includes expectations of nurturing assistance beyond the hours of paid care. However, gender-based assumptions and values were also reflected in the comments of home support workers as well.

> It disturbs me when a client with a capable daughter is receiving services. (Woman, age 41, employed in home care four years)

For home support workers, the negotiation of relationships in the home thus included a broad array of issues, from couple and gender dynamics, to agency policies and guidelines, to concerns about safety and isolation, to the blurring of the boundaries between paid and unpaid labour.

Perspectives of Family Members: Supplementing Care and Training Workers

When family members made explicit reference to the impact of home care workers on their parent's lives or on their own, it was to extol the benefits of home care in terms of how it facilitated their ability to continue in employment themselves, or to note how it had improved their own relationship with their parent and more positively focus the time they spent together:

> When I don't have to worry about basic home living for my elderly relatives, more time can be spent with them giving moral and emotional support. (Daughter, age 42, parents receiving home care two years)
>
> Home care allowed my wife to provide emotional support rather than be a full-time cook and housekeeper. (Man, aged 79, receiving home care three years)

In the blurring of boundaries between the public and the private sphere, "women who are paid carers may find themselves teaching women, in minutes, how to do what took them years of training to learn, making it more difficult to distinguish both the work and the workers" (Armstrong and Armstrong, 2004: 27). There was certainly evidence of this in the accounts of family members as they described, for example, being taught to insert a catheter, so that they could, as unpaid carers, assist with a medical procedure previously done by trained professionals.

Several home support workers acknowledged the vital role of family members in "training" them to provide better care. Most instances of informal carers providing such "training" were reported in terms of wives and daughters demonstrating to the home support worker their skills in knowing how to work with the client. However, husbands too showed the workers how their wives liked to be helped to walk, or have their food cut and served. Thus, in cases where formal training is inadequate to the task, or where it requires idiosyncratic knowledge of the client or environment, the unpaid and "informal" (typically female) carer or family member may train the paid "formal" carer. In the context of care in the home, the blurring of the public and private spheres of responsibility takes many forms.

Summary and Conclusions

This article has discussed a variety of ways in which home care workers are positioned at the centre of a web of contacts bridging the private world of family, providing care to an old person and the public world of services (care, health, welfare benefits). Working at the "unregulated" end of the home care continuum, these women are poorly paid, have minimal training and their labours are largely invisible in the context of public discourse about home care.

The qualitative data informing this article are derived from verbatim accounts of home support workers, elderly clients, and family members of clients as they describe the context of "home" as the site of care. Home support workers identified as problematic the balancing of agency guidelines and the unmet needs of elderly clients. For elderly clients, a key issue was the negotiation of relationships with successive "strangers" entering the private sphere of their home. Other elderly clients noted issues of negotiation of longer-term relationships with home support workers as employee and/or friend.

The accounts of workers, clients, and family members indicate the particular relevance of gender to the meaning of home, to issues of territory and control, to the relationship between care work (especially body work) and space, and to issues of security and isolation.

In situating home at the nexus of the private and the public spheres, this article has also considered what Giddens (1991) has called the distanciated relations that shape the contingent nature of home support work and of the provider–client interaction within the private sphere of the home. Framed within the context of governmental home care policies and agency guidelines, for elderly clients "the worker embodies both what the system can and cannot do for them" (Bowdie and Turwoski, 1986: 44). For workers, employer policies and regulations often challenge their ability to address the unmet needs of clients—and may contribute to a blurring of the boundaries between paid and unpaid care work.

The gendered lens of this researcher's autobiography was the catalyst for the conceptualization of home as situated at the nexus of the private and public spheres when home is the site of care. Several of the themes identified, such as the relationship between gendered care and the gendering of space, and the contingent nature of the worker–client relationship, reflect my experience of home care in my family biography.

Caught in the midst of policy debates about the future and funding of home care, there are elders and those who care for them, often struggling to respond to the immediacy of needs in the context of a system down-sizing or in flux. The challenges at the heart of these debates unwittingly enter their lives in the form of case managers, home care professionals and, most typically, poorly paid, educated, and often immigrant women employed as home support workers . . . The practices and procedures, and rules and regulations forged by governments and implemented by agencies in response to these policy debates enter the most intimate and private spheres of their personal spaces, when community-based care is, in the words of Armstrong and Armstrong (2004), brought "closer to home."

Acknowledgements

The author acknowledges the support of a visiting professorship awarded by the British Academy in the writing of this article. Sara Arber provided valuable insights that encouraged a refocusing of this article. I also thank Judith Phillips, Carolyn Rosenthal, and especially Joanie Sims-Gould for their helpful and constructive comments and contributions to my thinking about these issues.

References

Armstrong, P., and H. Armstrong. 2004. "Thinking It Through: Women, Work and Caring in the New Millennium," in K.R. Grant, C. Amaratunga, P. Armstrong, M. Boscoe, A. Pederson, and K. Willson, eds., *Caring For/Caring About: Women, Home Care and Unpaid Caregiving*, pp. 5–43. Aurora, Ontario: Garamond Press.

Aronson, J. 2004. "'Just Fed and Watered': Women's Experiences of the Gutting of Home Care in Ontario," in K.R. Grant, C. Amaratunga, P. Armstrong, M. Boscoe, A. Pederson, and K. Willson, eds., *Caring For/Caring About: Women, Home Care and Unpaid Caregiving*, pp. 167–83. Aurora, Ontario: Garamond Press.

Bowdie, R., and A. Turwoski. 1986. "The Problems of Providing Services to the Elderly in Their Own Homes," in A.O. Pelham and W.F. Clark, eds., *Managing Home Care for the Elderly*, pp. 31–46. New York: Springer.

Campbell, L.D., and A. Martin-Matthews. 2003. "The Gendered Nature of Men's Filial Care," *Journal of Gerontology: Social Sciences* 58B(6): S350–S358.

Després, C. 1991. "The Meaning of Home: Literature Review and Directions for Future Research and Theoretical Development," *The Journal of Architectural and Planning Research* 8(2): 96–114.

Dill, A.E.P. 1991. "Transformations of Home: The Formal and Informal Process of Home Care Planning," in J.F. Gubrium and A. Sankar, eds., *The Home Care Experience: Ethnography and Policy*, pp. 227–51. Newbury Park, CA: Sage.

Giddens, A. 1991. *The Consequences of Modernity*. Cambridge: Polity Press.

Hagestad, G.O. 1996. "On-Time, Off-Time, Out of Time? Reflections on Continuity and Discontinuity from an Illness Process," in V.L. Bengtson and B. Neugarten,eds., *Adulthood and Aging: Research on Continuities and Discontinuities*, pp. 204–28. New York: Springer.

Karner, T.X. 1998. "Professional Caring: Homecare Workers as Fictive Kin," *Journal of Aging Studies* 12(1): 69–82.

Katz, C., and J. Monk. 1993. *Full Circles: Geographies of Women over the Life Course*. London and New York: Routledge.

Martin-Matthews, A., and L.D. Campbell. 1995. "Gender Roles, Employment and Informal Care," in S. Arber and J. Ginn, eds., *Connecting Gender and Ageing*, pp. 129–43. Milton Keynes: Open University Press.

Martin-Matthews, A., and J.E. Phillips. 2003. "Home Care Work in Canada and England: Comparative Perspectives of Home Care Workers on Relationship Issues in the Provision of Home-Based Services to Elderly Persons," paper presented at the annual conference of the Gerontological Society of America, San Diego.

Martin-Matthews, A., and S. Wakefield. 1993. *Report of the Homemaker Services to the Elderly: Provider Characteristics and Client Benefit*. Toronto: Ontario Ministry of Community and Social Services.

Ray, R.E. 1999. "Researching to Transgress: The Need for Critical Feminism in Gerontology," *Journal of Women and Aging* 11(2/3): 171–84.

Rowles, G., and H. Chaudury, eds. 2005. *Home and Identity in Late Life: International Perspectives*. New York: Springer.

Rubenstein, R.L. 1990. "Culture and Disorder in the Home Care Experience: The Home as Sickroom," in J.F. Gubrium and A. Sankar, eds., *The Home Care Experience: Ethnography and Policy*, pp. 37–57. Newbury Park, CA: Sage.

Shanas, E., and M.B. Sussman. 1977. *Family, Bureaucracy and the Elderly*. Durham,NC: Duke University Press.

Shapiro, E. 2002. *The Health Care Transition Fund Synthesis Series: Home Care*, Cat. H13-6/2002-2. Ottawa: Minister of Public Works and Government Services Canada; at: www.hc-sc.gc.ca

Shapiro, E. 2003. "The Romanow Commission Reports and Home Care," *Canadian Journal on Aging* 22(1): 13–17.

The Home Care Sector Study Corporation. 2003. *Canadian Home Care Human Resources Study: Synthesis Report*. Toronto: Home Care Sector Study Corporation; at: www.homecarestudy.ca

Twigg, J. 2004. "The Body, Gender and Age: Feminist Insights in Social Gerontology," *Journal of Aging Studies* 18(1): 59–73.

Von Hof, T. 1991. "Homemaker Services to the Elderly: Impact on Family Caregivers," unpublished MSc. thesis, Department of Family Studies, University of Guelph, Ontario.

Chapter 23

Overview

Scott Coltrane picks up the concept of "doing gender" and applies it to the unpaid work that keeps families going. He seeks out heterosexual couples who identify themselves as sharing unpaid work between both parents, and then examines the concept of "shared parenting" to determine who really does what.

The couples in his study describe shared parenting as something to which they are consciously aspiring, with the commitment to shared parenting arrived at after long discussion, often before children actually enter the picture. They are strongly supportive of the idea that men and women should have equal rights and responsibilities. However, the day-to-day work of household labour often goes undiscussed, with couples describing themselves as falling into roles that feel "natural."

When Coltrane tracks who actually carries out household labour, he finds that, contrary to the professed equality in these couples, women tend to carry out more daily work than men. Often, this division of labour takes the form of a "manager/helper" dynamic, in which the mother takes charge of organizing the task, even if the father actually carries out the labour. Perhaps this division of labour is reinforced by the feedback these couples receive outside the home, where the fathers are singled out, whether positively or negatively, as unusual or atypical fathers. Establishing a truly equitable parenting situation turns out to be much more complex than making a philosophical commitment to gender equality.

Household Labour and the Routine Production of Gender

Scott Coltrane

Motherhood is often perceived as the quintessence of womanhood. The everyday tasks of mothering are taken to be "natural" expressions of femininity, and the routine care of home and children is seen to provide opportunities for women to express and reaffirm their gendered relation to men and to the world. The traditional tasks of fatherhood, in contrast, are limited to begetting, protecting, and providing for children. While fathers typically derive a gendered sense of self from these activities, their masculinity is even more dependent on *not* doing the things that mothers do. What happens, then, when fathers share with mothers those tasks that we define as expressing the true nature of womanhood?

This chapter describes how a sample of 20 dual-earner couples talk about sharing housework and childcare. Since marriage is one of the least scripted or most undefined interaction situations, the marital conversation is particularly important to a couple's shared sense of reality. I investigate these parents' construction of gender by examining their talk about negotiations over who does what around the house; how these divisions of labour influence their perceptions of self and other; how they conceive of gender-appropriate behaviour; and how they handle inconsistencies between their own views and those of the people around them. Drawing on the parents' accounts of the planning, allocation, and performance of childcare and housework, I illustrate how gender is produced through everyday practices and how adults are socialized by routine activity.

Gender as an Accomplishment

Candace West and Don Zimmerman (1987) suggest that gender is a routine, methodical, and recurring accomplishment. "Doing gender" involves a complex of socially guided perceptual, interactional, and micropolitical activities that cast particular pursuits as expressions of masculine and feminine "natures." Rather than viewing gender as a property of individuals, West and Zimmerman conceive of it as an emergent feature of social situations that results from and legitimates gender inequality. Similarly, Sarah Fenstermaker Berk (1985: 204, emphasis in original) suggests that housework and child care

> can become the occasion for producing commodities (e.g., clean children, clean laundry, and new light switches) and a reaffirmation of one's *gendered* relation to the work and to the world. In short, the "shoulds" of gender ideals are fused with the "musts" of efficient household production. The result may be something resembling a "gendered" household-production function.

. . . By investigating how couples share childcare and housework, I explore (1) the sorts of dyadic and group interactions that facilitate the sharing of household labour; (2) how couples describe the requirements of parenting and how they evaluate men's developing capacities for nurturing; and (3) the impact of sharing domestic labour on conceptions of gender.

The Sample

To find couples who shared childcare, I initially contacted schools and day care centres in several suburban California communities. Using snowball-sampling techniques, I selected 20 moderate- to middle-income dual-earner couples with children. To compensate for gaps in the existing literature and to enhance comparisons between sample families, I included couples if they were the biological parents of at least two school-aged children, they were both employed at least halftime, and both identified the father as assuming significant responsibility for routine childcare. I observed families in their homes and interviewed fathers and mothers separately, at least once, and as many as five times. I recorded the interviews and transcribed them for coding and constant comparative analysis.

The parents were primarily in their late thirties and had been living together for an average of 10 years. All wives and 17 of 20 husbands attended some college and most couples married later and had children later than others in their birth cohort. The median age at marriage for the mothers was 23; for fathers, 26. Median age at first birth for mothers was 27; for fathers, 30. Fifteen of 20 fathers were at least one year older than their wives. Median gross annual income was $40,000, with three families under $25,000 and three over $65,000. Sixteen of the couples had two children and four had three children. Over two-thirds of the families had both sons and daughters, but four families had two sons and no daughters, and two families had two daughters and no sons. The children's ages ranged from four to fourteen, with 80 per cent between the ages of five and eleven and with a median age of seven.

Mothers were more likely than fathers to hold professional or technical jobs, although most were employed in female-dominated occupations with relatively limited upward mobility and moderate pay. Over three-quarters held jobs in the "helping" professions. . . . Sample fathers held both blue-collar and white-collar jobs. Like most dual-earner wives, sample mothers earned, on average, less than half of what their husband's did, and worked an average of eight fewer hours per week. Eleven mothers (55 per cent), but only five fathers

(25 per cent) were employed less than 40 hours per week. In nine of 20 families, mothers were employed at least as many hours as fathers, but in only four families did the mother's earnings approach or exceed those of her husband.

Developing Shared Parenting

Two-thirds of the parents indicated that current divisions of labour were accomplished by making minor practical adjustments to what they perceived as an already fairly equal division of labour. A common sentiment was expressed by one father who commented:

> Since we've both always been working since we've been married, we've typically shared everything as far as all the working—I mean all the housework responsibilities as well as child care responsibilities. So it's a pattern that was set up before the kids were even thought of.

Nevertheless, a full three-quarters of the couples reported that the mother performed much more of the early infant care. All of the mothers and only about half of the fathers reported that they initially reduced their hours of employment after having children. About a third of the fathers said they increased their employment hours to compensate for the loss of income that resulted from their wives taking time off work before or after the births of their children. . . .

About half of the fathers referred to the experience of being involved in the delivery and in early infant care as a necessary part of their assuming responsibility for later childcare. Many described a process in which the actual performance of care-taking duties provided them with the self-confidence and skills to feel that they knew what they were doing. They described their time alone with the baby as especially helpful in building their sense of competence as a shared primary caretaker. One man said,

> I felt I needed to start from the beginning. Then I learned how to walk them at night and not be totally p.o.'ed at them and not feel that it was an infringement. It was something I *got* to do in some sense, along with changing diapers and all these things. It was certainly not repulsive and in some ways I really liked it a lot. It was not something innate, it was something to be learned. I managed to start at the beginning. If you *don't* start at the beginning then you're sort of left behind.

. . . While all fathers intentionally shared routine childcare as the children approached school age, only half of the fathers attempted to assume a major share of daily infant care, and only five couples described the father as an equal caregiver for children under one year old. These early caregiving fathers described their involvement in infant care as explicitly planned:

> She nursed both of them completely, for at least five or six months. So, my role was—we agreed on this—my role was the other direct intervention, like changing, and getting them up and walking them, and putting them back to sleep. For instance, she would nurse them but I would bring them to the bed afterward and change them if necessary, and get them back to sleep. . . . I really initiated those other kinds of care aspects so that I could be involved. I continued that on through infant and toddler and preschool classes that we would go to, even though I would usually be the only father there.

This man's wife offered a similar account, commenting that "except for breast-feeding, he always provided the same things that I did—the emotional closeness and the attention."

Another early caregiving father described how he and his wife "very consciously" attempted to equalize the amount of time they spent with their children when they were infants: "In both cases we very consciously made the decision that we wanted it to be a mutual process, so that from the start we shared, and all I didn't do was breastfeed. And I really would say that was the only distinction." His wife also described their infant care arrangements as "equal," and commented that other people did not comprehend the extent of his participation:

> I think that nobody really understood that Jennifer had two mothers. The burden of proof was always on me that he was literally being a mother. He wasn't nursing, but he was getting up in the night to bring her to me, to change her poop, which is a lot more energy than nursing in the middle of the night. You have to get up and do all that, I mean get awake. So his sleep was interrupted, and yet within a week or two, at his work situation, it was expected that he was back to normal, and he never went back to normal. He was part of the same family that I was. . . .

Practicality and Flexibility

[All] . . . families identified practical considerations and flexibility as keys to equitable divisions of household labour. Most did not have explicit records or schedules for childcare or housework. For example, one early-involved father reported that practical divisions of labour evolved "naturally":

> Whoever cooks doesn't have to do the dishes. If for some reason she cooks and I don't do the dishes, she'll say something about it, certainly. Even though we never explicitly agreed that's how we do it, that's how we do it. The person who doesn't cook does the dishes. We don't even know who's going to cook a lot of the time. We just get it that we can do it. We act in good faith.

. . . Most couples reported that they spent little time planning or arguing about who was going to do what around the house. Typical procedures for allocating domestic chores were described as "ad hoc," illustrated by one mother's discussion of cooking:

> Things with us have happened pretty easily as far as what gets done by who. It happened without having to have a schedule or deciding—you know—like cooking. We never decided that he would do all the cooking; it just kind of ended up that way. Every once in a while when he doesn't feel like cooking he'll say, "Would you cook tonight?' "Sure, fine." But normally I don't offer to cook. I say, "What are we having for dinner?"

In general, divisions of labour in sample families were described as flexible and changing. One mother talked about how routine adjustments in task allocation were satisfying to her: "Once you're comfortable in your roles and division of tasks for a few months then it seems like the needs change a little bit and you have to change a little bit and you have to regroup. That's what keeps it interesting. I think that's why it's satisfying."

Underlying Ideology

While ad hoc divisions of labour were described as being practical solutions to time shortages, there were two major ideological underpinnings to the sharing of housework and childcare: child-centredness and equity ideals. . . .

Couples were child-centred in that they placed a high value on their children's well-being, defined parenting as an important and serious undertaking, and organized most of their non-employed hours around their children. For instance, one father described how his social life revolved around his children:

> Basically if the other people don't have kids and if they aren't involved with the kids, then we aren't involved with them. It's as simple as that. The guys I know at work that are single or don't have children my age don't come over because then we have nothing in common. They're kind of the central driving force in my life.

While about half of the couples (11 of 20) had paid for ongoing out-of-home childcare, and three-quarters had regularly used some form of paid childcare, most of the parents said that they spent more time with their children than the other dual-earner parents in their neighbourhoods. One father commented that he and his wife had structured their lives around personally taking care of their children:

> An awful lot of the way we've structured our lives has been based around our reluctance to have someone else raise our children. We just really didn't want the kids to be raised from 7:30 in the morning 'til 4:30 or 5:00 in the afternoon by somebody else. So we've structured the last ten years around that issue.

. . . Concerning women's rights, 80 per cent of fathers and 90 per cent of mothers agreed that women were disadvantaged in our society, but only two mothers and one father mentioned equal rights or the women's movement as motivators for sharing household labour. Most did not identify themselves as feminists, and a few offered derogatory comments about "those women's libbers." Nevertheless, almost all parents indicated that no one should be forced to perform a specific task because they were a man or a woman. This implicit equity ideal was evidenced by mothers and fathers using time availability, rather than gender, to assign most household tasks.

Divisions of Household Labour

Contributions to 64 household tasks were assessed by having fathers and mothers each sort cards on a five-point scale to indicate who most often performed them (see Table 23.1). Frequently performed tasks, such as meal preparation, laundry, sweeping, or putting children to bed, were judged for the two weeks preceding the interviews. Less frequently performed tasks, such as window washing, tax preparation, or car repair, were judged as to who typically performed them.

Some differences occurred between mothers' and fathers' accounts of household task allocation, but there was general agreement on who did what.

Table 23.1 shows that in the majority of families, most household tasks were seen as shared. Thirty-seven of 64 tasks (58 per cent), including all direct childcare, most household business, meal preparation, kitchen clean-up, and about half of other housecleaning tasks were reported to be shared about equally by fathers and mothers. Nevertheless, almost a quarter (15) of the tasks were performed principally by the mothers, including most clothes care, meal planning, kin-keeping, and some of the more onerous repetitive housecleaning. Just under one-fifth (12) of the tasks were performed principally by the fathers. These included the majority of the occasional outside chores such as home repair, car maintenance, lawn care, and taking out the trash. As a group, sample couples can thus be characterized as sharing an unusually high proportion of housework and childcare, but still partially conforming to a traditional division of household labour. . . .

Managing versus Helping

Household divisions of labour in these families also can be described in terms of who takes responsibility for planning and initiating various tasks. In every family there were at least six frequently performed household chores over which the mother retained almost exclusive managerial control. That is, mothers noticed when the chore needed doing and made sure that someone adequately performed it. In general, mothers were more likely than fathers to act as managers for cooking, cleaning, and childcare, but over half of the couples shared responsibility in these areas. In all households the father was responsible for initiating and managing at least a few chores traditionally performed by mothers.

Based on participants' accounts of strategies for allocating household labour, I classified twelve couples as sharing responsibility for household labour and eight couples as reflecting manager–helper dynamics. Helper husbands often waited to be told what to do, when to do it, and how it should be done. While they invariably expressed a desire to perform their "fair share" of housekeeping and child-rearing, they were less likely than the other fathers to assume responsibility for anticipating and planning these activities. Manager–helper couples sometimes referred to the fathers' contributions as "helping" the mother.

When asked what they liked most about their husband's housework, about half of the mothers focused on their husband's self-responsibility: voluntarily doing work without being prodded. They commented, "He does the everyday stuff" and "I don't have to ask him." The other mothers praised their husbands for particular skills with comments such as "I love his spaghetti" or "He's great at cleaning the bathroom." In spite of such praise, three-fourths of the mothers said that what bothered them most about their husband's housework was the need to remind him to perform certain tasks, and some

Table 23.1 Household tasks by person most often performing them

Mother More	Father and Mother Equally	Father More
Cleaning		
• Mopping • Sweeping • Dusting • Cleaning bathroom sink • Cleaining toilet	• Vacuuming • Cleaning tub/shower • Making beds • Picking up toys • Tidying living room • Hanging up clothes • Washing windows • Spring cleaning	• Taking out trash • Cleaing porch
Cooking		
• Planning menus • Grocery shopping • Baking	• Preparing lunch • Cooking dinner • Making snacks • Washing dishes • Putting dishes away • Wiping kitchen counters • Putting food away	• Preparing breakfast
Clothes		
• Laundry • Hand laundry • Ironing • Sewing • Buying clothes	• Shoe care	
Household		
	• Running errands • Decorating • Interior painting • General yardwork • Gardening	• Household repairs • Exterior painting • Car maintenance • Car repair • Washing car • Watering lawn • Mowing lawn • Cleaning rain gutters
Finance, Social		
• Writing or phoning relatives/friends	• Deciding on major purchases • Paying bills • Preparing taxes • Handling insurance • Planning couple dates	• Investments

(*Continued*)

Table 23.1 *(Continued)*

Mother More	Father and Mother Equally	Father More
Children		
• Arranging baby-sitters	• Waking children • Helping children dress • Helping children bathe • Putting children to bed • Supervising children • Disciplining children • Driving children • Taking children to doctor • Caring for sick children • Playing with children • Planning outings	

Note: Tasks were sorted separately by fathers and mothers according to relative frequency of performance: (1) Mother mostly or always, (2) Mother more than father, (3) Father and mother about equal, (4) Father more than mother, (5) Father mostly or always. For each task a mean ranking by couple was computed with 1.00–2.49 = Mother, 2.50–3.50 = Shared, 3.51–5.0 = Father. If over 50 per cent of families ranked a task as performed by one spouse more than the other, the task is listed under that spouse, otherwise tasks are listed as shared. *N* = 20 couples.

complained of having to "train him" to correctly perform the chores. About a third of the fathers complained that their wives either didn't notice when things should be done or that *their* standards were too low. Although the extent of domestic task sharing varied considerably among couples, 90 per cent of both mothers and fathers independently reported that their divisions of labour were "fair."

Some mothers found it difficult to share authority for household management. For instance, one mother said, "There's a certain control you have when you do the shopping and the cooking and I don't know if I'm ready to relinquish that control." Another mother, who shares most childcare and housework with her husband, admitted that "in general, household organization is something that I think I take over." In discussing how they divide housework, she commented on how she notices more than her husband does:

> He does what he sees needs to be done. That would include basic cleaning kinds of things. However, there are some detailed kinds of things that he doesn't see that I feel need to be done, and in those cases I have to ask him to do things. He thinks some of the details are less important and I'm not sure, that might be a difference between men and women.

. . . Many mothers talked about adjusting their housecleaning standards over the course of their marriage and trying to feel less responsible for being "the perfect homemaker." By partially relinquishing managerial duties and accepting their husband's housecleaning standards, some mothers reported that they were able to do less daily housework and focus more on occasional, thorough cleaning or adding "finishing touches." A mother with two nursing jobs, whose husband delivered newspapers, commented:

> He'll handle the surface things no problem, and I get down and do the nitty gritty. And I do it when it bugs me or when I have the time. It's not anything that we talk about usually. Sometimes if I feel like things are piling up, he'll say "Well, make me a list," and I will. And he'll do it. There are some things that he just doesn't notice and that's fine: he handles the day-to-day stuff. He'll do things, like for me cleaning off the table—for him it's getting everything off it; for me it's putting the tablecloth on, putting the

> flowers on, putting the candles on. That's the kind of stuff I do and I like that; it's not that I want him to start.

This list-making mother illustrates that responsibility for managing housework sometimes remained in the mother's domain, even if the father performed more of the actual tasks.

Responsibility for managing childcare, on the other hand, was more likely to be shared. Planning and initiating "direct" childcare, including supervision, discipline and play, was typically an equal enterprise. Sharing responsibility for "indirect" childcare, including clothing, cleaning, and feeding, was less common, but was still shared in over half of the families. When they cooked, cleaned, or tended to the children, fathers in these families did not talk of "helping" the mother; they spoke of fulfilling their responsibilities as equal partners and parents. For example, one father described how he and his wife divided both direct and indirect child care:

> My philosophy is that they are my children and everything is my responsibility, and I think she approaches it the same way too. So when something needs to be done, it's whoever is close does it . . . whoever it is convenient for. And we do keep a sense of what the other's recent efforts are, and try to provide some balance, but without actually counting how many times you've done this and I've done that.

In spite of reported efforts to relinquish total control over managing home and children, mothers were more likely than fathers to report that they would be embarrassed if unexpected company came over and the house was a mess (80 per cent versus 60 per cent). When asked to compare themselves directly to their spouse, almost two-thirds of both mothers and fathers reported that the mother would be more embarrassed than the father. Some mothers reported emotional reactions to the house being a mess that were similar to those they experienced when their husbands "dressed the kids funny." The women were more likely to focus on the children "looking nice," particularly when they were going to be seen in public. Mothers' greater embarrassment over the kemptness of home or children might reflect their sense of mothering as part of women's essential nature.

Adult Socialization through Childrearing

. . . Usually the father was described as being transformed by the parenting experience and developing increased sensitivity. This was especially true of discourse between parents who were trying to convert a more traditional division of family labour into a more egalitarian one. A self-employed construction worker said his level of concern for child safety was heightened after he rearranged his work to do half of the parenting:

> There's a difference in being at the park with the kids since we went on the schedule. Before it was, like, "Sure, jump off the jungle bars." But when you're totally responsible for them, and you know that if they sprained an ankle or something you have to pick up the slack, it's like you have more investment in the kid and you don't want to see them hurt and you don't want to see them crying. I find myself being a lot more cautious.

The wife of the construction worker quoted above commented that she had not anticipated many of the changes that emerged from sharing routine childcare.

> I used to worry about the kids a lot more. I would say in the last year it's evened itself out quite a bit. That was an interesting kind of thing in sharing that started to happen that I hadn't anticipated. I suppose when you go into this your expectations about what will happen—that you won't take your kids to day care, that they'll be with their dad, and they'll get certain things from their dad and won't that be nice, and he won't have to worry about his hours—but then it starts creeping into other areas that you didn't have any way of knowing it was going to have an impact. When he began to raise issues about the kids or check in on them at school when they were sick, I thought, "Well, that's my job, what are you

> talking about that for?" or, "Oh my god. I didn't notice that!" Where did he get the intuitive sense to know what needed to be done? It wasn't there before. A whole lot of visible things happened.

Increased sensitivity on the part of the fathers, and their enhanced competence as parents, was typically evaluated by adopting a vocabulary of motives and feelings similar to the mothers', created and sustained through an ongoing dialogue about the children: a dialogue that grew out of the routine child care practices. Another mother described how her husband had "the right temperament" for parenting, but had to learn how to notice the little things that she felt her daughters needed:

> When it comes to the two of us as parents, I feel that my husband's parenting skills are probably superior to mine, just because of his calm rationale. But maybe that's not what little girls need all the time. He doesn't tend to be the one that tells them how gorgeous they look when they dress up, which they really like, and I see these things, I see when they're putting in a little extra effort. He's getting better as we grow in our relationship, as the kids grow in their relationship with him.

Like many fathers in this study, this one was characterized as developing sensitivity to the children by relying on interactions with his wife. She "sees things" which he has to learn to recognize. Thus, while he may have "superior" parenting skills, he must learn something subtle from her. His reliance on her expertise suggests that his "calm rationale" is insufficient to make him "maternal" in the way that she is. Her ability to notice things, and his inattention to them, serves to render them both accountable: parenting remains an essential part of her nature, but is a learned capacity for him. Couples talked about fathers being socialized, as adults, to become nurturing parents. This talking with their wives about childcare helped husbands construct and sustain images of themselves as competent fathers. . . .

[S]haring childcare and housework helped fathers understand its drudgery. One father who is employed as a carpenter explained how assuming more responsibility for housework motivated him to encourage his wife to buy whatever she needs to make housework easier.

> It was real interesting when I started doing more housework. Being in construction, when I needed a tool, I bought the tool. And when I vacuum floors, I look at this piece of shit, I mean I can't vacuum the floor with this and feel good about it, it's not doing a good job. So I get a good vacuum system. So I have more appreciation for housecleaning. When I clean the tubs, I want something that is going to clean the tubs; I don't want to work extra hard. You know I have a kind of sponge to use for cleaning the tubs. So I have more of an appreciation for what she had to do. I tell her "If you know of something that's going to make it easier, let's get it."

Most sample fathers reported that performance of childcare, in and of itself, increased their commitment to both parenting and housework. All of the fathers had been involved in some housework before the birth of their children, but many indicated that their awareness and performance of housework increased in conjunction with their involvement in parenting. They reported that as they spent more time in the house alone with their children, they assumed more responsibility for cooking and cleaning. . . .

Gender Attributions

Approximately half of both mothers and fathers volunteered that men and women brought something unique to childcare, and many stressed that they did not consider their own parenting skills to be identical to those of their spouse. One mother whose husband had recently increased the amount of time he spent with their school-aged children commented: "Anybody can slap together a cream cheese and cucumber sandwich and a glass of milk and a few chips and call it lunch, but the ability to see that your child is troubled about something, or to be able to help them work through a conflict with a friend, that is really much different." A list-making mother who provided less childcare and did less housework than her husband described herself as "more intimate and gentle," and her husband as "rough and out there." Like many others she emphasized that mothers and fathers provide "a balance" for their children. She described how she had to come to terms with her expectations that her husband would "mother" the way that she did:

> One of the things that I found I was expecting from him when he started doing so much here and I was gone so much, I was expecting him to mother the kids. And you know, I had to get over that one pretty quick and really accept him doing the things the way he did them as his way, and that being just fine with me. He wasn't mothering the kids, he was fathering the kids. It was just that he was the role of the mother as far as the chores and all that stuff.

A mother who managed and performed most of the housework and childcare used different reasoning to make similar claims about essential differences between women and men. In contrast to the mothers quoted above, this mother suggested that men could nurture, but not perform daily childcare:

> Nurturance is one thing, actual care is another thing. I think if a father had to—like all of a sudden the wife was gone, he could nurture it with the love that it needed. But he might not change the diapers often enough, or he might not give 'em a bath often enough and he might not think of the perfect food to feed. But as far as nurturing, I think he's capable of caring. . . . If the situation is the mother is there and he didn't have to, then he would trust the woman to.

This mother concluded, "The woman has it more in her genes to be more equipped for nurturing." Thus many of the manager–helper couples legitimated their divisions of labour and reaffirmed the "naturalness" of essential gender differences. . . .

However, the parents who were the most successful at sharing childcare were the most likely to claim that men could nurture like women. Those who sustained manager–helper dynamics in childcare tended to invoke the images of "maternal instincts" and alluded to natural differences between men and women. In contrast, more equal divisions of household labour were typically accompanied by an ideology of gender *similarity* rather than gender difference. The direction of causality is twofold: (1) those who believed that men could nurture like women seriously attempted to share all aspects of child care, and (2) the successful practice of sharing child care facilitated the development of beliefs that men could nurture like women.

Normalizing Atypical Behaviour

Mothers and fathers reported that women friends, most of whom were in more traditional marriages or were single, idealized their shared-parenting arrangements. About two-thirds of sample mothers reported that their women friends told them that they were extremely fortunate, and labelled their husbands "wonderful," "fantastic," "incredible," or otherwise out of the ordinary. Some mothers said that women friends were "jealous," "envious," or "amazed," and that they "admired" and "supported" their efforts at sharing domestic chores.

Both mothers and fathers said that the father received more credit for his family involvement than the mother did, because it was expected that she would perform childcare and housework. Since parenting is assumed to be "only natural" for women, fathers were frequently praised for performing a task that would go unnoticed if a mother had performed it:

> I think I get less praise because people automatically assume that, you know, the mother's *supposed* to do the childcare. And he gets a lot of praise because he's the visible one. Oh, I think that he gets far more praise. I can bust my butt at that school and all he has to do is show up in the parking lot and everybody's all *gah gah* over him. I don't get resentful about that—I think it's funny and I think it's sad.

While the fathers admitted that they enjoyed such praise, many indicated that they did not take these direct or implied compliments very seriously.

> I get more credit than she does, because it's so unusual that the father's at home and involved in the family. I realize what it is: it's prejudice. The strokes feel real nice, but I don't take them too seriously. I'm sort of proud of it in a way that I don't really like. It's nothing to be proud of, except that I'm glad to be doing it and I think it's kind of neat because it hasn't been the style traditionally. I kind of like that, but I know that it means nothing.

These comments reveal that fathers appreciated praise, but actively discounted compliments received from those in dissimilar situations. The fathers' everyday parenting experiences led them to view parenthood as drudgery as well as fulfillment. They described their sense of parental responsibility as taken-for-granted and did not consider it to be out of the ordinary or something worthy of special praise. . . .

Thus fathers discounted and normalized extreme reactions to their divisions of labour and interpreted them in a way that supported the "natural" character of what they were doing. . . .

Because fathers assumed traditional mothering functions, they often had more social contact with mothers than with other fathers. They talked about being the only fathers at children's lessons, parent classes and meetings, at the laundromat, or in the market. One father said it took mothers there a while before they believed he really shared a range of household tasks.

> At first they ask me, "Is this your day off?" And I say, "If it's the day off for me, why isn't it the day off for you?" "Well, I work 24 hours a day!" And I say, "Yeah, right. I got my wash done and hung out and the beds made." It takes the mother a couple of times to realize that I really do that stuff.

. . . Fathers tended to be employed in occupations predominantly composed of men, and in those settings were often discouraged from talking about family or children. Several fathers reported that people at their place of employment could not understand why they did "women's work," and a few mentioned that co-workers would be disappointed when they would repeatedly turn down invitations to go out "with the boys" for a drink. One of three self-employed carpenters in the study said that he would sometimes conceal that he was leaving work to do something with his children because he worried about negative reactions from employers or co-workers:

> I would say reactions that we've got—in business, like if I leave a job somewhere that I'm on and mention that I'm going to coach soccer, my son's soccer game, yeah. I have felt people kind of stiffen, like, I was more shirking my job, you know, such a small thing to leave work for, getting home, racing home for. I got to the point with some people where I didn't necessarily mention what I was leaving for, just because I didn't need for them to think that I was being irresponsible about their work, I mean, I just decided it wasn't their business. If I didn't know them well enough to feel that they were supportive. I would just say, "I have to leave early today"—never lie, if they asked me a question. I'd tell them the answer—but not volunteer it. And, maybe in some cases, I feel like, you know, you really have to be a little careful about being too *groovy* too, that what it is that you're doing is just so wonderful. "I'm a father, I'm going to go be with my children." It isn't like that, you know. I don't do it for what people think of me; I do it because I enjoy it.

Some fathers said co-workers perceived their talk of spending time with their children as indications that they were not "serious" about their work. They reported receiving indirect messages that *providing* for the family was primary and *being with* the family was secondary. Fathers avoided negative workplace sanctions by selectively revealing the extent of their family involvement.

Many fathers selected their current jobs because the work schedule was flexible, or so they could take time off to care for their children. For instance, even though most fathers worked full-time, two-thirds had some daytime hours off, as exemplified by teachers, mail carriers, and self-employed carpenters. Similarly, most fathers avoided extra, work-related tasks or overtime hours in order to maximize time spent with their children. One computer technician said that he was prepared to accept possible imputations of non-seriousness:

> I kind of tend to choose my jobs. When I go to a job interview, I explain to people that I have a family and the family's very important to me. Some companies expect you to work a lot of overtime or work weekends, and I told them that I don't have to accept that sort of thing. I may not have gotten all the jobs I ever might have had because of it, but it's something that I bring up at the job interview and let them know that my family comes first.

. . . Over half of the study participants also indicated that their own mothers or fathers reacted negatively to their divisions of labour. Parents were described as "confused," "bemused," and "befuddled," and it was said that they "lack understanding" or "think it's a little strange'. One mother reported that her parents and in-laws wouldn't "dare to criticize" their situation because "times have changed," but she sensed their underlying worry and concern:

> I think both sides of the family think it's fine because it's popular now. They don't dare—I mean if we were doing this thirty years ago, they would dare to criticize. In a way, now they don't. I think both sides feel it's a little strange. I thought my mom was totally sympathetic and no problem, but when I was going to go away for a week and my husband was going to take care of the kids, she said something to my sister about how she didn't think I should do it. There's a little underlying tension about it, I think.

Other study participants reported that disagreements with parents were common, particularly if they revolved around trying to change childrearing practices their own parents had used.

Many couples reported that initial negative reactions from parents turned more positive over time as they saw that the children were "turning out all right," that the couple was still together after an average of 10 years, and that the men were still employed. This last point, that parents were primarily concerned with their son's or son-in-law's provider responsibilities, highlights how observers typically evaluated the couple's task sharing. A number of study participants mentioned that they thought their parents wanted the wife to quit work and stay home with the children and that the husband should "make up the difference." Most mentioned, however, that parents were more concerned that the husband continue to be the provider than they were that the wife made "extra money" or that the husband "helped out" at home.

> In the beginning there was a real strong sense that I was in the space of my husband's duty. That came from his parents pretty strongly. The only way that they have been able to come to grips with this in any fashion is because he has also been financially successful. If he had decided, you know, "Outside work is not for me, I'm going to stay home with the kids and she's going to work." I think there would have been a whole lot more talk than there was. I think it's because he did both and was successful that it was okay.

Another mother noted that parental acceptance of shared parenting did not necessarily entail acceptance of the woman as provider:

> There is a funny dynamic that happens. It's not really about childcare, where I don't think in our families—with our parents—I don't get enough credit for being the breadwinner. Well they're still critical of him for not earning as much money as I do. In a way they've accepted him as being an active parenting father more than they've accepted me being a breadwinner.

Here again, the "essential nature" of men is taken to be that of provider. If the men remain providers, they are still accountable as men, even if they take an active part in childcare.

Discussion

. . . As Sara Ruddick (1982) has noted, the everyday aspects of child care and housework help share ways of thinking, feeling, and acting that become associated with what it means to be a mother. My findings suggest that when domestic activities are equally shared, "maternal thinking" develops in fathers, too, and the social meaning of gender begins to change. This de-emphasizes notions of gender as personality and locates it in social interaction.

To treat gender as the "cause" of household division of labour overlooks its emergent character and fails to acknowledge how it is, in fact, implicated in precisely such routine practices.

References

Berk, S.F. 1985. *The Gender Factory*. New York: Plenum.

Ruddick, S. 1982. "Maternal Thinking," in B. Thorne and M. Yalom, eds., *Rethinking the Family*, pp. 76–94. New York: Longman.

West, C., and D.H. Zimmerman. 1987. "Doing Gender," *Gender & Society* 1: 125–51.

PART VII
The Gendered Classroom

Along with the family, educational institutions—from primary schools to secondary schools, colleges, universities, and professional schools—are central arenas in which gender is reproduced. Students learn more than the formal curriculum—they learn what the society considers appropriate behaviour for men and women. And for adults, educational institutions are gendered workplaces, where the inequalities found in other institutions are also found.

From the earliest grades, students' experiences in the classroom differ by gender. Boys are more likely to interrupt, to be called upon by teachers, and to have any misbehaviour overlooked. Girls are more likely to remain obedient and quiet and to live up to (or down to) teachers' expectations. However, most of the gendering work of schools is done outside the classroom and the formal curriculum. Ellen Jordan and Angela Cowan explore the ways in which children's unstructured play re-creates gender stereotypes. The informal curriculum can also be resisted, changed, and negotiated, as Marilyn Iwama demonstrates in her poetic memoir of how food and memories of food shaped children's experiences in notorious educational institutions that also served as places of confinement: the residential school system and the internment camps for Japanese Canadians in the Second World War.

Most of you who are reading this book have left primary and secondary schooling behind, and are currently immersed in postsecondary education. Your experiences as students may resonate with the work of both Tracey Lindberg and Brenda Beagan, who investigate everyday life in and out of the classroom. Lindberg and Beagan examine different types of education, but both find that the experience of being a student is profoundly shaped not just by gender but also by other social identities. Gender is by no means the only factor that shapes students' experiences of belonging or not belonging in school but works in combination with other aspects of personal identity based in social categories such as race, class, and sexuality.

Questions for Critical Thought

1. Educational institutions include not only classrooms and curriculums but also locker rooms, cliques, playgrounds, and other sites of informal education about what gender means. What did you learn about gender at school outside the classroom?
2. One proposed solution to the problem of gender polarization in education is same-sex schools. Would you send your son or daughter to a same-sex school? What would be some of the advantages? What about disadvantages?
3. Jordan and Cowan identify "warrior narratives" as one form of unstructured dramatic play among young children. Can you identify any other such narratives from your own experiences with children's play? Is there a gendered form of play specific to girls?
4. If young children's play reinforces gender stereotypes, should parents or educators be concerned? Should we try to explicitly "teach" gender equality?
5. Do you have memories associated with food, as the participants in Iwama's study do? If so, does gender play a role in these memories?
6. Is there a connection between gender inequities and other kinds of "micro inequities," as discussed by both Beagan and Lindberg?
7. Have you observed "micro inequities" in your own academic setting? Is there a distinction between inequities and simple rudeness or insensitivity?
8. Did you have any teachers or professors who influenced the way you see gender? If so, how did they achieve this?
9. What do you think are the most effective means of challenging gender biases in schools?
10. How might your educational experiences have been different if you were born into a different gender category?

Chapter 24

Overview

Bad guys, good guys, superheroes, and villains—these are iconic elements of little boys' imaginative play. Ellen Jordan and Angela Cowan connect these preschool games to much wider questions about the "narratives of masculinity," which boys absorb and recreate through their play. These narratives are in turn connected, Cowan and Jordan argue, to ideas about political organization and political economy that depend on the idea of "warriors"—powerful men who use any means at their disposal to keep enemies at bay.

The enactment of warrior narratives in contemporary schoolyards poses dilemmas for early childhood educators. On the one hand, teachers generally do not wish to encourage violent play; on the other hand, they want to encourage creativity and imagination. And children are drawn to these warrior narratives, seeking opportunities to act them out. Jordan and Cowan depict how kindergarten children import these warrior narratives into their play, using whatever objects are close at hand. The Doll Corner, meant to the be the site of nonviolent domestic play, becomes the site of *bricolage*, in which objects are converted from one use to another and used in fighting and violent imaginative play.

For young boys, resistance to the no-fighting, no-violence rules of their kindergarten becomes part of the masculinity narratives they act out. Jordan and Cowan suggest that this resistance over time becomes tempered by other aspects of hegemonic masculinity, such as rationality and responsibility, enabling boys to acquire masculine identities that are not entirely bound up with warriordom.

Warrior Narratives in the Kindergarten Classroom: Renegotiating the Social Contract?

Ellen Jordan and Angela Cowan

Since the beginning of second-wave feminism, the separation between the public (masculine) world of politics and the economy and the private (feminine) world of the family and personal life has been seen as highly significant in establishing gender difference and inequality (Eisenstein, 1984). Twenty years of feminist research and speculation have refined our understanding of this divide and how it has been developed and reproduced. One particularly striking and influential account is given by Carole Pateman in her book *The Sexual Contract* (1988).

Pateman's broad argument is that in the modern world, the world since the Enlightenment, a "civil society" has been established. In this civil society, patriarchy has been replaced by a fratriarchy, which is equally male and oppressive of women. Men now rule not as fathers but as brothers, able to compete with one another, but presenting a united front against those outside the group. It is the brothers who control the public world of the state, politics, and the economy. Women have been given token access to this world because the discourses of liberty and universalism made this difficult to refuse, but to take part, they must conform to the rules established to suit the brothers. . . .

This is now widely accepted as the way men understand and experience their world. On the other hand, almost no attempt has been made to look at how it is that they take these views on board, or why the public/private divide is so much more deeply entrenched in men's lived experience than in women's. . . . A major site where this occurs is the school, one of the institutions particularly characteristic of the civil society that emerged with the Enlightenment (Foucault, 1980: 55–7). The school does not deliberately condition boys and not girls into this dichotomy, but it is, we believe, a site where what Giddens (1984: 10–13) has called a "cycle of practice" introduces little boys to the public/private division. . . .

In this article, we focus on a particular contest, which, although never specifically stated, is central to the children's accommodation to school: little boys' determination to explore certain narratives of masculinity with which they are already familiar—guns, fighting, fast cars—and the teacher's attempts to outlaw their importation into the classroom setting. We argue that what occurs is a contest between two definitions of masculinity: what we have chosen to call "warrior narratives" and the discourses of civil society—rationality, responsibility, and decorum—that are the basis of school discipline.

By "warrior narratives," we mean narratives that assume that violence is legitimate and justified when it occurs within a struggle between good and evil. There is a tradition of such narratives, stretching from Hercules and Beowulf to Superman and Dirty Harry, where the male is depicted as the warrior, the knight-errant, the superhero, the good guy (usually called a "goody" by Australian children), often supported by brothers in arms, and always opposed to some evil figure, such as a monster, a giant, a villain, a criminal, or, very simply, in Australian parlance, a "baddy." There is also a connection, it is now often suggested, between these narratives and the activity that has come to epitomize the physical expression of masculinity in the modern era: sport (Duthie, 1980; Crosset, 1990; Messner, 1992). It is as sport that the physicality and desire usually lived out in the private sphere are permitted a ritualized public presence. Even though the violence once characteristic of the warrior has, in civil society and as part of the social contract, become the prerogative of the state, it can still be re-enacted symbolically in countless sporting encounters. The mantle of the warrior is inherited by the sportsman.

The school discipline that seeks to outlaw these narratives is, we would suggest, very much a product of modernity. Bowles and Gintis have argued that "the structure of social relations in education not only inures the student to the discipline of the work place, but develops the types of personal demeanour, modes of self-presentation, self-image, and social-class identifications which are the crucial ingredients of job adequacy" (1976: 131). The school is seeking to introduce the children to the behaviour appropriate to the civil society of the modern world.

An accommodation does eventually take place, this article argues, through a recognition of the split between the public and the private. Most boys learn to accept that the way to power and respectability is through acceptance of the conventions of civil society. They also learn that warrior narratives are not a part of this world; they can only be experienced symbolically as fantasy or sport. The outcome, we will suggest, is that little boys learn that these narratives must be left behind in the private world of desire when they participate in the public world of reason.

The Study

The school where this study was conducted serves an old-established suburb in a country town in New South Wales, Australia. The children are predominantly Australian born and English speaking, but come from socioeconomic backgrounds ranging from professional to welfare recipient. We carried out this research in a classroom run by a teacher who is widely acknowledged as one of the finest and most successful kindergarten teachers in our region. She is an admired practitioner of free play, process writing, and creativity. There was no gender definition of games in her classroom. Groups composed of both girls and boys had turns at playing in the Doll Corner, in the Construction Area, and on the Car Mat.

The research method used was non-participant observation, the classic mode for the sociological study of children in schools (Burgess 1984; Thorne 1986; Goodenough 1987). The group of children described came to school for the first time in February 1993. The observation sessions began within a fortnight of the children entering school and were conducted during "free activity" time, a period lasting for about an hour. At first we observed twice a week, but then settled to a weekly visit, although there were some weeks when it was inconvenient for the teacher to accommodate an observer.

The observation was non-interactive. The observer stationed herself as unobtrusively as possible, usually seated on a kindergarten-sized chair, near one of the play stations. She made pencil notes of events, with particular attention to accurately recording the words spoken by the children, and wrote up detailed narratives from the notes, supplemented by memory, on reaching home. She discouraged attention from the children by rising and leaving the area if she was drawn by them into any interaction. . . .

In looking at the patterns of accommodation and resistance that emerge when the warrior narratives that little boys have adapted from television encounter the discipline of the classroom, we believe we have uncovered one of the cyclical practices of modernity that reveal the social contract to these boys.

Warrior Narratives in the Doll Corner

In the first weeks of the children's school experience, the Doll Corner was the area where the most elaborate acting out of warrior narratives was observed. The Doll Corner in this classroom was a small room with a glass-panelled door opening off the main area. Its furnishings—stove, sink, dolls' cots, and so on—were an attempt at a literal re-creation of a domestic setting, revealing the school's definition of children's play as a preparation for adult life. It was an area where the acting out of "pretend" games was acceptable.

Much of the boys' play in the area was domestic:

> Jimmy and Tyler were jointly ironing a tablecloth. "Look at the sheet is burnt, I've burnt it," declared Tyler, waving the toy iron above his head. "I'm telling Mrs Sandison," said Jimmy worriedly. "No, I tricked you. It's not really burnt. See," explained Tyler, showing Jimmy the black pattern on the cloth (23 February 1993). . . .

On the other hand, there were attempts from the beginning by some of the boys and one of the girls to use this area for non-domestic games and, in the case of the boys, for games based on warrior narratives, involving fighting, destruction, goodies, and baddies.

> The play started off quietly, Winston cuddled a teddy bear, then settled it in a bed. Just as Winston tucked in his bear, Mac snatched the teddy out of bed and swung it around his head in circles. "Don't hurt him, give him back," pleaded Winston, trying vainly to retrieve the teddy. The two boys were circling the small table in the center of the room. As he ran, Mac started to karate chop the teddy on the arm, and then threw it on the floor and jumped on it. He then snatched up a plastic knife, "This is a sword. Ted is dead. They all are." He sliced the knife across the teddy's tummy, repeating the action on the bodies of two stuffed dogs. Winston grabbed the two dogs, and with a dog in each hand, staged a dog fight. "They are alive again" (10 February 1993).
>
> Three boys were busily stuffing teddies into the cupboard through the sink opening. "They're in jail. They can't escape," said Malcolm. "Let's pour water over them." "Don't do that. It'll hurt them," shouted Winston, rushing into the Doll Corner. "Go away, Winston. You're not in our group," said Malcolm (12 February 1993).

The boys even imported goodies and baddies into a classic ghost scenario initiated by one of the girls:

> "I'm the father," Tyler declared. "I'm the mother," said Alanna. "Let's pretend it's a stormy night and I'm afraid. Let's pretend a ghost has come to steal the dog." Tyler nodded and placed the sheet over his head. Tyler moaned, "ooooOOOOOOOAHHHH!!!" and moved his outstretched arms toward Alanna. Jamie joined the game and grabbed a sheet from the doll's cradle, "I'm the goody ghost." "So am I," said Tyler. They giggled and wrestled each other to the floor. "No! you're the baddy ghost," said Jamie. Meanwhile, Alanna was making ghostly noises and moving around the boys. "Did you like the game? Let's play it again," she suggested (23 February 1993).

In the first two incidents, there was some conflict between the narratives being invoked by Winston and those used by the other boys. For Winston, the stuffed toys were the weak whom he must protect knight-errant style. For the other boys, they could be set up as the baddies whom it was legitimate for the hero to attack. Both were versions of a warrior narrative.

The gender difference in the use of these narratives has been noted by a number of observers (Paley, 1984; Clark, 1989; Thorne, 1993). Whereas even the most timid, least physically aggressive boys—Winston in this study is typical—are drawn to identifying with the heroes of these narratives, girls show almost no interest in them at this early age. The strong-willed and assertive girls in our study, as in others (Clark, 1990; Walkerdine, 1990), sought power by commandeering the role of mother, teacher, or shopkeeper, while even the highly imaginative Alanna, although she enlivened the more mundane fantasies of the other children with ghosts, old widow women, and magical mirrors, seems not to have been attracted by warrior heroes.[1]

Warrior narratives, it would seem, have a powerful attraction for little boys, which they lack for little girls. Why and how this occurs remains unexplored in early childhood research, perhaps because data for such an explanation are not available to those doing research in institutional settings. Those undertaking ethnographic research in preschools find the warrior narratives already in possession in these sites (Paley, 1984; Davies, 1989). In this research, gender difference in the appeal of warrior narratives has to be taken as a given—the data gathered are not suitable for constructing theories of origins; thus, the task of determining an explanation would seem to lie within the province of those investigating and theorizing gender differentiation during infancy, and perhaps, specifically, of those working in the tradition of feminist psychoanalysis pioneered by Dinnerstein (1977) and Chodorow (1978). Nevertheless, even though the cause may remain obscure, there can be little argument that in the English-speaking world for at least the last hundred years—think of Tom Sawyer playing Robin Hood and the pirates and Indians in J.M. Barrie's *Peter Pan*—boys have built these narratives into their conceptions of the masculine.

Accommodation through Bricolage

The school classroom, even one as committed to freedom and self-actualization as this, makes little provision for the enactment of these narratives. The classroom equipment invites children to play house, farm, and shop, to construct cities and roads, and to journey through them with toy cars, but there is no overt invitation to explore warrior narratives.

In the first few weeks of school, the little boys un-self-consciously set about redressing this omission. The method they used was what is known as *bricolage*—the transformation of objects from one use to another for symbolic purposes (Hebdige, 1979). The first site was the Doll Corner. Our records for the early weeks contain a number of examples of boys rejecting the usages ascribed to the various Doll Corner objects by the teacher and by the makers of equipment and assigning a different meaning to them. This became evident very early with their use of the toy baby carriages (called "prams" in Australia). For the girls, the baby carriages were just that, but for many of the boys they very quickly became surrogate cars:

> Mac threw a doll into the largest pram in the Doll Corner. He walked the pram out past a group of his friends who were playing "crashes" on the Car Mat. Three of the five boys turned and watched him wheeling the pram toward the classroom door. Mac performed a sharp three-point turn; raced his pram past the Car Mat group, striking one boy on the head with the pram wheel (10 February 1993).
>
> "Brrrrmmmmmm, brrrrrmmmmm," Tyler's revving engine noises grew louder as he rocked the pram back and forth with sharp jerking movements. The engine noise grew quieter as he left the Doll Corner and wheeled the pram around the classroom. He started to run with the pram when the teacher could not observe him (23 March 1993).

The boys transformed other objects into masculine appurtenances: knives and tongs became weapons, the dolls' beds became boats, and so on.

> Mac tried to engage Winston in a sword fight using Doll Corner plastic knives. Winston backed away, but Mac persisted. Winston took a knife but continued to back away from Mac. He then put down the knife, and ran away half-screaming (semi-seriously, unsure of the situation) for his teacher (10 February 1993). . . .

This mode of accommodation was rejected by the teacher, however, who practised a gentle, but steady, discouragement of such bricolage. Even though the objects in this space are not really irons, beds, and cooking pots, she made strong efforts to assert their cultural meaning, instructing the children in the "proper" use of the equipment and attempting to control their behaviour by questions like "Would you do that with a tea towel in your house?" "Cats never climb up on the benches in *my* house." It was thus impressed upon the children that warrior narratives were inappropriate in this space.

The children, our observations suggest, accepted her guidance, and we found no importation of warrior narratives into the Doll Corner after the first few weeks. There were a number of elaborate and exciting narratives devised, but they were all, to some degree, related to the domestic environment. For example, on April 20, Justin and Nigel used one of the baby carriages as a four-wheel drive, packed it with equipment and went off for a camping trip, setting out a picnic with Doll Corner tablecloths, knives, forks, and plates when they arrived. On May 18, Matthew, Malcolm, Nigel, and Jonathan were dogs being fed in the Doll Corner. They then complained of the flies, and Jonathan picked up the toy telephone and said, "Flycatcher! Flycatcher! Come and catch some flies. They are everywhere." On June 1, the following was recorded:

> "We don't want our nappies [diapers] changed," Aaron informed Celia, the mum in the game. "I'm poohing all over your clothes mum," Mac declared, as he grunted and positioned himself over the dress-up box. Celia cast a despairing glance in Mac's direction, and went on dressing a doll. "I am too; poohing all over your clothes mum," said Aaron. "Now mum will have to clean it all up and change my nappy," he informed Mac, giggling. He turned to the dad [Nigel], and said in a baby voice, "Googoo; give him [Mac] the feather duster." "No! give him the feather duster; he did the longest one all over the clothes," Mac said to Nigel (1 June 1993).

Although exciting and imaginative games continued, the bricolage virtually disappeared from the Doll Corner. The intention of the designer of the Doll Corner equipment was increasingly respected. Food for the camping trip was bought from the shop the teacher had set up and consumed using the Doll Corner equipment. The space invaded by flies was a domestic space, and appropriate means, calling in expert help by telephone, were used to deal with the problem. Chairs and tables were chairs and tables, clothes were clothes and could be fouled by appropriate inhabitants of a domestic space, babies. Only the baby carriages continued to have an ambiguous status, to maintain the ability to be transformed into vehicles of other kinds.

The warrior narratives—sword play, baddies in jail, pirates, and so on—did not vanish from the boys' imaginative world, but, as the later observations show, the site gradually moved from the Doll Corner to the Construction Area and the Car Mat. By the third week in March (that is, after about six weeks at school), the observer noticed the boys consistently using the construction toys to develop these narratives. The bricolage was now restricted to the more amorphously defined construction materials.

> Tyler was busy constructing an object out of five pieces of plastic straw (Clever Sticks). "This is a water pistol. Everyone's gonna get wet," he cried as he moved into the Doll Corner pretending to wet people. The game shifted to guns and bullets between Tyler and two other boys. "I've got a bigger gun," Roger said, showing off his square block object. "Mine's more longer. Ehehehehehehehehe, got you," Winston yelled to Roger, brandishing a plastic straw gun. "I'll kill your gun," Mac said, pushing Winston's gun away. "No Mac. You broke it. No," cried Winston (23 March 1993).
>
> Two of the boys picked up swords made out of blue- and red-colored plastic squares they had displayed on the cupboard. "This is my sword," Jamie explained to Tyler. "My jumper [sweater] holds it in. Whichever color is at the bottom, well that's the color it shoots out. Whoever is bad, we shoot with power out of it." "Come on Tyler," he went on. "Get your sword. Let's go get some baddies" (30 March 1993).

The toy cars on the Car Mat were also pressed into the service of warrior narratives:

> Justin, Brendan, and Jonathan were busy on the Car Mat. The game involved police cars that were chasing baddies who had drunk "too much beers." Justin explained to Jonathan why his car had the word "DOG" written on the front. "These are different police cars, for catching robbers taking money" (4 March 1993).
>
> Three boys, Harvey, Maurice, and Marshall, were on the Car Mat. "Here comes the baddies," Harvey shouted, spinning a toy car around the mat. "Crasssshhhhh everywhere." He crashed his car into the other boys' cars and they responded with laughter. "I killed a baddie everyone," said Maurice, crashing his cars into another group of cars (24 May 1993).

The boys were proposing a new accommodation, a new adaptation of classroom materials to the needs of their warrior narratives.

Classroom Rules and Resistance

Once again the teacher would not accept the accommodation proposed. Warrior narratives provoked what she considered inappropriate public behaviour in the miniature civil society of her classroom. Her aim was to create a "free" environment where children could work independently, learn at their own pace, and explore their own interests, but creating such an environment involved its own form of social contract, its own version of the state's appropriation of violence. From the very first day, she began to establish a series of classroom rules that imposed constraints on violent or disruptive activity. . . .

One of the outcomes of these rules was the virtual outlawing of a whole series of games that groups of children usually want to initiate when they are playing together, games of speed and body contact, of gross motor self-expression and skill. This prohibition affected both girls and boys and was justified by setting up a version of public and private spaces: The classroom was not the proper place for such activities, they "belong" in the playground.[2] The combined experience of many teachers has shown that it is almost impossible for children to play games involving car crashes and guns without violating these rules; therefore, in this classroom, as in many others (Paley, 1984), these games were, in effect, banned.

These rules were then policed by the children themselves, as the following interchange shows:

> "Eeeeeeheeeeeeheeeeh!" Tyler leapt about the room. A couple of girls were saying, "Stop it Tyler" but he persisted. Jane warned, "You're not allowed to have guns." Tyler responded saying, "It's not a gun. It's a water pistol, and that's not a gun." "Not allowed to have water pistol guns," Tony reiterated to Tyler. "Yes, it's a water pistol," shouted Tyler. Jane informed the teacher, who responded stating, "no guns, even if they are water pistols." Tyler made a spear out of Clever Sticks, straight after the banning of gun play (23 March 1993). . . .

As time passed, the games became less visible. The warrior narratives were not so much acted out as talked through, using the toy cars and the construction materials as a prompt and a basis:

> Tyler was showing his plastic straw construction to Luke. "This is a Samurai Man and this is his hat. A Samurai Man fights in Japan and they fight with the Ninja. The bad guys who use cannons and guns. My Samurai is captain of the Samurai and he is going to kill the sergeant of the bad guys. He is going to sneak up on him with a knife and kill him" (1 June 1993).
>
> Malcolm and Aaron had built boats with Lego blocks and were explaining the various components to Roger. "This ship can go faster," Malcolm explained. "He [a plastic man] is the boss of the ship. Mine is a goody boat. They are not baddies." "Mine's a steam shovel boat. It has wheels," said Aaron. "There it goes in the river and it has to go to a big shed where all the steam shovels are stopping" (11 June 1993).

It also became apparent that there was something covert about this play. The cars were crashed quietly. The guns were being transformed into water pistols. Swords were concealed under jumpers and only used when the teacher's back was turned. When the constructed objects were displayed to the class, their potential as players in a fighting game was concealed under a more mundane description. For example:

> Prior to the free play, the children were taking turns to explain the Clever Stick and Lego Block constructions they had made the previous afternoon. I listened to Tyler describe his Lego robot to the class: "This is a transformer robot. It can do things and turn into everything." During free play, Tyler played with the same robot explaining its capacities to Winston: "This is a terminator ship. It can kill. It can turn into a robot and the top pops off" (23 March 1993).

Children even protested to one another that they were not making weapons, "This isn't a gun, it's a lookout," "This isn't a place for bullets, it's for petrol."

The warrior narratives, it would seem, went underground and became part of a "deviant" masculine subculture with the characteristic "secret" identity and hidden meanings (Hebdige, 1979). The boys were no longer seeking accommodation but practising hidden resistance. The classroom, they were learning, was not a place where it was acceptable to explore their gender identity through fantasy.

This, however, was a message that only the boys were receiving. The girls' gender-specific fantasies (Paley, 1984; Davies, 1989) of nurturing and self-display—mothers, nurses, brides, princesses—were accommodated easily within the classroom. They could be played out without contravening the rules of the miniature civil society. Although certain delightful activities—eating, running, hugging, and kissing (Best, 1983)—might be excluded from this public sphere, they were not ones by means of which their femininity, and thus their subjectivity, their conception of the self, was defined.

Masculinity, the School Regime, and the Social Contract

We suggest that this conflict between warrior narratives and school rules is likely to form part of the experience of most boys growing up in the industrialized world. The commitment to such narratives was not only nearly 100 per cent among the boys we observed, but similar commitment is, as was argued above, common in other sites. On the other hand, the pressure to preserve a decorous classroom is strong in all teachers (with the possible exception of those teaching in "alternative" schools) and has been since the beginnings of compulsory education. Indeed, it is only in classrooms where there is the balance of freedom and constraint we observed that such narratives are likely to surface at all. In more formal situations, they would be defined as deviant and forced underground from the boys' first entry into school.

If this is a widely recurring pattern, the question then arises: is it of little significance or is it what Giddens (1984) would call one of the "cyclical practices" that reproduce the structures of our society? The answer really depends on how little boys "read" the outlawing of their warrior narratives. If they see it as simply one of the broad constraints of school against which they are continually negotiating, then perhaps it has no significance. If, on the other hand, it has in their minds a crucial connection to the definition of gender, to the creation of their own masculine identity, to where they position particular sites and practices on a masculine to feminine continuum, then the ostracism of warrior narratives may mean that they define the school environment as feminine. . . .

. . . We would argue, rather, that the regime being imposed is based on a male ideal, an outcome of the Enlightenment and compulsory schooling. Michel Foucault has pointed out that the development of this particular regime in schools coincided with the emergence of the prison, the hospital, the army barracks, and the factory (Foucault, 1980). Although teachers in the first years of school are predominantly female, the regime they impose is perpetuated by male teachers (Brophy, 1985), and this preference is endorsed by powerful and influential males in the society at large. The kind of demeanour and self-management that teachers are trying to inculcate in the early school years is the behaviour expected in male-dominated public arenas like boardrooms, courtrooms, and union mass meetings.[3]

Connell (1989) and Willis (1977) provide evidence that by adolescence, boys from all classes, particularly if they are ambitious, come to regard acquiescence in the school's demands as compatible with constructing a masculine identity. Connell writes:

> Some working class boys embrace a project of mobility in which they construct a masculinity organized around themes of rationality and responsibility. This is closely connected with the "certification" function of the upper levels of the education system and to a key form of masculinity among professionals. (1989: 291)

Rationality and responsibility are, as Weber argued long ago, the primary characteristics of the modern society theorized by the Enlightenment thinkers as based on a social contract. This prized rationality has been converted, in practice, into a bureaucratized legal system where "responsible" acceptance by the population of the rules of civil society obviates the need for individuals to use physical violence in gaining their ends or protecting their rights, and where, if such violence is necessary, it is exercised by the state (Weber, 1978). In civil society, the warrior is obsolete, his activities redefined bureaucratically and performed by the police and the military.

The teacher in whose classroom our observation was conducted demonstrated a strong commitment to rationality and responsibility. For example, she devoted a great deal of time to showing that there was a cause and effect link between the behaviour forbidden by her classroom rules and classroom accidents. Each time an accident occurred, she asked the children to determine the cause of the accident, its result, and how it could have been prevented. The implication throughout was that children must take responsibility for the outcomes of their actions.

> Mac accidentally struck a boy, who was lying on the floor, in the head with a pram wheel. He was screaming around with a pram, the victim was

playing on the Car Mat and lying down to obtain a bird's eye view of a car crash. Mac rushed past the group and collected Justin on the side of the head. Tears and confusion ensued. The teacher's reaction was to see to Justin, then stop all play and gain children's attention, speaking first to Mac and Justin plus Justin's group:

T.: How did Justin get hurt?
M.: [No answer]
T.: Mac, what happened?
M.: I was wheeling the pram and Justin was in the way.
T.: Were you running?
M.: I was wheeling the pram.

The teacher now addresses the whole class:

T.: Stop working everyone, eyes to me and listen. Someone has just been hurt because someone didn't remember the classroom rules. What are they, Harvey?

(Harvey was listening intently and she wanted someone who could answer the question at this point).

H.: No running in the classroom.
T.: Why?

Other children offer an answer.

Chn.: Because someone will get hurt.
T.: Yes, and that is what happened. Mac was going too quickly with the pram and Justin was injured. Now how can we stop this happening next time?
Chn.: No running in the classroom, only walk (10 February 1993).

Malcolm, walking, bumped Winston on the head with a construction toy. The teacher intervened.

T.: [To Malcolm and Winston] What happened?
W.: Malcolm hit me on the head.
M.: But it was an accident. I didn't mean it. I didn't really hurt him.
T.: How did it happen?
M.: It was an accident.
W.: He [Malcolm] hit me.
T.: Malcolm, I know you didn't mean to hurt Winston, so how did it happen?
M.: I didn't mean it.
T.: I know you didn't mean it, Malcolm, but why did Winston get hurt?
Chn.: Malcolm was running.
M.: No I wasn't.
T.: See where everyone was sitting? There is hardly enough room for children to walk. Children working on the floor must remember to leave a walking path so that other children can move safely around the room. Otherwise someone will be hurt, and that's what has happened today (23 February 1993).

This public-sphere masculinity of rationality and responsibility, of civil society, of the social contract is not the masculinity that the boys are bringing into the classroom through their warrior narratives. They are using a different, much older version—not the male as responsible citizen, the producer, and consumer who keeps the capitalist system going, the breadwinner, and caring father of a family. Their earliest vision of masculinity is the male as warrior, the bonded male who goes out with his mates and meets the dangers of the world, the male who attacks and defeats other males characterized as baddies, the male who turns the natural products of the earth into weapons to carry out these purposes.

We would argue, nevertheless, that those boys who aspire to become one of the brothers who wield power in the public world of civil society ultimately realize that conformity to rationality and responsibility, to the demands of the school, is the price they must pay. They realize that although the girls can expect one day to become the brides and mothers of their pretend games, the boys will never, except perhaps in time of war, be allowed to act out the part of warrior hero in reality.

On the other hand, the school softens the transition for them by endorsing and encouraging the classic modern transformation and domestication of the warrior narrative, sport (Connell, 1987; Messner, 1992). In the school where this observation was conducted, large playground areas are set aside for lunchtime cricket, soccer, and basketball; by the age of seven, most boys are joining in these games. The message is conveyed to them that if they behave like citizens in the classroom, they can become warriors on the sports oval.

Gradually, we would suggest, little boys get the message that resistance is not the only way to live out warrior masculinity. If they accept a public/private division of life, it can be accommodated within the private sphere; thus, it becomes possible for those boys who aspire to respectability, figuring in civil society as one of the brothers, to accept that the school regime and its expectations are masculine and to reject the attempts of the "resisters" to define it (and them) as feminine. They adopt the masculinity of rationality and responsibility as that appropriate to the public sphere, while the earlier, deeply appealing masculinity of the warrior narratives can still be experienced through symbolic re-enactment on the sports field.

Conclusion

We are not, of course, suggesting that this is the only way in which the public/private division becomes part of the lived awareness of little boys. We do, however, believe that we have teased out one strand of the manner in which they encounter it. We have suggested that the classroom is a major site where little boys are introduced to the masculinity of rationality and responsibility characteristic of the brothers in civil society; we have been looking at a "cycle of practice" where, in classroom after classroom, generation after generation, the mode of masculinity typified in the warrior narratives is first driven underground and then transferred to the sports field. We are, we would suggest, seeing, renegotiated, for each generation and in each boy's own life, the conception of the "social contract" that is characteristic of the era of modernity, of the Enlightenment, of democracy, and of capitalism. We are watching, re-enacted, the transformation of violence and power as exercised by body over body, to control through surveillance and rules (Foucault, 1977, 1984), the move from domination by individual superiors to acquiescence in a public sphere of decorum and rationality (Pateman, 1988).

Yet, this is a social *contract*, and there is another side to the bargain. Although they learn that they must give up their warrior narratives of masculinity in the public sphere, where rationality and responsibility hold sway, they also learn that in return they may preserve them in the private realm of desire as fantasy, as bricolage, as a symbolic survival that is appropriate to the spaces of leisure and self-indulgence, the playground, the backyard, the television set, the sports field. Although this is too large an issue to be explored in detail here, there may even be a re-enactment in the school setting of what Pateman (1988) has defined as the sexual contract, the male right to dominate women in return for accepting the constraints of civil society. Is this, perhaps, established for both boys and girls by means of the endemic misogyny—invasion of girls' space (Thorne, 1986, 1993), overt expressions of aversion and disgust (Goodenough, 1987; D'Arcy, 1990), disparaging sexual innuendo (Best, 1983; Goodenough, 1987; Clark, 1990)—noted by so many observers in the classrooms and playgrounds of modernity? Are girls being contained by the boys' actions within a more restricted, ultimately a private, sphere because, in the boys' eyes, they have not earned access to the public sphere by sharing their ordeal of repression, resistance, and ultimate symbolic accommodation of their gender-defining fantasies?

Notes

The research on which this article is based was funded by the Research Management Committee of the University of Newcastle. The observation was conducted at East Maitland Public School and the authors would like to thank the principal, teachers, and children involved for making our observer so welcome.

1. Some ethnographic studies describe a "tomboy" who wants to join in the boys' games (Best, 1983; Davies, 1989; Thorne, 1993), although in our experience, such girls are rare, rarer even than the boys who play by choice with girls. The girls' rejection of the warrior narratives does not appear to be simply the result of the fact that the characters are usually men. Bronwyn Davies, when she read the role-reversal story *Rita the Rescuer* to preschoolers, found that many boys identified strongly with Rita ("they flex their muscles to show how strong they are and fall to wrestling each other on the floor to display their strength"), whereas for most girls, Rita remained "other" (Davies, 1989: 57–8).
2. This would seem to reverse the usual parallel of outdoor/indoor with public/private. This further suggests that the everyday equation of "public" with "visible" may not be appropriate for the specialized use of the term in sociological discussions of the public/private division. Behaviour in the street may be more visible than what goes on in a courtroom, but it is nevertheless acceptable for the street behaviour to be, to a greater degree, personal, private, and driven by "desire."
3. There are some groups of men who continue to reject these modes of modernity throughout their lives. Andrew Metcalfe, in his study of an Australian mining community, has identified two broad categories of miner, the "respectable," and the "larrikin" (an Australian slang expression carrying implications of nonconformism, irreverence, and impudence). The first are committed to the procedural decorums of union meetings, sporting and hobby clubs, welfare groups, and so on; the others relate more strongly to the less disciplined masculinity of the pub, the brawl, and the racetrack (Metcalfe, 1988). This distinction is very similar to that noted by Paul Willis in England between the "ear'oles" and the "lads" in a working-class secondary school (Willis, 1977). It needs to be noted that this is not a *class* difference and that demographically the groups are identical. What distinguishes them is, as Metcalfe points out, their relative commitment to the respectable modes of accommodation and resistance characteristic of civil society of larrikin modes with a much longer history, perhaps even their acceptance or rejection of the social contract.

References

Anyon, J. 1983. "Intersections of Gender and Class: Accommodation and Resistance by Working-class and Affluent Females to Contradictory Sex-role Ideologies," in S. Walker and L. Barton, eds., *Gender, Class and Education*. Barcombe, Sussex: Falmer.

Best, R. 1983. *We've All Got Scars: What Girls and Boys Learn in Elementary School*. Bloomington: Indiana University Press.

Bowles, S., and H. Gintis. 1976. *Schooling in Capitalist America: Educational Reform and the Contradictions of Economic Life*. London: Routledge and Kegan Paul.

Brophy, J.E. 1985. "Interactions of Male and Female Students with Male and Female Teachers," in L.C. Wilkinson and C.B. Marrett, eds., *Gender Influences in Classroom Interaction*. New York: Academic Press.

Burgess, R.G., ed. 1984. *The Research Process in Educational Settings: Ten Case Studies*. Lewes: Falmer.

Chodorow, N. 1978. *The Reproduction of Mothering: Psychoanalysis and the Sociology of Gender*. Berkeley: University of California Press.

Clark, M. 1989. "Anastasia Is a Normal Developer because She Is Unique," *Oxford Review of Education* 15: 243–55.

———. 1990. *The Great Divide: Gender in the Primary School*. Melbourne: Curriculum Corporation.

Connell, R.W. 1987. *Gender and Power: Society, the Person and Sexual Politics*. Sydney: Allen and Unwin.

———. 1989. "Cool Guys, Swots and Wimps: The Interplay of Masculinity and Education," *Oxford Review of Education* 15: 291–303.

Crosset, T. 1990. "Masculinity, Sexuality, and the Development of Early Modern Sport," in M.E. Messner and D.F. Sabo, eds., *Sport, Men and the Gender Order*. Champaign, IL: Human Kinetics Books.

D'Arcy, S. 1990. "Towards a Non-sexist Primary Classroom," in E. Tutchell, ed., *Dolls and Dungarees: Gender Issues in the Primary School Curriculum*. Milton Keynes: Open University Press.
Davies, B. 1989. *Frogs and Snails and Feminist Tales: Preschool Children and Gender*. Sydney: Allen and Unwin.
Dinnerstein, M. 1977. *The Mermaid and the Minotaur: Sexual Arrangements and Human Malaise*. New York: Harper and Row.
Duthie, J.H. 1980. "Athletics: The Ritual of a Technological Society?," in H.B. Schwartzman, ed., *Play and Culture*. West Point, NY: Leisure.
Eisenstein, H. 1984. *Contemporary Feminist Thought*. London: Unwin Paperbacks.
Foucault, M. 1977. *Discipline and Punish: The Birth of the Prison*, A. Sheridan, trans. New York: Pantheon.
———. 1980. "Body/power," in C. Gordon, ed., *Power/Knowledge: Selected Interviews and Other Writings 1972–1977*. Brighton: Harvester.
———. 1984. "Truth and Power," in P. Rabinow, *The Foucault Reader*. New York: Pantheon.
Genovese, E.E. 1972. *Roll, Jordan, Roll: The World the Slaves Made*. New York: Pantheon.
Giddens, A. 1984. *The Constitution of Society. Outline of the Theory of Structuration*. Berkeley: University of California Press.
Goodenough, Ruth Gallagher. 1987. "Small Group Culture and the Emergence of Sexist Behaviour: A Comparative Study of Four Children's Groups," in G. Spindler and L. Spindler, eds., *Interpretive Ethnography of Education*. Hillsdale, NJ: Lawrence Erlbaum.
Hebdige, D. 1979. *Subculture: The Meaning of Style*. London: Methuen.
Messner, M.E. 1992. *Power at Play: Sports and the Problem of Masculinity*. Boston: Beacon.
Metcalfe, A. 1988. *For Freedom and Dignity: Historical Agency and Class Structure in the Coalfields of NSW*. Sydney: Allen and Unwin.
Paley, V.G. 1984. *Boys and Girls: Superheroes in the Doll Corner*. Chicago: University of Chicago Press.
Pateman, C. 1988. *The Sexual Contract*. Oxford: Polity.
———. 1989. "The Fraternal Social Contract," in *The Disorder of Women*. Cambridge: Polity.
Thorne, B. 1986. "Girls and Boys Together . . . But Mostly Apart: Gender Arrangements in Elementary Schools," in W.W. Hartup and Z. Rubin, eds., *Relationships and Development*. Hillsdale, NJ: Lawrence Erlbaum.
———. 1993. *Gender Play: Girls and Boys in School*. New Brunswick, NJ: Rutgers University Press.
Walker, J.C. 1988. *Louts and Legends: Male Youth Culture in an Inner-city School*. Sydney: Allen and Unwin.
Walkerdine, V. 1990. *Schoolgirl Fictions*. London: Verso.
Weber, M. 1978. *Selections in Translation*. W.G. Runciman, ed. and E. Matthews, trans. Cambridge: Cambridge University Press.
Willis, P. 1977. *Learning to Labour: How Working Class Kids Get Working Class Jobs*. Farnborough: Saxon House.

Chapter 25

Overview

Warrior narratives are one form of "school stories." Marilyn Iwama looks at a very different form of storytelling about schools, in her poetic description of how adults remember their experiences in two notorious educational institutions that also served political purposes: the residential schools to which First Nations children were sent from the late nineteenth century well into the second half of the twentieth century, and the internment camps in which Japanese Canadians were imprisoned during the Second World War.

Iwama uses the image of the medicine wheel, with four directions corresponding to four different aspects of life, to organize her meditations on the meanings of food. Within the residential schools and internment camps, food was laden with emotional and symbolic significance. The participants' memories encompass the meager rations that were made available by the institutions, the subversion and secrecy through which boys and girls supplemented their rations, and the nostalgic memories of home evoked by thinking about different foods.

Food was also gendered, with men and women recalling different memories of finding, sharing, and consuming food. Girls might be assigned to take part in cooking and serving food to others, while boys, perhaps enacting a form of masculinity, might steal food or lead protests against the quality or quantity of the food. Using food as an analytic lens, Iwama posits that these places of hardship became also places where gender was enacted and created by children.

"At Dawn, Our Bellies Full": Teaching Tales of Food and Resistance from Residential Schools and Internment Camps in Canada

Marilyn Iwama

I didn't know then that what I really wanted none of us would ever have. I wanted an unbroken line between me and the past. I wanted not to be fragments and pieces left behind by fur traders, soldiers, priests, and schools.

—Linda Hogan, *Solar Storms*

Our nations are reclaiming. We are breaking the silence that for so long has been our history. Everywhere, Indigenous peoples are taking positive steps to address their experiences. We are shedding pain and healing spirit. . . . Each story given, as a gift, is an act of resistance. An act of healing.

—Linda Jaine, *The Stolen Years*

I am going to talk about stories of food and resistance that women have written about two places of confinement in Canada—Indian Residential Schools and the Japanese Canadian, or Nikkei, internment camps of the Second World War. For this purpose, I rely primarily on two texts that offer adult recollections of childhood confinement: Constance Deiter's *From Our Mothers Arms: The Intergenerational Impact of Residential Schools in Saskatchewan* and *A Child in Prison Camp* by Shizuye Takashima. *From Our Mothers' Arms* is a collection of interviews that Deiter conducted with members of her family who attended Residential School. In the prose poem *A Child in Prison Camp,* Takashima tells the story of her own confinement in the internment camp at New Denver.

Because the transformative process of restoring humanity is essentially educative, these narratives have value as pedagogical tools. In the process of their telling, the stories construct a body of cultural experience. As teaching tools, the stories instruct the hearer in the means of revitalizing cultures once threatened with extinction by official programmes of assimilation and genocide. The stories of *A Child in Prison Camp* and *From Our Mothers' Arms* return cultural knowledge to individuals by placing food in narratives of transformation, abundance, service, and struggle. Their telling resituates the storyteller and the listener within community. In this way, "community becomes a Story that is a collection of individual stories" (Cajete, 1994: 169).

I have several reasons for considering narratives of internment with the help of the sacred circle (Fig. 25.1). Two points require emphasis here. The first regards the universality of the sacred circle, its function in the perception of "the continuity and interconnectedness of events and conditions of all living beings" (Calliou, 1995: 52). When Black Elk (1988) received his great vision, he saw "the whole hoop of the world" (43):

> And while I stood there I saw more than I can tell and I understood more than I saw; for I was seeing in a sacred manner the shapes of all things in the spirit, and the shape of all shapes as they must live together like one being. And I saw that the sacred hoop of my people was one of many hoops that made one circle, wide as daylight and as starlight, and in the center grew one mighty flowering tree to shelter all the children of one mother and one father. And I saw that it was holy. (43)

While the sacred circle is a central component in an aboriginal world view, the view is of all the world, able to accommodate and comprehend the stories of all those who people the world.

Secondly, because the circle is sacred, it requires far more than an intellectual appreciation or grasp of its meaning. The sacred circle is not simply an idea, nor is it to be taken lightly. Full understanding of the circle is reached after years of apprenticeship with elders, after years spent (l)earning wisdom. Because knowledge of my First Nations heritage came to me in my middle years, I approach the sacred circle with the tentative step of a young child and the certainty of faith. There is no authority in my words.

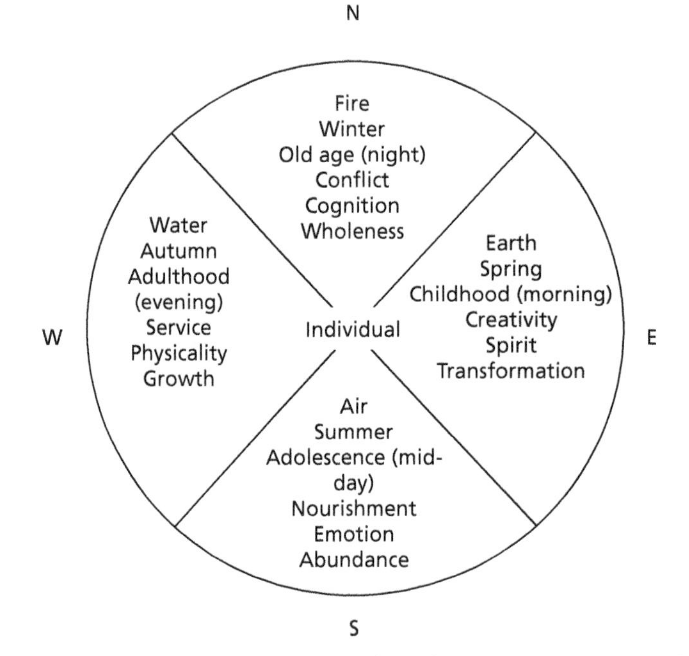

Figure 25.1 The Sacred Circle. Adapted from Bopp (1984), Calliou (1995), Dyck (1998), Hampton (1995), Sun Bear and Wabun (1980), and Weenie (1998).

> Do I really want to talk about this?
>
> I wear whiteness like a skin. After being raised white and educated white, after coming to terms with being white in a not-so postcolonial world, I learned about the Cree in me. One of my first emotions at the news was happiness. I'd been carrying a generous share of white guilt, yet experiencing the "rebound racism" that comes with being married to "a person of colour" and mothering mixed-blood kids in a "white" society (Frankenberg, 1993). I was wary of my Eurasian children thinking I didn't understand what it was like to be the racial underdog. After all, these days trying to be white is out, and trying to be native is in (Taylor, 1998).
>
> Just about the time my new Buffy St. Marie album was wearing out, the sobering significance of my "new" identity—and the fact that it had been kept from me—hit home. Like a child with a new toy, I was blind to the discomfort some members of my family were experiencing about what was, to me, a reason for celebration. I tried to rally these reluctant ones to celebrate our heritage. But I also wondered why I hadn't questioned earlier the contradiction between our family story of whiteness and the other story that was now so obvious to me in the family photo album.

Simply surviving uprootings is one kind of resistance. But many children in the camps and schools also resisted in other imaginative ways, often choosing food as the focus and channel of their resistance. Residential School food was strange; it was of poor quality, and it simply was not enough to keep the students healthy. Children stole food from school kitchens and gardens. In some schools, there was a thriving black market economy in stolen food. Girls who were assigned to kitchen duties had their own subversions; a favourite hiding spot for booty was the voluminous legs of the bloomers they were forced to wear. Parents and children demanded better and more food. In spite of Residential School, First Nations peoples kept their food practices alive, even if it was only, for a time, in memory.

Removing children from their homes was central to realizing assimilation: confinement interrupted the transmission of culture in each nation. Traditional food practices went underground, and students were nourished by their food only in memory or during family visits. At Christmas or summer vacation, mothers and grandmothers would stuff the little ones with bannock and jam and hot tea and roast meat and potatoes and fresh sweet berries. Back in school, the children comforted themselves by calling up memories of this feasting. As adults, they began recalling it on the page.

Geographical displacement was also a key to the assimilation of Canadian Nikkei. Many Nikkei who were sent to the camps were leaving the relative comfort and security of Powell Street in Vancouver. Powell Street was the place where Nikkei lived closely together "for the sake of mutual protection and the human need of companionship" (Kitagawa, 1985: 218). The neighbourhood was also the only source of Japanese food. A similar cultural enclave thrived in the Vancouver neighbourhood of Kitsilano. For Nikkei, removal to the internment camps meant a life of exile lived in a strange climate, among strange neighbours—without the familiar food of home. Their stories of clearing the land for gardens, foraging in the woods for berries and mushrooms, and generally "making do" are thus tales of resistance and survival, pedagogical tales of individuals finding their place in community, and of communities making a home.

East

On the sacred circle, east is the place of springtime and childhood, the home of fire and the creative spirit, the place of transformation. In the lives of peoples who have known a history of exclusion and discrimination, wintertime stories of struggle and conflict predominate, but tales of springtime do exist:

> But anyways, some of us used to just sit under the oak trees and these acorns would fall down. Then we would pretend that they were nuts and they were very nice you know. They tasted good. And sometimes when the boys were

> picking tomatoes and digging potatoes and all that, they'd be throwing these tomatoes at us and green tomatoes. Oh they were good, good to eat. It was just a great treat. (Deiter, 1999: 46)

Segregated by gender in Residential School, the children manage to transform both their roles and the nature of the food at their disposal. Acorns become tasty nuts and tomatoes become toys as the children's creative play evokes the playtime of home. Through their inventiveness, the children provide for their own nutritive needs and create a space for play.

As she prepares to leave the internment camp at New Denver, Shizuye Takashima's indecision over whether or not to pack a dusty old Christmas treat signals another transformative moment. The treat is a shoe filled with candies. The nuns who teach at the makeshift high school have transformed this utilitarian object into a "treasure chest" filled with candy and decorated with sparkling "gold rice" (71). Shizuye's older sister Yuki receives the gift at her school party and passes it on to the younger girl. After two years on the shelf, the gift retains its symbolic power for Shizuye, who writes that she "can still feel the love which the kind Sisters/put into it just when we needed love so much" (1).

Structurally, the Catholic Church supported the internment by commissioning nuns to assist its operation. But the individual actions of these nuns also situate them in the east, that "place of beginnings and enlightenment, and a place where new knowledge can be created or received to bring about harmony and right relations" (Calliou, 1995: 67). The physical transformation that the nuns create (shoe into treasure chest, rice into gold), in turn creates—or at least enables—a chain of transformations. The receiver becomes a giver, jailers become liberators, and prisoners children: "All of the Sisters and/Father looked so happy, and we could feel this/happiness. They really try to make us feel/warm, you know" (71–72).

In the camps and in the schools, children learned to be adept at distinguishing between the appearance of kindness and its genuine manifestations: "Sister Cloutier, in her understanding way, proceeded to give me a few pointers on the facts of life. I felt affection for the first time in that school. I shall always remember her" (Moine, 1975: n.p.). Children came to recognize the respect that motivates the cycle of transformations, the respect that is necessary for the construction of right relations (Calliou, 1995: 67).

Temporally speaking, the springtime of culture, education, and growth ought to happen in childhood. Communities socialize children into the ways of their group through the right functioning of families and other educational systems. However, for peoples who have lived the "parenthetical" existence of confinement, the transmission of culture is interrupted (*Four Women of Egypt*). For First Nations and Nikkei children, the experience of confinement based on ideas of race created in individuals a sense of cultural shame. To the degree that these projects were successful, childhood education in cultural practices and values was replaced by a process of re-socialization, whereby individuals must acquire knowledge of their cultures in a springtime of adulthood.

South

Significantly, it is the recollection of the lack of nurturing food in Residential School that triggers memories of abundance back home:

> The boys gardened and everything else and they looked after the farming and so on. And one thing about it, you know, they grew their own meat but mostly sheep. And that wasn't very, not at all inviting to see the gruel, always looked like that thing there. The stew [laughs and points to a floor mat] . . . the grey pan of top of the floor. Yeah, and it was never tasty. Just bits of lamb floating in this white, off-white gravy, you know. So it was really, it wasn't appetizing at all. But, you had to eat something or just go hungry.
>
> I think that the only time where we really ate [was at home] you know. One of my sisters is a very good cook. And she used to bake. She'll start Wednesday baking and so on. My father had a truck and we'd pick up people along the

> way and go to a picnic or something you know. Create your own sports day and so on, and by the time you got over there it was dinnertime and everybody was out in the field playing ball or football. That was our outing during those days. But there was also gardening, picking weeds, and not getting paid for it you know. Long rows of gardens. (Deiter, 1999: 41–42)

At the centre of this recollection of want by Bette Spence is a summertime of being released from barrenness into the freedom of abundance and contentment within community. Where Residential School food is a tasteless necessity to ease physical hunger, the food of summer vacation typifies plenitude. By honouring their respective kinship roles (sister cooks, father drives, everyone plays) the family participates in the construction of tradition (picnic and sports day). And because group play coincides with eating, sister's cooking feeds individual bodies as it nourishes the communal one. Where food in Residential School isolates the children from tradition, the summertime food of family and home affirms the children's place in community.

So it is for Takashima in the happy days of summer that she recalls. The intertwining memories of summertime food and the occasions for its eating prompt strong emotional reactions in her. Summer in Vancouver means swimming in the sea and hunting for baby crabs "for fun," not for eating, as Father hunts (57). Summer is for berry picking and walking "happily through the woods" (82). And during the summer that water first came to the camp at New Denver, even the simple washing of rice is a time for smiles (52). Takashima's happy recollections, like Spence's, record the right relations of kinship. Crab collecting and berry picking just for fun are the height of childhood abandon. As mimicry, the activities also teach children the adult responsibility of providing food for the family.

West

The emotional freedom of summer yields to the physical rationality of autumn in the west. Here is that adult place of introspection and insight, of service:

> Did you eat fresh vegetables?
>
> *Bette:* Not at the hospital. Not at the residential school. We did have potatoes. I don't remember any other vegetable except for maybe onion in the darn lamb stew. You know, it wasn't appetizing at all.
>
> So what happened to the vegetables that came from the garden?
>
> *Bette:* That's the part I don't know. I've been trying to remember what they did with them. So they must have stewed them. Most of the time they put them in the stew. Stew all the time. We just seemed to have stew all the time. On Sundays it was kind of special. They would have roast and potatoes and things you know, but that's about it. The most stewing place you ever came across you know [*laughter*]. Sometimes for dessert [we had] rice pudding or tapioca you know. And to this day I don't eat tapioca. "Oh, you're going to eat fish eyes you know," and we'd always say, "Yuck." (Deiter, 1999: 42)

Spence's narrative shifts from the emotional freedom of summers at home to the rational process of trying to understand just how the abundance of harvest at Residential School disappeared. Many of the schools had large gardens that could easily have fed the children well. Staff sold some of the produce funds for the various schools. Some of the food went to staff dining rooms; little made its way to student tables. For those children who were forced to harvest the gardens and crops and bottle the rich cream from the schools' dairy cows, the lack was especially difficult to bear.

In the camps, autumn was also the time for interned Nikkei to harvest vegetables they had managed to grow. Unlike the children in Residential School, Nikkei children were generally confined with their parents and enjoyed their continued guidance and care, however qualified or difficult internment made the delivery of that care: "Father enters the house. 'Well, another fall./It's getting cold. Did you pick the corn, Yuki?'/He rubs his hands. 'Yes, it's near the sink./Peel it, Shichan. Do I have to tell you each time?'/Yuki scolds me, so I start to peel the fresh corn" (64). Nonetheless, life in the internment camps abbreviated childhood for Nikkei children, just as the harsh rigours of Residential School forced a premature ageing and loss of innocence on First Nations children. As she peels the cobs, the knowledge that one living thing is food for another displaces Shizuye's childlike delight at the ordered beauty of the "lovely" plant. For big sister Yuki (one reading of this name means "snow"), the early autumn of rationality precipitates the acquisition of adult knowledge and responsibilities: "Yuki watered them so often. Father says:/'I guess that's the last of it.' Yuki begins to cook./'Are we ever going to have electricity?' she asks./Father says, angry, 'We're working on it now'" (65).

Eleanor Brass remembers how she and her fellow students discovered a hidden cache of summer's abundance at the File Hills School and took justice into their own hands:

> While I was at school, they kept barrels of apples in the attic. I don't remember them ever giving us any to eat so they must have been for the staff only. Somehow we found out about these apples so we discovered a way to steal them at night and take them to our beds to eat. The boys had easy access; they crawled across a small roof to the attic and took pillowcases to carry the apples back to their dorm. As each barrel became empty we turned it upside down.
>
> One day a member of the staff went up to get some apples and found all the barrels empty. Now we were in big trouble. We were all sent to bed immediately after supper and every night so many of us were called down to the office to get a strapping. When it came to my turn, I was scared. (Deiter, 1999: 31)

In the west, the emotional gives way to the physical, the irrational to the rational. In Residential School, the west is a poignantly paradoxical place where children parent children. Brass's narrative shows us how physical hunger forced the children to assuage their bedtime hunger and, perhaps, ease the loneliness of an empty bed. At the very least, the children's thievery redefines punishment as reward. That is, being sent to bed early because of their "crime" meant that the children could eat sooner from their cache of "stolen" apples.

This enforced adulthood demanded that children somehow discover a supplemental source of nutrition, devise a way of procuring the food, and hide their "thievery" from staff members. For First Nations, then, the Residential School system created an artificial need that taught the children that criminal behaviour was a way of life: "It was survival, but we used to have to learn to steal and lie, and be sneaky" (Deiter, 1999: 53). The necessity of deceit is a major theme in Inez Deiter's narrative. As testimonial, it bears witness to the real crime of Residential School. As theory, it provides a guidepost for reading student narratives and understanding the social implications of Residential School life in the lives of adult survivors.

North

Isolation and hunger are two of the strongest memories of the winter of Residential School, that night "that demands that we understand survival" (Hampton, 1995: 33). Understanding the northern winter of the sacred circle helps the reader appreciate the despair that children experienced: "Morale was very low. It was depressing. People would complain about the food. The food wasn't very good, watery porridge, and applesauce, mutton, and we didn't care for those. While I was in Onion Lake [school] somebody burned the school down" (Deiter, 1999: 54). Story after story reiterates this theme of insufficient, poor food. Many schools "mysteriously" burned down (Moine, 1975; Jaine, 1993; Deiter, 1999).

This is not to say that the children's experiences with food in Residential School were singularly defeating. Overwhelmingly, narratives of Residential School life tell how this wintering place of struggle and conflict was also a place where transformation was possible:

> One time the older kids demanded a change in the routine. When the supervisors wouldn't

> listen, the older kids rebelled. They broke into the kitchen and threw pork everywhere. The also destroyed the supervisor's supply of food, which was different from the food given to us. Some older boys brought us ice cream during the raid. We had never tasted ice cream! (Bell, 1993: 11–12)

For many reasons, food is a logical tool in the prisoner's rebellion (Ellman, 1993). In Residential School, food was a primary means of control and discipline and a primary symbol of want. Although the children who rebelled with Rosa Bell were chronically underfed, the point of their rebellion is not to feed their physical hunger. After all, the children destroy the nutritive meat and other coveted staff food and eat only the ice cream. On the surface, this might appear as "normal" childhood fancy. However, the children's destructive behaviour in the kitchen—and their choice of treat—have greater symbolic meaning. By refusing the nutrition they lack, and destroying the centre of food production, the students break the symbolic link between food and discipline, thereby challenging the larger system of order and authority within the school:

> The rebellion was successful and a meeting was held to discuss the changes. I felt scared and excited at the same time. Normally we weren't allowed to talk with the boys. There was a fence dividing the playground. The fences came down in the fourth year I was there. Males and females were then allowed to talk to one another. (Bell, 1993: 12)

Having made food the vehicle, rather than the goal of their protest, the rebel students transform legislated insufficiency into excess, discipline into chaos, and helplessness into autonomy. Bell's winter story teaches the teller and the listener that struggle is not the cause of renewal and transformation, but the source (Cajete, 1994).

Food was also a significant disciplinary tool throughout the uprooting and internment of Nikkei. In the temporary "housing" of the livestock buildings at Hastings Park in Vancouver, officials managed those imprisoned by regulating the quality and quantity of food provided. Like the Residential School diet, food at Hastings Park was of poor quality and radically different from the diet most Nikkei were accustomed to. One woman describes it to Shizuye's mother as "pigs' food" (9). And again, it is only when the inmates complain and finally refuse to eat that the diet improves (Ono, 1942; Takashima, 1971). Throughout *A Child in Prison Camp,* Takashima joins food with suffering to create a poignant symbol of want and struggle. In their empty house, Shizuye and her mother perch on the few packed boxes and drink fragrant green tea (11). As they wait for the train to remove them to British Columbia's interior, the children are overcome with hunger (14). When they finally arrive at New Denver, food prices are inflated and storekeepers unkind (19).

The north is also a place of vitality and mystery (Hampton, 1995; Weenie, 1998). It is in these dark days of struggle and want that the Nikkei who were interned create plenty through their own imaginative and determined efforts. They clear the land and plant gardens. They invent substitute ingredients in order to approximate their familiar diet. By invoking magic and spirits, Takashima shows the reader how Nikkei tapped the dormant plenitude of winter.

Considered together, narratives of experience in Residential Schools and internment camps constitute an encyclopedia of the foodways of various peoples. As projects of assimilation and genocide, confinement blocked the overt passage of knowledge from one generation to the next. Confinement separated children from the nurturing familiarity of home; it fractured the communities in which culture flourished. The recollection of that lack—all that evocative narrative detail about not trapping and not hunting and not smelling and eating the delicious food of home—has created a reservoir of cultural knowledge. Out of this reservoir flows the teaching that harmonizes the individual with his or her culture, the pedagogy that is "right" because it "effectively accomplishes this feat from the perspective of the culture it is designed to serve" (Cajete, 1994: 179).

Acknowledgements

The title is from *Blue Marrow*, by Louise Bernice Halfe. I should like to acknowledge the collaboration of Janis Brass, for her expertise in genealogy, and her support in finding and hearing the answers to many difficult questions. Thank you, Constance Deiter and Shizuye Takashima, for your interest in the project, and for your comments and suggestions. I also acknowledge the support of the Social Sciences and Humanities Research Council of Canada, and the Centre for Research in Women's Studies and Gender Relations, UBC. Thank you, especially, to those who have offered their stories: Rosa Bell, Eleanor Brass, Inez Deiter, Elizabeth Spence, Shizuye Takashima, the mothers and grandmothers.

References

Bell, R. 1993. "Journeys," in L. Jaine, ed., *Residential Schools: The Stolen Years*. Saskatoon: University of Saskatchewan Extension Press.

Black Elk. 1988. *Black Elk Speaks: Being the Life Story of a Holy Man of the Oglala Sioux. As Told through John G. Neihardt*. Lincoln: University of Nebraska Press.

Bopp, J., M. Bopp, L. Brown, and P. Lane Jr. 1984. *The Sacred Tree*. Lethbridge: Four Worlds Development Press.

Cajete, G. 1994. *Look to the Mountain: An Ecology of Indigenous Education*. Durango: Kivaki Press.

Calliou, S. 1995. "Peacekeeping Actions at Home: A Medicine Wheel Model for a Peacekeeping Pedagogy," in M. Battiste and J. Barman, eds., *First Nations Education in Canada: The Circle Unfolds*. Vancouver: UBC Press.

Deiter, C. 1999. *From Our Mothers' Arms: The Intergenerational Impact of Residential Schools in Saskatchewan*. Toronto: United Church Publishing House.

Dyck, L. 1998. "An Analysis of Western, Feminist and Aboriginal Science Using the Medicine Wheel of the Plains Indians," in L. Stiffarm, ed., *As We See . . . Aboriginal Pedagogy*. Saskatoon: University of Saskatchewan Extension Press.

Ellman, M. 1993. *The Hunger Artists: Starving, Writing and Imprisonment*. Cambridge, MA: Harvard University Press.

Four Women of Egypt. 1999. Knowledge Network, Vancouver. 13 December. Television Documentory.

Frankenberg, R. 1993. *White Women, Race Matters: The Social Construction of Whiteness*. Minneapolis: University of Minnesota Press.

Hampton, E. 1995. "Towards a Redefinition of Indian Education," in M. Battiste and J. Barman, eds., *First Nations Education in Canada: The Circle Unfolds*. Vancouver: UBC Press.

Jaine, L. 1993. *Residential Schools: The Stolen Years*. Saskatoon: University Extension Press.

Kitagawa, M. 1985. *This is My Own: Letters to Wes and Other Writings on Japanese Canadians, 1941–1948*. R. Miki, ed. Vancouver: Talonbooks.

Moine, L. 1975. *My Life in a Residential School*. Regina: Provincial Chapter I.O.D.E. & Provincial Library.

Ono, Y. 1942. *Diary*. Vancouver: UBC Special Collections.

Takashima, S. 1971. *A Child in Prison Camp*. Montreal: Tundra Books.

Taylor, D.H. 1998. *Funny, You Don't Look Like One*. Penticton: Theytus Books.

Weenie, A. 1998. "Aboriginal Pedagogy: The Sacred Circle Concept," in L. Stiffarm, ed., *As We See . . . Aboriginal Pedagogy*. Saskatoon: University of Saskatchewan Extension Press.

Chapter 26

Overview

Tracy Lindberg moves from the educational institutions of childhood to those of adulthood in her examination of the experiences of nine First Nations women in law school. For these women, the intersection of gender and racial categories produces experiences that are challenging, disturbing, and sometimes inspiring. They recount being subject to snap judgments and assessment of their fitness to be in law school based on their appearance and their self-identification. In addition to biased comments, the students also have to navigate within a school environment in which certain presumptions are made about First Nations women and about gender relations in First Nations communities. Professors and faculty members do not curb these negative experiences and in some cases actually contribute to them.

In addition to navigating the racialized and gendered biases in their law school, the students have to contend with gender differences within the community of First Nations students. Can men speak about issues of inequality to women? Should women talk about the "family differences" between men and women in their communities in white-dominated spaces such as the university, or should First Nations men and women maintain a united front against institutionalized racism? Can women carry out the responsibilities of being good members of their home communities while at the same time meeting the heavy demands of law school?

Although the women in Lindberg's study find their educational experience marred by institutionalized racism and exclusion, they also draw strength from their identities as Aboriginal women and from their acceptance of the challenge of bringing their perspectives and knowledge into a white-dominated, male-dominated educational system. They speak of frustration but also of hope and courage.

What Do You Call an Indian Woman with a Law Degree? Nine Aboriginal Women at the University of Saskatchewan College of Law Speak Out

Tracey Lindberg

I write this paper with an unsteady hand and with my heart beating in my head.[1] It is a very difficult thing to do—to evaluate legal education as it has affected First Nations women in the College of Law. I feel liberated since I am finally able to write as I want to with heart, spirit, and mind. I speak as an Indian. I speak as a woman. I speak as an Indian woman. I begin with a story.

I didn't go to Grace Adam's funeral. I didn't think I could talk to her family. She had four daughters and one son—the most giving and the strongest person, and a very lonely person. I'm not quite sure where I fit in. All I know is that they loved everyone, cared for the Earth, and celebrated the Creator.

She was an amazing woman, you know—one of the first Indian women in the province of Saskatchewan to graduate from Lebret Residential School, one of the first Indian women to obtain a university degree, one of the best teachers in the province. She was the closest many of us had come to meeting pure goodness. This woman typified for me what education for First Nations people could be like. She studied hard, learned new information, and adapted it to apply understandings of "Indianness." Learning was not limited to her formal education. She continued learning for the rest of her life. Her time spent at university was just a part of it. She taught her children traditional values and skills and let them learn formal education when they entered their learning phase. She was the most Indian person I had ever met. She worked hard in a world filled with much more enmity toward Indian woman than I will ever know. She always gave, constantly worked for change, and believed each person had value.

I want so much to describe effectively the story of being an Indian woman in a non-Indian, male educational setting. I want the story to be true and strong. I want it to reflect that I am here because of Grace Adam. My daughters may come here because of me. My story involves much beauty and celebration. Yet, it is written with somewhat more cynicism and bitterness than existed three years ago when I first began this journey.

First Nations women are best at telling the stories of our first days:

> I overhead two women in the back of Torts discussing who was and was not Indian in the classroom. The assessment was based purely on physical attributes. More distressing and painful than that was the fact that we were objectified and examined like some foreign entity in "their" class. I was hurt, alone and labeled by women I was to spend the next three years with. I remember that every time I speak with either of them.

Nine Aboriginal women,[2] including myself, have chosen to share our experiences in law school. I am fortunate to be the person compiling and presenting these experiences. The majority of Aboriginal women in the College of Law at the University of Saskatchewan are over 25 years of age. Three of the respondents are Métis women. The remainder are Treaty Indian women representing Indian Nations. Many have children. The few of us without partners or children are a distinct minority. The support system we provide for each other extends to the community as well. Many of us have met previously (through the Native Law Summer Program, employment, and political or social organizations). This support has been an undeniable factor in our continued success and presence in law school.

> I am fortunate because I know I can rely on the other Indian people I met through the summer program. It is not academic support. The presence of other Indian people in the college makes me feel visible. I thought I would vanish in law school . . . somehow become White. With other Aboriginal people here I am constantly reminded that I am here for many important and good reasons.

The contributors to this article co-operated with the knowledge that their statements and understandings would be compiled and presented as an assessment of legal education in Saskatchewan as it affects Aboriginal women. Our comments have been edited as little as possible to ensure that the truth, beauty, and, at times, rawness, are fully evident. It may hurt to read these pages. This pain is reflective of the anger and silent screaming that some of us have had to bear and suppress. These pages are also filled with support, strength, and wisdom. It will feel good to read them. Of the women polled, the majority state that they are glad to be law students. We offer our comments, critiques, and feelings not as a negative allegory of our experiences, but as an expression of our understandings of legal education. As "outsiders" (Sheppard and Westpahl, 1992), we are able to see patterns of belief or behaviour that are difficult to detect for those immersed in the college.

Our view necessarily includes a careful examination of the accommodation of Aboriginal women in the curriculum, class teachings, materials, and understandings of law school.[3] The comments were solicited by questionnaires distributed by hand to each Aboriginal woman in the college. Participants were given the option of answering anonymously or meeting with the author to discuss their responses. Most chose to discuss the questionnaire in person.

We leave the following words to you and to your interpretation. The onus of learning about Indian and Aboriginal peoples too often comes to lie on those who are being defined. We hope our words will aid in your learning. We will facilitate your knowledge, but you must take responsibility for your own education.

Aboriginal women come to law school for a variety of reasons:

> [I came to law school] on a dare from someone.

> I was particularly optimistic. I came here to change everyone's views about Indians. I mean it. I would change professorial teaching styles, the textbooks, non-Indian students and even the laws! I was going to teach the world about an alternative mode of justice. I guess I really didn't come here to learn.

> I came to law school because I've always wanted to be a lawyer. If I am going to make a difference in the world—a law degree will help me.

> For career reasons. A law degree offers many choices.

> Because of the way I was treated by males in the justice system.

> I was arrested once protesting at Indian Affairs. When I was being photographed and fingerprinted I asked the officer in charge why this process was being used. He said, "Because you'll be back." I kept that in my head while I wrote the *LSAT* and when I applied to law school.

There are times when as Aboriginal women, we find ourselves alienated from the learning processes. Many of the Aboriginal women interviewed found that, in part, the alienation was related to perceptions of their race based on physical attributes:

> I am able to be perceived as an Aboriginal person. This affects me in two very major ways: I cannot be a member of the very real boys club; I am to be an expert on all Aboriginal groups and all Aboriginal concerns.

> I am perceived and received as a First Nations female. Therefore, my interaction is based on who I am.

> [Other's perception of me as a First Nation member] has kept me from interacting with certain people in the college. You get vibes from some people so you in turn treat them as invisible as well. Once you do that I find some of these people take notice and are annoyed by it, probably because I am not a visible minority.

> I find that my look limits somewhat the people who associate with me. It is not chic or trendy to befriend an Aboriginal. I enter each situation open to new ideas and people. I request the same. I find that I do not receive this. I think there are probably all sorts of stereotypes and concerns that come with this brown skin. We are all affirmative action, we are all from reserves on a scholarship, who had a great GPA. I feel proud of how I look but I am distressed at being a brown page in their [other law students'] previously written book of experiences. I sometimes feel like I am on the outside looking in.

In many situations, we associate with, and locate near, other Aboriginal people. In many cases, the group that provides the most support includes Aboriginal peoples. The majority of

Aboriginal women at the College of Law do not separate gender from origin. Aboriginal women make up a strong portion of the circle. We perform an important role in racial and cultural self-determination. Therefore, issues of racism and community wellness are often our major concern.

Sisterhood in the college, in many cases, is a secondary concern to nationhood. As Aboriginal people, we find ourselves in the position of being a bridge between two worlds. Our interaction, therefore, takes place with many people of differing world views, including Aboriginal and non-Aboriginal people. Since our support within the college varies, some of us interact principally with other Aboriginal students.

Aboriginal women in the college find it difficult to stay connected. Many of us study with, or socialize predominantly with, Aboriginal males in the college. Many of the males are single with no dependants or have partners who assume the childcare responsibilities. We associate with other Aboriginal people in situations where we need support: exam periods, community and family concerns, and assignment due dates. This behaviour is known as taking comfort into the room with you (Monture, 1986).

> The support I received from Aboriginals whether male or female is moral and personal. [We are all concerned with] how to make the system work for us and who and what can work for us (the oppressed).

> I find myself drawn to minority group members (lesbians, gays, other First Nations members). I was never a very strong feminist, but there is merit to a somewhat common oppressive background. I find the Aboriginal men found their voices a lot easier than Aboriginal women in the college. I have only been present during one incident of an Aboriginal woman speaking out in class. It seems like we are the first to be asked for our opinions on Aboriginal issues and dismissed in many other situations.

> In my Advanced Constitutional Law class the professor announced we were to have a discussion the next day on First Nations constitutional concerns. As he read the reading list I felt more and more depressed and I couldn't figure out why. Another woman in class asked why all the assigned readings were written by non-Aboriginal males. I wanted to hug her. She made sure that I didn't disappear in that class.

> There is a general sense that we [all law students] share a common experience, but I received support specifically from both Aboriginal men and women both academically and personally and I cherish it.

> My main support in the college from Aboriginals has come from Aboriginal men. We keep each other sane at exam time and can discuss issues of race and even gender that are lacking in class. Aboriginal women are important to my life at law school and in general—but there is no one woman who has been a support group for school. They are good friends and good sounding boards for life though.

I have been told that women were created out of the bone of a buffalo—this is how integral Aboriginal women are to life. We were created with strength in mind—sinewy and rare. We were not made as a mate for one person, nor are we made from one person. Our strength supports all life. Because of this, we have distinct roles as Aboriginal women. We each have the same responsibilities to protect the children and their children.

However, every Aboriginal woman does not consider this gender differentiation—this feminine side of the earth—to mean that we must join together for that reason alone.

> I feel that Aboriginal women in law school are not as connected to one another as they should be; outside of law school, I have managed to maintain contact and communication with the Aboriginal organizations and attend and participate in events such as conferences, social events and so forth.

> There are so few of us that it is hard to bond just on the basis of race. All people of all cultures have interesting and complicated histories. I think we tend to connect with the people who are the most like us. This includes more than race and gender. While I certainly fell connected to all the Aboriginal students, as a single female with no dependants I share many traits and characteristics of other single females in the college.

> I am connected to some Aboriginal students and not to others—applies to women or men.

> In some classes I sit with Aboriginal students . . . our interaction is distinct because of shared experiences and confidences.

Another reason identified for this strong affiliating with Aboriginal people lies in the fact that almost all of the Aboriginal women interviewed found that non-Aboriginal students' knowledge of Aboriginal issues and understandings was quite low. This is the result of an education system that does not convey the understandings, needs, and legal positions of Aboriginal peoples and systems to the people who most need to understand it—non-Aboriginal students.[4]

In my world, you have to deal with Aboriginal people every day. I do not understand why this is not so in a college professing to be on the cutting edge of society. Aboriginal women possess untold stories and understandings. We come from areas where there is a 100 per cent Aboriginal population. We come from homes where families raised eight children. We have concepts of property and self-determination that could make others richer through the telling. I think that as Aboriginal women we have a story that is both the same as, and different from, shared. Most of us have found that the majority of the college's students are empathetic and open-minded towards Aboriginal issues, and we believe that they are "fertile ground" for planting new seeds of knowledge about Aboriginal people.

> I have found two people in the college who are constantly trying to understand, to really get around the concept of Aboriginal rights. They do this not for curiosity, for classroom purposes, or to settle their fears. They do this because they respect Aboriginal people and accept that the responsibility for keeping Aboriginal peoples and issues alive is their concern as well.

> I have heard the only two women on a hockey trip called "clan mothers" as a joke in the college newspaper. I just found the objectification so thoughtless and unkind. . . . I couldn't bring myself to mention it.

Most people recognize that a great deal of this knowledge deficit could be minimized if professors, administrators, and other staff realized that teaching from a variety of perspectives is beneficial to classroom settings. In many Aboriginal communities, elders and teachers bear a great responsibility of ensuring that the people/students are well prepared for life. This includes stories of other cultures, their understandings, and the importance of respect for all people. What kind of lives are Aboriginal law students being prepared for?

> I have had two completely awful contacts with college professors. In the first, one of my professors was unable to defuse a potentially damaging conversation about Aboriginal women. One of the students commented that "Indian men only hit Indian women when they are drunk." This was said in a jovial and accepting tone. Several other women in the class spoke for me as I was incoherent with weariness and pain. In the second situation, a professor questioned two of eleven presentations in a class belligerently and very condescendingly. The two presentations were both on issues of Aboriginal title that adopted a point of view that differed with that of the professor. Only one faculty member was sympathetic to my concern. Other comments I received from the faculty were "Professor X is one of the most sympathetic professors in the college," "Professor X is just brusque," and the advice I received was to "write your best paper" based

> on the presentation. Although the professor was approached eventually, I am disillusioned with the process of taking professors to task for their behaviour.

The general impression was that there were some "informed" professors, yet many others who were unable to convey to their classes that Aboriginal issues were often distinct and very much a reality. In the few instances where Aboriginal issues were discussed, the possibility of a female interpretation was often ignored. We found ourselves immersed in invisibility. Aboriginal issues and concerns, we believe, would be considered more seriously and addressed more frequently if there was an Aboriginal faculty member on staff.

This problem of little or no attention to gender resulted in two widely talked about class discussions in the College of Law last year. In one discussion, Aboriginal men spoke for all Aboriginal people, necessitating the request by Aboriginal women in the class that there be an opportunity for the concerns of Aboriginal women to be expressed by themselves. The other discussion, which took place in a small-group seminar class on Aboriginal law, involved a similar exclusion of Aboriginal women from the debate. In each situation, the distinct concerns of Aboriginal women were initially addressed only by Aboriginal men. In response, Aboriginal women found their voices and insisted that there were distinct issues that affected Aboriginal women.

The issue of gender differences in Aboriginal communities has become a subject that both Aboriginal and non-Aboriginal people prefer not to discuss. The truth is that women have always had a separate and equal position in politics, labour, and familial tasks. Equality as an ideal has different meanings for Aboriginal people. Aboriginal women are an essential and important part of the circle, the continuity of life. We are a part of fire, of water. We are elemental and essentially intrinsic to the continuance of life. We have our roles, different and the same, which match perfectly with those of our men. Yet somehow we are overlooked. We are elemental, and we need to reclaim our place. We are women. We are Aboriginal. But to draw a sharp line between these two characteristics makes sense only in theorists' minds.

> Aboriginal politics demands a role for Aboriginal women. I think that the Aboriginal community is slow to get the message of the importance of women's roles and involvement in society and especially in politics. As with everything else, women see problems and solutions from a different perspective—which is just as valid and as important. We need a voice, and a political voice often carries farther.

> I never see us as a Women's Struggle. Sisterhood, to me, most often will be secondary to nationhood. We have an unclaimed seat at the circle of Aboriginal politics. This is something we have tried and tried to discuss with other Aboriginal people. It seems the only time that Aboriginal political issues come to the forefront is when there is perceived infighting. I hope that Aboriginal issues from a women's perspective will soon be addressed. I am not yet willing to confer authority upon women's groups to speak for us.

It is widely recognized that many non-Aboriginal people do not think about, understand, or define reality in the same way that some Aboriginal people do (Monture, 1986). Certain situations and class discussions include introductory information that introduces and explains differing perspective. For example, in an environmental law class, it is made clear that corporations have different perspectives than other entities in society. The corporations' perspective is often alluded to. However, though this courtesy is extended to a fictional entity, it is not extended to Aboriginal people very often. It is even more rarely extended to Aboriginal women. As Aboriginal women, we enter our criminal law classes with the knowledge that the majority of female offenders in this province are Aboriginal women. We also recognize that there Aboriginal women prisoners are pre-judged as "violent, uncontrollable, and unmanageable" in some prisons (Sugar and Fox, 1990). Yet I have never heard an introductory lecture on systemic discrimination. There are many ways for a professor to convey that Aboriginal women don't matter and that includes silence (Boyle, 1986).[5] I have never once heard the term "institutionalized racism," cross a professor's lips. Yet I sit, I read, and I wonder each time we discuss an Aboriginal offender: what is everyone in this room thinking? It is not a good feeling. I feel indignant, angry, and afraid. I hope everyone in the room who is aware of these issues knows that I am Indian. I want no one to notice me and everyone to notice me. I hope no one will make a painful statement. It is an open wound to my being. This is my personhood (Monture, 1986), and we are dismembering it. Its main organs are taken out: the facts, the issues, and the ratio.

It is difficult to find the strengths in a college where many of us feel alienated, separate, and invisibly brown. Many of us only participate in seminar or limited-enrolment classes. Theory classes also encourage different perspectives, and many upper-year Aboriginal women feel comfortable speaking out in these classes. Large classes where the professor uses a Socratic teaching style were widely criticized as intimidating [and] uncomfortable.

There is a great deal of uncertainty that surrounds us as Aboriginal in law school. We have few predecessors to look for advice. None of us are second-generation lawyers. Some of us are the daughters and granddaughters of trappers. Coming to law school is similar to moving to a foreign country, learning a new culture and language. We proceed by trial and error. As a result, we are often quiet, sometimes ill at ease, and occasionally frightened.

> In property when Aboriginal title was starting I did not know how the class would respond; I felt responsible for the whole Aboriginal people—but it turned out okay and there was no need to defend my people.

> I am never comfortable when called upon. It doesn't matter how well I am prepared. I will offer information when I feel there is a point that needs to be raised. I never speak just to comment on a case or give my opinion. It there is an alternate way to interpret a situation I will try to bring that up.

> I try really hard to make sure I am prepared. This whole "lazy Indian" image really is alive and at work in this college. It is especially evident in the statements I have heard regarding Aboriginal people in the part-time program.

We find ourselves making choices based on a complex set of values. These values, it seems, are based upon how connected we are with the Aboriginal communities of interest to which we belong. In turn, this connection is based on our goals for the future. In establishing goals, all the Aboriginal women who responded stated that their connection to their communities of interest was central in goal determination and occupational choice:

> I will work in any capacity to facilitate the advancement of Aboriginal self-determination. I hope this does not leave me in an urban centre, but realistically it might. I want to take my information and training and better educate myself in traditional learning (teachings of the community, elders, and other involved in self-determination).

> I plan to stay in Saskatoon and work with the community here.

> If not to my reserve, to other Native communities.

> I feel best about speaking at Bridging Week in front of all the first year students. I told them that I know we are called squaws and that when some people see us they think "squaw." I am proudest of telling them to see people, not colours, and to think Indian person—not Indian. I have tried my best to eradicate labeling and naming.

It is very evident among most of my Aboriginal women colleagues that law school is a portion of their lives and not the entirety of it.

We are very proud of balancing family, partners, careers, community, and studies. The balance most of us accomplish is welcome and sometimes difficult to achieve. All but one of the respondents have familial support and obligations in addition to their studies. Balancing becomes an implicit and important part of our lives as family and community shift positions in our web of responsibilities.

> I feel terribly guilty for not committing any time to social or cultural concerns (like I did before law school).

> I had to miss conferences, ceremonies, and elders talks that I love to go to—for something that I am not even sure that I like.

> [I make time for] spiritual and extended family, children's social well-being, which call for frequent trips to Regina and rez. Lots of time, money, and support are required, not to mention family emergencies.

> [There is pressure on an Aboriginal woman that there is not on an Aboriginal man], women are still expected to do it all but I need a wife too. Not in the sexual sense but someone to do all or at least some of my duties.

> Considering the funding conditions put on me by Indian Affairs I have no choice but to go full-time to get full funding. Otherwise it would be full-time work and part-time studies.

Overt racism is something that few of the Aboriginal women had actually seen, heard, or experienced from law school peers. Yet a very strong majority of the women interviewed believed that there were racial slurs and understandings at work in the College of Law.

> I heard one male student jokingly saying that he was from [an urban centre with a very high Aboriginal population] and that because he was from that town it was okay if he transgressed the limits of the law because it was all relative. He stated that he could not be penalized because "he only shot one or two Indians." I did not say a word. It is too scary to approach someone who feels confident enough about that belief to say it in a normal tone of voice.

> I am quite sure there are [racist statements] in the college.

> I am not likely to be made privy to the confidences of people who dislike other people on the basis of skin colour. My friends have told me of a few instances. It is hard to sleep sometimes.

Yet, as Aboriginal women we have an ongoing responsibility to seven unborn generations of children. This responsibility includes making sure that they do not have to bear this weight. It includes ensuring that barriers that existed for us as Aboriginal women are knocked down so that our children do not have to break them down. It is in this spirit that the Aboriginal women in the University of Saskatchewan College of Law mad their recommendations in the questionnaire.

There is a perception in law school that Aboriginal people in law school are not there on our merits. We are taking the spot of deserving candidates. We are lower achievers and undeserving of a position in the college. All people should compete for spaces on the same basis. These prejudiced views extend to and touch every Aboriginal woman who goes to law school. Patricia Monture wrote of this sentiment:

> Remembering back to my first day of law school, I was confronted in the lounge by another student, who with some hostility explained that perhaps one of his friends was not present because of me. And this made him angry because the only reason I could have reached the hallowed halls of the law school was by virtue of a special access program. (Monture, 1990)

I have found this to be true in my experience as well.

Many of the legal concepts that we learn in law school are contrary to Aboriginal traditional notions of justice. All of the contributors to the questionnaire are in agreement that the Canadian legal system has a duty to respect Aboriginal peoples. This respect can be fostered by:

> displaying genuine commitment to and support of our dreams and aspirations of self-determination and by the willingness to listen to and implement the innovative idea conveyed by First Nations people in response to issues that directly affect us as a nation.

There is also concern regarding the exclusion of Aboriginal people and, particularly, Aboriginal women, from the curriculum. In my first year, my only memorable experiences with Aboriginal people in the justice system were confined to a duress defence (because Aboriginal people are, of course, unable to fully comprehend the complexities of a contract) and a drug-trafficking offence. As future lawyers, we all depend narrowly on our experiences in law school as a basis for future understanding and learning. I trust the ability of others to exclude information that is culturally biased, but I question all people's abilities to include information that is excluded. This includes hypotheticals that incorporate Aboriginal women as well as Aboriginal men. I have been present in two classes where there were serious attempts to linguistically include women in hypotheticals (Boyle, 1986). My pride and the feelings of inclusion were very strong. I felt my invisibility by exclusion warp for a moment. I was the same as, and different from, every person in the room. I felt included and important. It is such a small thing, but it chips away at the massive base of oppression.

We are always Aboriginal. We are always women. We are not allowed the luxury of turning our pain on and off (Monture, 1986).[6] But we bear it and we proceed. More importantly, we succeed. Many of the Aboriginal women currently in law school still consider themselves very attuned to the needs and goals of the Aboriginal community. In addition, there are more Aboriginal women in the University of Saskatchewan College of Law at this time than in any year in recent memory. We succeed in the management of studies, community interaction, and family. There can be no greater success story than that.

The essence of this paper is this: we have accepted the responsibility of educating ourselves. We have risen to the challenge of remaining Aboriginal in the search for knowledge in a system that challenges our make-up. We respect the wisdom that we have gained. We honour the teachers who have tried to change a vision of their world in order to include other worlds. We have found ourselves immersed in a value system that is strange and foreign to many of us. We have struggled academically, personally, and in innumerable other ways to include, or at least to respect, your vision of the world. It is your turn.

True success in law school includes ensuring that parity, fairness, and respect are maintained at all times. It is your turn to ensure that the infliction of racism, the appropriation of pain, and the disrespect of alternative viewpoints and understandings ends. Patricia Monture wrote of this responsibility:

> When are those of you who inflict racism, who appropriate pain, who speak with no knowledge or respect when you ought to listen and accept, going to take hard looks at yourself instead of at me. How can you continue to look at me to carry what is your responsibility? And when I speak and the brutality of my experience hurts you, you hide behind your hurt. You point the finger at me and you claim I hurt you. I will not carry your responsibility anymore. Your pain is unfortunate. But do not look at me to soften it. Look to yourself. (1986: 168)

We persevere and we struggle on. For many of us, the most difficult aspect of our experience is dealing with the ignorance of others. For Aboriginal women who are law students, as it was for Grace Adam, the struggle is a hard-fought one. We do not, in all cases, reject our legal education. We do, however, refuse to bear the burdens of a system that will not evolve. We continue to break the path initially walked by women like Grace Adam—our Women.

Notes

1. Because there are so few of us, many Aboriginal academics and professionals must play multiple roles in the achievement of our goals. Telling this story was important enough that I wanted to undertake to gather the stories, but I also wanted to be one of the voices that was heard. I do not profess to be impartial as I am a participant. I do not profess to be apolitical as this is personal and, as such, politicized.
2. The phrase "Aboriginal women" is utilized throughout this article to indicate the distinct and multi-facial component and also the cultural affinity, of the respondents. This may yield a certain homogeneity that is by no means indicative of our multiplicity of experiences, understandings, or feelings about law school. However, the term does encompass the unity of nations that binds the respondents together.
3. This examination is based, in great part, on the approach taken by Catherine Weiss and Louise Melling, "The Legal Education of Twenty Women," *Stanford Law Review* 40 (1988): 1299. We adapted and revised the questionnaire used in that article (Ibid., Appendix A at 1360). In particular, we employed terms of racial specificity and of race/gender duality. . . .
4. Mari Matsuda has written that "a system that ignores outsiders' perspectives artificially restricts and stultifies the scholarly imagination." Mari Matsuda, "Affirmative Action and Legal Knowledge: Planting Seeds in Plowed-Up Ground" *Harvard Women's Legal Journal* 2 (1988): 1–3.
5. Boyle discusses silence after a pro-woman comment is made. I think it is relevant that complete silence regarding any issue that concerns all students dismisses certain defined groups of people.
6. At a conference that Monture attended, she heard of a discussion where an individual stated that "the pain of minority people is like television, we can turn it on and off as we want to." This is a luxury that Aboriginal people are usually not allowed.

References

Boyle, C. 1986. "Teaching Law as If Women Really Mattered or What about the Washroom?," *Canadian Journal of Women and the Law* 2(1): 96–99.

Matsuda, M. 1988. "Affirmative Action and Legal Knowledge: Planting Seeds in Plowed-Up Ground," *Harvard Women's Legal Journal* 2: 1–3.

Monture, P.A. 1986. "Ka-Nin-Geh-Heh-E-Sa-Nonh-Yah-Gah," *Canadian Journal of Women and the Law* 2(1): 159–61.

———. 1990. "Now That the Door Is Open: First Nations and the Law School Experience" *Queen's Law Journal* 15: 179–205.

Sugar, F., and L. Fox. 1990. "Nistum Peyako Seht'wanin Iskwewak: Breaking Chains," *Canadian Journal of Women and the Law* 3(2): 465–69.

Sheppard, C., and S. Westpahl. 1992. "Equity and the University: Learning from Women's Experience," *Canadian Journal of Women and the Law* 5(1): 8.

Weiss, C., and L. Melling. 1988. "The Legal Education of Twenty Women," *Stanford Law Review* 40: 1299.

Chapter 27

Overview

Like Lindberg, Brenda Beagan focuses on postsecondary education and the experiences of students who find themselves excluded or limited by the biases of others. Also like Lindberg, Beagan takes an intersectional perspective, examining race, class, and sexuality along with gender. Although the composition of medical schools has changed tremendously in the last few decades, attitudes and behaviours often lag behind changes in the composition of the student body.

Beagan focuses on "micro inequities": the small, daily interactions between people that add up to create a hostile or uncomfortable environment for those who do not share the same social status as the dominant group. These micro inequities are not as blatant as overt discrimination or harassment, and thus they are more difficult to address or uproot. However, they both reflect and reinforce a hierarchy in which some medical students are constantly reminded that they do not really "fit" into the medical school environment, while others are able to study and work without infringement.

Although medical school is in theory a meritocracy, in which only academic and professional skills count, in reality, barriers still exist that hamper the full participation of some groups of people. The gender barriers are not the same as barriers related to class, sexual orientation, or race, all of these different barriers come together to create an environment that is permeated by inequality on the level of small everyday interactions.

Micro Inequities and Everyday Inequalities: "Race," Gender, Sexuality, and Class in Medical School[1]

Brenda Beagan

. . .

Over the [last] 40 years the profile of the typical North American medical school class [has] changed considerably. By 1993, 42 per cent of medical students in the United States were women (Bickel and Kopriva, 1993). In Canada, women's proportion of medical school classes increased from 9 per cent in 1957–8 to 49 per cent by 1997–8 (Association of Canadian Medical Colleges, 1998). By 1991–2 African American, Native American, Mexican American, Puerto Rican, other Hispanic, and Asian or Pacific Islander students made up 27 per cent of all medical students in the United States (Jonas et al., 1992; c.f., Foster, 1996). In Canada statistics on the "race" of medical students are not available. As well, medical students are somewhat older and better educated upon entry than they were in previous years (Gray and Reudy, 1998: 1047). Evidence also indicates there are more openly-identified gay/lesbian/bisexual medical students. There are currently gay and lesbian student caucuses in medical schools, a Canadian gay and lesbian medical student e-mail list, a gay and lesbian committee of the American Medical Student Association (Oriel et al., 1996), and recent journal articles addressing the concerns of gays and lesbians in medicine (Wallick et al., 1992; Rose, 1994; Cook et al., 1995; Oriel et al., 1996; Druzin et al., 1998; Klamen et al., 1999; Risdon et al., 2000).

In short, the medical student population is far less homogeneous than when Becker et al. (1961) conducted their research 40 years ago.[2] What is the impact of this increased diversity in the student population? Linda Grant (1988) suggests that who you are when you enter medicine affects the extent to which you "fit in" during medical school. She argues that all schools have their own "latent culture," which dictates the boundaries of appropriate behaviour: "Those who share the latent culture have a sense of belonging; those who do not may feel alienated and marginal" (Grant, 1988: 109).

Current research supports this position. Women medical students, for example, perceive more gender discrimination than do male students and are substantially more likely to be sexually harassed by clinicians, faculty, and/or patients (Grant, 1988; Dickstein, 1993; Hostler and Gressard, 1993; Komaromy et al., 1993; Bickel, 1994; Moscarello et al., 1994; Schulte and Kay, 1994; Bickel and Ruffin, 1995; Bergen et al., 1996). Studies have documented "micro inequities" (Haslett and Lipman, 1997) based in gender, including gender-exclusive language, absence of parental leave policies, gender-biased illustrations in medical texts, sexist jokes in class and at school social events, male students being called doctor while women are not, women being mistaken for nurses, being called "girls," being ignored by instructors (Dickstein, 1993; Lenhart, 1993; Bickel, 1994; Kirk, 1994; Mendelsohn et al., 1994; Guyatt et al., 1997). Taken together all of these factors lead to a gendered climate in medical school that may cause women to feel less welcome, more marginal.

Similarly, racial or ethnic harassment and discrimination have been experienced by 20 per cent of medical students (Baldwin et al., 1991) and 23 per cent of residents (Baldwin et al., 1994) in the United States.[3] There is less evidence about the more subtle processes that might construct a racialized medical school climate, nevertheless, one recent ethnography of a British medical school depicts a high degree of racial segregation in extracurricular activities, suggesting the marginalization of students of colour (Sinclair, 1997). Not surprisingly, perhaps, racialized minority students tend to have higher attrition rates than white students, take longer to complete undergraduate training, and are more likely to switch specialties or drop out of residency programs (Lee, 1992; Babbott et al., 1994; Campos-Outcalt et al., 1994; McManus et al., 1996).

Class-based cultural norms that may predominate in medical training remain under-examined. In a Canadian study with 80 medical students one of the two who self-identified as working-class joked that the hardest thing for him to learn at medical school was "the wine and cheeses" (Haas and Shaffir, 1987: 23).

Recent investigations into the impact of sexual orientation in medical school suggest that homophobic attitudes are as prevalent among medical students and faculty members as in the general population (Klamen et al., 1999). Thus students who identify as gay, lesbian, or bisexual may feel more marginalized in medical school than do heterosexually identified students. National surveys found 40 per cent of general internists and 50 per cent of internal medicine residents witnessed homophobic[4] remarks by fellow physicians, nurses, other health care workers, and patients (Cook et al., 1995; vanIneveld et al., 1996). An American study found that although 67 per cent of family practice residency program directors showed attitudes supportive to gay men and lesbians, 25 per cent would rank residency applicants lower if they were known to be gay or lesbian (Oriel et al., 1996). In addition, 46 per cent of the gay/lesbian/bisexual students surveyed had experienced discrimination based on sexual orientation during medical school, and most hid or planned to hide their homosexuality during their residency application process.

Most medical schools today have an institutional commitment to equality, which has led to the reduction or eradication of overt discrimination in admissions (Cole, 1986) and to the establishment of policies and procedures to address harassment and discrimination. Even in the absence of blatant discrimination, however, an institution may have an overall climate that welcomes some participants more than others. The research presented here sought to investigate the micro-level interactional processes through which the dominant culture of an institution may be conveyed, with attendant messages of inclusion and exclusion. This study did not set out to determine the *existence* of social inequalities based on gender, "race," class, and sexual orientation; instead it explicates processes through which, in one particular educational institution, such inequalities are enacted.

Research Methods and Participants

In this study, three complementary strategies were employed: A survey of an entire third-year class (123 students) at one medical school; interviews with 25 students from that class; and interviews with 23 faculty members from the same medical school.[5] In a traditional medical curriculum the third year is a key transition point for students as they move out of the classrooms and into the hospital wards and clinics (Becker et al., 1961; Coombs, 1978; Broadhead, 1983; Haas and Shaffir, 1987; Konner, 1987). The increased interactions with staff and patients reflect the students back to themselves as "doctors" (Coombs, 1978: 227; Konner, 1987; Shapiro, 1987). Such interactions can simultaneously enforce gendered and racialized notions of who fits best with common ideas of "doctor" by refusing to reinforce some students' emerging self-conceptions as physicians (Gamble, 1990; Rucker, 1992; Dickstein, 1993; Lenhart, 1993; Bickel, 1994; Kirk, 1994; Mendelsohn et al., 1994; Blackstock, 1996).

The characteristics of students who completed the survey are indicated in Table 27.1. . . .[6]

The purposive sample of faculty members and administrators tended to be male and of European heritage—not unlike the majority of faculty in this school. The length of time working at this medical school ranged from 3 to 29 years, averaging 15 years. Five were academic faculty, teaching the basic sciences;[7] the rest were clinical faculty.[8] Ten faculty members had administrative positions.

Everyday Inequalities and Micro Inequities

The notion of everyday inequalities is useful for understanding the micro-level processes through which inequities of racism, sexism, heterosexism, and classism are experienced and perpetuated in Canadian society, where most citizens express commitment to democratic principles of justice, equality, tolerance, and fairness. Studying the contrasts between America and the Netherlands, Dutch sociologist Philomena Essed developed the concept of "everyday racism," a form of racism distinctively structured in "practices that infiltrate everyday life and become part of what is seen as 'normal' by the dominant group," even in the context of formal commitment to equality (1991: 288). . . .

In their case study of women in law, Haslett and Lipman (1997) outline instances of hostile humour, isolation, diminishing, devaluation, and discouragement that cumulatively exclude women, rendering them less confident and productive. As was the case with everyday racism, the power of these practices, which Haslett and Lipman term "micro inequities," lies in their repetition and "aggregate burden."

> Taken individually, each instance of an innuendo or hostile humor may strike one as being minor and not worth "calling someone on it"; however, the daily, cumulative burden of continuously experiencing such micro inequities is significant . . . Over time . . . micro inequities constitute a formidable barrier to performance, productivity, and advancement. (Haslett and Lipman, 1997: 51)

The individually trivial nature of such practices makes them particularly difficult to address effectively.

Table 27.1 Characteristics of the samples

Characteristic	Student survey sample (*N* = 72)	Student interviews sample (*N* = 25)	Faculty interviews sample (*N* = 23)
Gender			
Female	36 (50%)	14 (56%)	5 (22%)
Male	36 (50%)	11 (44%)	18 (78%)
Age			
Mean age	27 years	28 years	51 years
Range	24–40 years	23–40 years	36–67 years
Race/Ethnicity*			
Euro-Canadian	38 (53%)	18 (72%)	23 (100%)
Asian	15 (21%)	6 (24%)	
South Asian	6 (8%)		
Jewish	2 (3%)	1 (4%)	
Aboriginal	1 (1%)		
Not given	10 (14%)		
First Language			
English	52 (72%)	23 (92%)	21 (91%)
Not English	20 (28%)	2 (8%)	2 (9%)
Social class background**			
Upper/Upper-Middle	36 (50%)	14 (56%)	
Lower-Middle	23 (32%)	6 (24%)	
Working/Poor	11 (15%)	5 (20%)	
Other	2 (3%)		
Sexual orientation			
Heterosexual	71 (99%)	24 (96%)	13 (56%)
Homosexual	1 (1%)	1 (4%)	2 (9%)
Unknown			8 (35%)

* Includes "Canadian," British, Scottish, Irish, American, German, Scandinavian, Polish, Italian, Portuguese, Oceanic. Asian includes Chinese, Japanese, Korean, Taiwanese, Indonesian, Malaysian. South Asian includes Indian, Punjabi, Pakistani.

** Self-described

The perpetuation of structural arrangements of inequality is accomplished through "ongoing, everyday, taken-far-granted practices that are rooted in cultural habit" (O'Brien, 1998: 25). Understanding, then, demands inquiry focused on the interactional processes that perpetually alter or counter existing structural arrangements. Inquiry must focus on the ways even those of us committed to equality practice inequality in our everyday interactions. . . .

Everyday Racism

In interviews, both faculty and students generally indicated that "race" and racism really are not issues in medical school. Nonetheless, many students then went on to describe racist incidents, most of which occurred during rural practice placements or elective rotations in other schools: "People there were quite racist against Natives."

> *Mark*[9]: Last summer when we did a rural practice elective out in the community I heard a few things about East Indian students who had trouble with the more redneck kind of attitudes. Older, white people in the communities might say something offensive.

In keeping with the notion of everyday racism, overt racist incidents were not very common, yet "race" appears to affect the extent to which students feel they fit in during medical school, with 45 per cent of "minority" students indicating they "fit in" well, compared with 58 per cent of non-minority students. Racialized minority students were slightly more likely than others to agree that "race" affects how students are treated by other medical staff, and that it affects the degree of respect from patients. The day-to-day importance of "race" and culture were also highest for minority students. Furthermore, 25 per cent of students who identified as members of minority groups indicated that their racial or cultural background had a negative effect on their experiences at medical school, compared to only 4 per cent of non-minority students. Interestingly, minority students were also more likely to indicate that their race/culture had a positive impact; in contrast 84 per cent of non-minority students experienced their race as neutral. In interviews students explained that being Chinese is often an advantage in a city with a large Chinese patient population.

The most apparent form of everyday racism was racist jokes. About half (52 per cent) of the survey respondents indicated they heard "offensive jokes" in medical school; the most common category of such jokes was those concerning "race or ethnicity" (see Table 27.2).[10] For example:

> *Sean:* This guy had gone through the windshield of his car and they made some comment about, "Oh, he was DWC. And I said, what's DWC? And they said, "Driving While Chinese." And that was the first day I was there. And that's on the wards, and walking along the halls, so anybody could hear it. One of the residents said that to a doctor and the doctor laughed and said, "Oh, that was a good one. I never heard that before."

Table 27.2 Survey findings concerning offensive jokes

Question: What type of jokes do you hear in medical school that you find offensive?

Jokes about:	Frequency
Ethnic/racial groups	22
Gender	19
Particular patient types	19
Gays and lesbians	14
Height or weight	12
Religious groups	10
Cadavers	7
"Crude" topics	3
Age	2

As Nancy indicates, it can be very awkward for students to deal with racist comments when they come from attending physicians or senior residents who are in a position of power over students.

> *Nancy:* We had a Native man come in and told us he wasn't feeling well or whatever. And we went into the other room and the doctor said, "So do you think this is a dumb Indian or a smart Indian?" And I went, "What?!" . . . This is a person I'm supposed to be learning from so I can't say, "What kind of a stupid questions are you asking me here?!" I've got to be with him for another three weeks and try and get a reference letter out of him, so I can't cut him down.

Two white students suggested they heard more overt racism than did students from racialized minority groups, since they were "included in all the jokes" and were assumed to be like-minded because they are white: "I was supposed to be one of them."

Everyday Sexism

Neither male nor female students, on average, thought gender had much impact on their experiences of medical school, although the day-to-day importance of gender was greatest for women. Women also demonstrate more polarization than men; 54 per cent of women said gender is important to how they think about themselves, while a significant minority (23 per cent) said it was very unimportant. A certain ambiguity became apparent in the interviews, where most students stated that gender is really not an issue in medical school; classes are almost exactly gender balanced and everyone gets treated similarly. Having said this, however, most women and some men then went on to give examples of how gender does make a difference, ranging from quite blatant sexism and sexual harassment to a more subtle climate of gendered expectations that may make things intangibly easier for male students.

One woman was in a small clinical group with three male classmates; they were greeted every day by the attending physician with, "Good morning, gentlemen." Again, in the terms of everyday sexism, this minor, perhaps trivial incident may have a cumulative effect over time, conveying a repeated message of marginalization. Other students described incidents of outright sexual harassment. For example, when one woman was serving as a model patient for a demonstration the male clinician inappropriately fondled and commented on her buttocks in front of the whole class.

Far more subtle is the impact of an overall gendered climate, a series of gendered assumptions and expectations that can make life in medical school more comfortable and inviting for male students. One woman described "low-level slightly irritating stuff," that is "just somehow not inclusive or something, or not valuing me the way I would." For example, students confront a lingering societal assumption that doctor *equals* man. Two male students suggested this assumption facilitates rapport with patients and eases their way through the medical hierarchy.

> *Mark:* Perhaps I bond better with the students and the residents and the staff members just because I come from the same background as the other doctors do. . . . I've often felt, because I fit like a stereotyped white that patients might see me as a bit more trustworthy. A bit more what they'd like to see. Who they want to see.

This assumption that doctors are male may be reinforced by the fact that women students are less likely to be called doctor by other health care staff or by patients. Both students and faculty reported that women students and clinicians are still frequently mistaken for nurses. Fifty-seven per cent of the women surveyed were occasionally or regularly called doctor by someone other than family or friends, compared with 78 per cent of the men; 14 per cent of the women were *never* called doctor compared with 0 per cent of the men, Again, though being called "Miss" while your male peers are called "doctor" is in itself trivial, the effect can be cumulative. Perhaps consequently, almost half (6 of 14) of the women students interviewed indicated that they do not identify themselves as medical students in casual social settings outside school lest they be seen as putting on airs. None of the male students indicated this.

Constructing a professional appearance is another key element of medical socialization (Beagan, 2001), and one that is highly gendered. Both male and female survey respondents had concerns about their appearances. While male students dealt with those concerns by shaving, wearing a shirt with a collar, perhaps adding a tie, women's concerns were both more extensive and more complex. Women worried about style, accessories, body shapes, hair and make-up, about looking well-dressed without appearing too provocative, too feminine, or simply incompetent: "Is it professional enough? Competent looking? . . . I do not want to appear sexy on the job" (Survey comment, female). In the interviews, both women students and clinicians talked about dressing to earn respect; deliberately constructing an image that conveys desired messages. In contrast, the men took this for granted.

One of the most obvious areas where gender affects medical education is in students' choice of future career directions. Women were under-represented among those considering anesthesiology, surgery, and internal medicine, all highly paid specialties. Women were over-represented among those considering obstetrics and gynecology, psychiatry, family medicine, and pediatrics, some of the lowest paid fields of medicine. Some faculty members argued that unless there are active moves to keep women out of specific specialties gender is not an issue. Indeed for 89 per cent of male students, gender was *not* an important consideration when choosing their future specialty; for 43 per cent of women it *was* an important or very important factor (see Table 27.3). . . .

. . . [S]everal women students ruled out surgery because they could not see how the long hours and intense call schedule would fit with having a family. Women rated parental and marital status as far more important considerations in career choice than did male students (see Table 27.3). Virtually every woman interviewed had concerns about fitting together career and family life, which guided them away from some specialties and toward others.

> *Nancy:* I worry about balancing my family life. I worry about when I'm going to have children. How I'm going to put my children and my husband into a full-time career, with him having a full-time career. I don't want to have children who know their nanny better than they know

Table 27.3 Gender-related concerns in specialty considerations

Question: How important are the following factors to you in choosing your future specialty? (1 = Not important, 5 = Very important)

	1	2	3	4	5
Gender					
Female %	26	14	17	31	12
Male %	67	22	8	3	0
$\lambda = 0.26$					
Parental status					
Female %	9	3	11	23	54
Male %	19	14	14	31	22
$\lambda = 0.17$					
Marital or relationship status					
Female %	9	3	6	37	46
Male %	19	6	17	36	22
$\lambda = 0.14$					

> me. I'm in that position that I think a lot of women are in, of wanting to be able to do it all and feeling inadequate when you can't. Wanting to be a full-time mom and have a nice house and be able to keep it up and do the grocery shopping and do the laundry and still work full-time and be there for all your patients and also be a good wife to your husband. And I know something's got to give and I'm not sure where it's going to be. I hope it's not my children.

While the women students were almost universally concerned with how a career would fit with expected family roles, virtually none of the men interviewed had thought about this.

Again, as was the case with everyday racism, the point is not that women face unusually high levels of sexism in medical school. Rather, this research illustrates the subtle processes of everyday sexism, interactional processes that construct the role of medical student or physician as somewhat more suited to a man than a woman. Women have to work to construct a professional appearance, to look feminine yet competent, to earn respect.

Women students choose career paths that avoid overly masculinized environments, opting for lower paid specialties that will allow them to be good wives and mothers without sacrificing their careers. When attending physicians routinely call women medical students "Miss" while addressing their male peers as "doctor," and when patients routinely call women students "nurse," those trivial incidents occur *on top* of a pattern of micro inequities (Haslett and Lipman, 1997), as part of daily processes of gendering medicine.

Everyday Heterosexism

The experience of being identifiably gay or lesbian in this medical school seemed to depend a great deal on the dominant tone of each class. Being openly gay might lead to isolation one year, while the next entering class might be very supportive of an openly gay classmate. The two clinicians interviewed who identified as gay said their sexual orientation had been a source of difficulty and marginalization for them in medical school. They had to decide how "out" to be, and how much to suppress that part of their identity. They both see gay and lesbian students today facing similar struggles.

The one gay student who responded to the survey noted that his sexual orientation is a source of great stress. One aspect of that stress is homophobia expressed by other medical personnel. Students and physicians indicated that jokes about gays and lesbians were common.

While there are some sanctions for staff who make harassing comments, homophobic comments from patients leave students with little recourse. One clinician indicated that students just have to learn to handle it.

> *Dr F.:* As a physician you will be called the "F-word" [fag]. You will be told that you're going to get punched if you don't leave. And if you're gay or of different orientation, they might tell you, "Hey, you take it in the ass and I'm not gonna talk to you." It will happen. And I think it's part of [students'] education—how to deal with it.

As was the case with racist jokes and comments, students are placed in a particularly awkward position when homophobic jokes or slurs come from their patients.

Students may also face some degree of homophobia from their classmates.[11] Two students identified their heterosexuality as an advantage, commenting that it would be difficult to be gay or lesbian in their class.

> *Robin:* I see huge homophobia. I'm not gay, but out of a hundred and twenty people, statistically there's gonna be a few gay or lesbian people in my class. And no one will admit to it. . . . They obviously don't feel comfortable saying that. . . . One of my colleagues in first year had someone scribble "fag" on his nametag on his desk. . . . I think people try to avoid standing out in any way and I guess one way to stand out is to be gay.

It only takes a few instances such as that described by Robin to have an effect. Even if just a few students are vocally homophobic, that may be sufficient to cause gay and lesbian students in the class to feel unsafe.

Students and faculty who identified as gay described leading highly segregated lives during medical school, keeping their school lives separate from their lives in gay and lesbian communities. Several faculty members argued that this segregation and "closeting" is a necessary survival strategy, as being out can be costly in terms of desired jobs. One gay clinician described a student coming out gradually by his third year of medical school, "then slipping back in during fourth year, because he was afraid—and, I hate to say it . . . my feeling is that he's probably right. If he were gay and out he probably wouldn't get into a surgical residency" (c.f. Oriel et al., 1996). Even if the risks of being out are more perceived than real, one clinician pointed out that "you're giving up an awful lot if you're wrong, if you feel that, 'Gee they would accept me,' and find out they won't." Finally, one faculty member suggested sexual orientation may even influence residency choices, as he sees gay and lesbian students trying to identify which fields might be safest for them to be out (c.f., Risdon, Cook, and Willms, 2000). Again, this process, like the process of women students choosing not to enter surgery, is one of self-elimination. The realm of the possible becomes defined through cultural habit, excluding some options from consideration.

> *Jason:* What I've experienced is a lot of—not overt homophobia, well, a *little* overt homophobia, especially by a vocal sect in the class. . . . Among the teaching faculty there's some homophobia, just underneath the surface. They never come out and say it, they're always politically correct, but you know it's there. Fellow students—I guess that's one of the reasons why I also feel more distant from a lot of people in the class. . . . If somebody talks about what they did on the weekend, if I did party I'm not going to tell them that I went to one of the gay bars.

Again, what is described here is not an unusually high degree of homophobia or heterosexism, nor even a set of hostile practices *intended* to exclude, discriminate, or harm. It is, rather, the experience of not quite fitting in with the dominant culture that surrounds you, of being marginalized. Everyday heterosexism, like everyday racism and sexism, is not life-threatening—although gay and lesbian students never know when it might be accompanied by a more virulent homophobia. From the simple assumption that everyone around you is heterosexual, to teasing about (hetero)sex at school social gatherings, to laughing at or making homophobic jokes, to not challenging homophobic remarks, to declining residency applications from openly gay students (Oriel et al., 1996), again the micro inequities of everyday heterosexism consist of the repetition of numerous small practices.

Everyday Classism

In Canada, the extremes of poverty and wealth are mitigated by our redistributive social welfare system. Widely accessible student loans mean university education—including medical education—and subsequent upward mobility are available to anyone willing to incur that level of debt. But social class is not just about money. Class also operates on the more subtle level of cultural capital and social capital: knowing the right people, being able to make the right sort of small talk, having the right hobbies and playing the right sports, knowing the right fork to use, and having the right clothes, accent, and demeanour.

Students from working class or impoverished families also described a significant struggle to construct the professional appearance expected in medicine. The "right look" felt wrong for them. One woman noted that the very first time she felt she actually belonged in medical school was during a third-year elective in a clinic for low-income patients: "I had the thrill of my lifetime at the Clinic. I could just dress in what's in my closet and not feel bad about it. And I could talk my natural way. And I *totally* fit in over there!"

There was considerable agreement among students and faculty that students from upper- or upper-middle-class backgrounds, especially the children of doctors, find it easiest to fit in at medical school and may adopt a student physician identity more readily. A third (31 per cent) of the students surveyed agreed that, "students who come from upper-class backgrounds find it easier to fit in during medical training"—a belief held most strongly by students from working-class and impoverished family backgrounds. Poor and working-class students were more likely to believe their class background had a negative impact during medical school. One student wrote simply: "I cannot relate to many of my classmates who come from very wealthy, Anglo-Saxon backgrounds" (Survey comment).

Two clinicians who came from working-class families said they never fit in during medical school and they continue to feel marginalized as physicians.

> *Dr P.:* [One] reason that I had a very difficult time [in medical school] is that I come from a working-class family, the only person in my extended family to finish high-school, to go to university. . . . That puts me in a very difference spot than the upper-middle-class white male, whose father was a doctor, who like the medical school, who was part of the "in group" at the school and who is now part of the "in group" as faculty.

One clinician was moved to tears during our interview when she recognized that the extreme isolation she felt as a working-class medical student 30 years ago has never really lessened.

Conclusions

This research in a single Canadian medical school illustrates the complexity of everyday racism, classism, sexism, and heterosexism. Well beyond blatant forms of discrimination (practices already targeted by formal anti-discrimination policies and procedures) more covert and more subtle forms of marginalization maintain and reproduce an institutional climate that is more welcoming to some participants than others. Micro-level everyday practices of inclusion and exclusion cumulatively convey messages about who does and who does not truly belong. The interactional processes of everyday inequalities maintain hierarchies even within this group of relatively elite students and faculty.

As Jodi O'Brien (1998) suggests, the practices of everyday inequalities are often mindless, unknowing, and habitual. The power of these micro inequities is that they are seen as normal, natural, or acceptable. The majority of the participants in this research would say that gender, "race," sexual orientation, and class are not issues in their medical school. In a society imbued with belief in meritocracy, these students and faculty have made it very near the top. They have a vested interest in denying categorically based injustices in favour of individual merit and equal opportunity. Yet the fact that the micro inequities illustrated here are at odds with the equality of opportunity expressly endorsed by the institution does not make them less damaging for marginalized and alienated students.

In contrast it suggests that ensuring equality of opportunity is not enough. Simply getting in to a school, an occupation, or a profession in which members of your social group have historically been under-represented, does not ensure that your experience there will be equitable. There may still be significant barriers to full participation. In his examination of a Canadian aboriginal teacher education program, Rick Hesch (1994: 201) argues that although students construct the program to meet their own needs as best they can, they do so in the face of "fundamentally punishing conditions" that serve to limit their achievements. Those punishing conditions arise in the intersection of institutional expectations about students' roles with socio-cultural expectations about their private lives; there is a privileging of particular class-based and Eurocentric forms of knowledge that implicitly marginalizes them or pushes them toward assimilation. Similarly, although medical education provides an avenue for members of subordinated social groups to achieve upward mobility, in doing so they confront an institution that privileges particular cultural habits and knowledge forms. It simultaneously reproduces the inclusions and exclusions of racism, sexism, heterosexism, and classism. That institutional climate is maintained through daily subtle practices whose effects taken individually may be considered trivial, but taken cumulatively convey a message about who does and who does not belong. What remains to be seen in further research is what impact—if any—these micro inequities and everyday inequalities and their messages of marginality have on medical practitioners in their work lives.

Notes

1. I would like to thank Bethan Lloyd for comments on earlier versions of this work, and the anonymous CJS reviewers for their detailed reading and helpful comments. The research was supported by doctoral fellowships from the Social Sciences and Humanities Research Council of Canada, and the Izaak Killam Memorial Foundation.
2. Yet even very recent research has failed to problematize the impact of social differences among students, perpetuating the image of a generic medical student (e.g., Sinclair, 1997).
3. This research is bolstered by a growing body of personal accounts about racism in medical school (Gamble, 1990; Rucker, 1992; Blackstock, 1996). Research on the experiences of racialized minority students in Canada is virtually non-existent.
4. By "homophobia" I mean fear and hatred of or, more mildly, hostility and condemnation directed toward people known or believed to be gay, lesbian, or bisexual. By "heterosexism" I mean the overwhelming assumption that the world is and must be heterosexual, and the systemic display of power and privilege that establish heterosexuality as the irrefutable norm—by extension establishing homosexuality as deviance. Heterosexism centres on oblivion about/denial of the very existence of gays and lesbians. Homophobia is a more active form of intolerance and hostility.
5. The medical school where the research was conducted is not identified. This was an agreement made with the administration of the school in order to gain access to the research site. That decontextualizes the research and leaves the degree of generalizability to other medical schools an empirical question. The school followed a traditional undergraduate curriculum and was located in a large Canadian city with a racially and ethnically diverse population.
6. Subjective assessment of class photos shows that since the early 1980s about 30 per cent of each class at this school would be considered "visible minority" students.
7. They represented anatomy, biochemistry, physiology, and pharmacology.
8. Their clinical areas included renal, pulmonary, pediatrics and pediatric oncology, medical genetics, family practice, surgery, neurology, ethics, internal medicine, infectious disease, endocrinology, anesthesia, and psychiatry.
9. All names used are pseudonyms.
10. Unfortunately, we cannot know from the data whether they had heard one such joke or heard them daily.
11. Again, whether the level of homophobia in medical school is higher or lower than in the rest of the society is not the point. The point is simply that students who identify as, or are identified as, gay or lesbian have distinctive experiences in medical school in part because they have to deal with homophobia from patients, staff, faculty, and classmates. It makes their experience of school different from that of students identified as heterosexual.

References

Association of Canadian Medical Colleges. 1998. *Canadian Medical Education Statistics* 20.

Baldwin, D.C., Jr, S.R. Daugherty, and B.D. Rowley. 1994. "Emotional Impact of Medical School and Residency," *Academic Medicine* 69 Supplement: S19–21.

Baldwin, D.C., S.R. Daugherty, and E.J. Eckenfels. 1991. "Student Perceptions of Mistreatment and Harassment during Medical School: A Survey in 10 United States Schools," *Western Journal of Medicine* 155: 140–5.

Beagan, B.L. 2001. "'Even If I Don't Know What I'm Doing I Can Make It Look Like I Know What I'm Doing': Becoming a Doctor in the 1990s," *Canadian Review of Sociology and Anthropology* 39(3): 275–92.

Becker, H.S., B. Geer, A.L. Strauss, and E.C. Hughes. 1961. *Boys in White: Student Culture in Medical School*. Chicago: University of Chicago Press.

Benokraitis, N.E., ed. 1997a. *Subtle Sexism: Current Practice and Prospects for Change*. Thousand Oaks, CA: Sage.

———. 1997b. "Sex Discrimination in the 21st Century," in N.V. Benokraitis, ed., *Subtle Sexism: Current Practice and Prospects for Change*, pp. 5–33. Thousand Oaks, CA: Sage.

Bergen, M.R., C.M. Guarino, and C.D. Jacobs. 1996. "A Climate Survey for Medical Students," *Evaluation and the Health Professions* 19: 30–47.

Bickel, J. 1994. "Special Needs and Affinities of Women Medical Students," in E.S. More and M.A. Milligan, eds., *The Empathetic Practitioner: Empathy, Gender and Medicine*, pp. 237–49. New Brunswick, NJ: Rutgers Press.

Bickel, J. and A. Ruffin. 1995. "Gender-Associated Differences in Matriculating and Graduating Medical Students," *Academic Medicine* 70: 552–9.

Bickel, J., and P.R. Kopriva. 1993. "A Statistical Perspective on Gender in Medicine," *Journal of the American Medical Women's Association* 48: 141–4.

Blackstock, D.G. 1996. "A Black Woman in Medicine," in D. Wear, ed., *Women in Medical Education: An Anthology of Experience*, pp. 75–80. New York, SUNY Press.

Broadhead, R. 1983. *The Private Lives and Professional Identities of Medical Students*. New Brunswick, NJ: Transaction.

Cassel, J. 1996. "The Woman in the Surgeon's Body: Understanding Difference," *American Anthropologist* 98: 41–53.

Cole, S. 1986. "Sex Discrimination and Admission to Medical School, 1929–1984," *American Journal of Sociology* 92: 549–67.

Cook, D.I., L.E. Griffith, M. Cohen, G.H., Guyatt, and B. O'Brien. 1995. "Discrimination and Abuse Experienced by General Internists in Canada," *Journal of General Internal Medicine* 10: 565–72.

Coombs, R.H. 1978. *Mastering Medicine*. New York: Free Press.

Dickstein, L.J. 1993. "Gender Bias in Medical Education: Twenty Vignettes and Recommended Responses," *Journal of the American Medical Women's Association* 48: 152–62.

Druzin, P., I. Shrier, M. Yacowar, and M. Rossognol. 1998. "Discrimination against Gay, Lesbian and Bisexual Family Physicians by Patients," *Canadian Medical Association Journal* 158: 593–7.

Essed, P. 1991. *Understanding Everyday Racism: An Interdisciplinary Theory*. New York: Sage.

Foster, H.W. 1996. "Reaching Parity for Minority Medical Residents: A Possibility or a Pipe Dream?," *Journal of the National Medical Association* 88: 17–21.

Frehill. L.M. 1997. "Subtle Sexism in Engineering," in N.V. Benokraitis, ed., *Subtle Sexism: Current Practice and Prospects for Change*, pp. 117–35. Thousand Oaks, CA: Sage.

Gamble, V.N. 1990. "On Becoming a Physician: A Dream Not Deferred," in E.C. White, ed., *The Black Women's Health Book: Speaking for Ourselves*, pp. 52–64. Seattle, WA: Seal Press.

Grant, L. 1988. "The Gender Climate of Medical School: Perspectives of Women and Men Students," *Journal of the American Medical Women's Association* 43: 109–19.

Gray, J.D., and J. Reudy. 1998. "Undergraduate and Postgraduate Medical Education in Canada," *Canadian Medical Association Journal* 58: 1047–50.

Guyatt, G.H., D.J. Cook, L. Griffith, S.D. Walter, C. Risdon, and J. Liukus. 1997. "Attitudes toward the Use of Gender-Inclusive Language Among Residency Trainees," *Canadian Medical Association Journal* 156: 1289–93.

Haas, J., and W. Shaffir. 1987. *Becoming Doctors: The Adoption of a Cloak of Competence*. Greenwich, CT: JAI Press.

Haslett, B.B., and S. Lipman. 1997. "Micro Inequities: Up Close and Personal," in N.V. Benokraitis, ed., *Subtle Sexism: Current Practice and Prospects for Change*, pp. 34–53. Thousand Oaks, CA: Sage.

Hesch, R. 1994. "Cultural Production and Cultural Reproduction in Aboriginal Preservice Teacher Education," in L. Erwin and D. MacLennan, eds., *Sociology of Education in Canada: Critical Perspectives on Theory, Research and Practice*, pp. 200–19. Mississauga: Copp Clark Longman.

Hostler, S.L., and R.R.P. Gressard. 1993. "Perceptions of the Gender Fairness of the Medical Education Environment," *Journal of the American Medical Women's Association* 48: 51–4.

Jonas, H.S., S.A. Etzel, and B. Barzansky. 1992. "Educational Programs in US Medical Schools," *Journal of the American Medical Association* 268: 1083–90.

Kirk, J. 1994. "A Feminist Analysis of Women in Medical Schools," in B.S. Bolaria and H.D. Dickenson, eds., *Health, Illness, and Health Care in Canada,* 2nd edn, pp. 158–82. Toronto: Harcourt Brace.

Klamen, D.L, L.S. Grossman, and D.R. Kopacz. 1999. "Medical Student Homophobia," *Journal of Homosexuality* 37: 53–63.

Komaromy, M., A.B. Bindman, R.J. Haber, and M.A. Sande. 1993. "Sexual Harassment in Medical Training," *The New England Journal of Medicine* 328: 322–6.

Konner, M. 1987. *Becoming a Doctor: A Journey of Initiation in Medical School*. New York: Viking.

Lenhart, S. 1993. "Gender Discrimination: A Health and Career Development Problem for Women Physicians," *Journal of the American Medical Women's Association* 4, 8: 155–9.

Mendelsohn, K.D., L.Z. Neiman, K. Isaacs, S. Lee, and S.P. Levison. 1994. "Sex and Gender Bias in Anatomy and Physical Diagnosis Text Illustrations," *Journal of the American Medical Association* 272: 1267–70.

Moscarello, R., K.J. Margittai, and M. Rissi. 1994. "Differences in Abuse Reported by Female and Male Canadian Medical Students," *Canadian Medical Association Journal* 150: 357–63.

O'Brien, J. 1998. "Introduction: Differences and Inequities," in J. O'Brien and J.A. Howard, eds., *Everyday Inequalities: Critical Inquiries*, pp. 1–39. Malden, MA: Blackwell.

Oriel, K.A., D.J. Madlon-Kay, D. Govaker, and D.J. Mersey. 1996. "Gay and Lesbian Physicians in Training: Family Practice Program Directors' Attitudes and Students' Perceptions of Bias," *Family Medicine* 28: 720–5.

Risdon, C., D. Cook, and D. Willms. 2000. "Gay and Lesbian Physicians in Training: A Qualitative Study," *Canadian Medical Association Journal* 162: 331–4.

Rose, L. 1994. "Homophobia among Doctors," *British Medical Journal* 308: 586–7.

Rucker, C.S. 1992. "Wrestling with Ignorance," *Journal of the American Medical Association* 267: 2392.

Schulte, H.M., and J. Kay. 1994. "Medical Students' Perceptions of Patient-Initiated Sexual Behavior," *Academic Medicine* 69: 842–6.

Shapiro, M. 1987. *Getting Doctored: Critical Reflections on Becoming a Physician*. Toronto, ON: Between the Lines.

Sinclair, S. 1997. *Making Doctors: An Institutional Apprenticeship*. New York: Berg.

vanIneveld, C.H., D.J. Cook, S.L. Kane, and D. King. 1996. "Discrimination and Abuse in Internal Medicine Residency," *Journal of General Internal Medicine* 11: 401–5.

Wallick, M.M., K.M. Cambre, and M.H. Townsend. 1992. "How the Topic of Homosexuality Is Taught at US Medical Schools," *Academic Medicine* 67: 601–3.

PART VIII
The Gendered Workplace

Perhaps the most drastic social change in industrial countries in the twentieth century was the entry of women into the workplace. The nineteenth-century ideology of "separate spheres"—the breadwinner husband and the homemaker wife—has slowly and steadily evaporated. While only 20 per cent of women, and only 4 per cent of married women, worked outside the home in 1900, more than 75 per cent did so by 1995, including 60 per cent of married women. The increase in employment amongst women with children has been even more dramatic—in 1976 only 31 per cent of women with children under six years old worked outside the home, while in 2012, 68 per cent did (Statistics Canada, 2012). Despite the collapse of the doctrine of separate spheres—work and home—the workplace remains a dramatically divided world where women and men rarely do the same jobs in the same place for the same pay. Occupational sex segregation, persistent sex discrimination, and wage disparities are all significant problems faced by working women. These disparities are least evident at the beginning of men's and women's working lives, widening slowly as time goes by and as other life events, particularly childbearing, exert different pressures on women and on men. This section, thus, should be read in conjunction with the section on the gendered family in order to appreciate the double impact of work life and family life in shaping differences and inequalities. Men and women are distributed non-randomly through the workforce, with different genders clustered in different sectors and different types of jobs. This clustering leads to certain jobs and sectors acquiring gendered reputations as "men's work" or "women's work."

In the last four decades women have made significant inroads into career areas that were formerly bastions of masculinity, such as medicine or law. Men, however, have been much less likely to "desegregate" women-dominated occupations such as nursery-school teaching or cosmetology. For those men who do enter women-dominated fields, negotiating the pitfalls of being the "wrong" sex for the job means finding one's professional way through a minefield of gender and sexuality, as Joan Evans discusses. The male nurses in Evans's work judge themselves, and are judged by others, by their adherence to or deviation from a feminized norm of caring.

At the other end of the spectrum, the firefighters interviewed by Shelley Pacholok inhabit an occupational world characterized by the hallmarks of stereotypical masculinity—risk, danger, strength, and protecting others. However, as Pacholok demonstrates, masculinity is not embedded in the work itself, but is constructed through discourse and representations as the different groups of firefighters talk about their work and rank themselves against their peers.

Workplace experiences are marked by race and class (among other social categories), which combine with gender to produce distinctive forms of masculinity and femininity.

Paid work provides both identity and subsistence to many, if not most, Canadians. However, for people with disabilities, employment can be a fraught issue. Both the work itself and the culture of the workplace can create barriers for those with physical impairments. Susan Lee investigates the experiences of women with disabilities, arguing that *under*-employment, and not just unemployment, can be hazardous to their financial, physical, and psychological health.

For most people, "work" and "home" are separate, and the challenges in one realm do not dominate life in the other. However, for some workers, their home *is* their workplace. Bernadette Stiell and Kim England examine the lives of live-in domestic workers, for whom the wall dividing home from work has collapsed. Although these female workers live in close quarters with their same-gender employers, hierarchies based on class and racial categories overshadow their physical proximity and their shared gender identity.

References

Statistics Canada. 2012. Employment Rates in Canada. www4.hrsdc.gc.ca/.3ndic.1t.4r@-eng.jsp?iid=13

Questions for Critical Thought

1. Are you currently training for a particular type of work, or do you have a particular career in mind? Do you expect that your gender will influence your success in this career?

2. If you work with people of different genders, whether in a part-time or full-time job, how do you think gender affects workplace experiences? If your workplace is dominated by one gender, why is that the case?
3. Why do you think women still make less money in their paid jobs than men? Is it because of individual choices or systematic barriers? Or both? Or neither?
4. The men nurses that Evans studied were clearly considered unusual for working in a field dominated by women. Are there any kinds of work that you think would be difficult for you, or that you would not want to take, because of your gender?
5. What workplaces have you encountered as a worker, customer, or visitor that are dominated by one sex or the other? What workplaces have you encountered that are more equally divided between the sexes?
6. How would you react if you encountered a man doing a "feminized" job such as nursing? Would you react differently if you encountered a woman doing a "masculinized" job such as firefighting?
7. Many of the readings in this chapter emphasize relations and interactions amongst co-workers in the workplace, whether it is a home (Stiell and England) or a hospital (Evans) or a fire department (Pacholok). How important are these relations or interactions to your own job satisfaction? How do ideas about gender get reinforced or resisted through these connections between co-workers?
8. Disability has been described as an identity that we will all assume at some point in our lives (unless we die young and healthy). How would your work life or job prospects be changed if you became disabled?
9. Paid work is important because it provides income, but the studies here suggest that paid work also contributes to individuals' sense of identity and selfhood. Do you think you are what you do for money? What are the impacts on identity and selfhood of not working for pay?
10. As Stiell and England suggest, the division between "work" and "home" is not always straightforward. How do you distinguish between these two spheres? In what ways is home like work or work like home?

Chapter 28

Overview

Do nurses treat their patients as sexual objects? This question seems absurd, yet the men nurses in Joan Evans's study have to negotiate their way around the suspicion that their interactions with patients are sexualized, rather than strictly professional. The fact that they are men doing work that has historically been associated with women means that they are vulnerable to biases against men who undertake caregiving work, deviating from hegemonic practices of masculinity. The nurses in this study believe that they are as capable of caregiving as any woman, even if their styles of caregiving are different, inflected by their masculine socialization.

Despite their dedication to their work, these men nurses have to develop ways to reassure patients of their professionalism and competence, especially when it comes to "high-touch" tasks such as assisting with labour and delivery or bathing patients. The nurses developed a repertoire of gendered strategies, such as engaging in "buddy-buddy" humour with male patients or trading off tasks with female nurses to avoid close physical proximity with female patients.

Gender biases intertwine with stereotypes about sexuality for these nurses, who report concerns that patients might think they are gay, having chosen a profession more commonly associated with women. The dilemmas of the male nurse thus illustrate the combined impacts of homophobia and sexism.

Cautious Caregivers: Gender Stereotypes and the Sexualization of Men Nurses' Touch

Joan A. Evans

Introduction

Caring for and about others is historically associated with women and nursing, and more than any other quality it captures the process and goal of nurses' work (MacDougall, 1997). Despite this association, men are now entering the profession in record numbers (Halloran and Welton, 1994; Zurlinden 1998) and challenging the stereotype that men are inappropriate in the caregiver role or incapable of providing compassionate and sensitive care. The nursing literature suggests that the desire to be of help and care for others is a major reason men chose nursing as a career (Taylor et al., 1983; Skevington and Dawkes, 1988; Galbraith, 1991; Cyr, 1992; Kelly et al., 1996; MacDougall, 1997). Once in the profession, however, prevailing gender stereotypes of men as sexual aggressors and men nurses as gay, negatively influence the ability of men nurses to develop comfortable and trusting relationships with their patients (Mathieson, 1991; Lodge et al., 1997). The sexualization of men nurses' touch provides insight into how gender stereotypes create discomfort and suspicion on the part of patients. This, in turn, impacts on men nurses' perceptions of their own safety while performing intimate and caregiving tasks. This situation ultimately impacts on the ability of men nurses to perform the very work they came into nursing to do.

The Study

Aim

The overall aim of this research was to explore the experience of men nurses and the gendered and sexed relations that structure different experiences for women and men in the same profession. The definition of masculinity used in this study is based on Connell's (1987) sociology of masculinity work. Meanings of masculinity are demonstrated through practices that capture the performative nature of gender. Connell's definition moves us away from the essentialist notion that a relatively stable masculine essence exists that defines men and differentiates them from a feminine essence that defines women (Petersen, 1998).

When theorizing about men and masculinity, we now talk of masculinities, rather than masculinity (Connell, 1987, 1995; Hearn and Morgan, 1990) because masculinity is not uniform. This concept is reflected in the notion of hegemony and the dominance in society of certain forms and practices of masculinity. Men nurses, by virtue of their participation in "women's work," may not measure up to the hegemonic standard as evidenced by the stigma of homosexuality that surrounds them.

Method

Participants

Eight men Registered Nurses practising in the province of Nova Scotia, Canada, were selected to participate in this research using a convenience sampling technique. Because men are a highly visible minority in nursing, demographic data have been purposefully kept vague to protect the identities of the participants. Their ages ranged from late-twenties to mid-fifties, and years of nursing practice ranged from 7 to 32 years. Areas of nursing practice included community health nursing, mental health nursing, medical-surgical, and general duty nursing. Three participants were in a leadership role; two had a baccalaureate degree. Six participants were married, and two lived with a partner. One participant was an "out" gay man. Data were collected in 1998 in two rounds of semi-structured interviews.

Findings

The theme of men nurses as cautious caregivers emerged as one of four themes that characterized the experience of participants. The findings presented offer insight into the experience of men in nursing, but are not intended to be generalizable.

Affirmation of Caring

The participants in this research affirmed the importance of caring and traits such as compassion, empathy, and honesty as those that gave meaning to their lives as nurses. They generally also supported the perception that men and women nurses' caring styles were not the same. As one participant noted, "We have our ways of getting it across without putting that female bent or lean on it." Participants did not agree, however, on the ways in which women's and men's expressions of caring differed and they expressed conflicting opinions about whether men nurses were more task-orientated, more gentle, or more caring. One participant characterized the difference between women and men nurses by describing women's caring as "warm fuzzies" and more "touchy feelie." These were not necessarily negative descriptors; however, most participants commented that men nurses generally used touch less than their women colleagues.

For most participants, humour and camaraderie were identified as important expressions of their caring practice. Humour in particular, added warmth and helped patients relax and feel more comfortable with them as men. Despite an acknowledgment that humour needed to be patient-specific, its character and purpose was different when it was used with men patients and in the presence of men only. In such instances, humour was described as important in relieving male anxiety. It was also a comfortable approach to men patients and a way to be more of a friend or "buddy" to them. Men patients in turn joked with men nurses and enjoyed the freedom of sharing things with another man that a woman might find inappropriate or offensive. The masculine nature of such humour is evidenced by its "male only" character as "when a female staff would come in, we wouldn't continue on with it."

The Problematic Nature of Men Nurses' Touch

Touch was one expression of caring that all participants identified as important, if not central, to their practice as nurses. Touch was also acknowledged, however, to be a practice that sometimes did not come naturally to them as men. One participant described his hands as "rough hands" before he became a nurse. Another spoke of the newness of touching people "because that wasn't part of my existence to that point." Despite the newness of some caring expressions, touching and comforting others was acknowledged to be rewarding for participants and patients.

Whether the purpose of touch is to perform a procedure or provide comfort, an overriding theme is that for men nurses touching patients, particularly women patients, is potentially dangerous. Participants voiced concern that women patients might be uncomfortable and/or misinterpret their touch—a situation that in turn might lead to accusations of inappropriate behaviour or sexual molestation. The fear of misunderstandings and accusations related to touching patients resulted in participants being cautious and vigilant: "I have to be careful what I'm doing . . . because of the possibility of somebody saying that I did something wrong, or rape, or I touched her wrong—that's always there." Another participant commented that: "You are very vulnerable, particularly if you're alone—and even in a ward situation. You have to be very careful that you assess the situation and know that this might be an inappropriate place to touch."

The perception that men nurses are unable to defend themselves against patient accusations of inappropriate behaviour compounded participants' sense of themselves as vulnerable caregivers. As pointed out by one participant, "It's my word against theirs." Another participant who acknowledged the difficulty of defending himself commented that there were situations where he deemed it was too unsafe to touch.

Assessing When It Is Safe to Touch

Knowing when it is safe to touch and what the touch should consist of is based on a careful assessment of each patient situation. When the patient was a man, decisions regarding touch were guided by an accepted masculine norm, or what one participant referred to as a "code" of understanding. This code is illustrated by the comment, "Large men don't wash a healthy man's back–code."

How far participants could go before violating the "code" or crossing the line was dependent on the illness acuity of the male patient. As one noted, "If you are sick, you don't mind a guy being there, you don't care who is doing anything." It was also influenced by the age of the patient as participants generally described feeling more comfortable with older men who were less "macho" and more receptive to expressions of compassion. They were less comfortable touching young people, particularly teens, who they perceived were more preoccupied with the possibility that a man nurse might be gay.

Participants commented that despite it being acceptable for women nurses to touch men and women patients, it was not as acceptable for men nurses to do the same. This aura of unacceptability was noted to impact not only on patients' perceptions of men nurses' touch, but also women nurses' perceptions. One participant commented that a woman colleague reported him to a supervisor when he reassured a distraught, partially dressed woman patient by putting his hand on her shoulder. Another was accused of molesting a newborn boy by the father who discovered him changing the baby's diaper. Incidents such as these left a lasting impression and reminded participants that touching patients was potentially dangerous work.

Strategizing to Protect Oneself from Accusations

As a result of the fear of being wrongfully accused of inappropriate touch, participants described six strategies they used to reduce this risk.

Strategy no. 1: Taking the time to build trust before touching. This was particularly important when interacting with women patients.

Strategy no. 2: Maintaining a degree of formality by shaking the hand of a patient. This set the tone of the interaction and provided an opportunity to assess patient comfort.

Strategy no. 3: Projecting the traditional image of a nurse to legitimize the role of men as nurses. This included wearing a white uniform.

Strategy no. 4: Working in teams with women colleagues in situations deemed to be unsafe. Such situations included checking female patients on night shifts, entering a room with teenage girls, or performing a procedure on a female that required intimate touching.

Strategy no. 5: Delegating tasks that required intimate touching of women patients. Participants traded off tasks with women nurses to ensure patient comfort and their own safety.

Strategy no. 6: Modifying procedural techniques to minimize patient exposure and the need for intimate touching. One participant commented that he might try to convince a female patient that the best intramuscular injection site was the thigh, "not the butt."

Discussion

Going against the Grain: Men Caregivers

Despite research that suggests men choose careers in nursing to help others (Taylor et al., 1983; Skevington and Dawkes, 1988; Cyr, 1992; Kelly et al., 1996; MacDougall, 1997), men nurses tend to gravitate to nursing specialties that require less intimate patient touching (Williams, 1989, 1995; Kauppinen-Toropainen and Lammi, 1993). The participants in this study support this tendency, and only two currently worked at the bedside in a role that required intimate caregiving. The remaining six, despite having worked at the bedside, were now in positions that required less touching and more psychological patient care. In some of these positions, however, participants continued to express vulnerability. This was especially so for those in psychiatry: "Touch takes on a whole new meaning that it didn't have in medicine or in med-surg. . . . It's never straight forward here. If I have someone who I know has a full-blown personality disorder, I won't even be caught in the same room alone with them."

In order to avoid uncomfortable situations, men nurses distance themselves from traditional nursing roles and the caring ideology of nursing (Egeland and Brown, 1989; Kauppinen-Toropainen and Lammi, 1993). They are also tracked into elite specialty and leadership positions considered more congruent with prevailing notions of masculinity (Williams, 1995; Evans, 1997). The result is that power and prestige tend to be associated with small numbers of men in the profession (Porter, 1992; Ryan and Porter, 1993; Villeneuve, 1994). At the heart of this situation are gender stereotypes and the belief that men are inappropriate in caregiver roles.

Feminization of Caring

Participant accounts draw attention to differences between societal and nursing expectations of men in relation to expressions of caring. They spoke of the newness of touching with caring hands and learning to feel comfortable touching others. The need to learn to care and/or develop comfort with expressions of caring previously not practised is supported in the nursing literature. In a study of 20 men nursing students in a baccalaureate nursing program, Paterson et al. (1996) found that men nursing students feared they would never be able to touch clients or openly display emotions because they had learned all their lives that such behaviours were effeminate and emasculating (32). Similarly, Streubert (1994) reported that men nursing students were confronted with the task of having to learn caring skills that were unique to them. They consequently struggled with the need to consciously divest themselves of their macho image as they learned to express caring in sensitive and demonstrative ways that women educators and nurses expected (Paterson et al., 1996).

Research conducted by Okrainec (1994) further highlights the notion that men and women judge the caring practices of men against a feminine norm. Okrainec surveyed 117 men and 121 women nursing students in the province of Alberta, Canada, and reported that 25 per cent of both men and women felt that women were superior in caring; 20 per cent of men and 25 per cent of women rated women superior to men in terms of empathy (104); and 50 per cent of men and 66 per cent of women rated women superior to men in ability to express feelings (103). Differences in perceptions between women and men students are noteworthy, given Okrainec's comment that most men and women nursing students thought that a caring attitude was equal in both sexes.

In the absence of an acknowledgment that expressions of caring include a wide range of possible behaviours that reflect the personalities of individual nurses and specifics of each client situation, theorizing about caring will be likely to continue to be based on stereotypical notions of masculine and feminine behaviours. Even more problematic, men nurses' expressions of caring will continue to be conceptualized as unique or special because they either fall outside the masculine stereotype, or conversely, within the feminine one. The implication of such stereotyping is that it perpetuates an artificial separation of the masculine and feminine and polarizes masculinity and femininity.

Maintaining Masculinity

For men in patriarchal culture, perpetuating the polarization of masculinity and femininity is an important practice of masculinity, as the maintenance of masculinity is predicated on the separation of all that is male and masculine from all that is female (Williams, 1989). Williams (1989) and Kauppinen-Toropainen and Lammi (1993) suggest that, for men nurses, this separation is accomplished by emphasizing different caring styles as a means of distinguishing the contribution of men nurses from that of women.

Maintaining Masculinity through Humour

Participants in this study demonstrate how humour as a practice of caring also constitutes a practice of masculinity. Participants commented that many of the jokes they shared with men clients were bawdy and sexist in nature and not appropriate for women. In this context, the practice of humour and its "male only" character can be understood to be an important means of (re)affirming masculinity. This conclusion is supported by ethnographic research about the role of humour in young men in two British schools. Researchers Kehily and Nayak (1997) suggest that humorous exchanges among young men have an unfeminine and exclusively "straight" character to them and are constitutive of heterosexual masculine identities. As such, humorous exchanges among men can also be conceptualized as practices of male bonding, as "men recognize and reinforce one another's bona fide membership in the male gender" and remind one another that "they were not born women" (Frank, 1992: 57).

Sexualization of Men Nurses' Touch

Men learn early in their nursing career that, despite being in an occupation that requires compassion and caring, touch as an expression of that compassion and caring exposes them to the risk of misinterpretation and accusations of inappropriate behaviour (Glasper and Campbell, 1994; Paterson et al., 1996). Unlike women's touch, which is considered a natural extension of women's traditional caregiver role, men's touch is surrounded with suspicion that implies that men nurses' motives for touching are not care-oriented, but sexual in nature.

Participants in this study were well aware of their vulnerability when they touched patients. Similarly, Streubert (1994) found that men nursing students dreaded how women clients might feel about having them as nurses. They consequently struggled with learning appropriate ways to care and touch that would avoid the problem of clients thinking that a man was seducing them (Paterson et al., 1996). Several practices described by participants indicate that, with experience, men nurses can and do develop strategies that allow them to care for patients and ensure their own safety. Such strategies reflect the notion that men who see themselves operating outside the hegemony of masculinity are fine-tuned to the necessary practices to protect themselves (Frank, 1992).

The sexualization of men nurses' touch is particularly evident in the area of obstetric nursing, where the nature of touch is extremely intimate. Situations in which obstetric or gynecological women patients refuse to be cared for by men nurses or men nursing students provide valuable insight into the sexualized character of men nurses' touch. An ethnographic study by Morin et al. (1999) of 32 women obstetric patients revealed that most women were accepting of men nurses. Those women who refused them, however, cited reasons that were often sexual in nature.

An interesting observation by Morin et al. (1999) is that men nurses who are older, married, and have children are generally more accepted as caregivers by women patients (85). This can be attributed to perceptions by women patients that such qualities make men nurses sexually safer and hence more comfortable to be around. Continuing with this line of theorizing, it follows that practices which contribute to the perception of men nurses as sexually safe would be employed by them to put women patients at ease. This conclusion may be evidenced by men nurses' practice of wearing a traditional nurse uniform. Mangan (1994) suggests that the nursing uniform strengthens and promotes the image of men as conforming to the expectations of the larger nursing group. This association may be important in helping men nurses project a genuine desire to care for others as one means of reducing the risk of accusations of inappropriate touch.

Discussion

Gender Stereotypes: A No-Win Situation

The need for men nurses to project conformity in relation to a traditional nursing image may not apply to all patient populations. In situations where men nurses provide intimate care to men, sexual safety for men patients may depend on the degree to which men nurses project hegemonic masculinity. The nurse uniform, because it projects a feminine image, may consequently have a negative influence on the acceptance of men nurses by men patients. It is interesting to note that only two of the participants in this research wore a nurse uniform. Both worked at the bedside in positions that required intimate patient touching.

For most participants, the need to minimize suspicions of gayness and project a masculine identity with men patients was facilitated by a "code" of understanding among men that was grounded in the heterosexist or homophobic principle that men do not touch other men without a legitimate need. The concept of need, as pointed out by participants, was complex and depended on factors such as patient age and illness acuity. They mentioned that they were more comfortable touching men who were acutely ill because they were too sick to care about what anyone did to them. They also found that older men were more comfortable being touched by another man because they were less macho.

Men Nurses as Failed Caregivers

The stigma associated with the stereotype of men nurses as gay is compounded by the stereotype that gay men are also sexual deviants and sexual predators (Levine, 1992). In situations where men nurses provide intimate care to children, the sexualization of men's touch consequently assumes a more sinister character that fuels suspicion that men nurses are pedophiles. Glasper and Campbell (1994) suggest that any intimate procedure conducted by men nurses on children is now suspicious as a result of a British nurse being convicted of sexually assaulting a child in his care. An interesting observation in light of this situation is that the behaviour of one man nurse has not been attributed to an individual deviation, but to all men nurses as a group.

The notion of blaming all men nurses for the transgressions of a few is also raised by Bush (1976). She notes the tendency of some patients to blame individual men nurses when they are perceived to fail in the performance of a technical skill. When a man nurse is perceived to fail in an affective area, however, men nurses as a group are blamed. This situation can be understood as a consequence of traditional gender stereotypes and the belief that men are inappropriate and unable to function as well as women in caring roles.

Conclusion

The gendered nature of men nurses' caring interactions reveals the ways in which gender stereotypes create contradictory and complex situations of acceptance, rejection, and suspicion of men as nurturers and caregivers. Here the stereotype of men as sexual aggressors creates suspicion that men are at the bedside for reasons other than a genuine desire to help others. When this stereotype is compounded by the stereotype that men nurses are gay, the caring practices of men nurses are viewed with suspicion in situations where there is intimate touching, not only of women patients, but of men and children as well. In each of these patient situations, men nurses are caught up in complex and contradictory gender relations that situate them in stigmatizing roles vulnerable to accusations of inappropriate touch.

Gender relations are complex and do not lend themselves to "quick fixes" or recommendations that are easily implemented. The challenge in nursing is to acknowledge the power and pervasiveness of gender relations and the role they play in all nurses' lives. The answer to reducing the suspicion that surrounds men nurses' caring practice lies in challenging prevailing gender stereotypes that situate men in deviant positions when they do not conform to the hegemonic masculine standard. This challenge cannot be taken up by women nurses or men nurses alone. Meaningful change will need to be grounded in an ethos of alliance-building between women nurses and men nurses. This alliance-building needs to begin with dialogue in our nursing classrooms and workplaces if we are to begin to reveal the gendered nature of our thinking, our practices, and our institutions in the interests of revaluing caring and interpersonal skills that challenge hegemonic masculinity.

References

Connell, R.W. 1987. *Gender and Power. Society, the Person and Sexual Politics*. Stanford, CA: Stanford University Press.

———. 1995. *Masculinities*. Cambridge: Polity.

Cyr, J. 1992. "Males in Nursing," *Nursing Managements* 23: 54–5.

Egeland, J., and J. Brown. 1989. "Men in Nursing: Their Fields of Employment, Preferred Fields of Practice and Role Strain," *Health Services Research* 24: 693–707.

Evans, J. 1997. "Men in Nursing: Issues of Gender Segregation and Hidden Advantage," *Journal of Advanced Nursing* 26: 226–31.

Frank, B. 1992. "Straight/Strait Jackets for Masculinity: Educating for 'Real' Men," *Atlantis* 18: 47–59.

Galbraith, M. 1991. "Attracting Men to Nursing: What Will They Find Important in Their Career," *Journal of Nursing Education* 30: 182–6.

Glasper, A., and S. Campbell. 1994. "Beyond the Clothier Inquiry," *Nursing Standard* 8: 18–19.

Halloran, E., and J. Welton. 1994. "Why Aren't There More Men in Nursing," in J. McCloskey and H. Grace, eds., *Current Issues in Nursing*, 4th edn, pp. 683–91. Toronto: Moshy.

Hearn, J., and D. Morgan. 1990. "Men, Masculinities and Social Theory," in J. Hearn and D. Morgan, eds., *Men, Masculinities and Social Theory*, pp. 1–18. Boston: Unwin-Hyman.

Kauppinen-Toropainen, K., and J. Lammi. 1993. "Men in Female-dominated Occupations: A Cross Cultural Comparison," in C. Williams, ed., *Doing "Women's Work,"* pp. 91–112. London: Sage.

Kehily, M.J., and A. Navak. 1997. "Lads and Laughter: Humor and the Production of Heterosexual Hierarchies," *Gender and Education* 9: 69–87.

Kelly, N., M. Shoemaker, and T. Steele. 1996. "The Experience of Being a Male Student Nurse," *Journal of Nursing Education* 35: 170–4.

Levine, M. 1992. "The Status of Gay Men in the Workplace," in M. Kimmel and M. Messner, eds., *In Men's Lives,* 2nd edn, pp. 251–66. Toronto: Maxwell MacMillan Canada.

Lodge, N., J. Mallett, P. Blake, and I. Fryatt. 1997. "A Study to Ascertain Gynecological Patients' Perceived Levels of Endorsement with Physical and Psychological Care Given by Female and Male Nurses," *Journal of Advanced Nursing* 25: 893–907.

MacDougall, G. 1997. "Caring—A Masculine Perspective," *Journal of Advanced Nursing* 25, 809–13.
Mangan, P. 1994. "Private Lives," *Nursing Times* 90: 60–4.
Mathieson, E. 1991. "A Question of Gender," *Nursing Times* 87: 31–2.
Morin, K., B. Patterson, B. Kurtz, and B. Brzowski. 1999. "Mothers' Responses to Care Given by Male Nursing Students During and After Birth," *Image: Journal or Nursing Scholarship* 31: 83–7.
Okrainec, G. 1994. "Perceptions of Nursing Education Held by Male Nursing Students," *Western Journal or Nursing Research* 16: 94–107.
Paterson, B., S. Tschikota, M. Crawford, M. Saydak, P. Venkatesh, and T. Aronowitz. 1996. "Learning to Care: Gender Issues for Male Nursing Students," *Canadian Journal of Nursing Research* 28: 25–39.
Petersen, A. 1998. *Unmasking the Masculine: Men and "Identity" in a Skeptical Age*. London: Sage.
Porter, S. 1992. "Women in a Women's Job: The Gendered Experience of Nurses," *Sociology of Health and Illness* 14: 510–27.
Ryan, S., and S. Porter. 1993. "Men in Nursing: A Cautionary Comparative Critique," *Nursing Outlook* 41: 262–7.
Skevington, S., and D. Dawkes. 1988. "Fred Nightingale," *Nursing Times* 84: 49–51.
Streubert, H. 1994. "Male Nursing Students' Perceptions of Clinical Experience," *Nurse Educator* 19: 28–32.
Taylor, E., R. Dwiggins, M. Albert, and J. Dearner. 1983. "Male Nurses: What They Think About Themselves—and Others," *RN* 46: 61–4.
Villeneuve, M. 1994. "Recruiting and Retaining Men in Nursing: A Review of the Literature," *Journal of Professional Nursing* 10: 217–28.
Williams, C. 1989. *Gender Differences at Work: Women and Men in Nontraditional Occupations*. Berkeley, CA: University of California Press.
———. 1995. "Hidden Advantages for Men in Nursing," *Nursing Administration Quarterly* 19: 63–70.
Zurlinden, J. 1998. "Are Men a Step Higher on the Nursing Ladder of Success?," *Nursing Spectrum* 10A: 4–5, 12.

Chapter 29

Overview

The wildfires that nearly destroyed the city of Kelowna, BC, in 2003 form the dramatic backdrop to Shelley Pacholok's investigation of how work intersects with gender to produce particular accounts of oneself. While the nurses in Evans' study face challenges because their work is not typically masculine, the firefighters interviewed by Pacholok hold jobs that are perhaps the epitome of hegemonic masculinity, involving physical bravery, protection, danger, and strength. Nonetheless, even within this group Pacholok finds evidence of different strategies of masculine self-presentation. Pacholok argues that even though the firefighters do not explicitly invoke the concept of masculinity, the qualities they ascribe to themselves and to other firefighters are related to dominant cultural narratives about gender.

Pacholok draws on the concept of multiple masculinities to examine the differentiation between groups of firefighters, as structural firefighters (who work in towns protecting buildings and populated areas) are more able to partake in the myth of the hero than their counterparts in wildland firefighting, whose work takes place far from admiring observers and media. The structural firefighters, who are most visible in their hegemonically masculine work, reap both symbolic and material rewards from being hailed as heroes. The wildland firefighters define themselves in contrast to their urban counterparts, seeing themselves as superior in the exercise of qualities such as risk-taking, aggression, and control of the situation.

Pacholok reminds us that while we may typically think of masculinity as something that is opposed to femininity, in fact masculinity may be constructed through contrasts men draw between themselves and other men. Masculinity is not simply the difference between men and women.

Gendered Strategies of the Self: Navigating Hierarchy and Contesting Masculinities

Shelley Pacholok

In the summer and autumn of 2003 wildfires in British Columbia, Canada, caused widespread damage to forests, wildlife, animal habitat, homes, suburban neighbourhoods, and tribal lands, the likes of which were unparalleled in recent decades. From a monetary and safety perspective the costs were enormous. The cost of battling with fires in British Columbia was $6 million per day in August 2003 (CTV, 2003). Also, tragically, one air tanker and one helicopter crashed, killing three firefighters. . . .

During this natural disaster firefighters were forced to contend with two challenging situations. First, by and large they felt that they lost the battle against the fire, something that they stressed they were not accustomed to. The occupational culture of firefighting values winning—defined as controlling or exterminating fire and preventing losses to property and other valued resources. Because millions of dollars of property and resources were destroyed, the firefighters' occupational identities were threatened by the losses. They were also faced with a social hierarchy in which some firefighting groups were granted more prestige, rewards and status than other groups. . . .

Theorizing Masculinities

Contemporary theoretical approaches to gender relations, and masculinity in particular, provide a number of pertinent insights. Firstly, differences among men shape the ways they experience and enact gender. Masculinity is profoundly influenced by social structures such as race, class, age, and sexuality, and these structures affect men in different ways. In addition, masculinity is historically and culturally contingent. So there is not one pattern of masculinity found everywhere, rather there are masculinities (Connell, 1995; Kimmel, 1994). In addition, some masculinities are deemed culturally superior to others; hegemonic masculinity is the most honoured or desired at a particular time and in a particular setting. Hegemonic masculinity cannot exist unless there are subordinated Others (that is, women and marginalized men) who are constructed as deficient in some way. As a result, hegemonic masculinity upholds power and status inequalities both between men and women, and among men (Connell, 1995, 2000).

The main patterns of contemporary hegemonic masculinity in Western societies include the connection of masculinity with toughness and competitiveness, the subordination of women, and the marginalization of gay men (Connell, 1995). In addition, appropriately masculine men are supposed to (a) remain calm and reliable in a crisis, and hold their emotions in check, (b) be aggressive and take risks, (c) repudiate anything even remotely related to femininity, and (d) strive for power, success and wealth (for example, see Brannon, 1976; Goffman, 1963; Kimmel, 1994).

While few men actually meet all these normative standards, hegemonic masculinity is the benchmark against which all men are measured. Moreover, according to Kimmel (1994), it is other men who do the evaluating:

> We are under the constant careful scrutiny of other men. Other men watch us, rank us, grant our acceptance into the realm of manhood. Manhood is demonstrated for other men's approval. It is other men who evaluate the performance. (p. 130)

A further theoretical insight is that hegemonic masculinity cannot be reduced to a simple model of cultural control, as the notion of hegemony implies an active struggle for dominance (Connell and Messerschmidt, 2005). Therefore, while hegemonic masculinity is the standard against which all other masculinities are measured, the position at the top of the hierarchy is never secure and is always contestable (Connell, 1995). . . . Herein lies the key to understanding why firefighters with high status construct superior selves: ascendancy is never guaranteed; therefore, they must continually work to maintain their status vis-à-vis other men and prove that they are, in fact, appropriately masculine and therefore superior. . . .

. . . Because hegemonic masculinity is relational it requires actors to draw boundaries and create superior selves that delineate "us" (superior men) from "them" (marginalized Others). . . .

Method

Sample

. . . [K]ey informants were identified through newspaper accounts of the fires. These informants were located and contacted by phone or e-mail. They were asked to participate in the study and also asked to provide the names of additional firefighters who were then contacted for interviews. I used this snowball technique to generate the remainder of the interview contacts.

Because the Okanagan Mountain Park fire was an interface fire, a number of different groups of firefighters were involved in the firefighting efforts. Four groups of firefighters fought on the front lines of the fire: (a) structural firefighters, (b) wildland firefighters, (c) pilots, and (d) heavy equipment operators.

Data Collection

Between June and December 2004 I travelled to Kelowna to do fieldwork on three separate occasions. I conducted informal observations at a number of sites including four City of Kelowna fire halls, three branch offices of the forestry department, two air tanker centres, and one helicopter base.

I also completed in-depth interviews with firefighters and informal interviews with a number of other people involved in the firefighting efforts (for example, fire centre dispatchers). . . .

. . . [I]nterviews took place in a wide variety of settings including coffee shops, outdoor parks, workplaces, and homes. However, most interviews were conducted at the participant's place of work. The interviews lasted from just over 30 minutes to two and a half hours, with the typical interview lasting from one to one and a half hours. . . .

To document the newspaper coverage of the fire I conducted archival work at the Kelowna library. I examined all the fire-related articles in the two major local newspapers, *The Kelowna Daily Courier* and *Capital News* from 20 August to 25 September 2003. I also retrieved articles from electronic news sources. The newspaper accounts revealed that a number of people in administrative positions played key roles in the event. For example, it became clear that relations with the media had implications for the ways in which the hierarchy emerged. . . .

Findings

Over the course of the fire and in the weeks and months that followed, a social hierarchy became apparent—one in which City of Kelowna firefighters received more recognition, rewards, and status from the media and the public than other firefighting groups.[1] This generated a great deal of animosity between the firefighters. While these were largely unsolicited, I heard numerous disparaging comments that were often, although not exclusively, directed at the City of Kelowna firefighters, especially the fire chief, who was a favourite target.

In addition, firefighters from all groups made a concerted effort to frame their own work group as superior (that is, the ones who put themselves in the most danger, worked the hardest under the most difficult conditions and were the most skilled, did the best job, and so on), while simultaneously positioning the other groups as inferior. The following quote from Greg,[2] a veteran forestry firefighter who was a supervisor during the fire, is representative of comments I heard from many of his colleagues. Greg revealed his frustration at what he felt was unfair recognition of the City of Kelowna firefighters and the lack of praise for forestry firefighters and equipment operators who were "really" the ones who took on the most important and dangerous firefighting tasks:

> I think the role, and what was accomplished by our people, on the ground, doesn't get the attention that it deserves. And I think that has a real psychological impact on our firefighters, and our equipment operators. I think that the glory all goes to the [structural] fire departments. . . . Our guys are out there, and I'm not just saying this, this isn't biased, this is my personal observation from the first 10, 12 days of the Okanagan fire. . . . Our staff, our crews, the forest service crews, were the last people out, after the fire department had left. Our guys were the ones who held and maintained that fire guard on the south side. It wasn't the [Kelowna] fire department who did that. . . . It was our front line folks and equipment operators that put in that [fire] guard, that worked through the heat and the dust and the hot and the dry. It's our people who do all of that. Those equipment operators chug away, day and night sometimes, 24 hours a day, and they get very little recognition. The glory all goes to the [Kelowna] fire department. And that in itself has a huge impact to the morale. And somehow the credit has to go where it rightfully belongs. . . .

The Making of Heroes

Based on newspaper accounts, it appears that structural firefighters (especially the fire chief) did receive considerably more print media coverage than any other groups or individuals who were involved in the firefighting efforts. . . .

. . . [M]ost of the firefighter personal interest stories were about structural firefighters and, most often, the Kelowna fire chief. While there were several articles about wildland firefighters, equipment operators and pilots, for the most part they appeared near the end of the fire. For example, over two weeks after the fire started one headline in the *Kelowna Daily Courier* exclaimed, "Unsung heroes: heavy equipment operators have put their lives on the line fighting the Okanagan Mountain blaze, but respect has been hard to find" (Poulsen, 2003b). Even the army, brought in to provide support services to the front line firefighters, such as putting out hot spots and performing mop-up duties, received a relatively large share of media coverage.

Chris, . . . a crew leader employed by a wildland firefighting contract company, . . . noted that, as a result of the unequal coverage, the public gave more credit to the structural firefighters than the wildland firefighters. . . .

According to Chris structural firefighters not only fared better than wildland firefighters in terms of media coverage, they won another important battle—the recognition, support, and adoration of the public. Chris was not alone in his sentiments: numerous other wildland firefighters were also critical of the coverage provided by the media. . . .

The Media as Reputational Entrepreneurs: Firefighters and Heroic Masculinity

. . . Both during the fire and in the weeks that followed, the print media covered numerous human interest stories about firefighters. Both of the local newspapers drew on dominant cultural discourses and symbols of heroism in these stories.

Many framed firefighters as heroes, either explicitly (through the use of the word hero), or implicitly (by referring to firefighters as courageous, selfless, and so on). In addition, the *Daily Courier* printed pull-out posters that read, "Thanks for being our heroes!" and urged readers to "show your gratitude and display this poster in your window." The media have been involved in the business of hero-making for more than two centuries (Houchin Winfield, 2003), and this event was no exception.

Again, many of these stories involved the Kelowna fire chief and, to a lesser degree, the structural firefighters who worked for him. Perhaps, in light of the valorization of structural firefighters as heroes in the wake of 9/11 (Langewiesche, 2002; Lorber, 2002), which occurred only two years before the fire, it was strategic for the media to portray structural firefighters as heroes. They want to generate and retain interest and are successful only to the extent that their readers identify with the principal characters and settings (Fine and White, 2002). . . .

Embedded in the heroism rhetoric were hegemonic constructions of masculinity. It is no secret that media representations enforce and reproduce culturally dominant gender norms, symbols, ideologies, and stereotypes (Dworkin and Wachs, 2000; Howard and Prividera, 2004). Since the use of conventional categories and familiar roles conveys stability, this may be especially true during times of crisis (Lorber, 2002). In addition, the media have a vested interest in supporting culturally dominant conceptions of manliness because they want readers to connect with the characters in their stories, as noted above.

Following are several examples that illustrate the ways in which the media implicitly championed hegemonic masculinity in their coverage of the fire. Two days after Black Friday one headline declared, "Hard fought battle: for every home lost, firefighters saved two, says weary fire chief" (Plant, 2003). The body of the article was punctuated by references to the danger that firefighters placed themselves in ("the fire prompted fierce firefighting that could have turned deadly"), including injuries sustained. It also relayed an incident where firefighters were trapped by the flames; however, the reporter was quick to note that "once [the] flames died down, the men fought their way back in and put out spot fires." Several days later, *Capital News*, reporting on the story of the trapped firefighters, printed the following headline, "Training and experience kept trapped firefighters calm" (Watters, 2003). Another headline in the *Daily Courier* exclaimed, "Hot stuff: studly forest fire point men are not just a couple of hosers" (Seymour, 2003).

These are only several examples among many in which the media implicitly referenced culturally dominant ideals of masculinity such as strength, aggression, courage in the face of danger, heterosexuality, and stoicism. As in other tragedies, the media used this event to protect and articulate dominant gender narratives (Projansky, 1998). The media . . . evoked and perpetuated the parameters of manhood that ultimately provided a context of support for the dynamic reproduction of hegemonic masculinity.[3] Here we can see how the collective actions of the media worked to (re)-inscribe symbolic boundaries around hegemonic masculinity, which ultimately allowed the gendered strategies of self invoked by structural firefighters to take hold. I elaborate on this process in the following section.

On the whole the public appeared to embrace the new heroes. They enthusiastically participated in a yellow ribbon campaign, posted signs of gratitude around the city, attended public events to honour firefighters, supported a number of fundraising causes, and donated a generous amount of time and money to the firefighting efforts.

Wildland firefighters, on the other hand, often expressed mixed emotions about the hero atmosphere that permeated the town, as they did not feel that the praise was necessarily directed at them (despite the fact that there were some signs and media stories that targeted non-structural firefighters). When asked how he felt about seeing the signs, Josh, a 22-year-old wildland firefighter in his third season as a crew member, remarked:

> Um, yeah, we saw [the signs] every time we drove in. And, like here at the [forestry] base there's somewhat, there's some animosity between us and the KFD, the Kelowna fire

> department. . . . Like, because they stopped the fire when it was all in the houses, they kind of got the glory. And it's, like, we all know, we couldn't do anything when it's in that kind of [forest conditions]. . . . So it was, kind of, like, well we did all this work and, despite our efforts, this is going to happen and you can't stop it. You know, we had posters and stuff but as it started kind of slowing down we were kind of, you know, we were back to doing our job and those guys are still kind of in the glory.

So, according to Josh, not only did the structural firefighters receive more credit because they were battling with house fires, they stayed in the limelight when the wildland firefighters went off to fight forest fires in other areas. . . .

In contrast, most of the structural firefighters seemed to recognize that the heroism narrative was directed at them. One newly recruited firefighter, Jeff, maintained that being called a hero was a great "morale booster"; however, he quickly added, "I don't think there's anyone who wants to be called a hero or anything, like it's just, you know that's what we're paid to do." All the structural firefighters denied being heroes and gave the trite answer that what they did was just "part of the job." . . .

> If somebody goes in to save a child or a mother or a grandmother, then I that's the risk that we run. We pull people out of burning buildings. We did it the other day, where we pulled a guy out, maybe 5 months ago, out of a burning building, right. Risking their [sic] lives, it's what we do, right? . . .
>
> It's nice to be recognized, but I don't know what the definition of hero is. We, the guys out here, do really dangerous, successful, heroic deeds nearly every day.

So while the structural firefighters claimed to reject the hero label, a hero-like narrative was woven into many of their accounts of their regular duties. The heroism rhetoric that was disseminated through the local media exacerbated the hierarchy among firefighters, as it favoured the fire chief and other structural firefighters. In addition, the hierarchy was perpetuated by the perceptions of the firefighters themselves. Many wildland firefighters seemed to believe that the media praise was directed solely at the structural firefighters and their chief. The structural firefighters, while denying that they were heroes, viewed their job as one that requires selfless acts on a regular basis.

Contesting Credibility

In navigating the status hierarchy that was exacerbated by the organization of the firefighting efforts and the media coverage of the fire, the firefighters constructed boundaries in an attempt to distinguish their group from the others. . . .

They accomplished this by adopting a measuring stick of firefighting competence that was variously deemed to include remaining calm in a crisis, using aggressive tactics, controlling emotions, and exterminating fire (the latter two criteria falling under the more general category of "repudiating the feminine" below). The firefighters drew on these criteria to demonstrate that their group was superior to other firefighting groups. Because these standards are analogous to culturally dominant ideals of masculinity, undermining firefighting competence simultaneously undermined the masculine integrity of the targeted group. These strategies are indicative of the importance of hegemonic masculinity to firefighters, as workers often judge members of other groups to be deficient in respect to the criteria they value most (Lamont, 2000).

The firefighters' gendered strategies of self not only reinforced occupational boundaries but created boundaries that delineated the difference between "us" (the competent firefighters and "real" men) and "them" (inferior firefighters and subordinate men). Ultimately, these tactics were attempts to erode the credibility of the firefighting group to which they were directed. . . .

Calm and Reliable in Crisis

According to Josh, the young wildland firefighter who remarked earlier that the structural firefighters "got all the glory," the wildland crew leaders were calm under pressure, while the structural firefighters fell apart:

> We had some [crew leaders] . . . who have both seen huge fire. But nothing like this. And they were just rock solid. They said, "No worries, get in [the vehicles], we'll get you all through." Everybody else was panicked. Like the Kelowna Fire department was just wiggy.

One of the crew leaders that Josh was referring to, Chris, explained that there were two occasions when he instructed structural firefighters to leave an area for safety reasons and, due to their ignorance of forest fire behaviour, they resisted. However, according to Chris, there were other times when they "took off" when it was safe, which resulted in the loss of houses:

> There were times when the structure guys again . . . the times they would leave an area when it was safe, and then homes would go. And you'd say, "Well, where the hell did they go?" So then you get on the radio and you start telling them, "No, you guys, it is safe there. I know what the fire is doing, I know where it is, and I know what it's going to do. If you're there right now you can save a couple." But no, of course they weren't.

Structural firefighters used similar tactics to portray wildland firefighters in an unflattering manner. For example, this structural firefighter seemed to genuinely delight in relaying a story where wildland firefighters apparently pulled back from the front line of the fire while the structural firefighters stayed:

> And I remember we were up in the Rimrock area when the fire broke through. . . . So we're sitting there, and we know it's coming because you can hear it, the heat, the wind, the smoke, the dust, everything. The forestry guys you know, they're all in there. And then all of the sudden we heard these whistles. And that's an emergency signal for the forestry to get the hell out. So all of these whistles, you can just hear them going right across the mountain side, and we're kind of listening and then we're like, "What the hell is that?" And it looked like rats jumping off a burning ship [chuckles]. These guys were running as hard as they could out of the forest, by us, and down the hill and they're gone. . . .

Mark's narrative positions his group as the competent firefighters—the real men who stayed to fight the fire. In contrast, according to Mark, the wildland firefighters ran away when things got bad. . . . Structural firefighters, rational, fearless, and calm under pressure, were ready to take on the fire, and ultimately, as Mark noted later in the interview, it was these men who put it out. . . .

. . . [C]laiming that wildland firefighters ran away, as Mark did, is a serious insult that directly undermines their credibility, both as firefighters and as men.

Aggression and Risk Taking

Greg, the wildland supervisor who earlier criticized the media coverage of the fire, explained that it was actually his people who put themselves in harm's way:

> While the fire department did a great job on the structure side of it, and I don't want to take anything away from anyone, anywhere on the structural side, but when it came to the actual front line of those fires and the people who put themselves at risk, it was our people under there.

In this passage Greg discursively positions his crew (and himself, by association) as the real firefighters—the men who put themselves at risk and got the job done. One wildland firefighter went public with this claim, stating that structural firefighters disappeared when the blaze was burning near his property: "I hate to be cynical, but I don't have a good word to say about them. You need passion and adrenaline to fight a fire. Their tolerance of risk was minimal" (Poulsen, 2003a). . . .

Many structural firefighters also talked about the perils associated with their job, but they tended to view risk and danger as an everyday part of their job, as their discourse about heroism indicated.

In both cases the implication is that firefighting competence requires taking risks, and (implicitly) those who are willing to take those risks are the most masculine.

Repudiating the Feminine

Firefighters also accomplished competence negatively; that is, they inferred that other firefighters were incompetent by associating them with characteristics stereotypically associated with femininity. Undermining masculinity is often achieved by implying that the person in question has qualities associated with femininity (for example, see Iacuone, 2005). This tactic is apparent in all the following narratives, although the discourse varied by occupational group. It is well established that masculinity construction is intertwined with the occupational settings in which men labour (Cheng, 1996; Collinson and Hearn, 1996; Meyer, 1999; Pierce, 1995; Prokos and Padavic, 2002). Since each group of firefighters worked in different occupations, they sometimes used disparate discourses to distance themselves from femininity or liken others to women.

One veteran firefighter, Richard, who had recently moved into an administrative position, explained the differences between structural and wildland firefighters in the following way:

> [The wildland firefighters'] job is more containment. Structural firefighters are aggressive, we don't take loss very well. Forestry firefighters are more tactical, they're more like army guys. They're willing to take some losses to get some gains, if that makes sense to you? I mean, they're willing to give up 100 acres of wildland and burn it themselves to stop the fire. Where we would never burn the house down to save another house. We would try and save that house and we would try and save the other house. That's the mental make-up of a structural firefighter versus a forestry guy, right? Forestry guys are like, okay, we'll build a guard here of dirt, and then we'll burn all this off so it doesn't come here, right. So we'll sacrifice some, to get some. Where structural firefighters are not about sacrificing anything.

Here structural firefighters are portrayed as aggressive, uncompromising, and unwilling to lose, and forestry firefighters as less aggressive (maybe even passive) and prepared to lose (at least some of the time). Clearly this rhetoric positions structural firefighters as better firefighters, while equating the mental make-up of wildland firefighters with characteristics typically associated with femininity, such as passivity (Adler et al., 1992; Gonick, 2006). Richard points to firefighting tactics specific to each occupation and uses these as resources to construct the competence and masculinity of structural firefighters as superior to that of wildland firefighters. . . .

Several forestry firefighters' accounts pointed to the mental state of structural firefighters and an emotional display by the fire chief, in a way that challenged their masculinity. In a well-publicized statement to the media the fire chief broke down in tears while relaying the events of Black Friday. . . .

In a similar vein one of the heavy equipment operators ridiculed structural firefighters who took stress leave or were otherwise having difficulty dealing with the fire. As emotions (except perhaps anger) are equated with femininity (Bird, 1996; Rubin, 2004), they are something to be disparaged. Wildland firefighters' accounts revealed disdain for public displays of emotion and their caustic remarks called into question the fire chief's masculinity.

Discussion

These findings indicate that the status hierarchy that became evident over the course of the Okanagan Mountain Park fire was due, at least in part, to the structural organization of the firefighting efforts and the ways in which the media covered the fire. The central location of the main fire hall and the fact that structural firefighters fought the fire within the city limits meant that they were more accessible to the media and, in turn, received more favourable media coverage. The media cultivated narratives consistent with hegemonic masculinity and heroism. Heroism did not appear to resonate with wildland or structural firefighters but the narratives of structural firefighters were often saturated with hero-like imagery.

In an effort to maintain their place at the top of the hierarchy structural firefighters reinforced the boundary between themselves and other groups by discursively positioning others, especially wildland firefighters, as less competent and implicitly as less manly. Wildland firefighters, equipment operators, and pilots attempted to secure their place at the top of the hierarchy using similar tactics. These strategies were attempts to diminish the credibility of the out-group in question. . . .

What was most notable in my study was that the structural firefighters, who had a relatively high social status, also employed strategies of the superior self. The fact that the structural firefighters used these strategies at all provides evidence to support Connell's (1995) claim that hegemonic masculinity is not statically reproduced, but rather, is always contested. If hegemonic masculinity is a given these tactics would not be required for those with the most power and status.

However, because the positions at the top of the gender hierarchy are never secure, even those with power (in this case, structural firefighters) are compelled to engage in practices that refute the integrity of those they perceive as Other. It is only by theorizing gender—masculinity dynamics that involve active struggles for dominance and the constant need to prove one's masculinity—that we can explain why the firefighters responded to the status hierarchy in the ways that they did.

We also saw that gendered strategies of self are not only used individually to construct superior selves, they are collective efforts that serve a collective end: defining and imposing boundaries between groups. The boundary work of the media, which bounded the parameters of heroism and manhood, enabled the structural firefighters' claims to competence and hegemonic masculinity to take hold. If it appears that groups are essentialized as a result of strategies of self and boundary work, it is because that is precisely their intent. Essentializing is "the making of doctrinal claims that certain good or bad traits inhere in all who share an identity" (Schwalbe and Mason-Schrock, 1996, p. 124). Each group of firefighters attempted to demonstrate that their group was populated by exemplars of masculinity and firefighting competence because they wanted to show that their group members were all of a certain character and quality, while others were not. . . .

Such symbolic "credibility contests" (Lamont and Molnar, 2002, p. 179) involving claims to hegemonic masculinity have symbolic and material implications for inequality. Symbolically, men who embody hegemonic masculinity are given honour, prestige, and authority (Connell, 1995). Materially, men who best exemplify this ideal are granted political and material resources. For example, men at the top of the gender hierarchy earn, on average, higher salaries than women and marginalized men, and are more likely to have political power; resources that can then be used to further their own agendas.

In other words, there are material rewards for those who win symbolic battles. Groups that can claim hegemonic masculinity are able to use their status to gain material resources. In this case, structural firefighters were able to convert their collective social capital into material rewards. With the help of their union representative, the fire chief, and the media, the structural firefighters successfully rallied the public and city hall and secured a pay raise less than one year after the fire.[4] The firefighters deliberately referred to the fire and their status as heroes to argue that they deserved a salary increase.[5] The fire chief, who became a local and national celebrity, also reaped many rewards. He was featured on the cover of a prominent national magazine, received an honorary degree and numerous gifts and awards, was invited to do public speaking engagements all over the country, and was asked to run for political office (which he declined).

Importantly, there were also costs associated with being on, or striving for, the top. Research indicates that hegemonic masculinity comes at a personal cost to men who wholeheartedly embrace it. For example, impoverished emotional relationships (Kaufman, 2001; Rubin, 2004), dysfunctional sexual relations (Gerschick and Miller, 2001), risk-taking (Courtenay, 2000; Iacuone, 2005), and negative health outcomes (Sabo, 2004) have been linked to hegemonic masculinity construction. . . .

Consistent with these findings, many firefighters noted that the fire and its aftermath was a difficult experience. In addition, there were long-term consequences for some. Several were on stress leave at the time of the interviews, at least one firefighter resigned, one senior member retired shortly after the fire, the fire chief retired two years later (at the age of 56), some were having marital difficulties, a number were on medication to reduce stress, and a least two senior firefighters were diagnosed with post-traumatic stress disorder. There were also a handful of firefighters who chose to leave their jobs a year or more after the fire, citing the fire as one reason for their decision. . . .

Acknowledgements

I would like to thank Steve Lopez, Tim Curry, Townsand Price-Spratlen, Liana Sayer, numerous other colleagues at the Ohio State University, and three anonymous reviewers for comments and suggestions that helped further develop the ideas in this article. This research was supported by the Social Sciences and Humanities Research Council of Canada.

Notes

1. There were also divisions in these groups. However, due to space limitations these intra-group divisions are not discussed here.
2. All names are pseudonyms.
3. I am indebted to an anonymous reviewer for this idea.
4. The wildland firefighters' organization also received some resources (such as more crew positions) as a result of the fire. However, I was told by a number of people that these were primarily resources that had been cut in recent years and had simply been reinstated.
5. Some firefighters expressed discomfort with this strategy, but it was one that the group utilized nonetheless.

References

Adler, P., S. Kless, and P. Adler. 1992. "Socialization to Gender Roles: Popularity among Elementary School Boys and Girls," *Sociology of Education* 65(3): 169–87.

Altheide, D. 2001. *Creating Fear: News and the Construction of Crisis*. New York: Aldine De Gruyter.

Alvesson, M. 1998 "Gender Relations and Identity at Work: A Case Study of Masculinities and Femininities in an Advertising Agency," *Human Relations* 51(8): 969–1005.

Barrett, F. 1996. "The Organizational Construction of Hegemonic Masculinity: The Case of the US Navy," *Gender, Work & Organization* 3(3): 129–42.

Berg, B.L. 2001. *Qualitative Research Methods for the Social Sciences*, 4th edn. Needham Heights, MA: Allyn and Bacon.

Bird, S. 1996. "Welcome to the Men's Club: Homosociality and the Maintenance of Hegemonic Masculinity," *Gender & Society* 10(2): 120–32.

Bourdieu, P. 1990. *The Logic of Practice*. Stanford, CA: Stanford University Press.

Brannon, R. 1976. "The Male Sex Role—and What It's Done for Us Lately," in R. Brannon and D. David, eds., *The Forty-nine Percent Majority*, pp. 1–40. Reading, MA: Addison-Wesley.

Brod, H. 1994. "Some Thoughts on Some Histories of Some Masculinities: Jews and Other Others," in H. Brod and M. Kaufman, eds., *Theorizing Masculinities*, pp. 82–96. Thousand Oaks, CA: Sage.

Canadian Press. 2003. "Fire Razes More Than 200 Homes in Kelowna, B.C." Available online at www.ctv.ca/servlet/ArticleNews/print?band=genericandarchive=CTVNewsanddate=2. Last consulted 15 February 2004.

CHBC TV. 2003. "Fire Cools a Little." Available online at www.chbc.com.news/articles_files/6812/news_14_6812.shtml. Last consulted 15 February 2004.

Cheng, C. 1996. *Masculinities in Organizations*. Thousand Oaks, CA: Sage.

Cmap Tools. n.d. Home page. Available online at http://cmap.ihmc.us. Last consulted 27 March 2009.

Collinson, D., and J. Hearn. 1996. *Men as Managers, Managers as Men*. London: Sage.

Connell, R.W. 1995. *Masculinities*. Berkeley, CA: University of California Press.

Connell, R.W. 2000. *The Men and the Boys*. Berkeley, CA: University of California Press.

Connell, R.W. 2001. "Introduction and Overview," *Feminism and Psychology* 11(1): 5–9.

Connell, R.W., and J.W. Messerschmidt. 2005. "Hegemonic Masculinity: Rethinking the Concept," *Gender & Society* 19(6): 829–59.

Cornwell, B., T.J. Curry, and K. Schwirian. 2003. "Revisiting Norton Long's Ecology of Games: A Network Approach," *City and Community* 2(2): 121–42.

Courtenay, W. 2000. "Constructions of Masculinity and Their Influence on Men's Well-being: A Theory of Gender and Health," *Social Science and Medicine* 50(10): 1385–401.

CTV. 2003. "Support from Public Keeps B.C. Fire Crews Going." Available online at www.ctv.ca/servlet/ArticleNews/print?brand=genericandarchive=CTVNewsanddate=2. Last consulted 15 February 2004.

Curry, T. 1986. "A Visual Method of Studying Sports: The Photo-elicitation Interview," *Sociology of Sport Journal* 3(3): 204–16.

Drew, J. 2004. "Identity Crisis: Gender, Public Discourse, and 9/11," *Women and Language* 27(2): 71–7.

Dworkin, S., and F. Wachs. 2000. "The Morality/Manhood Paradox," in J. McKay, M.A. Messner, and D.F. Sabo, eds., *Masculinities, Gender Relations, and Sport*, pp. 47–66. Thousand Oaks, CA: Sage Publications.

Fine, G.A. 1996. "Reputational Entrepreneurs and the Memory of Incompetence: Melting Supporters, Partisan Warriors, and Images of President Harding," *American Journal of Sociology* 101(5): 1159–93.

Fine, G.A., and R. White. 2002. "Creating Collective Attention in the Public Domain: Human Interest Narratives and the Rescue of Floyd Collins," *Social Forces* 81(1): 57–85.

Fisher, K. 1997. "Locating Frames in the Discursive Universe," *Sociological Research Online* 2(3).

Fothergill, A. 2004. *Heads above Water: Gender, Class, and Family in the Grand Forks Flood*. Albany, NY: State University of New York Press.

Fuchs Epstein, C. 1992. "Tinkerbells and Pinups: The Construction and Reconstruction of Gender Boundaries at Work," in M. Lamont and M. Fournier, eds., *Cultivating Differences: Symbolic Boundaries and the Making of Inequality*, pp. 232–56. Chicago, IL: University of Chicago Press.

Gerschick, T., and A.S. Miller. 2001. "Coming to Terms: Masculinity and Physical Disability," in M.S. Kimmel and M.A. Messner, eds., *Men's Lives*, pp. 392–406. Boston, MA: Allyn and Bacon.

Gieryn, T.F. 1983. "Boundary Work and the Demarcation of Science from Non-science: Strains and Interest in Professional Ideologies of Scientists," *American Sociological Review* 48(6): 781–95.

Glaser, B.G. 1992. *Emergence vs. Forcing. Basics of Grounded Theory Analysis*. Mill Valley, CA: Sociology Press.

Glaser, B.G., and A.L. Strauss. 1967. *The Discovery of Grounded Theory: Strategies for Qualitative Research*. Chicago, IL: Aldine.

Goffman, B. 1963. *Stigma; Notes on the Management of Spoiled Identity*. Englewood Cliffs, NJ: Prentice-Hall.

Gonick, M. 2006. "Between 'Girl Power' and 'Reviving Ophelia': Constituting the Neoliberal Girl Subject," NWSA *Journal* 18(2): 1–23.

Grewal, I. 2003. "Transnational America: Race, Gender and Citizenship after 9/11," *Social Identities* 9(4): 535–61.

Harper, D. 2000. "Reimagining Visual Methods," in N.K. Denzin and Y.S. Lincoln, eds., *Handbook of Qualitative Methods*, 2nd edn, pp. 717–32. Thousand Oaks, CA: Sage.

Heritage Society of British Columbia. 2004. "Rebuilding the Myra Canyon Trestles." Available online at www.heritagebc.ca/nl_article4.htm. Last consulted 15 February 2004.

Hill Collins, P. 2000. *Black Feminist Thought*, 2nd edn. New York: Routledge.

Holstein, J.A., and J.F. Gubrium. 1997. "The Active Interview," in D. Silverman, ed., *Qualitative Research: Theory, Method and Practice*, pp. 140–62. London: Sage.

Houchin Winfield, B. 2003. "The Press Response to the Corps of Discovery: The Making of Heroes in an Egalitarian Age," *Journalism and Mass Communication Quarterly* 80(4): 866–83.

Howard, J.W., and L. Prividera. 2004. "Rescuing Patriarchy or Saving 'Jessica Lynch': The Rhetorical Construction of the American Woman Soldier," *Women and Language* 27(2): 89–97.

Iacuone, D. 2005. "'Real Men Are Rough Guys': Hegemonic Masculinity and Safety in the Construction Industry," *The Journal of Men's Studies* 13(2): 247–66.

Jeffreys, S. 2007. "Double Jeopardy: Women, the US Military and the War in Iraq," *Women's Studies International Forum* 30(1): 16–25.

Kaufman, M. 2001. "The Construction of Masculinity and the Triad of Men's Violence," in M.S. Kimmel and M.A. Messner, eds., *Men's Lives*, 5th edn, pp. 4–18. Needham Heights, MA: Allyn and Bacon.

Kimmel, M.S. 1994. "Masculinities as Homophobia: Fear, Shame, and Silence in the Construction of Gender Identity," in H. Brod and M. Kaufman, eds., *Theorizing Masculinities*, pp. 119–41. Thousand Oaks, CA: Sage.

Lamont, M. 1992. *Money, Morals, and Manners: The Culture of the French and American Upper-Middle Class*. Chicago, IL: University of Chicago Press.

Lamont, M. 2000. *The Dignity of Working Men: Morality and the Boundaries of Race, Class, and Immigration*. Cambridge, MA: Harvard University Press.

Lamont, M., and V. Molnar. 2002, "The Study of Boundaries in the Social Sciences," *Annual Review of Sociology*, 28: 167–95.

Langewiesche, W. 2002. *American Ground: Unbuilding the World Trade Center*. New York: North Point Press.

Lois, J. 2003. *Heroic Efforts: The Emotional Culture of Search and Rescue Volunteers*. New York: New York University Press.

Lorber, J. 2002. "Heroes, Warriors, and Burqas: A Feminist Sociologist's Reflections on September 11," *Sociological Forum* 17(3): 377–96.

Meyer, S. 1999. "Work, Play, and Power: Masculine Culture on the Shop Floor; 1930–1960," *Men and Masculinities* 2(2): 115–34.

Miller, J., and B. Glassner. 1997. "The 'Inside' and the 'Outside': Finding Realities in Interviews," in D. Silverman, ed., *Qualitative Research: Theory, Method and Practice*, pp. 99–112. London: Sage.

Ministry of Forests Protection Branch. 2003a. "Fire Review Summary for Okanagan Mountain Fire." Available online at www.for.gov.bc.ca/protect/reports/2003review/okanagan%5Ffire%5Freview%5Fk50628.pdf. Last consulted 20 January 2004.

Ministry of Forests Protection Branch. 2003b. "Large Wildfires." Available online at www.for.gov.bc.ca/protect/reports/LargeFires.htm Last consulted 1 October 2004.

Ministry of Forests Protection Branch. 2004. "Interface Fires and Safety." Available online at www.for.gov.bc.ca/protect/FAQ/interface.htm#32. Last consulted 1 October 2004.

Monaghan, L. 2002. "Embodying Gender, Work and Organization: Solidarity, Cool Loyalties and Contested Hierarchy in a Masculinist Occupation," *Gender, Work & Organization* 9(5): 504–36.

Pacholok, S. 2007. "Masculinities in Crisis: A Case Study of the Mountain Park Fire." Unpublished PhD. Sociology Department, The Ohio State University: Columbus.

Peterson, A. 2003. "Research on Men and Masculinities: Some Implications of Recent Theory for Future Work," *Men and Masculinities* 6(1): 54–69.

Pierce, J. 1995. *Gender Trials: Emotional Lives in Contemporary Law Firms*. Berkeley, CA: University of California Press.

Plant, D. 2003. "Hard Fought Battle," *Okanagan Sunday*, Kelowna.

Poulsen, C. 2003a. "Fire Actions under Scope," *The Daily Courier*, Kelowna.

Poulsen, C. 2003b. "Unsung Heroes: Heavy Equipment Operators Put Their Lives on the Line Fighting the Okanagan Mountain Blaze, But Respect Has Been Hard to Find," *The Daily Courier*, Kelowna.

Projansky, S. 1998. "Girls Who Act Like Women Who Fly: Jessica Dubroff as Cultural Troublemaker," *Signs: Journal of Women in Culture and Society* 23(3): 771–808.

Prokos, A., and I. Padavic. 2002. "'There Oughtta Be a Law Against Bitches': Masculinity Lessons in Police Academy Training," *Gender, Work & Organization* 9(4): 439–59.

Rubin, L. 2004. "The Approach–Avoidance Dance: Men, Women, and Intimacy," in M.S. Kimmel and M.A. Messner, eds., *Men's Lives*, 5th edn, pp. 409–15. Boston, MA: Allyn and Bacon.

Sabo, D.F. 2004. "Masculinities and Men's Health: Moving Toward Post-Superman Era Prevention" in M.S. Kimmel and M.A. Messner, eds., *Men's Lives*, 5th edn, pp. 347–61. Boston, MA: Allyn and Bacon.

Schwalbe, M., and D. Mason-Schrock. 1996. "Identity Work as Group Process," in B. Markovsky, M. Lovaglia, and R. Simon, eds., *Advances in Group Processes*, pp. 115–49. Greenwich, CT: JAI Press.

Seymour, R. 2003 "Hot Stuff," *The Daily Courier*, Kelowna.

Sherman, R. 2005. "Producing the Superior Self: Strategic Comparison and Symbolic Boundaries among Luxury Hotel Workers," *Ethnography* 6(2): 131–58.
Sherman, R. 2006. *Class Acts*. Berkeley, CA: University of California Press.
Strauss, A., and J. Corbin. 1998. *Basics of Qualitative Research: Techniques and Procedures for Developing Grounded Theory*. Thousand Oaks, CA: Sage.
Strauss, A.L. 1987. *Qualitative Analysis for Social Scientists*. Cambridge: Cambridge University Press.
Watters, A. 2003. "Training and Experience Kept Trapped Firefighters Calm," *Capital News*, Kelowna.
Wetherell, M., and N. Edley. 1999. "Negotiating Hegemonic Masculinity: Imaginary Positions and Psycho-discursive Practices," *Feminism and Psychology* 9(3): 335–56.

Chapter 30

Overview

How does disability affect paid work? The most obvious answer is that it restricts the type of work one can do. Yet as Susan Lee points out in her study of ten women with disabilities, the impact of physical impairment on work goes beyond simply locking disabled people out of the workplace. Using a feminist disability framework, she investigates the experience of *under*-employment and its impacts on the women's physical and psychological health. Because paid work is closely tied to identity, one of the consequences of being chronically underemployed is a diminished sense of self, especially if one is unable to support oneself through paid work.

Biases and stereotypes about disabled people also create micro inequities and difficulties in workplace culture for women who are physically disabled, similar to the gender-related biases discussed by Beagan and Lindberg in Part VII.

Lee argues that many of the barriers faced by disabled women reside not in the disability itself but in the norms, practices, and environments of workplaces. She calls for the adoption of a social, as well as medical, model of disability, which recognizes that ability and disability, like gender, are primarily social constructions built on physiological scaffolding.

Women's Perspectives on Disability, Underemployment, and Health

Susan S. Lee

Underemployment, which can be defined as "all dimensions of the wasted ability of the workforce, as they apply to either job holders or the unemployed" (Livingstone, 2004: 55), is a chronic feature of the labour market and affects all segments of the population. While one-quarter of the working-age non-disabled population is underemployed, nearly half of disabled persons are underemployed due to unemployment or involuntary part-time employment (Canada, 2009). Thus, disabled Canadians are underrepresented in the workforce; they also experience underemployment in the form of underutilized skills or unmet potential in the job market. Underemployment also affects annual income and lifetime earnings. Disabled persons are less likely than nondisabled persons to be employed in full-time, full-year work; of disabled Canadians who are employed, only about half (54.7 per cent) are employed year-round (Canada, 2009). Reduced income due to part-time or undervalued work is related to health concerns; employment and income are closely linked to health status for everyone but especially those with disabilities. Significantly more employed disabled adults (37.2 per cent) than unemployed disabled adults (25.1 per cent) self-rate their health as "very good" or "excellent" (Canada, 2009). Disabled women are more likely than disabled men to be without work for the entire year (Canada, 2009). When they have paid employment, disabled women earn approximately $11,000 less than disabled men (average $24,720 versus $36,240, respectively, in 2006) (Canada, 2009). . . .

My research . . . explor[es] how women with physical impairments understand and address health experiences resulting from underemployment. In this paper, I review the two theoretical frameworks that guided my analytic approach—the social model of disability and feminist disability research—and present a critical interpretive textual analysis of a series of interviews I conducted with underemployed disabled women about their experiences of disability, underemployment, and health in a Canadian context. These narratives illustrate experiences of underemployment including marginalized identities, lost opportunities, limited income, and wasted energy, as well as the physical, mental, emotional, and social dimensions of health. The findings provide insights into how Canadian workplaces have constructed disability, which may inform methods to advance social justice, both inside and outside the work contexts.

Theoretical Frameworks

My perspective has been informed by the social model of disability (Oliver, 1996; UPIAS, 1976) and feminist disability researchers (Fawcett, B., 2000; Hall, 2011; Garland-Thomson, 2011a). According to the social model of disability, society constructs barriers for disabled persons: attitudes, policies, physical facilities, technology, learning environments, work opportunities, and cultural representations. These barriers are disabling, so in this sense, disabilities reside outside the individual: "impairment" is the individual condition, and "disability" is socially constructed. Accordingly, the phrases "disabled person" or "disabled women" that I use in this paper reflect an understanding that the person is being "disabled" by society. This differs from the individual or medical model of disability, in which a disabled person is considered to embody a medical condition: a diseased body that needs to be diagnosed, treated, and returned to the normative state. . . .

Research Methods

I investigated the effects of underemployment through qualitative interviews with disabled members of the involuntary part-time or precarious work force. The narratives I discuss here are from 10 disabled women . . . Semi-structured interviews were conducted with adults (18 years and older) who had a physical and/or visible impairment/s, had worked outside the home for at least five years, and spoke English. Physical and visible impairments were used as selection criteria because these impairments are more obvious than others and may be more likely to reveal instances of discrimination by employers. A five-year term of employment was selected because this period should be sufficient to allow promotions or to reveal a lack thereof. Interviews were conducted in-person and were recorded. First, interviewees were provided with a working definition of underemployment: "all dimensions of the wasted ability of the workforce, as they apply to either job holders or the unemployed" (Livingstone, 2004: 55). Next, they were asked questions including: What does underemployment mean to you? Could you provide a couple of stories or examples? Based on these examples, how did these scenarios make you feel? What did you do about the situations? How has underemployment impacted your health? The interviews were transcribed and the data were subjected to critical interpretive textual analysis to investigate the social phenomenon of underemployment. . . .

Experiences of Underemployment

. . .

Marginalized Identities

Disclosure is a complex decision. A number of interviewees reported that disclosing their impairment/s was not always in their best interest to land a job. Patsy (aged 57, a self-described "WASP" or White Anglo-Saxon Protestant with a Ph.D. in education) described juggling work as a line cook, program director, and university lecturer, and frequently being on the receiving end of exclusionary practices. She had an auto-immune condition and used a cane and wheelchair for mobility purposes, and attributed underemployment to attitudes toward impairments that often begin with an employer's reaction to an interviewee's self-identification during the initial hiring processes. She expressed concern that self-identification can elicit negative consequences:

> how you self-identify when you're applying for a position and perhaps self-identifying as a person with a disability. But, I found that it doesn't always work to my advantage. You know because if that's known then they're less likely to hire me. I mean if I appear to have a fully able-body, and have great energy and all that stuff, they'll hire me. Then I can tell them later that they're with a crip.

Patsy understood the consequences of disclosure: if she presented herself as a fully able-bodied individual who can fit into the normative, dominant culture of able-bodied others, then the hiring process was less of a barrier. She had thought carefully about her social relations with potential employers and chose non-disclosure as an effective strategy to access a job interview and possible employment.

Larissa (a 58-year-old Ukrainian Canadian) had a visible impairment and did not have the choice of disclosure or non-disclosure: she identified as blind and said her blindness was congenital. She had a Master of Arts in English and American literature and worked as a writer and consultant; at the time of the interview, she was working on a contract for a women's directorate, gathering and managing information to produce educational resources for the public. Larissa would have preferred full-time work to contract work. Her experience reveals how underemployment appears in different forms; Larissa felt she was treated differently than others and that her opinions were not valued in meetings; she said, "I feel that I am a token blind person." In recalling the definition of underemployment by Livingstone (2004), her knowledge and skills were being wasted since she was not able to use them in her current employment. Larissa did not want to just sit and get paid an honorarium; she wanted to be acknowledged for her ability to contribute to meaningful discussions, rather than simply be a statistic to obtain government funding. Although she was hired for her expertise and lived experiences with blindness, she was simultaneously excluded because she was not necessarily valued as a spokesperson with knowledge and experiences to share with her work colleagues.

These scenarios point to identities that are marginalized: "disabled identities" that are often perceived as inferior to the dominant non-disabled culture. Whether individuals refrain from disclosure out of fear, or disclose with the anticipation of negative attitudes or consequences, these acts are often connected to the experiences of underemployment.

Lost Opportunities

Although many of the interviewees had degrees, including Master's and Doctoral degrees, many were working in contract jobs, and sometimes not even in their field of study. Margaret (aged 46) had multiple degrees, including a Master's in special education and a certificate as a music teacher. She had multiple sclerosis with multiple mobility impairments and used a power wheelchair, a walker, a quad cane, and a manual wheelchair, and struggled to find work in her respective fields. At the time of the interview, she said she was underemployed as a teacher and accessibility consultant:

> Fully qualified teacher, master's degree, extra qualifications in special education and ESL, variety of teaching subjects and levels, will work for food. (long pause) That's me. I consider that underemployed.

Apart from obtaining employment, interviewees said that moving up the ladder through promotions was also challenging. Rachel (aged 49) had been working as a receptionist for a government agency for more than 20 years, and has felt the missed opportunities since she has applied for various jobs over the years. She has had a visual impairment since birth. She said that job mobility was challenging because employers were not willing to accommodate her needs and did not invest in their current employees, commenting "I am good at what I am doing. I can do more but there are restrictions." Without access to tools such as a scanner recorder, she said she was not able to increase her job responsibilities to gain the experiences that would demonstrate to future supervisors that she is capable of more.

Many of these women are well-educated: their educational backgrounds qualified them for positions as educators in higher education, consultants in specialized fields, and senior level government workers. However, they were all underemployed, working part-time (often outside their field of expertise), and many were forced to work multiple jobs to pay for basic needs such as food and shelter.

Limited Incomes

As a result of part-time work or shortened careers, many interviewees had limited income. Marpes (aged 53) had a visual impairment and worked as a receptionist at a non-government agency in addiction services. She said, "Underemployment for me is fewer hours, between five and 10 hours per week. Not enough pay. Lack of accommodations." At the time of this interview, she had been working in the same job for over seven years; a lack of accommodations (more current computer software technology) meant that she was unable to pursue a full-time job opportunity within the same organization. Apart from the immediate income needed for basic needs (food, clothing, and shelter), Larissa, the writer and consultant, said:

> The biggest concern of all is that the money that was supposed to go into investment for my old age that would look after the care that I may need is pretty much gone. I have had to take a bit every month out of my retirement savings.

Living in poverty makes it difficult to meet the immediate needs of food, clothing, shelter, and often, even medications. Limited income can force individuals to accept lower standards in food (limited variety of foods, or needing to use food banks) and shelter (ranging from owning a home to renting low-income housing). Changes in income can dictate what can and cannot be afforded even to meet the most basic needs and immediate financial needs leave little room for retirement savings.

Wasted Energies

Underemployment also leads to wasted energy for individuals who have little to spare. Many disabled women spend a lot of time trying to negotiate their work contexts so that they can fulfill their job responsibilities. Remi (a 50-year-old East Indian) was a university researcher with a Doctorate in education, and low vision from birth. She said she needs to take time during working hours to educate her supervisor and colleagues about the accommodations she needed: if the accommodations were not appropriate, they would be a waste of money for her employer, and useless to herself. Persons with low vision or other visual impairments may require different kinds of accommodations. Employers are not always pleased to receive accommodation requests. This was obvious in the case of

Anita (a 58-year-old) who had worked in the field of education for 26 years as a high school teacher, department head, and curriculum developer. She had muscular dystrophy for more than 42 years, and used braces, a walker at home, and a scooter for mobility. She was forced to retire early from her career as an educator due to a lack of accommodations, in what she has described as a "hostile" and "indifferent" environment. She tried to negotiate accommodations with her principal, but was told that she had to continue with her more physical role as a classroom teacher, rather than working as a cooperative education teacher. She said, "My lack of accommodations while employed negatively impacted my health, and caused my disability to progress more rapidly." Energies used to educate and inform current supervisors about accommodations are necessary to ensure the work environment is adjusted to the needs of the employee, but when these energies are expended and are not accommodated, they are simply wasted—and employees try to do their best with minimal accommodation.

Health Implications of Underemployment

. . .

Physical Health

Underemployment often involves working long hours to compensate for low paying jobs, which can have a direct impact on physical health. Patsy forced herself to adapt to the challenging physical environment and long shifts as a line cook in a kitchen restaurant. Unfortunately, the physical toll of being asked to work long hours deleteriously affects Patsy's health. This kind of inflexible environment can push employees with impairments beyond their physical limits. Anita also commented that her work as a teacher was physically taxing:

> Part of the medical diagnosis is physical stress on the muscle will cause it to deteriorate at a faster rate and I knew that, so I was actually taking on a workload that I knew ultimately if I continued, would cause my disease to progress more rapidly.

Due to the lack of accommodations, the physical stress on her body worsened Anita's medical condition. She requested a less physically taxing position as a cooperative education teacher instead of her role as a high school classroom teacher, but was declined.

Mental Health

Patsy explained how she was stressed both physically and mentally as a result of underemployment, which exacerbated her existing health condition:

> So I never know where the next job is coming from, and I, I've never had a steady job because I work professionally. So the stress of constantly looking for work and working at a variety of different jobs is both physically and emotionally challenging when you've already got disabilities to deal with.

Underemployment undervalues individuals by affecting self-esteem and mental health. Mental health issues are further complicated by the lack of funds for the basic physiological needs of food and shelter. Patsy preferred "working professionally." She was reluctant to stop working in multiple professions, as the alternative would be to access the Ontario Disability Support Program (ODSP). ODSP funding would provide her with an income similar to that of her multiple, low-paying jobs, but she chose to work professionally and maintain her professional identity. Mary (aged 41) also juggled multiple jobs to balance her income with her living expenses. She was self-employed as a registered massage therapist, copy editor, transcriber, and restaurant server; she had an honours bachelor degree in English literature and a certificate in massage therapy. She said she had been blind from birth, and used a white cane for navigation. With reference to her underemployment, she said:

> I think it's affected my mental health at different times in my life, feeling that my potential is untapped, and that I am not a regular functioning member of society is something that can

> eat away at you mentally. . . . It's been a factor in depression for me occasionally, that I'm not supporting myself, that I have too much spare time, that I can't seem to make a success in my professional life.

These stories help illustrate how underemployment affects mental health via low-paying jobs, untapped potentials, work intensification, and technological changes. Mental health is closely linked with other factors such as emotional health, as discussed in the next section.

Emotional Health

Margaret described the emotional impact of underemployment and how she sometimes accepted food in exchange for her services. Margaret wanted to work and was qualified to work in her field, but her precarious employment forced her to accept less than the regular rate for her specialized skills in special education and English as a second language. She referred to these payments as "honorariums," which generally do not reflect a competitive pay rate and are often a fraction of the standard rate. Margaret's payment needed to be in the form of honorariums because she received ODSP; she was limited in what she could charge for her services without jeopardizing her limited government funding. According to Margaret, the rate of tutoring (at the time of the interview) was \$15–\$20, while she received \$5–\$10 worth of items, such as "a couple cans of soup, that's five dollars, for the same two hours of work." This was one way for her to handle the structural barriers related to ODSP funding. Other interviews also referred to their precarious employment and the accompanying minimal income:

> I would once in a while hire a cleaning lady. I can't do that. Now it makes me more dependent on other people. You feel less of a person because not only are you disabled, now you are underemployed and feel unemployable. (Larissa)
>
> Emotionally it's quite draining because you are not getting to exercise your potential, and you are sitting at home and not doing something. You get a reactive depression, especially, if you are supporting yourself. (Remi)

The worry during constant job seeking, dependence on others, and concern with career potentials can spiral into emotion problems such as stress, dependency, and depression, all of which are also related to social health.

Social Roles

Underemployment affects the social roles of disabled women inside and outside of work contexts. Remi, the university researcher, emphasised the need for social networks at work:

> We are oppressed because we cannot network. We are oppressed because people do not understand. The attitudes are really towards persons with disabilities. We are underemployed, and they are not changing in a hurry.

Networking at work-related social functions can help reduce underemployment, but if no deliberate moves are made to provide accommodations or support, the disabled employee will remain marginalized, will not be recognized for promotions, or may not even retain his/her job. A shortened career can affect the social dimension of health; according to Anita:

> If you are prematurely taken out of the work force, or you never get into the work force, and you add to that a disability. Socially you are extremely isolated, because the disability brings an amount of disability with it just because it's a disability.

All these disabled women experienced significant negative impact to their health, as revealed by an investigation of the interconnected physical, mental, emotional, and social dimensions.

Discussion and Suggestions

. . . The narratives of the disabled women helped clarify their lived experiences and the health impact of underemployment; these were both characterize by marginalized identities, lost opportunities, limited incomes, and wasted energies. The social model of disability can help identify specific social conditions such as structural, environmental, and attitudinal barriers that lead to underemployment. The interviewees' narratives revealed structural barriers including the lack of training opportunities for disabled employees and the restrictions imposed on employment opportunities by the ODSP. Environmental barriers included hiring practices, inaccessible physical environments, poor compliance to accessibility legislation, and low wage in certain sectors of employment. Canadian census comparative data from 2001 to 2006 revealed that the average salary for working-age disabled adults has not increased ($30,490 in 2001 to $30,380 in 2006), while wages for working-age non-disabled adults increased from an average salary of $35,670 in 2001 to $38,150 in 2006 (Canada, 2009).

Negative attitudes towards disabled individuals are prevalent in the workplace: employers and co-workers often either ignore the presence of disabled persons or include them only as token representatives as they perform their job responsibilities. Individuals with "token" status may stay in the same job for a long time, as they do not have access to the informal networks within an organization and miss opportunities for socializing with important contacts for job mobility. Jones (1997) found that "in-group" employees could access the sponsorship, role modelling, and mentoring of supervisors, and were rewarded with challenging job assignments and decision-making situations, while "out-group" employees were not able to access these opportunities. Another study found that disabled workers received fewer promotions (12 per cent) than non-disabled workers (31 per cent) (Officer, 2009). According to the lived experiences of the disabled women in the study discussed here, these women also encountered attitudes in the workplace that did not respect their knowledge, skills, and abilities for their current jobs nor their needs to be accommodated for social functions. Many of these persons ignored the benefits of diverse identities within the workplace. This kind of negative attitude contributes to the underemployment that is prevalent among disabled persons: Officer (2009) found that approximately one-third (34 per cent) of disabled persons reported a performance gap in that they were not able to use their skills or knowledge on the job, while nearly half (47 per cent) reported a subjective gap in their "fit" to their job and limited options for a better one or to fully realize their job potential. The limited ability to apply their skills acts as a barrier to career advancement. . . .

The disabled women in the current study spoke about the negative impact of underemployment on the multiple dimensions of health: physical, mental, emotional, and social. They reported feeling anxiety about their precarious work and constant job searches. Participants with invisible impairments also had to make decisions about disclosure, which contributed to stress about how employers might perceive their potential as capable employees compared to non-disabled candidates. A previous study also found that disabled job candidates were reluctant to disclose their impairment, although co-workers and managers preferred full disclosure (Church et al., 2008). Many disabled employees do not disclose their impairment due to potential stigma by work colleagues, and may go to great efforts to hide their impairments: taking work home, disguising physical changes, and scheduling medical appointments outside work hours (Wallace & Fenwick, 2010; Duckett, 2000).

Limited incomes from undervalued or part-time work severely affected the social class of the disabled women interviewed: they shared stories of using food banks and second-hand clothing stores, which affected their self-worth. More importantly, their inability to meet the expectations of society by joining friends for social functions, fulfilling a grandmother's role, or contributing to society in a meaningful way through charities or within their particular profession affected their emotional well-being and self-identity. Along with their present difficulties, they were stressed about the future when they had already dipped into their retirement savings.

Employment, job security, and working conditions can all contribute to the social determinants of health. Moreover, when these social determinants of health intersect with social identities such as gender and impairment, and geographies such as lack of accessible transportation, these factors become "synergies of oppression" whereby individuals are experiencing negative impacts greater than any single factor that they would face (McGibbon & McPherson, 2011). Within the dominant culture, lower employment incomes, part-time work, and career positions (Canada, 2009) among disabled persons and especially disabled women highlight how these populations are oppressed by: "every-day practices, not necessarily motivated by maleficient intentions, but those which place people in certain groups where they are disadvantaged and suffer from injustice" (Takala, 2009: 124).

Oppression is linked to the dominant social practice of making disabled persons "other" to the majority of non-disabled persons: disabled persons become "objects of our experience instead of regarding them as subjects of experience with whom we might identify" (Wendall, 1996: 60). This dominant social practice then leads to fear and/or rejection of disabled persons. Thus, the cycle of poor health and underemployment needs to be broken to pave the way for an improved state of well-being for disabled women who aspire to use their knowledge, skills and talents in fulfilling employment scenarios and to be contributing citizens to society. . . .

The Body

The social model of disability critiques the social context in terms of structural, environmental, and attitudinal barriers, but it tends to exclude the body because it stresses the need for change at the social level rather than at the individual levels (Oliver, 1996; UPIAS, 1976). However, within a feminist disability framework, the body is considered the site of knowledge and experiences (Fawcett, B. 2000; Garland-Thomson, 2005; Hall, 2011; Linton, 1998; Wendall, 1996). According to Garland-Thomson, "Inequality occurs not purely from prejudicial attitudes but is an artifact of material configurations misfitting with bodies" (2011b: 602). She also commented that: "One of the fundamental premises of disability politics is that social justice and equal access should be achieved by changing the shape of the world, not changing the shape of our bodies" (2011b: 597).

Her theory of "fits" and "misfits" refers to "harmony" or "disjunctures" in terms of the flexibility of the environment to adapt to varied bodies. The paradigm shift will require re-imagining the relationships between the social environment and the individual, and avoiding a simple focus on either the social barriers or the individual impairment. In the real world, efforts can focus on how the requested accommodations fit the disabled employee. Disabled employees and their employers can ask questions like: Is there accessible access to the work site? Is the workspace accessible? Are the computer software and hardware appropriate for the individuals' needs to be able to work? If the answer is "no," then changes need to be made to the social environment, not the individual. Anything less raises the concern that "to misfit into the public sphere is to be denied full citizenship" (Garland-Thomson, 2011b: 601).

Along with this need to fit the social environment to the individual, it is important to consider social relations between employees. Embodied experiences can also provide knowledge and skills that can inform this discussion beyond accessible accommodations; Lindgren noted that a "focus on the body in trouble can contribute to the feminist project of revaluing bodily experience and to the development of more nuanced and inclusive theories of the body" (2004: 147). When embodied experiences are valued more, disabled employees will feel more welcome to bring their perspectives to invited discussions. Work relationships can then start to change, encouraging different perspectives during work collaborations and fostering more networking opportunities by inviting disabled colleagues to social functions. Regular interpersonal communications between disabled and non-disabled individuals can provide opportunities for improved understanding; unfamiliarity encourages fear and exclusion, whereas familiarity and a desire for embodied knowledge among different individuals can encourage respect and inclusion.

Activism

The interviewees felt this project was an opportunity to expose their social relations within organizations and to pave the way for activism. Their stories are critical ways of "making public private miseries and of viewing self-defined need as publicly actionable" (Fawcett, B. 2000: 43). One dominant concern of participants was the attitude of employers and employees. Actions such as asking for accommodations, knowing their rights, and educating work colleagues are ways for disabled women to exert the presence of disability into work contexts that have often operated in the absence of awareness about disability. More flexible hours can ensure disabled women have the energy to work and manage their family life. Previous research demonstrated how disabled women with children had the additional responsibility of juggling childcare; it also revealed that disabled women spent more time doing household tasks and preparing meals, resulting in less energy and time to pursue paid employment. Specifically, 50 per cent of disabled women compared to 70 per cent of disabled men received assistance with meal preparation (Fawcett, G., 2000). By educating employers and exerting their rights in the workplace, disabled women can begin to influence change.

Activism can be practised alongside allies, including non-disabled individuals who support the goals and rights of disabled individuals. Working with rather than working for is a necessary principle for a disability rights movement addressing the concerns of disabled women. To realize change, every employee must commit to individual efforts toward equity and inclusion, thereby supporting the organization's ability to embrace disabled employees who can provide valued skills and different perspectives. Company policies, procedures, facilities, and programs should incorporate the opinions of disabled persons, and with the insights and guidance of disabled persons, disability awareness training can address social barriers such as attitudes stemming from fear or assumptions about disability. This training will also provide a forum to initiate dialogue and open up space for change during various stages of employment: recruitment, retention, and promotion. Employees need to be aware of their rights to accommodations according to human rights legislation. While adherence to legislation can often provide a minimum level of change, a solid commitment to equity can compel and inspire paradigm shifts that address human rights—including women's and disability rights. This change needs to be above and beyond the minimum standards in the dominant culture, and needs to be acceptable to the individuals who embody difference and desire to enter the workplace. The ability to pursue a fulfilling career with competitive pay can go a long way in addressing the physical, mental, emotional, and social health of disabled women. A move toward integration, as recommended by Garland-Thomson (2011b), can eventually transform workplaces into more inclusive ones. These transformed workplaces can then pave the way for the transformation of society: from one that excludes disabled persons to a more inclusive and equitable environment.

Conclusions

This paper contributes to the literature about women's perspectives on disability, underemployment, and health. As a public medium, this paper represents the lived experiences of underemployed, disabled women through their own voices and narratives; it also represents an activist's resistance to the normative, taken-for-granted way of being and behaving in an unjust society. The narratives of disabled women demonstrated that underemployment has a negative impact on the multiple dimensions of health: physical, mental, emotional, and social. The social model of disability can identify the causes of underemployment, which can be attributed to structural, environmental, and attitudinal barriers resulting in marginalized identities, lost opportunities, limited incomes, and wasted energies. The feminist disability model focuses on the primacy of identity, the body, and activism, and can further explain how disabled women can act as change agents to structure their quests for paid employment, fulfilling careers and self-actualization. More insights into these social and embodied factors can support disabled women in their search for paid employment within a work culture that respects and accommodates individual differences. A commitment to equity in attitudes and real-world work situations will encourage dialogue between disabled and non-disabled persons to erase this socially constructed divide, to foster respect for disability rights, and to create workplace accommodations that better fit our embodied differences. Only then, can there be a greater movement toward employment equity and a reduction in underemployment.

References

Canada. 2009. *Advancing the Inclusion of Persons with Disabilities 2009.* Retrieved June 7th, 2012, from www.esdc.gc.ca/eng/disability/arc/federal_report2009/fdr_2009.pdf

Church, K, C. Frazee, M. Panitch, T. Luciani, and V. Bowman. 2008. "Doing Disability at the Bank: Discovering the Work of Learning/Teaching Done by Disabled Bank Employees," in D.W. Livingstone, K. Mirchandani, and P.H. Sawchuk, eds., *The Future of Lifelong Learning and Work*, pp. 147–53. Rotterdam/Taipei: Sense Publishers.

Duckett, P.S. 2000. "Disabling Employment Interviews: Warfare to Work," *Disability & Society* 15(7): 1019–39.

Fawcett, B. 2000. *Feminist Perspectives on Disability.* Essex, England: Pearson Education, Ltd.

Fawcett, G. 2000. *Bringing Down the Barriers: The Labour Market & Women with Disabilities in Ontario.* Ottawa: Canadian Council on Social Development.

Garland-Thomson, R. 2011a. "Integrating Disability, Transforming Feminist Theory," in K.Q. Hall, ed., *Feminist Disability Studies*, pp. 13–47, Bloomington, IN: Indiana University Press.

Garland-Thomson, R. 2011b. "Misfits: A Feminist Materialist Disability Concept," *Hypatia* 26(3): 592–609.

Garland-Thomson, R. 2005. "Feminist Disability Studies," *Signs* 30(2): 1557–87.

Hall, K.Q. 2011. "Reimagining Disability and Gender through Feminist Disability Studies," in K.Q. Hall, ed., *Feminist Disability Studies*, pp. 1–10, Bloomington, IN: Indiana University Press.

Jones, G.E. 1997. "Advancement Opportunity Issues for Persons with Disabilities," *Human Resource Management Review* 7(1): 55–76.

Lindgren, K. 2004. "Bodies in Trouble: Identity, Embodiment, and Disability," in B.G. Smith and B. Hutchison, eds., *Gendering Disability*, pp. 145–65. New Brunswick, New Jersey, and London: Rutgers University Press.

Linton, S. 1998. *Claiming Disability: Knowledge & Identity*. New York: New York University Press.

Livingstone, D.W. 2004. *The Education-jobs Gap: Underemployment or Economic Democracy*, 2nd edn. Toronto: Garamond Press.

McGibbon, E., and C. McPherson. 2011. "Applying Intersectionality and Complexity Theory to Address the Social Determinants of Women's Health," *Women's Health & Urban Life* 10(1): 59–86.

Officer, S. 2009. "Struggling to Remain Employed: Learning Strategies of Workers with Disabilities and the Education-Job Match," in D.W. Livingstone, ed., *Education & Jobs: Exploring the Gap*, pp. 226–48. Toronto: University of Toronto Press.

Oliver, M. 1996. *Understanding Disability: From Theory to Practice*. New York: St. Martin's Press.

Takala, T. 2009. "Gender, Disability and Personal Identity," in K. Kristiansen, S. Vehmas, and T. Shakespeare, eds., *Arguing about Disability Philosophical Perspectives*, pp. 124–33. London and New York: Routledge.

UPIAS. 1976. *Fundamental Principles of Disability*. London: Union of Physically Impaired Against Segregation. Available on the Disability Archive: www.leeds.ac.uk/disabilitystudies/archiveuk/index.

Wallace, J., and T. Fenwick. 2010. "Transitions in Working Dis/Ability: Able-ing Environments and Disabling Policies," in P. Sawchuk and A. Taylor, eds., *Challenging Transitions in Learning and Work: Reflections on Policy & Practice*, pp. 309–24. Rotterdam/Taipei: Sense Publishers.

Wendall, S. 1996. *The Rejected Body: Feminist Philosophical Reflections on Disability*. Great Britain: Routledge.

Chapter 31

Overview

We often take for granted that work is one place, and home is another. What happens when the distinction between work and home collapses? Bernadette Stiell and Kim England interviewed 18 live-in caregivers who reside (or are expected to be present) in the homes of their employers. This all-female workforce must navigate the expectation that they will become "one of the family," while at the same time attempting to protect their own autonomy and personal space. Not only do these workers live in their workplaces, but the caregiving work they do is very similar to the unpaid domestic work that is stereotypically undertaken by wives and mothers. Thus, ideas about gender permeate the workplaces of these live-in caregivers and are reflected in their experiences in their employers' homes.

The workers and their employers, usually also female, interact in an asymmetry of power, in which the employer can exert effective control over the employee but in which emotional ties and expressions are often expected by the employer. The caregivers resent the ideology of "personalism," according to which they are treated as friends and confidantes when it is convenient for their employers yet simultaneously exploited. Stiell and England connect this to the pervasive idea that women are intrinsically supportive and nurturing, and should bring these qualities into their paid work.

Racial and ethnic difference are also factors when it comes to gender norms. The caregivers who are most similar to their employers in sharing a racial identification as white report more equitable and respectful relations with their employers than those who do not share this identity. Once again, gender intersects with other social categories, such as race and ethnicity, to produce different experiences for different people. Thus, the racial privilege accorded to white people in general shapes the content of the gendered relationship between caregiver and employer.

Domestic Distinctions: Constructing Difference among Paid Domestic Workers in Toronto[1]

Bernadette Stiell and Kim England

Have you seen the movie *Mary Poppins*? There's a song that says that if you can find the good things, then everything else is ok. What she says is actually amazing. The kids love it too. It's my theme song to keep me going sometimes. That is our song, the nanny song. "You find the fun and the job's a game." That's exactly it, "a spoonful of sugar helps the medicine go down," that's it literally, and figuratively speaking. A pat on the back goes a long way. But I didn't get that at all. That's the reason why I was unhappy [with her previous employer]. (Silke, a 30-year-old German woman employed as a "domestic worker" in Toronto.)

Silke came to Toronto in 1986 to work as a nanny. She is one of more than 90,000 women who have arrived in Canada over the past 15 years under two federal government programs (the Foreign Domestic Movement program, 1981–92, and the Live-in Caregivers Program, 1992 to the present). These programs require that domestic workers/caregivers be "live-ins" at their employer's homes for their first two years in Canada. Silke had a difficult relationship with her employer, partly as a result of the contradictions and ambiguities associated with her "workplace" being her employer's "home." In this paper we explore how paid domestic workers in Toronto, including Silke, negotiate the dynamics of their employer–employee relation.

As in Canada as a whole, live-in paid domestic work in Toronto is usually the work of migrant or immigrant women, especially "third world" women of colour. However, most employers are white. Thus, our investigation of the employer–employee work relation hinges on an exploration of difference and diversity. Recent discussions in feminist studies stress the simultaneous and inseparable operation of various social relations of difference. In other words, social relations of difference are not merely additive; instead the experience of one transforms the experience of the others. Taken together, gender, "race"/ethnicity, class, and so on form interlocking, relational systems of oppression and privilege within which there are a multiplicity of identities, which in turn gain meaning in relation to other identities (Spelman, 1988; hooks, 1989; Hill-Collins, 1990; McDowell, 1991; Kobayashi and Peake, 1994; Ruddick, 1996). In this paper we explore the experiential pluralities of women in paid domestic work.

Toward a Household Geography of Paid Domestic Work

Blurring the "Public"/"Private" and "Home"/"Work" Divides

Since 1981, Canada's federal policies have strictly stipulated that foreign domestic workers can only enter Canada if they "live-in" for two years. Various advocacy groups have lobbied to remove the live-in requirement, but the government insists that the demand is only for live-in domestic workers, and that live-out jobs in domestic work can be easily filled by workers already in Canada (Employment and Immigration Canada, 1991, 1992). Live-in domestic work represents a peculiar form of paid employment and employer–employee relations. First and foremost, the domestic worker's "workplace" is her employer's home, with its high degree of personalism in a "private" (as opposed to the more usual "public") domain of work. So, live-in paid domestic work blurs the boundaries between "home" and "work" and "public" and "private," which in turn complicates the employer–employee relation. Secondly, the work relation is shaped by intimacy, affective labour, ideologies of the family, as well as public discourse about "good mothering." It is a work relation summarized by the notion that it is a "labour of love" and that paid domestic workers are Like One of the Family (Childress, 1956).[2] Thirdly, that the boundary of public and private is blurred and even undefined, means that live-in domestic work can lead to exploitation (Rollins, 1985; Colen, 1989; Arat-Koç, 1992; Ng, 1993; Bakan and Stasiulis, 1994; Gregson and Lowe, 1994; Thornton-Dill, 1994). For example, Arat-Koç and Villasin (1990) found that 65 per cent of the domestic workers they surveyed in the Toronto area were routinely required to work overtime, 44 per cent of whom received no compensation.

When an employee is legally required to live-in as part of her job, work relations are complicated by antagonisms and ambiguities based on the merging of public "work" and private "home" spheres, and the emotional complexities of trying to simultaneously maintain both a personal relationship and a work relationship.

The literature on the experience of paid domestic workers highlights a set of commonalities. It tends to be characterized by oppressive material conditions, including isolation, loneliness, powerlessness, and invisibility. Even for the live-out domestic workers (who form the focus of many non-Canadian studies), exploitation is a frequent experience, imposed by long working hours, unpaid overtime, and limited time off. For some domestic workers, working in what they see as a low-status occupation means that stigma, low self-esteem, and low self-worth are also relatively common. In part, these experiences relate to the asymmetrical power relations between the domestic worker and her employer (Cock, 1980; Gaitskell et al., 1984; Rollins, 1985; Glenn, 1986, 1992; Bradshaw-Camball and Cohen, 1988; Colen, 1989; Romero, 1992; Thornton-Dill, 1994; Mattingley, 1996). The characteristics and experiences of domestic work are further exacerbated when the domestic worker is "living in." Certainly, significant improvement in work experience is reported when the "live-in" arrangement is removed (Colen, 1989; Romero, 1992). This is clearly the case in the US where the trend towards live-out, "day-work," multiple employers and more formal work schedules has decreased the intensity of isolation, dependence, and exploitation which are still features of live-in domestic work in Canada.

In Canada, at least, there is evidence that strongly suggests that paid domestic work has become racialized. Key to the process of racialization is the ideology that a domestic worker's relative worth is judged relative to the poverty (or wealth) of her country of origin. European women seem to be accorded more prestige than "third world" women. Moreover, it seems that Europeans may receive higher pay, better treatment, and be regarded as "nannies" in the strictest sense of doing mainly childcare. "Third world" women may receive less pay and be treated less well, while being deemed "domestics" who are expected to do extensive housework as well as childcare (Arat-Koç, 1992; Bakan and Stasiulis, 1994, 1995).

Employer–Employee Relations

Previous studies indicate that women are more likely to hire domestic workers if they are unable to negotiate an equitable division of domestic labour with their male partners (Rollins, 1985; Hertz, 1986; Arat-Koç, 1992; Ng, 1993; Gregson and Lowe, 1994). In other words, despite the growth in women's employment, women continue to be largely responsible for domestic work whether as paid domestic workers, or as "managers" of domestic workers they hire. However, the gender commonality between employer and employee is often marked by myriad differences. For example, that immigrant women of colour are over-represented among domestic workers is naturalized as their being predisposed to domestic work (Rollins, 1985; Glenn, 1992; Macklin, 1992; Ng, 1993; Bakan and Stasiulis, 1995). Macklin (1992) demonstrates this point with the example of Mary, the white Canadian employer of Delia, a Filipina domestic worker:

> Mary [can] objectify Delia in various ways that are influenced, but not precluded, by gender. For example, Mary can hardly claim that Delia is ideally suited to domestic work because she is a woman without impugning herself, but she can fall back on Filipino women being "naturally" hard working, subservient, loyal, tidy housekeepers, and "good with children." In this context, race, ethnicity, and culture conjoin with sex to create a sub-category of women whose subordination other women can rationalize by projecting onto them the stereotypical "feminine" qualities that patriarchy has used against women generally. (1992: 754)

Of course, not all employer–employee relations in paid domestic work are exploitative and abusive. Bradshaw-Camball and Cohen (1988) suggest that the range and variety of employer–employee relations can be placed along two intersecting continua: one representing the domestic worker's "sense of self-worth," the other representing the employer's "concern with equity and fairness." So, for instance, potentially exploitative work relations may result from an employer with little "concern with equity and fairness" employing a domestic worker with a low "sense of self-worth." The employer's and domestic worker's location on these continua are mediated by issues of identity. Employers of domestic workers in Toronto are more likely to be white and middle-class and, most commonly, anglophone. On the other hand, domestic workers are frequently of a different "race"/ethnicity, country of origin, immigration/citizenship status, and language, and these differences can alter the complexion of employer–employee relations.

In this paper, we take the first word/third world dichotomy as a starting point. However, we want to avoid an over-emphasis on the fixed and oppositional categories of black/white dichotomy of "race." This is particularly important in the case of foreign domestic workers in Canada, because if the more subtle differences of language are not accentuated, Filipinas might not be differentiated from Afro-Caribbeans (the two largest groups of foreign domestic workers in Canada). In light of the diversity among Canada's foreign domestic workers, we look at a number of groups of paid domestic workers in Toronto. Our analysis highlights the simultaneous operation of systems of difference (gender, "race"/ethnicity, class, language, and so on) that texture the experience of paid domestic workers, and emphasizes that within these interlocking systems there are a range of locations with varying degrees of power and marginality.

Background to the Study

The empirical portion of our paper is based on our collaborative analysis of 18 lengthy, in-depth interviews conducted by Bernadette with women who were, or had been, paid domestic workers in Toronto (see Table 31.1; the women are identified by pseudonyms). The women were reached through notices in the offices of INTERCEDE and "snowballing." The women interviewed came from nine countries of origin—Canada, England, France, Germany, Hungary, Eire, Jamaica, Philippines, and Thailand. In no way do we contend that this small sample is representative of all domestic workers in Toronto; rather, we believe these 18 women reflect

Table 31.1 Characteristics of domestic workers interviewed

Pseudonym	Country of Origin	"Race"	First Language	Age (years)	Marital Status	Children	Year of arrival	Immigration Status	Live-in or Live-out
Barb	Canada	White	English	24	Single	0	N/A	Citizen	Live-in
Kath	England	White	English	22	Single	0	1989	Open	Live-in
Karen	England	White	English	23	Single	0	1993	Temp	Live-in
Sue	England	White	English	23	Single	0	1993	Temp	Live-in
Maryse	France	White	French	27	Single	0	1991	Temp	Live-in
Ingrid	Germany	White	German	29	Single	0	1991	Temp	Live-out
Silke	Germany	White	German	30	Single	0	1986	Landed	Live-out
Alena	Hungary	White	Hungarian	26	Single	0	1991	Open	Live-in
Anna	Hungary	White	Hungarian	27	Divorced	0	1990	Open	Live-out
Maggie	Eire	White	English	29	Single	0	1986	Landed	Live-in
Cynthia	Jamaica	Non-white	English	30	Single	0	1991	Temp	Live-in
Felicity	Jamaica	Non-white	English	35	Married	2	1992	Temp	Live-in
Edith	Philippines	Non-white	Tagalog	50s	Single	0	1986	Landed	House-keeper
Joan	Philippines	Non-white	Tagalog	32	Married	1	1987	Landed	Cashier[*]
Jocie	Philippines	Non-white	Tagalog	34	Single	0	1989	Open	Live-in
Naomi	Philippines	Non-white	Tagalog	28	Single	0	1991	Open	Live-in
Wilma	Philippines	Non-white	Tagalog	30	Single	0	1990	Open	Cashier[*]
Amy	Thailand	Non-white	Thai	30	Single	0	1989	Landed	Cashier[*]

* Woman with open/landed immigrant status who no longer works as a paid domestic worker.

some of the diverse identities and experiences of this varied group of workers. The majority of the women were in their twenties and thirties, and all but two were single (the two who were married were also the only ones with children). One was Canadian, five were landed immigrants; of the others, five were on open permits (an immigration status between a temporary work permit and landed immigrant), and seven were on temporary work permits. Most of the women were live-ins, but three were live-outs and another three (who were no longer on temporary work permits) had recently left paid domestic work.

I (Bernadette) conducted the interviews, and quickly realized that my own identity was a significant factor in the subtle and not too subtle interactions between myself and the participants. My country of origin (England), language and accent (southeast English), "race" and culture (British West Indian), education (graduate student at the University of Toronto), and, of course, gender, all to some extent affected the negotiation of the "betweenness" of the researcher–researched relationship. I was able to relate with great ease with the English and Irish women. We chatted quite generally about our shared experience of being "Anglos" in Canada. There were also partial points of connection between the Jamaican women and myself in terms of a shared "West Indian" identity—they disclosed a number of experiences and opinions that I do not believe they would have so readily revealed to a Canadian or white English interviewer. At the same time, however, there were occasions when I realized they had assumed rather too much common ground and I was unable to appreciate fully the more subtle nuances of everything they said because I am not Jamaican. Perhaps the greatest social distance was between the Filipina women and myself, which was in part due to a lack of shared language fluency and my unfamiliarity with their culture (all the interviews were conducted in English).

Employer–Employee Relations and the Construction of Difference

A number of major themes emerged from the interviews regarding the relationship between the paid domestic workers and their middle-class employers. In particular, we look at the domestic workers' experiences of living-in, being "one of the family" and the degree of respect, dignity, and self-worth they feel. We not only consider these experiences around issues of class and "race"/ethnicity, but in terms of domestic workers' immigration/citizenship status, country of origin (or nationality), and language.

Living-in

> Living-in means you are on call 24 hours a day. Living-in means if (the employers) feel like going to a party at 10 o'clock, then that's ok, the nanny's there. And you don't get paid for that. (Felicity, Jamaican)

More than any other issue that emerged from the interviews, the living-in requirement was unanimously cited as being especially problematic. However, this was not the case for every woman interviewed. As a white, anglophone Canadian, Barb was not required to live-in. She saw living-in as an opportunity to live away from her parents that enabled her to continue living in a comfortable middle-class home (something she could not afford if she was in a different occupation). Regardless of their motivations for coming to Canada or their long-term immigration goals, all the women who entered Canada as domestic workers/caregivers were legally required to live-in their employer's home for their first two years in Canada. Corroborating previous studies, we found that regardless of their identities, most of the women interviewed felt that they had experienced some level of exploitation through excessively long working hours, overtime without pay, restricted days off, or performing tasks outside their contract—all of which they attributed wholly or partially to their living-in. As Joan (Filipina) and Felicity (Jamaican) put it:

> When you live-in they can demand a lot, because they see that you're there. In the night, if they want something to eat or drink, they will call you. As long as they are awake, then

> you have to stay awake with them too. (Joan, Filipina)

> I knew it wasn't going to be easy living in someone else's home. What I didn't prepare myself for was the subtle abuses. . . . Living-in means they come in at 5:30 pm, but you keep the kids until they've finished supper. Then you clean up, after you clean up, they might decide they want to go for ice cream or coffee, but you are still working. When you even mention that you're supposed to get overtime pay, they say "You're a trouble-maker." They say no one has ever asked for that before. (Felicity, Jamaican)

Although exploitation was a general feeling, it is interesting to observe the ways in which different groups of domestic workers experienced these problems and how they were able to deal with them. One important issue was the perceived need to remain in an unsuitable job. When the English NNEB-trained[3] nannies reported enduring poor working or living conditions it was usually in their first job, which was often arranged before their arrival in Canada. These jobs often fell short of their expectations, but they remained with these employers in the pursuit of a good reference for their next job. As Kath described:

> My first job changed, that's why I was only there for a year. It was awful. They changed a lot of things once I got here . . . they wanted a housekeeper and they took the car away from me, extended my hours, but that just wasn't on. When I tried to talk to them about it they said they'd deal with it later, but later never came. When you're at college they drum it into you that you have to do your first year, you have to get that experience and then a good reference. They don't tell you how easy it is to get another job over here. So I stuck it out, I was unhappy, but I did it. (Kath, English)

For a number of the "third world" women, it was their desire to apply for landed immigrant status that may have led them to put up with intolerable conditions and treatment from their employers. In a number of instances, domestic work provided much-needed remittance to support children and relatives in their homeland. Changing jobs entailed bureaucratic delays, considerable expense, and could reduce their chances of being viewed as reliable and hard-working when they came to submit their application for landed-immigrant status. Lack of freedom to change jobs, negotiate with employers or even complain about their treatment was expressed by a number of "third world" women, including Cynthia and Jocie:

> Each time you have to change jobs, you pay Immigration $100. . . . It doesn't look good on your record—that's why a lot of people take the abuse, you can't be bothered changing this and that. And then the probability of you meeting someone who is decent is 0.000000 up to infinity 1. (Cynthia, Jamaican)

> There's less problem [with Filipinas], because they don't complain. Even though they get into trouble, they just stay quiet. You know why? Because they don't want to get bad record from government. They want their immigration status. (Jocie, Filipina)

For most, living-in contributed to the feelings of isolation and loneliness associated with their job. Joan (a Filipina carer of an elderly couple) remarked that "when you live-in, you feel lonely, when you don't see anybody, just this old couple"; and Amy (Thai) said that: "My first employer never made me feel as if their home was mine. I missed my family. I became very lonesome and they wouldn't allow my friends to visit." Many of the domestic workers said that they felt like an intruder in their employer's house. For example, paid domestic workers are often segregated to selected areas of the household at specific times of the day—a practice that Romero (1992) terms "spatial deference" (also see Glenn, 1992). Cynthia (Jamaican) illustrated this concept when she talked of her employer's insistence on family privacy extending to making Cynthia wait until they had finished eating the meal that she had prepared, before "crawling out of my room to get something to eat." Of course, "spatial deference" highlights the use of space to reinforce the invisibility expected of domestic workers when their services were not required; and the "non-person," invisible identity domestic workers are expected to assume emphasizes the significance of geography at the household scale.

Typically, the women resented living-in because it often engendered a feeling of being trapped and also impinged upon their independence as adults. This was summed up by Joyce (Filipina): "I'm living under someone else's rules" and Ingrid (German): "I don't have to tell them where I'm going or what I'm doing all the time, but they ask anyway." Such feelings were exacerbated by the family's lack of respect for the domestic worker's privacy and space, especially when they have to share a bathroom, or if their bedrooms are all on the same floor. Immigration Canada states that employers should "provide accommodation which ensures privacy, such as a private room with a lock on the door," for which room and board is deducted monthly (Employment and Immigration Canada, 1992). Six of the women said that in at least one job they had bedroom doors without locks, which sometimes resulted in members of the family entering without knocking. Generally, living-in was less resented in more equitable, respectful employer–employee relationships, and the more privacy and freedom the women had, the more content they tended to be living-in. Once in a "good job," compromises were less frequent and usually compensated, and/or appreciated.

"Like One of the Family"?

> You're supposed to feel so privileged to be part of their family that you overlook everything else. (Cynthia, Jamaican)

The interviews indicated that "living-in" was an almost uniformly problematic experience for the women, but that the experience of being "like one of the family" was less even. The emotional involvement of domestic workers in private households can result in mutual friendships with the employers. Rollins (1985) even uses the term "maternalism" to convey the highly gendered and personal nature of this type of work relation, where women's supportive, nurturing roles alter the power dynamic. While nationality, "race"/ ethnicity, and class differences are very significant, the extent and way in which personalism is experienced obviously also depends on the personalities of the individual domestic worker and her employer. However, we think the interviews suggest that more equitable, mutually supportive, and respectful relationships were most often experienced where there was greater similarity in the identities of the domestic worker and her employer.

More than any other group, the white anglophones (Canadian, English, and Irish) reported having more informal and symmetrical relationships with their employers, sometimes describing their employers as "friends," or feeling that they are considered to be "like one of the family." As Barb (Canadian) told Bernadette:

> Sometimes we go from being like best friends to employer–employee. There's a line you can't cross when you're in this job. It's kinda weird, sometimes you're really good friends, and sometimes you can just say the wrong thing, if you are not in the friendship mode. (Barb, Canadian)

However, being "like one of the family" was also interpreted by some of the woman as a means of extracting further unpaid physical and affective labour, without the genuine caring and respect associated with familial relationships. Gregson and Lowe (1994) describe such relations as false kinship ties. Felicity expresses her disdain at what she felt were false displays of affection and kinship from her white employer:

> What I can't deal with is the idea that because I mop their floors, I'm stupid. They can do anything they want to me. They don't have to respect you, but they come with this disguise, "Oh, you're part of the family." They hug you. I don't want to be hugged! For God's sake, I'm your employee, treat me like an employee! I don't want to be hugged. But that's their way of trying to outsmart you. It's emotional blackmail.

> You're meant to think, "This nice white lady, she's hugging me." Then I'm supposed to take everything they dish out. I don't want that. I just want to be respected as a worker, with an employer–employee relationship. (Felicity, Jamaican)

Both Jamaican women with whom Bernadette spoke objected to what they considered to be a patronizing emotional association. Their comments also reflect Rollins' (1985) and Romero's (1992) observations that personalism across racial lines is often advantageous to the employer. Women of colour can become safe confidants for their middle class, white employers, as they each tend to have entirely different social networks. The inherent power relation means that the middle-class, white employer need not fear rebuttal, disapproval, or rejection.

Of course, no matter how symmetrical the employer–employee relationship, there still remains a status differential in terms of the work relation. Maryse (French) came to Canada as a nanny to learn English. In her first job she had difficulties based on her language ability. However, in her present job, class has emerged as a prominent factor in her relationship with her employer, who does not have a paid job outside the home:

> She's not from a rich family, but, because she's married to a neuro-surgeon, she feels she must live a good life . . . she's not a bad person, she's just snobby, and because of that it makes a big difference. She's a woman, she says "It's because I pay (you) I need everything, you have to give me everything." And she's really demanding. When she wants something, she wants it now. She's just like a spoilt kid. (Maryse, French)

We see the intersection of gender and class as very evident here. Asymmetric power relations are enforced because Maryse's employer feels that she should be able to purchase obedience through her husband's class position and her status as his wife. The gendered character of the domestic division of labour also comes into play as the employer sees herself as paying Maryse to do "her" chores. Moreover, it seems to us that the deference inherent in this type of work relation may have placed the employer in a position of power not otherwise available to her as a "housewife." This power differential seemed to have been internalized by Maryse who said: "You feel like a real slave. . . . I feel extremely humiliated sometimes. I know I shouldn't take it that way, but it's the way I feel."

The introduction of "race"/ethnicity differences into an already asymmetrical relationship multiplies the subtleties of those differences already inherent in class difference. Cynthia and Felicity (Jamaicans) both told Bernadette that they had experienced racism (as well as classism), often in quite overt and complex ways. Felicity maintained that racism was fundamental to explaining her situation, although she clearly understood that it is impossible to untangle "race" from other structures of differentiation.

> Sometimes when they treat you badly, it's because you're black, and they really just don't have any respect for you as a human being, no matter how educated, well-spoken, and no matter how good you are with the kids. But it's also because they pay you to be in their house that makes it even worse, you become nothing in their eyes. I can't tell you why, there are so many reasons, but they happen together, we come as one package. . . . They just abuse, abuse, abuse you. It doesn't matter how intelligent you may appear to be, they just look at you as a black helper. . . . Colour doesn't have any respect for class. They will still see you as a helper, no matter what. (Felicity, Jamaican)

In short, intimacy, affective labour, and a high degree of personalism often veil the asymmetrical class relation associated with paid domestic employment. However, we think the interviews also reveal that the class relation is constructed in relation to interlocking systems of "race"/ethnicity and gender.

Respect, Dignity, and Self-Worth

> I'm pretty well respected . . . what you say goes, and they're willing to come around to what you want. Well this one (her current employer), more than the first one. They know what you're capable of. She's always had NNEBs. She knows what to expect. (Kath, English)

Respect and dignity are fundamental to a person's feeling of self-worth and self-esteem, and are important in defining the dynamics of the social relations of paid domestic work. It does seem that the degree of respect experienced by different groups of domestic workers is highly variable and nuanced, with the overriding significant factor being the precise nature of each employer–employee relation—the attitude of the employer to her employee, and the ability of each domestic worker to be assertive in a given situation. The relative presence or absence of respect in the employer–employee work relation can also indicate the level of asymmetry in the power relation. Bradshaw-Camball and Cohen's (1988) concepts of the employer's "concern with equity and fairness" versus the employee's "sense of self-worth" are useful here.

As a white, anglophone Canadian, Barb shared the same citizenship and (at least in terms of her family background) class position as her employer. So, relative to the foreign domestic workers Bernadette interviewed, Barb experienced the most symmetrical power relations with her employer.

> My dad is not poor. I am not a poor person, I'm basically pretty privileged. My boss finds it weird that I'm on the same social scale as she is. I'm not impressed by the car she drives, or the house she lives in, so in a way that is different. I'm Canadian, I speak near-perfect English, and I'm educated . . . (our relationship) is pretty good. Having me was a bit of an adjustment because she was used to having a Filipina nanny, and to have someone who understands everything she says to me, and someone who's not going to fight her exactly, but not meekly let her walk all over me, was a big change for her. Sometimes we have our altercations over it. Other than that she really likes me, and I really like her. (Barb, Canadian)

Barb's confident and assertive personality must be placed in the broader context of her identity. Barb makes the interconnections between numerous systems of difference when explaining her reasonably symmetrical work relation. She does not stress her class background alone. Her country of origin (including its relative wealth), citizenship, language, and education intersect to construct her relatively privileged position. Indeed, the openly contested nature of this work relation appears to have presented more challenges for Barb's employer, who had been in a position of clear authority and control with her previous Filipina employee. As Barb put it: "The difference with me is that I have more choice, more freedom. Tomorrow if I think 'well, screw you,' I can walk out the door and go home." Barb became a nanny because she "loves kids," but she only saw her job as "something to do for now." We argue that Barb's secure social, economic, and political status as a Canadian, without immigration or employment restrictions, helped create a much more equitable power relation between her and her employer.

The other groups of foreign domestic workers seldom expressed the same level of friendship with, or respect from their employers. English language difficulties can distance non-anglophone domestic workers (even those from Europe) from the mutual respect or intimacy of personal friendship. Although they often talked about respect and mutuality, the non-anglophone domestic workers also talked of being made to feel "stupid" because of language and communication difficulties:

> These employers respect me, they respect what I have to say about the children, what I think should happen. They respect me (but sometimes) I think they must think that we are pretty stupid. . . . They really underestimated my intelligence, which is really insulting. (Silke, German)

However, it seemed to us that the non-anglophone Europeans often challenged their employers when they "underestimated their intelligence." As Anna (Hungarian) told Bernadette, "If your English is not that great, they think you're as stupid as your English is. But the first time you show that you are not, they know it!" We feel it is important to differentiate between East and West Europeans. For instance, Anna and Alena (Hungarians) experienced further degrees of isolation and alienation based on their transition from a socialist background to the Western culture of Canada. Alena felt that her employer had been especially neglectful of her responsibilities towards her foreign employee, and was insensitive to Alena's "culture shock." She felt that this, combined with her feelings of powerlessness and her employer's apparent lack of respect for her needs, prevented Alena from objecting to her employer's demands for emotional support:

> She's a single mother, when she comes home after a hard day, I am her spouse! When she talks to me about her troubles, all her hard times at work, somewhere behind that (is) "what an easy life you've got." Sometimes she wants to comfort me and say "I know how hard your day can be," but basically, I know what she thinks. Many times we ended up talking, imagine, I am desperate to get to my room. . . . I am willing to listen to her, but I'm very bothered by the fact that I'm paid there (and) she's still the boss actually, no matter how friendly she is. (And the) fact that she can use those things against you (in day-to-day confrontations and negotiations, or even with Employment and Immigration Canada), if I start talking about my problems. (Alena, Hungarian)

This situation is clearly not a mutually supportive emotional relationship. The asymmetric power relation is obvious, and it is only the emotional needs of the employer that are being met, with little consideration for the boundaries of the work relation, or Alena's personal needs.

"Race"/ethnicity differences further reinforced feelings of language inferiority, particularly if the employers did not seem to respect their employees efforts to learn English. Moreover, having their intellect demeaned was a particularly familiar experience for the Thai and Filipina women, as Amy (Thai) and Joan (Filipina) show:

> I didn't get on well with my employer. I couldn't speak English well. After seven months things got better, but they think you are stupid because you can't speak English, so they over-work you, they think you don't know the rules. . . . I was so upset when I heard them call me stupid. That made me determined to learn to speak English. (Amy, Thai)

The interviews are full of statements that illustrate that the stereotype of the uneducated, poor, "third world" domestic worker of colour, who cannot speak English is so persuasive and potent that it can lead to their educational achievements or middle-class background being discounted. Joan described her previous job:

> At my last employer, her daughter—she were talking to me, asking me about life in the Philippines. . . . And I was telling her, I never worked as a domestic back home. All of my family are educated, all the children and everything. And she felt that because she was not educated, she was just a high school graduate, working in Bell Canada, she felt like I am over her. She said to me, even though you are educated, they don't acknowledge your education here and you still belong to a poor country. That's what she told me! I don't say anything, because I think I hurt her feelings in some way. She had to find some way to put me down. I just don't say anything. I feel bad, but I just don't say anything. I just keep quiet. (Joan, Filipina)

It is evident that Joan disrupted and challenged the "third world domestic" stereotype. This family member reasserted an asymmetric power relation by reconstructing Joan as a "third world domestic" by discounting her worth, achievements and background as "inferior" to her own.

As with personalism, a "sense of self-worth" is dependent on a number of structural factors, including "race"/ethnicity, class, education, and training, as well as other factors such as personality, life experience, support networks, and family responsibilities. Similarly, the employer's "concern with equity and fairness" can also be related to her own and her employee's identity, personality, and life experiences. Overall, the interviews indicated to us that the white anglophones generally appeared to have a higher degree of confidence and a stronger "sense of self-worth," enabling them to be more assertive, while non-anglophones and women of colour experienced increasing degrees of difficulty in negotiating their position and gaining their employer's respect.

Conclusions

Our paper illustrates how paid domestic workers' experiences of the employer–employee relation are mediated through an interlocking, relational system of difference, particularly gender, class, "race"/ethnicity, immigration/citizenship status, and language. Commonalities of gender and occupation shared by domestic workers are cross-cut by locations of privilege and marginality in terms of class, citizenship/immigration status, "race"/ethnicity, country of origin, training, and language. The most privileged was the white, anglophone Canadian who experienced the most freedom, choice, and power, which meant she had a much more secure, symmetrical relationship with her employer compared to many of her foreign counterparts. Of the foreign domestic workers interviewed, the specific articulation of systems of difference led to a range of experiences of the extent of asymmetry in employer–employee power relations, with the greatest symmetry tending to be in those situations where the employee and employer held more similar positions in the social relations of difference.

However, we also want to emphasize that many of the women interviewed shared a number of common concerns. Almost all the domestic workers had, at some stage, experienced difficulties related to living-in, especially in dealing with employers who frequently demanded additional duties not stated on their contracts. But those who are less marginalized tended to be better able to negotiate these situations. Their locations in the systems of difference often related to their "sense of self-worth" in terms of their occupation and their experience of respect. One result tended to be that anglophone "nannies," unlike "third world" "domestic workers" were more likely to find jobs with better hours and less or no housework.

We have attempted to provide insights into the dynamic, complex, and interrelated character of the processes that shape employer–employee relations marked by the antagonisms, contradictions, and ambiguities associated with a "workplace" being someone else's "home." We have stressed that specific articulations of difference (as well as the specific context and the individual personalities involved) produce difference constellations of experiences of live-in paid domestic work.

Notes

1. We thank the staff and volunteers of Intercede for their time and access to their resources. We also thank women who participated in this research: they are identified by pseudonyms. We are grateful to Kevin Cox, Nancy Duncan, Linda McDowell, Lynn Staeheli, and the three reviewers for their helpful comments on an earlier version of this paper. Bernadette Stiell was partly funded by the Canadian Memorial Foundation.
2. Alice Childress's book is a fictional account that draws on lived experiences from the everyday lives of African American domestic workers.
3. The NNEB (National Nursery Examination Board) diploma is offered only in Britain. It is a two-year, postsecondary training program and is one of the most widely recognized qualifications in childcare.

References

Arat-Koç, S. 1992. "In the Privacy of Our Own Home: Foreign Domestic Workers as Solution to the Crisis of the Domestic Sphere in Canada," in M.P. Connelly and P. Armstrong, eds., *Feminism in Action: Studies in Political Economy*, pp. 149–75. Toronto: Canadian Studies Press.

Arat-Koç, S., and F. Villansin. 1990. "Report and Recommendations on the Foreign Domestic Movement Program." Submitted to the Ministry of Employment and Immigration on behalf of Intercede, Toronto Organization for Domestic Workers' Rights.

Bakan, A.B., and D. Stasiulis. 1994. "Foreign Domestic Worker Policy in Canada and the Social Boundaries of Modern Citizenship," *Science and Society* 58: 7–33.

———. 1995. "Making the Match: Domestic Placement Agencies and the Racialization of Women's Household Work," *Signs* 20: 303–35.

Bradshaw-Cambrall, P., and R. Cohen. 1988. "Feminists: Explorers or Exploiters," *Women and Environments* 11: 8–10.

Childress, A. 1956. *Like One of the Family*. Brooklyn, NY: Independence.

Cock, J. 1980. *Maids and Madams: A Study in the Politics of Exploitation*. Johannesburg: Raven Press.

Colen, S. 1989. "'Just a Little Respect': West Indian Domestic Workers in New York City," in E.M. Chaney and M.G. Castro, eds., *Muchachas No More: Household Workers in Latin America and the Caribbean*, pp. 171–94. Philadelphia: Temple University Press.

Employment and Immigration Canada. 1991. *Foreign Domestic Workers: Preliminary Statistical Highlight Report*. Ottawa: Employment and Immigration Canada.

———. 1992. *The Live-in Caregiver Program: Information for Employers and Live-in Caregivers from Abroad*. Ottawa: Employment and Immigration Canada.

Gaitskell, D., J. Kimble, M. Manconachie, and E. Unterhalther. 1984. "Class, Race, and Gender: Domestic Workers in South Africa," *Review of African Political Economy* 27/28: 86–108.

Glenn, E.N. 1986. *Issei, Nisei, War Bride: Three Generations of Japanese American Women and Domestic Service*. Philadelphia: Temple University Press.

———. 1992. "From Servitude to Service Work: Historical Continuities in the Racial Division of Paid Reproductive Labor," *Signs* 18: 1–43.

Gregson, N., and M. Lowe. 1994. *Servicing the Middle Classes: Class, Gender and Waged Domestic Work in Contemporary Britain*. London and New York: Routledge.

Hertz, R. 1986. *More Equal Than Others: Women and Men in Dual-career Marriages*. Berkeley, CA: University of California Press.

Hill-Collins, P. 1990. *Black Feminist Thought: Knowledge, Consciousness and the Politics of Empowerment*. London and New York: Routledge.

hooks, b. 1989. *Talking Back—Thinking Feminist, Thinking Black*. Boston: South End Press.

Kobayashi, A., and L. Peake. 1994. "Unnatural Discourse: 'Race' and Gender in Geography," *Gender, Place and Culture* 1: 225–43.

Macklin, A. 1992. "Foreign Domestic Worker: Surrogate Housewife or Mail Order Bride?," *McGill Law Journal* 37: 681–760.

Mattingley, D. 1996. "Domestic Service, Migration, and Local Labor Markets on the US–Mexican Border," PhD dissertation. Graduate School of Geography, Clark University, Worcester, MA.

McDowell, L. 1991. "The Baby and the Bath Water: Diversity, Deconstruction and Feminist Theory in Geography," *Geoforum* 22: 123–33.

Ng, R. 1993. "Racism, Sexism, and Immigrant Women," in B. Sadra, L. Code, and L. Dorney, eds., *Changing Patterns: Women in Canada*, pp. 279–301. Toronto: McClelland and Stewart.

Rollins, J. 1985. *Between Women: Domestics and Their Employers*. Philadelphia: Temple University Press.

Romero, M. 1992. *Maid in the USA*. London and New York: Routledge.

Ruddick, S. 1996. "Constructing Difference in Public Spaces: Race, Class, and Gender as Interlocking Systems," *Urban Geography* 17: 132–51.

Spelman, E. 1988. *Inessential Woman: Problems of Exclusion in Feminist Thought*. Boston: Beacon Books.

Thornton-Dill, B. 1994. *Across Boundaries of Class and Race: An Exploration of the Relationship between Work and Family among Black Female Domestic Servants*. New York: Garland Publishing.

PART IX
Gender and Media

The notion that Canadian society is saturated by media has become a cliché. Pop psychology and sociology abound with accounts of how media shape our beliefs and behaviours concerning gender. According to the most simplistic of these accounts, men and women mindlessly imitate the images of masculinity and femininity on their screens and pages, so that young women strive to be sexually provocative and skinny, while young men obsess over the macho trappings of violence.

The authors in this section go beyond this monkey-see-monkey-do approach to media and gender to examine how gender is constituted, represented, and differentiated in media products. There is much more to gender and media than simple imitation. Ideas about gender appear in ways that are not obvious or overt, and the "gendering" of media texts is often more complex than it appears at first.

Yasmeen Jiwani starts off with an examination of how Afghan women have been represented in mainstream Canadian media, which becomes a study of the intersecting cultural constructions of gender, racial category, and the "other." She suggests that the story of Canada's intervention in Afghanistan has been told through the media as a classic gender fable: the helpless, endangered maiden(s), rescued by the chivalric knight who can save them from the bad men. However, Jiwani points out that this is not only a story about gender, it is also a story about race and difference. Afghan women are made rescuable through their portrayal as passive, unable to save themselves, and culturally homogenous. These qualities differentiate them from the Canadian soldiers who fight the Taliban on their behalf. In a global context, this is a tale with neo-colonial implications, as Canada is positioned as not only symbolically masculine and heroic, but also as more "advanced" or "civilized" than Afghanistan. Jiwani is no apologist for the Taliban, but she is mindful of the pitfalls that lie in the ways this story gets told.

In contrast to the other articles in this section, which deal with the reinforcement of stereotypes about gender in the mainstream media. Alison Jacques examines what happens when these stereotypes are challenged. Her article examines media responses to a subculture driven by the explicit rejection and deconstruction of gender stereotypes: the "riot grrl" movements of the 1990s. She highlights the contradictions and ambivalences of this media treatment, in which opinion leaders such as *Rolling Stone* and *Seventeen* spread the word about the "grrls," while simultaneously repackaging the confrontational challenge of the movement into tame, non-threatening commodities.

Like Jiwani, Steven Jackson also addresses masculinized representations of Canada, but he does so through a rather different set of texts—beer advertisements. These will probably be familiar to everyone reading this textbook, but you may never before have thought of them as templates for masculinity. Jackson argues that these ads are not just offering up a "guidebook" for being masculine; they are offering a particularly *Canadian* vision of masculinity. In a globalizing world, in which much national distinctiveness is being erased, the creation of a distinct and self-conscious Canadian identity through gendered metaphors is noteworthy. This Canadian masculinity is not simply a way of being; it is also, inevitably, a commodity, which is bought and sold through buying and selling beer.

Questions for Critical Thought

1. The articles in this section deal primarily with "media 1.0," print and television. Do you find significant differences in the representation of gender in older media as compared to newer media, such as YouTube or Facebook?
2. Jiwani argues that the complex story of Afghanistan was streamlined into a simplistic narrative of good versus evil, with Canada positioned firmly on the side of good. Is it possible for mainstream media to tell complex stories? How might such as difficult and complicated story as Afghanistan be told better?
3. Do you consider yourself a creator of media content, or are you primarily a consumer? Are you an active or a passive consumer of media?
4. Are subcultural or countercultural movements like the one Jacques discusses inevitably co-opted by their incorporation into mass media? Do you know of any individuals or groups who successfully balanced subversion of gender stereotypes with mass appeal?

5. Do you consider yourself a critical consumer of media? What have you learned about gender from TV, Internet, social media, or print media?
6. Ads are often critiqued for their promotion of gender stereotypes, but Jackson argues that these gender stereotypes are also laden with connotations of other social categories, such as nationality. Are there any other media products you can think of which promote visions of "Canadianness"?
7. Why is beer advertising so strongly gendered, compared to (for example) ads for fast food or cars?
8. Can you recall media products you consumed as a child? How is children's media different from media targeted at adults, in terms of gender?
9. Should media be regulated in terms of the representation of gender? Should certain images or texts be censored or prohibited, or should anything be allowed?
10. If you have lived in different communities over the course of your life, have you noticed any difference in terms of the "mediascapes," and how gender is represented in different media products?

Chapter 32

Overview

Yasmin Jiwani turns a critical gaze on Canada's intervention in Afghanistan, reading it through a set of gendered metaphors. While she doesn't judge the rightness or wrongness of the intervention itself, she points out that the way in which it was conceptualized and presented in the mass media draws on stereotypes of powerful masculinity and vulnerable femininity. Jiwani argues that framing Afghan women as victims in need of rescue is a way of positioning Canada as an agent of "chivalric masculinity," coming to save endangered women. A few individual Afghan women are lauded for their courage or perseverance in the face of persecution by the Taliban, but "Afghan women" in general are described as passive or helpless. The benevolence of foreigners is needed to bring them out of their social and cultural captivity.

As Jiwani points out, this very gendered framing has several negative consequences. It distorts the reality of Afghan history by positioning the Taliban as the source of all problems, and it contributes to Islamophobia by implying that symbols of gender oppression such as the *burqa* are created by rigid adherence to Islam. It also implies that becoming like Western women is the ultimate goal for Afghan women, ignoring the possibility that their ideas of emancipation and liberation may not be the same as those held by Canadian women.

Jiwani doesn't minimize the challenges and constraints Afghan women are facing, nor does she condemn the empathy and concern that men and women around the world may feel for the women of Afghanistan. However, her piece is an important reminder of how media representations can produce overly simplistic gender dualities, like victim/hero, rescued/rescuer, or helpless maiden/chivalrous knight.

Helpless Maidens and Chivalrous Knights: Afghan Women in the Canadian Press

Yasmin Jiwani

> The knights of civilization aim to bring enlightened understanding to the further regions of the world still living in cruel and irrational traditions that keep them from developing the economic and political structures that will bring them a good life.
>
> —Iris Marion Young

Discourses of security depend on identifying a threat "out there" against which "we" can be defended. Although articulating a dominant ideological chord, such discourses are often rife with contradictions but inescapably anchored in a historical stock of knowledge. In the contemporary global context, the elimination of threat needs to be rationalized discursively if it is to obtain consent. . . . [As] Iris Marion Young argues . . . the state's civility assumes a chivalrous character, privileging a particular masculinist logic:

> In this patriarchal logic, the role of the masculine protector puts those protected, paradigmatically women and children, in a subordinate position of dependence and obedience. To the extent that citizens of a democratic state allow their leaders to adopt a stance of protectors toward them, these citizens come to occupy a subordinate status like that of women in the patriarchal household. (Young, 2003: 2)

Thus, according to Young, the two faces of the security state are constituted by a chivalric masculinity and a dominative masculinity that wages war against others "out there." It is this notion of chivalric masculinity that I wish to emphasize in this essay, for, as Young puts it, the "knights of civilization" redeem their dominative masculinity by being "good men" protecting their women within the homeland and rescuing helpless maidens outside it.

In this essay, I draw upon popular discourses that have circulated in the Canadian press, notably the *Globe and Mail*, to demonstrate constructions of Afghan women as quintessential innocent victims requiring rescue, wherein such a rescue mission produces and reproduces the chivalric code of masculinity that is the inverse of the hard power of the security state. Thus, conquest and containment (through profiling and security certificates) are legitimized through the soft power of intervention through rescue and aid leavened by civilizational discourses. I begin with a discussion situating representations of female victims of violence in the press, since a comparative examination of how different women are portrayed demonstrates their discursive construction as worthy or unworthy victims of rescue. Thereafter, I analyze the *Globe*'s representations of Afghan women derived from a search of the newspaper's archives over a seven-year period, paying particular attention to the kinds of frames that are deployed by the media to make "sense" of Afghan women as victims. I conclude by highlighting how the press works in concert with the state to secure consent for Canadian intervention in Afghanistan ("over there"), all the while occluding the reality of gendered violence ("over here") (S. Khan, 2001). In securing such consent, I argue, the security of Afghan women was imperilled as they were once again rendered objects of epistemic, material, and political violence (Ayotte and Husain, 2005).

Women As Victims in The News

. . . In her insightful analysis of the press coverage of women victims of violence, Marian Meyers argues that "news coverage of violent crimes reveals society's biases and prejudices. It tells us who is valued and who is not; whose life has meaning and whose is insignificant; who has power and who does not" (1997: 99). She adds that women are most likely to be represented as blameworthy victims of gender violence. In a similar vein, Ken Dowler, Thomas Fleming, and Stephen Muzzatti observe that women victims are often more heavily represented in the news, but that

> this newsworthiness is contingent on their social status: victims must be judged innocent, virtuous and honorable. Consequently, a paradox exists between victims who are "innocent" and those who are "blameworthy," a paradox rooted in patriarchal notions of femininity and gender stereotypes. (2006: 841)

It is this paradox that becomes evident in the reporting of differently racialized groups of women and their experiences of violence.

. . . Distinctions between worthy and unworthy victims are determined by race, class, gender, and sexuality, through which middle-class values and morality are asserted, naturalizing an "existing scheme of things" (1979: Hall 325–26). In a study of crime coverage concerning women in newspapers in Toronto, Scot Wortley (2002) observes that Black women who are victims of male violence are usually given less attention and that their stories are confined to the back pages. This echoes Dowler, Fleming, and Muzzatti's (2006) point that crime coverage depends on the status of the victim, wherein white, middle-class women as victims are more likely to be covered than their Black, working-class counterparts. In a similar vein, Warren Goulding (2001) argues that the murders of Aboriginal women in Canada scarcely generate any significant media coverage. In contrast, in previous research I have found that violence against women in the South Asian Canadian community has elicited far greater coverage in the Canadian press and that such coverage tends to invoke and articulate stereotypes about South Asian cultures and communities as exotic and deviant others (Jiwani, 2006). It would seem, then, that how and which stories about violence against women are covered depends not only on the status and race of the women, but also on cumulative knowledge that exists about particular groups of women along with the stereotypes, common sense notions, and historical experiences that inform such a stock of knowledge.

News coverage, bounded as it is within the parameters of values of newsworthiness, tends to focus on those stories that ideologically make "sense." To put it another way, stories are more likely to be told if they are considered to be relevant, timely, or unusual, and if they pertain to a conflict and/or involve elite nations and personalities. Hence, stories about honour killings (which are framed as emblematic of "exotic" cultures) are more likely to get press than those dealing with "home-grown" domestic violence (Narayan, 1997).

"Liberating Afghan Women"

The "rescue motif" has been a repeated feature of colonial discourse, invoked especially when it has suited colonial powers to invade, conquer, and subjugate the colonized (Abu-Lughod, 2002; Grewal, 2003; Macdonald, 2006). The burqa in Afghanistan, the chador in Iran, and the abaya in Saudi Arabia, not to mention similar forms of veiling in other Muslim states, have become iconic symbols of women's oppression under Islam. The mobilization of the US-led intervention into Afghanistan after 11 September, for example, has utilized this image to secure consent for war. Under the guise of a "rescue" mission, the intervention has been aimed explicitly, and especially rhetorically, at establishing democracy and equality in Afghanistan, and liberating Afghans from the yoke of Taliban tyranny (Hunt, 2002; Russo, 2006).

Eric Louw (2003) insightfully analyzes how the Pentagon has strategically utilized the trope of the oppressed Afghan women. He notes that the Pentagon's public relations strategy has involved searching the nongovernmental organization sphere for suitable discourses that could be brought in to harness the war effort. The issue of women's oppression under the Taliban had been circulating in these spheres since 1996. Yet it was not until 2001 that the Pentagon saw it as a cause worthy enough to mobilize its military intervention and revive flagging support for the war. Naturally, there have been other economic and politically motivated reasons for engaging in the war. Nevertheless, the use of women's bodies has served a useful ploy.

Charles Hirschkind and Saba Mahmood (2002) argue that Hollywood celebrities, in conjunction with the Feminist Majority Foundation in the United States, were the first to publicize the oppression of Afghan women in the West. From there, concern over Afghan women's oppression escalated after 11 September when US First Lady Laura Bush and Britain's Cherie Blair's respective and heavily publicized speeches heightened public attention. Thereafter, even Benetton, the popular clothing company, featured burqa-clad women on its website (an image that has since been removed). What has horrified the West is the Taliban's complete suppression of women's rights, including the right to wear lipstick and nail polish, reveal one's face, wear shoes that make any kind of noise, appear in public without the burqa and unaccompanied by a male relative, and participate in educational and social exchanges and work. . . .

What was largely elided in the media coverage that followed in the immediate aftermath of September 11 was that the Taliban's strictures were imposed largely on urban women (in Kabul, for instance), and that women's oppression was scarcely less prior to the Taliban takeover (Hirschkind and Mahmood, 2002). Sonali Kolhatkar notes that, after ousting the Soviet-backed regime in

Afghanistan, the US—and Saudi Arabia—financed Mujahadeen "instituted laws banning alcohol and requiring that women be veiled. Both of these new crimes were punishable by floggings, amputations, and public executions" (2002: 16).

Women's illiteracy rates were high before the Taliban gained control over Afghanistan; maternal death and infant mortality rates were equally high (Barakat and Wardell, 2002). The extreme economic deprivation faced by women prior to and after Taliban control has often been negated in press accounts, as is the fact that it was under Soviet occupation that women had enjoyed the most freedom and greater access to education and services.[1] Neither has much been made of the fact that the particular brand of Deobandi Islam that was exported (from Saudi Arabia) to Afghanistan at that time embodied the same literal interpretation of Islam as that imposed by the Taliban (see Entman, 2003; Kellner, 2003). However, as Robert M. Entman points out, this particular frame of analysis underscoring Saudi involvement, though attempted by various journalists in the United States, has not been able to dislodge the White House's preferred framing of the Taliban as the archetypal force of evil and of Osama bin Laden as the formidable villain (Agathangelou and Ling, 2004; Winch, 2005). That both the Taliban and Al-Qaeda have been considered synonymous and used rhetorically as instruments of evil and oppression obscures the reality that the Taliban would have continued to exercise its oppressive regime with or without bin Laden or Al-Qaeda (Ayotte and Husain, 2005).

Afghan Women in the *Globe and Mail*

A search of the Factiva database (2000–07) yielded 254 stories in the *Globe and Mail* that make some mention of Afghan women.[2] After discarding letters to the editor and articles that refer to Afghan women only in passing, 229 stories remain in the final corpus for my analysis. Not surprisingly, the concentration of stories dealing with Afghan women peaks in 2001–02. Thereafter, the number of stories declines, yet their significance does not. Throughout this seven-year period, the spectre of the victimized Afghan women surfaces repeatedly, often harnessed to Canadian benevolence and justification for the military intervention in Afghanistan. So much is this trope utilized that even when newspapers report on flagging support for the war, as evident in the results of popular opinion polls, retired Major-General Lewis MacKenzie has countered that pollsters have been asking the wrong questions. Instead, he opines, pollsters should ask the public the following:

> "Do you support beheading teachers in front of their class if they permit even one girl to attend?" "Do you support denying all Afghan women the right to visit a doctor, as there are no female doctors permitted by the Taliban and male doctors are not allowed to inspect female patients?" "Do you support the government's right to execute women by blowing out their brains in front of thousands of cheering onlookers in a football stadium because the victims were seen in the company of men other than their husbands?" "Do you support the actions of a suicide bomber who, just before he blows himself up beside elderly Muslims waiting to obtain papers for a once-in-a-lifetime pilgrimage to Mecca, picks up a child and presses her against his explosive vest before detonating himself?" (MacKenzie, 2006)[3]

Rather than interrogating this complicity, Canadian journalists, like their American counterparts, have belaboured the oppression of Afghan women. One popular columnist has gone so far as to describe Afghan women as "walking wombs" under Taliban reign:

> The women of Afghanistan are the most oppressed group of people in the world. Their country has been destroyed by wave on wave of war, and now they live under the tyranny of brutal misogynists. The Taliban believes that females are scarcely more than walking wombs, and they treat them worse than animals. If—when—the Taliban is overthrown, the women of Afghanistan will probably be better off. (Wente, 2001a)

. . . There are two issues here worthy of examination; first is the orientalist (Said, 1978) framing of Afghanistan and the justification for war; second is the notion of the oriental woman as needing to be saved. To be "saved," women have to be considered worthy of rescue. Afghan women are rendered worthy of this rescue (even though their situation has not changed for the better since then) by virtue of the construction of the Taliban as an ultra-patriarchal force representative of Islam. This reinforces stereotypical constructions about the barbaric nature of Islam and its subhuman treatment of women, a theme that resonates with orientalist literature and popular images of oppressed Muslim women (Rosenberg, 2002).

A Joyless, Monomaniacal Theocracy

Constructed as a misogynistic force of evil, the Taliban constitutes an aberrance that is institutionally grounded (through a specific interpretation of Islam), embodying what Geoffrey York calls a "joyless, monomaniacal theocracy" (2001b). Armed with weapons, reliant on the drug trade, and engaged in the sale of women as well as in their complete oppression, the Taliban is portrayed as an undifferentiated mass, a force that can be countered only with the enlightened force of the West. As one editorial opines, "The driving force is misogyny masquerading as faith and paternalistic protection" ("Women").

Afghan women's oppression is underscored at every turn. What seals their representation discursively as victims worthy of rescue are particular features interwoven through most of these stories. First and foremost is the consistent repetition, almost mantra-like, of the excesses of the Taliban. Thus, with every reference to the Taliban one finds some mention of the actions it has committed in the name of Islam to suppress women's rights and liberties. This continual reference effectively conjures associations among the burqa, Islam, the Taliban, and oppression, thereby creating a mediated template of fundamentalist Islam. Jenny Kitzinger observes that

> templates serve as rhetorical shorthand, helping journalists and audiences to make sense of fresh news stories. They are instrumental in shaping narratives around particular social problems, guiding public discussion not only about the past, but also the present and the future. (2000: 61)

What makes these stories particularly poignant in terms of summoning feelings of identification and empathetic, if not sympathetic, sentiment is that the Afghan women are constructed as victims through no fault of their own except in being women. Thus, in one particularly compelling article, Lauren Oates states, "The treatment of Afghan women under the Taliban was so excessive in its brutality that it has been dubbed 'gendercide' or 'gender apartheid'" (2006). This notion of "gendercide" is a powerful discursive move, as it suggests that, without the Taliban and their particular interpretation of Islam, Afghan women would not have been so oppressed—a point of view that camouflages previous US imperial interests and involvement in the region (Russo, 2006).

However, in the aftermath of the coalition forces entering Afghanistan, the lack of an immediate military success by NATO and Canadian forces, not to mention the absence of a widespread and joyous "liberation" of Afghan women through a massive public unveiling, has resulted in a reframing of the Taliban oppression template, such that Taliban excesses have become redefined in cultural and essentialist terms. In other words, the women have been positioned as culture-bound, and it has been implied that only through exposure to the West could they be sufficiently enlightened to undertake the task of their own liberation. . . .

"Rescue-ability," then, comes to be defined through terms that reveal how these women have become "ours" or more like us. The discarding of the burqa constitutes one such sign—and much has been made of it in the few instances in which women have publicly de-veiled themselves (Wente, 2001b).

Yet another sign of this "rescue-ability" can be read in terms of Afghan women's embracing of Western economic initiatives. For example, after the Taliban conceded defeat, one of the first business initiatives to be deployed in Afghanistan concerned the beautification of Afghan women, with major US cosmetic companies funding various programs (Ghafour, 2004a). This suggests how, through such enterprises, women can be cultivated into future consumers. Micro-credit endeavours have also received considerable media coverage because of their success among Afghan women, as evidenced in a telling example:

> Bibi Qutbi . . . lives on the side of a hill that surrounds Kabul, in a house carved out from the rock face. Ms Qutbi's husband is unemployed and her son is disabled. She is a tailor, who took out a $200 loan to import gold and silver thread from India.
>
> She is now a certified provider of hand-embroidered badges for police and military. She has a steady market and is training several other women to join her. Proceeds from her business support her family and go toward medical treatment. (Grant, 2007)

Thus, through the rescue mission (in the form of military intervention, micro-credit enterprises, and beauty schools), Afghan women are rendered more like "us." They demonstrate initiative and, in their embracing of Western ways, they prove their deservedness as victims worthy of saving and, in line with that, as potential consumers for Western goods.

The Heroic Afghan Women

The second aspect of the media discourse that underscores the worthiness of Afghan women as victims is evident in a combination of stories that stresses their resilience, agency, and resistance to the Taliban. Numerous stories detail the challenges they have faced, the individual risks they have undertaken, and their fearlessness in the face of death threats, beatings, executions, and the like. These first-person accounts of suffering are also marked by tropes of normalcy, situating these women as engaging in day-to-day activities, often emphasized by reference to their vocations. Here is one such example dating back to a news story published in 2000:

> Kabul—Her name is Fatima, and she was risking a beating. Defiantly, she stood outside, talking to a man. Her face was uncovered.
>
> Under Taliban rule, such openness by a woman is forbidden. But Fatima said she did not care. She was growing used to a life with some risk. Three months ago, she and a few other women decided to break the law. They opened a school for girls. . . .
>
> A teacher by training, she is in her 30s. She was dressed smartly in a black jacket and long skirt. Standing in an open courtyard, her cheeks had become rosy from the morning cold. She was wearing lipstick. (Bearak, 2000)

The heroism of Afghan women is a recurrent theme throughout the seven-year period examined here. Thus, through these news stories the audience learns about Afghan women such as Sima Samar, a physician living in exile who organized and managed clinics and schools of girls (York, 2002); Masooda Jalal, a presidential candidate who ran against Hamid Karzai in the elections held by the grand council in 2002 (MacKinnon, 2002) and in 2004 (Wente, 2004); Badrai, an illiterate Afghan woman who, despite threats against her, registered to vote in the election (Ghafour, 2004c); Malalai Joya, a populist hero who also ran for office (Ghafour, 2004b); Malalai Badahari, a counter-narcotics cop (Morarjee, 2005); Safia Ama Jan, provincial director for the Ministry of Women's Affairs who was killed by the Taliban (N. Khan, 2006); Rona Tareen (Blatchford, 2006), her successor; and countless other women whose heroic deeds are outlined in some detail in the *Globe*'s articles. What is interesting about these stories is that the women are named, individualized, and quoted directly. Not only are women in Afghanistan represented in such heroic terms, but so too are the fleeing women refugees whose stories of extreme hardship and distress make for a compelling read (see for example, York, 2001a).

Closer to home, Canadian women of Afghan origin are similarly described in this corpus of articles. For instance, Nelofar Pazira, author of *A Bed of Red Flowers* and featured in the film *Kandahar*, is quoted as saying, "For me, the issue of death is resolved. I am ready to die any moment if I have to. I'm not afraid of it. I look at the faces of those little Afghan girls I have seen starving,

I see myself in them" (McLaren, 2001). Pazira's statement can be read as a form of ventriloquism, echoing what "we" as the audience would expect of her. In her analysis of *Kandahar*, Weber remarks that President George W. Bush specifically wanted to view this film and encouraged all Americans to see it. Central to its strategic value is the United States appropriation of the film as a text that has "propelled occidental subjects to 'lift the veil' on Afghanistan and on Afghan women by viewing *Kandahar* as if it [has] positioned the feminine as a needy and wiling object of us rescue" (Weber, 2005: 360). . . .

Canadian Benevolence

The heroism and unflinching commitment of Afghan women is matched by Canadian benevolence, which ostensibly seems to bring out the best in people in Afghanistan. The corpus included numerous stories that detailed initiatives by individuals and their families in Canada to help support Afghan women. Sally Armstrong, author of *Veiled Threat: The Hidden Power of the Women of Afghanistan* (2003), in decrying Canada's vacillating commitment to military involvement in ensuring security and, thus, democracy (the two issues are interlinked in this news discourse), wrote,

> Canadians have done impressive work to deliver the promises made in Bonn. Two Calgary women started an organization called Women for Women in Afghanistan and raised $500,000 that goes directly to nurses' training, school kits, and an orphanage. A Toronto woman started a fundraiser called Breaking Bread for Women that has held more than 400 potluck suppers across Canada and raised half a million dollars to pay teachers in Afghanistan. A Winnipeg man brought together medical students from universities across Canada to restock the library at Kabul University's medical school; the Canadian military delivered the books, and a philanthropist in Vancouver paid the cost of sending a librarian to Kabul to train the library staff. (Armstrong, 2006)

That aside, news reports also detail the Canadian government's contributions to Afghanistan, including micro-loans to 135,000 Afghan women, special health project grants, and contributions by the Canadian International Development Agency. As well, the military's presence has been identified as a significant Canadian contribution.

In all these stories, Canadians' benevolence and noblesse oblige are highlighted. As General Rick Hillier, former chief of the Defence Staff, has reportedly stated, "We are in Afghanistan to help Afghans. . . . We're not there to build an empire, we're not there to occupy a country. We're there to help Afghan men, women, and children rebuild their families" (Den Tandt, 2006). In keeping with the gendered theme, Governor General Michaëlle Jean, during her visit to Afghanistan on International Women's Day, has been quoted as saying,

> The women of Afghanistan may face the most unbearable conditions, but they never stop fighting for survival. . . . Of course, we, the rest of the women around the world, took too long to hear the cries of our Afghan sisters, but I am here to tell them that they are no longer alone. And neither are the people of Afghanistan. (Friesen, 2007)

Canadian "rescue" efforts continue.

Conclusion

In their introduction to *Going Global: The Transnational Reception of Third World Women Writers*, Amal Amireh and Lisa Majaj outline the prevailing paradigms that organize relations between Third World and First World women: "[T]he 'saving brown women from brown men' model, the 'victims of culture' model, and the 'feminist by exposure to the *West*' model" (2000: 7). The burqa-Islam-Taliban-oppression template articulates these paradigms. First, the barbarism of the Taliban underscores the worthiness of Afghan women as victims by making explicit the imposed nature of the oppression. Second, the failure of the women to engage in massive and public de-veiling after the fall of the Taliban preempts any revelation of the hollow discourse of women's liberation being used by the United States and its allies (Arat-Koc, 2002). Culture becomes the focal point of attention, and the need for rescue is thus reframed as one of saving women from what Uma Narayan has described as "death by culture" (1997). Finally, the juxtaposition of Afghan heroines with the agency and commitment of diasporic Afghan women (from Canada, the United States, and elsewhere in the West) reaffirms the notion of Afghan women as inherently "like us"—fighting against oppression and thus worthy of our support. In this respect, although they are directly named and quoted, their voices echo Western assumptions. Culminating in this portrayal is the constant and repeated assertion that this oppression has been imposed first by Islam and then by a barbaric culture.

Acknowledgements

This research was made possible by funding from the Social Sciences and Humanities Research Council of Canada. I am especially indebted to Vivian Tabar and Alan Wong for their critical insights and editorial assistance. I would also like to acknowledge Reisa Klein and Meg Leitold for their research assistance.

Notes

1. Only one story celebrates women's achievements (as pilots) during the Soviet occupation in the *Globe*'s coverage during these seven years (see Smith, 2006).
2. The *Globe and Mail* is one of Canada's national dailies, regarded as a newspaper of record, influencing policy decisions and targeting a middle-class, educated readership.
3. The Canadian government has recognized the strategic value of this discursive move with the revelations from a report it had commissioned that declining support for the war could be shifted if the emphasis were put on "rebuilding," "enhancing the lives of women and children," and "peacekeeping" (Freeman, 2007). Thus, women and children have continued to play a significant role in harnessing support for Canada's continued military involvement in Afghanistan.

References

Abu-Lughod, L. 2002. "'Do Muslim Women Really Need Saving?': Anthropological Reflections on Cultural Relativism and Its Others," *American Anthropologist* 104(3): 783–90.

Agathangelou, A.M., and L.H.M. Ling. 2004. "Power, Borders, Security, Wealth: Lessons of Violence and Desire from September 11," *International Studies Quarterly* 48(3): 517–38.

Amireh, A., and L. Suhair Majaj, eds. 2000. *Going Global: The Transnational Reception of Third World Women Writers*. New York: Garland.

Arat-Koc, S. 2002. "Hot Potato: Imperial Wars or Benevolent Interventions? Reflections on 'Global Feminism' post September 11th," *Atlantis* 26(2): 433–44.

Armstrong, S. 2003. *Veiled Threat: The Hidden Power of the Women of Afghanistan*. Toronto: Penguin Canada.

———. 2006. "We've Forgotten Why We're Really in Afghanistan," *Globe and Mail*, 20 March.

Ayotte, K.J., and M.E. Husain. 2005. "Securing Afghan Women: Neocolonialism, Epistemic Violence, and the Rhetoric of the Veil," *NWSA Journal* 17(3): 112–33.

Barakat, S., and G. Wardell. 2002. "Exploited by Whom? An Alternative Perspective on Humanitarian Assistance to Afghan Women," *Third World Quarterly* 23(5): 909–30.

Bearak, B. 2000. "Afghan Women Run Risk for Education: In a Drafty Rundown Building, a

Kabul Girls' School Operates in Defiance of the Taliban," *Globe and Mail,* 10 March.

Blatchford, C. 2006. "Women's Director Who Faces Down Fear Gets a Quiet Boost from Canadian Team: Courage and Ruin in Afghanistan," *Globe and Mail*, 18 December.

Den Tandt, M. 2006. "PM Eyes Afghan Sojourn: With Many Wary of the Mission, Top Soldier Calls Potential Visit by Harper 'Heartening,'" *Globe and Mail*, 25 February.

Dowler, K., T. Fleming, and S.L. Muzzatti. 2006. "Constructing Crime: Media, Crime, and Popular Culture," *Canadian Journal of Criminology and Criminal Justice* 48(6): 837–50.

Entman, R.M. 2003. "Cascading Activation: Contesting the White House's Frame after 9/11," *Political Communication* 20(4): 415–32.

Freeman, A. 2007. "Change Tune on War, PM Told: Adopt Softer Vocabulary to Reassure Skeptical Public, Report Says," *Globe and Mail*, 13 July.

Friesen, J. 2007. "Jean Makes Surprise Visit to Afghanistan: Governor-General Praises Local Women and Those Serving in Canadian Military," *Globe and Mail*, 9 March.

Ghafour, H. 2004a. "Beauticians without Borders Teach Basics to Afghan Women," *Globe and Mail*, 24 February.

———. 2004b. "A Populist Hero Emerges from under the Rule of the Gun," *Globe and Mail*, 27 July.

———. 2004c. "Universal Suffrage Not without Suffering: Bombs, Land Mines, Executions and Threats Make Many Afghan Women Fearful of Voting," *Globe and Mail*, 2 July.

Goulding, W. 2001. *Just Another Indian*. Alberta: Fifth House.

Grant, T. 2007. "Small Loans, Big Dreams: A Microfinance Agency Run by an Expatriate Is Helping Afghan Women Achieve Financial Stability," *Globe and Mail*, 30 April.

Grewal, I. 2003. "Transnational America: Race, Gender and Citizenship after 9/11," *Social Identities* 9(4): 535–61.

Hall, S. 1979. "Culture, the Media and the 'Ideological Effect,'" in J. Curran, M. Gurevitch, and J. Woollacott, eds., *Mass Communication and Society*, pp. 315–47. London: Arnold in association with Open University Press.

Hirschkind, C., and S. Mahmood. 2002. "Feminism, the Taliban, and the Politics of Counter-insurgency," *Anthropological Quarterly* 75(2): 339–54.

Holland, P. 1996. "When a Woman Reads the News," in H. Baehr and A. Gray, eds., *Turning It On: A Reader in Women and Media*, pp. 195–200. London: Arnold.

Hunt, K. 2002. "The Strategic Co-optation of Women's Rights, Discourse in the 'War on Terrorism,'" *International Feminist Journal of Politics* 4(1): 116–21.

Jiwani, Y. 2006. *Discourses of Denial: Mediations of Race, Gender and Violence*. Vancouver: University of British Columbia Press.

Kellner, D. 2003. *From 9/11 to Terror War: The Dangers of the Bush Legacy*. Lanham: Rowman and Littlefield.

Khan, N. 2006. "Educator Shot Dead by Militants in Kandahar: Taliban Take Credit for Gunning Down Popular Afghan Women's-Rights Activist," *Globe and Mail*, 26 September.

Khan, S. 2001. "Between Here and There: Feminist Solidarity and Afghan Women," *Genders* 33. www.genders.org/g33/g33_kahn.html

Kitzinger, J. 2000. "Media Templates: Patterns of Association and the (Re)Construction of Meaning over Time," *Media, Culture & Society* 22(1): 61–84.

Kolhatkar, S. 2002. "The Impact of US Intervention on Afghan Women's Studies," *Berkeley Women's Law Journal* 17: 12–30.

Louw, P.E. 2003. "The 'War against Terrorism': A Public Relations Challenge for the Pentagon," *Gazette* 65(3): 211–30.

Macdonald, M. 2006. "Muslim Women and the Veil: Problems of Image and Voice in Media Representations," *Feminist Media Studies* 6(1): 7–23.

MacKenzie, L. 2006. "Remember the Taliban, and Stay the Course," *Globe and Mail*, 10 October.

MacKinnon, M. "Karzai's Plans Include Afghan Truth Commission: Newly Elected President to Move Slowly in Land Where Warlords Ruled for Years," *Globe and Mail*, 14 June.

McLaren, L. 2001. "'1 Am Ready to Die any Moment.' In Returning to Afghanistan in a Futile Attempt to Rescue Her Childhood Friend from the Taliban, the Ottawa Resident Risked Her Life," *Globe and Mail*, 20 October.

Meyers, M. 1997. *News Coverage of Violence against Women: Engendering Blame*. Thousand Oaks: Sage.

Morarjee, R. 2005. "Women Soldier against Drugs in 'the New Afghanistan,'" *Globe and Mail*, 23 April.

Narayan, U. 1997. *Dislocating Cultures: Identities, Traditions, and Third World Feminism*. New York: Routledge.

Oates, L. 2006. "Don't Share a Table with the Taliban: Women's Rights Would Be Negotiated out of Existence by Misogynists," *Globe and Mail*, 3 November.

Rosenberg, E.S. 2002. "Rescuing Women and Children," *Journal of American History* 89(2): 456–65.

Russo, A. 2006. "The Feminist Majority Foundation's Campaign to Stop Gender Apartheid," *International Feminist Journal of Politics* 8(4): 557–80.

Said, E. 1978. *Orientalism*. New York: Random House.

Smith, G. 2006. "Sisters Sailed from the Heavens," *Globe and Mail*, 21 August.

Weber, C. 2005. "Not without My Sister(s): Imagining a Moral American in Kandahar," *International Feminist Journal of Politics* 7(3): 358–76.

Wente, M. 2004. "'No One Wants to Be the First to Bring His Wife to Vote,'" *Globe and Mail*, 7 October.

———. 2001a. "The Taliban's Forgotten War on Women," *Globe and Mail*, 20 September.

———. 2001b. "Will We Sell Out Afghan Women?," *Globe and Mail*, 24 November.

Winch, S.P. 2005. "Constructing an 'Evil Genius': News Uses of Mythic Archetypes to Make Sense of Bin Laden," *Journalism Studies* 6(3): 285–99.

"Women and the Taliban." 2001. Editorial. *Globe and Mail*, 4 June.

Wortley, S. 2002. "Misrepresentation or Reality? The Depiction of Race and Crime in the Toronto Print Media," in B. Schissel and C. Brooks, eds., *Marginality & Condemnation: An Introduction to Critical Criminology*, pp. 55–82. Halifax: Fernwood.

York, G. 2002. "Holy War Engulfs Afghan Feminist," *Globe and Mail*, 7 August.

———. 2001a. "'The People Pay the Price.' Najla, an Afghan Mother of Six, Has Clung to Her Life in Kabul throughout Rocket and Missile Attacks, Droughts and the Rule of the Taliban. But When News of the Attack in New York Filtered down to Her Mud House, She Knew She Must Flee . . . ," *Globe and Mail*, 22 September.

———. 2001b. "Under the Hammer: No Pity, No Remorse; American Bombing Is Only Adding to the Repression of Life under a Joyless, Monomaniacal Theocracy," *Globe and Mail*, 1 November.

Young, I.M. 2003. "The Logic of Masculinist Protection: Reflections on the Current Security State," *Signs* 29(1): 1–25.

Chapter 33

Overview

Alison Jacques addresses a gendered movement that defines itself by opposition to the mainstream media and explicit rejection of the values and norms its adherents believe are embedded in these media.

The riot grrl movement is an amorphous and loosely bounded collection of musicians, writers, and artists who adopt a radical analysis of gender and a politically informed infusion of theory and activism into their cultural work. They have affiliations with the punk scene but are adamant that they are feminists, first and foremost.

However, keeping the mainstream media at a distance is tricky and problematic for the riot grrls. While media attention could dilute and commodify their message of radical empowerment, the mainstream media is also the best way to reach other girls and women who are not part of the tightly connected riot grrl networks. Jacques describes this as the "reach out/sell out" dilemma. Can messages of gender transformation be spread through the media? Or will these messages inevitably be distorted by the same forces that produce "moral panics" and negative stereotypes?

You Can Run but You Can't Hide: The Incorporation of Riot Grrrl into Mainstream Culture

Alison Jacques

The group of young punk feminists calling itself "riot grrrl" always struck me as a subculture built on contradiction. On the one hand, its call for a "Revolution Girl Style Now" is basically an angrier, more urgent version of the second-wave feminist assertion that "sisterhood is powerful." Springing from the male-dominated terrain of punk (and male-dominated society at large), riot grrrl promoted female empowerment, expression, and "girl love," and gave voice to many women's experiences that have traditionally been silenced. But, rather than taking the opportunity to spread its message and reach out to as many girls and women as possible through the mass media, riot grrrl opposed media coverage with a vehemence that verged on paranoia. Much of the group's energy was spent staying out of the spotlight, and its "revolution" was therefore limited to those in the know.

I am interested in the process by which a subculture is brought to the mainstream, and I will attempt in this paper to demonstrate that riot grrrl was subject to this process of incorporation despite its attempts to resist.

Riot Grrrl: Revolution, Whose Style?

The beginnings of the riot grrrl (RG) movement can be traced to 1990 when, according to Theo Cateforis and Elena Humphreys, young women in Olympia, Washington, "decided to react against that city's stagnant male-dominated punk scene" (1997: 320). In August 1991 the week-long International Pop Underground Convention in Washington, D.C., kicked off with Girl Day, which, in retrospect, was RG's "coming out" party. In 1992, the three-day national Riot Grrrl Convention was held in D.C., comprising a number of educational workshops on topics such as violence against women, fat oppression, and unlearning racism; performances by female bands and spoken word artists; and the "All-Girl All-Night Dance Party" (Cateforis and Humphreys, 1997: 320; Klein, 1997: 214).

Generally speaking, RG emerged as an American-based movement comprising young female punks who were fed up with the overwhelming maleness of punk rock, as well as being feminists who were fed up with sexism in general. The bands (e.g., Bikini Kill, Bratmobile, Heavens to Betsy) were on independent record labels. Media-savvy grrrls hooked up through self-published fanzines and word-of-mouth. Their lyrics and other writing centred on themes of sexual abuse, oppression, and body image. They attended and organized conventions and fundraisers around feminist issues. They adopted slogans like "Revolution Girl Style Now" and "Stop the J-Word jealousy from Killing Girl Love" (Klein, 1997: 213). They took the original punk do-it-yourself approach to music-making, encouraging female peers to pick up instruments and form bands. They were overwhelmingly white, mostly middle class, many were college educated, and a large proportion identified as queer. Membership of RG was relatively small when compared to that of other subcultures, such as punk or hip hop. According to the pop-cult web site alt.culture, RG numbers were "grossly over-inflated by a media titillated by the notion of a teenage girl army" ("rock women, 1999").

One must consider the context from which a subculture springs, as well as the context within which it is received by the mainstream, in order to avoid overstating its innovation—a tendency of early subculture theorists (see Clarke, 1997). As stated, RG was a musical and political subculture, born of punk rock and feminism. Riot grrrls were certainly not the first women in punk, nor were they the first feminists to make political music. But, as a group, they were the first to deliberately and explicitly fuse the two realms with such an aggressive, in-your-face style. A Bikini Kill performance, for example, was described as "not just a vague, fuck-society punk gesture, but a focused critique of the [patriarchal structure of the] punk scene itself" (White, 1995: 399). Several writers have noted a mid-'80s shift within punk toward a hardcore, misogynist scene that many females found hostile and unwelcoming (Cateforis and Humphreys, 1997; Gottlieb and Wald, 1994; Klein, 1997; Wald, 1998). Many riot grrrls were students or graduates of college Women's Studies programs, as well as being "daughters of seventies women's libbers" (White, 1995: 404)—feminist discourse and political action were familiar. In terms of the context within which RG was received—or, why the media would be "titillated by the notion of a teenage girl army"—I believe it is significant that rap music was gaining widespread popularity in the late 1980s; it is possible that angry white women seemed positively charming to the media compared to angry black men.

Antagonism between RG and mainstream media is well documented (see Cateforis and Humphreys, 1994; Gottlieb and Wald, 1994; Greenblatt, 1996; Klein, 1997). The most popular version of events is that distorted or dismissive press coverage of RG led the grrrls to establish a nationwide media blackout in 1992–93. After all, according to Kathleen Hanna (Bikini Kill singer and oft-touted RG leader), "we weren't doing what we did to gain fame, we were just trying to hook up with other freaks" (qtd. in Greenblatt, 1996: 25). However, neither RG nor the media were homogenous groups and, despite the call for a media blackout, there was no monolithic RG resistance to co-optation. The relationship between the two resembled both Hebdige's (1979) oppositional model and Thornton's (1994) co-operative model. For one thing, some riot grrrls didn't mind talking to the mainstream press, and did so (see Malkin, 1993); others continued to do interviews with underground publications like *Punk Planet* and *off our backs*. The "alternative," but-still-mainstream teen magazine *Sassy* promoted RG to some three million readers, demonstrating that "the media, beyond its function to control and contain this phenomenon, may also have helped to perpetuate it" (Gottlieb and Wald, 1994: 265). In addition, for a political movement that wanted to reach out to alienated girls, the media-blackout strategy closed RG off to girls in smaller centres and risked defining RG as an exclusive, insular movement. Indeed, Gottlieb and Wald advise that:

> If Riot Grrrl wants to raise feminist consciousness on a large scale, then it will have to negotiate a relation to the mainstream that does not merely reify the opposition between mainstream and subculture. (1994: 271)

Although this dilemma to remain "authentic" but risk elitism, or to reach a wider audience but to "sell out" exists in all subcultures, I believe it was especially prevalent for RG because of the movement's foundation in both punk rock and feminism. Depending on one's perspective, each can be seen to limit RG's ability to resolve the reach-out/sell-out dilemma. On the one hand, while feminist praxis ideally involves consciousness-raising and the fostering of women's diverse voices, punk tends to be an insular scene with a high degree of subcultural capital and disdain for outsiders and commercial success; on the other hand, while punk promotes a strong D.I.Y. ethic that opens itself to amateurs, feminism traditionally has been a vehicle primarily for educated, middle-class, white women (as was RG). Discussion of this dilemma implies that there was a real choice to be made, that the scene/music in question could take or leave the path to success. However, there is the distinct possibility that RG music was ultimately unsellable: the combination of punk's abrasive sound and low production quality with the grrrls' frank feminist lyrics may not have been as attractive to the media as the grrrls themselves. Judging by the fact that the media did not champion RG music, it seems the media felt riot grrrls were better seen and not heard. As one grrrl wrote in her zine, "The media didn't give a shit about any of the things any of the girls were saying, they just wanted to sell their paper [sic] with pictures of angry grrrls and riot grrrl fashion" (*channel seven,* 1994: 4). Ultimately, media attention turned to other female rockers—women whose anger was more palatable, like Alanis Morrisette and Liz Phair. Although RG chapters still exist around North America, and continue to start up worldwide, many of these grrrls "have no tangible connection with the women from the beginning" and the original musicians have moved on to new projects (Cateforis and Humphreys, 1997: 337).

Incorporation: Grrrl for Sale

Although RG bands were never featured on the cover of *Spin* or on the *Billboard* charts, I propose that the media did their best to neutralize the ideological threat posed by RG by co-opting and trivializing the movement's very name. As well, I will argue that a particular RG system of signification—namely, the words some grrrls wrote on their bodies—was commodified and mass-(re)produced in the form of slogan T-shirts. As Hebdige points out, of course, both ideology and commerce can be seen to "converge on the commodity form" (1979: 96). So, although I have classified appropriation of "grrrl" as an example of the ideological form of incorporation, dissemination of the word occurred in the marketplace; at the same time, while mass-production of girl-themed T-shirts represents the commodity form of incorporation, the display of words is a behaviour with significant symbolic value and, as such, is linked to the ideological form.

The Ideological Form (an Example)

The name "Riot Grrrl" is a deliberate manipulation of signs: the word "riot" implies protest and aggression; the word "girl" describes female childhood and is condescending when used to refer to a grown woman; the transformed word "grrrl" literally includes a growl that turns the sugar-and-spice connotations of "girl" upside-down. For the mass media, an industry that thrives on sound bites and buzz words, "grrrl" was a commercial dream come true. Through decontextualized adoption of this word, the media effectively trivialized its origins and, in so doing, minimized the otherness of RG. After initial reports on RG itself, the popular press used "grrrl" to refer to any independent, noisy (white) female rock musicians, such as Kim Gordon (of Sonic Youth), L7, and Courtney Love. Then it was spread to other genres. A 1993 *Rolling Stone* article on Natalie Merchant (of 10,000 Maniacs), for example, was called "Flower Grrrl." The term was also taken outside the music world into general pop-cultural terrain: also in 1995, a profile of a female athlete in *Seventeen* was called "Biker Grrrl"; in *Wired*, a story about a female computer whiz was called "Modern Grrrl" (Cateforis and Humphreys, 1997: 337). The very word with which a subculture had named its defiance was re-defined to encompass mass public femaleness. Once established as a trend, of course, it became destined for obsolescence. In 1996, a *Newsweek* article reported that "Female rage is all the rage" ("Where the wimps are," 1996: 80); by 1998, a *Time* feature on young feminists described "grrrl" as "that tiresome battle growl" (Labi, 1998: 55).

The Commodity Form (an Example)

Riot grrrls were "skilled creators of spectacle" (White, 1995: 405). Music and fashion are hard to separate in any case; with RG, as with punk, hip hop, and grunge, the name refers equally to sound and style. Many grrrls used their bodies to convey bold statements in two ways: first, through "punk fashion irony" and the juxtaposition of gendered signs (e.g., "1950s dresses with combat boots, shaved hair with lipstick, studded belts with platform heels") (Klein, 1997: 222); and second, through writing politically loaded words such as "rape," "shame" (Japenga, 1995: 30), "prophet" (France, 1993: 23), and "slut" on their arms and midriffs. I believe a line can be drawn from the words that riot grrrls wrote on their bodies in the early 1990s to popular girl-themed slogans printed on T-shirts in the mid- to late '90s. A 1993 story on RG in *Seventeen* stated that grrrls "like to 'accessorize' with black Magic Markers" (Malkin, 1993: 81). In 1993, *Rolling Stone* reported on this "new" trend, as publicly displayed by four (male) rock stars: Prince, Eddie Vedder, Shannon Hoon (of Blind Melon), Nuno Bettencourt (of Extreme)—adding, "Riot grrrls do it, too" ("Body talk," 1994: 16). So-called "alternative" shops were soon flooded with "baby tees"—tight-fitting T-shirts for girls—emblazoned with sassy, sexy words like "Tasty," "Tart," and "Maneater" (Heinrich, 1995: B1). More recently, Porn Star became a popular T-shirt moniker and, thanks (?) to the enormous popularity and ubiquity of the Spice Girls, circa 1997, malls were flooded with "girl power" merchandise from T-shirts to shoelaces and stickers.

T-shirts have long been popular public forums for political slogans and advertisements alike. Indeed, "girl power" (or "girls rule," "girls rock," and so on) is a message—a catchy slogan, to be exact: the nature of the medium—that girls should wear on their sleeves, so to speak. Giese argues that the wearers of such T-shirts are political in that they "are taking a risk by going public with their beliefs and are forcing everyone in sight to deal with those views" (1994: 20); however, as D'Andrade points out,

> For some people, it's a way to bypass the complexities of feminism—it's a lot easier to wear a "girls kick ass" T-shirt than to learn how to defend yourself physically. (1999: 21)

A "Girls Rule" T-shirt is probably no more or less a politically authentic statement than a "Save the Whales" bumper sticker, depending on its wearer and the context of its use. Still, it is important to remember that RG was deliberately anti–consumer culture; writing on oneself with a marker is not only a political, feminist action (first, in choosing to "deface" the feminine body, which is ideally a flawless object; second, in drawing attention to issues of women's oppression through the words), but displays the classic do-it-yourself ethic of punk. While anyone willing to mark herself has access to a felt pen and a range of words limited only to her imagination, a baby tee must be purchased at its marked-up retail cost. Whether or not its slogan is meant to be ironic, any critique of capitalism is, by definition, lost in its (mass) production.

Conclusion

Despite generalizations made for the purposes of this paper, RG was not a homogenous entity—nor was it self-contained. I suspect that many self-declared grrrls also reached beyond this movement in their tastes and style (and that other girls reached in), and it would be worthwhile to find out where RG intersected with other subcultures and the mainstream. As well, it would be interesting to compare the path of RG bands with that of women who attained commercial success in the mainstream music industry. After all, RG's inception—that is, pre-*Jagged Little Pill*, Lilith Fair, and the Spice Girls—preceded the amalgam of "women in rock" that peaked at the end of the 1990s. In particular, comparisons with the more visible major-label "angry women" (e.g., Hole, the contents of Women in Rock compilations) may determine whether "selling out" necessarily requires that women compromise a feminist stance. The contradiction with which I opened this paper rears its head again here: it may be true that riot grrrl remains an "authentic" and enormously empowering movement for thousands of girls, but there are millions more who might pay attention if the "Revolution Girl Style" were indeed televised.

References

"Body Talk." 1994. *Rolling Stone* 6 October: 16.

Cateforis, T., and E. Humphreys. 1997. "Constructing Communities and Identities: Riot Grrrl New York City," in K. Lornell and A.K. Rasmussen, eds., *Musics of Multicultural America: A Study of Twelve Musical Communities*. New York: Schirmer.

channel seven. 1997. [No issue no.].

Clarke, G. 1997 [1981]. "Defending Ski-Jumpers: A Critique of Theories of Youth Subcultures," in K. Gelder and S. Thornton, eds., *The Subcultures Reader*. London: Routledge.

D'Andrade, H. 1999. "The Buffy Effect," *Bitch* Summer: 18–21, 58.

"Flower Grrrl." 1993. *Rolling Stone* (8–22 July): 24–5.

France, K. 1993. "Grrrls at War," *Rolling Stone* (8–22 July): 23–4.

Giese, R. 1994. "To Die For! From Ribbon-Mania to Ghetto Flavas, the Fashion Industry Is Out to Accessorize Your Dissent," *This Magazine* (June): 17–22.

Gottlieb, J., and G. Wald. 1994. "Smells Like Teen Spirit: Riot Grrrls, Revolution and Women in Independent Rock," in A. Ross and T. Rose, eds., *Microphone Fiends: Youth Music and Youth Culture*. York: Routledge.

Greenblatt, C. 1996. "Unwilling Icons: Riot Grrrl Meets the Press," *Border/Lines* Dec.: 24–7.

Hebdige, D. 1979. *Subculture: The Meaning of Style*. London: Routledge.

Heinrich, Kim. 1995. "Tee Tease," *Calgary Herald*, 6 June: B1.

Japenga, A. 1995. "Punk's Girls Groups are Putting the Self Back in Self-Esteem," *New York Times*, 15 Nov.: 30.

Klein, M. 1997. "Duality and Redefinition: Young Feminism and the Alternative Music Community," in L. Heywood and J. Drake, eds., *Third Wave Agenda: Being Feminist, Doing Feminism*. Minneapolis: Univ. of Minnesota.

Labi, N. 1998. "Girl Power," *Time* (29 June): 54–6.

Malkin, N. 1993. "It's a Grrrl Thing," *Seventeen* (May): 80–2.

"rock women." 1999. alt.culture. www.altculture.com/aenries/r/rockxwx.html. Date accessed: 23 June 1999.

Thornton, S. 1994. "Moral Panic, the Media and British Rave Culture," in A. Ross and T. Rose, eds., *Microphone Fiends: Youth Music and Youth Culture*. New York: Routledge.

Wald, G. 1998. "Just a Girl? Rock Music, Feminism, and the Cultural Construction of Female Youth," *Signs: Journal of Women in Culture and Society* 23 (3): 585–610.

"Where the wimps are." 1996. *Newsweek* (29 April): 80.

White, E. 1995 [1992]. "Revolution Girl Style Now," in E. McDonnell and A. Powers, eds., *Rock She Wrote: Women Write about Rock, Pop, and Rap*. New York: Dell.

Chapter 34

Overview

Steven Jackson argues that beer, sports, and masculinity form a "holy trinity" of Canadian identity and that these three concepts become welded together through media and advertising. Focusing on iconic Molson ads, Jackson demonstrates how beer companies use sports to sell a version of masculinity that involves physical activity, outdoor recreation, camaraderie, and lots of beer. However, this is not simply any masculinity—this is a specifically *Canadian* articulation of masculinity. Two running ad campaigns, "The Rant" and "The Code," Jackson argues, are texts of gendered nationalism, selling a vision of masculinity in which any Canadian man can partake simply by buying beer. These advertising texts define hockey and beer-drinking as male spheres of action, in which an idealized form of Canadianness can be enacted.

Globalization, Corporate Nationalism, and Masculinity in Canada: Sport, Molson Beer Advertising, and Consumer Citizenship

Steven Jackson

Introduction

Within the context of globalization, nations have increasingly become the object of both production and consumption. Simply stated: "nation-branding has been incorporated into the project of nation building."[1] On one hand nations are being produced as branded tourist destinations or as sites of valuable material resources for either development or investment by international capital. On the other hand, nations, and their symbolic value, are increasingly being used by both global and local corporations as a means of aligning brands with national identity. . . . This is often achieved through a carefully orchestrated practice that involves corporations using the currency of "the nation," that is, its symbols, images, stereotypes, collective identities, and memories as part of their overall branding strategy.[2] To this extent, advertising, marketing, and the creative promotional industries more generally play a key role in producing and representing particular visions of the nation that link brands and commodities with aspects of contemporary social life, ultimately influencing individual and group identity formation. This paper examines the relationship between one global commodity (beer) as it is located within one particular national context (Canada) through one particular brand (Molson) in order to explore how the process of corporate nationalism engages with and shapes other identities including masculinity. Specifically, this paper seeks to advance our understanding of how the circuit of culture[3]—that is, the production, symbolic representation, and consumption of commodities—plays a key role in contemporary identity formation and citizenship.

The relationship between sport, alcohol, and masculinity has arguably achieved holy trinity status[4] offering us unique insights into the nature of the contemporary consumer citizen. This point has become particularly evident in the context of professional and corporatized sport where various organizations have become dependent on breweries that serve as either team owners and investors, direct team sponsors, or sponsors via the purchase of various forms of attendant advertising time and space.[5] Historically, the basis of the relationship between beer and masculinity (and herein it is also argued sport) was structured around and through assumptions about what men do, where they do it, when they do it, why they do it, and with whom they do it.[6] In short, sport and beer have been consumed by a male audience sharing the experience of watching male athletes perform hypermasculine activities as a means of confirming and defining their own maleness. . . . Beer advertising provides an ideal site of analysis because of the intense pressure on breweries and their allied advertising agencies to continually accommodate and nurture new, often marginalized, target markets while simultaneously reaffirming a dominant form of masculinity that is steeped in nationalism and offered through a nostalgic lens all within the context of a highly competitive marketplace. . . .

The Holy Trinity

Historically, sport has long been celebrated as a man's world based largely on its links with the military and nationhood.[7] However, amidst a wide range of social changes and the advancement of women's rights, including their access to education, employment, and the political sphere, sport has gained renewed prominence and significance at particular junctures.[8] Indeed, within the context of contemporary gender relations, we might consider sport to be one of the last frontiers of masculinity. There are few cultural institutions and practices outside of sport that are as clearly defined in terms of gender and accepted as exclusive male spaces. Consider, for example, that sport (1) provides the opportunity to perform sanctioned physical aggression; (2) provides a context for the demonstration of courage, commitment, and sacrifice; (3) helps reaffirm historical links with war and the military largely through popular discourse; (4) offers an exclusive space for men away from work and family; (5) provides a context where groups of men can engage in regular body contact without the fear of being labelled gay; and (6) offers a legitimated setting for male bonding and the consumption of alcohol and in particular beer. These factors reinforce sports' centrality in the holy trinity, a historically based, unique configuration of social institutions and practices, social identities and power relations that collectively form part of "a remarkably resilient bastion of hegemonic masculinity."[9] What role then do the production, representation, and consumption of beer play in articulating the holy trinity and corporate nationalism? To begin to address this question and its wider cultural implications, it is necessary to outline the social significance of beer and its promotional, symbolic representation via advertising.

Despite its seeming universality, the real power of beer (its production, representation, and its consumption) may lie in its taken-for-granted nature. It is this "naturalness" that enables beer to articulate with a range of other powerful social institutions, commodities, and social relations, thus reinforcing its elevated position. . . .

. . . The sheer economics of the industry point to the commodity's importance. For example, in the US, the alcohol industry spent $8.2 billion to air approximately 2.6 million commercials on television between 2001 and 2009; and expenditures increased 27 per cent over this period, leading to a 30 per cent increase in alcohol ad exposure.[10] Furthermore, highlighting both the significance of sport and its highly gendered consumer base, it is worth noting that almost three-fifths of television spending are typically allocated to sports programming.[11] Overall this confirms that:

> [s]port offers a unique avenue for the drinks industry to reach its most lucrative target audience of males aged between 16 and 35. The increasingly global nature of sports brands, whether belonging to competitions or clubs, makes them even more attractive to an industry

> which itself is consolidating across national boundaries into "super-breweries."[12]

This quote reveals the more contemporary configuration and manifestation of the holy trinity by emphasizing the relationship between media, advertising, sport, and male consumers. How and why then do advertisers seek to reach men through beer advertising, and what are the possible consequences for society, gender relations, and contemporary forms of citizenship?

According to Strate,[13] there are five basic questions that can guide explorations of what it means to be a man in contemporary society: What kinds of things do men do? What kinds of settings do men prefer? How do men relate to each other? How do boys become men? How do men relate to women? Further, Strate asserts that beer advertisements may provide valuable insights into these questions given that "no other industry's commercials focus so exclusively and so exhaustively on images of the man's man."[14] To this end, Strate suggests that the power and pervasiveness of beer advertising's representations are such that they serve as a virtual "manual on masculinity":

> The manifest function of beer advertising is to promote a particular brand, but collectively the commercials provide a clear and consistent image of the masculine role; in a sense, they constitute a guide for becoming a man, a rulebook for appropriate male behavior, in short, a manual on masculinity.[15]

Confirming Strate's sentiments and referring to some of the wider socializing effects of beer and its promotion, McCracken[16] asserts that:

> Beer is no mere incident of masculinity . . . beer is crucial to the way in which young men present themselves to other males. Beer is not just one of the things that happens to be invested with maleness in our culture; it is at the very heart of the way maleness is constructed and experienced.

Clearly, beer is not just a commodity that is symbolically used and consumed to perform and confirm masculinity. Rather, its extensive promotional representations through advertising may also serve as both mirrors and systems of surveillance where men evaluate themselves and other men. The next section explores one particular beer brand, *Molson Canadian*, as perhaps the quintessential example of the articulation between the holy trinity and corporate nationalism in Canada. At this point, the paper explores how Molson brewery has endeavoured to link beer consumption with both national and masculine identities in Canada highlighting a particular manifestation of how spheres of consumption and citizenship are increasingly intertwined.

Molson Beer Advertisements: Manuals of Masculinity for Canadian Males

Founded in 1786, Molson is the oldest brewery in North America and, after merging with Coors (US) in 2005, is now part of the world's fifth largest "super-brewery." Through careful management of the family-owned trademark, including links with a wide range of sport leagues, teams, venues, and events, Molson emerged as "one of the few brands in Canada with the heritage and ubiquity needed to become an icon."[17] In 1994, Molson created one of the most definitive examples of corporate nationalism with the launch of their "I am Canadian" slogan and campaign that was tagged to their "Canadian" brand of beer. This marketing strategy gave Molson the advantage they needed to retain their market share over their number one rival in Canada, Labatt's.[18] However, Molson's next marketing campaign entitled "This is where we get Canadian" resulted in a loss of market share and was eventually abandoned. Undertaking what is best described as a brand soul search, Molson carefully reviewed its position using a range of market research techniques including surveys, qualitative observation, and focus groups to gain insight into what young people, and young men in particular, felt about Canada, nationalism, and national identity.[19]

With the market research completed on Sunday, March 26, 2000, Molson purchased a single television advertising spot during the Academy Awards. What quickly became an advertising phenomenon both within and outside Canada, "The Rant" (see narrative below) seemed to capture people's imaginations. Of particular note with respect to this analysis is the fact that sport played a key role in the campaign during the spring of 2000. Although Labatt's Breweries held the sponsorship rights to one of the longest running and highest rating sporting programmes on television, *Hockey Night In Canada*, Molson strategically maintained team sponsorships with all six Canadian franchises of the National Hockey League (NHL) and was thus able to gain brand exposure via signage and other promotions. Perhaps most significant was the live performance of "Joe" Canadian (played by actor Jeff Douglas) who performed "The Rant" live at NHL games in both Toronto and Ottawa during the playoffs. Although the "The Rant" campaign has been described and analyzed by others,[20] it is included here briefly as it serves as an important point of departure for understanding future Molson advertising campaigns.

Molson's "The Rant" Campaign

> I am not a lumberjack or a fur trader. I don't live in an igloo or eat blubber or own a dogsled. And I don't know Jimmy, Sally, or Susie from Canada although I'm certain they're really, really nice. I have a Prime Minister, not a President. I speak English and French, not American. I pronounce it about, not "aboot." I can proudly sew my country's flag on my backpack. I believe in peacekeeping not policing, diversity not assimilation, that the beaver is a truly proud and noble animal. A toque is a hat, a chesterfield is a couch, and it is pronounced "Zed," not "Zee," "Zed." Canada is the second largest land mass, the first nation of hockey, and the best part of North America. My name is Joe and I AM CANADIAN! Thank You.[21]

Drawing upon a wide range of stereotypes, the commercial is a humble salute to many self-proclaimed positive features of being Canadian: friendly, polite, bilingual, multicultural, champions at ice hockey, and advocates of peace. Of equal importance the entire advertisement is an illustration of how identity is defined out of difference, in this case to Canada's southern neighbour the US. The advertisement was widely celebrated both for its humour and its ability to capture/articulate a piece of the Canadian popular imagination. However, it did have its critics. According to Millard, Riegel, and Wright,[22] "The Rant" was both antagonistic and paradoxical for a nation that espouses modesty:

> The rant was an overtly, even belligerently, patriotic message that struck a chord in a country that . . . is supposed to be distinguished . . . by its absence of overt patriotism. . . . The rant was . . . the most spectacular manifestation of the wider trend towards loud nationalism in Canada. Canadians are now in effect, shouting about how quiet they are . . . in paradoxical contrast to the "loud American."[23]

"The Rant" was created by Glen Hunt of the advertising firm Ben Simon Ben Darcy.[24] Strikingly, while much of advertising is about storytelling, "The Rant" is partly autobiographical. Hunt had worked in New York and fell victim to many jokes about Canada and being Canadian, which included stereotypes about toques, beavers, and how certain words are pronounced. Hence, the ad was based, in part, on his own experience and taken in this context: it can be seen as both Canadian pride and a critique of America. Notably, and in keeping with the expectations of Canadian generosity, Hunt signed over the rights to "The Rant" to Molson for $2.

Despite the number of Molson campaigns that have been created and aired since 2000, "I am Canadian" remains the brand's signature tagline. Just under a decade after "The Rant," Molson launched a multi-platform campaign titled "The Code" mirroring, in many ways, various aspects of "The Rant." At this juncture, it is worth reiterating a key point about the social significance of beer to reinforce the multiple ways in which it shapes human interaction, social relations, and national identity and citizenship. As such, the production, representation, and consumption of Molson, like any other beer and its associated brand, are important because:

> drinking is a historical and contemporary process of identity formation, maintenance, and reproduction and transformation. Its importance to scholars of national identity and ethnicity is not principally in its role in grand state policies and the loftier ideals of the nation (although there too alcohol has played a role). Rather, drinking is the stuff of everyday life, quotidian culture which at the end of the day may be as important to the lifeblood of the nation as are its origin myths, heroes, and grand narratives.[25]

Molson's "The Code" Campaign

In 2008, Molson returned to the link between their brand and national identity with a series of advertisements referred to as "The Code." Similar to the "The Rant," "The Code" campaign draws upon a pastiche of Canadian stereotypes, involves a bit of national self-mocking, and is male dominated. The focus on men and masculinity in "The Code" campaign, however, is much more explicit. Moreover, central to "The Code" campaign is a commitment to linking the Molson brand to both masculinity and nationalism. Throughout the campaign, this occurs rather effortlessly given that it makes repeated reference to the sport of ice hockey—a gendered cultural institution and practice in Canada that conspicuously articulates nationalism and masculinity.[26] From this, it is suggested that masculinity itself emerges from and is performed within particular national contexts just as national identity may emerge from and be performed within particular contexts of masculinity. Hence, the way in which *masculine nationalisms*—where masculinity is socially constructed in and through different types of national spaces and practices (ice hockey in Canada, football/soccer in Europe, the UK, and South America, and rugby in New Zealand and South Africa)—and *national masculinisms*—where particular characteristics or significations of nationality define masculinity (e.g., military, drinking cultures)—are produced, represented, and consumed within beer advertising and, arguably, corporate nationalism is paramount to this analysis.

Four television advertisements were produced for "The Code," series and these were strategically released to air during the 2008 NHL playoffs. The appeal to men is fully acknowledged by Molson, as brand director Michael Shekter explains:

> The strategy for [Molson] Canadian has not changed in years. The purpose of these ads is to reflect the role that Molson Canadian plays in the Canadian beer environment. It stands up for what it means to be a Canadian guy.[27]

In each advertisement, the audience hears dramatic music and a strong, serious, deep male voiceover accompanied by a series of fast-paced images corresponding to the dialogue. The narratives for all four advertisements (along with website links for viewing) are given below. To achieve consistency of brand communication, they all begin with "There is an unwritten code in Canada" and they all end with "This is our beer, Molson Canadian."

> "The Code 1"[28]
>
> There's an unwritten code in Canada. If you live by it, chances are: You've left your coat on some pile, and knew it wouldn't get stolen. You've never made a move on your buddy's girlfriend. You know that on a road trip the strongest bladder determines the pit stops. You've kept all your hockey trophies. You've replaced someone's pint if you've knocked theirs over. If your buddy's in trouble, you've got his back. You've clapped for a dancer even though she shouldn't be a dancer. You've used a blow torch to curve your stick. You've used your arm as an ice-scraper, and, you've grown a beard in the post-season. This is our beer, Molson Canadian.
>
> "The Code 2"[29]
>
> There's an unwritten code in Canada. If you live by it, chances are: You have a hockey scar somewhere. You've gone on a road trip with a car that had no business going on a road trip. You're proud to know a girl who got jiggy with a pro hockey player. You feel kinda bad

reclining your seat in an airplane. You've used a cheesy pick-up line because your buddy dared you. You fill your friend's pint before your own. You think hockey tape can fix anything. You've gotten kicked out of somewhere, and, you've turned down a booty call in the post-season. This is our beer, Molson Canadian.

"The Code 3"[30]

There's an unwritten code in Canada. If you live by it, chances are: You've driven an hour for 19 minutes of ice time. You've been to a bar that starts with Mc or ends in Annigan's. You appreciate a woman who's into sports. You'll call anyone with goalie equipment, a friend. You know what a J-stroke is. And sometimes, figure skating is worth watching. You know the sippy cup lid isn't as dumb as it sounds. You've worn a canoe as a hat. You've assembled a barbecue, and, they're not dents, they're goals. This is our beer, Molson Canadian.

"The Code 4"[31]

There's an unwritten code in Canada. If you live by it, chances are: You've overcome bad directions to find your friend's cottage. You know what happens on the ice stays on the ice. You've come face to face with some type of freaky bird. You hold a pint with all five fingers. And, it's never okay to rub another man's rhubarb. You know the last box in is the first to get unpacked. Your soap smells like soap. You've guess-timated a phone number. You've cooked with a flashlight and you recycle. This is our beer, Molson Canadian.

Throughout the ads, a range of fleeting signifiers are used to communicate the rules or "codes" of Canadian masculinity. Yet, despite their diversity, there are some common themes throughout the ads including Canadian politeness and demonstrations of male strength and courage. Furthermore, there are two key signifiers of masculinity in each advertisement: relationships with women and dedication to sport. Here, women occupy marginal, sexually infused, positions as strippers, desperate amorous girlfriends, and prospective one-night stands, although humour or Canadian courtesy is used to neutralize any insult or offence that might be taken. References to sport are evident throughout the series, not only with respect to the context of the NHL playoffs within which the ads were aired but also in regard to the demarcated meaning of hockey to Canadian males whether it be through long-standing traditions (growing a beard during the playoffs, using a blowtorch to curve your hockey stick, driving long distances just to play a game) or the nonchalant parading of real or metaphorical badges of competition (keeping old hockey trophies, displaying a hockey scar).

Reminiscent of Strate's[32] "manual of masculinity" mentioned earlier, "The Code" certainly provides a series of defining characteristics and/or guidelines for Canadian men.

However, the opening catchphrase "There's an unwritten code in Canada" suggests that these rules are not formal and explicit; rather there is a subtle expectation that they are known. To this extent, the codes infer hegemony, whereby they are the widely represented, accepted, and reproduced commonsense, modus operandi for many Canadian males. As Williams[33] notes:

> Because the code is unwritten, and hence lost, the advertisement goes on to list not what the code states, but what the effects of following it look like; this allows you to know you're doing your job as a Canadian man without memorizing a bunch of rules and stuff.

According to Aaron Starkman, creative director at Zig Advertising, the agency credited with developing the campaign, "We wanted to continue to exemplify the values of the young Canadian guy in a heroic way . . . This year's commercials are more honed in on beer occasions."[34] Thus, according to this cultural intermediary, it was not simply about representing both masculinity and national identity but celebrating it and articulating it with particular "beer moments," which are often highly gendered or exclusive male spaces or zones. And, in light of various discussions and debates about a contemporary crisis of masculinity,[35] these exclusive male spaces and zones serve as the means to enable the construction, negotiation, and even the evaluation of masculinities.[36] . . .

Conclusion

The holy trinity and its particular nation-based manifestations offer—for a number of reasons—a unique site through which the complexities and contradictions of contemporary identity formation can be explored. First, both masculinity and national identity have been commodified, that is, while they may operate as subjectivities that we embody, they are increasingly available through various forms of consumption thus confirming the articulation of the citizen-consumer. For example, with respect to masculinity specifically, Edwards[37] asserts that: "masculinities now are not so much something possessed as an identity as something marketed, bought—and sold . . . across the world of visual media culture more generally." Evidence of this reveals that men are investing more of their identity into consumption. According to Holt and Thompson's[38] compensatory consumption thesis, "Men use the plasticity of consumer identity construction to forge atavistic masculine identities based upon an imagined life of self-reliant, premodern men who lived outside the confines of cities, families, and work bureaucracies." Yet, an exploration of the observation that males are increasingly seeking to find or express their masculinity through consumption warrants attention. . . .

. . . This paper has examined the power of both beer and sport as commodities steeped in masculinity and nationalism as illustrated through two of Molson's "I am Canadian" campaigns. In addition, the paper has highlighted potential implications for the reproduction of a particular form of national hegemonic masculinity through the articulation of the holy trinity (sport, beer, and masculinity) and national identity. Future cross-cultural research examining the articulation of the holy trinity in other national contexts will provide further insights into the similarities and differences in how local/national cultures embrace or resist particular global campaigns including those that reproduce inequities with respect to citizenship, identity, and human rights.

Acknowledgements

The author would like to thank the guest editor and Sarah Gee for their helpful feedback on this paper and the anonymous reviewers of earlier versions of this paper.

Notes

1. Huang, "Nation-Branding and Transnational Consumption," 3.
2. Jackson, "Reading New Zealand."
3. See du Gay et al., *Doing Cultural Studies*.
4. Wenner and Jackson, *Sport, Beer, and Gender*.
5. Collins and Vamplew, *Mud, Sweat and Beers*.
6. Strate, "Beer Commercials."
7. Burstyn, *Rites of Men*.
8. Messner, *Sport, Men and Gender*.
9. Sabo and Jansen, "Prometheus Unbound," 211.
10. Center on Alcohol Marketing and Youth, *Youth Exposure to Television Advertising*.
11. Center on Alcohol Marketing and Youth, *Youth Exposure to Television Advertising*
12. Collins and Vamplew, *Mud, Sweat and Beers*, 123–4.
13. Strate, "Beer Commercials."
14. Strate, "Beer Commercials," 78.
15. Strate, "Beer Commercials," 78.
16. McCracken, "Value of the Brand," 131.
17. "Molson Canadian," 2.
18. Labatt's Breweries belongs to Anheuser-Busch InBev, "one of the world's top-5 consumer products companies, that manages a portfolio of well over 200 beer brands and holds the No. 1 or No. 2 market position in 19 countries."
19. For a range of reasons that may never quite fully be understood, there was a strong sense of

Canadian nationalism (re)emerging at the beginning of the new millennium.

20. Cf. MacGregor, "I am Canadian"; and Manning, "I AM CANADIAN Identity."
21. B. Garfield, "Blame Canada and Molson for Brilliant Rant at States," 8 May 2000, www.adage.com/news_and_features/ad_review/archives/ar20000508.html
22. Millard, Riegel, and Wright, "Here's Where We Get Canadian."
23. Millard, Riegel, and Wright, "Here's Where We Get Canadian," 15.
24. It has been suggested that Molson got the idea for the "I am Canadian" campaign from a song by David Hook titled "I'm Canadian," which can be traced back to at least 1994 and whose lyrics contain many of the references in the beer commercial.
25. Wilson, *Drinking Cultures*, 12.
26. Gee, "Mythical Ice Hockey Hero"; and Whitson and Gruneau, *Artificial Ice*. This is despite the enormous success of the Canadian Women's ice hockey team in the Olympics and World Championships and the massive growth of female ice hockey in Canada.
27. J. Lloyd, "New Molson Canadian Platform Is in the Code," April 15, 2008, www.marketingmag.ca/brands/new-molson-canadian-platform-is-in-code-13820
28. www.youtube.com/watch?v=XAwg71Gg9ek
29. www.youtube.com/watch?v=i4cIDO1w4Bw&NR=1
30. www.youtube.com/watch?v=aQL0Q6EvdH0
31. www.youtube.com/watch?v=TRvwWcUsrE8&NR¼1
32. Strate, "Beer Commercials."
33. "Williams Reviews That New Molson Canadian Advertisement," January 13, 2009, http://maxandwilliams.wordpress.com/2009/01/13/williams-reviews-that-new-molson-canadianadvertisement/
34. Lloyd, "New Molson Canadian Platform."
35. Atkinson, *Deconstructing Men & Masculinities*; Clare, *On Men*; Edwards, *Cultures of Masculinity*; and Gee, "Mythical Ice Hockey Hero."
36. West, "Negotiating Masculinities."
37. Edwards, *Cultures of Masculinity*, 43.
38. Holt and Thompson, "Man-of-Action Heroes," 426.

References

Atkinson, M. 2011. *Deconstructing Men and Masculinities*. Toronto: Oxford University Press.

Burstyn, V. 1999. *The Rites of Men: Manhood, Politics, and the Culture of Sport*. Toronto: University of Toronto Press.

Center on Alcohol Marketing and Youth. 2009. *Youth Exposure to Television Advertising on Television, 2001–2009*. Baltimore, MD: John Hopkins Bloomberg School of Public Health.

Clare, A. 2000. *On Men: Masculinity in Crisis*. London: Chatto & Windus.

Collins, T., and W. Vamplew. 2002. *Mud, Sweat and Beers: A Cultural History of Sport and Alcohol*. Oxford: Berg.

du Gay, P., S. Hall, L. Janes, H. Mackay, and K. Negus. 1997. *Doing Cultural Studies: The Story of the Sony Walkman*. London: Sage in association with The Open University Press.

Edwards, T. 2006. *Cultures of Masculinity*. New York: Routledge.

Gee, S. 2009. "The Mythical Ice Hockey Hero and the Contemporary Crisis of Masculinity: The National Hockey League's 'Inside the Warrior' Advertising Campaign," *Sociology of Sport Journal* 26(4): 578–98.

Holt, D., and C. Thompson. 2004. "Man-of-Action Heroes: The Pursuit of Heroic Masculinity in Everyday Consumption," *Journal of Consumer Research* 31: 425–40.

Huang, S. 2011. "Nation-Branding and Transnational Consumption: Japan-Mania and the Korean Wave in Taiwan," *Media, Culture & Society* 33(1): 3–18.

Jackson, S.J. 2004. "Reading New Zealand Within the New Global Order: Sport and the Visualisation of National Identity," *International Sport Studies* 26(1): 13–29.

Lloyd, J. 2008. "New Molson Canadian Platform is in the Code," April 15, *Marketing Magazine*. www.marketingmag.ca/brands/new-molson-canadian-platform-is-in-code-13820

MacGregor, R.M. 2003. "I am Canadian: Canadian Identity in Beer Commercials," *Journal of Popular Culture* 37(2): 276–86.

Manning, E. 2000. "I AM CANADIAN Identity, Territory and the Canadian National Landscape," *Theory and Event* 4(4): https://muse.jhu.edu/journals/theory_and_event/v004/4.4manning.html

McCracken, G. 1993. "The Value of the Brand: An Anthropological Perspective," in D.A. Aaker and A.L. Biel, eds., *Brand Equity and Advertising*, pp. 125–42. Hillside, NJ: Lawrence Erlbaum.

Messner, M. 1992. *Sport, Men and Gender: Sports and the Problem of Masculinity*. Boston, MA: Beacon Press.

Millard, G., S. Riegel, and J. Wright. 2002. "Here's Where We Get Canadian: English Canadian Nationalism and Popular Culture," *The American Review of Canadian Studies* 32(1): 11–34.

Molson Canadian. 2001. *Canadian Advertising Success Stories*. Toronto: Canadian Congress of Advertising.

Sabo, D., and S.C. Jansen. 1998. "Prometheus Unbound: Construction of Masculinity in Sports Media," in L. Wenner, ed., *Mediasport*, pp. 202–20. London: Routledge.

Strate, L. 1992. "Beer Commercials: A Manual on Masculinity," in S. Craig, ed., *Men, Masculinity and the Media*, pp. 78–92. London: Sage.

Wenner, L., and S.J. Jackson. 2009. *Sport, Beer, and Gender: Promotional Culture and Contemporary Social Life*. Zurich: Peter Lang.

West, L.A. 2001. "Negotiating Masculinities in American Drinking Subcultures," *Journal of Men's Studies* 9: 371–92.

Whitson, D., and R. Gruneau. 2006. *Artificial Ice: Hockey, Culture and Commerce*. Peterborough, ON: Broadview Press.

Wilson, T. 2005. *Drinking Cultures*. Oxford: Berg.

PART X
The Gender of Violence

From early childhood to old age, violence is perhaps the most obdurate, intractable gender difference we have observed. In Canada, a 2005 study of police apprehension rates found that women constituted only 18 per cent of those apprehended for crimes against persons. As the level of violence involved in the crime increases, the gender imbalance increases. At the higher end of the spectrum of physical violence, the study concluded that "female rates for homicide, attempted murder, and sexual assault were negligible" (Statistics Canada, 2008: 4). "Men are always and everywhere more likely than women to commit criminal acts," write criminologists Michael Gottfredson and Travis Hirschi (1990: 145).

But how are we to understand this connection between men and violence? Peggy Reeves Sanday argues that it's not a question of men being innately prone to violence. She connects levels of violence to levels of gender inequality, arguing that the more unequal a society, the more rape happens. By locating the origins of rape in male domination—profound separation between masculine and feminine social spheres, low levels of male involvement in child care, women's dependence on men—Sanday lays to rest the argument that rape is simply an inevitable hazard of a gendered society. Along similar lines, Russell Dobash, R. Emerson Dobash, and their colleagues use a gendered power analysis to explain why men batter the women they say they love in far greater numbers than women hit men.

However, gender alone is not the whole story in domestic violence. As Sepali Guruge, Nazilla Khanlou, and Denise Gastaldo demonstrate, this violence does not arise from the simple fact of maleness. The authors track the important influences that ethnicity and economic class, as well as the stresses and insecurities of international migration and "outsider" status in Canada, have on gender violence. Further, gender violence is not limited to attacks on women by men (or vice versa). Violence is also implicated in the social organization of gender when it is used to enforce the rigid gender binary, by punishing those who dare to step outside it, such as transgender people. Viviane Namaste coined the term "genderbashing" to describe the violence perpetrated on transgender individuals and argues that this form of violence is still largely invisible to the general public, even as violence against lesbians and gay men receives more and more attention.

References

Gottfredson, M., and T. Hirschi. 1990. *A General Theory of Crime*. Stanford, CA: Stanford.

Statistics Canada. 2008. "Female Offenders in Canada," *Juristat* 28: 1. Available online at www.statcan.gc.ca/pub/85-002-x/85-002-x2008001-eng.pdf.

Questions for Critical Thought

1. Do you live in or have you experienced a rape-prone culture?
2. How successful do you think a fraternity like the one described in Sanday's article would be on your campus?
3. What do you think it would take to reduce rates of gendered violence in Canada? Are you optimistic or pessimistic about the possibility that Canada could become a "rape-free society"?
4. Do you agree with the statement that the only thing that will stop male violence is a radical change of heart among men?
5. Dobash and colleagues jump into the heated debate about the gender division of domestic violence and argue that marital violence is more often visited on women by men than on men by women. Why is this such a contentious and controversial topic in the media, in the world of academic research, and in the world of policy-making?
6. What defines violence? Are there some acts that are considered violent and unacceptable in some contexts but acceptable in others? Where would you draw the line between acceptable and unacceptable conduct, especially with respect to intimate or domestic relationships?
7. How is racism connected to gendered violence, according to Guruge et al.? Can you see any other connections between other forms of violence and gender violence?

8. How can we account for the extreme violence visited on people who don't conform to norms of what a man or a woman "should" look or act like, as described by Namaste? How is "genderbashing" connected to the violence perpetrated against women?

9. Have you known individuals who were subjected to violence because they didn't conform to stereotypical expectations for their gender? How did the people around them react to this violence?

10. Most of these readings deal with physical violence, yet psychological or emotional violence is arguably equally damaging. How does non-physical violence differ from the physical kind?

Chapter 35

Overview

Is rape inevitable? Are human beings simply hardwired for sexual violence? Peggy Reeves Sanday, a leading American scholar of sexual violence, thinks not. She argues, based on intensive study of societies across the globe, that cultural variables shape the frequency and acceptability of sexual violence. Sanday believes that a "rape-free society"—one in which rape is both very rare and heavily penalized—is possible.

Unfortunately, many societies, both large and small, adhere to values that permit or even encourage sexual violence. Sanday's study of all-male university fraternities indicates that activities such as unbridled consumption of alcohol, male bonding through sexual bragging, and the constant availability of pornography are associated with higher rates of perpetration of sexual crimes. These factors vary from one campus to another and so does the incidence of rape, indicating that rape is not an inevitable outcome of campus life. Sanday contrasts "rape-free campus cultures" with "rape-prone" ones, using the example of QRS, an actual fraternity that does not adhere to rape-friendly values. QRS members prize values such as friendship with women and accountability amongst men, making their fraternity an example of how cultural change can bring about changes in sexual violence.

Rape-Prone versus Rape-Free Campus Cultures[1]

Peggy Reeves Sanday

In *Fraternity Gang Rape* (Sanday, 1990) I describe the discourse, rituals, sexual ideology, and practices that make some fraternity environments rape-prone. The reaction of fraternity brothers to the book was decidedly mixed. Individuals in some chapters were motivated to rethink their initiation ritual and party behaviour. In sarcastic opinion pieces written for campus newspapers other people dismissed the book on the grounds that I was "out to get" fraternities. As recently as December 1995, a young man wrote a letter to the editor of *The Washington Post* criticizing me for allegedly connecting hate speech and sexual crimes on college campuses with "single-sex organizations." Having set me up as the avenging witch, this young man then blames me for perpetuating the problem. My "[a]cross-the-board generalizations," he claimed "only make it more difficult for supportive men to become involved and stay active in the fight against these attacks."

It is one of the tragedies of today's ideological warfare that this writer finds such an easy excuse to exempt himself from participating in the struggle to end violence against women. To make matters worse, his rationalization for opting out is based on a trumped-up charge. In the Introduction to my book, I carefully note that I am dealing with only "a few of the many fraternities at U. and on several other campuses." I state the case very clearly:

> The sexual aggression evident in these particular cases does not mean that sexual aggression is restricted to fraternities or that all fraternities indulge in sexual aggression. Sexist attitudes and the phallo-centric mentality associated with

"pulling train" have a long history in Western society. For example, venting homoerotic desire in the gang rape of women who are treated as male property is the subject of several biblical stories. Susan Brownmiller describes instances of gang rape by men in war and in street gangs. Male bonding that rejects women and commodifies sex is evident in many other social contexts outside of universities. Thus, it would be wrong to place blame solely on fraternities. However, it is a fact also that most of the reported incidents of "pulling train" on campus have been associated with fraternities. (Sanday, 1990: 19)

As an anthropologist interested in the particulars of sexual ideologies cross-culturally, I am very wary of generalizations of any sort. In 1975 I was very disturbed to read Susan Brownmiller's claim in the opening chapter of *Against Our Will* (1975) that rape is "a conscious process of intimidation by which all men keep all women in a state of fear" (15). This statement was inconsistent with the compelling argument she presents in subsequent chapters that rape is culturally constructed and my own subsequent research on the sociocultural context of rape cross-culturally, which provided evidence of rape-free as well as rape-prone societies.

In this chapter, I will briefly summarize what we know about rape-prone fraternity cultures and contrast this information with what a rape-free context might look like. Since the available data are sparse my goal here is mostly programmatic, namely to encourage studies of intra-campus and cross-campus variation in the rates and correlates of sexual assault.

Rape-Prone Campus Environments

The concept of rape-free versus rape-prone comes from my study of 95 band and tribal societies in which I concluded that 47 per cent were rape-free and 18 per cent were rape-prone (Sanday, 1981). For this study I defined a rape-prone society as one in which the incidence of rape is reported by observers to be high, or rape is excused as a ceremonial expression of masculinity, or rape is an act by which men are allowed to punish or threaten women. I defined a rape-free society as one in which the act of rape is either infrequent or does not occur. I used the term "rape-free" not to suggest that rape was entirely absent in a given society but as a label to indicate that sexual aggression is socially disapproved and punished severely. Thus, while there may be some men in all societies who might be potential rapists, there is abundant evidence from many societies that sexual aggression is rarely expressed.

Rape in tribal societies is part of a cultural configuration that includes interpersonal violence, male dominance, and sexual separation. Phallocentrism is a dominant psycho-sexual symbol in these societies and men "use the penis to dominate their women" as Yolanda and Robert Murphy say about the Mundurucu (Sanday, 1981: 25). Rape-prone behaviour is associated with environmental insecurity and females are turned into objects to be controlled as men struggle to retain or to gain control of their environment. Behaviours and attitudes prevail that separate the sexes and force men into a posture of proving their manhood. Sexual violence is one of the ways in which men remind themselves that they are superior. As such, rape is part of a broader struggle for control in the face of difficult circumstances. Where men are in harmony with their environment, rape is usually absent.

In *Fraternity Gang Rape* I suggest that rape-prone attitudes and behaviour on American campuses are adopted by insecure young men who bond through homophobia and "getting sex." The homoeroticism of their bonding leads them to display their masculinity through heterosexist displays of sexual performance. The phallus becomes the dominant symbol of discourse. A fraternity brother described to me the way in which he felt accepted by the brothers while he was a pledge.

> We . . . liked to share ridiculously exaggerated sexual boasting, such as our mythical "Sixteen Kilometre Flesh-Weapon." . . . By including

> me in this perpetual, hysterical banter and sharing laughter with me, they showed their affection for me. I felt happy, confident, and loved. This really helped my feelings of loneliness and my fear of being sexually unappealing. We managed to give ourselves a satisfying substitute for sexual relations. We acted out all of the sexual tensions between us as brothers on a verbal level. Women, women everywhere, feminists, homosexuality, etc., all provided the material for the jokes. (Sanday, 1990: 140–1)

Getting their information about women and sex from pornography, some brothers don't see anything wrong with forcing a woman, especially if she's drunk. After the 1983 case of alleged gang rape I describe in the book, one of the participants—a virgin at the time—told a news reporter:

> We have this Select TV in the house, and there's soft porn on every midnight. All the guys watch it and talk about it and stuff, and [gang banging] didn't seem that odd because it's something that you see and hear about all the time. I've heard stories from other fraternities about group sex and trains and stuff like that. It was just like, you know, so this is what I've heard about, this is what it's like. . . . (Sanday, 1990: 34)

Watching their buddies have sex is another favourite activity in rape-prone campus environments. A woman is targeted at a party and brothers are informed; they then hide out on the roof outside the window, or secret themselves in a closet, or look through holes in the wall. Since the goal is to supply a live pornography show for their buddies, the perpetrators in these cases may easily overlook a woman's ability to consent. They certainly don't seek her consent to being watched. It is assumed that if she came to the house to party she is prepared for anything that might happen, especially if she gets drunk. On some campuses I have been told that this practice is called "beaching" or "whaling."

Taking advantage of a drunk woman is widely accepted. As a group of brothers said in a taped conversation in which they discussed the young woman in the 1983 case:

> "She was drugged."
> "She drugged herself."
> "Yeah, she was responsible for her condition, and that just leaves her wide open . . . so to speak." [laughter]. (Sanday, 1990: 119)

In a 1990 talk show—on which I appeared with a victim of gang rape—a young man from a local university called up and admitted that the goal of all parties at his fraternity was "To get 'em drunk and go for it." In 1991, I read an article entitled "Men, Alcohol, and Manipulation," in a campus newspaper from still another university. The author reported hearing several members of a fraternity talking with the bartender about an upcoming social event as follows:

Brother 1: Hey, don't forget—make the women's drinks really strong.
Bartender: Yeah, I won't forget. Just like usual.
Brother 2: We need to get them good and drunk.
Bartender: Don't worry, we'll take care of it.
Brother 3: That'll loosen up some of those inhibitions.

This is the kind of discourse I would classify as rape-prone.

Getting a woman drunk to have sex in a show staged for one's buddies is tragically evident in the testimony heard in the St John's sex case tried in Queens, New York, in 1991–2. This case involved six members of the St John's University lacrosse team, who were indicted for acts ranging from unlawful imprisonment and sexual abuse to sodomy. A seventh defendant pleaded guilty and agreed to testify for immunity (see Sanday, 1996, for a description of the case and the subsequent trial). From the testimony in the case and interviews with the complainant and members of the prosecution team, I reconstructed the following scenario.

A young, naive woman student, whom I call Angela (pseudonym), accepted a ride home from school from a male friend, Michael. On the way, he stopped at the house he shares with members of the St John's lacrosse team to get gas money and invited her inside. At first she refused to go in but upon his insistence accepted the invitation. Inside she met his roommates. Left alone in the third floor bedroom, she accepted a drink from Michael:

> The drink tasted terrible. It was bitter and stung her throat. When she asked what was in it, Michael said he put a little vodka in it. When she explained that she never drank, because drinking made her sick, Michael didn't listen. Then she tried to tell him that she hadn't eaten anything since lunch, but this did not move him. "Vodka is a before dinner drink," he explained, insisting that she drink it.
>
> Finally, she gave in to his pressure and downed the contents of the first cup in a few gulps because of the bitter taste. When she finished, Michael went over to the refrigerator and brought back a large container, which he said was orange soda with vodka. He placed the container on the floor beside her feet. When Michael poured another cup, she told him, "But Michael, I couldn't finish the first one. I don't think I will be able to finish another." Michael said again: "It's only vodka. It can't do anything to you, Angela." He also said, "You know, Angela, in college everyone does something, something wild they can look back on."
>
> "Something wild?" Angela asked quizzically.
>
> "Something wild," Michael said again. "Something you can look back on and talk about later in life." With the beer can that he was holding in his hand but never drank from, he hit her cup and said, "Here's to college life." Later, Angela blamed herself for accepting the drinks from Michael. She was caught between wanting to please the host and wanting to assert her own needs. She had tried to please him by finishing the first drink. Now, she drank the second.
>
> Then, he poured a third drink. When she balked at drinking this one, he started getting upset and annoyed. He told her it was a special drink, made just for her. He accused her of making him waste it. He started pushing the drink up to her mouth. He put his hands over the cup and pushed it to her lips. He said, "Oh Angela, don't make me waste it. It's only vodka. A little vodka can't do anything to you."
>
> By now, Angela felt dizzy and her hands were shaking. She felt lost, unable to move. She had spent a lifetime doing what she was told to avoid being punished. Here was Michael upset with her because she didn't want the drink he had made for her. She thought to herself, "If he wants me to drink it, I'll drink it for him." After she drank most of the third cup, Michael went to put the container back. Her head was spinning and she began to feel really sick, like she was going to vomit. She tried to tell Michael that she was sick, but he didn't seem interested in how she was feeling.
>
> Michael sat next to her and massaged her shoulder. She would never forget his pseudo-seductive voice. She hardly knew him, and here he was talking to her like he really cared for her. It was so obviously a put-on, she was shocked by the insincerity. He kept telling her, "You need to relax. You are too tense. If you relax, you will feel better." She tried to get up but she was too weak and she fell back down. (Sanday, 1996: 11–12)

Testimony in the case revealed that after Angela passed out from Michael's drinks, three house members stood on the landing and watched as Michael engaged in oral sodomy. After Michael left the house, these three took their turns while visitors invited over from another lacrosse team house watched. At the trial these visitors testified that they left the room when Angela woke up and started screaming. One of the lead prosecutors speculated that they left because they realized only then that she was not consenting. They did not understand that the law applies to using drugs and alcohol as it does to using force.

Cross-Campus Variation in Rape and Sexual Coercion

In his paper, Boeringer reports that 55.7 per cent of the males in his study at a large southeastern university obtained sex by verbal harassment (i.e., "threatening to end a relationship unless the victim consents to sex, falsely professing love, or telling the victim lies to render her more sexually receptive," the variable labelled Coercion). One-quarter of the males in Boeringer's study reported using drugs or alcohol to obtain sex (Drugs/Alcohol) and 8.6 per cent of the sample reported at least one use of force or threatened force to obtain sex (Rape).

Schwartz and Nogrady found a much lower incidence of sexual coercion and assault at their research site, a large mid-western university. These authors (private communication) reported that 18.1 per cent of the 116 males in their sample reported some form of unwanted sex: sex by pressure (6.9 per cent); forced sex play/attempted rape (5.2 per cent); or completed rape (6.0 per cent). Of the 177 women interviewed 58.6 per cent reported some form of unwanted sex; sex by pressure (24.1 per cent); forced sex play/attempted rape (14.4 per cent); and completed rape (20.1 per cent).

The effect of fraternities is quite different on the two campuses. Boeringer found that fraternity men reported a higher overall use of coercion short of physical force to obtain sex. According to Boeringer, "fraternity members engage in significantly greater levels of sexual assault through drugging or intoxicating women to render them incapable of consent or refusal" (9). Fraternity members are also more likely than independents to use "non-assaultative sexual coercion," or verbal pressure. "While not criminal in nature," Boeringer points out, "these verbally coercive tactics are nonetheless disturbing in that they suggest a more adversarial view of sexuality in which one should use deceit and guile to 'win favours' from a woman" (10). From his study, Boeringer concludes that "fraternity members are disproportionately involved in some forms of campus sexual aggression." Like the prosecutor in the St John's case mentioned above, he suggests that in all likelihood the process of "working a yes out" which I describe (Sanday, 1990: 113) is viewed by fraternity members as a "safer path to gaining sexual access to a reluctant, non-consenting woman than use of physical force" (12).

Schwartz and Nogrady found no effect of fraternity membership. The most important predictor of sexual victimization in their study involves alcohol. It is not drinking per se that they found important, but whether or not a male perceives that his friends approve of getting a woman drunk for the purpose of having sex (the Approve variable). Also important is whether a male reports that he has friends that actually engage in this behaviour (the Get Drunk variable). The drinking variable that is the most influential in predicting a man's reported sexual assault is the intensity of his drinking—that is, the number of drinks he consumes when he goes out drinking (Drinks). Thus, the authors conclude that "the level of the perceived male peer support system for exploiting women through alcohol, plus the amount of alcohol actually consumed by men when they drink, are the primary predictors of whether they will report themselves as sexual victimizers of women."

The differences reported by Boeringer and Schwartz and Nogrady suggest not only that fraternities vary with respect to rape-prone behaviours but also that campuses vary with respect to overall rates of sexual assault. The latter result suggests that we need to look at cross-campus variation as well as at intra-campus variation. There are several problems that need to be addressed before either intra-campus or cross-campus variation can be established. First, in studying intra-campus variation we must be careful in reaching conclusions about the effect of such factors as drinking intensity or fraternity membership because the dependent variable is frequently lifetime prevalence rates rather than incidence in the past year.

Regarding cross-campus variation, there is the problem of comparability of studies. Boeringer (private communication), for example, measures prevalence rates in his study, while Schwartz and Nogrady (private communication) measure incidence. Since incidence rates are always lower, we cannot conclude that the campuses studied by these authors are much different. Additionally, as noted by Schwartz and Nogrady as well as by Koss (1993), victimization rates from one study to another may not be comparable because of different methodologies, definitions, questions, and sampling procedures.

Nevertheless, some trends can be noticed. The available evidence against variation is seen in the fact that Koss's 15 per cent completed rape prevalence rate in the national study of 32 campuses is replicated by other studies of college students on particular campuses. Koss and Cook (1993: 109) note, for example, that estimates of completed rape frequency in the 12 per cent range have been reported for two campuses and estimates "as high or higher than 12 per cent for unwanted intercourse have been reported in more than 10 additional studies lacking representative sampling methods." According to these authors "there are no studies that have reported substantially lower or higher rates of rape among college students."

Evidence for variation comes from Koss's analysis of the relationship of prevalence rates to the institutional parameters used to design the sample (Koss, 1988). She found that rates varied by region and by governance of the institution. Rates were twice as high at private colleges and major universities (14 per cent and 17 per cent respectively) than they were at religiously affiliated institutions (7 per cent).

Ethnicity of the respondent (but, interestingly not the respondent's family income) was also associated with prevalence rates. More white women (16 per cent) reported victimization than did Hispanic (12 per cent), black (10 per cent), or Asian women (7 per cent). These figures were almost reversed for men. Rape was reported by 4 per cent of white men, 10 per cent of black men, 7 per cent of Hispanic men, and 2 per cent of Asian men. Prevalence rates reported by men also differed by region of the country. More men in the Southeast region (6 per cent) admitted to raping compared with men in the Plains states (3 per cent) and those in the West (2 per cent) (Koss, 1988).

Intriguing evidence for cross-campus variation in rape rates and related variables comes from Koss's national study of 32 campuses. Using Koss's data I looked at prevalence and incidence rates for each of 30 campuses in her study (2 campuses were excluded because of the amount of missing information). The results show a wide discrepancy when campuses are compared. For example the campus percentages of males admitting that they have used alcohol or force to obtain sex (Koss's 1988, 11 rape variables) range from 0 to 10 per cent. Campus percentages of males who admit to perpetrating unwanted sex in the past year (as opposed to since the age of 14) range from 6 to 22 per cent. The latter percentages are higher because I computed them using all the sexual experience questions (excluding the two authority questions). Since the latter percentages are based on a question that measures incidence ("How many times in the past school year?") the results provide a measure of an dependent variable that can be compared with drinking intensity.

The Koss survey includes two questions that might be taken as measures of drinking intensity. Both questions are asked in such a fashion as to measure drinking intensity in the past year. One asks "How often do you drink to the point of intoxication or drunkenness?"; the other asks "On a typical drinking occasion, how much do you usually drink?" The campus percentages of males checking the most extreme categories of the first question (1–2 or more times a week) ranges from 1 to 24 per cent. The campus percentages of males checking the most extreme categories of the second question (more than 5 or 6 cans of beer or other alcoholic beverages) ranges from 6 to 71 per cent. Since all studies—Schwartz, Boeringer, Koss, and Gaines (1993)—are unanimous on the effect of drinking, this information, perhaps more than any other, is suggestive of variation in the rape-prone nature of campus environments.

The Concept of a Rape-Free Society

Assuming that we could identify campuses on which both males and females reported a low incidence of rape and/or unwanted sex, the next question would be whether there is a significant difference in the sexual culture on these campuses compared to the more rape-prone campuses. My cross-cultural research which demonstrated differences in the character of heterosexual interaction in rape-free as opposed to rape-prone societies would suggest that the answer to this question is yes. The outstanding feature of rape-free societies is the ceremonial importance of women and the respect accorded to the contribution women make to social continuity, a respect which places men and women in relatively balanced power spheres. Rape-free societies are characterized by sexual equality and the notion that the sexes are complementary. Although the sexes may not perform the same duties or have the same rights or privileges, each is indispensable to the activities of the other.

Since 1981 when this research was published, I have spent approximately 24 months (extended over a period of 14 years) doing ethnographic research among the Minangkabau, a rape-free Indonesian society. I chose the Minangkabau because of social factors that conformed with my profile of rape-free societies. The Minangkabau are the largest and most modern matrilineal society in the world today. Women play an undisputed role in Minangkabau symbol system and daily life, especially in the villages. Among the most populous of the ethnic groups of Indonesia, the Minangkabau are not an isolated tribal society in some far off corner of the world. Banks, universities, and modern governmental buildings are found in two of the major cities of West Sumatra, the traditional homeland of the Minangkabau people. At the major universities, it is not uncommon to find Minangkabau PhDs trained in the United States. People own cars and travel by bus throughout the province. Most children go to local schools and, increasingly, many attend college.

The challenge facing me when I went to West Sumatra was first to find out whether the incidence of rape was low and, if so, to crack the cultural code that made it so. In the early years there was ample evidence from police reports and from interviews conducted all over the province that this was a rape-free society. Ethnographic research conducted in several villages provided confirmation. This research demonstrated that women are the mainstays of village life. The all-important family rice fields are inherited through the female line. Husbands live in their wives' houses. It is believed that this is the way it should be, because otherwise in the event of a divorce women and children would be left destitute. The main reason given for the matrilineal inheritance of property is that since women bear the infant and raise the child it is in keeping with the laws of nature to give women control of the ancestral property so that they will have the wherewithal to house and nurture the young.

Missing from the Minangkabau conception of sexuality is any show of interest in sex for the sake of sex alone. Sex is neither a commodity nor a notch in the male belt in this society. A man's sense of himself is not predicated by his sexual functioning. Although aggression is present, it is not linked to sex nor is it deemed a manly trait. The Minangkabau have yet to discover sex as a commodity or turn it into a fetish.

There is a cultural category for rape, which is defined as "forced sex" and is punishable by law. Rape is conceived as something that happens in the wild, which places men who rape beyond the pale of society. In answer to my questions regarding the relative absence of rape among them compared to the United States, Minangkabau informants replied that rape was impossible in their society because custom, law, and religion forbade it and punished it severely. In the years that I worked in West Sumatra, I heard of only two cases of rape in the village where I lived. One case involved a group of males who ganged up on a young, retarded woman. In this case the leader of the group hanged himself the next day out of fear of avenging villagers. The rest of the assailants went to jail. The second case involved a local woman and a Japanese soldier during the Japanese occupation of the Second World War and after. To this day people remember the case and talk about the horror of the Japanese occupation.

In the past few years, Indonesia's entrance into the global economy has been accompanied by an amazing shift in the eroticization of popular culture seen on TV. In 1995 the signs that this culture was filtering into Minangkabau villages were very evident. To the extent that commodification and eroticization breaks down the cultural supports for its matrilineal social system, the Minangkabau sexual culture will also change. Indeed, today in the provincial capital some argue that the Minangkabau are not rape-free.

During my last field trip in 1995, I heard of many more reports of rape in the provincial capital. In the early 1990s, for example, there was a widely publicized acquaintance gang rape of a young woman by a group of boys. Interviewing court officers in the capital, I was told that this was the only case of its kind. Compared with similar cases in the United States, such as the St John's case, the outcome was still very different. While the St John's defendants were either acquitted or got probation after pleading guilty, all the defendants in the Sumatran case were convicted and sent to jail. But, one may well ask whether the criminal justice system will continue to convict defendants as tolerance for sexual coercion begins to permeate popular beliefs.

Rape-Free Campus Cultures

A rape-free campus is relatively easy to imagine, but equally hard to find. Based on anecdotal information one candidate comes to mind. On this campus everyone—administrators, faculty, and students—are on a first-name basis, which makes the atmosphere more egalitarian than most campuses. Decision making is by consensus and interpersonal interaction is guided by an ethic of respect for the individual. Those who are disrespectful of others are ostracized as campus life is motivated by a strong sense of community and the common good. No one group (such as fraternities, males, or athletes) dominates the social scene. Sexual assault is a serious offence treated with suspension or expulsion. Homophobic, racist, and sexist attitudes are virtually nonexistent. Individuals bond together in groups drawn together by mutual interests, not to turn against others. Interviews suggest that the incidence of unwanted sex on this campus is low; however, this must be corroborated by a campus-wide survey.

For information on a rape-free fraternity culture I turn to a description offered by a student who wrote a mini-ethnography on his fraternity for a class project. Another brother in the same fraternity corroborated his description after reading the ethnography and adding additional information. In the following, the fraternity is referred to by the pseudonym QRS. With their permission, the fraternity brothers are identified by name.

Noel Morrison and Josh Marcus recognize that fraternities on their campus (called U.) "propagate sexist attitudes and provide a breeding ground for insecure acts of sexism, racism, and homophobia." According to Noel, U.'s fraternities "tend to be self-segregating entities which seek to maintain the inferior social position of women and minority students through exclusion" and social intolerance. QRS, however, consciously fights against this norm.

QRS is one of the oldest fraternities at U., going back at least 100 years. It was like all other fraternities at U. until 1977 when it was almost forced to disband due to insufficient numbers. At that time, a group of nine first-year males pledged as a group knowing that their numbers would give them control of house decisions. They exercised this control by rewriting the house constitution and initiation rituals. Today the brothers are proud to say that they are "not a real fraternity." Interestingly, although both Joel and Noel treasure their lives in QRS (because of the fun, companionship of respected friends, and community the house offers), both feel that fraternities should be abolished.

Partly as a defence mechanism and partly to underscore their difference, QRS brothers stigmatize members of other fraternities as "jarheads." The word "jarhead" is used to refer to the "loud, obnoxious, sexist, racist, homophobic" members of U.'s fraternities. Most of the brothers in QRS do not participate in the campus inter-fraternity council and prefer to see themselves as "a group of friends," rather than as a fraternity, and their house as "a place to have concerts." Parties are always open to anyone and are either free to everyone or everyone pays, contrary to parties at other houses in which men pay and women are admitted for free.

At QRS heavy drinking is not a requisite for membership and is not a part of initiation. There are no drinking games and binge drinking does not occur. While some brothers drink to get drunk more than once a week, most don't. At parties there are always brothers who watch out for women or house members who have had too much to drink. Josh stressed that "it is clearly not acceptable for someone to take advantage of a drunk woman, because that's rape." There is no talk in the house about getting a girl drunk to have sex, he says. Members are very aware that where there is heavy drinking someone can be taken advantage of. If a female passes out or is very drunk she is watched or escorted home. Both Josh and Noel remember an incident during a party in the fraternity next door, in which several members of QRS came to the aid of a young woman whose shirt was above her waist and who had passed out on their porch, left there perhaps by friends from the party who had deserted her. Their intervention may have saved her life. When they were unable to get her to talk, they took her to the emergency room of a nearby hospital only to learn that she was in a coma and her heart had stopped. Fortunately, they were in time and she responded to treatment.

Women are not seen as sex objects in the house, but as friends. Unlike other fraternities at U., there is no distinction drawn between "girlfriends" and friends and there are no "party girls." Noel says that when he was rushing he would often hear women referred to as "sluts" in other fraternities. However, at QRS this is unheard of. According to Josh, a brother who acted "inappropriately" with a woman would be severely reprimanded, perhaps even expelled from the fraternity. The brothers are not afraid of strong women. There are women's studies students who are regulars at the house, along with outspoken feminists and activists. Noel quotes one of them:

> I guess there're a few brothers who make sexist jokes, but I don't know how seriously people take them. I remember last year in the middle of mid-terms I was studying late at night and was feeling sick and tired, and in a span of about five minutes, four people offered their beds to me, not as a sexual thing at all, but just because they cared.

One QRS brother started the Men's Association for Change and Openness (MACHO) and is an active participant in U's student peer-counselling group for sexual health. One brother displays a "Refuse and Resist" sticker on his door, proclaiming, "Date rape: cut it out or cut it off." In a 1993 pamphlet advertising QRS as the site of the National Anarchist gathering, the brothers wrote, "Although QRS is a frat, it is generally a friendly place, along with being a safe haven for women."

Most interesting about QRS is its acceptance of homosexuality and bisexuality. Homophobia does not become the basis for males to prove their virility to one another. Because of its openness about sex and acceptance of homosexuality, QRS has earned the reputation on campus of being "the gay frat" or "faggot house." Josh comments on this reputation and what it means to him:

> QRS's attitudes about homosexuality are complex, but fundamentally tolerant and respectful. Some brothers revel in rumours that we are the "gay frat." It is rumoured that a few years ago a few of the brothers were involved sexually, and one of our most involved alumni is homosexual.

Although most fraternities have had or have a few homosexual brothers, this honest acceptance of homosexuality is unusual. QRS brothers are proud of being called the "gay frat." Evidence of this is the humorous statement in the letters given prospective pledges offering bids, which ends with the phrase "we are all gay."

Conclusion

The first step in the struggle against "hidden rape," which began in the late '60s with consciousness-raising groups (see Sanday, 1996: Chapter 8), was to recognize the problem and speak out against it. The next step was to change outmoded rape laws and assess the causes and frequency of sexual violence against women. Mary Koss's national survey of 1985 demonstrated that one in four women will experience rape or attempted rape in her lifetime. Since the '80s many other surveys have replicated her findings. The search for causes has been the subject of numerous studies. . . .

The next step is to go beyond the causes and study solutions. One approach would be to find naturally occurring rape-free environments on today's college campuses. QRS is one example. No rape-free campuses have been identified by research, yet I have heard descriptions from students that lead me to believe that such campuses exist. Identifying such campuses and seeking out environments like QRS is the next step for research. In this paper I have identified the kinds of problems such research must address. First, it is necessary to obtain incidence as well as prevalence data. Secondly, we need more subtle measures of the kinds of socio-cultural correlates that have been discussed in this paper: drinking intensity; using pornography to learn about sex rather than talking with one's partner; bragging about sexual conquests; setting women up to display one's masculinity to other men; heterosexism; homophobia; and using pornography as a guide to female sexuality. Finally, we need to develop a consensus on the criteria for labelling a campus either rape-free or rape-prone. If at least one in five women on a given campus say they have experienced unwanted sex in the last year, I would label the campus rape-prone. However, others may want to propose different criteria. Once a consensus is reached, the movement to make our campuses safe for women might include identifying rape-free and rape-prone campuses.

Note

1. This article has benefited from the comments of Mary P. Koss. I am also grateful to Koss for supplying me with the data on her 1986 study of 32 campuses. Martin D. Schwartz and Scot B. Boerginer graciously supplied me with additional data from their studies and answered my many questions. Noel Morrison played an important role by giving me permission to summarize his description of his fraternity. John Marcus, a brother in the same fraternity, was also helpful in corroborating Noel's observations and supplying a few of his own.

References

Brownmiller, S. 1975. *Against Our Will: Men, Women, and Rape*. New York: Simon and Schuster.

Koss, M.P. 1988. "Hidden Rape: Sexual Aggression and Victimization in a National Sample of Students in Higher Education," in A.W. Burgess, ed., *Rape and Sexual Assault II*, pp. 3–25. New York: Garland.

———. 1993. "Rape: Scope, Impact, Interventions, and Public Policy Responses," *American Psychologist* (October): 1062–9.

Koss, M.P., and J.A. Gaines. 1993. "The Prediction of Sexual Aggression by Alcohol Use, Athletic Participation, and Fraternity Affiliation," *Journal of Interpersonal Violence* 8: 94–108.

Koss, M.P., and S.L. Cook. 1993. "Facing the Facts: Date and Acquaintance Rape Are Significant Problems for Women," in R.J. Gelles and D.R. Loseke, eds., *Current Controversies on Family Violence*, pp. 104–19. Newbury Park, CA: Sage.

Sanday, P.R. 1981. "The Socio-cultural Context of Rape: A Cross-Cultural Study," *Journal of Social Issues* 37: 5–27.

———. 1990. *Fraternity Gang Rape: Sex, Brotherhood and Privilege on Campus*. New York: New York University Press.

———. 1996. *A Woman Scorned: Acquaintance Rape on Trial*. New York: Doubleday.

Chapter 36

Overview

One of the most common myths about gendered violence is that women and men are equally likely to perpetrate it. This myth has a superficial appeal to logic—neither women nor men are angels, so bad behaviour by one gender is likely to resemble bad behaviour by the other.

Unfortunately, as Dobash and colleagues point out, the data simply don't support this belief. The Conflict Tactics Scale (CTS) is often used to suggest that men and women perpetrate violence at equal rates, but the CTS obscures gender differences in the frequency and severity of the violence. The resulting research has been taken out of context, suggesting a false equivalence of male-perpetrated violence with female-perpetrated violence.

Dobash et al. are not interested in minimizing or playing down the wrongness of violence, whether perpetrated by men or by women. In either case, it is unacceptable. However, they argue that in order to understand the gendered dynamics of violence, context matters. Contextual accounts of violence reveal a pattern in which men, as a group, tend to mete out more severe violence more frequently than women, as a group. This does not mean women are non-violent, but it does mean that the social construction of masculinity is key to any efforts to contain or prevent violence.

The Myth of Sexual Symmetry in Marital Violence

Russell P. Dobash, R. Emerson Dobash, Margo Wilson, and Martin Daly

Long denied, legitimized, and made light of, wife-beating is at last the object of widespread public concern and condemnation. Extensive survey research and intensive interpretive investigations tell a common story. Violence against wives (by which term we encompass de facto as well as registered unions) is often persistent and severe, occurs in the context of continuous intimidation and coercion, and is inextricably linked to attempts to dominate and control women. Historical and contemporary investigations further reveal that this violence has been explicitly decriminalized, ignored, or treated in an ineffectual manner by criminal justice systems, by medical and social service institutions, and by communities. Increased attention to these failures has inspired increased efforts to redress them, and in many places legislative amendments have mandated arrest and made assault a crime whether the offender is married to the victim or not.

A number of researchers and commentators have suggested that assaults upon men by their wives constitute a social problem comparable in nature and magnitude to that of wife-beating. Two main bodies of evidence have been offered in support of these authors' claims that husbands and wives are similarly victimized: (1) self-reports of violent acts perpetrated and suffered by survey respondents, especially those in two US national probability samples; and (2) US homicide data. Unlike the case of violence against wives, however, the victimization of husbands allegedly continues to be denied and trivialized. "Violence by wives has not been an object of public concern," note Straus and Gelles (1986: 472). "There has been no publicity, and no funds have been invested in ameliorating this problem because it has not been defined as a problem."

We shall argue that claims of sexual symmetry in marital violence are exaggerated, and that wives' and husbands' uses of violence differ greatly, both quantitatively and qualitatively. We shall further argue that there is no reason to expect the sexes to be alike in this domain, and that efforts to avoid sexism by lumping male and female data and by the use of gender-neutral terms such as "spouse-beating" are misguided. If violence is gendered, as it assuredly is, explicit characterization of gender's relevance to violence is essential. The alleged similarity of women and men in their use of violence in intimate relationships stands in marked contrast to men's virtual monopoly on the use of violence in other social contexts, and we challenge the proponents of the sexual symmetry thesis to develop coherent theoretical models that would account for a sexual monomorphism of violence in one social context and not in others. . . .

The Claim of Sexually Symmetrical Marital Violence

Authoritative claims about the prevalence and sexual symmetry of spousal violence in America began with a 1975 US national survey in which 2,143 married or cohabiting persons were interviewed in person about their actions in the preceding year. Straus (1977–8) announced that the survey results showed that the "marriage licence is a hitting licence," and moreover that the rates of perpetrating spousal violence, including severe violence, were higher for wives than for husbands. He concluded:

> Violence between husband and wife is far from a one way street. The old cartoons of the wife chasing the husband with a rolling pin or throwing pots and pans are closer to reality than most (and especially those with feminist sympathies) realize. (Straus, 1977–8: 447–8)

In 1985, the survey was repeated by telephone with a new national probability sample including 3,520 husband–wife households, and with similar results. In each survey, the researchers interviewed either the wife or the husband (but not both) in each contacted household about how the couple settled their differences when they had a disagreement. The individual who was interviewed was presented with a list of eighteen "acts" ranging from "discussed an issue calmly" and "cried" to "threw something at him/her/you" and "beat him/her/you up," with the addition of "choked him/her/you" in 1985 (Straus, 1990a: 33). These acts constituted the Conflict Tactics Scales (CTS) and were intended to measure three constructs: "Reasoning," "Verbal Aggression," and "Physical Aggression" or "Violence," which was further subdivided into "Minor Violence" and "Severe Violence" according to a presumed potential for injury (Straus, 1979; Straus and Gelles, 1990a). . . .

According to both surveys, rates of violence by husbands and wives were strikingly similar. The authors estimated that in the year prior to the 1975 survey 11.6 per cent of US husbands were victims of physical violence perpetrated by their wives, while 12.1 per cent of wives were victims of their husbands' violence. In 1985, these percentages had scarcely changed, but husbands seemed more vulnerable: 12.1 per cent of husbands and 11.3 per cent of wives were victims. In both surveys, husbands were more likely to be victims of acts of "severe violence": in 1975, 4.6 per cent of husbands were such victims versus 3.8 per cent of wives, and in 1985, 4.4 per cent of husbands versus 3.0 per cent of wives were victims. . . .

Others have endorsed and publicized these conclusions. For example, a recent review of marital violence concludes, with heavy reliance on Straus and Gelles's survey results, that "(a) women are more prone than men to engage in severely violent acts; (b) each year more men than women are victimized by their intimates" (McNeely and Mann, 1990: 130). One of Straus and Gelles's collaborators in the 1975 survey, Steinmetz (1977– 8), used the same survey evidence to proclaim the existence of "battered husbands" and a "battered husband syndrome." She has remained one of the leading defenders of the claim that violence between men and women in the family is symmetrical. Steinmetz and her collaborators maintain that the problem is not wife-beating perpetrated by violent men, but "violent couples" and "violent people." Men may be stronger on average, argues Steinmetz, but weaponry equalizes matters, as is allegedly shown by the nearly equivalent numbers of US husbands and wives who are killed by their partners. The reason why battered husbands are inconspicuous and seemingly rare is supposedly that shame prevents them from seeking help. . . .

A corollary of the notion that the sexes are alike in their use of violence is that satisfactory causal accounts of violence will be gender-blind. Discussion thus focuses, for example, on the role of one's prior experiences with violence as a child, social stresses, frustration, inability to control anger, impoverished social skills, and so forth, without reference to gender. This presumption that the sexes are alike not merely in action but in the reasons for that action is occasionally explicit, such as when Shupe et al. (1987: 56) write: "Everything we have found points to parallel processes that lead women and men to become violent. . . . Women may be more likely than men to use kitchen utensils or sewing scissors when they commit assault, but their frustrations, motives and lack of control over these feelings predictably resemble men's."

In sum, the existence of an invisible legion of assaulted husbands is an inference that strikes many family violence researchers as reasonable. Two lines of evidence—homicide data and the CTS survey results—suggest to those supporting the sexual-symmetry-of-violence thesis that large numbers of men are trapped in violent relationships. These men are allegedly being denied medical, social welfare, and criminal justice services because of an unwillingness to accept the evidence from homicide statistics and the CTS surveys.

Violence against Wives

Any argument that marital violence is sexually symmetrical must either dismiss or ignore a large body of contradictory evidence indicating that wives greatly outnumber husbands as victims. While CTS researchers were discovering and publicizing the mutual violence of wives and husbands, other researchers—using evidence from courts, police, and women's shelters—were finding that wives were much more likely than husbands to be victims. After an extensive review of extant research, Lystad (1975) expressed the consensus: "The occurrence of adult violence in the home usually involves males as aggressors towards females." This conclusion was subsequently supported by numerous further studies of divorce records, emergency room patients treated for non-accidental injuries, police assault records, and spouses seeking assistance and refuge. Analyses of police and court records in North America and Europe have persistently indicated that women constitute 90–95 per cent of the victims of those assaults in the home reported to the criminal justice system.

Defenders of the sexual-symmetry-of-violence thesis do not deny these results, but they question their representativeness: these studies could be biased because samples of victims were self-selected. However, criminal victimization surveys using national probability samples similarly indicate that wives are much more often victimized than husbands. Such surveys in the United States, Canada, and Great Britain have been replicated in various years, with essentially the same results. Beginning in 1972 and using a panel survey method involving up to seven consecutive interviews at six-month intervals, the US National Crime Survey has generated nearly a million interviews. Gaquin's (1977–8) analysis of US National Crime Survey data for 1973–5 led her to conclude that men "have almost no risk of being assaulted by their wives" (634–5); only 3 per cent of the violence reported from these surveys involved attacks on men by their female partners. Another analysis of the National Crime Survey data from 1973 to 1980 found that 6 per cent of spousal assault incidents were directed at men (McLeod, 1984). Schwartz (1987) re-analyzed the same victimization surveys with the addition of the 1981 and 1982 data, and found 102 men who claimed to have been victims of assaults by their wives (4 per cent of domestic assault incidents) in contrast to 1,641 women who said they were assaulted by husbands. The 1981 Canadian Urban Victimization Survey and the 1987 General Social Survey produced analogous findings, from which Johnson (1989) concluded that "women account for 80–90 per cent of victims in assaults or sexual assaults between spouses or former spouses. In fact, the number of domestic assaults involving males was too low in both surveys to provide reliable estimates" (1–2). The 1982 and 1984 British Crime Surveys found that women accounted for all the victims of marital assaults. Self-reports of criminal victimization based on national probability surveys, while not without methodological weaknesses, are not subject to the same reporting biases as divorce, police, and hospital records.

The national crime surveys also indicate that women are much more likely than men to suffer injury as a result of assaults in the home. After analyzing the results of the US National Crime Surveys, Schwartz (1987: 67) concludes, "There are still more than 13 times as many women seeking medical care from a private physician for injuries received in a spousal assault." This result, again, replicates the typical findings of studies of police or hospital records. For example, women constituted 94 per cent of the injury victims in an analysis of the spousal assault cases among 262 domestic disturbance calls to police in Santa Barbara County, California; moreover, the women's injuries were more serious than the men's. Berk et al. (1983: 207) conclude that "when injuries are used as the outcome of interest, a marriage license is a hitting licence but for men only." Brush (1990) reports that a US national probability sample survey of over 13,000 respondents in 1987–8 replicated the evident symmetry of marital violence when CTS-like questions about acts were posed, but also revealed that women were much more often injured than men (and that men downplayed women's injuries).

In response, defenders of the sexual-symmetry-of-violence thesis contend that data from police, courts, hospitals, and social service agencies are suspect because men are reluctant to report physical violence by their wives. For example, Steinmetz (1977–8) asserts that husband-beating is a camouflaged social problem because men must overcome extraordinary stigma in order to report that their wives have beaten them. Similarly, Shupe et al. (1987) maintain that men are unwilling to report their wives because "it would be unmanly or unchivalrous to go to the police for protection from a woman" (52). However, the limited available evidence does not support these authors' presumption that men are less likely to report assaults by their spouses than are women. Schwartz's (1987) analysis of the 1973–82 US National Crime Survey data found that 67.2 per cent of men and 56.8 per cent of women called the police after being assaulted by their spouses. One may protest that these high percentages imply that only a tiny proportion of the most severe spousal assaults were acknowledged as assaults by respondents to these crime surveys, but the results are nonetheless contrary to the notion that assaulted men are especially reticent. Moreover, Rouse et al. (1988), using "act" definitions of assaults which inspired much higher proportions to acknowledge victimization, similarly report that men were likelier than women to call the police after assaults by intimate partners, both among married couples and among those dating. In addition, a sample of 337 cases of domestic violence drawn from family court cases in Ontario showed that men were more likely than women to press charges against their spouses: there were 17 times as many female victims as male victims, but only 22 per cent of women laid charges in contrast to 40 per cent of the men, and men were less likely to drop the charges, too. What those who argue that men are reluctant or ashamed to report their wives' assaults overlook is that women have their own reasons to be reticent, fearing both the loss of a jailed or alienated husband's economic support and his vengeance. Whereas the claim that husbands under-report because of shame or chivalry is largely speculative, there is considerable evidence that women report very little of the violence perpetrated by their male partners.

The CTS survey data indicating equivalent violence by wives and husbands thus stand in contradiction to injury data, to police incident reports, to help-seeking statistics, and even to other, larger, national probability sample surveys of self-reported victimization. The CTS researchers insist that their results alone are accurate because husbands' victimizations are unlikely to be detected or reported by any other method. It is therefore important to consider in detail the CTS and the data it generates.

Do CTS Data Reflect the Reality of Marital Violence?

The CTS instrument has been much used and much criticized. Critics have complained that its exclusive focus on "acts" ignores the actors' interpretations, motivations, and intentions; that physical violence is arbitrarily delimited, excluding, for example, sexual assault and rape; that retrospective reports of the past year's events are unlikely to be accurate; that researchers' attributions of "violence" (with resultant claims about its statistical prevalence) are based on respondents' admitting to acts described in such an impoverished manner as to conflate severe assaults with trivial gestures; that the formulaic distinction between "minor" and "severe violence" (whereby, for example, "tried to hit with something" is definitionally "severe" and "slapped" is definitionally "minor") constitutes a poor operationalization of severity; that the responses of aggressors and victims have been given identical evidentiary status in deriving incidence estimates, while their inconsistencies have been ignored; that the CTS omits the contexts of violence, the events precipitating it, and the sequences of events by which it progresses; and that it fails to connect outcomes, especially injury, with the acts producing them.

. . . That the CTS is widely used cannot be gainsaid, but whether it is reliable or valid is questionable.

Problems with the Interpretation of CTS Responses

With the specific intention of circumventing imprecision and subjectivity in asking about such abstractions as "violence," the CTS is confined to questions about "acts." Respondents are asked whether they have "pushed" their partners, have "slapped" them, and so forth, rather than whether they have "assaulted" them or behaved "violently." This focus on "acts" is intended to reduce problems of self-serving and biased definitional criteria on the part of the respondents. However, any gain in objectivity has been undermined by the way that CTS survey data have then been analyzed and interpreted. Any respondent who acknowledges a single instance of having "pushed," "grabbed," "shoved," "slapped," or "hit or tried to hit" another person is deemed a perpetrator of "violence" by the researchers, regardless of the act's context, consequences, or meaning to the parties involved. Similarly, a single instance of having "kicked," "bit," "hit or tried to hit with an object," "beat up," "choked," "threatened with a knife or gun," or "used a knife or fired a gun" makes one a perpetrator of "severe violence."

Affirmation of any one of the "violence" items provides the basis for estimates such as Straus and Gelles' (1990b: 97) claim that 6.8 million husbands and 6.25 million wives were spousal assault victims in the United States in 1985. Similarly, estimates of large numbers of "beaten" or "battered" wives and husbands have been based on affirmation of any one of the "severe violence" items. For example, Steinmetz (1986: 734) and Straus and Gelles (1987: 638) claim on this basis that 1.8 million US women are "beaten" by their husbands annually. But note that any man who once threw an "object" at his wife, regardless of its nature and regardless of whether the throw missed, qualifies as having "beaten" her; some unknown proportion of the women and men who are alleged to have been "beaten," on the basis of their survey responses, never claimed to have been struck at all. Thus, the "objective" scoring of the CTS not only fails to explore the meanings and intentions associated with the acts but also has in practice entailed interpretive transformations that guarantee exaggeration, misinterpretation, and ultimately trivialization of the genuine problems of violence.

Consider a "slap." The word encompasses anything from a slap on the hand chastizing a dinner companion for reaching for a bite of one's dessert to a tooth-loosening assault intended to punish, humiliate, and terrorize. These are not trivial distinctions; indeed, they constitute the essence of definitional issues concerning violence.

Almost all definitions of violence and violent acts refer to intentions. Malevolent intent is crucial, for example, to legal definitions of "assault" (to which supporters of the CTS have often mistakenly claimed that their "acts" correspond; e.g., Straus, 1990b: 58). However, no one has systematically investigated how respondents vary in their subjective definitions of the "acts" listed on the CTS. If, for example, some respondents interpret phrases such as "tried to hit with an object" literally, then a good deal of relatively harmless behaviour surely taints the estimates of "severe violence." Although this problem has not been investigated systematically, one author has shown that it is potentially serious. In a study of 103 couples, Margolin (1987) found that wives surpassed husbands in their use of "severe violence" according to the CTS, but unlike others who have obtained this result, Margolin troubled to check its meaningfulness with more intensive interviews. She concluded:

> While CTS items appear behaviorally specific, their meanings still are open to interpretation. In one couple who endorsed the item "kicking," for example, we discovered that the kicking took place in bed in a more kidding, than serious, fashion. Although this behavior meets the criterion for severe abuse on the CTS, neither spouse viewed it as aggressive, let alone violent. In another couple, the wife scored on severe physical aggression while the husband scored on low-level aggression only. The inquiry revealed that, after years of passively accepting the husband's repeated abuse, this wife finally decided, on one occasion, to retaliate by hitting him over the head with a wine decanter. (1987: 82)

By the criteria of Steinmetz (1977–8: 501), this incident would qualify as a "battered husband" case. But however dangerous this retaliatory blow may have been and however reprehensible or justified one may consider it, it is not "battering," whose most basic definitional criterion is its repetitiveness. A failure to consider intentions, interpretations, and the history of the individuals' relationship is a significant shortcoming of CTS research. Only through a consideration of behaviours, intentions, and intersubjective understandings associated with specific violent events will we come to a fuller understanding of violence between men and women. Studies employing more intensive interviews and detailed case reports addressing the contexts and motivations of marital violence help unravel the assertions of those who claim the widespread existence of beaten and battered husbands. Research focusing on specific violent events shows that women almost always employ violence in defence of self and children in response to cues of imminent assault in the past and in retaliation for previous physical abuse. Proponents of the sexual-symmetry-of-violence thesis have made much of the fact that CTS surveys indicate that women "initiate" the violence about as often as men, but a case in which a woman struck the first blow is unlikely to be the mirror image of one in which her husband "initiated." A noteworthy feature of the literature proclaiming the existence of battered husbands and battering wives is how little the meagre case descriptions resemble those of battered wives and battering husbands. Especially lacking in the alleged male victim cases is any indication of the sort of chronic intimidation characteristic of prototypical woman battering cases.

Any self-report method must constitute an imperfect reflection of behaviour, and the CTS is no exception. That in itself is hardly a fatal flaw. But for such an instrument to retain utility for the investigation of a particular domain such as family violence, an essential point is that its inaccuracies and misrepresentations must not be systematically related to the distinctions under investigation. The CTS's inability to detect the immense differences in violence between stepparents and birth parents, as noted above, provides strong reason to suspect that the test's shortcomings produce not just noise but systematic bias. In the case of marital violence, the other sorts of evidence reviewed in this paper indicate that there are massive differences in the use of confrontational violence against spouses by husbands versus wives, and yet the CTS has consistently failed to detect them. CTS users have taken this failure as evidence for the null hypothesis, apparently assuming that their questionnaire data have a validity that battered women's injuries and deaths lack.

Homicides

The second line of evidence that has been invoked in support of the claim that marital violence is more or less sexually symmetrical is the number of lethal outcomes:

> Data on homicide between spouses suggest that an almost equal number of wives kill their husbands as husbands kill their wives (Wolfgang, 1958). Thus it appears that men and women might have equal potential for violent marital interaction; initiate similar acts of violence; and when differences of physical strength are equalized by weapons, commit similar amounts of spousal homicide. (Steinmetz and Lucca, 1988: 241)

McNeely and Robinson-Simpson (1987: 485) elevated the latter hypothesis about the relevance of weapons to the status of a fact: "Steinmetz observed that when weapons neutralize differences in physical strength, about as many men as women are victims of homicide."

Steinmetz and Lucca's citation of Wolfgang refers to his finding that 53 Philadelphia men killed their wives between 1948 and 1952, while 47 women killed their husbands. This is a slender basis for such generalization, but fuller information does indeed bear Steinmetz out as regards the near equivalence of body counts in the United States: Maxfield (1989) reported that there were 10,529 wives and 7,888 husbands killed by their mates in the entire country between 1976 and 1985, a 1.3:1 ratio of female to male victims.

Husbands are indeed almost as often slain as are wives in the United States, then. However, there remain several problems with Steinmetz and Lucca's (as well as McNeely and Robinson-Simpson's) interpretation of this fact. Studies of actual cases lend no support to the facile claim that homicidal husbands and wives "initiate similar acts of violence." Men often kill wives after lengthy periods of prolonged physical violence accompanied by other forms of abuse and coercion; the roles in such cases are seldom if ever reversed. Men perpetrate familicidal massacres, killing spouse and children together; women do not. Men commonly hunt down and kill wives who have left them; women hardly ever behave similarly. Men kill wives as part of planned murder-suicides; analogous acts by women are almost unheard of. Men kill in response to revelations of wifely infidelity; women almost never respond similarly, though their mates are more often adulterous. The evidence is overwhelming that a large proportion of the spouse-killings perpetrated by wives, but almost none of those perpetrated by husbands, are acts of self-defence. Unlike men, women kill male partners after years of suffering physical violence, after they have exhausted all available sources of assistance, when they feel trapped, and because they fear for their own lives.

A further problem with the invocation of spousal homicide data as evidence against sex differences in marital violence is that this numerical equivalence is peculiar to the United States. Whereas the ratio of wives to husbands as homicide victims in the United States was 1.3:1, corresponding ratios from other countries are much higher: 3.3:1 for a 10-year period in Canada, for example, 4.3:1 for Great Britain, and 6:1 for Denmark. The reason why this is problematic is that US homicide data and CTS data from several countries have been invoked as complementary pieces of evidence for women's and men's equivalent uses of violence. One cannot have it both ways. If the lack of sex differences in CTS results is considered proof of sexually symmetrical violence, then homicide data must somehow be dismissed as irrelevant, since homicides generally fail to exhibit this supposedly more basic symmetry. Conversely, if US homicide counts constitute relevant evidence, the large sex differences found elsewhere surely indicate that violence is peculiarly symmetrical only in the United States, and the fact that the CTS fails to detect sex differences in other countries must then be taken to mean that the CTS is insensitive to genuine differences.

A possible way out of this dilemma is hinted at in Steinmetz and Lucca's (1988) allusion to the effect of weapons: perhaps it is the availability of guns that has neutralized men's advantage in lethal marital conflict in the United States. Gun use is indeed relatively prevalent in the US, accounting for 51 per cent of a sample of 1,706 spousal homicides in Chicago, for example, as compared to 40 per cent of 1,060 Canadian cases, 42 per cent of 395 Australian cases, and just 8 per cent of 1,204 cases in England and Wales (Wilson and Daly, 1990). Nevertheless, the plausible hypothesis that gun use can account for the different sex ratios among victims fails. When shootings and other spousal homicides are analyzed separately, national differences in the sex ratios of spousal homicide remain dramatic. For example, the ratio of wives to husbands as gunshot homicide victims in Chicago was 1.2:1, compared to 4:1 in Canada and 3.5:1 in Britain; the ratio of wives to husbands as victims of non-gun homicides was 0.8:1 in Chicago, compared to 2.9:1 in Canada and 4.5:1 in Britain (Wilson and Daly, 1990). Moreover, the near equivalence of husband and wife victims in the US antedates the contemporary prevalence of gun killings. In Wolfgang's (1958) classic study, only 34 of the 100 spousal homicide victims were shot (15 husbands and 19 wives), while 30 husbands were stabbed and 31 wives were beaten or stabbed. Whatever may explain the exceptionally similar death rates of US husbands and wives, it is not simply that guns "equalize."

Nor is the unusual US pattern to be explained in terms of a peculiar convergence in the United States of the sexes in their violent inclinations or capabilities across all domains and relationships. Although US data depart radically from other industrialized countries in the sex ratio of spousal homicide victimization, they do not depart similarly in the sex ratios of other sorts of homicides (Wilson and Daly, 1990). For example, in the United States, as elsewhere, men kill unrelated men about 40 times as often as women kill unrelated women.

Even among lethal acts, it is essential to discriminate among different victim–killer relationships, because motives, risk factors, and conflict typologies are relationship-specific. Steinmetz (1977–8; Steinmetz and Lucca, 1998) has invoked the occurrence of maternally perpetrated infanticides as evidence of women's violence, imagining that the fact that some women commit infanticide somehow bolsters the claim that they batter their husbands, too. But maternal infanticides are more often motivated by desperation than by hostile aggression and are often the result of acts of neglect or abandonment rather than by assault. To conflate such acts with aggressive attacks is to misunderstand their utterly distinct motives, forms, and perpetrator profiles, and the distinct social and material circumstances in which they occur.

How to Gain a Valid Account of Marital Violence?

How ought researchers to conceive of "violence"? People differ in their views about whether a particular act was a violent one and about who was responsible. Assessments of intention and justifiability are no less relevant to the labelling of an event as "violent" than are more directly observable considerations like the force exerted or the damage inflicted. Presumably, it is this problem of subjectivity that has inspired efforts to objectify the study of family violence by the counting of "acts," as in the Conflict Tactics Scales.

Unfortunately, the presumed gain in objectivity achieved by asking research subjects to report only "acts," while refraining from elaborating upon their meanings and consequences, is illusory. As noted above, couples exhibit little agreement in reporting the occurrence of acts in which both were allegedly involved, and self-reported acts sometimes fail to differentiate the behaviour of groups known to exhibit huge differences in the perpetration of violence. The implication must be that merely confining self-reports to a checklist of named acts cannot allay concerns about the validity of self-report data. We have no more reason to suppose that people will consensually and objectively label events as instances of someone having "grabbed" or "hit or tried to hit" or "used a knife" (items from the CTS) than to suppose that people will consensually and objectively label events as instances of "violence."

If these "acts" were scored by trained observers examining the entire event, there might be grounds for such behaviouristic austerity in measurement:

whatever the virtues and limitations of behaviouristic methodology, a case can at least be made that observational data are more objective than the actors' accounts. However, when researchers have access only to self-reports, the cognitions of the actors are neither more nor less accessible to research than their actions. Failures of candour and memory threaten the validity of both sorts of self-report data, and researchers' chances of detecting such failures can only be improved by the collection of richer detail about the violent event. The behaviouristic rigour of observational research cannot be simulated by leaving data collection to the subjects, nor by active inattention to "subjective" matters like people's perceptions of their own and others' intentions, attributions of loss of control, perceived provocations and justifications, intimidatory consequences, and so forth. Moreover, even a purely behaviouristic account could be enriched by attending to sequences of events and subsequent behaviour rather than merely counting acts.

Enormous differences in meaning and consequence exist between a woman pummelling her laughing husband in an attempt to convey strong feelings and a man pummelling his weeping wife in an attempt to punish her for coming home late. It is not enough to acknowledge such contrasts (as CTS researchers have sometimes done), if such acknowledgements neither inform further research nor alter such conclusions as "within the family or in dating and cohabiting relationships, women are about as violent as men" (Straus and Gelles, 1990b: 104). What is needed are forms of analysis that will lead to a comprehensive description of the violence itself as well as an explanation of it.

In order to do this, it is, at the very least, necessary to analyze the violent event in a holistic manner, with attention to the entire sequences of distinct acts as well as associated motives, intentions, and consequences, all of which must in turn be situated within the wider context of the relationship.

The Need for Theory

If the arguments and evidence that we have presented are correct, then currently fashionable claims about the symmetry of marital violence are unfounded. How is it that so many experts have been persuaded of a notion that is at once counterintuitive and counterfactual? Part of the answer, we believe, is that researchers too often operate without sound (or indeed any) theoretical visions of marital relationships, of interpersonal conflicts, or of violence.

Straus (1990a: 30), for example, introduces the task of investigating family violence by characterizing families as instances of "social groups" and by noting that conflicts of interest are endemic to groups of individuals, "each seeking to live out their lives in accordance with personal agendas that inevitably differ." This is a good start, but the analysis proceeds no further. The characteristic features of families as distinct from other groups are not explored, and the particular domains within which the "agendas" of wives and husbands conflict are not elucidated. Instead, Straus illustrates family conflicts with the hypothetical example of "Which TV show will be watched at eight?" and discusses negotiated and coerced resolutions in terms that would be equally applicable to a conflict among male acquaintances in a bar. Such analysis obscures all that is distinctive about violence against wives, which occurs in a particular context of perceived entitlement and institutionalized power asymmetry. Moreover, marital violence occurs around recurring themes, especially male sexual jealousy and proprietariness, expectations of obedience and domestic service, and women's attempts to leave the marital relationship. In the self-consciously gender-blind literature on "violent couples," these themes are invisible.

Those who claim that wives and husbands are equally violent have offered no conceptual framework for understanding why women and men should think and act alike. Indeed, the claim that violence is gender-neutral cannot easily be reconciled with other coincident claims. For example, many family violence researchers who propose sexual symmetry in violence attribute the inculcation and legitimation of violence to socializing processes and cultural institutions, but then overlook the fact that these processes and institutions define and treat females and males differently. If sexually differentiated socialization and entitlements play a causal role in violence, how can we understand the alleged equivalence of women's and men's violent inclinations and actions?

Another theoretical problem confronting anyone who claims that violent inclinations are sexually monomorphic concerns the oft-noted fact that men are larger than women and likelier to inflict damage by similar acts. Human passions have their own "rationality," and it would be curious if women and men were identically motivated to initiate assaults in contexts where the expectable results were far more damaging for women. Insofar as both parties to a potentially violent transaction are aware of such differences, it is inappropriate to treat a slap (or other "act") by one party as equivalent to a slap by the other, not only because there is an asymmetry in the damage the two slaps might inflict, but because the parties differ in the responses available to them and hence in their control over the dénouement. Women's motives may be expected to differ systematically from those of men wherever the predictable consequences of their actions differ systematically. Those who contend that women and men are equally inclined to violence need to articulate why this should be so, given the sex differences in physical traits, such as size and muscularity, affecting the probable consequences of violence.

In fact, there is a great deal of evidence that men's and women's psychologies are not at all alike in this domain. Men's violent reactions to challenges to their authority, honour, and self-esteem are well known; comparable behaviour by a woman is a curiosity. A variety of convergent evidence supports the conclusion that men (especially young men) are more specialized for and more motivated to engage in dangerous risk-taking, confrontational competition, and interpersonal violence than are women. When comparisons are confined to interactions with members of one's own sex so that size and power asymmetries are largely irrelevant, the differences between men and women in these behavioural domains are universally large.

We cannot hope to understand violence in marital, cohabiting, and dating relationships without explicit attention to the qualities that make them different from other relationships. It is a cross-culturally and historically ubiquitous aspect of human affairs that women and men form individualized unions, recognized by themselves and by others as conferring certain obligations and entitlements, such that the partners' productive and reproductive careers become intertwined. Family violence research might usefully begin by examining the consonant and discordant desires, expectations, grievances, perceived entitlements, and preoccupations of husbands and wives, and by investigating theoretically derived hypotheses about circumstantial, ecological, contextual, and demographic correlates of such conflict. Having described the conflicts of interest that characterize marital relationships with explicit reference to the distinct agendas of women and men, violence researchers must proceed to an analysis that acknowledges and accounts for those gender differences. It is crucial to establish differences in the patterns of male and female violence, to thoroughly describe and explain the overall process of violent events within their immediate and wider contexts, and to analyze the reasons why conflict results in differentially violent action by women and men.

References

Barling, J., and A. Rosenbaum. 1986. "Work Stressors and Wife Abuse," *Journal of Applied Psychology* 71: 346–8.

Berk, R.A., S.F. Berk, D.R. Loseke, and D. Rauma. 1983. "Mutual Combat and Other Family Violence Myths," in D. Finkelhor, R.J. Gelles, G.T. Hotaling, and M.A. Straus, eds., *In the Dark Side of Families*, pp. 197–212. Beverly Hills, CA: Sage.

Brush, L.D. 1990. "Violent Acts and Injurious Outcomes in Married Couples: Methodological Issues in the National Survey of Families and Households," *Gender and Society* 4: 56–67.

Gaquin, D.A. 1977–8. "Spouse Abuse: Data from the National Crime Survey," *Victimology* 2: 632–43.

Gelles, R.J., and J.W. Harrop. 1991. "The Risk of Abusive Violence among Children with Nongenetic Caretakers," *Family Relations* 40: 78–83.

Johnson, H. 1989. "Wife Assault in Canada." Paper presented at the Annual Meeting of the American Society of Criminology, November, Reno, NV.

Jouriles, E.N., and K.D O'Leary. 1985. "Interspousal Reliability of Reports of Marital Violence," *Journal of Consulting and Clinical Psychology* 53: 419–21.

Lystad, M.H. 1975. "Violence at Home: A Review of Literature," *American Journal of Orthopsychiatry* 45: 328–45.

Margolin, G. 1987. "The Multiple Forms of Aggressiveness between Marital Partners: How Do We Identify Them?", *Journal of Marital and Family Therapy* 13: 77–84.

Maxfield, M.G. 1989. "Circumstances in Supplementary Homicide Reports: Variety and Validity," *Criminology* 27: 671–95.

McLeod, M. 1984. "Women against Men: An Examination of Domestic Violence Based on an Analysis of Official Data and National Victimization Data," *Justice Quarterly* 1: 171–193.

McNeely, R.L., and C.R. Mann. 1990. "Domestic Violence is a Human Issue," *Journal of Interpersonal Violence* 5: 129–32.

McNeely, R.L., and G. Robinson-Simpson. 1987. "The Truth about Domestic Violence: A Falsely Framed Issue," *Social Work* 32: 485–90.

Rouse, L.P., R. Ereen, and M. Howell. 1988. "Abuse in Intimate Relationships: A Comparison of Married and Dating College Students," *Journal of Interpersonal Violence* 3: 414–29.

Schwartz, M.D. 1987. "Gender and Injury in Spousal Assault," *Sociological Focus* 20: 61–75.

Shupe, A., W.A. Stacey, and L.R. Hazelwood. 1987. *Violent Men, Violent Couples: The Dynamics of Domestic Violence*. Lexington, MA: Lexington Books.

Steinmetz, S.K. 1977–8. "The Battered Husband Syndrome," *Victimology* 2: 499–509.

———. 1986. "Family Violence: Past, Present, and Future," in M.B. Sussman and S.K. Steinmetz, eds., *Handbook of Marriage and the Family*, pp. 725–65. New York: Plenum.

Steinmetz, S.K., and J.S. Lucca. 1988. "Husband Battering," in V.B. Van Hasselt, R.L. Morrison, A.S. Bellack, and M. Hersen, eds., *Handbook of Family Violence*, pp. 233–46. New York: Plenum Press.

Stets, J.E., and M.A. Straus. 1990. "Gender Differences in Reporting Marital Violence and Its Medical and Psychological Consequences," in M.A. Straus and R.J. Gelles, eds., *Physical Violence in American Families*, pp. 151–65. New Brunswick, NJ: Transaction Publishers.

Straus, M.A. 1977–8. "Wife-beating: How Common, and Why?", *Victimology* 2: 443–458.

———. 1990a. "Measuring Intrafamily Conflict and Violence: The Conflict Tactics (CT) Scales," in M.A. Straus and R.J. Gelles, eds., *Physical Violence in American Families*, pp. 29–47. New Brunswick, NJ: Transaction Publishers.

———. 1990b. "The Conflict Tactics Scales and Its Critics: An Evaluation and New Data on Validity and Reliability," in M.A. Straus and R.J. Gelles, eds., *Physical Violence in American Families*, pp. 49–73. New Brunswick, NJ: Transaction Publishers.

Straus, Murray A., and Richard J. Gelles. 1986. "Societal Change and Change in Family Violence from 1975 to 1985 as Revealed by Two National Surveys," *Journal of Marriage and the Family* 48: 465–80.

———. 1987. "The Costs of Family Violence," *Public Health Reports* 102: 638–41.

Straus, M.A., and R.J. Gelles, eds. 1990a. *Physical Violence in American Families*. New Brunswick, NJ: Transaction Publishers.

———. 1990b. "How Violent are American Families? Estimates from the National Family Violence Resurvey and Other Studies," in M.A. Straus and R.J. Gelles, eds., *Physical Violence in American Families*, pp. 95–112. New Brunswick, NJ: Transaction Publishers.

Szinovacz, M.E. 1983. "Using Couple Data as a Methodological Tool: The Case of Marital Violence," *Journal of Marriage and the Family* 45: 633–44.

Wilson, M., and M. Daly. 1990. "Who Kills Whom in Spouse-killings? On the Exceptional Sex Ratio of Spousal Homicides in the United States," *Criminology* 30: 189–212.

Wolfgang, M.E. 1958. *Patterns in Criminal Homicide*. Philadelphia, PA: University of Pennsylvania Press.

Chapter 37

Overview

Sepali Guruge and colleagues take up the concern of the previous chapter with the contexts of gendered violence. In their research on intimate partner violence in a Tamil immigrant community, they describe their theoretical approach as "feminist postcolonial"—while noting the gender imbalance in the violence, they also situate it within global inequalities and asymmetries, such as the civil war that forced Tamil families from their homes, bringing violence into family life. The researchers adopt an ecosystemic approach that examines variables at different levels of social life, from the "micro" world of the couple relationship, to the "meso" world of the extended family and community, to the "macro" world of global changes and dynamics that disrupted life in Sri Lanka and created the condition for movement to Canada.

The move from one set of circumstances in Sri Lanka to a very different world in Canada is also connected to stressors and pressures that find expression at times in violence against family members. Changes in social networks, different expectations of marriage in Sri Lanka and in Canada, and the everyday racism experienced in Canadian life form the social context within which violence occurs.

Guruge et al. do not lay all the blame for intimate partner violence on the experience of immigration and dislocation—as they note, some women experienced this violence even before immigration, while other couples move to Canada and handle the stresses and conflicts that result without resorting to violence. However, they argue that intimate partner violence cannot be understood by simply focusing on incidents of violence, instead the micro, meso, and macro influences must be examined.

Intimate Male Partner Violence in the Migration Process: Intersections of Gender, Race, and Class

Sepali Guruge, Nazilla Khanlou, and Denise Gastaldo

Introduction

Intimate partner violence is the threat of, and/or actual, physical, sexual, psychological, or verbal abuse by a current or former spouse or non-marital partner, as well as coercion, or the arbitrary deprivation of liberty that can occur in public or private life (United Nations [UN] 1993). Intimate male partner violence (IMPV) is widely acknowledged as a critical health issue for women worldwide; however, relatively little is known about its production in diverse settings and contexts. Data compiled by the World Health Organization (WHO) (2000) for IMPV across many countries has suggested that the percentage of women who had ever been physically assaulted by a male intimate partner ranged from 5.1 per cent to 67 per cent. In addition to other limitations, these statistics do not include other forms of abuse such as emotional and sexual abuse, and thus do not accurately demonstrate the prevalence and seriousness of the issue. The recent WHO (2006) study addressing some of these concerns showed that the prevalence of diverse forms of IMPV ranged from 15 per cent to 71 per cent across 10 countries (n = 24,000) and rates of lifetime IMPV varied widely, as did women's responses to IMPV, with many factors affecting the production of IMPV. The findings reinforced the need to develop context-specific knowledge about this issue.

Background

IMPV as a Global Health Issue

The IMPV is a significant cause of morbidity and mortality for women worldwide (Heise et al. 1994), the most common physical injuries being multi-site contusions and soft tissue injuries (Muellman et al. 1996). Chronic physical health conditions linked to IMPV include neck and back pain, arthritis, headaches and migraines, hypertension, unexplained dizziness, sexually transmitted infections, chronic pelvic pain, gynecological symptoms, and gastrointestinal problems (Ratner, 1995; Campbell and Lewandowski, 1997; Coker et al., 2000). Mental health problems include depression, acute and chronic symptoms of anxiety, symptoms consistent with post-traumatic stress disorder, substance use/dependence and thoughts of suicide (Eby et al., 1995; Ratner, 1995; Eischbach and Herbert, 1997).

IMPV in the Canadian Context

The 1993 *Violence against Women Survey*, well known in Canada, in which 12,300 randomly selected women were interviewed, showed that 51 per cent had been physically or sexually assaulted at least once since the age of 16 years, 29 per cent had been physically abused, and 8 per cent had been sexually assaulted by a male intimate partner (Rodgers, 1994). According to the more recent (2000) *General Social Survey* (GSS) of over 14,000 women (over 15 years) from 10 provinces, approximately 37 per cent of women who had ever been married or ever had a male live-in intimate partner had experienced IMPV at least once. The attempts to assess IMPV prevalence in immigrant households through secondary analysis of GSS data (e.g., Hyman, 2002; Ahmad et al., 2005) were constrained by the survey's limitations. Among others, it excluded those who did not speak Canada's two official languages.

Interest in IMPV in the post-migration context has recently increased in Canada. We consider this a positive move, given that more than 200,000 immigrants and refugees arrive annually, women make up about half of this number, and lack of attention to this topic limits the resources and policy attention devoted to it.

Theorizing IMPV

Numerous theories have been offered to explain why IMPV occurs. In general, they can be divided into those focusing on the individual level (e.g., based on biological and psychological explanations) and those emphasizing the relationship at the micro-, meso- or macro-systemic levels (e.g., based on social and gender perspectives). Most theories have not explored the intersectionality of migration, race, culture, gender, and class in understanding IMPV.

To overcome these limitations, we used a post-colonial feminist perspective in this study. A review of some key post-colonial feminist authors' (Memmi, 1967; hooks, 1984; Jayawardena, 1986; Minh-Ha, 1989; Collins, 1990; Mohanty, 1991) work indicates that there is no single post-colonial feminist perspective. However, all these perspectives emphasize the importance of understanding the historical construction of women in and from low- and middle-income countries and its consequences, and the need to recognize, as well as construct, knowledge from their perspective (Spivak, 1988; McClintock, 1995).

An ecosystemic framework was also used in this study. Ecosystemic frameworks help reveal how people and their environments are understood in the context of their continuous and reciprocal relationships (Loue and Faust, 1998; Germain and Bloomm, 1999). The factors considered are ontogenic (the individual history of the partners); micro-systemic (the family setting in which the abuse occurs); meso-systemic (the social networks in which the family participates); and macro-systemic (the culture and society-at-large).

Using an ecosystemic framework, situated in a postcolonial feminist perspective, avoids the creation of simplistic views of IMPV as relating to particular groups or to people with particular characteristics. The relevance of the two together in addressing post-migration IMPV has been discussed elsewhere (see Guruge and Khanlou, 2004).

Migration and Displacement of Sri Lankan Tamils

The estimated 188 million people living in Sri Lanka in 1998 (UN, 1999) represented several different ethnic groups. As each group struggled to overcome damage from a colonial past and ongoing neo-colonialism, new forms of domination and exploitation evolved within the country. For 25 years, civil war raged between the Sri Lankan government and the Liberation Tigers of Tamil Eelam, a militant/separatist group fighting for full independence and a separate homeland for Tamils. Since 1983, many Tamils have fled the war to countries such as India, Australia, Norway, Germany, England, and the United States of America (USA). Canada is the home to the largest Sri Lankan Tamil community outside Sri Lanka.

The Study

Aim

This paper is a report of a study of Sri Lankan Tamil Canadian immigrants' perspectives on factors that contribute to IMPV in the post-migration context.

Design

An exploratory qualitative descriptive design was used.

Participants

Combining opportunity, snowball, and purposive sampling strategies, we recruited participants from October 2004 to May 2005. The data were collected through individual interviews with 16 community leaders in health and settlement work (Set 1); four focus groups with women (6–12 in each group) and another four with men (4–6 in each group) from the general Tamil community (Set 2); and individual interviews with six women who had experienced IMPV (Set 3). The purpose of selecting these groups was to capture the phenomenon from diverse viewpoints (Schensul et al., 1999). For example, community leaders were better suited to exploring macro-systemic factors, community members had knowledge of meso-factors, and abused women were better qualified to discuss their individual situations. Similarly, we wanted to hear from women and men, and women with an abuse history and those without. The underlying premise was that topics such as male violence against women cannot be understood fully by only hearing abused women's stories; we must also understand the viewpoints of the oppressors (Anderson and Hill Collins, 1995) if we are to challenge the status quo, especially along the lines of multiple sites of oppression.

Data Collection

Interviews and focus groups were, on average, two hours long. The first author conducted all individual interviews (in Sets 1 and 3) ($n = 22$), except for one interview that required an interpreter. The (Set 2) focus groups with women and men were conducted in Tamil, respectively by a female and male community leader. The first author co-facilitated all eight focus group discussions ($n = 41$). The focus groups conducted in Tamil created a space for participants to voice in their own language the concerns of importance to them. According to the post-colonial feminist perspective, the idea of giving voice to those who might not be heard (e.g., due to language differences), guided this study. The individual and group discussions were guided by exploratory, open-ended questions (see Tables 37.1 and 37.2). The interviews were transcribed verbatim, and focus groups were translated and transcribed.

Table 37.1 Examples of individual interview questions posed

What do you think about Tamil men's and women's relationships in Sri Lanka/Canada?
What do you think about wife abuse in the Tamil community? Why do you think it happens in Sri Lanka/Canada? (probe about gender, culture, class)
How do you think what happens at home between a husband and wife is influenced by their friends, family, and neighbours? (probe about gender, culture, class, race)
How are the couples influenced by what is happening in Canadian culture and society? (probe about gender, culture, class, race)

Table 37.2 Examples of focus group questions asked

Please tell me about your experience about coming to live in Canada.
What was it like to build a new life here?
What would have been helpful to you and your family in getting settled in Canada?
What leads to conflicts among Tamil couples living in Canada?
How do they resolve these conflicts?
Wife abuse happens in every community and culture. Why do you think it happens in the Tamil community?
How does being in Canada shape why/how wife abuse happens?

Ethical Considerations

Ethics approval was obtained from the appropriate university. All potential participants were informed, both via consent form and verbally, of their right to refuse to participate or answer any questions or to terminate participation at any time. Focus group participants were also made aware, in advance, of who the facilitators were. At the beginning of focus group sessions, participants were asked to respect each other's information and not to disclose identifying information about themselves. Focus group facilitators and the transcriptionists signed a confidentiality agreement.

Findings

The participants represented the demographics of the Sri Lankan Tamil community in Canada in terms of age (range = 24–70 years), education (range = elementary school to university), length of stay in Canada (range = 1–20 years), and religion (most were Hindu) (see also Tables 37.3, 37.4, 37.5). Their conceptualizations of the production of IMPV are presented under four themes.

Experiences of Violence Pre-migration and during Border-Crossing

Participants in all three sets spoke about their experiences during the civil war. Many lost homes, businesses, and employment. They spoke about frequent roadside checking, bomb threats, and sounds of sirens and having to run to bunkers. Young men were arrested and tortured; some disappeared and/or died in prison. Participants from Set 1 connected men participating in, witnessing, or being victims of war violence with intolerance, anger, suspicion, and aggression at home:

> Husbands being separated from wives (. . .) have been taken out for interrogation . . . having to always suspect another person, whether he is an enemy or not. (Set 1, Participant 6)
>
> The children grow up seeing people fighting and killing, you know. Anger and aggression becomes an acceptable way of expressing discontent with something. Which is what you have often when you come to a new place. (Set 1, Participant 10)

The second quote also implies that learned behaviour can affect how a person manages discontent or

Table 37.3 Demographic characteristics of community leaders

Characteristic	
Gender	10 women, 6 men
Age group	6 (in their 30s), 5 (in their 40s), 5 (over 50 years)
Birth city	9 (Jaffna)
Decade left Sri Lanka	1 (1970s), 8 (1980s), 4 (1990s), 3 (2000s)
Lived in a third country	10
Years in Canada	1.5–20: 6 (1–5 years); 2 (6–10 years); 6 (11–15 years); 2 (16–20 years)
Level of education	Grade 10–University
Work type in Canada	Health or settlement sectors (*n* = 16)

Table 37.4 Demographic characteristics of focus group participants

Focus group	1 (*n* = 8)	2 (*n* = 6)	3 (*n* = 12)	4 (*n* = 5)	5 (*n* = 6)	6 (*n* = 4)
Gender	Women	Men	Women	Men	Women	Men
Age range (years)	30–63	41–50	27–65	25–62	24–69	35–69
Birth city	Jaffna	Jaffna	Jaffna	Jaffna	Jaffna	Jaffna
Years in Canada	1–10	2–12	2–11	1–11	2–11	8–18
Level of education	8–13	8–13	10–13	10–13	<8–Univ.	1.3–Univ.
Arranged marriage	All	3	8	2	4	2
Second session	Yes (*n* = 7)	–	–	–	–	Yes (*n* = 4)

Table 37.5 Demographic characteristics of abused women participants

Characteristic	
Age	25–70 years
Birth city	Mostly Jaffna (*n* = 5)
Years in Canada	3–12
Level of education	Grade–University
Length of marriage	2–50 years
Arranged marriage	Yes (*n* = 5)
Worked outside home in Sri Lanka	Yes (*n* = 5)
Currently employed	Yes (*n* = 3)
Number of children	0–5

anger. Overall, participants perceived that psychological stress and trauma from the war influenced men negatively.

Conflicts and wars increase violence against women, which is the case in Sri Lanka. In all three sets, participants spoke about the vulnerability of girls and women. Parents often feared for their daughters' safety and attempted to send them out of the country:

> Unfortunately a friend of mine . . . disappeared. My family was worried that I was going to disappear. So they proposed [a marriage for] me to (. . .) from (. . .). I didn't want to marry that time. I wanted to study and get a good job, but I didn't feel safe. We hear all kinds of things happening to girls. I was missing my friend and that had a very bad effect on me. My family was scared and started to react. That is how I ended up in this situation. (Set 3, Participant 5)

Because of the country's situation, this participant agreed to marry a man who later became abusive. There had not been enough time to investigate her potential husband's background, the usual procedure in arranged marriages.

Violence was reported to occur also during border-crossing. Although Canada has made considerable efforts to accept refugees, current immigration policies make the process difficult for Tamils. For example, Tamils are unable to register with the United Nations High Commissioner for Refugees (UNHCR) to obtain refugee status while still living in Sri Lanka (Fuglerud 1999), and they cannot apply for a Canadian visa, for example, if they have lost necessary documents during displacement or cannot easily replace them because villages have been destroyed or evacuated. Further, family sponsorship applications in Canada are often delayed. These problems drive Tamils to other ways of reaching safety or reuniting with family members, including hiring agents who bring them to Canada, often breaking international laws. The following illustrates some of the complexity of border-crossing:

> It is because of the civil war we had to leave the country. I came here through the US. Until then, I have never been to a jail. But there, they put me in jail for a month. I was very much affected mentally due to this, as we didn't commit any crime. (Set 2, Participant 2)

Some participants highlighted evidence of violation of people's rights by those in authority in various countries as well as the unacceptable daily life conditions that some Tamils had to endure to reach their final destination. While the hope of a new home and safer place drive people to such travel, uncertainty, fear, anxiety, and stress associated with these steps were identified by participants as having a negative psychological impact on people, both short- and long-term. According to most, these incidents also shaped how people view others, and whether or not they would seek help from others, for example to cope better with post-migration stressors, especially from those in authority, such as health care professionals, settlement workers and child welfare officers.

Gender Inequity in the Marital Institution

Coming from a patriarchal society, participants had learned gender roles in childhood and adulthood from family, neighbours, schools, workplaces, and society-at-large. In Sri Lanka men were the primary breadwinners; they often did not do household work but were responsible for household repairs and physically demanding work, such as lifting and moving. Although gendered responsibilities varied over time, among families, and across socio-economic groups, women were primarily responsible for cooking, cleaning, and child-rearing.

After migration, Tamil men who came alone were forced to assume household tasks. However, according to participants, most men continued to perceive household responsibilities as women's domain. Most single men returned to Sri Lanka to find a suitable wife who would fulfil such expectations:

> As soon as their mother, wife, or sisters come, men expect the women to work for them. There are exceptions. (Set 1, Participant 5)

In the new context, some couples successfully negotiated household responsibilities based on who could do the tasks better/more easily, who was available at a particular time of day, and who enjoyed doing the task. Such change was perceived to be more common among those who immigrated at a younger age:

> He is a young guy . . . very much a short-tempered guy. . . . I saw a change in him. He told me, "I am helping my wife." She has two kids. "I am a truck driver, and she is alone, so I have to come back and clean for her . . . so I decided to take local trips instead of long-distance trips." (Set 1, Participant 4)

Others changed because they had no choice—owing to their work commitments, timing, and so on—allowing for a more equal distribution of work between the couple. In contrast, some husbands held their wives responsible for household work even if they worked outside the home as many hours as he did and contributed equally to the family income.

Participants in Sets 1 and 2 spoke about a general perception in the community that some disciplining of the women was justified, especially to prevent bigger problems. The reasons presented included incomplete household work, suspected or real extramarital affairs, refusing husbands' requests for sex, arguing or complaining, and asking for things such as money or tasks to be completed at "inappropriate times." These were also the justifications used by the abusive husbands of participants in Set 3. These expectations/perceptions/responses were also shaped by the changes in post-migration social networks.

Changes in Social Networks and Supports

The Tamils were used to a social structure and networks that often strongly influenced their lives in Sri Lanka. Such networks often provided instrumental, informational, emotional, and psychological support, especially to new couples, young families, and those who were dealing with life challenges. However, post-migration social networks are usually smaller or non-existent, especially for women who often arrive sponsored by their husbands. According to most participants, even if family members were in Canada, the values that governed the expected/perceived/given support have changed since coming to a more individualistic society:

> Relationships are much tighter back home. It is not the same here. Even when we have relatives here, we would think about interfering or not [in people's personal lives by trying to help them]. (Set 2, Participant 4)

The changes in the quantity and quality of support have also changed due to the extremely busy lives they lived in Canada.

The resulting lack/loss of support has increased the household responsibilities of both spouses and their reliance on each other for support. While the latter has positive effects, such as increased communication and shared decision making between the couple without the influence or interference of family, sole reliance on one person causes tremendous stress. A participant highlighted a possible scenario:

> When there is pregnancy, when there is childbirth, they have no one to care for them, and that is the time when they need family the most. That is when the husband might feel stressed out (. . .) and move out. (Set 1, Participant 7)

Overall, participants emphasized that increases in stress resentment, and arguments about the quantity and quality of household work each spouse did contributed to conflict and abuse. If the woman's family was not in Canada, the husband also had more power over her (especially if his family was living with them or nearby). In some cases, the husband's family was reported to be the instigator or the abuser. Women's family members also were perceived to reinforce patriarchal practices. Participants in Set 2, for example, spoke about the indirect and direct pressure women themselves placed upon other women to adhere to such patriarchal practices. This idea was confirmed by a participant in Set 1:

> My mum tells me, "Your husband is coming, now, you're talking with me, why don't you go greet your husband and serve him food?" My

> mother-in-law immediately stops whatever she is doing and serves food for her son. But she never told me [directly] "Oh, you are his wife, you have to go and do things." (Set 1, Participant 3)

These changes in social networks and supports were perceived to be particularly negative for women who were not fluent in English or not in paid employment, as they were more isolated and further dependent on their husbands.

Perceptions of Changes in Social Status and Privilege: Gender and Race Lenses

Immigration to a new country is often imbued with changes in socioeconomic status and privileges. A negative change in this regard is more likely for immigrants from low- and medium-income countries who move to high-income nations. According to most of our women participants, their husbands and other men in their community often were stuck in jobs that they began as stepping stones to better jobs that never materialized because of racism in the employment sector in Canada. Their accounts implied that immigrants are being used as a source of cheap labour:

> [Canada] needs people for its economy. They need people to clean their offices, clean toilets, deliver newspapers, and wash dishes in restaurants, because not that many white Canadian people want to do these low-paying, low-status jobs. . . . So there is no real motivation for [the] government to invest in these people [immigrants] in a way that they become successful. Then who will do these types of jobs? (Set 1, Participant 1)

This participant's perception of the new forms of colonization taking place in immigrant-receiving countries in the West was in line with the perceptions of most others in Sets 1 and 2. Tamil men's downward mobility in professional and economic status led to loss of social status at home, and within their extended families, the Tamil community, and larger Canadian society. As can be gleaned from the next excerpt, patriarchal ideological values dictated that men assume the responsibilities of paying off family debts, sponsoring their wives and children for immigration, financially supporting their extended families in Sri Lanka, and paying dowries for their sisters and daughters to be married:

> I borrowed money from an uncle to come here. I was worried if I could give back the loan if I get deported. Also, my siblings were back home. I was the eldest. In our culture, as you know, the girls have to be married off by the boys and we need to give dowry for that and only then we can get married. So these were all pressures on me. I have an elder sister [who needed to be married off] and I was crying about that situation. (Set 2, Participant 6)

Across interviews, participants agreed that, as part of arranged-marriage customs in Sri Lanka, women almost always married men of equal or higher educational and professional status and then enjoyed the associated living standard. One woman commented on the implications of husbands' status change on family dynamics:

> Here a woman lawyer can marry a chef and it is not a problem at home. But our society is set up to say that women should always marry up or someone who is doing a better job or is better than you professionally. So, when we come here, things become upside down. You don't know what it does to the family . . . not just to the man. (Set 1, Participant 15)

Inability to fulfil these responsibilities as well as expectations associated with their previous status demoralized men; some became depressed or turned to alcohol. In some cases, couple conflict ensued.

Discussion

Study Limitations

The study sample was limited to those who, in Canada, belonged to the lower-middle class and working class and were under 65 years of age, and it is possible that those outside these criteria might perceive IMPV differently. To avoid placing them at risk, we did not speak with women who were living with abusive husbands; thus, their voices are absent from this study. The presence of community leaders as focus groups facilitators might have limited the openness with which participants spoke about the issues.

Factors Influencing Post-migration IMPV

Participants' accounts revealed a complex range of factors that influenced IMPV after migration, presented here according to the ecosystemic framework. All were specifically connected to the intersectionality of gender, race, and class, and were congruent with post-colonial thought.

Individual-level factors

The individual-level factor that we found to be key to IMPV was pre-migration exposure to war and multiple trauma. Men who experienced or engaged in violence were perceived to have mental health problems, such as low tolerance for stress (e.g., job loss) and various stimuli (e.g., loud noise at home), and symptoms of anxiety and depression. They were perceived to be more suspicious of their wives because they had learned to distrust people in general. Chambion (1989) and Penalosa (1986) noted that immigrant men's previous exposure to violence could be connected to aggressive or violent behaviour towards their wives. In a recent study by Gupta et al. (2009) involving a group of immigrant men to the USA, a statistically significant relationship between pre-migration exposure to political violence and IMPV perpetration in the post-migration context was found. However, there is limited literature on this topic.

Micro-level factors

Key micro-level factor influencing the production of IMPV post-migration included the changes in husband's and wife's socio-economic statuses. These changes contributed to two scenarios of post-migration family power imbalance. In the first, some husbands gained control, authority, and power within their families after migration—for example, by being sole breadwinner or through their wife's isolation and/or lack of English skill. Other researchers have also reported this scenario (e.g., Abraham's 1999, 2000 studies of South-Asian immigrants). In the second scenario, some husbands' power and authority decreased owing to the deskilling and deprofessionalization they experienced. Wives' greater access to paid (albeit low status and low paid) employment post-migration, and their relatively increased earnings, led some husbands to reassert their authority through violence. Other researchers in the USA and Canada (e.g., Krulfeld, 1994; Kulig, 1994; Morrison et al., 1999; Oxman-Martinez et al., 2000; Min, 2001; Tang and Oatley, 2002) have noted similar findings. An important contribution of our study to the literature is the recognition that the two scenarios can co-exist within the same community.

Meso-level factors

The most important meso-level factor affecting the post-migration production of IMPV was the change in social networks and supports. In Canada, Tamil couples might have no family members to help with day-to-day life, and thus rely heavily on each other. Under economic and time constraints, this situation leads to stress, resentment, and conflict. Hyman et al. (2004) reported similar findings in their study with Ethiopian-immigrant married couples in Toronto, and in their follow-up study (Hyman et al., 2006) with divorced women and men from the same community. McSpadden and Moussa (1993) also found that loss of extended family support and advice led to marital conflict among Canadian Ethiopian immigrants.

As in other communities, Tamil women are often held as the bearers of the community values and beliefs. As such, even when family members were available in Canada, they often enforced patriarchal norms and practices. Husbands' family involvement (in the absence of women's families) was noted to be particularly negative for the woman when couple conflicts occurred. Women's sole reliance on husbands and their families also increased the likelihood of a woman being abused by her husband's relatives, mainly female in-laws. Similar findings were noted in the USA among "Asian-Americans" (Huisman, 1996), "Asian-Indians" (Mehotra, 1999), and Mexicans (Morash et al., 2000). The Tamil community further enforced, both subtly and overtly, patriarchal rules and practices, even when some such practices were reported to have changed/are changing

What Is Already Known about This Topic

- Numerous factors explain the production of intimate male partner violence, with little consensus on its etiology.
- Etiological theories of violence have included psychological explanations, biological differences, sociological perspectives, and feminist approaches.
- Some etiological theories explain intimate male partner violence at an individual level, while others look to the family for an explanation, and some operate at the societal level.

What This Paper Adds

- Rather than being caused by one or several factors operating within a single level of society, intimate male partner violence is produced by a complex and interrelated set of factors operating at individual, family, community, and societal levels in the pre-migration, border-crossing, and post-migration contexts.
- Production of post-migration intimate male partner violence involved experiences of violence in the pre-migration and border crossing contexts; gender inequity in the marital institution; and post-migration changes in social supports as well as in socioeconomic status and privilege.
- Women who had been married and lived with their husbands in Sri Lanka experienced wife abuse only after coming to Canada; thus, the relevance of the post-migration context in the production of intimate male partner violence should not be underestimated.

in Sri-Lanka. Overall, this situation gave men an upper hand over the rest of the family.

Macro-level factors

Our findings, along with those of a number of previous studies, show that post-migration factors operating at the macro-level of society, including economic insecurity resulting from non-recognition of professional/educational credentials, workplace deskilling, and racial/ethnic discrimination—added to patriarchal pressure for men to meet family and social responsibilities—pushed men to self- and family destructive behaviours such as alcohol and other addictions, and to infidelity (Perilla et al., 1994; Rhee, 1997; Morash et al., 2000; Tran and Des Jardins, 2000) as well as to engaging in abusive behaviours (George & Ramkissoon, 1998; Perry et al., 1998; Moghissi & Goodman, 1999; Abraham, 2000). In other words, our findings along with these other studies findings illuminate the connection between the social inequities and their impact on individual men and their families (i.e., how gender and class intersected with race to create conflicts and abuse post-migration). Our findings thus can be used to contest uni-factoral explanations of IMPV, such as patriarchy.

Conclusion

Post-colonial feminist perspectives are useful in understanding post-migration IMPV, which is produced by the interaction of multiple forms of inequities that men and women experience before migration, while crossing borders, and after migration that are created in the intersection of several forms of neo-colonial oppressive relations, such as racism, classism, and sexism. While we did not explore the reproduction of IMPV in this study—that is, IMPV that began before migration and continued after couples reunited, it is noteworthy that women in this study who had married and lived with their husbands in Sri-Lanka experienced abuse only after coming to Canada. Thus, we propose that post-migration IMPV can only be explained by such plurality of factors that capture the complexity of immigrants' lives in diaspora and displacement.

Acknowledgements

We acknowledge the contribution of Dr Shahrzad Mojab, thesis committee member, and Dr Ruth Gallop, co-supervisor and thesis committee member, during the project development phase of the study.

Funding

The first author gratefully acknowledges the financial support she received for her work from the Canadian Institutes of Health Research in the form of a Doctoral Fellowship (2003–2006) and a New Investigator Award (2008–2013) in the area of Gender and Health.

Conflict of Interest

No conflict of interest has been declared by the authors.

Author Contributions

SG, NK, and DG were responsible for the study conception and design. SG performed the data collection. SG performed the data analysis. SG was responsible for the drafting of the manuscript. SG, NK, and DG made critical revisions to the paper for important intellectual content. SG and NK obtained funding. NK and DG supervised the study. SG, NK, and DG provided other contributions.

Contribution to the Paper

This paper is based on SG's doctoral dissertation defended in December 2006 at the Faculty of Nursing, University of Toronto. NK and DG supervised SG's thesis. SG drafted the paper, and NK and DG critically revised it.

References

Abraham, M. 1999. "Sexual Abuse in South Asian Immigrant Marriages," *Violence Against Women* 5: 591–618.

Abraham, M. 2000. "Isolation as a Form of Marital Violence: The South Asian Immigrant Experience," *Journal of Social Distress and the Homeless* 9: 221–36.

Ahmad, F., M. Ali, and D.E. Stewart. 2005. "Spousal Abuse among Canadian Immigrant Women," *Journal of Immigration Health* 7: 239–46.

Anderson, M.L., and P. Hill Collins. 1995. *Race, Class, and Gender: An Anthology*, 2nd edn. Belmont, CA: Wadsworth.

Bryman, A. 2001. *Social Research Methods*. New York: Oxford University Press.

Campbell, J., and L. Lewandowski. 1997. "Mental and Psychical Health Effects of Intimate Partner Violence on Women and Children," *Psychiatric Clinics of North America* 20: 353–74.

Chambion, A. 1989. "Refugee Families' Experiences: Three Family Themes—Family Disruption, Violent Trauma, and Acculturation," *Journal of Strategic and Systemic Therapies* 8: 3–13.

Coker, A.L., P.H. Smith, F. Bertea, M.R. King, and R.E. McKeown. 2000. "Physical Health Consequences of Physical and Psychological Intimate Partner Violence," *Archives of Family Medicine* 9: 451–57.

Collins, P.H. 1990. *Black Feminist Thought: Knowledge, Consciousness, and the Politics of Empowerment*. New York: Routledge.

Eby, K., I. Campbell, C. Sullivan, and W. Davidson. 1995. "Health Effects of Experiences of Sexual Violence for Women with Abusive Partners," *Health Care for Women International* 16: 563–76.

Fischbach, R., and B. Herbert. 1997. "Domestic Violence and Mental Health: Vorrelates and Conundrums within and across Cultures," *Social Science and Medicine* 45: 1161–76.

Fuglerud, O. 1999 *Life on the Outside: The Tamil Diaspora and Long Distance Nationalism*. London: Pluto.

George, U., and S. Ramkissoon. 1998. "Race, Gender and Class: Interlocking Oppressions in the Lives of South Asian Women in Canada," *Affilia* 13: 102–19.

Gerbert, B., A. Bronstone, S. Pantilat, S. McPhee, M. Allertun, and J. Moe. 1999. "When Asked, Patients Tell: Disclosure of Sensitive Health-risk Behaviours," *Medical Care* 37: 104–11.

Germain, C.B., and M. Bloom. 1999. *Human Behaviour in the Social Environment*, 2nd edn. New York: Columbia University Press.

Gupta, J., D. Acevedo-Garcia, D. Hemenway, M.R. Decker, A. Raj, and J.G. Silverman J.G. 2009. "Premigration Exposure to Political Violence and Perpetration of Intimate Partner Violence among Immigrant Men in Boston," *American Journal of Public Health* 99: 462–69.

Guruge, S., and E. Collins. 2008. *Working with Women: Issues and Strategies for Mental Health Professionals*, 1st edn. Toronto: Centre for Addiction and Mental Health.

Guruge, S., and D. Gastaldo. 2008. "Violencia en la pareja e inmigración: ?Cómo ser parte de la solución? [Violence in couples and immigration: How to be part of the solution?]" (Editorial), *Presencia* 8. Retrieved from www.index-f.com/presencia/n8/p8801.php on 10 January 2009.

Guruge, S., and N. Khanlou. 2004. "Intersectionalities of Influence: Researching Health of Immigrant and Refugee Women," *Canadian Journal of Nursing Research* 36: 32–47.

Heise, L.L., J. Pitanguy, and A. Germain. 1994. *Violence Against Women: The Hidden Health Burden: World Bank Discussion Papers (No. 255)*. Washington, DC: International Bank for Reconstruction and Development/World Bank.

hooks, b. 1984. *Feminist Theory: From Margin to Center*. Boston: South End.

Huisman, K.A. 1996. "Wife Battering in Asian American Communities: Identifying the Service Needs of an Overlooked Segment of the U.S. Population," *Violence Against Women* 2: 260–83.

Hyman, I. 2002. "Immigrant and Visible Minority Women," in D.E. Stewart, A. Cheung, L.E. Ferris, I. Hyman, M. Cohen, and I.J. Williams, eds., *Ontario Women's Health Status Report*, pp. 338–58. Toronto: Ontario Women's Health Council.

Hyman, I., S. Guruge, R. Mason, N. Stuckless, J. Gould, T. Tang, H. Teffera, and G. Mekonnen. 2004. "Post Migration Changes in Gender Relations among Ethiopian Immigrant Couples in Toronto," *Canadian Journal of Nursing Research* 36(4): 74–89.

Hyman, I., S. Guruge, R. Mason, N. Stuckless, J. Gould, T. Tang, H. Teffera, and G. Mekonnen. 2006. *Post Migration Changes in Gender Relations in the Ethiopian Community in Toronto: Phase II*. Centre of Excellence for Research on Immigration and Settlement, Toronto, Canada. Retrieved from http://ceris.metropolis.net/Virtual%20Library/RFPReports/Hyman_PhaseII2004.pdf on 9 June 2006.

Jayawardena, K. 1986. *Feminism and Nationalism in the Third World*. London: Zed Books.

Krulfeld, R.M. 1994. "Changing Concepts of Gender Roles and Identities in Refugee Communities," in L.A. Camino and R.M. Krulfeld, eds., *Reconstructing Lives, Recapturing Memory: Refugee Identity, Gender and Culture Change*, pp. 71–4. Washington, DC: Gordon and Breach.

Kulig, J. 1994. "Old Traditions in a New World: Changing Gender Relations among Cambodian Refugees," in L.A. Camino and R.M. Krulfeld, eds., *Reconstructing Lives, Recapturing Memory: Refugee Identity, Gender and Culture Change*, pp. 129–46. Washington, DC: Gordon and Breach.

Lincoln, Y.S., and E. Guba. 1985. *Naturalistic Inquiry*. Newbury Park, CA: Sage.

Lofland, J., and L.H. Lofland. 1995. *Analyzing Social Settings: A Guide to Qualitative Observation and Analysis*, 3rd edn. Belmont, CA: Wadsworth.

Loue, S., and M. Faust. 1998. "Intimate Partner Violence among Immigrants," in S. Loue, ed., *Handbook of Immigrant Health*, pp. 521–44. New York: Plenum Press.

McClintock, A. 1995. *Imperial Leather*. New York: Routledge.

McLoughlin, F., and K. Grumbach. 1999. "Screening and Intervention for Intimate Partner Abuse: Practices and Attitudes of Primary Care Physicians," *Journal of the American Medical Association* 282: 468–474.

McSpadden, L.A., and H. Moussa. 1993. "I Have a Name: The Gender Dynamics in Asylum and in Resettlement of Ethiopian and Eritrean Refugees in North America," *Journal of Refugee Studies* 6: 203–25.

Mehotra, M. 1999. "The Social Construction of Wife Abuse: Experiences of Asian Indian Women in the United States," *Violence Against Women* 5: 619–40.

Memmi, A. 1967. *The Colonizer and the Colonized*. Boston: Beacon Press.

Min, P. 2001. "Changes in Korean Immigrants' Gender Role and Social Status, and Their Marital Conflicts," *Sociological Forum* 16: 301–20.

Minh-Ha, T.T. 1989. *Woman, Native, Other: Postcolonial Feminism*. Indianapolis: Indiana University Press.

Moghissi, H., and M.J. Goodman. 1999. "'Cultures of Violence' and Diaspora: Dislocation and Gendered Conflict in Iranian-Canadian Communities," *Humanity and Society* 23: 291–318.

Mohanty, C.T. 1991. "Under Western Eyes: Feminist Scholarship and Colonial Discourses," in C.T. Mohanty, ed., *Third World Women and the Politics of Feminism*, pp. 51–80. Bloomington: Indiana University Press.

Montalvo-Liendo, N. 2008. "Cross-cultural Factors in Disclosure of Intimate Partner Violence: An Integrated Review," *Journal of Advanced Nursing* 65(1): 20–34.

Morash, M., H.N. Bui, and A.M. Santiago. 2000. "Cultural-specific Gender Ideology and Wife Abuse in Mexican-descent escent Families," *International Review of Victimology* 7: 67–91.

Morrison, F., S. Guruge, and K.A. Snarr. 1999. "Sri Lankan Tamil Immigrants in Toronto: Gender, Marriage Patterns, and Sexuality," in G.A. Kelson and D.L. DeLaet, eds., *Gender and Immigration*, pp. 144–60. New York: New York University Press.

Muellman, R.L., P.A. Lenaghan, and R. A. Pakieser. 1996. "Battered Women: Injury Locations and Types," *Annals of Emergency Medicine* 28: 486–92.

Oxman-Martinez, J., S. Abdool, and M. Loiselle-Leonard. 2000. "Immigration, Women and Health in Canada," *Canadian Journal of Public Health* 91: 394–95.

Penalosa, F. 1986. *Central Americans in Los Angeles: Background, Language and Education* (Occasional Paper 21). Los Angeles: Spanish Speaking Mental Health Research Center.

Perilla, J., R. Bakeman, and K. Norris. 1994. "Culture and Domestic Violence: The Ecology of Abused Latinas," *Violence and Victims* 9: 325–39.

Perry, C.M., M. Shams, and C.C. DeLeon. 1998. "Voices from an Afghan Community," *Journal of Cultural Diversity* 5: 127–31.

Ratner, P. 1995. "Indicators of Exposure to Wife Abuse," *Canadian Journal of Nursing Research* 27: 31–46.

Rhee, S. 1997. "Domestic Violence in the Korean Immigrant Family," *Journal of Sociology and Social Welfare* 24: 63–77.

Rodgers, K. 1994. "Wife Assault in Canada: The Findings of a National Survey," *Juristat Service Bulletin*, Canadian Centre for Justice Statistics 14(9): 1–21.

Schensul, S.L., J.J. Schensul, and M.D. LeCompte. 1999. *Essential Ethnographic Methods*. Walnut Creek, CA: Altamira Press.

Spivak, G.C. 1988. "Can the Subaltern Speak?," in C. Nelson and L. Grossberg, eds., *Marxism and the Interpretation of Culture*, pp. 271–313. Chicago: University of Illinois Press.

Tang, T.N., and K. Oatley. 2002. *Transition and Engagement of Life Roles among Chinese Immigrant Women*. Paper presented at American Psychological Association Annual Convention, Chicago.

Tran, C.G., and K. Des Jardins. 2000. "Domestic Violence in Vietnamese Refugee and Korean Immigrant Communities," in J.L. Chin, ed., *Relationships among Asian American Women*, pp. 71–96. Washington, DC: American Psychological Association.

Tuhiwai Smith, F. 2001. *Decolonizing Methodologies: Research and Indigenous People*. Dunedin: University of Otago Press.

United Nations. 1993. *Declaration on the Elimination of Violence against Women*. Canada–USA New York: Women's Health Forum, p. 6. Retrieved from www.hc-sc.gc.ca/canusa/papers/canada/english/violence.htm on 1 February 2005.

United Nations. 1999. *Consideration of Reports Submitted by States Parties under Article 18 of the Convention on the Elimination of All Forms of Discrimination Against Women: Third and Fourth Reports*.

World Health Organization. 2000. *Prevalence of Violence against Women by an Intimate Male Partner*. Retrieved from www.who.int/violence_injury_prevention/vaw/prevalence.htm on 11 June 2006.

World Health Organization. 2006. *Multi-country Study on Women's Health and Domestic Violence against Women. Summary Report: Initial Results on Prevalence, Health Outcomes and Women's Responses*. Geneva, Switzerland: World Health Organization.

Chapter 38

Overview

Not all gendered violence involves heterosexuals. Vivian Namaste makes the case that homophobic violence—attacks on gay, lesbian, queer, or transgender individuals—can be understood as a form of gendered violence. Namaste claims that attacks on these people are a manifestation of social intolerance for anyone who does not fit into rigid gender categories so that men who appear to other men to be effeminate are vulnerable to being targeted and attacked with slurs, whether or not they are actually homosexual. It is the gender-bending, not the sexuality, which is at the heart of "gay-bashing" or "queer-bashing."

However, in some official accounting, only crimes committed against gay men and women in areas known to be queer-friendly, such as Montreal's Gay Village, are tallied as "official" attacks on sexual minorities. The attacks on transgender sex workers in neighbouring areas do not get counted as homophobic crimes, yet Namaste argues that both types of violence are manifestations of the same hatred for individuals who do not conform to expectations for their gender. Separating "gay-bashing" from attacks on transgender individuals results in an underestimate of the true extent of gendered violence.

Genderbashing: Sexuality, Gender, and the Regulation of Public Space

Viviane K. Namaste

In North America, violence against lesbians, gay men, and bisexuals is escalating at an alarming rate. A survey conducted in 1986–7 by the Philadelphia Lesbian and Gay Task Force reports that violence against lesbians and gay men in that city had doubled since 1983–4 (as cited in Valentine, 1993: 409). The United States National Gay and Lesbian Task Force (NGLTF) documents that incidents of violence against sexual minorities increased 127 per cent from 1988 to 1993 (NGLTF, 1994: 1).

Though scholars (Comstock, 1991; von Schultess, 1992; Valentine, 1993) and community activists (Hendricks, 1993) have increasingly addressed the issue of violence against lesbians and gay men, there remains very little reflection on the function of gender within these acts of aggression. In this chapter, I argue that a perceived transgression of normative sex/gender relations motivates much of the violence against sexual minorities, and that an assault on these "transgressive" bodies is fundamentally concerned with policing gender presentation through public and private space. I also consider the implications of this research for transsexual and transgendered people. Given that the perception of gender dissidence informs acts of queerbashing, we can deduce that those individuals who live outside normative sex/gender relations will be most at risk for assault. Finally, I examine some of the ways in which educational strategies on violence separate gender and sexuality, and thus prevent a political response that accounts for the function of gender in queerbashing. Specific examples are taken from briefs presented in November 1993 to the Quebec Human Rights Commission's public hearing in Montreal on violence and discrimination against lesbians and gay men (Demczuk, 1993; Hendricks, 1993; Namaste, 1993; Pepper, 1993).[1] I demonstrate the ways in which gender and sexuality are separated, and thus how the issue of gender is foreclosed by certain gay male community activists.

Limits of Tolerance: Gender Norms and Gender Transgressions

"Gender" refers to the roles and meanings assigned to men and women based on their presumed biological sex (Mackie, 1983). It is a social function, neither timeless nor historical. For example, we generally associate the colour pink with girls and femininity and the colour blue with boys and masculinity. There is nothing inherent in either of these colours that links them to a particular gender: pink, or turquoise, could just as easily designate masculinity. Gender is also about what men and women are supposed to do in the world—men wear pants, have short hair, can grow beards, and are considered more physically aggressive than women. Women can wear skirts, have longer hair, wear makeup, and are judged to be emotional. In Western societies, it is thought that there are only two genders—men and women (Ortner and Whitehead, 1981).

"Sexuality," in contrast, refers to the ways in which individuals organize their erotic and sexual lives. This is generally categorized into three separate areas: heterosexuals—individuals who have sexual relations with members of the opposite sex; homosexuals—those who have sexual relations with members of the same sex; and bisexuals—people who relate erotically to both men and women (Kinsey, Pomeroy, and Martin, 1948).

In Western societies, gender and sexuality get confused. For example, when a 15-year-old boy is assaulted and called a "faggot," he is so labelled because he has mannerisms that are considered "effeminate." He may or may not be gay, but he is called a "queer" because he does not fulfill his expected gender role. A young girl can be a tomboy until the age of 11 or so, but she must then live as a more "dainty," "feminine" person. If she does not, she may be called a "dyke"—again, regardless of how she actually defines her sexual identity. In both examples, the presentation of gender determines how these youths are received by their peers. When people shout "faggot" at a 15-year-old boy, they really mean that he is not a "masculine" man. Gender and sexuality are collapsed. As Rubin points out, the merging of gender and sexuality enables some feminist theorists to write about erotic desire (Rubin, 1984: 307).

The fusion of gender and sexuality has distinct implications for the problematic of violence. The connotations of the pejorative names used against individuals who are assaulted—names like "sissy," "faggot," "dyke," "man-hater," "queer," and "pervert"— suggest that an attack is justified not in reaction to one's sexual identity, but to one's gender presentation. Indeed, bashers do not characteristically inquire as to the sexual identity of their potential victims, but rather make this assumption on their own. On what basis do "queerbashers" determine who is gay, lesbian, or bisexual?

Joseph Harry's research suggests that gender should be considered an important variable in queerbashing incidents (1982, 1990). Harry found that groups of assailants involved in these crimes relied on gender cues to ascertain sexual identity. If they judged a potential victim to be "effeminate," for example, he was subject to attack. A related study confirms this hypothesis: 39 per cent of men surveyed who behaved in a "feminine" manner had been physically assaulted, compared with 22 per cent of men who were "masculine" and only 17 per cent of men who conducted themselves in a "very masculine" fashion (Harry, 1982). According to this survey, males who are classified as "effeminate" are more than twice as likely to experience physical violence than males whose gender presentation corresponds to social norms. A study of anti-lesbian abuse in San Francisco indicates that 12 per cent of lesbians surveyed had been punched, kicked, or otherwise physically assaulted (von Schultess, 1992). Significantly, the only justification offered related to gender:

> [F]ourteen of the women said that the only explanation for incidents they had experienced was the fact that they had short hair and were wearing trousers and in most cases were in the company of another woman. (Valentine, 1993: 409)

Women and men who transgress acceptable limits of self-presentation, then, are among those most at risk for assault. Assaults against men judged to be "effeminate" or women deemed "masculine" reveal the ways in which gender and sexuality are intertwined. Gender is used as a cue to locate lesbians and gay men. Though the perceived transgression of gender norms motivates bashing, this affects men and women differently. The gendered construction of space—both public and private—figures centrally in these acts of aggression.

Transsexual and Transgendered People and Violence

Despite the variety of gender identities available in transgender networks, and despite the prevalence of transgendered people in other cultures, most people in Western societies assume that there are only two sexes (males and females) and two genders (men and women) (Ortner and Whitehead, 1981; Devor, 1989; Bullough and Bullough, 1993; Herdt, 1994; Feinberg, 1996). For transsexual and/or transgendered people, this poses a significant problem: a person must choose the gender to which he/she belongs and behave accordingly. Because most people believe that there are only "men" and "women," transgendered people need to live as one or the other in order to avoid verbal and physical harassment. In transgendered communities, this is known as the need to pass. Passing is about presenting yourself as a "real" woman or a "real" man—that is, as an individual whose "original" sex is never suspected.[2] Passing means hiding the fact that you are transsexual and/or transgendered. Most people go to extraordinary lengths to live undetected as transsexuals. Electrolysis, voice therapy, the binding of breasts, mastectomy, and plastic surgery are some of the more common means employed to ensure that people pass successfully.

Given the cultural coding of gender into a binary framework, a high incidence of violence directed against TS/TG people is not surprising. Although there is very little data available on transgendered people as victims of violence, a 1992 study showed that 52 per cent of MTF transsexuals and 43 per cent of FTM transsexuals surveyed in London, England, had been physically assaulted (Tully, 1992: 266). Contrast these members with data from a 1989 American telephone poll, which revealed that 7 per cent of lesbians and gay men were victims of assault in the previous year (NGLTF, 1994). Although these samples represent two different countries, the statistical difference of violent incidents against gay/ lesbian and transgender individuals is remarkable and certainly suggests that gender plays a crucial role in the attacks generally referred to as "gaybashing."

Although gender plays a central role in incidents of queerbashing, a collapse of gender and sexuality precludes a consideration of how this violence specifically affects transgendered people. Dorian Corey notes that contemporary gay antiviolence activists do not recognize the different ways aggression is, and has historically been, directed against transgendered people and gays:

> When the closet doors were shut [for gays, in the past], drag queens, of course, were out there anyways. We never had a closet. Let's face it, when you put on a dress and hit the world, you're declaring what you are. . . . These children that are supposedly straight looking, they're the ones getting bashed, so now [in the 1990s] they're protesting. The girls were always getting their asses kicked. It's just a thing of who you are and what you are. (as quoted in Enigma, 1992: 35–6)

Transsexual activists have suggested that one of the ways we can respond to the function of gender in violence is by naming it directly. As an activist button proclaims, "transsexuals get queerbashed too." Activists also insist that we need to speak of *genderbashing*, not gaybashing. This discourse separates gender and sexuality, since their collapse prevents an appreciation of the specificity of violence against transsexual and transgendered people.

Sex Work and Transsexual/Transgendered Public Space

"Transsexual and transgendered public space" refers to urban areas known for their transsexuals and transvestites, such as the Meat District on the border of New York's Greenwich Village, Santa Monica Boulevard in Los Angeles, or the Tenderloin in San Francisco. While gay male public space is defined through the presence of gay businesses and bars, transsexual public space reflects the areas of the city frequented by transsexual and transvestite sex workers.

Since gender and sexuality are not the same, it is not surprising that most cities have separate geographic areas known for transgendered people and lesbians/gays. Pat Califia articulates the differences between gay ghettoes and sex worker areas:

> Gay ghettos operate differently than other types of sex zones. They are more likely to be residential districts for gay men as well as places where they can find entertainment. Although johns still enter gay ghettos in quest of pleasurable activities not available within the nuclear family, they have better luck scoring if they camouflage themselves as residents of the area. (1991: 14)

Because transgender areas are not tied to a notion of a resident (as in the case of gay ghettos), the ways in which the space can be defined varies. Although certain sections of the city are known for their transsexuals and transvestites, these people are usually only visible at night. New York's Meat Market District is so named because of its many meat-packaging warehouses. When these businesses close at the end of the day, transgendered sex workers come out to earn their livelihoods, and thus transform the meaning of the term "meat" into one with explicit sexual connotations. Time of day and geographic space converge to establish a public transgender identity. For example, a Toronto sex worker interviewed in David Adkin's film *Out: Stories of Lesbian and Gay Youth* refers to the area where transgender prostitutes solicit clients as "trannie town" (Adkin, 1993).

As Califia demonstrates, the recent emergence of gay ghettos has separated sexual minorities from transsexual prostitutes. Although bars catering to transgendered people are extremely rare, they are usually located in sex worker districts rather than in gay villages. In Montreal, for example, the transsexual/transvestite bar Café Cléopâtra is situated near the corner of Sainte-Catherine and Saint-Laurent streets, in the heart of the red-light district.[3] The bar is widely known for its prostitutes—it is a space not only where transgendered people can socialize, but where they can also earn their livings. Montreal police observe the establishment regularly. While recent years have not witnessed any official raids on the bar, it is common of officers to walk in, "do the rounds," and inspect bar patrons, sex workers, and their prospective clients.[4]

This police harassment of transgendered people relates to the laws against prostitution. In Canada, prostitution is entirely legal, but soliciting clients is not (*Pocket Criminal Code of Canada*, 1987: 118–19). Individual officers have enormous scrutiny in the interpretation of what constitutes "solicitation": it may be a verbal agreement about sexual acts in exchange for financial compensation, or it may be a smile or glance directed at an undercover officer. While the latter instance would probably not be considered "solicitation" in a court of law, officers still have the power to charge individuals with the crime and place them in custody at night (Scott, 1987). It is the communication of sexual desire that is criminalized in Canada, not sexual desire or its enactment per se. Not surprisingly, this legislation does not affect all sex workers equally. Cathy, the operator of an escort service, remarks that street prostitutes—those most visible in the public eye—are most affected by this law: "escort services . . . have enjoyed . . . tolerance as we go tiptoeing around in the night, not bothering communities because we're not standing in people's front yards" (1987: 88–91). Research indicates that police use the soliciting law to harass prostitutes, following them down the street in a patrol car or stopping to talk with them during their work (Hankins and Gendron, n.d.).

Limits of Antiviolence Activism: Opposing Gender and Sexuality

Much of the activist response to violence against sexual and gender minorities has centered on the gay village of a particular city (see Hendricks, 1993). As most gay men are assaulted in areas demarcated as "gay": this focus is useful. Yet such a strategy forecloses an investigation of gender and ignores the different experiences of lesbians, bisexual women, and transgendered people with respect to public space and violence. By emphasizing sexual identity, this discourse establishes an antiviolence agenda that is, at best, only somewhat useful. Consider the text of an educational poster produced by Montreal's police department (Service de police de la communauté urbaine de Montreal, or SPCUM): "Being lesbian, gay, or bisexual is not a crime. Bashing is." The slogan—which also appears on buttons produced by antiviolence activists in Toronto—addresses the perpetrators of violence directly, and in that, it is to be commended. Despite this direct address, however, the poster does not engage the cognitive processes at work that perpetrators use to determine who is gay, lesbian, or bisexual. In this discourse, identity is mobilized as the ground upon which acts of violence are established. People are bashed because they are gay, lesbian, or bisexual. But we have already seen that bashing occurs due to the perception of potential victims, and that compulsory sex/gender relations figure centrally in these acts of interpretation. In this light, educational materials that address the perpetrators of violence should focus on the interpretive processes these people use to locate queerbashing victims. Because gender is the primary mechanism through which this takes place, there is a desperate need for posters, pamphlets, and presentations that outline the ways in which a binary gender system is upheld, as well as the power relations concealed within it. Through a stress on being, rather than on the perception of doing, the SPCUM poster reifies sexual identity and prevents a proper investigation of gender in the problematic of violence.

Implicitly, gender and sexuality are juxtaposed. This opposition can be witnessed in the brief presented by the SPCUM to the Quebec Human Rights Commission in association with its public hearings on violence and discrimination against lesbians and gay men (November 1993). In their brief to the commission, the SPCUM presented data on the prevalence of crime in District 33—the geographic area that includes (but is not limited to) the gay village. The borders of the village (René-Lévesque and Ontario, Amherst, and Papineau) were compared to a similar section of the city—that demarcated by the streets René-Lévesque and Ontario (north/south axis) and Amherst and Saint-Laurent (east/west). The SPCUM was interested in comparing these two sections of District 33 in order to evaluate the frequency of violent incidents (thefts, sexual assault, harassment). The areas are proportional in size, each comprising about 20 per cent of the district. Moreover, they share certain similarities in terms of the businesses, bars, and people present:

> Tous deux sont dans l'axe de la rue Ste-Catherine, rue très fréquentée de jour comme de nuit et où l'on retrouve divers commerces, restaurants, bars, et salles d'amusement. On y retrouve également des activités reliées à la vente et la consommation de stupéfiants, à la prostitution masculine et féminine contrôlée, en partie, par deux groupes des motards criminels. [Both include Sainte-Catherine Street, which is busy both day and night, and where one can find a variety of businesses, restaurants, bars, and amusement halls. One can also find activities related to the sale and consumption of drugs, as well as male and female prostitution, which is controlled, in part, by two groups of criminal bikers.] (SPCUM, 1993)

The SPCUM data indicates that between November 1991 and October 1993, a total of 1,454 crimes were recorded for the gay village—approximately 18 per cent of the total number of reported crimes in District 33 (1993: 10–11). Given that the gay village comprises 20 per cent of the district, the study implies that incidents of violence and crime correspond proportionately to geography. (However, the brief does not address the population of the gay village in relation to that of the entire district, thus associating violence with city space rather than demographics.)

The SPCUM offers comparative data to legitimate this figure. The section of District 33 to which the gay village is compared indicates 2,774 incidents of violence over the same time period, a statistic that amounts to 34 per cent of the violence in the total district (1993: 11). Since the comparison territory is relatively equal in size to that of the gay village, it is suggested that violence and crime occur more frequently in this area than in the section of the city known to be populated by gay men. By demonstrating the ways in which crime in the gay village is statistically below the proportional incidents of violence in District 33, the SPCUM attempts to dismiss activists who point to increased instances of bashing in Montreal's gay village. (The results of the SPCUM study are presented in Figure 38.1.)

There are, of course, tremendous differences in the data on violence collected by police departments and that collected by lesbian and gay community groups (Comstock, 1991; NGLTF, 1994). What is perhaps even more remarkable about the research presented by the SPCUM, however, is the way in which it forces a separation between sexuality and gender in terms of public space. The comparative section of District 33—that area bordered by Saint-Laurent, Amherst, Ontario, and Réne-Lévesque—is well known as the city's sex worker district. The city's only transsexual/transvestite bar is located here, and streets in this region are also frequented by TS/TG prostitutes.

Although the SPCUM maintains that both the gay village and this comparative section are homes to prostitutes, they do not account for the gendered breakdown of this activity. Field research conducted in the summer of 1993 indicates that most male prostitutes work in the gay village, toward Papineau; directly on its borders (Parc Lafontaine, located just above Amherst and Ontario); or in an adult cinema at the corner of Sainte-Catherine and Amherst. In contrast, most female prostitutes work on the corner of Saint-Laurent and Sainte-Catherine, on Saint-Denis, or on side streets in the vicinity. Transgendered

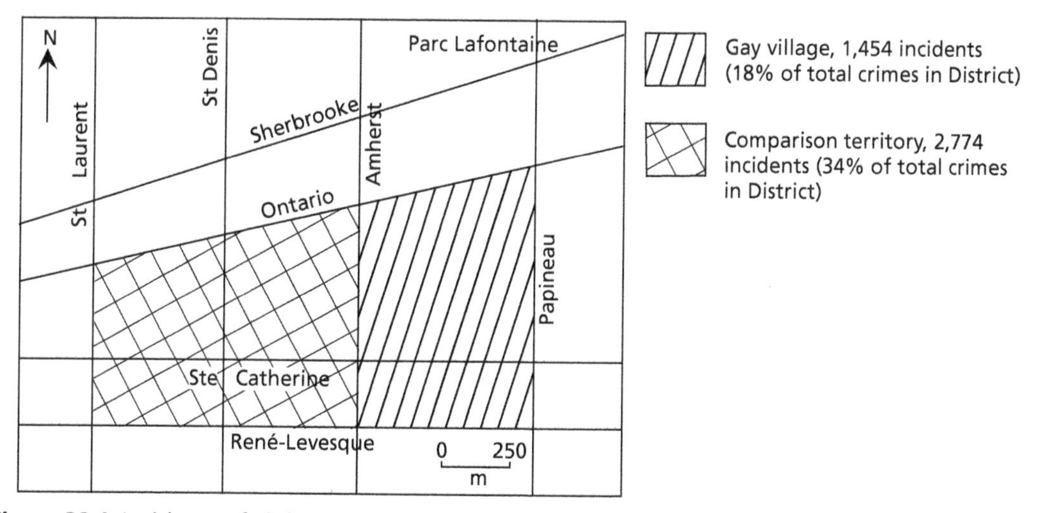

Figure 38.1 Incidents of violent crimes in two sections of Police District 33, Montreal, November 1991–October 1993. (Source: SPCUM, 1993: 10–11.)

prostitutes can also be found in this area. (The geographic location of sex workers in District 33 is depicted in Figure 38.2).

Regarding incidents of violence, most TS/TG prostitutes work in an area with a much higher frequency of criminal acts than the gay village (34 per cent versus 18 per cent). Although these statistics do not necessarily indicate that more transgendered people (proportionally) are victims of violence than gay men, it is certainly fair to stipulate that they work in an area known for criminal activities. To present this region as a comparative sample against the gay village is, then, to juxtapose gender and sexuality. While the SPCUM attempts to dispel fears about the high incidence of violence in gay space, it offers no examination of the role gender plays either in this site or its comparative territory. Because gender is not signalled as a factor in the discussion of District 33—along with other variables including poverty and homelessness—the SPCUM assumes that crime does not vary according to the gendered dimension of public space. The focus accorded to sexuality and the gay ghetto makes it impossible to address the violence that is directed against TS/TG people—whether they are in the gay village, a sex worker zone, or elsewhere.

Conclusion

The theoretical issues presented here, especially the relations between gender and sexuality, raise additional questions as to the collection and interpretation of evidence on gendered violence. What implications does the presence of TS/TG people in public space hold in terms of violence? Do bashers drive into these areas, looking to assault a transsexual woman or a transvestite prostitute, as they often drive into gay villages in search of queerbashing victims (Comstock, 1991: 49)? Are transgendered people of colour assaulted more frequently than those who are white? What happens when transgender prostitutes enter areas demarcated as "gay"? Are these people subject to assault because of an association between prostitution and AIDS, and if so, how does this relate to increased violence against those perceived to be HIV-positive (NGLTF, 1994)? Since much of the data on queerbashing indicates that it is often perpetrated by young males, usually in groups (Comstock, 1991: 65), are transgendered youth most at risk for assault? What are the specific methodological difficulties involved in collecting data on violence against transgendered people? Will these people be reluctant to report the assaults they experience

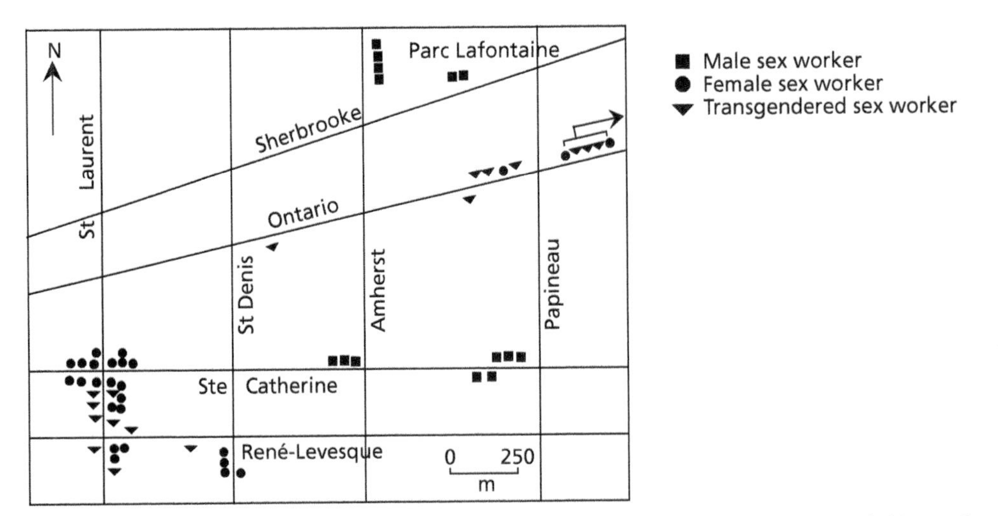

Figure 38.2 Sex-worker presence according to gender in Police District 33, Montreal, November 1991–October 1993. Note: more sex workers can be found further east on Ontario. (Source: field research.)

to the police, as are many lesbians, gay men, and bisexuals? Given that transsexuals are incarcerated according to their "original," biological sex (e.g., an MTF person is placed in an all-male jail), can we expect transsexuals to consider police and law enforcement officials in a favourable light?[5] Do transgendered people even inform gaybashing hotlines when they are assaulted, or do they not consider themselves part of these communities? How can we record incidents of genderbashing for the collection of hate crime statistics?[6] These are only a few of the questions that a more detailed, empirical study of violence against transgendered people would address.

In recent years, the issue of violence has received increased attention in the communities of the sexually marginalized, as well as within the academy. Although some of the research emphasizes the role of gender in violence (Harry, 1990; von Schultess, 1992; Valentine, 1993), it has yet to explore the implications of this issue for transgendered individuals and communities. The definition of public space is intimately linked to culturally sanctioned gender identities. This has profound implications for people who live outside normative sex/gender relations: "ordinary" public space as well as regions known as gay ghettoes are sites where the gender potential of being verbally abused, and/or physically assaulted, is remarkably high. Furthermore, although gender and sexuality are conventionally confused, such that "effeminate" men and "masculine" women are "gaybashed" irrespective of their sexual identities, the variables of gender and sexuality can also be juxtaposed. Such an opposition can be quite explicit, as when middle-class gay men struggled to evict transgendered prostitutes from Vancouver's West End (Arrington, 1987). A separation of gender and sexuality can also be more subtle, as in the discourse on violence proposed by many gay male activists that privileges sexuality over gender, and hence develops a political response that is only valid for urban, middle-class gay men.

Taking up the issue of violence against sexual and gender minorities, this chapter has attempted to illustrate how some of the responses to violence preclude an adequate conceptualization of gendered aggression. Through a literature review on gender and violence, as well as a preliminary analysis on the geographic location of Montreal prostitutes in 1992, I have argued that the discourse of violence against sexual minorities excludes transsexual women. Furthermore, the briefs presented to the Quebec Human Rights Commission offer an engaging case study of how the social relations of gender are textually coordinated in one institution, such that transsexuals are beyond consideration.

Notes

1. Copies of these briefs are available from the Commission des droits de la personne et de la jeunesse, 360 Saint-Jacques, Montreal, QC, H2Y 1P5, Canada.
2. The issue of "passing" has been examined from an ethnomethodological perspective within sociology. See Harold Garfinkel, *Studies in Ethnomethodology* (Englewood Cliffs, NJ: Prentice-Hall, 1967); and Kessler and McKenna, *Gender: An Ethnomethodological Approach* (New York: John Wiley and Sons, 1978).
3. For more on the geographic area of Montreal's red-light district, see Daniel Proulx, *Le Red Light de Montreal, 1945–1970* (Montreal: Boreal, 1994); and Thérèse Limonges, *La Prostitution à Montreal: Comment, pourquoi certaines femmes deviennent prostituées: Étude sociologique et criminologique*. (Montreal: Édit de l'homme, 1967).
4. Montreal police entered Café Cléopâtra with a video camera, for instance, on 13 November 1997. See Viviane Namaste, "Évaluation des besoins: Les travesty(e)s et les transsexuel(le)s au Quebec à l'égard du vih/Sida." Report submitted to the Centre Québécois de Coordination sur le SIDA, Montreal, May 1998. (A copy of this report is available through ASST(e)Q in care of CACTUS, 1626 rue Saint-Hubert, Montreal, QC, H2L 3Z3.)
5. For more on transgendered people in prison, see James Tee, *Health Issues of the HIV + MTF Transgendered Prison Population* (Toronto: PASAN—Prisoners' AIDS Support Action

Network [489 College St, Suite 405, Toronto, ON, M6G 1A5, 416-920-9567], 1997); Maxine Petersen, Judith Stephens, Robert Dickey, and Wendy Lewis, "Transsexuals within the Prison System: An International Survey of Correctional Services Policies," *Behavioral Sciences and the Law* 14 (1996): 219–29; and Ann Scott, "A Brief on HIV/AIDS in the Transgendered Prison Population." Presentation at the International Foundation for Gender Education conference, Toronto, 27 March 1998. Also see Ann Scott and Rick Lines, "HIV/AIDS in the Male-to-Female Transsexual and Transgendered Prison Population: A Comprehensive Strategy. A Brief from PASAN" (Toronto: May 1999).

6. Documenting hate crimes against gays and lesbians is difficult because the violence must be clearly accompanied by anti-gay epithets. For instance, if a man is stabbed in the gay village and his wallet stolen, he will be considered the victim of a robbery unless the assailants called him derogatory insults relating to his perceived sexuality (see SPCUM, "Mémoire sur la discrimination et la violence envers les gais et les lesbiennes." Brief presented to the Quebec Human Rights Commission, November 1993. [Copy available for consultation at the Commission des droits de la personne et de la jeunesse, 360 Stain-Jacque, Montreal, QC, H2Y 1P5.]). In the case of violence against transgendered people, this criterion for documentation is questionable, since many MTF transsexuals are called "faggot." Programmatically, we should not have to wait until bashers decry transgendered people with the proper vocabulary before we have an adequate manner of recording such genderbashing incidents.

References

Adkin, D. 1993. *Out: Stories of Lesbian and Gay Youth*. Montreal: National Film Board of Canada.

Arrington, S. 1987. "Community Organizing," in L. Bell, ed., *Good Girls/Bad Girls: Sex Trade Workers and Feminists Face to Face*, pp. 104–8. Toronto: Women's Press.

Bullough, B., and V. Bullough. 1993. *Cross Dressing, Sex, and Gender*. Philadelphia: University of Pennsylvania Press.

Califa, P. 1991. "The City of Desire: Its Anatomy and Destiny," *Invert* 2(4): 13–16.

Cathy. 1987. "Unveiling," in L. Bell, ed., *Good Girls/Bad Girls: Feminists and Sex Trade Workers Face to Face*, pp. 88–91. Toronto: Women's Press.

Comstock, G. 1991. *Violence against Lesbians and Gay Men*. New York: Columbia University Press.

Demczuk, I. 1993. "Des droits à reconnaître. Hétérosexisme et discrimination envers les lesbiennes." Brief presented to the Quebec Human Rights Commission, November 1993.

Devor, H. 1989. *Gender Blending: Confronting the Limits of Duality*. Bloomington: Indiana University Press.

Enigma, A. 1992. "Livin' Large: Dorian Corey," *Thing* 8: 35–6.

Feinberg, L. 1996. *Transgender Warriors: Making History from Joan of Arc to RuPaul*. Boston: Beacon Press.

Hankins, C., and S. Gendron. n.d. *Project Prostitution: Rapport sur les entretiens de groupes réalisés à la maison Tanguay*. Montral: Centre d'études sur le sida, Unité de santé publique, Hôpital général de Montreal.

Harry, J. 1982. "Derivative Deviance: The Cases of Extortion, Fag-Bashing and the Shakedown of Gay Men," *Criminology* 19: 546–63.

———. 1990. "Conceptualizing Anti-gay Violence," *Journal of Interpersonal Violence* 5: 350–8.

Hendricks, M. 1993. "Lesbian and Gay Community Relations with the M[ontreal] U[rban] C[ommunity] Police." Brief presented for the group Lesbiennes et Gais contre la violence to the Quebec Human Rights Commission, November 1993.

Herdt, G., ed. 1994. *Third Sex, Third Gender: Beyond Sexual Dimorphism in Culture and History*. New York: Zone Books.

Kinsey, A., W. Pomeroy, and C.E. Martin. 1948. *Sexual Behavior in the Human Male*. Philadelphia: W.B. Saunders Company.

Mackie, M. 1983. *Exploring Gender Relations*. Toronto: Butterworths.

Namaste, K. 1993. "Transgenders and Violence: An Exploration." Brief presented to the Quebec Human Rights Commission, November 1993.

National Gay and Lesbian Task Force (NGLTF). 1994. *Anti-gay/lesbian Violence, Victimization, and Defamation in 1993*. Washington, DC: NGLTF Policy Institute.

Ortner, S., and H. Whitehead, eds. 1981. *Sexual Meanings: The Cultural Construction of Gender and Sexuality*. Cambridge, UK: Cambridge University Press.

Pepper, D. 1993. "Community Based Responses to Bias Crimes: Some Critical Steps." Brief presented to the Quebec Human Rights Commission, November 1993. *Pocket Criminal Code of Canada*. 1987. Toronto: Carswell.

Rubin, G. 1984. "Thinking Sex: Notes Towards a Radical Theory of the Politics of Sexuality," in C. Vance, ed., *Pleasure and Danger: Exploring Female Sexuality*, pp. 267–319. Boston: Routledge and Kegan Paul.

Scott, V. 1987. "C-49: A New Wave of Oppression," in L. Bell, ed., *Good Girls/Bad Girls: Sex Trade Workers and Feminists Face to Face*, pp. 100–3. Toronto: Women's Press.

SPCUM. 1993. "Mémoire sur la discrimination et la violence envers les gais et les lesbiennes." Brief presented to the Quebec Human Rights Commission, November 1993.

Tully, B. 1992. *Accounting for Transsexuality and Transhomosexuality*. London: Whiting and Birch.

Valentine, G. 1993. "(Hetero)Sexing Space: Lesbian Perceptions and Experiences of Everyday Spaces," *Environment and Planning D: Society and Space* 11: 409.

von Schultess, B. 1992. "Violence in the Streets: Anti-lesbian Assualt and Harassment in San Francisco," in G. Herek and K. Berril, eds., *Hate Crimes: Confronting Violence Against Lesbians and Gay Men*, pp. 65–77. London, UK: Sage.

PART XI
Social Movements

When most people think of gender and social activism, they picture suffragists marching for women's right to vote in the 1920s, or perhaps the "women's lib" movement of the 1960s and 1970s (in which, by the way, no bras were ever burned—the torching of lingerie was a media invention). These movements were about redistributing power between the genders, through political, economic, domestic, and cultural actions. Some may also think of the men's movement, which began in the 1980s, in which men too found themselves questioning repressive and confining norms of gender.

Some critics have tried to write off feminism as "over and done with," now that Western women have the same legal rights and many of the same opportunities as their male counterparts. However, Candis Steenburgen argues that rumours of feminism's death are greatly exaggerated. While younger feminists today may differ from their foremothers in their tactics and in some aspects of their goals, she contends; the questioning, transformative spirit of earlier feminism lives on.

Far from being marginalized, feminism in Canada has become institutionalized, with feminist organizations carrying out invaluable work in society, from running shelters for survivors of domestic violence to advocating for training programs to help women become skilled in trades. However, this work is always at risk of being derailed by shifting political currents, as Kathleen Rodgers and Melanie Knight describe. The institutional survival of feminist movements is a tremendous challenge to activists.

In addition to social movements that focus on women, the world has seen a blossoming of social activism to transform masculinity. Erin Casey and her co-authors offer a panoramic, global view of men's movements, examining common challenges, inspiration, and achievements across diverse cultures and societies. The intersection of gender with other identities and contexts emerges as a key focus for men's activism across the world.

The term "gender and social movements" does not refer only to social movements *about* transforming gender. Activists for a variety of causes *do* gender in the course of advocating for their goals. Miya Narushima looks at groups of activists who push the gendering of social movements to the point of absurdity—which is precisely their intent. She profiles the Raging Grannies, older women activists for international peace, economic redistribution, and other causes, who adopt an exaggerated "little old lady" persona, with accompanying songs and performances, to draw attention to their causes and to deflect negative responses through humour. The Grannies deftly deploy gender as a political tactic, and turn stereotypes on their heads.

Questions for Critical Thought

1. Have you ever participated in any social movement? (Or perhaps you currently consider yourself a proponent of a particular cause.) If so, what drew you to take part? Was there anything gendered about the movement, or about your participation?
2. Do you consider yourself a feminist? Why or why not? Have you encountered self-defined feminists in your own life?
3. What do you think the current political climate in your home province is like for gender activism? What are some of the current gender issues where you live?
4. Steenbergen argues that the current generation of feminists is a "third wave" that is significantly different from earlier waves of activists. What are the strengths and limitations of the "wave" metaphor? Can you think of other areas of social life in which generational differences might be conceptualized as "waves"?
5. Why do you think the media are eager to proclaim feminism dead?
6. What should the role of the government be in promoting gender equality? Should governments (federal, provincial, municipal) take active roles and advocate for change?
7. Why do you think men's gender activism has centred on issues of gender violence? What makes this topic compelling for so many men?
8. What do you think are the most effective ways to accomplish social change? How do you balance the effectiveness of working within the system against protest

movements that are based outside the system, like the movements the Raging Grannies support?

9. Can you imagine a Raging Grandpas group? What stereotypes about masculinity might lend themselves to the sort of comic exaggeration the Grannies have taken on?

10. Between Steenburgen, Rodgers and Knight, and Narushima, we have examples of activism across the lifespan. How do life events affect people's ability or willingness to engage in social change movements? How are the social movements of young people different from those of older ones?

Chapter 39

Overview

Are we in a post-feminist moment, when all the battles have been won and feminism itself is outdated? Not according to Candis Steenbergen, who argues that feminism remains relevant and attractive to up-and-coming generations of women. Despite efforts by media pundits and others to pronounce feminism dead, Steenburgen says, young women continue to find value in the work of their feminist forebears and to create new priorities and areas of struggle. Steenburgen uses the concept of feminist generations—or waves—to distinguish young feminists today from earlier ones. The current third wave of feminists is powerfully concerned with sexuality and the commodification of women's bodies, spurred by the ever-growing sexualization of advertising and media, as well as by advances in queer theory and LGBTQ activism.

Not all third wave feminists share the same agenda, nor do they agree on a "party line" that dictates what they should believe and do. However, this internal diversity is also a source of strength and vitality for contemporary Canadian feminism.

Feminism and Young Women: Still Alive and Kicking

Candis Steenbergen

Efforts to define "feminism" and attempts to determine the boundaries of the "women's movement" have always been problematic. Characterizing a feminist (or worse: the feminists) has been even harder. "Feminism," as Geraldine Finn has noted, "does not speak with one voice" (1982: 299). Feminists have always expressed their desire for social, political, economic, and cultural change in a variety of milieus. Feminist activity has always assumed a wide range of forms: from militant political activism, to silent volunteerism, to academic research and writing, to the creation of works of art, to so much more. Feminist historians acknowledge that the women's movement in Canada has always had a "diverse, complex, and shifting reality," and agree that feminists have never followed a unified political ideology (Adamson, Briskin, and McPhail, 1988: 9). While all feminisms share certain characteristics, significant differences in political strategy, in vision, in attitudes towards men, in understanding the roots of women's oppression, and in setting priorities also typify the Canadian women's movement ideology (Adamson et al., 1988; Hamilton, 1996).

Feminism itself has altered and evolved over time as the intricacies of women's positions in society have changed (Wine and Ristock, 1991; Adamson et al., 1988). In the early moments of the contemporary women's movement, second-wave feminists identified, named, analyzed, and resisted women's oppression, particularly as it existed in the private lives of "ordinary" women. The decade that followed has been called "a phase of expansion and consolidation," a period in which the women's movement grew in size and visibility, as well as in organizational and strategic terms (Tremblay, 1993).[1]

In the 1980s, many of the battles fought by the mainstream women's movement concentrated on institutional policy and political change. The strategies adopted by the women's movement through all three decades were employed in reaction to the political conditions of their struggles. But they were also the result of constant internal checks and balances performed by and among women of strikingly different political persuasions (Hamilton, 1996).[2]

Feminism in the last decade has been no different. By the early 1990s, the battlegrounds for feminist struggles had altered again. As early as 1993, Manon Tremblay noted that:

> Over the course of the last few years, the feminist movement has devoted itself primarily to fighting to maintain what women have gained in a climate of political conservatism, of financial austerity, and of the affirmation of a neo-conservative right wing. In addition, the antifeminist undercurrent which is currently developing in the West has led to the belief that the feminist movement has lost its raison d'etre with women now having achieved equality with men. (1993: 276)

At the beginning of the new century, Tremblay's "undercurrent" is a commonly heard reproach of feminism and its proponents. The "diversified, multifaceted, and enriched" nature of feminist activities has been re-interpreted (and perpetuated by popular media) as demonstrative of an antiquated, ineffectual, "splintered and fragmented" women's movement (Hamilton, 1996: 80). The evidence supporting those charges has been even more unsettling. The arrival of a number of North American publications in the very recent past—written predominantly by young, female iconoclasts—incited reports of the arrival of the next generation of feminists: self-proclaimed "dissidents" who herald the coming of feminism's last breath.

In the United States, "feminism's daughters" appeared in the form of Katie Roiphe's *The Morning After: Sex, Fear and Feminism* (1993), Christina Hoff Sommers' *Who Stole Feminism? How Women Have Betrayed Women* (1994), Rene Denfeld's *The New Victorians: A Young Woman's Challenge to the Old Feminist Order* (1995), and—of course—Danielle Crittenden's *What Our Mother's Didn't Tell Us: Why Happiness Eludes the Modern Woman* (1999), and Wendy Shalit's *A Return to Modesty: Discovering the Lost Virtue* (1999), to name just a few. Almost perfectly paralleling the introduction of Ally McBeal to the television-consuming public, the entrance of these young voices—all straight, white, and well-educated voices, I should add—announced the "coming-of-age" of the heirs of the sexual revolution and the new faces of feminism. Women have made it, they say. Get over it.

Canada has not been without similar voices. In 1992, Amy Friedman published *Nothing Sacred: A Conversation with Feminism*. Using Queen's University as a model, the American-born author asserted that feminism had mutated and that she was no longer comfortable identifying with what the movement had become. Over the last 30 years, she argued, feminism has grown terrified of recognizing differences among women, and has not retained the sacredness of the personal. Individual stories, she asserted, now served only as "fodder for a statistical mill" (42). Friedman's agitation with academic feminism was multifaceted: she "deplored [the] sloppy, inaccurate, lazy language" used by proponents, was angered by the promotion of "female knowledge as distinct from male knowledge," and was dismayed by the apparent feminist belief in "ultimate solutions" for the atrocities of the world against women (42, 44, 58). She stated:

> The new feminist rhetoric . . . was beginning to sound like other versions of revolutionary fanaticism, and revolutionary fanaticism, we all know, has sparked some of the most heinous regimes in humankind's history. No matter who the enemy. (1992: 60)

According to Friedman, feminism lost sight of its original goals and fixated on romanticized images of women as powerless victims, encouraged self-pity, and sought to gain strength in martyrdom.

In 1995, Canadian journalist Kate Fillion published *Lip Service: The Truth about Women's Darker Side in Love, Sex, and Friendship*. Fillion discussed the myth of female moral superiority, and attempted to deconstruct a number of existing stereotypes, including "woman as victim," and "woman as saint." She stated that women today adhere to conflicting paradigms:

> Self-determination is what women want, but the myth of female moral superiority tells us that women cannot be actors in their own right. Apparently, women are too pure to harbor negative feelings and too virtuous to make mistakes. Agency—having some control over one's own life—is confused with happy endings. When things turn out well, women are given full credit, but when something goes wrong, we are absolved of responsibility. (1995: 318)

Based on her own observations and a handful of interviews, Fillion denounced feminists for attempting to achieve sexual liberation through the perpetuation of dangerous dichotomies and through the preservation of an age-old sexual script, and argued that, consequently, "the common language used to discuss sexuality in the public arena . . . [has been] predicated on women's passivity and oppression" (1995: 223).

The next year, Donna LaFramboise (also a journalist) published *The Princess at the Window: A New Gender Morality*. LaFramboise attacked "establishment feminism," that group of "people who are recognized by society at large as legitimate feminist spokespersons" (1996: 8). Citing Ann Landers, *Ms*, Marilyn French, and Catherine MacKinnon, LaFramboise asserted that "the lunatic fringe has taken over mainstream feminism" (1996: 33). Arguing that highly questionable ideas have been elevated to feminist dogma, she claimed that feminism has become extremist, self-obsessed, arrogant, and intolerant. LaFramboise was alarmed by the speed at which such "sloppy thinking" has permeated the rhetoric of popular culture and has influenced public policy, and stated that traditional methods of examining women's issues have become obsolete (1996: 48). LaFramboise argued that feminism has perpetuated the myth of female martyrdom, stated that feminists have deliberately maintained such fictions to ensure its survival, and differentiated between "a feminism that informs one's opinions and a feminism that dictates how one should think" (1996: 323).

Friedman, Fillion, and LaFramboise presented limited analyses of feminisms past shortcomings and future directions. All three generalized "North American feminism" as a unit based upon their own observations, anecdotes, conversations with friends, content analyses of newspaper columns, and a variety of studies on white, heterosexual, able-bodied, educated, middle- to upper-class women. All of the authors were former students (or graduates) of women's studies departments, and all three targeted the work of feminists in the academy, yet all failed to illustrate an in-depth knowledge of feminist theory or of the history of the women's movement. All of the authors used items from the popular press, provided snippets of contentious quotations from select feminist theorists (mostly American ones), and relied heavily upon personal interviews. All three expressed concern for the current state of feminism, and all provided instances in which mainstream second-wave praxis has "failed," but none provided viable alternatives. All three viewed tolerance and flexibility as key elements of future strategies for the women's movement, yet none succeeded in achieving a sound blend of analysis, theory, and practice.

Feminist commentators were swift in their criticism of the three Canadian-published books, their authors, and their American counterparts. One reviewer attacked their "highly selective, blinkered vision," and stated that their texts were little more than "in-your-face rant[s]" supported by "extraordinarily inflated ideas" about the prevalence and influence of feminism in Canada (Hurley, 1996). Myrna Kostash attacked Fillion for presenting second-wave feminism as "a monolithic movement reducible to a single tendency," and suggested that this new generation believes that feminism is anti-male, and that "mainstream feminists hate the very idea of sex with men" (1996: 13). By the year 2000, the presence of a new generation of women, concerned with little more than individual gain, the consumption of material goods, and the exertion of their own enlightened power, was branded into the public mind. The image of the "new modern woman" of the millennium was a "bad girl," one who has rejected the "tyranny of contemporary sexual politics" brought about by feminism and who has been aggressively taking matters into her own hands (Dennis, 1992: 3).

As the last decade's media frenzy suggests, a new generation of women has emerged, aggressively analyzing, rethinking, and challenging the assumptions and strategies of feminism's diverse histories and theories. Unfortunately (but not surprisingly), the popular press pinpointed the wrong group of women. A third wave has appeared within the women's movement; a generation of young women actively addressing the complexities of women's everyday experiences and the personal and structural relations affecting them. Their critiques—as varied as the feminisms that have come before—are intended to further the feminist cause, not to slander the movement or its proponents.

Despite the mass visibility of post-feminists, young feminist women—raised with feminism as a familiar concept since their birth; the beneficiaries of many of the successes of the women's movement; and those who know that there are still challenges remaining and obstacles to be jumped for women—exist and work and resist in the millennium. And, like the "popular kids" of their age group, many of them are vigorously engaged in exploring the intersections of sexualities, sexual pleasure, and feminism—and challenging some of the feminist strategies of the past as a result. The differences between the two, however, are significant. For one thing, most young women with legitimate concerns and critiques of feminism and the women's movement have not lined bookstore shelves with mass-market bestsellers, done the talk-show circuit, or made countless headlines. Instead, their voices appear in independently produced zines, in book reviews hidden in the backs of journals, on walls and across public advertisements, in non-mainstream publications, and in other, less conspicuous (and less financially rewarding), spaces. Third-wave feminists also understand and recognize that there is no feminist monolith, or any feminist "establishment" trying to take all the fun out of sex.[3] As well, young women see the historical specificity of the women's movement's engagement with and inquiries into issues of sexuality and body politics. They might not be thrilled with the way things turned out and want to revisit older strategies and theories (and question and confront those who pursued them), but most have the rationale not to blindly point fingers.

Women's sexual freedom was one of the key feminist goals of the late 1960s and early 1970s, and women's right to sexual pleasure and to control their own bodies symbolized their right to social equality.[4] Women formed woman-centred collectives and organizations and utilized public spaces as forums to speak about, challenge, and try to resolve, sexual discrimination and lingering post-war repression.[5] One objective was to denounce and dispel the inaccuracies of "those heterosexual practices predicated on the assumption of the priority of a male sexual urge and a male right to sexual pleasure" (Hamilton, 1996: 65). Activists sought to expose the double standard that celebrated men for "sowing their wild oats" and divided women as "whores" and "virgins." In public and in the home, feminists challenged socially enforced domesticity,

> To wrest control away from the state, the medical establishment, institutionalized religion, pharmaceutical companies, advertisers, pornographers, institutionalized censorship, [and] the violence of men. (Pierson, 1993: 98)

The struggle for reproductive rights, the revelatory discovery of the clitoris as a site of sexual response, and the publication of woman-centred journals, created "a thrilling sense of new possibilities" for women (Tiefer, 1995: 115).

By the mid-1970s, mainstream feminist praxis had turned its attention away from the personal aspects of sexuality and focused predominantly on legal, political, and social policy making and change, and in that climate "it was virtually impossible for lesbian, bisexual, or heterosexual feminists to claim the right to sexual pleasure" (Ross, 1995: 113). Concentrating instead on policy-based issues that they could mobilize around and effectively influence, the now "mainstream" feminist movement became focused on male sexual violence, the legalities of the Divorce Act, pornography, and the political and legal battles regarding rape and sexual assault. The sexuality debates had begun to change, and analyses of sexual danger rapidly superseded discussions of women's personal empowerment, pleasure, and desire.[6]

When the next generation of women came of age in the late 1980s and 1990s, sexuality was again a hot topic—one that pervaded (and continues to drench) virtually all facets of popular culture, the media, and mass-market advertising. The growth and intellectual development of young women today has been marked by a greater overall awareness of sex, sex identities, and sexualities, and a resurgent interest in the role that sexual identity plays in their everyday lives. The establishment of women's studies in schools, the inclusion (albeit paltry) of feminist and queer theory in other fields of study, and strong and vocal lesbian and gay voices have all contributed to their awareness. Young women also grew up with an expansion of cultural influences: music videos, cable TV, improved satellite communications, the Internet, and specialty magazines; all of which have affected and shaped their outlook. Advertising specifically and pop culture generally have become increasingly sexualized and young feminists have acknowledged that "as women became more powerful in real life, their clothes got tighter and shorter in the make-believe-it's-real world of television" (Timson, 1995: 52). In many ways, post-feminism emerged at an opportune moment in history: feeding off of the backlash of the '80s and utilizing the public fixation with and consumption of sexuality to their advantage.

The desire to analyze body image, self-esteem, desire, sexuality, and sexual pleasure has been strong in third-wave writings to date. To many, those pursuits have revolved around continual self-analysis and personal negotiation, an attempt to reconcile the desire to create their own version of "femininity," and the fear of betraying their allegiance to feminism and the struggle for female empowerment. For some, that has translated into a strong defiance of pre-constructed notions of what constitutes a "beautiful" female body and activism against fat-phobia. For others, it has meant indulging in beauty culture: fashion magazines, makeup, hair products, and slinky fashions previously viewed as fodder for the male gaze:

> For me, being a femme means that I take pride in wearing just the right shade of lipstick, drawing the perfect black line above my eye-lashes, keeping my legs smooth, and smelling good. Being a femmenist means knowing I am just as attractive when I don't wear makeup, shave, or put on perfume. (delombard, 1995: 29–30)

Young feminists are conscious of the use of sexuality and sexualized images of women in the media that consistently support and perpetuate traditional sex roles and sexual identities, and actively strive to make sense of manipulative media techniques in their work. A number of young feminist scholars, writers, artists, activists, and critics of the mass media have attempted to link their connection (and attraction) to the hyper-sexualized culture of consumerism and consumption with their identities as women, sexual beings, and feminists. The editors of *BITCH: Feminist Response to Pop Culture* explain the rationale:

> We are supposedly living in a new age—one that some have dubbed post-feminist. Feminism is over, they say. Just get over it. But television demonstrates that most people still think what a woman is wearing is more important than what she's thinking. Magazines that tell us, both implicitly and explicitly, that female sexual urges are deviant while reminding us that maintaining our sex appeal is the only way to wring commitment out of a man, without which our lives will be sad and incomplete in spite of dazzling careers and intense friendships. Billboards urge us to fork over our hard-earned cash for the glittery, overpriced wares of companies that depend on our unhappiness and dissatisfaction for their profits.

The negotiation between the attractive, processed, advertised, and consumable version of female sexuality and the difficulties of translating it into a lived reality has been substantial in third-wave analyses to date. In many respects, the approach has been to acknowledge the mixed messages pervading popular culture and account for the "problem desires" that often result. Not surprisingly, the craving for sexual empowerment has paralleled young women's questioning of reality, of the sexual revolution, and—necessarily—of their feminist "brand."

While young feminist perspectives regarding sexuality have just begun to emerge, much of the writing to date begins from a location similar to pro-sex feminists: where the early second-wave feminists left off. Early feminist writings that emphasized women's sexual freedom did not ignore the existence of sexual danger in many women's lives. Instead, they argued that women's sexual freedom could not occur without a more thorough sense of women's realities as well as a realization of the need for social, economic, and political rights.[7] It's just that one ended up absorbing the other. The complex sexual context of the current time has made a reconnection of the two necessary and unavoidable, and young women's activism has reflected that. In organizations and campus centres, young feminists have created pamphlets, how-to manuals, and newsletters on everything from surgical operations to enhance, sculpt, or rejuvenate the vagina, to tips on body piercing and tattooing, to info on the morning-after pill, to AIDS awareness.[8] Third-wave reactions to body politics coalesce neatly with the intentions of early second-wave discussions on the body.

In response to the often contradictory conditions surrounding women's sexual lives, young women have sought to combine radical perspectives on sexual theory with the everyday occurrences of women's lived experiences. That has translated, so far, into a reinterpretation of both personal and collective identities, an interrogation of the women's movement of the past and of the current period, as well as the creation of new visions for the future. Mariana Valverde has noted that there have traditionally been two genres used by women to talk about sex: the intellectual application of a number of abstract theoretical frameworks to women's sexual experiences and desires, and "the confessional." The new generation of feminists values both, and has been actively attempting to combine the two strategies in a concerted effort to work through the "lived messiness" of women's lives. The potential that explorations of women's sexuality has is "infinite and incalculable," but the myriad of problems, issues, and concerns facing young women also indicates that their "sexual project is just beginning" (Crosbi, 1993: xii).

Of course, the issues of sexuality and body politics covered herein are only fragments of the kinds of work that young women are currently engaged in. Like the waves that came before, the third is as difficult to define and as arduous to label and their activism has been as problematic—or more so—to pinpoint. Like their forerunners, their feminisms come in myriad forms: they don't all adhere to the "feminist" label, they don't follow a single agenda, they don't necessarily agree, and they don't share the same political motivations, priorities, or dreams. Their realities are as diverse, fluid, and complicated as the environment in which they resist. Whether feminism's "third wave" overshadows post-feminist ideology in the public's eye remains to be seen, but a number of things are certain. The new generation of young feminists is emerging, reacting, and acting within a particular moment in history, just as the feminisms of the past have changed in reaction to the ideological, social, cultural, and political climates within theirs. The future of feminism in Canada is not post-feminism; it is a strongly supported, vigorously active, dynamic group of young women who are determined to flex and bend their feminisms with where the world takes them, pushing the women's movement into the next century.

Notes

1. Tremblay notes that the 1970s marked the institutionalization of the women's movement with the establishment of state organizations like the Canadian Advisory Council on the Status of Women.
2. Hamilton noted that "feminists disagreed not only on the explanations for women's inequality, oppression, and subordination, but also on the means to transform their situation" (1996: 54).

3. For a satirical look at one woman's quest for "the feminist establishment" (and for a job therein) see Kamen (1996).
4. The feminist interest in sexuality and sexual pleasure certainly didn't begin in the 1960s. It has always been at the forefront of feminist inquiries. For a thorough look at sexuality in the post-war years, see Adams (1997).
5. The contemporary gay liberation movement emerged from the New Left as a unified force during this period (see Kinsman, 1996).
6. These discussions continued at the grassroots level. Mainstream feminists, the more visible, public "face" of the women's movement, switched their focus to more political, policy-based issues.
7. It should be noted that Valverde (1995), Kinsman (1996) and Ross (1995) have all illustrated that pro-sex feminism, gay/lesbian cultural formations, and the pursuit of sexual pleasure through "alternative" means have always existed in Canada, and they did not dissipate when the mainstream women's movement began to target violence and policy issues more actively in the mid-1970s. They just didn't get props.
8. See AGENDER (Carleton University) and Challenge the Assumptions! Both illustrate a concern articulated in the mid-1980s, expressed in McCooey (1986).

References

Adams, M.L. 1997. *The Trouble with Normal*. Toronto: University of Toronto Press.

Adamson, N., L. Briskin, and M. McPhail. 1988. *Feminist Organizing for Change*. Toronto: Oxford University Press.

Bellafante, G. 1998. "Feminism: It's All About Me!," *Time Magazine* 151(25), 29 June: 48–56.

BITCH: *Feminist Response to Pop Culture* www.bitch-magazine.com/mission.html.

Connell, R.W. 1997. "Sexual Revolution," in L. Segal, ed., *New Sexual Agendas*. New York: New York University Press.

Crittenden, D. 1999. *What Our Mothers Didn't Tell Us: Why Happiness Eludes the Modern Woman*. New York: Simon & Schuster.

Crosbie, L. 1993. *The Girl Wants To*. Toronto: Macfarlane, Walter and Ross.

delombard, j. 1995. "Femmenism," in R. Walker, ed., *To Be Real: Telling the Truth and Changing the Face of Feminism*, pp. 21–33. New York: Doubleday.

Denfeld, R. *The New Victorians: A Young Woman's Challenge to the Old Feminist Order.* New York: Warner Books.

Dennis, W. 1992. *Hot and Bothered*. Toronto: The Penguin Group.

Fillion, K. 1995. *Lip Service: The Truth about Women's Darker Side in Love, Sex, and Friendship*. Toronto: Harper Collins Publishers.

Finn, G. 1982. "Conclusion," in A. Miles and G. Finn, *Feminism in Canada*, pp. 299–306. Montreal: Black Rose Books.

Friedman, A. 1992. *Nothing Sacred: A Conversation with Feminism*. Canada: Oberon Press.

Greenglass, E.R. 1982. *A World of Difference: Gender Roles in Perspective*. Toronto: John Wiley and Sons.

Greer, G. 1999. *The Whole Woman*. London: Bantam-Dell-Doubleday.

Hamilton, R. 1996. *Gendering the Vertical Mosaic*. Toronto: Copp Clark Ltd.

Hurley, C. 1996. "Feminists Bashing Feminism: The Princess at the Window," *The New Brunswick Reader* 17.

Kamen, P. 1996. "Acquaintance Rape: Revolution and Reaction," in N.B. Maglin and D. Perry, eds., *"Bad Girls"/"Good Girls": Women, Sex & Power in the Nineties*, pp. 137–49. New Brunswick: Rutgers University.

Kamen, P. 1998. "Paradigm For Sale," in Might Magazine, ed., *Shiny Adidas Track Suits and the Death of Camp: The Best of Might Magazine*. New York: Boulevard Books.

Kinsman, G. 1996. *The Regulation of Desire: Homo and Hetero Sexualities*. Montreal: Black Rose Books.

Kostash, M. 1980. *Long Way from Home*. Toronto: James Lorimer and Co.

Kostash, M. 1996. "Dissing Feminist Sexuality," *Canadian Forum* (September 1996): 13–17.

LaFramboise, D. 1996. *The Princess at the Window: A New Gender Morality*. Toronto: Penguin Books.

LaFramboise, D. 1999. "Freedom, Baby," *The National Post*, 18 March: A18.
McCooey, S.J. 1986. "Help Yourself," *Herizons* 4(1): 39.
Parr, J. 1995. *A Diversity of Women*. Toronto: University of Toronto Press.
Pierson, R.R. 1993. "The Politics of the Body," in R.R. Pierson, M.G. Cohen, P. Bourne, and P. Masters, eds., *Canadian Women's Issues: Volume 1: Strong Voices, Twenty-five Years of Women's Activism in English Canada*, pp. 98–122. Toronto: James Lorimer & Company, Publishers.
Roiphe, K. 1993. *The Morning After: Sex, Fear and Feminism*. Boston: Little Brown & Company.
Ross, B. 1995. *The House That Jill Built*. Toronto: University of Toronto Press.
Segal, L. 1994. *Straight Sex: Rethinking the Politics of Pleasure*. Berkeley: University of California Press.
Shalit, W. 1999. *A Return to Modesty: Discovering the Lost Virtue*. Toronto: HarperCollins Canada.
Sommers, C.H. 1994. *Who Stole Feminism? How Women Have Betrayed Women*. New York: Simon & Schuster.
Tiefer, L. 1995. *Sex Is Not a Natural Act and Other Essays*. Boulder: Westview Press.
Timson, J. 1995. "Bimbo-Watch: Resistant to Feminism, She Just Won't Go Away," *Maclean's* 27: 52.
Traas, W. 1999. "Splitting Hairs: Creative Expression vs. Self-Normalization in Women's Hair Care." Diss. Brock University.
Tremblay, M. 1993. "Gender and Society: Rights and Realities," in D. Thomas, ed., *Canada and the United States: Differences That Count*. Peterborough: Broadview Press.
Valverde, M. 1984. "If Freud Were a Woman . . .," *Broadside* 5(6): 9.
Whelehan, I. 1995. *Modern Feminist Thought*. New York: New York University Press.
Wine, J.D., and J.L. Ristock. 1991. *Women and Social Change*. Toronto: James Lorimer and Company.

Chapter 40

Overview

Social movements don't take place in a vacuum. In Canada, activists and advocates for gender equality have at times benefited from being able to access the resources of the federal government to pursue transformative goals. However, any alliance with the state is unpredictable and fraught with potential peril, as Kathleen Rodgers and Melanie Knight demonstrate.

The authors show how changes in funding and policy priorities by the federal government effectively "knocked the wind out of" some of the most active and effective organizations advocating for women. When funding disappears, organizations and individuals must rebalance their priorities and retool their agendas or risk disappearing entirely. Some seek alliances with other social movements, some redesign their activities in order to appeal to potential private funders, or re-direct existing monies to the tasks of simply keeping the lights on, at the expense of transformative work.

Federal policies and priorities thus influence the growth of social movements, whether they enable or constrain that growth. Canadian gender activists continue to face dilemmas over the costs and benefits of their ties to the federal government.

"You Just Felt the Collective Wind Being Knocked Out of Us": The Deinstitutionalization of Feminism and the Survival of Women's Organizing in Canada

Kathleen Rodgers and Melanie Knight

> After all of the assaults we have suffered over the years with the chipping away at the funding and program mandates and all of that, this was like the axe in the chest . . . you just felt the collective wind being knocked out of us . . . it was a palpable feeling of defeat.[1]

Introduction

Consistent mobilization, protests, and lobbying efforts by the Canadian Women's Movement during the late twentieth century resulted in the creation of one of the most elaborate sets of government mechanisms for achieving gender equality in the world (Brodie and Bakker, 2007). These institutionalized relationships between the movement and the Canadian state began to unravel, however, in the mid-1980s, a trajectory punctuated by regular cuts to funding for women's organizations. Thus, in 2006, when Canada's ruling federal Conservative Party made a number of dramatic budgetary moves . . . their actions served to cement the decades-long erosion and delegitimization of the women's movement (Brodie, 2007). This . . . comprehensive assault on the movement and its accomplishments took the form of the dismantling of the institutional mechanisms that had financially supported the movement and provided a platform for movement demands. . . .

First we contextualize recent events by providing a brief historical overview of the movement and second, based on interviews with feminist activists across the country, we attempt to "take stock" of the contemporary movement, at the national level, in the wake of this ideological and fiscal decision-making. In particular, we examine how feminist organizations struggle to negotiate the pressures of diminished and inadequate funding and changing relations with the state. . . . We argue that the long-term erosion of funds to the women's movement has indeed eroded the national organization infrastructure of the movement that developed throughout the 1970s and 1980s and that this will have an impact on the ability of feminists to launch campaigns, gain attention, and, ultimately, protect existing gains. At the same time, however, we demonstrate that activists are reconceptualizing feminist activism in Canada, maintaining networks, and developing strategies that may allow the movement to survive until a new grievance crystallizes.

Data and Methods

. . . We conducted interviews with 30 representatives of national and provincial women's organizations across Canada, with the exception of Quebec.[2] Our criteria of inclusion were national and provincial women's organizations who conduct advocacy and service provision work. . . .

Canadian Feminism within Shifting National and International Contexts, 1970–2010

Within Canada, the feminist movement has been an important force for progressive social change for more than 40 years. The trajectory for this second wave of the women's movement was established in the early 1970s with the issuing of the report on the Royal Commission on the Status of Women. Indeed, as "the first success of second wave feminism" the Commission's report acted to outline shared grievances for the various ideological and political elements within the movement, provided a benchmark for establishing the equality of women in Canada and, with the creation of the Minister responsible for the Status of Women, ultimately established a platform for advancing women's concerns within the Canadian state (Black, 1992). At the outset, this trajectory appeared to indicate a promising future for Canadian feminism, as well as Canada's ideological commitment to human rights and equality, more generally. The relationship between second wave feminism and the Canadian state has not, however, remained conciliatory, and the Canadian state's commitment to advancing and protecting equality has not persisted, eroded by successive waves of fiscal and ideological attacks on the movement. . . .

Beginning in the 1980s . . . the prominent role of feminism within the Canadian state began to erode as it came under attack from a number of political and ideological forces. As Bashevkin (1996: 213) argues, while Canadian feminism appeared to have great influence at the outset of the 1980s, the election of Brian Mulroney in 1984 "set the stage for increasingly polarized ties between parliamentary actors and extra-parliamentary feminism." Indeed, as the wave of neoliberalism that began to sweep the world in the 1980s hit Canada, the process of "downsizing the state and its administration after 40 years of state expansion" began (Clark, 2002: 782). Brodie and Bakker (2007: 34) argue that the progressive "delegitimization" of the women's movement coincided with the "ascendancy of *neo-liberal governing practices*" (emphasis added). Figure 40.1[3] demonstrates that as part of this project, funding to feminist organizations through the Women's Program (Bashevkin, 1994; Briskin and Eliasson, 1999). Additional hallmarks of neoliberal reforms also began to shape the grant process: a shift away from long-term core funding to contract funding, greater focus on measurable outcomes and most recently, market competition was established in the functioning of SWC as for-profit organizations became eligible to apply for the funds.

It would be wrong to suggest that ideologies of fiscal restraint manifest in these cuts were the sole factor shaping state responses to Canadian feminists. It was in the 1980s that not only fiscal cuts were implemented but ideological decisions also began to redirect the Women's Program. For instance, Bergqvist and Findlay (1999) describe how directors of the Women's Program were

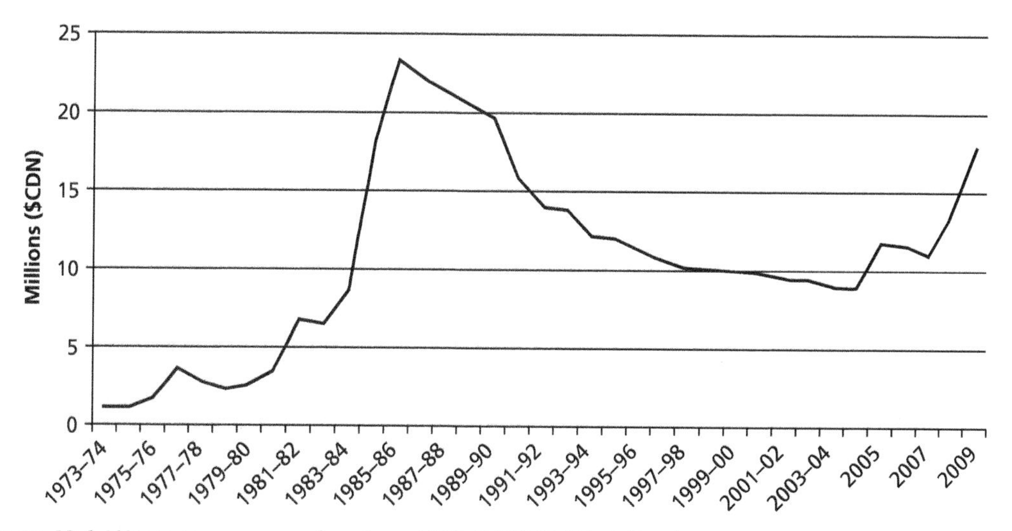

Figure 40.1 Women's program funding, 1973–2009 (2010 dollars)

instructed to exclude lesbian projects and those related to abortion reform. Indeed, the decision to reform the Women's Program in the 1980s, was also influenced by the neoconservative ideology characteristic of Ronald Reagan and Margaret Thatcher in the 1980s (Bashevkin, 1994), but also active in Canada via a number of virulent and influential conservative countermovements (Erwin, 1988; Steuter, 1992). In particular, two interconnected countermovements, the pro-family and anti-abortion movements have made ongoing attempts to undermine many feminist concerns. Limiting sex education, opposing policies ensuring universal childcare and pay equity, undermining Canadian abortion law (as well as opposing the liberalization of laws surrounding homosexuality) have been central elements in their agenda (Erwin, 1988; Steuter, 1992).

Moreover, the lobbying efforts of these conservative movements have successfully made inroads into shaping the Canadian approach to equality. Erin Steuter (1992) argues that during the 1980s, the pro-family organization REAL (Realistic, Active and for Life) Women that formed in 1983, had a particularly influential role in shaping the policies of the Conservative Party of Canada and their erosion of the capacities of the Women's Program. She provides the example of the creation of the child care tax credit, "a policy REAL had been pressing" (Steuter, 1992: 300). Moreover, it was at this point that REAL Women really began to challenge the Women's Programme, successfully demanding that the eligibility rules of the program be changed to allow for the funding of groups that promoted traditional roles for women (Dobrowolosky and Jenson 2004: 164–6). . . .

An important qualification to the assertion that Canada's domestic women's movement has been in steady decline . . . is the observation that . . . in an era of globalization, women's activism has shifted "upward" to focus on "new forms of cooperation among women" (Gabriel and MacDonald, 1994: 535.) In Canada, this trend was particularly notable in the wake of transnational mobilization against the North American Free Trade Agreement (NAFTA) as women's organizations in Canada, Mexico, and the United States protested against what they saw as the specific effects of the trade agreement on women. To capture this increasing interaction between women's groups from different countries, scholars refer to the idea of "transnational feminist networks" (TFNs). As Valentine Moghadam (2005) explains, one example of the outcomes of the creation of such networks among women's organizations is the 2000 World March of Women which was launched in Quebec but which was a coordinated global campaign against the poverty and violence experienced by women. But as Moghadam notes, feminists working in TFNs and on issues of a transnational nature face the same funding constraints faced by domestic organizations. Indeed, fiscal constraints on domestically oriented Canadian organizations undermine the ability of Canadian feminists to contribute to global feminist campaigns. . . .

Institutionalization, State Funding and Social Movement Communities

Research on social movements has long demonstrated the centrality of financial security to an organizational infrastructure and therefore. social movement growth, stability, and success. . . .

Thus, one of the keys to the development of such organizations and the positive functions that they provide is the availability of resources and the ability to acquire them. Movement organizations are often able to do so as their demands become "institutionalized," in the form of stable government structures, practices, and relationships. In Canada, the institutionalization of feminism that followed the Royal Commission on the Status of Women generated . . . funds to organizations that would encourage the flourishing of feminist ideas both inside and outside of the government. [Some] scholars view foundation support for social insurgents as a means of "channeling" or "moderating" the radical elements of movements. This occurs as activists meet the professional and administrative demands of foundations in order to obtain funding (Jenkins, 1998). Such a dynamic, may have the effect of diffusing dissent in favour of more traditional forms of organizing and political engagement that meet the approval of funding bodies. In the case of Canadian feminism, the movement remained composed of a diverse spectrum of organizations in the wake of institutionalization.

However, dependence on federal funding did become a major thread of concern within the movement Thus, state funding, when it becomes available, is an attractive avenue for activists as it may, for a time, become a dependable flow of revenue, more stable and more easily obtained than fees or donations (Staggenborg, 1988, Gamson, 1990; Clement, 2007) but the ease of obtaining these funds represses attempts to develop alternative funding-raising efforts and may privilege some forms of political work over others. . . .

For instance, the National Action Committee on the Status of Women (NAC), once a coalition of over 700 organizations at its height, struggled with internal concerns that it was dependent on state funding. Choosing to resist a move to alternative sources of funding, NAC's resources declined when government funding began to drop in the 1980s. As one of our respondents observed about the dependency of women's groups on government funding in Canada,

> We became complacent and have this sense of entitlement around government funding . . . if you look at other parts of the world, it is quite a unique position we have been in over these years. And so I think we need to be innovative and think about other ways to fund this work and not let that be the determining factor about whether we fail or succeed.

Importantly, social movement scholars have also argued that an over-reliance on elite funding sources detracts movement organizers from mobilizing resources from *within* the movement's adherents (Minkoff, 2002). And while elite sources may be easier to obtain and facilitate the formalization and professionalization of organizations, the absence of grassroots funding places movements at risk of becoming disconnected from their mass base, the foundation of their legitimacy and protest capacity, and from mounting ongoing protests. . . .

Findings

In our exploration of he more long-term retraction of state funding on women's organizing in Canada, three broad themes have emerged. In the first section we discuss the direct impact of funding cuts on the organizational capacities of advocacy and research organizations, and in the second, we examine some of the strategies activists use to negotiate the new environment. In the process, we examine not only the impact of the funding cuts themselves but also some of the additional dynamics reshaping the movement. Because we are sensitive to the idea that formal organizations are not the only repositories for movement ideas, we then explore the role of the broader social movement community in responding to the current political and economic context.

Shifting Organizational Capacities: Advocacy, Research, and Services-based Organizations in Flux

The literature . . . highlights three interrelated observations: first, that stable organizations are key to activists' ability to mobilize constituents, to launch ongoing campaigns, and to garner media attention. Second, the existence of stable sources of funding is crucial to the ongoing maintenance of such organizations. And finally, despite the centrality of this funding to such organizations, there are many risks for movements and organizations that rely on official sources of funding. . . .

However, because of the relative ease of securing these monies, funding opportunities for women's organizations have been readily accepted, . . . making government funding an important dynamic of the women's movement in Canada.[4] The removal of this funding raises questions about the ongoing stability of the organizational infrastructure of the movement. Given the importance of organizational stability to movements' capacity to engage in contentious behaviour, this brings into question the ability of the movement to mobilize constituents, shape policy, mount protests, garner media attention, to engage in transnational activism, and otherwise advance women's equality concerns.

... [I]n the two rounds of funding decisions following the mandate changes, funding was not continued for at least 30 organizations, several of whom are longstanding feminist organizations in Canada.[5] National and provincial-level advocacy and research organizations such as Women's Future Fund, Canadian Research Institute for the Advancement of Women, the Legal Education and Action Fund, the National Organization of Women and the Law, New Brunswick Pay Equity Coalition, the Alberta Network of Immigrant Women, and the Centre for Equality Rights in Accommodation, are all organizations founded in the 1970s or '80s, that have been prominent voices in provincial and federal policy processes. Interviews with representatives from some of these organizations have confirmed that the loss of these funds has resulted in the dramatic decline of their capacity to conduct their work. . . .

Although number-counting appears relevant to this issue, it also draws attention away from the magnitude of these cuts on the broader organizational infrastructure and capacity of the movement. . . . [T]he closure or reduced capacity of many longstanding women's organizations has resulted in a lack of basic technological and human infrastructure for advancing their agenda. Basic necessities such as fax, phone, computers, or photocopiers are fundamental tools for activist organizations, as are the expertise of staff members in conducting research, crafting grant proposals, and engaging with authorities and the media.

For some of those organizations that remain, they do so in name only. Indeed, a number of organizations that had previously had large offices with several staff members were now reduced to a single individual working in temporary, borrowed spaces or from their homes. The National Association of Women and the Law (NAWL), provides an apt example of the trend. Once an organization sustained by membership fees, grants from Status of Women, the Ministry of Justice, and the Court Challenges Program, it had at one time a central office in Ottawa with fulltime staff including an executive director and a director of reform. At its height NAWL was the main feminist voice on legal reform, active on landmark cases involving the rights of Aboriginal women, incarcerated women, and immigrant women. Like other organizations having lost stable government funding, by 2010 it was reduced to one staff member working from her home. Throughout the 1980s and 1990s the women's movement in Canada developed organizations, such as NAWL, with specialized capacities for engaging in social change at a national level. As other like NAWL have closed, respondents expressed their concern that the movement is losing human capital—research and writing skills, organizational memory, media savvy—as women of a feminist orientation have left women's organizations to find gainful employment elsewhere. The greater concern associated with this trend was that this outward transfer of skills is leading to a leadership vacuum and a lack of intergenerational transfer to a subsequent wave of feminist activists. Leading to de-professionalization, the departure of paid feminists has therefore, renewed the importance of the role of volunteers within organizations.

The declining professional capacity of individual organizations such as NAWL has meant that the specialized functions played by these organizations have been diminished. Pamela Cross of NAWL reflects on the far-reaching impact of this decline:

> We have tried to maintain some amount of visibility . . . because we hear from women's organizations across the country that there is a huge gap that has been created by the loss of NAWL as a functioning organization. Many, many women's organizations that themselves didn't have the capacity to do this kind of legal research and writing relied heavily on NAWL to produce material that they then used in their work. And no one is producing that material now.

In this way, the reduced professional capacity of singular organizations also has more far reaching implications in terms of the representation of the concerns of the movement in judicial, policy, and political processes. One key theme related to this, cited by several of our interviewees has been the lack of up-to-date research available on issues related to women's equality. For example, one respondent explained that in her attempts to give a presentation to a parliamentary standing committee on the subject of women in nontraditional occupations, the only data she was able to obtain was out of date, impeding her ability to make an effective case on behalf of women in an under-represented occupation.[6] . . .

There are also many locally based or service-based organizations that have alternative sources of funding or were not completely funded by Status of Women, and have not therefore been as badly damaged by the loss of funding. These organizations are impacted by the "trickledown" effects of these changes to the organizational infrastructure of the movement. In a number of instances [participants] stated that because of the absence or diminished capacity of these organizations, when they needed research on particular subject, this was not available (research on violence and aboriginal women were both provided as examples). In this sense, the erosion of some key organizations sets off a series of domino-like effects that leave local, regional, provincial, and other national-level organizations without the basic tools they need to engage in their own advocacy work. . . . Moreover, the national level organizations developed the specialized role of advocating in national and international arenas; in the absence of the organizations, the local and regional groups lacked the capacity to take over this role, leaving local organizations "dangling" without a prominent voice in Ottawa.

The reduced capacity of the women's movement to carry out the most mundane daily demands of professionalized social change work also has important implications for mobilizing adherents to the movement Many participants we spoke with mentioned not being able to produce and distribute materials to members and supporters, not being able to maintain a website or lacking the capacity to respond to calls from journalists. . . .

One measure of a movement's ability to engage in such mobilization and of its effectiveness more broadly is its ability to garner ongoing media attention. The role of well-funded movement organizations in attracting media attention is well-established (Hackett and Carroll, 2004) because of the role that they play in orchestrating protest events and in developing well-coordinated media tactics. We therefore investigated media coverage of the women's movement in Canada's main national newspaper, the *Globe and Mail.* Using data from the *Globe and Mail,* this graph shows coverage of the "National Action Committee on the Status of Women," the most prominent national women's organization during the period under investigation and "women's groups"[7] between 1977 and 2010.[8] Accordingly, Figure 40.2 reveals significant coverage of NAC and "women's groups" in the 1980s and early 1990s, but as the main national voice of feminism fell away so too did the broader movement's capacity to attract interest from the main national newspaper.

The graph supports two complimentary hypotheses. First, it signals the real decline in protest events, reflecting the fact that as movements become institutionalized, the inclination of activists toward protest becomes diminished. Second, the

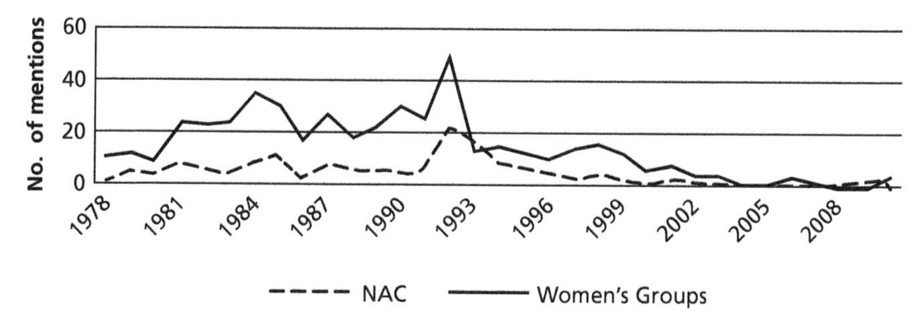

Figure 40.2 Media coverage of the Women's Movement, *Globe and Mail*, 1978–2010

graph also reflects the fact that as the organizational capacity of a movement declines so too does its capacity to garner media attention, in part as a result of a decreased capacity to coordinate protest.

The women's movement in Canada has had a historically troublesome relationship with the mass media as journalists have chosen to focus on conflict within feminist organizations and on the personal details of the lives of individual leaders, marginalizing feminist issues and delegitimizing the movement among the public (Black, 1992; Goddu, 1999; Dobrowolosky, 2008). But, in the case of the Canadian Women's Movement, the loss of NAC in the 1990s also created a national leadership void, an observation that one respondent reflected on: "NAC nurtured a certain kind of feminist or strong woman leadership and what's fostering that now? I don't know that there is anything that's fostering that now."[9] Thus, while the movement had already suffered from negative media framing, the loss of this organizational infrastructure meant that the movement lacked the resources to successfully "re-frame" feminism in Canada.

Agency and Resistance: Strategies for Survival

Although the above section suggests an important decline in the capacity of women's organizations and their ability to influence policy and attract media attention, our respondents also outlined strategies for adaptation and survival; while some organizations have disappeared and others have declined, others have managed to survive by transforming the purpose of their organizations, re-connecting to their mass base, and/or going online. Laurie and Bondi (2005: 5) have argued that in situations where activists have experienced fiscal and ideological constraints, they are nonetheless able to find ways to subvert the constraints, "re-thinking the parameters of political agency." We have similarly found that women's organizations began to see the proverbial "writing on the wall" and very often transformed themselves in such a way as to continue their research and advocacy work under another guise.

A prominent strategy adopted by feminist activists hit hard by cuts to funding was to develop a service-orientation that would allow them to compete for project-based, outcome focused and market funding while maintaining the basic functions or principles of the organization. One of our respondents described how, when no longer able to secure SWC funding for her antiviolence education initiative, using the networks she had developed in her advocacy work, her organization took on the role of providing research for a provincial government. The funds that came from this service-provision provided her with the means to maintain the operations of her antiviolence work.[10]

In a slightly different kind of transformation, following the closure of the women's advocacy organization she led, long-time feminist activist Shari Graydon developed an organization called *Media Action* and a sister organization called Informed Opinions.[11] Together the two organizations conduct media analysis and provide training workshops, keynote presentations, and editing support to "experts in making their ideas and knowledge more accessible to print, broadcast, and online information media."[12] In this way, the organization is not explicitly an advocacy or research organization but remains committed to feminist principles:

> Our goals are to bridge the gender gap in public commentary and enhance the quality of public discourse by expanding the diversity of perspectives that inform Canada's policies and priorities in all realms—from finance, health and education to technology, business and the environment.[13]

But while some organizations closed or adopted service-provision as a means of supporting their work, the leaders of other organizations chose to re-connect to their mass-base of constituents in order to re-create the organization. The Legal Education and Action Fund (LEAF) is a good example of an organization which, when it lost the majority of its government funding in the late 1990s, was forced to downsize significantly. In response, the new leadership of the organization chose to renew organizational operations by using elite fundraising techniques, soliciting funds from individuals, and growing its membership base.

Now at over 5000 members, LEAF boasts a budget larger than when it originally lost funding.

And still other organizations re-organized to find space within receptive institutions. Canadian Research Institute for the Advancement of Women, for instance, is a well-respected research institute that formed in 1975 and had long held Status of Women funding with the goal of promoting feminist research on issues pertaining to federal government policy. CRIAW lost core funding in 1990 but continued to attract project funding until 2006 when, based on its status as a research organization, it was no longer eligible. In 2010, CRIAW reaffirmed its role as an important research institute when it carved out a new space within the University of Ottawa, having been awarded a major research grant from the Social Sciences and Humanities Research Council (SSHRC).

In some cases financial pressures forced the closure of physical offices and women's organizations such as DAWN: the Disabled Women's Activist Network, survived following the loss of their SWC funding in the 1990s but only in as much as they are now active entirely online. But while this sampling of strategies suggests that activists are able to "carve out" space within the new financial constraints, each scenario presents new considerations for movements. In the case of Internet activism, for instance, Nimijean and Rankin (2008) caution that women's movements "face barriers that transcend" internet activism. Or, for organizations that adopt a service oriented approach, this may allow them to maintain viability but it also limits their education, advocacy, and other activist activities.

Moving beyond Movement and Organizational Boundaries: Movement Survival in Coalitions and the Social Movement Community

While the social movement literature has documented the importance of stable organizations in ensuring the capacity of movements to mobilize constituents, engage in protest, and to attract media attention, we also point to the idea that movement activity exists beyond organizational boundaries, both in terms of coalitions and "social movement communities." . . . In the case of the women's movement, the "social movement community" refers to women's activist organizations but also to women's centres, unions, shelters, women's studies departments, women's caucuses, and others which support the goal of the advancement of women's equality.

Our respondents identified numerous ways in which the broader social movement community has supported the work of women's advocacy following the decline in federal funding. Perhaps the most notable contribution has been financial and in-kind support from ideologically aligned organizations. As women's organizations have struggled with the day-to-day realities of the loss of staff, office space and the accompanying practical necessities for carrying out business, member-funded organizations (both women's organizations and otherwise) that have been less reliant on state funding have stepped in to provide sizeable donations and in-kind support Canadian labor unions, in particular, including the Communication, Energy and Paper Workers Union of Canada (CEP) and the Canadian Labour Congress (CLC) have provided large amounts of money to maintain several organizations and have also provided in-kind support, such as office-space, the use of a staff member or photocopying equipment.[14] In this sense, while unions have long been supporters of feminist organizations, the decline of state funding has served to "activate" networks within the movement community, causing the director of the women's caucus in one union to observe that they were now working with women's groups to an extent that she "never would have anticipated."[15]

The most recent round of cuts was aimed directly at the advocacy and research organizations that have played a historically central role in the movement. But . . . service structures had long been important mobilizing centres for the movement. As the most recent attack took place, new political importance was placed on rape crisis centers and shelters. That this occurred is not entirely surprising; Dookie (2004) reports that while in 1975 there was a meager 18 emergency women's shelters in Canada, by 2000 there were 508. Consequently, throughout the 1990s, such locales became the organizational basis for mobilizing constituents on feminist issues. "Take Back the Night" marches, for instance, which are meant to demonstrate solidarity against violence against women are organized primarily out of rape crisis centres and have been important events for maintaining a sense of pan-Canadian feminist activism. Indeed, long-time feminist activist Lee Lakeman explained that although there was very much a shift toward service-based organizations, these structures had "acted as repositories of feminist ideas" and a mobilizing base for collective action when other core organizations came under attack. Women's shelters, she explained were not only politicized spaces but, when other organizations had begun to close their offices, shelters, women's centres, and rape crisis centers also became the physical meeting places for mobilizing responses.

Adding to the complexity of this picture, while service-based organizations had indeed taken on this central role as advocacy organizations faltered, transformations to the service-based structures themselves had also begun to take place beginning in the 1980s (Bonisteel and Green, 2005; O'Connor, 2005). By the end of the 1990s, Joyce Hancock explained, even though the organizational base of the women's movement in Canada "had become very much a service oriented structure," a process of co-optation was affecting these structures to the point that with their growing acceptance of government funding, "we weren't setting our own agenda." As part of this trend, government expectations of professionalization were altering the nature of shelters. Government-funded shelters were expected to hire "professional, not activist, leadership," she explained, forcing many shelters to "leave behind feminist-inspired organizational structures and principles in favour of structures and mandates that met with the expectations of bureaucratic criteria." . . .

Formal coalition-work has been the other means by which activists have responded to the attacks on the movement and have managed to remain active. As a reflection of their concern about the 2006 funding cuts, there was an initial series of angry protests across the country when the cuts and changes were originally announced.[16] These outbursts were generally short-lived and limited to the immediate fallout. The widespread anger that emerged in response to the original cuts and changes in 2006 did, however, result in the creation of some broad-based coalitions. The Ad Hoc Coalition for Women's Equality and Human Rights that formed specifically in reaction to changes to SWC is the most prominent example. More recently, organizations from a broad spectrum of social justice fields, including human rights, humanitarian, and women's groups, known as "Voices" have formed to organize to create a broad based pro-democracy movement garnering support from more than 180 social justice organizations across the country. . . .

In this sense, the government decision-making has served to mobilize, echoing Brodie's contention that this neoliberal ideology can serve as a "call to arms." However, in the case of the women's organizations, their reduced capacity has also affected the strength of these coalitions and their potential to engage in meaningful campaigns. One respondent observed that "people told me at meetings of the [Ad Hoc] coalition that they would like to attend the meetings but they did not have the capacity . . . "[17] Similarly, another commented that "When you can't mobilize your community to go to Ottawa and present information, that's a huge issue. We have the information, it's well researched, the recommendations are valid and when you can't do that it cuts you off at the knees and so you can't create change."[18]

Thus, while the renewed alliances above have kept several national organizations viable, these dynamics also presented new considerations for some activists; the representatives of several women's organizations that had accepted financial and in-kind support from unions and other organizations feared that this would simply result in another kind of cooptation, changing the agenda of organizations that had no choice but to accept the support. One respondent, for instance made this observation:

> We would not want to be operating forever with our sole source of funding being union any more than we would ideally want our sole source of funding to be the government. No matter how much you support unions, unions like any other entity have their own agenda. And I think there is a problem if all of our work is union funded because does it make us then susceptible to be swayed in a particular direction or focus on a particular area of research. Perhaps more importantly, would that become the public perception.[19]. . .

Conclusion

While recognizing the ideological underpinnings of recent federal policy changes, the goal of this paper has been to investigate the effects of dominant fiscal currents on women's organizing in Canada. The response of women's organizations and other ideologically aligned organizations to this new context highlights the ability of women's organizations to adapt by coalition building and by carving out spaces for survival. . . .

While national women's organizations are in decline, they have been adapting to an increasingly repressive political and economic context. This echoes the findings of scholars using the concept of social movement community to demonstrate that even where movements become less visibly active, movements rarely fade away completely. In *Whatever Happened to the Women's Movement*, Staggenborg and Taylor (2005) address this precise question in the American context. They make the argument that the ideas of the women's movement remain present and relevant within institutions such as political parties, related movements, women's studies departments, and unions even where its visibility has declined. Moreover, other scholars have suggested that in this global era, activism and the nation state are being decoupled, shifting activism to the transnational level.

But neither of these conclusions is very comforting for advocates of women's rights in Canada. Because, while many Canadian feminists have certainly shifted their focus to more transnational issues, the domestic nation state is still central to political outcomes and as such, Canadian activists remain constrained by fiscal constraints at home.

Moreover, despite the reality stated by many activists that while Canadian women have "come a long way," issues such as the wage gap, pay equity, child care, support for antiviolence initiatives, support for immigrant and visible minority women are still outstanding and require intervention at the federal level.

Finally, the movement also faces systematic attempts to dismantle the gains that have been made. For instance, in addition to the cuts to funding discussed in this paper, recent media attention has been focused on the fact that the terms "gender" and "gender-based violence" have been quietly removed from Canadian foreign policy documents.[20] The absence of a strong organizational base may restrict the possibilities for responding to such attacks. Our findings suggest that while feminism has lost a great deal of direct influence within Canadian decision-making processes, it is also undergoing a period of adaptation. What is clear is that the kind of pan-Canadian movement supported by federal funds that characterized the 1970s and '80s is a historical artifact. The subsequent decade will indicate the shape that women's organizing will take in light of these ongoing battles.

Notes

1. Participant No. 6, April 9, 2010.
2. At this point in time, women's organizations in Quebec will not be interviewed as provincial and federal funding guidelines will most likely differ from the rest of Canada and will be beyond the scope of this preliminary study. A comparative analysis with a scholar conducting work in Quebec is currently underway.
3. Note that although the graph shows an increase in funds in 2007, this accompanied a dramatic shift in the eligibility requirements for the grants. The funds were now available to a much wider pool of candidates (for-profit

organizations, most notably) and the research and advocacy organizations that were central to the women's movement were now disallowed from applying.
4. NAC discussed this precise issue in the early 1990s. Some within the organization wanted to move away from government funds while others resisted this change (Rebick, 2005).
5. This information was obtained from the Ad-Hoc Coalition on Equality.
6. Participant No. 11.
7. We determined that the *Globe and Mail* rarely used the terms "women's movement," "feminism, or "feminist movement" to refer to organized feminism. The term "women's groups" was almost invariably used to refer to the collective actions of feminist or women's organizations. We also investigated coverage of several other feminist organizations, past and present. The coverage was negligible.
8. This graph does not evaluate the nature of the coverage of the groups. For such an analysis consult Freeman (2001).
9. Participant No. 16.
10. Participant No. 2.
11. Media Action was formerly called Media Watch.
12. Website www.informedopinions.org/?q=node/2 November 15, 2010.
13. Website www.informedopinions.org/?q=node/2 November 15, 2010.
14. A representative from the CEP, for example, estimated that when in-kind services were included, they diverted approximately 100,000 to women's groups (Participant 5).
15. Participant No. 11.
16. Cf. "Women rally across Canada to protest Tory cuts," *CBC News online*. December 8, 2006; "That was then . . . this is now," *Ottawa Citizen* January 28, 2007; "Women set up "hotline' to PMO over Status of Women," *Ottawa Citizen*, December 7, 2006.
17. Participant No. 11.
18. Participant No. 10.
19. Participant No. 4.
20. See Michelle Collins, "Gender Equality, Child Soldiers and Humanitarian law are Axed from Foreign Policy language," The *Embassy Magazine*, 29 July 2009.

References

Bashevkin, S. 1994. "Confronting Neo-conservatism: Anglo-American Women's Movements under Thatcher, Reagan and Mulroney," *International Political Science Review* 15: 275.

Bashevkin, S. 1996. "Losing Common Ground: Feminists, Conservatives and Public Policy in Canada during the Mulroney Years," *Canadian Journal of Political Science* 29(2): 211–42.

Bergqvist, C., and S. Findlay. 1999. "Representing Women's Interests in the Policy Process: Women's Organizing and State Initiatives in Sweden and Canada, 1960s–1990s," in L. Briskin and M. Eliasson, eds., *Women's Organizing and Public Policy in Canada and Sweden*, pp. 119–46. Montreal and Kingston: McGill-Queen's University Press.

Black, N. 1992. "Ripples in the Second Wave," in C. Backhouse and D. Flaherty, eds., *Comparing the Contemporary Women's Movement in Canada and the United States in Challenging Times: The Women's Movement in Canada and the United States.* Montreal: McGill-Queen's Press.

Bonisteel, M., and L. Green. 2005. *Implications of the Shrinking Space for Feminist Anti-violence Advocacy. Accessed July, 2011, from Paper presented at the 2005 Canadian Social Welfare Policy Conference*, Fredericton, New Brunswick. www.awcca.GJ/pdf/ShrinkingFeministSpace.pdf

Briskin, L., and M. Eliasson. 1999. *Women's Organizing and Public Policy in Canada and Sweden.* Montreal: McGill-Queens Press.

Brodie, J. 2007. "We Are All Equal Now: Contemporary Gender Politics in Canada," *Feminist Theory* 9(2).

Brodie, J., and I. Bakker. 2007. *Canada's Social Policy Regime and Women: An Assessment of the Last Decade.* Ottawa: Status of Women Canada. www.swccfc.gc.ca/pubs/pubspr/0662450870/200703_9780662450870_1_e.html

Clark, D. 2002. "Neoliberalism and Public Service Reform: Canada in Comparative Perspective," *Canadian Journal of Politcal Science* 35: 771–93.

Clement, D. 2007. *Canada's Rights Revolution: Social Movements and Social Change, 1937–1982.* Vancouver: UBC Press.

Dobrowolosky, A. 2008. "The Women's Movement in Flux: Feminism and Framing, Passion and Politics," in M. Smith, ed., *Group Politics and Social*

Movements in Canada, pp. 159–80. Peterborough: Broadview Press.

Dobrowolosky, A., and J. Jenson. 2004. "Shifting Representations of Citizenship," *Canadian Politics of Women and Children in Social Politics* (2): 11.

Dookie, I.J. 2004. "Canada," in K. Malley-Morrison, ed., *International Perspectives on Family Violence and Abuse*, pp. 431–49. Malwah, NJ: Erlbaum.

Erwin, L. 1988. "What Feminists Should Know about the Pro-family Movement in Canada: A Report on a Recent Survey of Rank-and-file Members," in P. Tancred-Sheriff, ed., *Feminist Research: Prospect and Retrospect*. Montreal: McGill-Queen's University Press.

Freeman, B. 2001. *The Satellite Sex: The Media and Women's Issues in English Canada 1966–1971*. Waterloo, ON: Wilfrid Laurier University.

Gabriel, C., and L. MacDonald. 1994. "NAFTA, Women and Organising in Canada and Mexico: Forging a 'Feminist Internationality,'" *Journal of International Studies* 23(3): 535–82.

Gamson, W. 1990. *The Strategy of Social Protest*. Homewood, IL: Dorsey Press.

Goddu, J. 1999. "'Powerless, Public-spirited Women,' 'Angry Feminists,' and 'the Muffin Lobby': Newspaper and Magazine Coverage of the Canadian Advisory Council on the Status of Women, the National Action Committee on the Status of Women, and REAL Women of Canada," *Canadian Journal of Communication* 24(1).

Hackett, R.A., and W.K. Carroll. 2004. "Critical Social Movements and Media Reform," *Media Development* XLXI(1): 14–19.

Jenkins, J.C. 1998. "Channeling Social Protest: Foundation Patronage of Contemporary Social Movements," in W.W. Powell and E.S. Clemens, eds., *Private Action and the Public Good*. New Haven, CT: Yale University Press.

Laurie, N., and L. Bondi. 2005. "Introduction," in N. Laurie and L. Bondi, eds., *Working the Spaces of Neoliberallsm: Activism, Professionalisation and Incorporation*. Oxford: Blackwell Publishing.

Minkoff, D. 2002. "Walking a Political Tightrope: Responsiveness and Internal Accountability in Social Movement Organizations," *Nonprofit Advocacy and the Policy Process*. Washington, DC: The Urban Institute.

Moghadam, V.M. 2005. *Globalizing Women: Transnational Feminist Networks*. Baltimore: The Johns Hopkins University Press.

Nimijean, R., and P. Rankin. 2008. "Can Movements 'Move' Online? Online Activism, Canadian Women's Movements and the Case of PAR-L," in M. Hammond Callaghan and M. Hayday, eds., *Mobilizations and Engagements: Social Movements in Canada*. Fernwood: Black Point.

O'Connor, J. 2005. "Rape Crisis: The Debate over Professionalised Services," *Herizons* 28–29.

Rebick, J. 2005. *Ten Thousand Roses: The Making of a Feminist Revolution*. Toronto: Penguin Canada.

Staggenborg, S. 1988. "The Consequences of Professionalization and Formalization in the Prochoice Movement," *American Sociological Review* 53: 585–606.

Staggenborg, S., and V. Taylor. 2005. "Whatever Happened to the Women's Movement?," *Mobilization: International Journal of Theory and Research About Social Movements and Collective Behavior* 10: 37–52.

Steuter, E. 1992. "Women against Feminism: An Examination of Feminist Social Movements and Anti-feminist Countermovements," *The Canadian Review of Sociology and Anthropology* 29(3).

Chapter 41

Overview

What does it mean to be an "ally" in the fight to end violence against women? Across the world, activist organizations grapple with this question as they work to engage men in the project of gender transformation. Such activist work is complex and sensitive, because antiviolence programming often calls into question the very bases of hegemonic masculinity, particularly its grounding in ideas about power and control. Male activists have to do nothing less than create alternative ways of being a man and bring into being new visions of masculinity in which violence against women is abhorrent and dishonourable. Such visions are not always welcomed, so men's antiviolence organizations often find themselves working to allay defensiveness and suspicion on the part of men they are seeking to engage.

This activist work also involves building coalitions with feminist organizations and women's groups who are engaged in the same struggles. Increasingly, consideration of intersectionality, and the ways in which ideas about masculinity are inflected by class, ethnicity, and cultural background, is paramount. In order to be effective, this form of gendered activism cannot take a "one size fits all" approach to analyzing and transforming gender. Attention to local contexts, local challenges, and local synergies is key to effective antiviolence work for men.

Context, Challenges, and Tensions in Global Efforts to Engage Men in the Prevention of Violence against Women: An Ecological Analysis

Erin A. Casey[1], Juliana Carlson[2], Cathlyn Fraguela-Rios[3], Ericka Kimball[4], Tova B. Neugut[5], Richard M. Tolman[5], and Jeffrey L. Edleson[6]

Global efforts to prevent and end gender-based violence increasingly include the proactive engagement of men and boys. Across a myriad of programs and approaches, this involvement typically entails engaging men in educational opportunities, fostering their awareness of violence against women, and nurturing their ability to cultivate nonviolence and gender equity in their families, peer groups, communities, and at broader societal and policy levels (Flood, 2011b). Consensus is emerging across practitioners, scholars, and policy makers that ending gender-based violence requires full community participation—and particularly the increased participation of men (Flood, 2005; World Health Organization [WHO] 2007).

While increasingly perceived as a vital element of ending violence, the process of engaging men in antiviolence work is fraught with complexities. As an "ally" movement (a conceptualization we employ in this article), engaging men involves mobilizing a socially privileged group to work toward dismantling a problem largely perpetuated from within its own ranks (Black et al., 2011). This carries fundamental tensions around engaging men in ways that do not reinforce or re-create gendered power inequities (Casey, 2010; Edwards, 2006) or that result in supplanting women's voices and leadership in antiviolence movements (Atherton-Zemon, 2009) while still attracting and sustaining male participation. Some of these tensions, particularly those involved in reaching out to and engaging *individual* men as antiviolence allies, are beginning to be described in existing literature (e.g., Casey, 2010; Funk, 2008). Less articulated are barriers to men's engagement that emerge at broader organizational and community levels, or the ways that these challenges vary regionally as men's antiviolence groups become a central part of global gender-based violence prevention efforts. Ultimately, the broad participation of men in reducing gender-based violence requires a strategic examination and negotiation of these inherent complexities, both to more successfully engage individual men and to enhance the sustainability and effectiveness of men's antiviolence efforts over time. The purpose of this article is, therefore, to present findings from a study of organizations around the world that work to engage men in gender-based violence prevention and to describe the multilevel challenges and dilemmas they encounter in these efforts.

Defining Men's Antiviolence Engagement

. . . Globally, many men's engagement programs are also informed by a pro-feminist analysis (Carlson et al., in press). This perspective ties gender-based violence to social, economic, and political inequities based on gender as well as to socially constructed notions of masculinity that link manhood to dominance and control (see e.g., Murnen, Wright, and Kaluzny, 2002). In feminist-informed programs, critically examining traditional assumptions about gender and particularly masculinity constitutes a central component of discussions with men regarding dismantling violence. In a global review of evaluated gender equity promotion programs, the WHO (2007) concluded that programs with the strongest impacts on men's behaviour and beliefs were those that explicitly addressed gender and masculinity-related norms. Simultaneously, critically exploring traditional masculinity and its associated privileges generates one of the fundamental tensions inherent in engaging men in antiviolence work—inviting men to reimagine closely held beliefs about their own gender means examining and perhaps working to shed the privileges that accrue to them based on gender.

Engaging Men in Violence Prevention: Challenges and Complexities

Linked to the fundamental gender-related tension identified above, an emerging literature identifies several complexities related to engaging individual men in gender-based violence prevention. For example, men may perceive gender-based violence prevention efforts as inherently antagonistic toward and blaming of men (Casey, 2010; see for review, Flood, 2011a), and may view gender-based violence as a "women's issue" with no relevance to their own lives (Crooks et al., 2007), or may perceive violence prevention to be associated with a feminist agenda with which they are uncomfortable or disagree (Casey, 2010). On the other hand, evidence suggests that many men see violence against women as an important problem and want to help, but may not know how to contribute (Crooks et al., 2007), or lack the skills or knowledge to take some kind of active stand against violence (Casey and Ohler, 2012). Furthermore, some men who become visible antiviolence allies or who speak up about the disrespectful behaviour of other men may encounter skeptical, negative, and/or homophobic reactions from their male peers (Berkowitz, 2004). Organizers of men's antiviolence projects and organizations have also found it difficult to sustain individual men's commitment to and involvement in the work over time (e.g., Funk, 2008). . . .

Reaching out to individual men occurs in larger organizational, community, and social environments, however, which can harbour both supports and challenges to the gender equity goals of violence prevention programs. This means that it is critical not only to articulate the complexities involved in reaching out to individual men but to examine the obstacles present in the settings and communities in which those efforts occur. Evidence from prevention fields more broadly suggests that prevention efforts that operate on multiple levels and that engage both individuals and their communities can be particularly effective in fostering lasting change (Wandersman and Florin, 2003; WHO, 2007). To date, however, most "tested" gender-based violence prevention programs operate almost exclusively at the individual level (Senn, 2011), circumscribing the knowledge base about the impact of multilevel approaches. To date, there has also been limited examination of how the larger contexts in which men's engagement occurs affect the process and outcomes of organizations that involve men in violence prevention.

To move toward addressing this gap, this study examines qualitative data from interviews with twenty-nine organizational representatives speaking on behalf of gender-based violence prevention programs around the world that involve men in their work. Specifically, this study aims to (1) provide an ecological description of challenges experienced by men's antiviolence organizations at individual, organizational, and community levels and (2) examine how these challenges manifest across different regional contexts. By more fully explicating the multilevel complexities involved in engaging men, we hope to move closer to conceptualizing ways to navigate them.

Method

Participant Recruitment

We sent e-mail invitations to participate in the Internet-based survey to relevant violence and prevention-related listserves, professional networks, and programs around the world, with the added invitation to forward the survey link to other potentially eligible parties. Participation eligibility was described as having part or all of the organizational mission dedicated to engaging men in violence prevention (operationalized as "men taking action to stop violence against women and children before it begins by advocating for and creating respectful relationships"). The first survey was conducted over a two-month period ending in June 2010 and was provided in English. One hundred and sixty-five programs around the world responded to the first survey and 104 of these provided contact information and consent to be recontacted for the research described here.

We . . . recontacted forty-eight organizations by e-mail to invite a program representative to participate in our in-depth interview for this study (these invitations included forty-six organizations from the first phase of the project, and two additional referrals contacted to increase global representation). . . .

Sample

Twenty-nine organizational representatives (twenty-one male and eight female) participated in the interviews. Nineteen organizations either did not respond to the invitation to participate or did not follow up to schedule an interview. Descriptive information about participating organizations is provided in Table 41.1. . . .

Results

Organizational representatives described five core challenges related to designing, implementing, or sustaining efforts to engage men in the prevention of violence against women: (1) negotiating issues of gender, (2) intersectionality, (3) sustainability, (4) legitimacy, and (5) ideological inclusivity. Here, we operationalize these challenges as "tensions," as they often involve arbitrating among competing priorities and/or multiple constituencies or ideologies. Influencing these tensions are two larger themes. The first is the influence of context. In this study, although programs of different types and in different regions often described navigating similar tensions, the specific manifestations of these challenges were bound by local cultural, political, economic, and social structures—encompassed in our subsequent employment of the term context. Second and related, all tensions could be conceptualized as manifesting across multiple ecological levels of analysis, with implications for working with individual men, but also with impacts at organizational, community, and sometimes national levels. . . .

Gender

Not surprisingly, the most common tension described by program staff centres on navigating the role of gender in violence prevention and in creating strategies for inviting men's participation. Twenty-five program informants (86 per cent) representing every region of the world spoke about the gendered complexities inherent in engaging men to address a topic long seen as a "woman's issue," a process that inevitably involves examining gender roles, men's own past behaviour, and men's power. Participants noted that the movement to engage men is both rooted in and further complicated by the historical leadership of and struggle by women and women's organizations in efforts to end violence, and their long-standing work to gain access to sufficient resources and recognition of the problem of violence against women. Although the tensions posed by sorting out the role of gender in violence prevention are nuanced and multifaceted, two strong, major subthemes related to

Table 41.1 Participating organization characteristics

Characteristics	*N* (%) of Sample
Region	
Africa	7 (24%)
Australia	5 (17%)
Central/South America	3 (10%)
Europe	3 (10%)
North America	7 (24%)
South Asia/Southeast Asia/Middle East	4 (14%)
Type of organization	
Stand-alone agency (mostly nonprofits)	16 (55%)
Unit or program within a larger, multiservice agency	5 (17%)
Regional or multinational coalition	5 (17%)
Program in a university setting	2 (7%)
Governmental organization	1 (4%)
Length of program history	
Less than two years	2 (7%)
2–5 years	12 (41%)
6–8 years	4 (14%)
8+ years	11 (38%)

gender emerged from the interviews: negotiating male privilege and having man-only spaces.

Male privilege

Eighteen program representatives (62 per cent) spoke about the inevitable tension involved in asking a privileged social group—men—to examine their deeply held beliefs about what it means to be a man as well as critically evaluate the sources of that very privilege. Participants noted that addressing male privilege entails the need to surface and examine assumptions linking traditional definitions of masculinity to power and authority over women. This can make it off-putting and difficult both to initially engage men and to convince them to sustain their participation. Program representatives cited homophobia, transphobia, and men's assumptions that antiviolence programs are inherently antimale as related barriers. For example, a program representative in South America felt that by surfacing issues of gender in his men's groups he was inescapably perceived as undermining fundamentally held beliefs:

> It's hard. It's hard to get men to . . . I mean, when you're inviting them, you're basically telling them there's something that they grew up their whole lives thinking they could do . . . "she's my wife, she's like an object so I can do with an object whatever I want to, she's mine." And for you to tell those men, "look . . . this is wrong, you need help, this has to stop" . . . it's quite an issue. (P21)

Other program staff talked about their struggle to navigate the simultaneous and yet conflicting needs to make participation palatable and inviting for men without colluding with or reinforcing the notions of male privilege that contribute to perpetuating the problem of gender-based violence in the first place. A program representative in North America lamented:

> . . . there are a lot of men doing it [sexual violence] and there are a lot of men that are sitting down watching all those guys do it and helping them do it. And we're [antiviolence groups] tiptoeing around them trying to figure out how we can say this so that they won't be offended. Right? Meanwhile, they're beating and raping women and making massive [money] at enormous rates and we're being entertained by it, both the depiction and the realities of it . . . and we're sitting around tiptoeing around men wanting to be polite with them. (P96)

On a macro level, program representatives identified institutionalized male power within governmental, media, criminal justice, religious, tribal, and other community institutions as a significant barrier. This socially embedded patriarchy not only reinforces notions of traditional masculinity and male privilege held by individual men, it also impedes prevention groups' efforts to garner resources, legitimacy, support, and membership. In a handful of cases, program staff reported experiences of being publicly ridiculed for their efforts:

> . . . one of the challenges is . . . because most of the men here do not think the time has come for men to talk about the rights of women . . . according to the newspaper, we're just a group of men battered, beaten by our wives. So we are going around telling men, crying around like babies who cannot handle their wives. I should have read [you] the editorial of that newspaper that actually called me, specifically, a "sissy" . . . They call me a "notorious sissy." (P30–Africa)

In this case, the disjuncture between this program representative's antiviolence work, and widely understood ideas in his community about the allocation of power across genders results in his own masculinity being publicly called into question. By implication, other men joining the group are at risk of similar treatment and of being defined as outside the norm—a tactic that organizational representatives across regions reported being used against their efforts. A similar experience with some unique implications was reported by a program informant in South Asia, who noted the danger involved in challenging gender norms upheld by religious leaders in some local communities: ". . . we are facing the religious leaders' influencing in our programs and threatening us—to we are spies of the global world, 'you are spies of the United States' and like this they say to us" (P34). Here, by attempting to "sensitize" local men about violence against women, this program was testing entrenched gender-based power structures, and in this case, being defined as outsiders to the state through accusations of collusion with "terrorist" entities.

Although programs in every region of the world reported navigating tensions related to negotiating the role of gender, the specific expression of those challenges were locally and culturally specific. Program representatives highlighted features of their local context/culture that they perceive to be tied up in constructions of gender and violence. For example, the previously mentioned program in an urban region of South Asia, and a program in rural North America both articulated the ways in which local notions of appropriate masculinity reinforced gendered power inequities and resistance to prevention efforts. However, the participant in South Asia attributed the stability of these norms to power structures within local religious and political institutions while the organization in rural North America cited economic forces that drove a long-standing division of labour and gender roles:

> Well, there is the hyper-masculine stereotype guy that goes out and shoots the buffalo or elk and brings enough for the family, and the wife is at home and he is working on the railroad or in the mine. It is a very frontier mentality here by and large as a society. . . . (P84)

A program informant in Australia perceived that a sports-focused culture feeds pockets of misogyny and disrespect for women in and around the context of sport:

> [Rugby] is a very, what we call in Australia a very "blokie" environment, it's not mitigated very much by the presence of women. There can be a culture, I don't know if you have the same thing

> with your football teams, but there can be quite a culture of disrespect with rugby. (P18) . . .

Man only spaces?

The second subtheme related to gender was articulated by nine programs (31 per cent), which included organizations in Africa, Asia, Europe, and North and South America. Program staff reported deliberating within their programs about the appropriateness of focusing only on men's engagement and creating spaces that were man-only or dominated by men. Many organizational representatives, including those that provide treatment services to perpetrators, felt that having gender-specific spaces was essential to facilitate the kind of atmosphere necessary for honest discussion and minimizing defensiveness. Others, however, expressed concern about fragmenting prevention efforts either along gender lines or by a proliferation of disconnected programs that communicate only minimally with one another. Program representatives were also mindful of the risk of reinforcing gendered inequities by creating man-only spaces or unnecessarily undermining the positive change and relationships that could be fostered by coeducational programming. Further, some program staff warned that engaging men (or "changing" men) should not be an end unto itself. Rather, participants suggested that inviting men's participation should be one strategy within a larger movement to promote norms of respect and equality within communities. For example, a program in Africa that focuses on engaging community members to foster localized activism related to violence and gender noted:

> Actually, our perspective has always been that we have to work with both men and women if we're about to create social change. How else can we do it? If we're in a community where men and women, together, make up the values of that community, how can we be working with just one group? We can't, and, I think [there are] dangerous results when we try . . . I think what we need to be saying is we need to talk about social change, talk about community mobilization, whatever language, but make it inclusive. (P47)

At organizational and community levels, this tension could take the form of suspicion from or conflict with victims' services organizations, feminist organizations, or other women's groups. While most of the program representatives in this study highlighted the importance of working collaboratively with and being accountable to women and women's organizations, some noted that their presence was nonetheless perceived by others as encroaching on hard-won territory. Given the historical difficulty of establishing violence against women as a critical issue, and of garnering resources to assist victims, the emergence of groups focused on engaging men holds the potential to raise concerns about the allocation of resources, ideological compatibility, and leadership sharing across organizations. A participant in Europe highlighted the tension caused by the rise of men's engagement efforts in her community:

> . . . we've got a big strategy at the government level for the past 10 years now, working on men's violence against women and children, funding a lot of women-only organizations. It [doing men's engagement work] seems to have led to quite a high degree of anger, fear and hostility. And there has been sort of two camps you know; the center feminist camp almost and then men. So trying to break through that particularly when we're working with abuse issues has been quite hard. (P36)

Intersectionality

Closely related to the issue of gender, ten programs (34 per cent) discussed how other aspects of identity and social position (and their intersections) complicate the conceptualization, implementation, and even prioritization of engaging men in gender-based violence prevention. These ten programs came from Africa, Asia, and North and South America. On an individual level, barriers which align with social position based on class, ethnicity, religion, and so on, within their national or regional context, render men themselves more vulnerable to multiple kinds of violence or impede their access to getting involved in antiviolence efforts. Program representatives noted that issues such as poverty, migration, racism, illiteracy, and food insecurity make the issue of violence against women less visible and a potentially lower concern for many men. "On the scale of things to worry about, domestic violence doesn't come very high on boys' . . . list of priorities" noted a program in South Asia (P27). Organizations identifying this tension largely either served a marginalized group within a specific national context (such as a specific ethnic minority group) or had programs focused exclusively on gender-based violence (many programs in the sample included other and sometimes multiple social and health issues within their organizational mission).

The specific nature and impact of intersectionality-related barriers was context specific. Many regions highlighted poverty-related barriers, such as the South American participant who noticed differential participation in his program, with the men who dropped out being "younger . . . they were poorer, they had less money than the men that were in the project" (P21). In another vein, a staff member from a program focused on engaging a culturally specific group of men in North America noted that societal racism undermined programmatic efforts to foster sustainability, and made more complex the nature of support and engagement needed by individual male participants. These same experiences may leave men feeling limited in their access to power and security, an experience at odds with many violence prevention strategies that ask men to critically evaluate their power and privilege. Further, for some men marginalized by racism and/or poverty, traditional avenues for performing and embodying hegemonic masculinity may be complicated or foreclosed. Some program informants suggested that this may increase risk of adhering to traditional gender roles, which allow men to align with at least one source of widely accepted "masculine" norms.

> . . . and this is an issue that I think goes beyond . . . the issue of gender-based violence, is the high degree of number of individuals who have left schools early, left secondary school early for a number of different factors, to generate income for their homes . . . and so there are a lot of young men here who are now unemployed. And so that is definitely challenging some of the dimensions of how do they define themselves in terms of masculinity. (P26–Central America)

On a macro level, program informants delineated a tension around highlighting and prioritizing the issue of gender-based violence when violence more generally is structurally embedded in communities and society. Further, these forms of violence, which across contexts might include poverty, genocide, racism, civil war, or multistate war, can serve to marginalize men who likely have important contributions to make to gender-based violence prevention efforts. A multicountry coalition noted the challenge of trying to support local communities in doing gender equity work while acknowledging the larger context of violence that simultaneously undermines a focus on violence against women and makes smaller scale prevention efforts feel inadequate or off target:

> . . . what is difficult for the field and for us is grappling with the intersectionality of violence . . . where we have all of these modifiers of identity. Identities constructed by ethnicity, class, race, and all this, and for people to understand violence as cross-cutting or intersecting those domains, and therefore, response changing is a big challenge because there's so much that's just targeted, short term—these short-term interventions that are like, "ok, we're going to work with just youth inside this classroom. We're going to tell them how to be better men and we're going to practice how to be better men and we're going to sing and dance and all this" and then, you walk outside the classroom and exactly the opposite messages are being reinforced through many ways. You know, like men understanding their own violence and experiences of violence like, just to say, in a place like [specific country] where violence is a tool to keep power hierarchies in place. (P106)

Among the many important tensions embedded in this participant's comments, two bear rehighlighting. First, the backdrop of the multiple ways in which men, themselves, experience violent marginalization (often in state-sanctioned ways), calls into question the legitimacy of prioritizing and focusing on men's violence against women. Here, "short-term," gender-focused prevention activities at the individual level can seem misplaced or inadequate in the face of broad-based political violence and/or violence experienced on the bases of other markers of identity. Second, this organizational representative notes that violence modelled, sanctioned, or even promoted on a broad scale can directly undermine and counteract efforts to support men in critically evaluating their own misuse of power. . . .

Sustainability

Twenty-one of the program informants (72 per cent) identified program sustainability as a continual tension. These organizations came from every region represented in the study. On an individual and organizational level, participants primarily operationalized sustainability as keeping men actively engaged in the vision, direction, and activities of the program in an ongoing way. Competing demands on individual men's time, difficulty nourishing momentum, a lack of tangible action, and skill deficits related to community organizing and facilitating were all cited as barriers to maintaining a vibrant, consistent, and active program once the initial recruitment of male participants was accomplished. An organizational representative from North America summed up these challenges:

> . . . people do not know how to organize and they don't know how to have a meeting and they don't know how to keep men in meetings, So that's another thing, if you're going to have men that are going to keep coming on this issue, you have to be either moving towards the action, and/or, generally, you have to be talking with them and sharing information about male socialization, manhood, power and violence. They'll keep coming back if you talk about that . . . and/ or you gotta be moving towards some kind of action so they feel like it's worth their time. (P96)

In some contexts, organizational representatives also noted that because men's engagement programming is relatively new and still developing, the pool of qualified and ideologically compatible workers is limited. A program representative in South Asia noted:

> Suffice it to say, you can't hire these people off the block. So for us, the most important thing is that the people we hire are actually sincere about the type of work we're doing. It's more important to be sincere about, you know, gender equality and domestic violence than it is about being a professional trainer or professional mentor. And so, my point is that we've only got one mentor at the moment, and the people that we would want to hire are few and far between. (P27)

At a broader level, program representatives' discussion of sustainability largely focused on funding. Across all regions of the world, the primary organizational level challenge to sustainability was a lack of funding and difficulty securing ongoing resources to continue to build on organizational accomplishments. For some programs, this was related to time constraints, the small size of the program, and the considerable effort needed to pursue stable funding sources. A handful of program representatives pinpointed the difficulty created by bureaucratic funding cycles for programs with ongoing support needs as a major hurdle in securing stability. Others noted additional funding challenges including the recession, and mismatches between the preventative focus of their organization with national or local funding priorities: "The main challenge is how to get funding for such programs, because lots of funding [is] going on developing economic projects like [unemployment]. Social programs get less funding than others" (P34, South Asia).

Legitimacy

Intricately connected to the notion of sustainability was the struggle to realize "legitimacy," a theme articulated by participants from every region except South America. Nine program representatives (31 per cent) spoke about striving to establish relevance and validity, both within their specific community contexts and with organizational peers and funders. For many organizations, this tension emerged from a perceived lack of tested models for effectively engaging men in violence prevention, coupled with a simultaneous cultural narrowness of models that are available. For example, a program in South Asia noted:

> . . . it's quite funny. So, all the manuals that we've come across talk about quite academic subjects of masculinity and discrimination and . . . you know violence and sort of human rights, and these sorts of things. So we've found as soon as you start talking about human rights and discrimination, violence and stuff like that to the boys we work with, you know, you lose fifty per cent of them straight away. (P27)

. . . Other program staff noted that the time and resources needed to conduct evaluations of their programs and outcomes created a barrier to rigorously evaluating their work and "proving" success. . . .

> [An agency] will come in and say, "OK, we've got three years and so much money. We need these outputs, we need these deliverables in three years. If you want to do it, we'll work with you." But it's very top down and rigid. That's simplifying things a lot but it tends to be that many service providing agencies are sort of tightening their belt and being driven by different impact and results evaluations where they have to show people are being motivated by these measurements that are . . . you know, within three years, that I think in prevention, it just doesn't fit. You know, you're not going to change much in three years in terms of behaviors and attitudes. (P106, Asia)

On the other hand, one South American program noted that a recent influx of funding for domestic violence services had sparked a troubling proliferation of fragmented programs whose "legitimacy" could not be evaluated: " . . . these groups are sort of popping up everywhere and no one actually knows what's going on. Who's doing those groups, what types of information do those people have, where did they get the information to actually do that?" (P21). Providing an apt summary of tensions related to establishing benchmarks for legitimacy, a North American program informant noted, "So that's the challenge, that we have to create these models so that people can begin adapting them and shifting them and changing them so we can get into some kind of, you know, some promising practices" (P96). In the shorter term, at least, negotiating legitimacy may therefore require programs to strike a balance between honouring the unique components relevant to localized communities with adopting evaluated models of prevention that appeal to funders and that can be brought to scale across communities.

A Big Tent

Finally, seven representatives (24 per cent) from all regions except Asia and Australia discussed the dilemma inherent in reaching out to more men and more diverse circles of men while trying to maintain a specific ideological purity (generally pro-feminist) related to anti gender-based violence work. This tension interacts with the aforementioned challenge of sustainability; as programs look to increase their membership, impact, and stability, they pull in a greater diversity of men and community partners. On a micro level, this means that individual men come in the doors of these organizations with a variety of ideas and worldviews related to gender, with unexamined sexist beliefs, and potentially with histories of their own use of violence. In striving to be inclusive, organizations may risk having their organizational focus on gender equity diluted or even co-opted. Some programs, such as this coalition in North America, intentionally worked toward building a "big tent," and in so doing, had to manage diverse agendas:

> I mean, it's really created some painful experiences within the organization because what we wanted to do was have this really big tent. Not naively, but hopefully so, so that any man could be involved with us and do this work with us and sit on our board of directors and all that kind of stuff. And, of course, what that has resulted in is we've had attempts by the fathers' rights groups to take over the board, we've had campaigns on the phone from across [the country] about the work we do. We've had attempts

to change what we call ourselves, that is pro-feminist . . . we've kind of stuck with it and have not done what other groups have done, which has been to become more restrictive about who can be involved. But it's been painful. (P25) . . .

Discussion

Negotiating Tensions: Implications for Future Practice and Research

. . . A central finding here is the simultaneous similarity across regions around the kinds of tensions men's organizing efforts are experiencing, alongside the role of context in shaping the location-specific manifestations of these tensions. On one hand, the relative uniformity with which organizations identified challenges related to navigating gender, legitimacy, and sustainability suggest there is much to be gained from cross-program and cross-region exchange about strategies for tackling these tensions, and for solidarity around the difficulty of doing so. For example, some programs reported experiences of having their members' masculinity publicly called into question, the impact of which may be mitigated by cross-program and international communication and support among men. Similarly, threats or challenges to an organization's perceived legitimacy in a specific governmental or funding context may be answered by evidence of the prevalence and level of acceptance of similar programs in other communities or countries. Indeed, the nascent existence of men's antiviolence engagement programs in every region of the world is a testament to the growing legitimacy and evidence base for this element of violence prevention. As a whole, the shared nature of many of the challenges surfaced here suggest that strategy sharing and testing across regions is a fruitful practice deserving of continued and enhanced support and that leadership resources in this regard exist across all regions of the world.

On the other hand, many of the tensions surfaced here play out in very contextually specific ways for each program. Context in this study can be described as the socially constructed local cultures which are situated in the economic, historical, and political environment of a community or region. It likely goes without saying that as strategies are shared cross-regionally, careful assessment of fit to local context and culture is critical. This also suggests that enhanced resources are needed for more localized evaluation of men's engagement efforts, to allow programs to simultaneously tailor their ally building activities, generate evidence of the importance and impact of their work, and contribute to the cross-regional knowledge base that could enhance legitimacy, effectiveness, and sustainability of men's engagement programs more broadly. . . .

Finally, the ways that intersecting social identities and experiences of violence both impede and can be leveraged in the successful engagement of men is an area critically in need of additional research. Coupled with the lack of men's engagement models in general, and culturally tailored models in particular, the intersecting sources of identity and marginalization of men is underaddressed within this work. Some gender-equity programs around the world address this, in part, by avoiding the silos of tackling single issues (such as solely intimate partner violence), and conceptualizing their work as addressing a range of related outcomes (sexual health, human rights, family economic security, etc.; WHO, 2007). Incorporating an intersectional analysis into antiviolence work may therefore be done through collaboratively addressing shared structural contributors to/risk factors for a range of health and equity issues that ultimately impact both men and women. . . .

Acknowledgements

The authors would like to thank the twenty-nine organizational representatives who volunteered their time to participate in this study. We also extend our thanks to the Mobilizing Men for Violence Prevention Global Advisory Committee, many of whom provided feedback on iterations of this analysis.

Declaration of Conflicting Interests

The author(s) declared no potential conflicts of interest with respect to the research, authorship, and/or publication of this article.

Funding

The author(s) disclosed receipt of the following financial support for the research, authorship, and/or publication of this article: This research was supported by the University of Minnesota, College of Education and Human Development, International Research Grant Program.

Notes

1. Social Work Program, University of Washington, Tacoma, WA, USA
2. School of Social Work, University of Minnesota, St Paul, MN, USA
3. School of Social Work, University of Washington, Seattle, WA, USA
4. Augsburg College Minneapolis, MN, USA
5. School of Social Work, University of Michigan, Ann Arbor, MI, USA
6. School of Social Welfare, University of California, Berkeley, CA, USA

References

Atherton-Zeman, B. 2009. "Minimizing the Damage—Male Accountability in Stopping Men's Violence against Women," *A Journal of the Battered Women's Movement* Spring: 8–13.

Black, M.C., K.C. Basile, M.J. Breiding, S.G. Smith, M.L. Walters, M.T. Merrick, J. Chen, and M.R. Stevens. 2011. *The National Intimate Partner and Sexual Violence Survey (NISVS): 2010 Summary Report.* Atlanta, GA: National Center for Injury Prevention and Control, Centers for Disease Control and Prevention.

Berkowitz, A.D. 2004. *Working with Men to Prevent Violence against Women: An Overview.* VAWnet: National Online Resource Center on Violence against Women. Accessed March 19, 2012. www.vawnet.org/applied-research-papers/?type=Prevention.

Carlson, J.C., E.A. Casey, J. Edleson, R. Tolman, T. Neugut, and E. Kimball. in press. "Strategies to Engage Men and Boys in Violence Prevention: A Global Organizational Perspective." *Violence against Women.*

Casey, E.A. 2010. "Strategies for Engaging Men as Anti-violence Allies: Implications for Ally Movements," *Advances in Social Work* 11: 267–82.

Casey, E.A., and K. Ohler. 2012. "Being a Positive Bystander: Male Anti-violence Allies' Experiences of 'Stepping up,'" *Journal of Interpersonal Violence* 27: 62–83.

Crooks, C.V., G.R. Goodall, R. Hughes, P.G. Jaffe, and L.L. Baker. 2007. "Engaging Men and Boys in Preventing Violence against Women: Applying a Cognitive-behavioral Model," *Violence against Women* 13: 217–39.

Edwards, K.E. 2006. "Aspiring Social Justice Ally Identity Development: A Conceptual Model," *NASPA Journal* 43: 39–60.

Flood, M. 2005. "Changing Men: Best Practice in Sexual Violence Education," *Women Against Violence* 18: 26–36.

Flood, M. 2011a. "Building Men's Commitment to Ending Sexual Violence against Women," *Feminism & Psychology* 21: 262–67.

Flood, M. 2011b. "Involving Men in Efforts to End Violence against Women," *Men and Masculinities* 14: 358–77.

Funk, R. 2008. "Men's Work: Men's Voices and Actions against Sexism and Violence," *Journal of Intervention and Prevention in the Community* 36: 155–71.

Murnen, S.K., C. Wright, and G. Kaluzny. 2002. "If 'Boys Will Be Boys,' Then Girls Will Be Victims? A Meta-analytic Review of the Research That Relates Masculine Ideology to Sexual Aggression," *Sex Roles* 46: 359–75.

Senn, C.Y. 2011. "An Imperfect Journey: Reflections on the Process to Develop an Effective Sexual Assault Resistance Programme for University Women," *Feminism & Psychology* 21: 121–37.

Wandersman, A., and P. Florin. 2003. "Community Interventions and Effective Prevention," *American Psychologist* 58: 441–48.

WHO (World Health Organization). 2007. *Engaging Men and Boys in Changing Gender-based Inequity in Health: Evidence from Programme Interventions.* Accessed March 19, 2012. www.who.int/gender/documents/Engaging_men_boys.pdf.

Chapter 42

Overview

Gendered activism is not restricted to movements that are focused on transforming gender. Miya Narushima examines one of the most intriguing actors in the Canadian political scene—the Raging Grannies—a loosely organized network of older women who use humour, parody, and funny hats to deliver pointed commentary on the issues of the day. The Grannies are women who are seeking to make a difference in the world they are passing on to their grandchildren, efforts that Narushima connects to the personal and social spaces that open up to women who have finished their years of earning and active child-rearing. The Grannies see themselves as elders with a special responsibility to use their years of wisdom and experience to work towards peace, environmental justice, and more open democracy, among other causes.

By using the gendered stereotype of the "little old lady," as well as costumes and props, the Grannies are able to get their message across through song and performance where more conventional political activists might fail. Although the Grannies' work has not been uniformly successful, they represent a creative way of bringing gender into social movements.

A Gaggle of Raging Grannies: The Empowerment of Older Canadian Women through Social Activism

Miya Narushima

Introduction: A Portrait of the Raging Grannies Movement

A Gaggle of Grannies
(Tune: "Side by Side")
Oh, We're just a gaggle of grannies
Urging you off of your fannies
We're telling you boys
We're sick of your toys
We want no more war
We know if you tried you could
Chretien [Canada's Prime Minister at the time of writing]
Change our country's direction
We're telling you now
We're angry and how
We want no more war
We really mean it
No more war
We'll say it nicely
No more war
We mean precisely
NO MORE WAR!
(Kingston Grannies, 2001)

"A Gaggle of Grannies" is a standard number sung by many Raging Grannies groups across Canada. As its lyrics depict, the Raging Grannies are groups of female social activists who are 50-plus. The history of their movement goes back to 1987, when 10 older women in a street theatre group in Victoria, British Columbia, paddled canoes to confront the big US nuclear-powered warship that had entered Canadian waters, while chanting protests songs in flamboyant "granny" duds with flowery hats (McLaren and Brown, 1991). Having successfully gained media attention and public interest, they branched out into other areas of social concern including the environment, mining, nuclear power, militarism, clear-cut logging, poverty, corporate greed, racism, sexism, and any forms of social and economic injustice.

Grannies are politically conscious but non-partisan. Their activism is largely community-based, i.e., each local group acts independently choosing the issues that they wish to work on. Yet, they are also linked nationally through the Internet, regular newsletters, annual regional meetings and the biannual nationwide assembly that they call their "Unconvention." All these help them spread their network to exchange songs and strategies, while informing a wide range of updated news and social issues. Grannies often collaborate with other advocacy groups in their local communities to organize larger-scale events and protests. As a street singing and theatre troupe, they are also frequently invited to perform in a variety of community gatherings and festivals. The financial support for their activism mainly comes from the donations received in these booked appearances. . . .

From its small beginnings, the "Raging Grannies" has become a viable political movement with chapters in more than 50 cities and towns across Canada, some in the US, and a few even in Greece and India. Why this rapid increase in popularity? Why "Raging Grannies"? What does this kind of social activism mean to women in late adulthood, and what are its implications for an aging and lifelong learning society? To find answers to these questions, I conducted a qualitative case study of this older women's movement in Canada, combining an extensive document analysis with four months of fieldwork with two Granny groups in Ontario. In the following article, divided into five sections, I begin with a brief description of the context of a greying Canadian society and its growing numbers of older women. Second, I summarize some theories regarding later life development, women's empowerment, and multiple roles from the critical gerontology and psychodrama perspectives. Then, I outline my research methodology and procedures, followed by a presentation of my findings and analysis. The final section discusses the implications of the Grannies' activism in the light of lifelong learning.

Context: The Aging Population and Older Women

In Canada, as in many other countries, older adults over 65 are the fastest growing segment of the population. Statistics Canada (Norland, 1994) has estimated that there will be more "seniors" than any other age group in the Canadian population in 30 years, by which time the ratio of Canadians over 65 will have almost doubled (to 22.4 per cent by 2030). This demographic shift, sometimes called "apocalyptic demography" (Robertson, 1999) or a "ticking time bomb," has raised worries that the younger generation will have to carry too many dependent elderly on their shoulders. By lumping "seniors" together by chronological age, however, this kind of demographic determinism overlooks various factors including socio-economic conditions, health, lifestyle, cohort difference, and gender, all of which affect an individual's aging. Given that most provinces in Canada still have a mandatory retirement system and that policy debate is monopolized by the premise of "older people" as post-productive service recipients, opportunities to utilize the skills and strengths of older people have been limited by structural factors and entrenched patterns of discourse. In a sense older people, regardless of gender, are alienated from the mainstream, while the social roles and cultural meaning of "old age" are neglected despite the aging population (Cole, 1992).

"Old age," however, is not a gender-neutral category—it requires a gender-specific perspective. Women's longer life expectancy means that they outnumber their male counterparts in late adulthood. The life expectancy of Canadian men in 1999 was 76.3 years compared to 81.7 for their female counterparts, for example, while the sex ratio of Canadians over 65 was 75 men per 100 women (Statistics Canada, 2002, quoted in McCarten, 2002). This means that so-called aging problems—i.e., chronic illness and frailty, poverty, loneliness, abuse, and so forth—also tend to be associated more with women. Consequently, older women are likely to be pathologized and denigrated as fragile, needy recipients of welfare and health care services. In a sense, senior women face the double-jeopardy of agism and sexism (Browne, 1998).

Partly because of this kind of stereotype, older women's potential for empowerment through collective political action remains largely overlooked. Preconceptions associating old age with social disengagement leads to a misperception of political behaviour among older adults. Yet, aging is not accompanied by a decline in political and social interest, and even greater "grey power" may develop in the years ahead, something Peterson and Somit's (1994) study of US seniors suggests. Contemporary older women can be seen as a pioneer cohort moving beyond the traditional gender stratification of society.

Research Method

This study . . . was divided into two phases. Phase I consists of document analysis including 40 microfilmed articles issued between 1988 and 2000 in various local newspapers in Canada, 116 websites (including one local Grannies group homepage), and about 200 songs collected in their song books. Based on the overview gained through phase 1, I then conducted face-to-face interviews along with participant observation of 15 women in two Grannies groups in Ontario between August and December in 2001. . . .

I selected these two groups because neither had been studied by other researchers or journalists, and for the practical reason that they were located in suburban cities within a range of my home in Toronto, which allowed me to make frequent visits for participant observation and interviews. Both groups were originally formed six to seven years ago and were similar in terms of the socioeconomic and cultural backgrounds of their members. One difference between the two groups was that one was larger (15 people) including more original members, while the other was smaller (7 people) and three of them had just joined when my fieldwork began. . . .

The racial and socioeconomic backgrounds of participants in my study were similar to those in Hill's (2000) study of Toronto Grannies. The 15 Grannies who I interviewed were middle-class (except for one farmer) white women whose ages ranged from mid-50s to mid-70s. Twelve were married, one divorced, and two were widows who lived by themselves. All but two were grandmothers. Four were still working full or part time (as a senior administrator in a university, a pharmacist, a writer, and an organic farmer), while the rest had retired from various occupations (e.g., teachers, social workers, nurses, lab technicians, secretaries, etc.). All participants spoke English as their first language although two had immigrated to Canada from other Commonwealth countries in their youth. Despite the commonalties, however, certain differences from Hill's 2000 group were noticeable. Half the Grannies in my study were facing health problems, either their own or those of close family members. In terms of my participants' history of social activism, about 60 per cent were veteran activists, whereas 40 per cent had got their feet wet in "activism" for the first time in retirement, although most had done community volunteering.

Face-to-face interviews were conducted at participants' homes, coffee shops, event sites, or workplaces depending on their preference. Each participant engaged in at least one formal videotaped interview, each of which was between 60 and 90 minutes long, semi-structured with open-ended questions. Grannies were asked to talk freely about why they joined the Grannies, what their experience was like, and how they thought it had changed them. Participant observations were conducted at each group's "gigs" or public appearances at various occasions (e.g., Hiroshima Remembrance Day, United Nations Day, The End of Sanctions on Iraq campaign, a Town Hall meeting for anti–World Trade Organization) as well as their monthly meetings. Since the period of my fieldwork spanned the events of September 11, most of the Grannies' gigs after the incident aimed at dampening pro-war sentiment. . . .

Theoretical Perspectives: Women's Later Life Development and Empowerment

. . . Theories of empowerment . . . add another dimension to our understanding of the Raging Grannies' activism, highlighting the social and collective aspect of older women and power. Taken together, the literature in women's studies (Miller, 1991; Surrey, 1991; Browne, 1998) and later life learning (Cusack, 2000; Jarvis, 2001) suggest that "power" for older women can be posited as the "capacity to move or to produce change," as "power emerging from interaction," or as the "increased ability to engage in critical thinking and leadership." Jarvis (2001: 125), from the perspective of later life learning, has advocated the importance of critical thinking in the empowerment of older adults by noting that "once older adults feel free to engage in critical thought, they are empowered."

Regarding the process of older women's empowerment, Cox and Parsons (1996), based on their social work practice, stressed the importance of a cohesive collective or group experience to problem solving. Their study (1996: 135) also suggested that older women need a safe environment for building relationships upon feelings of trust, reciprocity, and commonality, which are developed through continued interaction and a sense of belonging, acceptance, affirmation, and mutual aid. What these theories imply is that women's individual empowerment and the relational context through which this empowerment emerges must always be considered simultaneously.

"Raging Grannies" as a Self-Defined Social Role

The mission statement of the Raging Grannies movement included in their songbook goes as follows:

> We are enraged about the state of the Earth we are leaving for our precious grandchildren. We are raging against the system that has allowed this to happen and the institutions that perpetuate the atrocities against our planet. As grandparents, we have a responsibility to the children and grandchildren of the future, and it is not too late for us to act. (McLaren and Brown, 1991: 4)

"Earth," "responsibility," "children and grandchildren," "future," "act"—as these words imply, the Raging Grannies frame their activism as a symbolic extension of their roles as responsible and caring grandmothers who are concerned about the future of our planet and posterity. Most Grannies I interviewed are real-life grandmothers, and they underscored the point that they are acting on behalf of their grandchildren:

> I had not been socially active in this way, but I felt, at this point in time, it was time to do something. Because I had enough anger building in me over the years over things that should be happening or not happening. I have seen so many dreams and hopes fall in the dust and then resurrect themselves. And I don't feel so shattered when something doesn't work out. I have more of a long-term view now. I think if something doesn't happen in my lifetime, it may happen in the lifetime of my grandchildren. The idea is to make a better world for our grandchildren so that when they are growing up they will have not exactly an easier time, but a fuller life. (Granny M)

Given their passion with which they talk about issues that may harm their descendants, it is indisputable that the activism of the Grannies stems from a kind of grandmotherly love mixed with a ripened awareness about the world, and where priorities should be placed. This desire to leave a better world for future generations can be interpreted as a demonstration of a high degree of "generativity" and "gero-transcendence" in later life, reflecting Hill's (2000) study that found generativity at the core of the Granny psyche. Friedan (1993: 619), an advocate for social involvement in later life, suggested that "generativity is expressed in more mundane terms whenever [senior citizens'] talents are truly used as a community resource, or where they are allowed or encouraged to use their wisdom in work with younger people." In the current discourse on "old age" in Western societies, however, how much encouragement do older people—in particular, older women—really receive to cultivate their generativity while contributing their talents and wisdom as a broader community resource? This is the question confronted by the Raging Grannies. Indeed, the more I got to know them, the more I was convinced that their activism extends far beyond the "generative" acts of caring grandmothers.

The Raging Grannies can be understood as an older women's liberation movement. As Hill (2000) pointed out, their activism sends a strong feminist message about the oppression of women in a patriarchal system. My participants' "rage" about the social devaluation of older women was loudly echoed in comments like this:

> The grannies in our society opted to be silent. Now they talk more and more about elder abuse. I think of elders as elders in the traditional indigenous sense. Most often our society sees them in the malls or in church afternoon women's groups. Nobody expects them to really do anything for society. So I think that's another thing that we are deliberately taking on. You cannot shut us up in an old people's home, you cannot put us in a mall and expect us to buy a cup of coffee and we will be happy all day, because we know something is wrong here. (Granny L)

This comment reveals two things: an anger about the social stigma of "older women" as "being past, useless, and not really being involved" (Granny L), and their strong desire to keep involved in and contributing to society. Browne (1998) once posited that agism on top of sexism can radicalize older women, mobilizing them to fight against other forms of oppression and injustice. Given the Grannies' vehemence about the social denigration of "older women," Browne's (1998) hypothesis may be less idealistic than many assumed.

Despite the feminist nature of the Raging Grannies' movement, however, their activism exhibits a strong emphasis on caring as an affirmative feminine attribute.

Older Women
(Tune: "Merry Widow Waltz")
Let us celebrate the older woman now
To the troubles in her life
She will not bow
Earning every wrinkle
Striving to be strong
Sharing laughter, friendship
All the day is long
Older women overseas, newspapers show
War and sadness in their eyes
The truth they know
Fighting for their families
Willing peace to be
Standing tall while losing all
They call to me
Older women changed this land
They won the vote
Built careers, ran corporations
And we note
Took on politicians
So to change our laws
Fighting on for justice
They win our applause!
Here's to older women
All the things they do
Nurturing, supporting, caring
Their lives through
Wisdom comes with aging
Every grey hair won
Years unfold and still we feel
We've just begun.
(Southwest Ontario Grannies, 2000: 95–96)

This song portrays the struggles, sorrows, accomplishments of women who shared a certain period of history and culture, as well as their pride and solidarity. Above all, it depicts older women's endorsement of the "nurturing, supporting, and caring" activities that have formed the core of their identity and provide them with a sense of purpose and continuity in life. The Grannies I met often suggested that "care" was the central value generating their energy: "Well, 'raging' to me simply means being forceful about what we consider in need of correction and improvement. I think it's a good strong word that means that we really 'care'" (Granny H). This reminds us to avoid the simplistic dualism which sees women's caregiving as either all good or all bad, a position argued in the feminist analysis of gender-graded roles (Browne, 1998, Altschuler, 2001). After all, it is undeniable that caring has been essential part of these older women's self development across their entire life span (Gilligan, 1982; Caffarella and Olson, 1993; Browne, 1998; Price, 1998; Altschuler, 2001). Providing caring hands indeed seems to be a great source of joy and satisfaction for these older women. Given the importance of continuity in later life to cope with inevitable physical and social change (Atchley, 1999), the value of caring for older women should not be seen in black and white terms.

Given their emphasis on caring and nurturing, at first glance the Raging Grannies' image risks promoting the prevailing rhetoric of traditional gender roles. Ironically, however, it is these conventional norms that the Raging Grannies aim to break free of. By identifying themselves as "raging," these older women, who are biologically and economically in the post-productive period, are trying to extend their generative "caring" from the domestic to the social arena to establish a new social role as "caretakers of our planet" (DeShaw of Southwest Ontario Grannies, 2000: 5). Even more unconventional is the way they take advantage of the "granny" stereotype to achieve this goal. Like the Trojan Horse, they exploit the social perception of "sweet little old ladies" to gain entry to otherwise inaccessible places (McLaren and Brown, 1991). In fact, their group even made the "Anti-Canadian" list of the Royal Canadian Mounted Police for "acts of civil disobedience"! An 83-year-old Granny once confided that "a Granny isn't a grandmother. A Granny is a frame of mind" (Growe, 1998). Given that the social role can be "how you like to appear to the world, not simply how the world makes you appear" (Hopcke, 1995: 23), these words suggest that what a "Granny" is seeking is an alternative way of living and aging. Rather than withdrawing from society in retirement, the Grannies choose to engage in the world even more fully through their social and political commitment, in other words their "rage" or "care."

Grannies' Dual-Layered Mask Strategies

Mask 1: Strategic Humour and Absurdity

The Raging Grannies are known for their eye-catching style with their trademark outrageous "granny" garb and hats, and their parodic songs that match their lyrics with well-known folk, pop, rock, and hymn melodies. Although both the Grannies groups I observed followed this basic general pattern, each had its own unique style of protest. These and other groups' ingenuous strategies have been reported in local newspapers across Canada. To take a few examples, to demonstrate against the Gulf War one group sang anti-militaristic songs while literally knitting a web around a tank in front of an armoury (McLaren and Brown, 1993). To raise public awareness about the dangers of pesticide and herbicide, another group dressed up like big yellow dandelions and marched into a local Saturday farmers' market, where they sang and served organic dandelion dishes (*Hamilton Spectator*, 2000). One group even joined bicycle club riders to sing against urban pollution (Harper, 2000). As these episodes manifest, the Grannies' protest is unpredictable, witty, and funny, and even absurd at first glance.

The playfulness of their act, however, masks a serious intent. Their extravagant "granny" duds, mocking songs, and other overtly dramatic acts are all strategies to grab an audience's attention and get their progressive message across.

Sanctions Hokey Pokey
We say you can't have pens
We say you can't have toys
We say you can't have books
'Cause you're Iraqi girls and boys
The banned list also freezes
Drugs to cure diseases
Do we care whom this destroys? "No!"
The bombs the US dropped
Were topped off with a slick
Canadian uranium
To make your people sick
It gives your children cancer
Chemo could be the answer
But we'll make the sanctions stick!
(Peterborough Grannies, 2002)

After hamming up this song at an event called "End of Sanctions on Iraq Campaign," one Granny explained their strategic humour:

> Of course, you get some funny looks if you are walking around in this get-up and doing this (shrugs her shoulders). But it's entertaining, so people will take a lesson in that form. You can't just walk up to people and say, "What do you think of the sanctions on Iraq?" But if you are doing it in this way, it just warms people up and they will accept things that they probably wouldn't accept in other ways. In addition, people are less likely to attack "Grannies" than they would you. If you came across opinions you didn't like and the person was your grandmother, you would think "Well, it's OK." You are not going to jump up and down. If we laugh about it, they are not going to attack us for sure. (Granny B)

The Grannies know from their life experience that preaching or talking in a structured manner on serious matters is not necessarily the best way to raise people's awareness. Instead, they use music and laughter to evoke a gut response in their audience.

Despite their approach, however, the reaction from the audience is not always as they expected:

> We started to do our gig on New Year's Eve, something called the First Night in this city. And there is a big party in the malls downtown. For the first few years, they asked the Raging Grannies to sing. Because Grannies are funny, people would gather around to listen. But when they heard that we have serious messages, they would just dribble away. When we go to events where people are committed to social action, we get a great response. They like us. But generally speaking, I think most people think, "Aren't they cute? But aren't they crazy?" I haven't got time to think about it, but that's my sense. (Granny J)

Both the Granny groups I observed seemed to be well-respected and popular among fellow community activists in both cities, with many booked performances in various events organized by local organizations. Yet, their voluntary gigs on street corners tended to be either ignored or treated as a momentary curiosity by busy passers-by despite the Grannies' zealous efforts to get them to join in by offering song sheets and sometimes even homemade cookies. Hill's (2000) study and many other articles regard the Grannies' efforts to raise public awareness about social issues as effective without offering any supporting data. I do not completely disagree with their claims. Yet, my participant observations convinced me that the Grannies' activism has a stronger influence on the older women themselves than it does on the general public.

Mask 2: The Grannies' Act and Creative Self-expression

The strategic use of political satire works not only to draw public attention but also to provide a space for older women to freely express themselves in creative and enjoyable ways. The second layer of the Grannies' "mask" is that element of dramatic performance, symbolically implied by the fact that Grannies call their public appearances "gigs." It struck me that, in contrast with their outrageous and comical public image in media, many of the older women whom I met were unexpectedly gentle and rather shy when off-stage. Many mentioned the transformative influence of acting in costume:

> You need to be brave to do this, and I don't think I'm so much a brave person in public. Well, I tell you. When I dress up, like a lot of actresses say, I feel freer to sing and to speak out. It changes my personality a little. It's like make-up. When I dress up I feel I can act like a Granny (laughter). When I put on this costume, I'm braver and I'm overcoming my fear. (Granny N)

Like a "mask," the costume provides older women with the Raging Granny's persona, thus transforming the self. On the surface, it is paradoxical that older women need the "Granny" mask to make them feel "less themselves" (Granny B) to do their gigs, while the aim of their action is to express themselves through raising their voice and making themselves visible. Hopcke (1995), a clinical psychologist, provides a clue to how this works by noting that putting on a mask and ritual clothing unconsciously serves to help transform oneself by lifting one from the ordinary to the transcendent, and that such an obliteration of ordinary self immediately results in self-liberation. In this sense, the Grannies' flamboyance seems to provide a sense of playfulness and freedom that helps them break down the conventional behaviour of middle-class older women.

The Grannies also respond to the idea of using songs as a political weapon. Many of my participants included singing and writing poems, verses, and short stories among their hobbies. Granny M, who once was a music teacher and loves singing, commented:

> I know that I've been angry with a lot of things: health care is still falling apart, the environment, the treatment of women and so forth. These things create so much anger and frustration, like what can I do about it. Being a Granny is finding a way to control our fears and frustrations by channelling our anger into action. I find it very satisfying that we let out our emotions by writing a song and singing it loudly. (Granny M)

As this comment implies, art forms such as music, poetry, and drama make it easier and even "therapeutic" for older women to express their anger, frustration, and fear, providing a way to convert their negative emotions into positive actions. In addition, writing and singing protest songs requires a great deal of critical thinking to analyze the social issues based on their own daily experiences, and think about actions to address the problems. In this sense, to wear a "Granny" mask is not simply to obliterate or liberate older women through the play and joy mode; rather, it makes them take the role represented by the mask more seriously. Adopting a social persona means to become that person, that identity, and therefore take the responsibilities that come with the role (Hopcke, 1995).

The Sense of "Us" and Collective Empowerment

> **Rebel in Disguise**
> (Tune: "You're a Devil in Disguise," Elvis)
> I looked like a granny
> I felt like a granny
> I thought like a granny
> Then I got wise
> Now I'm a rebel in disguise
> Oh yes I am
> A rebel in disguise, Oh yeah
> A rebel in disguise
> I got off my fanny
> I joined Raging Grannies
> I learned it was canny
> To protest LOUD
> (Chorus) We are rebels in disguise
> Oh yes we are
> Rebels in disguise Oh Yeah
> Rebels in disguise
> We stand up for what's right
> Sing out, day or night
> We can fight a good fight
> When we're inspired.
> (Southwest Ontario Grannies, 2000: 13)

This song delineates the process of transition and liberation of an old woman who has joined the Raging Grannies. As one may have noticed, the subject of the verses shifts from "I" to "we" as the song goes on. In fact, this sense of "us," of connection, is a dominant characteristic of the Grannies' activism. Grannies always use "we" as subject when they are talking about their activities, not to mention in the lyrics of their songs. Four participants in my study joined their groups about the same time as I began my fieldwork. During the first month or so, they often used the third person "the Grannies" or "they" to mention their colleagues. Yet, they shifted to "we" or "other Grannies" in a relatively short period. At the same time, they were getting more involved in various aspects of Grannies' activities.

It is beyond the scope of this study to posit the extent to which the experience of Granny initiates resembles that of younger people in a similar situation. Yet, I assume there may be some differences between older and younger people in terms of the speed and the degree of adaptability. Most of the Grannies I interviewed, even new members, had been actively involved in different forms of social action (e.g., community volunteering, writing letters to politicians and newspapers, marching to support social causes, etc.) and had built up a large store of frustration and criticism throughout their lives. Therefore, although it may take more time and courage for older women to commit to this new type of activism, once they have joined, they quickly become active and devoted members. In contrast, youth may find it much easier to join a protest movement as an extension of their social network without fully grasping or even agreeing with its vision (Kilgore, 1999).

After all, it takes a lot of guts for older women to express their anger and political concerns in public or even in private, as these comments imply:

> Some of my friends don't want to be with me when I dress up like a Granny. They are much too proper. I don't know what they think, but they probably cannot acknowledge this foolishness. (Granny N)

> To come out with the Grannies has really almost saved my life, because I have good friends here and I can get some of this frustration out of my system from having to stay at home and not being able to speak out. Well, my husband doesn't agree with me politically at all. I always express my opinion (laughter), but he doesn't necessarily hear it. (Granny J)

For some Grannies, it was a kind of lifelong frustration they were breaking free of. They said that they had always felt isolated, or even guilty, for being critical of the social system in their rather conservative middle-class circles: "I am no longer a little boy crying in the wilderness. I am now in a shelter under the Granny umbrella. This is where I can think that many people think as the same as I do" (Granny O). As these comments testify, the sense of "us" provides socially conscious older women with a "shelter" where they can talk, free of any uneasiness, about their political concerns with other women who have similar inclinations and values.

This collective identity, however, is not something that springs up naturally—rather it is carefully cultivated. In fact, both groups in my study were making efforts to make their relationship non-hierarchical, mutually respectful, harmonious, encouraging, and co-operative. Each has a couple of core members who are veteran activists with a broad social network in their communities. These are the untitled leaders who lead and encourage other members who are less experienced. Old members often give a new member their extra Granny hats as a symbolic welcome gift. One of the leaders of one Granny group explained the principles of their "feminist inclusive approach":

> We don't blame people for not being at gigs and practices. We're not negative about members who aren't willing to take part in things. We really try to be inclusive and just keep that door as open as we can. If you come, great. If you cannot come, that's OK. So we try not to be judgmental. Because we are really busy people. And I think that really helps us. (Granny H)

Another Granny leader explained her group's collective decision-making process as follows:

> Our discussion is quite open. Of course, like any other group, we cannot assume everybody has the same way of thinking. There are certain things we agree on and there are other things we just don't agree on. When we disagree, we sit around and talk, and try to find a comfort level. Or we just say those who are interested join the gig. But we would also discuss it and go over some of the analysis about why some of us think it's important and why some are uncomfortable. (Granny E)

The safe environment of the Grannies' groups—characterized by collective decision-making and inclusive, non-judgmental relationships—fulfils many of the factors said to make older women's empowerment happen in a relational context (Cox and Parsons, 1996). Yet what kind of personal power have Grannies gained through their activism? To get a more concrete idea, I asked them whether their activism has led to any personal changes or rewards. Granny B, who had just joined the group one month earlier, explained her personal change in this way:

> I gained more self-confidence. It's just being able to declare who you are more freely. Even if nobody is listening, I'm stating who I am. Sometimes I compare it to . . . well, my daughter is gay, and she joined the gay pride parade and that was sort of the same feeling, I think. You declare to the world, this is who I am. That's very empowering. (Granny B)

For Granny R, who was suffering from a chronic illness:

> It [activism] gives me a voice. The voice that the Grannies have is a gentle voice. We are not pushing people or coercing them but giving them some fun with the lesson. Oh, I feel good about it. Besides, I have a nasty chronic disease, which means I'm often sick. But it's all right. Part of what Grannying does for me is that it makes me feel I can do things. I do push harder at things than if I wasn't sick. I think being sick may even be part of why I'm a Raging Granny. I'm fighting for myself. I need to have a life, not just lie around in bed. But I've never thrown up at a Granny gig yet (laughter). (Granny R)

Granny U, who got involved in social activism around the time she turned 60, reflects:

> It [activism] makes me much more aware of the power that individuals can have. Often people say, "Oh, well, we cannot do anything about that." That is not true. All movements started from one person's thought. That's the only way to start it and there is power in people. I think the power of people is greater than many believe. Now with globalization and lobby groups . . . it's very important for some of us to do something if there is any hope at all.

Although the answers vary depending on each woman's personal context, being a Granny has definitely affected their lives. It provides them with a sense of purpose, of contribution, and of mastery. It promotes self-help, self-acceptance, liberation, and the realization of their capacity to become an agent for change. All these can be considered essentials for psychosocial development and well-being in later life. They are also congruent with the concept of an alternative power for women advocated in the literature of both women's studies (Miller, 1991; Surrey, 1991; Browne, 1998) and later life learning (Cusack, 2000; Jarvis, 2001). The Raging Grannies' empowerment is an ongoing process through which both individuals and groups learn to be free from the conventional often internalized image of "old age," while realizing their "power within" and the "power in people" (Granny M). . . .

The example of the Raging Grannies suggests that it is important to generate more opportunities for older women to involve themselves in political community activism, a social and collective learning environment to help them cultivate their creativity, critical thinking, sense of self-liberation, and well-being in late adulthood. It also exemplifies how so-called women's attributes can be turned into an advantage for older women when they are properly included in a curriculum. In these unsettled times dominated by military might, corporate greed, environmental destruction and languishing welfare and public services, it is critical that older women be encouraged to broadcast their non-violent, harmonious, caring point of view.

Of course, some questions must be asked concerning the further development of the Grannies' activism. Why are members of the Grannies so homogeneous in terms of ethnicity and class? Would it be better if they included more inter-generational activities? In particular, how can they take their "mask" strategies one step further to better communicate their political message? Although by now Granny activities across Canada seem to have gained enough support in the media to be reported in a sympathetic way, these reports often focus on their amusing appearance rather than their message. In addition, the Grannies are, in a sense, still faceless due to their collective Granny mask. If the Raging Grannies cannot encourage a more diversified membership or find ways to take off their Granny masks when the occasion requires, then their movement will remain a shelter for socially conscious, creative, middle-class older women. Yet, the need to wear the Granny mask reflects what older women have to fight against in Canadian society. Until ordinary older women can express their social concerns unmasked, until their voices are taken seriously, the Grannies' gaggle will continue.

Acknowledgements

I would like to thank the Grannies I interviewed for their lenient collaboration and the Toyota Foundation, Tokyo, for their generous financial support for this study.

References

Altschuler, J. 2001. "Meaning and Centrality of Caring Activities among Older Women," *Journal of Women & Aging* 13(3): 79–99.

Atchley, R.C. 1999. *Continuity and Adaptation in Aging: Creating Positive Experiences*. Baltimore and London: The Johns Hopkins University Press.

Browne, C.V. 1998. *Women, Feminism and Aging*. New York: Springer.

Caffarella, R.S., and S.K. Olson. 1993. "Psychosocial Development of Women: A Critical Review of the Literature," *Adult Education Quarterly* 43: 125–51.

Cole, T.R. 1992. *The Journey of Life*. Cambridge, New York, Port Chester, Melbourne and Sydney: Cambridge University Press.

Cox, E.O., and R.R. Parsons. 1996. "Empowerment-oriented Social Work Practice: Impact on Late Life Relationships of Women," *Journal of Women & Aging* 8(3/4): 129–43.

Cusack, S. 2000. "Critical Educational Gerontology and the Imperative to Empower," in F. Glendenning, ed., *Teaching and Learning in Later Life: Theoretical Implications*, p. 61. Aldershot, Burlington, Singapore and Sydney: Ashgate Atena.

Erikson, E.H. 1983. *Childhood and Society*, 35th anniversary edn. New York and London: W.W. Norton & Company.

Evasuk, S. 1990. "Never Underestimate Granny Power," *The Toronto Star*, 2 April.

Friedan, B. 1993. *The Fountain of Age*. New York: Simon & Schuster.

Greer, G. 1991. *The Change: Women, Aging, and Menopause*. New York: Fawcett.

Growe, S.J. 1998. "Raging Grannies Try to Make World a Better Place," *The Toronto Star*, 14 November.

Gilligan, C. 1982. *In a Different Voice: Growth and Change in Adult Life*. New York: Simon & Schuster.

Hamilton Spectator. 2000. "Raging Grannies Protest against Pesticides: Virtues of Dandelions Touted over Chemicals," 11 July.

Harper, T. 2000. "Grannies Heckle Day," *The Toronto Star*, 29 October.

Hill, L.P. 2000 "The Raging Grannies: Personal Attributes of Older Women Involved in Popular Education for Social Change." Unpublished MA thesis, OISE/University of Toronto.

Hopcke, R.H. 1995. *Persona: Where Sacred Meets Profane*. Boston and London: Shambhala.

Jarvis, P. 2001. *Learning in Later Life: An Introduction for Educators & Carers*. London: Kogan Page.

Kilgore, D.W. 1999. "Understanding Learning in Social Movements: A Theory of Collective

Learning," *International Journal of Lifelong Education* 18(3): 191–202.

Kingston Grannies. 2001. Personal communication.

Kotre, J.N. 1984. *Outliving the Self: Generativity and the Interpretation of Lives*. Baltimore and London: The Johns Hopkins University Press.

Landy, J.R. 1990. "The Concept of Role in Drama Therapy," *The Arts in Psychotherapy* 17: 223–30.

Landy, J.R. 1993. *Persona and Performance: The Meaning of Role in Drama, Therapy, and Everyday Life*. London, Bristol, Pennsylvania: Jessica Kingsley.

Loevinger, J. 1976. *Ego Development*. San Francisco: Jossey-Bass.

McCarten, J. 2002. "Men Gain Ground in Numbers Game," *The Toronto Star*, 17 July.

McLaren, J., and H. Brown, eds. 1991. *The Raging Grannies Songbook*. Gabriola Island, BC & Philadelphia, PA: New Society.

Merriam, S.B. 1998. *Qualitative Research and Case Study Applications in Education: Revised and Expanded from Case Study Research in Education*. San Francisco: Jossey-Bass.

Miller, J.B. 1991. "The Development of Women's Sense of Self," in J.V. Jordan, A.G. Kaplan, J.B. Miller, I.P. Striver, and J.L. Surrey, eds., *Women's Growth in Connection: Writings from the Stone Center*, p. 11. New York and London: Guilford.

Moody, H.R. 1988. *Abundance of Life: Human Development Policies for an Aging Society*. New York: Columbia University Press.

Norland, J.A. 1994. *Profile of Canada's Seniors*. Ottawa: Ministry of Industry, Science and Technology, Statistics Canada, No. 96-312E.

Peterborough Grannies. 2001. Personal communication.

Peterson, S.A., and A. Somit. 1994. *The Political Behavior of Older Americans*. New York and London: Garland.

Price, C.A. 1998. *Women and Retirement: The Unexplored Transition*. New York and London: Garland.

Raging Grannies. 1997. Vow. Available online: http://reseau.chebucto.ns.ca/CommunitySupport/vow/songs.htm.

Robertson, A. 1999. "Beyond Apocalyptic Demography: Toward a Moral Economy of Interdependence," in M. Minkler and C.L. Estes, eds., *Critical Gerontology: Perspective from Political and Moral Economy*, p. 75. Amityville, NY: Beywood.

Southwest Ontario Grannies. 2000. *Raging Grannies' "Carry On" Song Book*. Collected by Southwest Ontario Grannies, spring 2000.

Surrey, J.L. 1991. "Relationship and Empowerment," in J.V. Jordan, A.G. Kaplan, J.B. Miller, I.P. Striver, and J.L. Surrey, eds., *Women's Growth in Connection: Writings from the Stone Center*, p. 163. New York & London: Guilford.

Thomas, A. 1992. "The Emergence of a New Leisure Class," in J.E. Thornton, ed., *Education in the Third Age: Canadian and Japanese Perspectives*, p. 39. Vancouver, BC: Faculty of Education, University of British Columbia.

Tornstam, L. 1994. "Gero-Transcendence: A Theoretical and Empirical Exploration," in L.E. Thomas and S.A. Eisenhandler, eds., *Aging and the Religious Dimension*, p. 203. Westport, CT: Auburn House.

Wilmot, C. 2000. "Don't Mess with These Nice Old Ladies!," *The Jamaica Gleaner*, 12 February. Available online: http://dev.go-jamaica.com/gleaner/20000212/cleisure/c3.html.

Withnall, A. 2000. "The Debate Continues: Integrating Educational Gerontology and Lifelong Learning," in F. Glendenning, ed., *Teaching and Learning in Later Life: Theoretical Implications*, p. 87. Aldershot, Burlington, Singapore and Sydney: Ashgate Arena.

Credits

Atkinson, Michael. "Exploring Male Femininity in the 'Crisis': Men and Cosmetic Surgery," *Body & Society*, March 2008, 14: 67, pp. 67–87. Reprinted by Permission of SAGE

Aujla, Angela. "Others in Their Own Land: Second Generation Asian Canadian Women, Racism, and the Persistence of Colonial Discourse," *Canadian Woman Studies/Les Cahiers De La Femme*, Vol. 20, No. 2, Spring 2000, pp. 41–7. Reprinted by permission of the author.

Beagan, Brenda. "Micro Inequities and Everyday Inequalities: 'Race', Gender, Sexuality, and Class in Medical School". Reprinted by permission of the *Canadian Journal of Sociology*.

Beres, Melanie. "'It Just Happens': Negotiating Casual Heterosexual Sex". This chapter originally appeared in Beres, M.A. (2006). From *Sexual Consent to Heterosexual Casual Sex among Young Adults Living in Jasper*. Unpublished Doctoral Dissertation, University of Alberta, Edmonton, Alberta, Canada. Reprinted by permission of the author.

Bordo, Susan. "The Body and the Reproduction of Femininity". From *Unbearable Weight: Feminism, Western Culture, and the Body*. Published by University of California Press. Copyright © 2004, The Regents of the University of California.

Buss, David M. "Psychological Sex Differences through Sexual Selection", *American Psychologist* 50(30): 164–71. Copyright © 1995 by the American Psychological Association. Reproduced with permission.

Casey, Erin A., Juliana Carlson, Cathlyn Fraguela-Rios, Ericka Kimball, Tova B. Neugut, Richard M. Tolmam, and Jeffrey L. Edleson. "Context, Challenges, and Tensions in Global Efforts to Engage Men in the Prevention of Violence against Women: An Ecological Analysis," *Men and Masculinities* 16 (2) 228–251. Reprinted by Permission of SAGE Publications.

Coltrane, Scott. "Household Labour and the Routine Production of Gender", *Social Problems* 36, 5 (1989): 473–90. University of California Press.

Dobash, Russell P., R. Emerson Dobash, Margo Wilson, and Martin Daly. "The Myth of Sexual Symmetry in Marital Violence", *Social Problems* 39, 1 (1992): 71–91. University of California Press.

Dominelli, Lena, Susan Strega, Chris Walmsley, Marilyn Callahan, and Leslie Brown. "'Here's my Story': Fathers of 'Looked After' Children Recount their Experiences in the Canadian Child Welfare System," *British Journal of Social Work*, 2011, 41, 351–67, by permission of Oxford University Press

Evans, Joan A. "Cautious Caregivers: Gender Stereotypes and the Sexualization of Men Nurses' Touch", *Journal of Advanced Nursing*, 40(4): 441–8. Published by Blackwell Publishing Ltd.

Fausto-Sterling, Anne. "The Five Sexes: Why Male and Female Are Not Enough", *The Sciences* (March/April 1993). The author of the 5 Sexes urges you to read the companion piece, *The Five Sexes Revisited* she wrote a decade later, so that you can have a more current sense of her thinking on the topic of intersexuality. The article is available at: https://www.researchgate.net/profile/Anne_Fausto-Sterling/publications/2

Gagné, Patricia, Richard Tewksbury, and Deanna McGaughey, "Coming Out and Crossing Over: Identity Formation and Proclamation in a Transgender Community", *Gender & Society* (Vol. 11, No. 4), pp. 478–508, copyright 1997 by Sociologists for Women in Society. Reprinted by Permission of SAGE Publications

Gillian Creese, "Gendered Diasporas Across Generations: The New African Diaspora in Vancouver", in Renata Seredynska-Abou, editor, *Diasporic Choices*. Oxford: Inter-disciplinary Press, 2013: 109–20.

Guruge, Sepali, Nazilla Khanlou, and Denise Gastaldo. "Intimate Male Partner Violence in the Migration Process: Intersections of Gender, Race, and Class", *Journal of Advanced Nursing*, Vol. 66, No. 1 (January 2010) 103–13. Reprinted by permission of John Wiley & Sons, Inc.

Iwama, Marilyn. "'At Dawn, Our Bellies Full': Teaching Tales of Food and Resistance From Residential Schools and Internment Camps in Canada," *Journal of Intercultural Studies*, 21: 3, 239–54 (2000). Reprinted by permission of the publisher (Taylor & Francis Ltd, http://www.tandfonline.com).

Jackson, S. J. "Globalisation, Corporate Nationalism and Masculinity in Canada: Sport, Molson Beer Advertising and Consumer Citizenship." *Sport in Society*, 17(7) 901–16. (2014). Taylor & Francis Ltd., www.informaworld.com

Jacques, Alison. "You Can Run but You Can't Hide: The Incorporation of Riot Grrrl into Mainstream Culture", *Canadian Women's Studies*, Vol. 20/21, No. 4/1 (2001), 46–51. Reprinted by permission of the author.

Jiwani, Yasmin. "Helpless Maidens and Chivalrous Knights: Afghan Women in the Canadian Press," *University of Toronto Quarterly*, Vol. 78, No. 2, Spring 2009, pp. 728–44. Reprinted with permission from University of Toronto Press (www.utpjournals.com)

Jordan, Ellen and Angela Cowan. "Warrior Narratives in the Kindergarten Classroom: Renegotiating the Social Contract?" *Gender & Society* (Vol. 9, No. 6), pp. 727–43, copyright 1995 by Sociologists for Women in Society. Reprinted by Permission of SAGE Publications.

Lee, Susan. "Women's Perspectives on Disability, Underemployment & Health," *Women's Health and Urban Life*, Vol 12 (1), pg 61–79. 2013. Reprinted with permission.

Lindberg, Tracey. "What Do You Call an Indian Woman with a Law Degree: Nine Aboriginal Women at the University of Saskatchewan College of Law Speak Out", *Canadian Journal of Women and the Law* 9 (1997): 301–35. Copyright © University of Toronto Press 1997. Reprinted with permission from University of Toronto Press (www.utpjournals.com).

Lorber, Judith. "Believing Is Seeing: Biology as Ideology", *Gender & Society* (Vol. 7, No. 4), pp. 568–81, copyright 1993 by Sociologists for Women in Society. Reprinted by Permission of SAGE Publications.

Martin-Matthews, Anne. "Situating 'Home' at the Nexus of Public and Private Spheres: Aging, Gender, and Home Support Work in Canada", *Current Sociology*, March 2007, Vol. 55(2): 229–49. Reprinted by Permission of SAGE

Mulé, Nick. "Same-Sex Marriage and Canadian Relationship Recognition: One Step Forward and Two Steps Back: A Critical Liberationist Perspective", *Journal of Gay and Lesbian Social Services*, 22: 74–90 (2010). Reprinted by permission of the publisher (Taylor & Francis Ltd, http://www.tandfonline.com).

Namaste, Viviane K. "Genderbashing: Sexuality, Gender, and the Regulation of the Public Space". From *Invisible Lives: The Erasure of Transsexual and Transgendered People*, by Vivian K. Namaste. University of Chicago Press.

Narushima, Miya. "A Gaggle of Raging Grannies: The Empowerment of Older Canadian Women through Social Activism", *International Journal of Lifelong Education*, Vol. 23, No. 1 (January 2004) 23–42. Reprinted by permission of the publisher (Taylor & Francis Ltd, http://www.tandfonline.com).

Pacholok, Shelley. "Gendered Strategies of the Self: Navigating Hierarchy and Contesting Masculinities", *Gender, Work, and Organization*, Vol. 16, No. 4 (July 2009), 471–500. Journal compilation © 2009 Blackwell Publishing Ltd.

Ranson, Gillian. "No Longer 'One of the Boys': Negotiations with Motherhood, as Prospect or Reality, among Women in Engineering", *Canadian Review of Sociology & Anthropology* 42(2) (2005): 145–66. Reprinted by permission of John Wiley & Sons, Inc.

Razack, Sherene H. "Gendered, Racial Violence and Spatialized Justice: The Murder of Pamela George", © 2002, in *Race, Space, and the Law: Unmapping a White Settler Society*, Sherene H. Razack, ed. (Toronto: Between the Lines, 2002) 121–56. Used with permission of the publisher.

Reeves Sanday, Peggy. "Rape-Prone versus Rape-Free Campus Cultures", *Violence against Women* (Vol. 2, No. 2), pp. 191–208, copyright 1996 by Sociologists for Women in Society. Reprinted by Permission of SAGE Publications.

Rodgers, Kathleen and Melanie Knight. "'You just felt the collective wind being knocked out of us': The Deinstitutionalization of feminism and the survival of women's organizing in Canada," *Women's Studies International Forum* 34 (2011) 570–581. With permission from Elsevier

Ruby, Tabassum F. "Listening to the Voices of Hijab", *Women's Studies International Forum* 29, 1 (2006): 54–66. With permission from Elsevier.

Sapolsky, Robert M. "Testosterone Rules". Reprinted by permission of the author.

Steenbergen, Candis. "Feminism and Young Women: Still Alive and Kicking", *Canadian Women's Studies*, Vol. 20, No. 4 (Winter–Spring 2001), 6–15. Reprinted by permission of the author.

Stiell, Bernadette and Kim England. "Domestic Distinctions: Constructing Difference among Paid Domestic Workers in Toronto", *Gender, Place, and Culture* 4 (1997): 339–60. Reprinted by permission of the publisher (Taylor & Francis Ltd, http://www.tandfonline.com).

Theberge, Nancy. "'It's Part of the Game': Physicality and the Production of Gender in Women's Hockey". *Gender & Society*, Sage Publications. Reprinted by Permission of SAGE Publications

Tsui, Lily and Elena Nicoladis, "Losing It: Similarities and Differences in First Intercourse Experiences of Men and Women". Reprinted with permission from *The Canadian Journal of Human Sexuality*. Published by the Sex Information and Education Council of Canada.

Wakewich, Pamela. "Contours of Everyday Life: Women's Reflections on Embodiment and Health over Time". Excerpted from *Women's Bodies/Women's Lives: Health, Well-being and Body Image*. Reprinted by permission of the author.

West, Candace and Don H. Zimmerman. "Doing Gender", *Gender & Society* (Vol. 1, No. 2), pp. 125–51, copyright 1987 by Sociologists for Women in Society. Reprinted by Permission of SAGE Publications.